Actuary's
Report
25 March
1813

In Compliance with the order of the Board of the 16th Instant the Actuary has given all the attention the shortness of the time would admit to the subject referred to him, and begs leave to report;

That from the general appearance of the Public Sentiment in the various conversations he has had with different persons it is likely that applications will be made to the Company for almost every species of Contract contemplated in their association, but they will all come under the Character of Assurances on lives, annuities, or, as the case of Survivorships, partake of both, and will be governed by the same principles viz: a combination of the casualties of life with the Interest of money.

Many institutions have been formed in Europe and more especially in England for like purposes of which we have a particular Account in the writings of Dr Price, Morgan, Bailey and many others of the most eminent and accurate Mathematicians in that Country or perhaps in the world, who have so completely analyzed and reduced the subject to rule, as to leave us little more to do than to attend strictly to their instructions. They have uniformly founded their calculations on the bills of mortality kept in different places whereby the average decrements of human life has been ascertained with a sufficient degree of exactness for practice and by common consent those in England have deduced theirs from the bills at Northampton, the propriety whereof the experience of many years has abundantly confirmed.

These Bills of mortality give the number dying with their respective ages, from which is composed a table of the probabilities of life, by placing in one column the whole number living

The first actuarial report ever written in North America (see p.4). (Courtesy of First Pennsylvania Bank of Philadelphia)

OUR YESTERDAYS:

the
HISTORY
of the
ACTUARIAL PROFESSION
in
NORTH AMERICA
1809-1979

E.J. MOORHEAD F.S.A.

Society of Actuaries
475 N. Martingale Road
Schaumburg, Illinois 60173

NOTICE

Library of Congress Cataloging-in-Publication Data

    Moorhead, E.J., 1910-
      Our yesterdays: the history of the actuarial profession in North America, 1809-1979/by E.J. Moorhead.
      437 p.   cm.
      Bibliography: p.
      Includes index.
      ISBN 0-938959-08-5
      1. Actuaries—United States—History.   2. Actuaries—Canada—History.
      I. Title.
    HG8782.M66 1989
    368'.01'097—dc20

                                     89-31624
                                     CIP

ISBN 0-938959-08-5

To actuaries of all lands
who have struggled mightily
to create and maintain
a profession worthy of
public trust

CONTENTS

List of Charts and Tables xiii

Foreword by the Council of Presidents xv

About the Author xvii

Author's Preface xix

Chapter I. 1809–1858: Beginnings 1

  Pioneers of Our First Half-Century 1

  The Tasks These Pioneers Faced 1

  Philadelphia: Cradle of Our Profession in North America 4

  Jacob Shoemaker, America's First Actuary 4

  Premiums Charged in Early Days 6

  Balance Sheets. Surplus Distribution. The Note System 8

  Two Exceptional Actuaries: Wright and Gill 9

  Pioneer Consulting Actuaries: Entz and Elliott 13

  The First Canadians: Baker and Cherriman 14

  Formation of the Institute of Actuaries 14

  Our Profession in 1858 14

Chapter II. 1859–1888: Steps Towards a Professional Body 17

  Communication Among Actuaries 17

  1859. The First American "Life Underwriters' Convention" 18

  1859. Elizur Wright's First Major Reform — Policy Valuations 19

  A Voice from Georgia 20

  1861. Elizur Wright's Second Major Reform — Surrender Values 22

  1861. The American Experience Table 24

  1862. The Contribution Plan of Surplus Distribution 24

  1866. The First Woman Actuary 27

  1866–1867. Two Tries for an Actuarial Organization 28

  1867. The Tontine Dividend System 33

  1870–1879. Life Company Failures Give Rise to Assessment Companies . . . 34

  Milestones in Supervision: 1868 — Canada; 1871 — United States 35

  1872. Furor Over Mutual Life Proposal to Reduce Premiums 37

  1881. The Thirty American Offices Table 38

  1885. Death of Elizur Wright 39

Our Profession in 1888   40

Appendix to Chapter II: Papers by North American Actuaries in Volumes
Earlier than 1889 of the *Journal of the Institute of Actuaries*   41

Chapter III. 1889–1918: The First Four Bodies **43**

The Decision to Launch a Professional Body   43

The Event of April 25–26, 1889   46

The *Transactions* and *Yearbook*   52

The Council, 1889–1909   54

The Actuarial Society's Motto   54

Enrollment of Overseas Members   55

Domestic Growth, 1890–1898   58

Classification of Members   58

International Congresses   60

The First Elected Women Members   62

Mortality Studies   63

The Armstrong Investigation, 1905   66

Complaints and Discipline   70

Preliminary Term Valuation   71

Founding of the American Institute of Actuaries —
Viewed from the Actuarial Society   72

How the American Institute of Actuaries Was Founded   74

Scottish Influence in Pre-merger Days   78

Legal Notes and Book Reviews, 1910   80

Influx of Canadian Actuaries   81

Actuarial Society Incorporation Study, 1911   82

Group Life Insurance Enters the Scene, 1911   82

Introduction to Pension Mathematics, 1914   83

The Casualty Actuarial (and Statistical) Society (of America), 1914   85

World War I   92

Death of Emory McClintock, 1916   95

Fraternal Actuarial Association, 1916   96

The Influenza Pandemic, 1918   100

Our Profession in 1918   101

Appendix to Chapter III: Papers by North American Actuaries
at the First through Seventh International Congresses of Actuaries   104

Chapter IV. 1919–1948: Fat Years and Lean Years **107**

Changing Attitudes and Directions   107

Clinging to the American Experience Table 108
Mortality and Related Studies 111
Non-Medical Insurance 113
Competitive Problems with Pricing and Product Design 113
Substandard Underwriting 115
The Library of the Actuarial Society 116
First Joint Meeting of Actuarial Society and American Institute, 1924 117
Death of David Parks Fackler, 1924 118
Tenth Anniversary of Casualty Actuarial Society, 1924 118
Tenth Anniversary of Fraternal Actuarial Association, 1926 120
International Meetings 121
Pensions 123
Aviation Risks 125
Arthur Pedoe's 1929 Paper, "The Actuarial Profession on the North
    American Continent" 126
Women Fellows in Our Profession's First Forty Years 128
Amendments to New York's Expense Limitation Statute 128
Depression Strikes, October 1929 131
The United States Social Security Act, 1935 138
Depression Days in Canada 144
The Canadian Association of Actuaries 145
Adoption of Modern Valuation and Nonforfeiture Standards 146
Recommendations of the First Guertin Committee, June 1939 147
The Work of the Second Guertin Committee 148
The 1941 CSO Table 149
The Standard Valuation Law 150
Actuarial Studies of Agency Questions 151
World War II 152
Anniversaries 153
Moving Toward Merger 156
Our Profession in 1948 159
Appendix to Chapter IV: Papers by North American Actuaries at the Eighth
    through Twelfth International Congresses of Actuaries 160

Chapter V. 1949–1964: Expansion and Fresh Directions **165**

Early Days of the Society of Actuaries 165
Influx of Fellows of the Institute and Faculty of Actuaries 168
Formation of the Conference of Actuaries in Public Practice (CAPP), 1950 . 169
Apprehensions of the Nuclear Era 173

Life Company Investments 175
The 1958 Commissioners Standard Ordinary Mortality Table 176
Beginning of a Product Revolution 177
Accident and Health Insurance 179
Increasing the Supply of Actuaries 180
Pensions 182
Social Security 189
International Congresses 190
Professional Conduct 191
Leaders in Income Tax Formulation 193
Mortality Studies 193
Certification of Actuaries 195
Challenges to Traditional Actuarial Prerogatives 196
Fraternal Actuarial Association 198
Society of Actuaries Library Moved to New York, 1963 199
End of "Legal Notes," 1964 200
Election Procedures, Society of Actuaries 200
Completing the Casualty Actuarial Society's First Half-Century 201
The Profession in Mexico 204
Our Profession in 1964 205
Appendix to Chapter V: Papers by North American Actuaries at the
     Thirteenth through Seventeenth International Congresses of Actuaries . . 207

Chapter VI. 1965–1979: A New Professional Structure **211**
A Journalist's View of the Profession 211
Two National Organizations Are Launched 212
Conference of Actuaries in Public Practice 221
American Society of Pension Actuaries 222
Casualty Actuarial Society 223
Expansion of Research 227
Newsletters 231
The Society of Actuaries Peers into Its Future 235
Public Expression of Professional Opinion 236
Birthday Celebrations 238
The New South Life Case 238
Minority Recruiting 239
Design and Pricing of Individual Life Insurance 240
Policy Cost Comparisons 241
Life Insurance Company Financial Statements 244

The Academy in the 1970s. 250
Independence of the Actuary 252
Elections in the Society of Actuaries 253
Council of Presidents, 1972 255
International Meetings 255
Trouble in the Old Age Survivors and Disability Insurance (OASDI) System . 256
Discipline 262
Pensions 263
Attempt at Consolidation of Actuarial Bodies 270
Farewell to the Fraternal Actuarial Association 271
First Joint Meeting of the Casualty Actuarial Society and Society of
    Actuaries, 1978 271
Life Insurance Reserves and Nonforfeiture Values 272
Committee Work on Statutory Minimum Nonforfeiture Benefits 272
Changes in Statutory Valuation Requirements 274
The First Woman President 276
Our Profession in 1979 276
Appendix to Chapter VI: Papers by North American Actuaries at the
    Eighteenth through Twentieth International Congresses of Actuaries . . . 279

Chapter VII. Actuarial Education **283**
Original Textbooks 283
Education and Examinations by Actuarial Bodies, 1897–1928 284
Tuition and Textbooks 292
Early University Courses in Actuarial Science 297
The Beginnings of Jointly Administered Examinations, 1928 299
New Directions, 1939–1949 301
Developments, 1949–1962. 306
Cooperation in Educational Requirements, Starting in 1963 308
The Rappaport/Plumley Paper, 1975 312
Steps Toward Linkages 313
Continuing Education 315
At the Twenty-First Congress: "The Training of the Actuary" 316
Trend of Student Population in the Late 1970s 316

Chapter VIII. Income Disability Benefits **319**
Advance Warnings. 319
Early Warnings 320
Report of Committee on Disability Experience, 1926 321

Actions Taken to Curb Disability Losses, 1927 to 1930 323
The Flight from Income Disability Coverage, 1932 324
The Pacific Mutual Life Case 326
Mutual Benefit Life, A Notable Contrast 326
The Experience in Canada 327
How the Noncancellable Contracts Fared 328

Chapter IX. How Actuaries Calculated **331**

Before the Mechanical Calculator Era 331
Babbage, Scheutz and Wright 333
Desk Calculators 334
Hollerith and Gore 337
Phillips, Berkeley and Finelli 340
Notation 347

Chapter X. The Profession in Wartime **349**

Introduction 349
Records of Members in Military Service 350
Commending Actuarial Talents to Wartime Authorities 352
Uses Made of Actuarial Skills in Two World Wars 353
Wartime Disruptions of the Profession's Activities 359
Anecdotes 360

Chapter XI. Administration and Finance **363**

Operations of the Actuarial Society of America 363
Operations of the American Institute of Actuaries 365
Operations of the Casualty Actuarial Society 367
Operations of the Fraternal Actuarial Association 368
Operations of the Society of Actuaries 368
Operations of the Conference of Actuaries in Public Practice 370
Operations of the Canadian Institute of Actuaries 371
Operations of the American Academy of Actuaries 372
Dues Scales of All Actuarial Bodies at Ten-Year Intervals 372

Chapter XII. Actuarial Clubs **373**

The British Example 373
The Actuaries Club 374
The Actuaries Club of New York 375
More Clubs Appear 376
The Actuaries Club of Hartford 377

The Senior Actuaries Club 378
The Regional Clubs 378
Clubs Serving Casualty Actuaries 380
Relationships Between Actuarial Societies and Clubs 380
Data from 1972 Committee Study 381

Chapter XIII. Thinking Statistically **383**

Views on Mathematical Statistics by North American Actuaries 383
The Influence of R.A. Fisher 385
Credibility and Experience Rating 385
Other Applications of Bayes' Theorem 387
Some North American Leaders in Statistical Approaches to
    Actuarial Problems 388
Hewitt's Story of Sinclair Lewis 389

Chapter XIV. Laughing at Ourselves **391**

The Light Side in the Casualty Actuarial Society 391
The Light Side in the Actuarial Society of America 394
The Light Side in the American Institute of Actuaries 398
The Light Side in the Society of Actuaries 399
The Light Side in the Canadian Institute of Actuaries 401
The Light Side in the Conference of Actuaries in Public Practice 404
The Light Side of Guest Presentations 404

Acronyms and Abbreviations **407**

Bibliography **411**

Index **417**

List of Charts and Tables

Chart I   The Trend of Population Mortality in the United States xxii
Chart II   Yields on Invested Assets of United States Life Insurance Companies . xxiii
Chart III   The Trend of the United States Consumer Price Index xxiv
I.1   Leading Actuaries of the Early Nineteenth Century 2
I.2   Mortality Experience of Mutual Life, February 1843 to February 1851 . 12
III.1   Charter Me mbers of Actuarial Society of America, 1889 51
III.2   Actuarial Society of America, Chart of Council Members, 1889–1909 . 56
III.3   Ratios of American Institute Fellows to Total Fellows of
            Actuarial Society and American Institute at Selected Dates 74
III.4   Charter Fellows of American Institute of Actuaries, 1909 76
III.5   Fellows and Associates of American Institute of Actuaries, 1909–1918   78
III.6   Percentages of Canadian Fellows to (United States + Canadian)
            Fellows, 1889–1945 81
III.7   Eighty Charter Fellows of the Casualty Actuarial Society 90
III.8   Changes in the Roster of Fellows of the Casualty Actuarial
            Society, November 7, 1914 to December 31, 1918 92
III.9   Charter Members of the Fraternal Actuarial Association 99
III.10   Fellows and Associates of Actuarial Society of America,1889–1918 . . 102
IV.1   Changes in the Roster of Fellows of the Casualty Actuarial
            Society, Calendar Years 1919 to 1924 120
IV.2   Women Who Became Fully Qualified Members of Any of the Four
            Actuarial Bodies before the End of 1929 130
IV.3   Percentages of Candidates Who Passed the Joint Actuarial
            Society/American Institute Examinations in College
            Algebra, 1929 to 1934 134
IV.4   Value of 1,000 q_x on Three Mortality Tables 149
IV.5   Numbers of Fellows of Actuarial Society of America and
            American Institute of Actuaries on Selected Dates 157
IV.6   Numbers of Fully Qualified Members by the Respective
            Standards of the Four Actuarial Bodies on December 31, 1948 . . . 159
V.1   Officers, Other Board Members, and Non-Board Senior Charter
            Members of the Conference of Actuaries in Public Practice,1950 . . 171
V.2   Values of 1,000 q_x by Four Mortality Tables at Decennial Ages 177
V.3   Numbers of Fellows and Associates of Society of Actuaries
            and Its Predecessors at Ten-Year Intervals, 1893–1983 181
V.4   Fellows and Associates of Society of Actuaries and Its
            Predecessors by Type of Employment on Selected Dates 181
V.5   Values of Gompertz's Constant in Selected Mortality Tables 194
V.6   Numbers of Senior Members of Four Actuarial Bodies, 1948 and 1964   205

VI.1   Rosters of Canadian Institute of Actuaries, November 1965 and June 1987 214

VI.2   OASDI Trust Funds, December 31, 1976–1982 261

VI.3   Mortality Rates Per 1,000 by American Experience and 1980 CSO Tables 274

VII.1   1908 Associateship Examination Subjects 286

VII.2   1908 Associateship Examination Results 286

VII.3   1908 Fellowship Examination Subjects 286

VII.4   Numbers and Percentages of Women Who Passed Associateship Examinations in 1919 and 1920 288

VII.5   Rosters of Associates of Actuarial Society of America and American Institute of Actuaries for Selected Periods, 1897–1923 290

VII.6   New Associates of Actuarial Society of America by Examination, 1937–1941 300

VII.7   Numbers of New Fellows of Society of Actuaries and Its Predecessor Bodies, 1946–1963 305

VII.8   Numbers of Students Who Passed the General Mathematics Examination, 1976–1988 317

VIII.1   Comparative Values of Disability Functions in Hunter's Tables (1911) and in Class 3 Experience (1926) 322

VIII.2   Disability Claim Rates and Disability Annuity Values in 1930 and Later Years Measured by 1926 Class 3 Yardsticks 325

VIII.3   Numbers of Companies That Had Entered, Withdrawn, and Remained Active in the Noncancellable Disability Field by Ends of Years 1919, 1924, 1929 and 1934 328

VIII.4   Net Premiums and Adjusted Loss Ratios on Noncancellable Disability Policies of Thirteen Selected Companies, 1925, 1928, 1932, 1933 and 1934 329

IX.1   Desk Calculators Used by North American Actuaries 335

X.1   Deaths from War and War-Related Causes among Members and Students of the North American Actuarial Bodies 351

XI.1   Income and Expenses of Actuarial Society of America in Three Selected Years 364

XI.2   Income and Expenses of American Institute of Actuaries in Two Selected Years 366

XI.3   Income and Expenses of Casualty Actuarial Society in Three Selected Years 368

XI.4   Maximum Dues Charged by North American Actuarial Bodies at Ten-Year Intervals, 1909–1979 372

FOREWORD BY THE COUNCIL OF PRESIDENTS

The actuarial profession has always had a strong sense of the importance of understanding its history in an effort to preserve its traditional values of integrity, commitment to excellence, vision and public spiritedness. This is exemplified by a series of publications, of which the present volume is an appropriate and definitive culmination. Earlier publications included "The Origin of the Society of Actuaries," by Reinhard A. Hohaus, *TSA* 1 (1949), and "Society of Actuaries—Its First Twenty Years," by Victor E. Henningsen, *TSA* 21 (1969), as well as "The First Fifty Years," by Dudley M. Pruitt, *PCAS* 51 (1964). The most comprehensive example previous to this volume is *From Actuarius to Actuary* by Robert B. Mitchell (September 1974) published to mark the twenty-fifth anniversary of the founding of the Society of Actuaries in 1949.

In 1983 the Council of Presidents of the principal actuarial organizations in North America began to consider appropriate ways for marking the one hundreth anniversary of the founding of the initial actuarial organization in North America, the Actuarial Society of America. It was concluded that a special anniversary meeting to be held in Washington in 1989 would be appropriate; that year would also mark the seventy-fifth anniversary of the founding of the Casualty Actuarial Society and the fortieth anniversary of the Society of Actuaries.

Dwight K. Bartlett III, then President of the Society of Actuaries, urged that an effort be made to produce a definitive historical work that would be of sufficient quality to do credit to the profession; it should be useful to actuaries who would want to know more about their history and also to a broader audience. He asked E. J. (Jack) Moorhead to serve as chairperson of a task force to develop a plan for producing such a volume.

Perhaps the single most important question presented by the task force for resolution by the Council of Presidents was: Who should be engaged as author of the book? Should the author be a professional writer, not an actuary, as was the case for *From Actuarius to Actuary*, or should the author be an actuary who had a reputation for considerable literary skills, a demonstrated talent for historical research and a high level of enthusiasm for the project? The decision was made easy for the Council by the availability of Jack Moorhead, since he fulfilled admirably all three criteria.

Mr. Moorhead has had great support from members of the profession and from the staffs of the actuarial organizations. It should be clear, however, that *Our Yesterdays* is uniquely the product of his efforts and talents. It justifies in all respects the confidence that the Council of Presidents had in Mr. Moorhead and should serve as a source of pride for the profession for years to come.

W. James MacGinnitie, President
American Academy of Actuaries

David L. Hewitt, President
Conference of Actuaries in Public Practice

Jacques Cloutier, President
Canadian Institute of Actuaries

Ian M. Rolland, President
Society of Actuaries

Kevin M. Ryan, President
Casualty Actuarial Society

March 1989

ABOUT THE AUTHOR

E. J. (Jack) Moorhead's career path to the prestigious post of historian for the actuarial profession in North America was almost entirely mapped out for him by three people: Ernest S. Moorhead, an Irish physician practicing in Winnipeg; Iris de Wet Moorhead, a former actuarial department employee at the Great-West Life; and Dwight K. Bartlett III, a New York City actuary.

Dr. Moorhead, having identified the actuarial profession in 1924 as a haven for introverts with some grasp of mathematics, advised his son that the position of an actuary should be his goal. In 1926, the doctor sent the boy to the University of Liverpool and, in 1929, took him to Staple Inn Hall in London to be enrolled in the Institute's correspondence course. Iris Moorhead in 1938 urged her husband to take a public speaking course, not foreseeing the lifetime of listening to his speeches and then eventually typing innumerable drafts of *Our Yesterdays* that would result. Mr. Bartlett obtained for Moorhead the post of chairman of a task force responsible for commissioning a centennial history, fully expecting that Moorhead would end up writing the book himself.

The professional career of Jack Moorhead, FSA, MAAA, AIA, spans fifty-five years. Mr. Moorhead was at Great-West Life from 1929 to 1945; at a predecessor of the Life Insurance Marketing and Research Association (LIMRA, at that time LISRB) from 1945 to 1948; at United States Life in New York City from 1948 to 1952; at New England Mutual Life from 1952 to 1967; and at Integon in Winston-Salem from 1967 till his retirement in 1972. Since 1972, he has participated in public interest activities including advisory work for the United States Senate Subcommittee on Antitrust and Monopoly, and two studies of the financial problems of the social security system.

Within the organized profession, he served the Society of Actuaries as chairman of the Committee on Papers, editor of *The Actuary*, and president (1969–1970) and served the American Academy of Actuaries as president (1973–1974). He has published several papers in the *Transactions*.

AUTHOR'S PREFACE

It is astounding—and cause for sorrow—that a comprehensive history of the actuarial profession in North America was not written long ago. Apparently no governing body even discussed such a project seriously until the early 1980s. The pioneer undertaking was that of Dudley M. Pruitt for the Casualty Actuarial Society in 1964 ("The First Fifty Years," *PCAS* 51, 148), but even Pruitt stated flatly, "this is not a history."

Walter S. Nichols (1841–1921) or Levi W. Meech (1821–1912) could surely have written first-class accounts of the struggles of pioneer actuaries in the years before 1889, but the Actuarial Society founders were strikingly chary about even mentioning those days. Henry H. Jackson (1884–1955) or James S. Elston (1889–1980) would have been pleased to record the facts and their interpretations thereof with respect to, say, the first forty years after 1889, but seemingly nobody thought to ask them. Robert Henderson (1871–1942) chose as the title of his 1923 presidential address "Prominent Names in Early Actuarial History," but, alas, the period he covered (*T.A.S.A.* 24, 1) ran only from 1623 to 1823 and contains only one passing reference to North America.

Down the years a rather thorough job was done of destroying or mislaying the documents that would have helped so much to throw light upon actuarial events and viewpoints during the nineteenth and early twentieth centuries. In the summer of 1984, Society of Actuaries Executive Director John E. O'Connor, a man to whom and to whose staff this project owes much, took this would-be author to a storage bin in rural Illinois where lay three cardboard cartons with the welcome word "History" scrawled upon them. But apart from a few intriguing personal papers of David Parks Fackler, the pickings in general were thin.

Except for a handful of instances, the Actuarial Society of America did not publish in its *Transactions* any reports of its informal discussions. And when a historical paper was written, it was usually allowed to go into the annals without discussion; this applies to Emory McClintock's essays on Charles Gill in 1913–1914, and in the present Society of Actuaries to Reinhard A. Hohaus' "The Origin of the Society of Actuaries" in 1949, to Victor E. Henningsen's "Society of Actuaries—Its First Twenty Years" in 1969, and to three papers by appointed historians in 1975 and 1977. Likewise there was no recorded discussion of Pruitt's CAS paper of 1964. These were damaging mistakes; it is every bit as important to garner viewpoints other than the author's on historical subjects as it is on papers devoted to any other subjects.

* * * * *

The fourteen chapters in this volume comprise two distinct sections: the first six chapters are chronological; the other eight deal with selected special subjects. Readers in the United Kingdom will notice, and I hope will accept as its intended compliment, adherence to the pattern used by Reginald C. Simmonds' *The Institute of Actuaries 1848–1948.*

In recognition that the paths chosen by our forebears were heavily influenced by the outside conditions that they faced, I append to this preface three ready-reference charts depicting major outside circumstances—mortality, interest yields, and costs-of-living—that confronted successive generations of actuaries. The following is a description of each of these charts; they have been designed so as to remove minor irregularities and thus to display trends.

CHART I: THE TREND OF POPULATION MORTALITY IN THE UNITED STATES.

The functions plotted are (A) (broken line) the unadjusted mortality rates per 1,000 for Massachusetts males at five-year intervals, 1860 to 1900, and (B) (solid line) the age-adjusted mortality rates per 1,000 for United States white males at two-year intervals from 1900 to 1982.

Source: *Historical Statistics of the United States—Colonial Times to 1970*, and, for years after 1970, *Monthly Vital Statistics Reports*.

CHART II: YIELDS ON INVESTED ASSETS OF UNITED STATES LIFE INSURANCE COMPANIES.

The function plotted is the yield, net of investment expense but before deducting federal income taxes, plotted at two-year intervals starting in 1876. From 1966 on, the investment experience excludes that arising from separate account business.

Source: American Council of Life Insurance.

CHART III: THE TREND OF THE UNITED STATES CONSUMER PRICE INDEX.

The function plotted is the value computed by this author of $(\sqrt[3]{B/A} - 1) \times 100$, where B is the Consumer Price Index (1967 = 100) in the year shown, and A is the corresponding value three years earlier. This, like the functions in Charts I and II, is plotted at two-year intervals, starting in this case in 1810.

Source: U.S. Government Reports.

The values plotted on all three charts are shown on page xxv.

Harry H. Panjer has kindly supplied me with as many of the corresponding figures for Canada as can be found. After comparing the Canadian trends with their United States counterparts, I have concluded that although the values themselves differ, the major trends are sufficiently similar to make the United States trendlines trustworthy for readers in either country.

* * * * *

My gratitude for the hard work and guidance accorded this project by a host of skilled and patient people is intense as I observe how poor a product this would be without them. I name just some of them here; others I hope will accept my thanks even though their names do not appear.

Susan L. Pasini, expert in style and in the mysteries of book production, edited the manuscript for printing, contributed many excellent ideas for format and wording and corrected author's mistakes along the way. Successive Society of Actuaries' Librarians, Joan I. Chapa and Donna L. Richardson, performed prodigious feats of search and research. Peggy J. Grillot patiently and capably converted heavily marked-up pages into word-processed neatness. Barbara Simmons took good care of liaison with designer Mark Becker and printer's representative George Gion. Linda M. Delgadillo, in her capacity as the Society's Director of Communications, contributed advice and kept a watchful eye on the calendar.

Iris Moorhead typed many hundreds of pages of successive drafts, mostly from her husband's dictation. She also cheerfully permitted one room of our home to be unavailable for any other activities between 1984 and 1989.

Edward F. Cowman was a surprise partner such as few authors ever find. His volunteer work in preparing a consolidated index to the *T.A.S.A., R.A.I.A.*, and *TSA* first brought him over this project's horizon. He prepared sub-indexes for my use and indexed the articles in twenty years of issues of *The Actuary* just in time to give me convenient access to that important source. To cap all this, he put his trusty computer to work compiling the index that graces this volume.

I have saved to the last an expression of heartfelt praise for the absolutely essential guidance given me by colleagues who served as constructive critics of drafts that have come to them since early 1986: Dwight K. Bartlett III, Geoffrey N. Calvert, Donald F. Campbell, Robert G. Espie, Frank L. Griffin, Charles G. Groeschell, Charles C. Hewitt, Colin E. Jack, Walter Klem, Edward A. Lew, Laurence H. Longley-Cook, Robert J. Myers, Murray Projector, Charles F. B. Richardson, Charles E. Rickards, Matthew Rodermund, Henry F. Rood, Walter L. Rugland and Julius Vogel. Some of these kindly read nearly all the chapters, while others helped with their own specialties. Every one of these mentioned and other highly qualified advisors shares in whatever success this history enjoys, and none of them is to blame for its shortcomings.

E. J. (Jack) Moorhead
Bermuda Run, North Carolina
January 1989

CHART I

THE TREND OF POPULATION MORTALITY
IN THE UNITED STATES

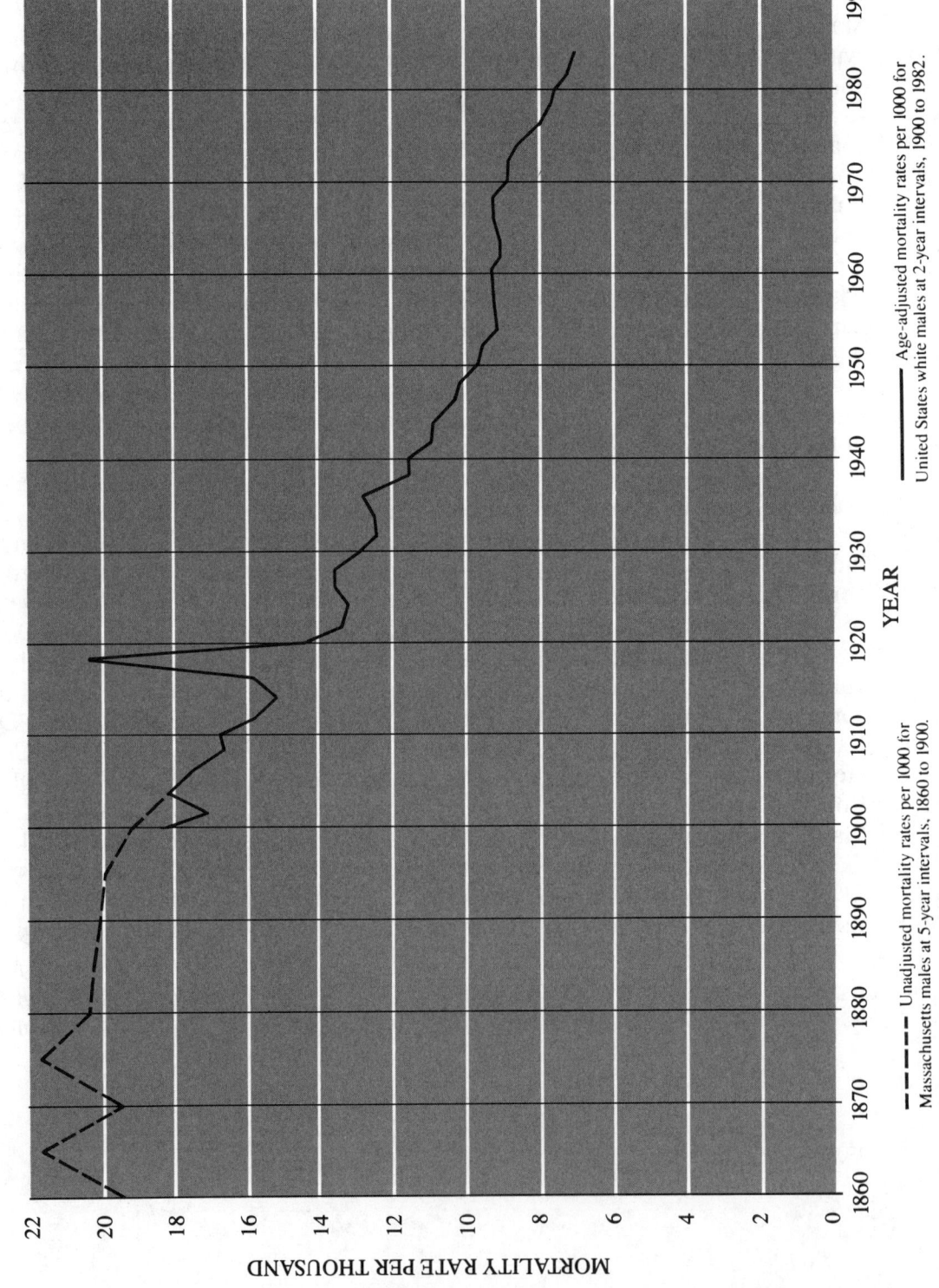

– – – Unadjusted mortality rates per 1000 for
Massachusetts males at 5-year intervals, 1860 to 1900.

——— Age-adjusted mortality rates per 1000 for
United States white males at 2-year intervals, 1900 to 1982.

YEAR

MORTALITY RATE PER THOUSAND

CHART II

**YIELDS ON INVESTED ASSETS OF UNITED STATES
LIFE INSURANCE COMPANIES**

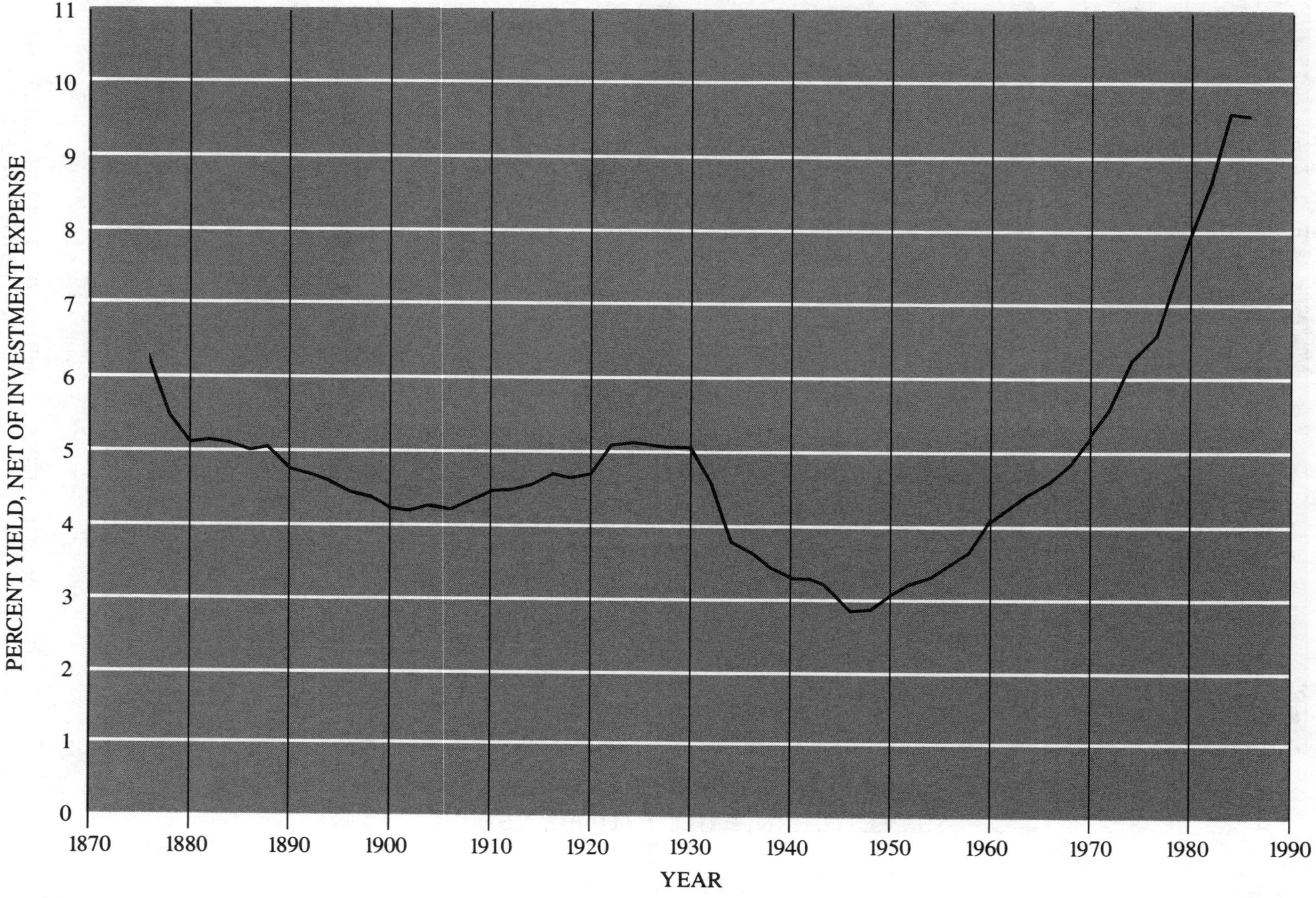

CHART III

THE TREND OF THE UNITED STATES
CONSUMER PRICE INDEX

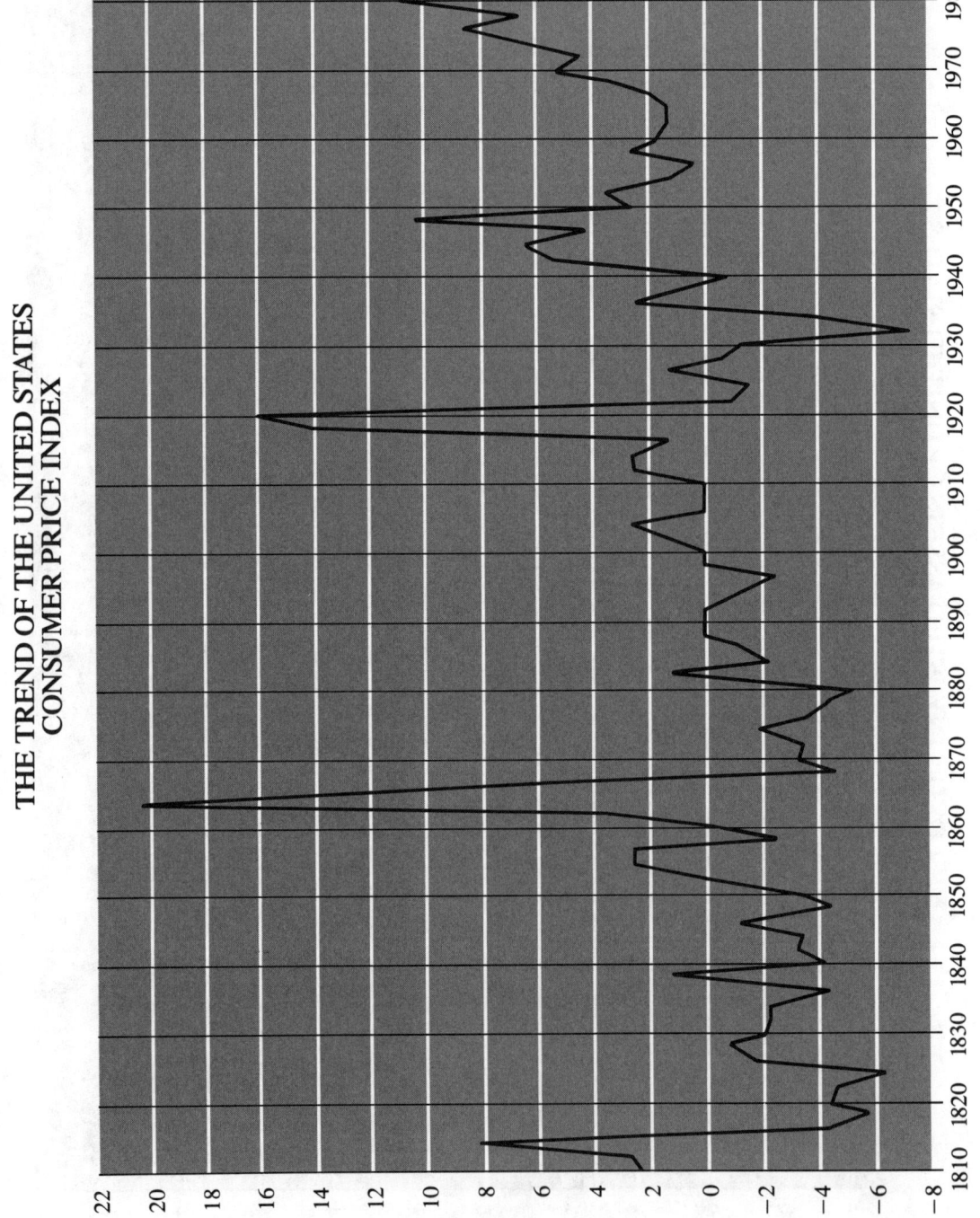

YEAR

PERCENTAGE COMPOUND ANNUAL CHANGE IN C.P.I.
OVER THE THREE YEARS ENDING AT THE DATE INDICATED.

VALUES PLOTTED IN READY-REFERENCE CHARTS
(I. MORTALITY; II. INVESTMENT YIELDS; III. CONSUMER PRICE INDEX CHANGES)

YEAR	I	II	III
1810			2.22
1812			2.76
1814			8.01
1816			-4.20
1818			-5.78
1820			-4.35
1822			-4.55
1824			-6.21
1826			-1.89
1828			-0.99
1830			-2.00
1832			-2.13
1834			-2.13
1836			-4.40
1838			1.06
1840			-4.09
1842			-3.23
1844			-3.34
1846			-1.20
1848			-2.44
1850			-3.71
1852			0.00
1854			2.60
1856			2.60
1858			-2.44
1860	19.3		-1.20
1862			3.57
1864			20.29
1865	21.7		
1866			5.95
1868			-4.55
1870	19.5		-3.28
1872			-3.45
1874	21.8		-1.89
1875			
1876		6.36	-3.85
1878		5.60	-4.22
1880	20.3	5.16	-3.23
1882		5.23	1.18
1884		5.15	-2.35
1885	20.2		
1886		5.07	-1.20
1888		5.11	0.00
1890	20.0	4.80	0.00
1892		4.78	0.00
1894		4.63	-1.25
1895	19.9		
1896		4.61	-2.53
1898		4.57	0.00
1900(A)	19.2		
1900(B)	18.4		0.00
1902	17.0	4.33	1.32
1904	18.1	4.31	2.60
1906	17.6	4.50	0.00
1908	16.6	4.26	0.00
1910	16.7	4.46	0.00
1912	15.7	4.55	2.41
1914	15.2	4.59	2.44
1916	15.8	4.69	3.26
1918	20.2	4.80	14.05
1920	14.2	4.72	16.04
1922	13.3	4.83	-1.04
1924	13.1	5.12	-1.52
1926	13.6	5.17	1.22
1928	13.6	5.09	-0.77
1930	12.8	5.05	-1.30
1932	12.3	5.05	-7.27
1934	12.5	4.65	-4.19
1936	12.8	3.92	2.27
1938	11.5	3.71	0.88
1940	11.6	3.45	-0.78
1942	10.9	3.44	5.47
1944	10.8	3.23	6.12
1946	10.2	2.93	4.14
1948	10.0	2.96	10.18
1950	9.6	3.13	2.53
1952	9.5	3.28	3.65
1954	9.0	3.46	1.14
1956	9.1	3.63	0.54
1958	9.1	3.85	2.59
1960	9.2	4.11	1.71
1962	9.0	4.34	1.24
1964	9.0	4.53	1.21
1966	9.2	4.73	1.96
1968	9.2	4.97	3.31
1970	8.9	5.34	5.16
1972	8.8	5.69	4.50
1974	8.4	6.31	6.78
1976	7.9	6.68	8.60
1978	7.6	7.39	6.61
1980	7.5	8.06	10.79
1982	7.1	8.87	9.97
1984	6.9	9.65	4.54
1986		9.64	3.24

Note 1. Year 1900, Column I: (A) is the unadjusted mortality rate per 1,000 for Massachusetts males, corresponding to all the values for earlier years. (B) is the age-adjusted mortality rate per 1,000 for United States white males, corresponding to all the values for later years.

Note 2. Years 1852 to 1910, Column III: The zero values do not represent complete stability of the Consumer Price Index; the CPI changes were so small that the values thereof computed many years later did not show what those small changes actually were.

Chapter I.
1809–1858: BEGINNINGS

It is remarkable that a science, which began with the consideration of games of chance, should be elevated to the rank of the most important subjects of human knowledge.

—Pierre Simon Laplace (1749–1827)

PIONEERS OF OUR FIRST HALF-CENTURY

Twenty-seven men practiced as company actuaries, consulting actuaries or teachers of actuarial science, for a minimum of five years each, during the actuarial profession's first half-century in North America. Historians have been divided on just when our profession should be considered as having come into existence. Some have dated it from eighteenth century attempts to design clergy pensions. At the opposite extreme, Emory McClintock, in *T.A.S.A.* 14 (1913) described Charles Gill as "The First Actuary in America," tantamount to dating us from 1849. Capsules of the careers of all twenty-seven actuaries can be found in *TSA* 36, 351–83.

Even though fire and marine insurance became established on this continent, as elsewhere, ahead of life insurance, all of these twenty-seven men practiced in the life field. The heyday of what are now called casualty actuaries lay many years in the future, this mainly for two reasons. First, life insurance and annuity contracts were long-term while non-life contracts were issued for short terms, three years or less, and the need for actuarial guidance was more easily perceived in calculating long-term than short-term contract rates. Second, non-life premium determination was viewed as more an art than a science as also was risk classification of fire and marine insurance applications.

Among these twenty-seven actuaries, thirteen, listed chronologically in Table I.1 by their entry into the actuarial sphere, were clearly the most influential.

THE TASKS THESE PIONEERS FACED

As one contemplates the characters of these men and the conditions that confronted them, it is difficult to see how David Parks Fackler, founder of the Actuarial Society of America, reached the conclusion he expressed in his reminiscences at the Society's twentieth anniversary meeting in May 1909 (*T.A.S.A.* 11, 10):

> [T]he problems for actuaries in this country inside of the insurance companies were generally very simple until after 1860. . . . It was not until our companies

Table I.1
LEADING ACTUARIES OF THE EARLY NINETEENTH CENTURY

Entry Year	Lifetime	Location	Claim to Fame
c.1792 Robert Patterson	1743–1824	Philadelphia	Teacher of elementary actuarial science at the University of Pennsylvania, who computed premiums for Presbyterian Ministers Fund.
1809 Jacob Shoemaker	1758–1822	Philadelphia	The first life company actuary on this continent.
1823 Nathaniel Bowditch	1773–1838	Boston	Renowned navigator who also shone as actuary of Massachusetts Hospital Life Insurance Company.
1830 William Bard	1778–1853	New York	President and actuary of New York Life & Trust (not same as present New York Life).
1836 John F. James	1802–1871	Philadelphia	First American actuary to undertake surplus distribution to policyholders.
c.1840 John F. Entz	1798–1872	New York	America's first consulting actuary.
1844 Elizur Wright	1804–1885	Boston	Immensely influential in establishing sound actuarial practices.
1847 Hugh C. Baker	1818–1859	Hamilton, Ontario	Canada's first life insurance actuary.
1848 Charles F. McCay	1810–1889	Athens, Georgia & Baltimore	Respected teacher and prolific writer on actuarial topics.
1848 Harvey G. P. Tuckett	c.1800–1854	Philadelphia	Crusading insurance journalist and consulting actuary from England.
1849 Charles Gill	1805–1855	New York	Actuary of the first major life company in the United States.
1849 Ezekiel B. Elliott	1823–1888	Boston & Washington	First U.S. government actuary.
c.1850 Nicholas De Groot	1810–1887	New York	An immigrant actuary who made valuable contributions from his experience in England.

began to issue policies more complex than the old-fashioned life or term policies that much need for trained actuaries was felt on this Continent.

If any of those thirteen pre-1860 actuaries listed had survived until 1909, one can picture him reminding Mr. Fackler, who had joined Mutual Life of New York as an eighteen-year-old gold medalist from City College in the fall of 1859, that Fackler's seniors had to overcome handicaps unique to their era, such as:

- Lack of opportunities to discuss their problems with their peers.

- Dependence upon books and papers written by and for English actuaries, mostly not written as textbooks, and far from uniform in notation.

- Absence of insured life mortality experiences, making it necessary to use tables derived from population statistics with unknown, although fortunately ample, safety margins.

- Uncertainty about existing surplus margins during many years when concepts of balance sheet preparation were faulty to the point that some companies even showed the face amounts of their policies in force as liabilities.

- Widespread public disapproval of life insurance, particularly prejudice against it on religious grounds.

- Low prestige of actuaries among life company officers and directors, severely hampering actuaries' efforts to gain acceptance of their recommendations.

- Prevalence of smallpox, cholera in port cities, and other causes of adverse mortality, especially troublesome in times when volumes of business were small.

- Woefully inadequate supporting legislation, jurisprudence, and regulation, giving the public reason to doubt that contract guarantees would be met at maturity.

In summary, an account of the first half-century of actuarial practice on this continent is mainly the story of individual, inexperienced mathematicians poring over books and figures in search of guidelines to discharge unfamiliar responsibilities.

An astute observer, Walter S. Nichols, speaking at the Second International Congress of Actuaries in 1898, analyzed the conditions of those early days thus (*T.A.S.A.* 5, 196):

> In Europe, life insurance was a natural growth in which the development of its scientific principles went hand in hand with their practical application. In America, it was an exotic introduced as a business known to be successful in England. . . . We borrowed our rates and contract forms from abroad, and with little knowledge of the principles at first, treated this business as an ordinary mercantile venture, requiring only the skill of the accountant to adjust the income and outgo of the company. . . . The actuary was almost unknown. . . . As in a bank or fire company, the cash in hand, after providing for the obligations, represented to the practical managers the surplus payments, which in true mercantile fashion should be returned as dividends.

PHILADELPHIA: CRADLE OF OUR PROFESSION IN NORTH AMERICA

Philadelphia's initial prominence in insurance was a natural consequence of its premier position in the eighteenth century as the financial, and for a time the political, capital of the United States. That city's entry into fire and marine insurance stemmed from the American Revolution when Lloyds of London ceased to be available to U.S. ships; the Insurance Company of North America, the oldest stock insurance company in the country, was formed to fill this gap. That company was briefly in life insurance when it wrote six term policies on sea captains, the first U.S. life policies. At about the same time, mutual fire insurance made its first start in Philadelphia. It was altogether natural that a respected Philadelphian and devout Quaker, Jacob Shoemaker, should launch the actuarial profession on this side of the Atlantic Ocean.

JACOB SHOEMAKER, AMERICA'S FIRST ACTUARY

The stock life insurance company, with the cumbersome name Pennsylvania Company for Insurances on Lives and Granting Annuities, that Jacob Shoemaker (1758–1822) helped to found, began operations in his home. Although it was to be dwarfed by the mutual life companies that sprang up in and after the 1840s, Shoemaker not only perceived his duties with admirable clarity but also passed on his traditions of prudence and fidelity to his four successors. Those successors, distinguished in their days, too, were:

1811–1828   Robert M. Patterson, son of Professor Robert Patterson.

1829–1835   Joseph Roberts, who died prematurely.

1835–1845   Sears C. Walker, more famous for his work in astronomy.

1845–1875   William B. Hill, also rated highly as a mathematician by the historian and early Actuarial Society member, J. A. Fowler.

In times when business panics repeatedly yielded their harvests of life company bankruptcies, the Pennsylvania Company remained a credit to its founder by faithfully discharging its liabilities until and after it ceased in 1872 to write new life insurance in favor of trust and banking activities.

Shoemaker's lasting memorial is an actuarial report (see frontispiece) that he presented to his Board of Directors in 1813. This document rests in the archives of the First Pennsylvania Bank in Philadelphia. As the following excerpts show, it was a credit to his objectives and reveals problems of a lonely actuary:

> In compliance with the orders of the Board of the 16th Instant, the Actuary has given all the attention the shortness of the time would admit to the subject referred to him and begs leave to report,

> That from the general appearance of the Public sentiment in the various conversations he has had with different persons it is likely that applications will be made to the Company for almost every species of contract contemplated in their association, but they will all come under the character of Assurances on lives, annuities, or, in the case of Survivorships, partake of both, and will be governed

by the same principles (viz.) a combination of the casualties of life with the Interest of money.

Many institutions have been formed in Europe and more especially in England for like purposes of which we have a particular account in the writings of Dr. Price, Morgan, [Francis] Baily and many others of the most eminent and accurate Mathematicians in that Country or perhaps in the World, who have so completely analyzed and reduced the subject to rule, as to leave us little more to do than to attend strictly to their instructions. They have uniformly founded their calculations on the bills of mortality kept in different places whereby the average decrement of human life has been ascertained with a sufficient degree of exactness for practice, and by common consent those in England have deduced theirs from the bills at Northampton, the propriety whereof the experience of many years has abundantly confirmed.

After outlining the data in a bill of mortality, Shoemaker continued:

On these principles the tables herewith submitted are constructed, and by comparing them with those of England the Board will be able to form a pretty correct judgment of the proportion of the mortality in the respective places, and from them and following facts and observations decide on the proper rule of their proceedings. They will no doubt remark the great difference their [*sic*] exists in the mortality at the middle ages (say from 20 to 40) between the general bills of the board of health in this City, and of those of Europe, and indeed from that formed from the records of the Society of Friends during the same period and in the same district. By the first a frightful picture indeed is exhibited of the fragility of our nature which if true in the general would shew Philadelphia instead of one of the healthiest of large cities, a gaping sepulchre not inferior to Batavia or the pestiferous settlements on the coast of Africa, and the census instead of exhibiting a population nearly doubling in 20 years, would only give a melancholy evidence of the necessity of immense immigration to prevent her utter extinction; happily however sufficient facts exist to prove that this external appearance is fallacious and that this City, as has been generally believed is as favourable to human longevity as any other town of its size.

Shoemaker went on to explain how the information in the bills can be used and to reconcile the findings with his thesis that they give no cause for alarm. Then came his summing-up, surely a fine blend of actuarial courage and caution:

If then these facts are truly stated, and the reasoning is a fair deduction from them it follows that the Company may safely govern themselves by the English tables, the rather because money may be improved at a much higher interest here than there, yet as this is quite a new attempt in this country it may be advizeable to make an addition of, say, 10PCent to their rates and if in experience the Directors should find them higher than is proper, they can make such deductions as they may judge proper and the safety of the institution will admit.

Philadelphia March 25, 1813.   (sgnd.) Jacob Shoemaker

PREMIUMS CHARGED IN EARLY DAYS

Throughout this first half-century, actuaries continued to suffer from the severe shortage of trustworthy information on insured life mortality, but matters did gradually improve.

As the American actuaries were alert to developments in England, it is likely that two major announcements from there were noticed. First, in 1825 came the news that a London actuary, Benjamin Gompertz (1779–1865), had postulated his now familiar law of mortality. Others had speculated that such a law would some day be found; Henry H. Jackson in 1932 (*T.A.S.A.* 33, 118) said that the eminent Edmond Halley had so hinted in 1693, though it is not easy to feel comfortable about this by reading Halley's paper which was reprinted in 1874 (*JIA* 18, 251).

The second news item brightened the horizon in 1843: publication of a major intercompany study, the Actuaries' Table, giving the data from seventeen companies in Great Britain. This was helpful though recognized as a risky standard; the committee had pointed out that the average duration of policies in that aggregate study was a mere eight and a half years.

The American actuaries knew that their premiums calculated from population tables were so high as to be suspect. In a report by the New York Life Insurance and Trust Company (William Bard, actuary) to the Chancellor of New York State in 1831, soon after that company had commenced business, the following words appear (*T.A.S.A.* 7, 231):

> It has been suggested that the company's tables are higher than the safety of the company requires. The subject is too important a one not to have attracted the serious attention of the trustees. If the tables are too high, it prevents insurance; upon the number of the insured depends the safety of the company. While it is few, the risk is great. It is decidedly [to] the interest, therefore, of the company to encourage insurances by making the tables as low as by any prudent calculation they can be made. The tables by which the company have been governed in their insurances, are the same with those which have been used for fifteen years in Boston and Philadelphia, and for one hundred years by the Equitable in London. The insurance of lives was a subject new to the trustees as well as to the State, and in the commencement of their operations they were unwilling to vary from what the experience of others deemed prudent in fixing the rate of insurance. Having been informed that the Philadelphia company proposed to lower their rates, the president of this company has had a correspondence with the actuary of the Philadelphia office on the subject of the rates which it would be prudent to adopt in this country. He has also received from the actuary of one of the offices in Paris, his manuscript calculations and observations on the rates used there.
>
> The trustees only wait the fulfillment of the promise of Mr. Roberts, the actuary in Philadelphia, to forward to them his views and corrected tables, to decide on the proper alteration in their own, if prudent to make any. The whole subject is at present under the consideration of the board.

The company in Boston was certainly the Massachusetts Hospital Life Insurance Company (Nathaniel Bowditch, actuary), whose 1823 rate book has recently been

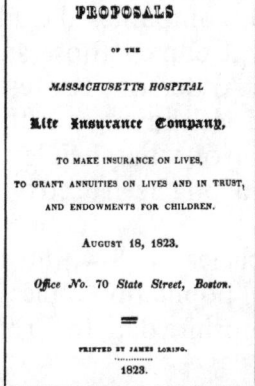

INSURANCE ON LIVES.

TABLE
Of the rates of insurance of one hundred dollars on a single life.

Ages	1 year.	7 years	For life	Ages	1 year	7 years	For life
				36	$2.03	$2.18	$3.37
10				37	2.07	2.24	3.45
to				38	2.12	2.30	3.54
14	$0.98	$1.18	$2.07	39	2.15	2.35	3.64
15	0.99	1.25	2.12	40	2.23	2.43	3.74
16	1.06	1.35	2.18	41	2.31	2.50	3.84
17	1.16	1.43	2.24	42	2.39	2.56	3.94
18	1.27	1.51	2.29	43	2.45	2.63	4.05
19	1.37	1.56	2.35	44	2.50	2.71	4.17
20	1.50	1.62	2.39	45	2.56	2.79	4.29
21	1.59	1.66	2.45	46	2.62	2.89	4.41
22	1.61	1.68	2.49	47	2.69	2.99	4.54
23	1.63	1.70	2.54	48	2.76	3.10	4.68
24	1.65	1.73	2.59	49	2.87	3.21	4.83
25	1.68	1.77	2.64	50	3.03	3.34	4.99
26	1.71	1.79	2.70	51	3.15	3.45	5.14
27	1.73	1.83	2.76	52	3.24	3.56	5.30
28	1.77	1.86	2.81	53	3.35	3.68	5.48
29	1.80	1.89	2.87	54	3.46	3.82	5.66
30	1.82	1.92	2.93	55	3.57	3.96	5.85
31	1.85	1.96	3.00	56	3.69	4.11	6.05
32	1.89	1.99	3.06	57	3.83	4.26	6.27
33	1.92	2.02	3.14	58	3.97	4.43	6.50
34	1.95	2.07	3.21	59	4.13	4.62	6.75
35	2.00	2.13	3.29	60	4.29	4.80	7.00

From this table it appears, that a person aged 31 years, by paying to the Company $1.85 may secure to his heirs one hundred dollars, if he should die within one year. This insurance may be renewed on the follow-
2

Massachusetts actuary Nathaniel Bowditch (Courtesy of the Peabody Museum of Salem, Mass.) and two pages from his 1823 rate book.

donated to the archives of the Society of Actuaries; the Philadelphia company was the Pennsylvania Company for Insurances on Lives and Granting Annuities (Joseph Roberts, actuary). An account of Bowditch by Dwight K. Bartlett III (*The Actuary,* June 1979) confirms that Bowditch's company and the Pennsylvania Company were using identical rates calculated on a variation of the Northampton Table. It tells us that Bowditch visited Philadelphia and, incidentally, was displeased by the relaxed habits of that company's actuary (probably Eugenius Nulty) who, in Bowditch's words, "attends daily from 9 to 2 at the office and then it is shut up."

In a 1911 paper (*T.A.S.A.* 12, 253), Solomon A. Joffe gave his analysis of these early premiums. He found that the rates that Bowditch calculated for Massachusetts Hospital Life, which Bard briefly adopted for New York Life and Trust, were those of the Northampton Table with 3% interest, loaded 10%. In April 1832, Bard's company adopted rates, for ages up to 55, calculated by the Carlisle Table at 4% interest, loaded 35%. Above age 55, the premiums previously in effect remained unchanged, producing, as Charles Gill pointed out twenty years later, something less than a neat junction.

Whether Bard's new rates were the same as those he had told New York State were under negotiation with the Pennsylvania Company is not known. It is likely that both companies adopted them and that most other U.S. companies did likewise; when Mutual Life of New York began business in 1843, it copied those same rates and continued to use them until 1853. Dr. Henry James Anderson, Professor of Mathematics at Columbia College in New York, was credited with having calculated these new rates, but it is not likely that he made the major decision on what their level ought to be; their merit was that they were close to the rates that had long been used by the Equitable of London.

New England Mutual, when it began issuing policies in 1844, did not follow the crowd; its premiums were based on a blend of several population tables, one of which had been compiled from Massachusetts and New Hampshire data by Professor Edward Wigglesworth of Harvard in 1789.

BALANCE SHEETS. SURPLUS DISTRIBUTION. THE NOTE SYSTEM.

If the two companies formed by religious orders—the Presbyterian Ministers Fund and the Episcopal Corporation—are left out of account, there were no mutual companies in North America until Mutual Life of New York and New England Mutual began business in the 1840s. There was no serious government supervision until the Massachusetts statute of 1858. Yet, financial statements were needed for internal information and soon for determining distributable surplus. So, the question of what liability should properly be declared for future death claims on in-force policies quickly arose.

In his encyclopedic 1939 paper (*R.A.I.A.* 28, 269), Clinton O. Shepherd quotes historian Charles K. Knight as saying:

> Prior to [1858] the principle of gross [premium] valuation, based for the most part on the Carlisle table and four per cent, appears to have been the basis, both in this country and in England. A few of our companies, however, reported reserves calculated on the net premium basis, and all of the better managed ones made some allowance for future expenses. . . . But beyond all doubt, all of them would have insisted, had it been necessary, that they could meet future liabilities on policies if their reserves plus the present value of future gross premiums due equalled the present value of outstanding insurances.

This last sentence meant that every actuary would assert to the adequacy of a policy reserve equal to the present value of the benefit calculated on the valuation table reduced by the value of 100% of future gross premiums on that same table, using the valuation interest rate. This seems absurd on the face of it, but the absence of any provision for future expenses was perhaps supportable in an era when expenses were relatively low, at least in established companies, and even more important, when no surrender values were guaranteed.

The premiums charged by the stock life companies were identical with those of the mutual companies—a fact which the public soon began to recognize as unreasonable. Only the Girard Life Insurance, Annuity and Trust Company of Philadelphia, founded in 1836 as a stock company but with a promise that its policyholders would share in its earnings, was free of this criticism. In fact, Girard Life's actuary, John F. James (1802–1871), in 1844 made a surplus distribution to policyholders before any mutual company did. The system he used was the British system, a uniform percentage bonus addition to the amount insured.

The majority of the companies, both stock and mutual, soon introduced a system of anticipating that some part of the contract premium might never be needed, by following the lead of New England Mutual in accepting some specified part of each premium in the form of an interest-bearing note—in effect, a form of policy loan although on a policy devoid of any guaranteed cash value.

It can be conceded that, used with restraint, such a system would have been practical. But the idea got out of hand. One company, for instance, is said to have accepted notes to the extent of one-half of each premium, anticipating that, by the time the fifth and later premiums became due, one note at a time could be repaid out of emerging profit and that the four notes always remaining would be cancelled at death via a post-mortem dividend. The plan broke down when profits were found insufficient to accomplish all this. In other companies, the premium notes became an inordinate part of the assets in their balance sheets, leading to bankruptcy especially during the financial panics and depressions that occurred several times in that century.

From this note system eventually emerged the annual dividend system which was made mandatory by the New York legislature in the aftermath of the 1905 Armstrong Investigation (discussed in Chapter III).

TWO EXCEPTIONAL ACTUARIES: WRIGHT AND GILL

Actuarial practice for many years, even up to the present, has been materially influenced by two diverse men of extraordinary character and ability who entered our profession in the 1840s: Elizur Wright in 1844 and Charles Gill in 1849.

Elizur Wright (1804–1885) made his name as a reformer—fighting first to abolish slavery, and then to make Massachusetts a leader in life insurance regulation.

His first life insurance connections were with Massachusetts Hospital Life and New England Mutual. From the latter company he managed to secure an agency contract containing a provision of his own design that demonstrates his remarkable imagination and his grasp of actuarial principles. Wright, himself an ardent temperance worker, realized two things: (1) that even though life companies were not knowingly insuring immoderate drinkers, the temperate policyholders in a mutual company must in the long run pay for the premature deaths among those whose intemperance had escaped notice or had developed after their policies had been issued, and yet (2) that the actuaries had no data from which to determine what premium rates would be appropriate for the genuinely temperate. His solution was to enter into an agreement with New England Mutual under which policies would be issued at regular rates. But the genuinely temperate would, in return for accepting a policy endorsement voiding their insurance if they ever used liquor as a beverage, be promised that if within four years from September 1845 a majority of them should elect to form a distinct company, New England Mutual would pay into that new company's coffers the excess of all premiums already paid over the cost of term insurance for the elapsed period.

In his printed brochure entitled "Total Abstinence Life Insurance," Wright predicted that when the time came New England Mutual would be found willing to

TOTAL ABSTINENCE LIFE INSURANCE.

SIR: Your attention is respectfully invited to the following remarks, the subject of which may be of interest to some of your friends, if not to yourself.

To a large portion of our fellow-citizens an adequate provision for a dependent family is an object yet to be attained, and one which causes no small anxiety. To procure food, clothing, and shelter for the present, while the husband and father's life is spared, is not so difficult. But what will become of the widow and fatherless if he should suddenly be removed, the victim of disease, or one of a hundred common accidents? Christian charity, we may trust, will not let them starve; but will it not let them suffer? Will the dying man commit his wife and little ones to Christian charity, with the most comfortable feelings, if he has not made all the provision for them which lay in his power? Is it undervaluing Christian charity to inculcate prudence and forethought? Would not the world be all the better, if each father, in regard to his own offspring, should follow out somewhat the aspiration, —

"Thy spirit, Independence, let me share,
Lord of the lion heart and eagle eye!"

It is one of the many important aspects of Life Insurance, that it puts it in the power of every man, in the receipt of a tolerable income or salary from his labor, to be independent, not only in regard to the present, but the future maintenance of his family. The saving of even half such a salary in a bank would not for many years meet the case. The man may die to-morrow, and leave no more than enough to settle for his funeral. Mutual Life Insurance effects the object at once. The moment the contract is sealed, by the payment of the first premium, the insurer has a little fortune secured in case of his death, no matter how soon it may occur. This is the happiest solution of a difficult problem in social life which civilization has ever presented. It secures the benefit of the associative or gregarious principle, on the one hand, without trenching upon the equally important principle of personal independence on the other.

The undersigned, having studied this subject attentively, and witnessed the happy, tranquillizing, and care-killing effect of Life Insurance upon English society, has been deeply impressed with the importance of having it more generally practised in our own country, where capital is less accumulated, and a larger proportion of families are dependent upon the productive energy of the father. It has appeared to him especially important, that it should become prevalent in its best form. The mutual plan is obviously preferable to that of insurance by stock companies; for, as safety cannot be attained without exacting premiums considerably beyond what would be sufficient to provide for the average mortality, the holders of the stock must evidently be, in general, winners in an operation which too much resembles gambling. On the mutual plan, this surplus is, from time to time, divided equitably among the insured; or rather, the share belonging to each is returned to him. But there is still this important defect in the mutual plan, as ordinarily practised. No provision is made against the voluntary abuse of health which insurance is effected. A policy will generally be made void by a suicide, according to the finding of a coroner's jury; but not by a suicidal neglect of the means of preserving health, or indulgence in alcoholic poisons. In regard to intemperance, in a community like this, it cannot fail to be seen, that pledged and thorough teetotallers must thus insure to a disadvantage in the long run. Suppose a mutual company to be composed of one half pledged, and one half unpledged men. They are all temperate, in the usual acceptation of the word, at first, for no prudent company will think of insuring immoderate drinkers. But in the usual course of things, a certain portion of the unpledged men (the reader may judge for himself how great) will, in twenty or thirty years, become intemperate, and shorten their lives thereby. The company loses all the premiums they would have paid had they attained their due age, and the compound interests upon them and the previous payments; and this loss falls mostly upon the pledged men, because they are alive to bear it.

The true mode of escaping this evil, is not to lower the rates for pledged men, or men insuring on condition of total abstinence, because there are no data from which to determine the real value of abstinence to life. But when a company, or a class, insure each other on this condition at the usual rates, the common fund being subject to no reduction by loss from the use of alcohol, the surplus will all come back to the insured in the shape of a reduction of premium, and they will at last enjoy the precise value of their total abstinence. The favorable reflex influence of such a plan upon the temperance cause, temperance men will not fail to appreciate. Every premium that is paid will increase the motive for strict adherence to the pledge. A policy on this condition will be a sort of diploma, more truly significant than those given by some literary bodies, testifying to the reality and sincerity of the holder's temperance professions. If he is accused of drinking, he may reply, "Prove it, and destroy my policy." A company on this plan has been in operation for five years in London, with happy results.

In order to make practical this improvement in Life Insurance, without unnecessary delay, the undersigned has effected the following

Arrangement with the New England Mutual Life Insurance Company.

That company will, when desired, issue for satisfactory lives, at their usual rates, policies containing the following clauses:—

"On condition that if the said ———— shall, at any time, use any intoxicating liquor as a beverage, this policy shall be void."

"———— upon the understanding and agreement, that whenever a majority of the persons insured by this company, upon the above condition of abstaining from the use of intoxicating liquors, shall, within four years from the 1st of September, 1845, express to the directors of this company, their election to withdraw as a new distinct company, such new company being ready to take all persons insured by this company upon such condition for the remaining term of their respective policies, at the same rate of premium, this policy shall, if said ———— or this company so elects, before or at the time for the payment of the then next premium, be surrendered and cancelled, and the excess of premium which shall have been paid on the policy, over what would have been paid on a policy for the period during which this policy shall have existed, shall be paid over to such new company."

This arrangement may possibly lead to an addition to the charter of the New England Company, conferring power to establish distinct classes for those insuring on distinct conditions, so that each class will pay its own losses and divide its own surplus, and the establishment of such distinct class for those insuring on the condition above cited. Such a class may be found to have some advantages over a distinct company.

1. The New England Company is already established on safe and sound principles, with an adequate guaranty capital, and the share of incidental expenses to each of the insured will be much less.

2. Two classes, — one pledged and the other not, — going on for a number of years, or generations, under the same board of direction, and subject to the same incidental expenses, will more accurately illustrate the value of total abstinence in its application to Life Insurance; — a consideration of great national importance.

But whether there shall be a willingness on the part of the New England Company to form such a class, or not, according to this arrangement the total abstinence insurers will have the power, whenever, within the specified time, they judge themselves sufficiently strong, to organize a distinct company, which will in this way be got up with the least expense, and with the advantage of insuring those who are ready to compose it, without a single moment's delay.

A company preferable to the New England does not, at present, exist within our reach. Insurance in it, in any way, is an excellent thing. Insurance in it under this arrangement gives a strong probability of something still better. The hearty support of the friends of temperance is confidently looked for, in a movement which tends to anchor that cause, and make it fast to one of the most permanent and beneficent moneyed institutions of civilized society. Let a thousand teetotallers at once come forward, and insure their lives for such sums as they can afford to pay the annual premium of, and they will truly form a standing army for total abstinence, whose loyalty to the principle can no more be called in question than that of the old National Guard to Napoleon. If the New England Company should not, then, show a disposition to procure the requisite authority, and form a total abstinence class, they may immediately step forward and procure a distinct charter for themselves, and have ample funds to commence insurance on their own basis.

The proposition now thrown out to the temperance public reflects great credit upon the liberality of the New England Company, and shows a disposition to aid the temperance cause which ought to secure the cordial cooperation of its special friends. The cost and labor of getting up a new company are very heavy. A guaranty capital must be looked up, for which interest must be paid while the company is weak; offices and officers are to be hired, and all the apparatus of a full-grown company, for a mere handful of insurers. This will inevitably exhaust the whole surplusage of premium, and perhaps more, for a few of the first years; and during that time the success of the company is problematical. By the plan of engrafting at once upon a sound stock, with the power of colonization when full grown, nothing can be lost in any case, and much may be gained.

Organization of the New England Mutual Life Insurance Company.

The subscribed guaranty fund, all of which is liable for the losses of the company, is $100,000, half of which is actually paid in. The company takes no premium notes, and its funds are carefully invested in the best cash securities. The following are the officers of the company:—

President — Hon. WILLARD PHILLIPS.

Directors — Robert Hooper, William Parsons, Charles P. Curtis, Francis C. Lowell, George H. Kuhn, William W. Stone, Robert B. Forbes, Peter Wainwright, Thomas A. Dexter, James Read, Otis Tufts.

Secretary — Jonathan Amory.

First page of Elizur Wright's 1845 brochure soliciting applications for "Total Abstinence Life Insurance" and also describing in detail the procedure for calculating the annual premium for $100 of whole life insurance at age 30. (Courtesy of Robert Hohertz, St. Louis, Mo.)

establish those temperate policyholders into a distinct class, making withdrawal to a new company unnecessary. This ingenious plan never came to fruition, and regrettably no record of the number who accepted the temperance endorsement has survived. The earliest American mortality study on total abstainers seems to be that given in 1895 by Emory McClintock (*T.A.S.A.* 4, 9).

Wright seems to have been, in 1844, the first American actuary to make a trip to England in search of life insurance knowledge, a visit which materially affected his subsequent objectives in improvement of company treatment of withdrawing policyholders.

Charles Gill (1805–1855) was an actuary for only six and a half years, immediately before his untimely death at age fifty. He had come to the United States from England in 1831 to continue his career in teaching, and to become a noted editor of an abstruse periodical, *Mathematical Miscellany*. In April 1849, Mutual Benefit Life Insurance Company appointed him its mathematician, but he soon moved across the Hudson River to answer the acutely felt need of the Mutual Life of New York for guidance in surplus ascertainment and distribution, mortality studies and premium revision. Mutual Life was just then establishing its position as the country's leading life insurance company, which it maintained for the next forty years. For some time Gill seems to have been employed by both the Mutual Life and the Mutual Benefit.

The only four-part paper ever printed in *T.A.S.A.* was Emory McClintock's "Charles Gill; The First Actuary in America," presented in the spring and fall of both 1913 and 1914. Possibly in deference to McClintock's seniority, that paper was received without discussion; otherwise a member, appropriately one from Philadelphia, might have gently suggested that "The First *Mutual Company* Actuary in America" would have been more accurate.

Gill's accomplishments were fruitful and wide-ranging despite his lack of previous actuarial experience.

In 1851 he presented to his Board a report on the company's mortality experience during its first eight years of existence. His whole report, printed in the final segment of McClintock's paper (*T.A.S.A.* 15, 258), is of historical interest as the first such investigation made on this continent; only the summary of results by numbers of policies is shown in Table I.2. The ratios of actual to expected deaths were not displayed in the original; they have been calculated for readers' convenience.

Gill was well aware that no more than tentative conclusions could be drawn from such small exposures. He not unnaturally described the experience on California risks as "startling," pointing out that lives whose average age was twenty-eight had experienced mortality applicable to seventy-year-olds. The Trustees had already discontinued selling policies in California; Gill congratulated them on their prudence.

In May 1851, the Board instructed Gill to make a trip to England to confer with the appropriate life company officers and to procure such books as he might deem necessary. The maximum expense authorized was $1,000, but Gill submitted a bill for only $483, $63 of which was for books. McClintock mentioned that Gill's trip happily coincided with the Great Exhibition at London's Crystal Palace, built for that event, remarking that Gill was the man to take full advantage of so golden an opportunity.

Table I.2

**MORTALITY EXPERIENCE OF MUTUAL LIFE,
FEBRUARY 1843 TO FEBRUARY 1851 BY NUMBERS OF POLICIES.
EXPECTED DEATHS BY CARLISLE MORTALITY TABLE.**

		Actual Deaths	Expected Deaths	Percent Actual/ Expected
I.	Eastern & "Middle States"	111	146.738	75.6%
II.	West of "Middle States" and North of the Southern Line of Virginia & Kentucky	30	30.103	99.7
III.	South of II but North of 32nd Parallel*	12	12.015	99.9
IV.	South of 32nd Parallel*	13	10.936	118.9
V.	California	26	4.744	548.1
	General Experience (which evidently included a small exposure not in I – V)	198	207.297	95.5

*Mutual Life was charging modest extra premiums to residents of Areas III and IV—one-quarter of 1% in Area III, one-half of 1% in Area IV.

One gratifying consequence was a December 1851 letter from the Institute of Actuaries announcing Gill's election as a Corresponding Member, the highest honor then available to an actuary outside the British Empire.

In June 1851, Gill submitted to the Institute a letter, "On The Determination of Surplus," which the editor of *JIA* printed, describing the procedure as "highly ingenious" though a bit complicated for British tastes. This letter, explaining how Gill arrived at the total surplus available for distribution as dividends, is reprinted in *T.A.S.A.* 15, 265.

In 1852, Gill seems to have been working with other New York actuaries, one being the actuary of United States Life, Nicholas De Groot, on proposals for improving methods used by companies in policy valuations. In that same year, Elizur Wright described the prevailing state of affairs thus:

> By some companies in this country, policies are carefully estimated and balanced against matured liabilities, yearly; by others, there is reason to believe, that liabilities have been rudely and lumpingly guessed at; and by others still, it is probable, that no such estimate has been made or attempted in one way or another. In this state of things, it is not without good reason that several state legislatures have interested themselves to guard their constituents against the mismanagement of life insurance companies.

This remark of Wright's was approvingly quoted in the *Transactions* of the First International Congress in 1895 (p. 376) in a report by the distinguished Actuarial Society charter member, Howell W. St. John.

In 1853, Gill wrote a follow-up mortality report embracing two more years of the company's experience. This time he compared the results with a mortality table of his own devising, consisting of a blend of British population and insured life data. That table he then used to compile a new premium scale which Mutual Life used for the next fifteen years until Gill's successor, Sheppard Homans, made another change using the later famous American Experience Table. Solomon A. Joffe in 1912 (*T.A.S.A.* 13, 80) gave a thorough analysis of Gill's historically important mortality table.

In 1854, the company increased its extra premiums for residents of the Gulf States (Area IV of Table I.2) to 5% of the basic premium, as a result of Gill's studies and recommendation.

Gill's completely unexpected death in October 1855 was recognized as an immense loss to the company, and indeed to the community and our profession. McClintock, remarking correctly that the longevity of Actuarial Society members had since shown it to be "hard to kill off an actuary," speculated on whether a contributing cause of Gill's death might have been his unpleasant relationship with the company's irascible president, Frederick S. Winston, a problem that also afflicted Homans a dozen years later. McClintock, expressing his conviction that Gill had "genius as distinguished from talent," concluded with these words: "He might have been a poet, but was merely a mathematician."

The Institute of Actuaries paid a remarkable tribute to Gill's character and accomplishments by reprinting in full (*JIA* 6, 216) a sketch of his life that had appeared in the *United States Assurance Gazette*.

PIONEER CONSULTING ACTUARIES: ENTZ AND ELLIOTT

The term *consulting actuary* came into use well before 1858, but those to whom it was applied were often moonlighting actuaries of established companies or college professors. Two genuine harbingers of the modern consulting actuarial fraternity, however, began practicing before 1858.

The first was John F. Entz (1798–1872) who had come from Switzerland to the United States as a boy and, in 1840, had opened an office as an accountant in New York City. Quickly his activities broadened into the actuarial field, and he took the trouble to become knowledgeable on European as well as American literature and practices.

Entz was a prolific writer of incisive articles in the insurance press, which although frequently critical of prevailing practices seem to have been well received by the life insurance establishment. His 1847 essay reporting enthusiastically on French and German tontine plans concluded with the words, "With some improvements, these plans ought to be imitated in this country, being, in my opinion, based upon sound and benevolent principles." This may have helped to influence the Equitable Life of New York to enter the tontine field in 1867.

The other consulting actuary of this period, Ezekiel B. Elliott (1823–1888), opened an office in Boston in 1849, announcing himself as the peculiar mix "actuary and electrician." In the 1850s he was consulting actuary to some Boston life companies and to the State of Massachusetts where he doubtless became acquainted with Elizur Wright. Elliott established his reputation as an authority in the field of vital statistics; years later (see Robert J. Myers' paper *TSA* 6, 488), he became the first United States Government Actuary, berthed in Washington, D.C.

THE FIRST CANADIANS: BAKER AND CHERRIMAN

Hugh C. Baker (1818–1859), who organized Canada Life Assurance Company on his own initiative in 1847, is acknowledged as the founder of Canadian life insurance, and Canada's first actuary. Thomas B. Macaulay, a charter member of the Actuarial Society, writing in 1900 (*T.A.S.A.* 6, 400) described Baker as possessed of sound judgment and good education, by no means a mere man of affairs (Baker had been a banker in Hamilton, Ontario) but one who made it his duty to understand the mathematical principles on which the success of his company depended.

Facts about Baker's initial decisions on premiums and policy provisions are lacking, but it is known that this stock life company had the benefit of strong backing from leading Ontario businessmen. Its volume of business was small, and it faced virtually no competition until after Baker's death in 1859 when Alexander G. Ramsay was recruited from Glasgow to succeed him.

In 1852, Baker became North America's first Fellow of the Institute of Actuaries.

John B. Cherriman (1823–1908) came to the University of Toronto from England in 1850 and by 1853 had been awarded the professorship of mathematics and philosophy. He was interested in life insurance mathematics and doubtless communicated that subject to his students. In 1871 he was appointed actuary of the newly organized Confederation Life Association in Toronto. In 1875 he accepted federal appointment as Canada's first Superintendent of Insurance and, in that same year, was elected a Fellow of the Institute of Actuaries (see Kenneth R. MacGregor's discussion, *TSA* 6, 501). His term as Superintendent lasted until 1885, whereupon he retired and returned to England.

FORMATION OF THE INSTITUTE OF ACTUARIES

The establishment of the Institute of Actuaries in London in 1848 was a development of immense value and stimulus to the profession in North America. The earliest direct effect was through the Institute's *Journal* (for a while called also the *Assurance Magazine*); not only did this give North American actuaries easy access to British developments, but also the *Journal's* columns were from the outset cordially receptive to papers and reports of professional activities from this continent. The Institute premises, especially after moving to Staple Inn Hall, were a mecca for Canadian and U.S. actuaries.

The same, though necessarily to a lesser extent, applies to the premises and (much later) the *Transactions* of the Faculty of Actuaries after the Scottish members of the Institute formed their own body in Edinburgh in 1856.

Our profession across the Atlantic was in its early days plagued with dissension within its own ranks and embarrassed by instability of many of its insurance companies, but its beneficial impact upon actuaries in North America was immediate and profound.

OUR PROFESSION IN 1858

At the close of this first half-century of our history, the number of practicing actuaries on this continent remained scattered and minuscule. Twenty-eight reasonably well-established life companies were functioning, one of these in Canada. The total roster of actuaries did not exceed a score.

The center of actuarial practice and thought had moved from Philadelphia to the New York/New Jersey area. But the time when actuaries would hold positions of major authority in their companies had not yet arrived.

Unfortunately, the voices of Bard, Tuckett, and Gill, any one of whom might have served as our profession's Hippocrates instructing actuaries in their responsibilities to the public, had been prematurely stilled by death. Large problems, with which the rising generation would be unable to cope, lay just ahead. Failure to solve them was to lead to vast expansion of assessment insurance, many life company failures, and eventually, restrictive legislation. It is noteworthy that Canada was relatively free of the mistakes that plagued the life companies in the United States. One saving grace perhaps was that Canadians did not consider it politically necessary to have a completely separate supervisory mechanism in each one of their provinces.

Chapter II.

1859–1888: STEPS TOWARDS A PROFESSIONAL BODY

Behold, how good and how pleasant it is for brethren to dwell together in unity!

—*Psalm 133: 1*

COMMUNICATION AMONG ACTUARIES

We have seen that in 1823, Boston actuary Nathaniel Bowditch visited actuary Joseph Roberts at the Pennsylvania Company; in 1831, New York actuary William Bard corresponded with Roberts. Elizur Wright visited actuaries in England in 1844, and Charles Gill did so in 1851. Communication between actuaries in person and by letter must have steadily increased as the insurance magazines and newspapers came into being and welcomed articles on actuarial subjects, even many that extensively employed algebraic and commutation symbols.

Papers by North American actuaries in the *Journal of the Institute of Actuaries*, listed in the appendix to this chapter, must also have generated letters to those authors.

An amusing example is a set of a dozen letters to Emory McClintock, handwritten by Elizur Wright on his personal letterhead identifying him as a consulting actuary at 39 State Street in Boston. All twelve have survived, presumably in McClintock's personal papers, and were entrusted by Walter Klem to the archives at John Hancock Mutual.

At the time, Wright was past his sixty-fifth birthday with a quarter-century of his insurance career behind him, while McClintock, at age twenty-eight, was less than two years into his actuarial career and was, moreover, associated with an extremely small life company. The text of the opening letter follows:

Boston, March 2, 1869

Emory McClintock Esq.

Act., Asbury Life Ins. Co.

Dear Sir,

Taking for granted you are the writer of the article signed E.M. on the 125th page of the Ins. Times of Feb. I hasten to thank you not only for showing how I missed some figures, and might have made my proofs less awkward, but for your ready appreciation of the principle I was driving at, in my remarks on surrender values. Having to write in haste, if at all, and thinking more of the end

17

than the means, I probably made more than one mistake in the figures, but your method is so much simpler that it will save me the trouble of correcting. If I had only been bright enough, I should have seen how transforming [algebraic into commutation symbols] would give me a table of two factors, that is, *yours,*—but I am rather glad I wasn't.

I admire both the ingenuity and industry displayed in your table on page 111. Being myself on the steepish part of the life-curve, when I see such coadjutors coming in, I feel something like old Simeon in the Temple.

With much respect,

Yours truly

[Signed] Elizur Wright

To receive such words from a famous and embattled actuary thirty-five years his senior must have been gratifying to McClintock.

In 1859, not many could have been seriously considering forming an organization along the lines of the then eleven-year-old Institute of Actuaries, but as Actuarial Society President Oscar B. Ireland remarked at that body's May 1903 meeting (*T.A.S.A.* 7, 460), some "had visions of some such an organization." He quoted from a letter written to trade paper editor Gilbert E. Currie by Elizur Wright:

I am too little acquainted with American actuaries to know whether or not they are ready to associate for mutual improvement, or what benefit is to be expected of such an association, if formed. One thing, however, is quite plain to me, that thought and labor are still required to bring to perfection the science and the methods of Insurance, and to make its benefits, as well as its difficulties and dangers, more generally understood. ... As deserts are more comfortably crossed by caravans than by solitary pilgrims, so the dry wearisomeness of the almost illimitable statistics required to perfect the business of Insurance may be relieved by sound co-operation. If an association can be formed on so broad a basis as to be free from the sway and the suspicion of private and personal interests, I shall be inclined to hope much good of it, and shall feel very proud if I can contribute, in any way, to promote its grand object.

The man who wrote these words must have been distressed if he ever knew, or guessed, that he himself was later to be regarded as a reason for postponing, rather than proceeding with, building the "caravan" of his striking illustration.

It should be recognized, however, that in 1859 it was the exception rather than the rule for members of a profession in the United States to band together. The American Medical Association had been organized in 1847, but the American Bar Association was not formed from state bodies until 1878, and the first professional body in the accounting field came on the scene in 1887.

1859. THE FIRST AMERICAN "LIFE UNDERWRITERS' CONVENTION"

An assembly in New York City of life company officials, many of whom were actuaries, on May 25–26, 1859, may reasonably be considered the forerunner of all insurance gatherings on this continent. Much of the work it proposed to undertake was either directly actuarial or of prime interest to actuaries. The editor of the *Journal of the Institute of Actuaries*, Charles Jellicoe, hailed it as an event of importance, reported its activities in *JIA* 8, 268, and hinted that the actuaries might thereby make a large addition to the international stock of actuarial knowledge.

One of its committees announced plans for an intercompany mortality study which, not surprisingly since Sheppard Homans was one of its three members, bore a striking resemblance to Charles Gill's studies described in Chapter I.

The assembly also recommended studies of premiums for substandard risks, lapsed policies, and interest rate trends.

One of the actuaries present, Lieutenant Lewis Merrill of Penn Mutual Life, presented his views on war mortality, predicting rashly (as was very soon demonstrated by the grim experience in the U.S. Civil War) that rating up the age by one or two years would meet the increased risk of death from wounds in battle.

The Convention adjourned with high resolves and expectations but after reassembling just once more in the following year abandoned this first attempt at cooperative data gathering.

1859. ELIZUR WRIGHT'S FIRST MAJOR REFORM—POLICY VALUATIONS

On the closing day of the 1858 Massachusetts legislative session, Elizur Wright finally succeeded in getting a law passed requiring the Commissioner of Insurance to calculate the reserves on all the policies of all the licensed companies. In 1859 Wright himself was appointed one of the state's two commissioners charged with accomplishing this new law's purpose. The decisions on what method and what mortality table and interest rate would be used were left to the Commissioners' discretion; Wright selected the net level premium method (a controversial decision of immense importance in actuarial history) using the Combined Experience (an 1843 British) Table with 4% interest. The role of the companies was simply to furnish the data; the insurance department had to calculate the reserves, a task that had been said to be prohibitively onerous for just a single company, let alone for the policies of all domestic and out-of-state companies. But Wright had invented an "Arithmeter" (pronounced consistently with the word *arithmetic*) to ease the work of calculation and did not shrink from drafting several of his many children to assist him.

Wright always insisted that, contrary to the view widely imputed to him, he did not regard the aggregate reserve by the net level premium method as a necessary test of company solvency. At the first convention of state insurance commissioners in New York City, May 1871, he expressed himself thus (*Proceedings,* p. 45):

> The valuation established by law, in Massachusetts, in 1858, the net valuation, has been considered by the public at large, and by a great many insurance men, as applied as a test of solvency of the company. That was not the intention of those who framed the law and applied this valuation. . . . The question which [the valuation] seeks [to] answer is not that of solvency in the sense of the market. It is rather whether the condition of solvency at present existing will continue until every pending contract is settled.

Clinton O. Shepherd in his 1939 paper (*R.A.I.A.* 28, 281) quoted Wright, more vehemently, on the same point. It may reasonably be said that Wright's test was considered by him to be of the "early warning" variety. He required, however, that a company failing his test should discontinue issuing policies in Massachusetts until the deficiency had disappeared, which any affected company naturally considered a penalty almost as severe as a declaration of bankruptcy.

Elizur Wright in his latter days as a consulting actuary.
(Courtesy of Christopher Wright, Washington, D.C.)

Wright promptly provoked an international actuarial controversy by demanding that an English company, the International Life Assurance Society, cease writing business in Massachusetts because of its inability to meet his standard; the Insurance Superintendent of New York, William Barnes, in his First (1860) Annual Report made the identical ruling for that state. The International's two actuaries, one of them the eminent W. S. B. Woolhouse, challenged this decision, enrolling the famous Harvard mathematician Professor Benjamin Peirce in support of their variant of a gross premium valuation. Wright, supported by Sheppard Homans, Nicholas De Groot (actuary of United States Life and son of a London actuary) and others, stuck to his guns. Later, International Life justified Wright's decision by becoming a financial casualty.

Although not an ideal example of the point at issue, because the offending company's valuation offset 100% of the value of future gross premiums (making no allowance for renewal expense) against the present value of the death benefit, this controversy was progenitor of outpourings of actuarial literature on both sides of the Atlantic on the relative merits of net and gross premium statutory valuations, and also of level premium versus modified preliminary term valuations. In considering the degree to which Elizur Wright bears responsibility for the dominance of the net level premium system in North America today, it should be remembered that Wright's political power existed only a few years and in but a single state. There was plenty of opportunity for the growing actuarial profession to influence change if it held, as the great British actuary Thomas B. Sprague did in 1870 (*JIA* 15, 411), that "the net-premium method of valuation is open to very serious objections."

A VOICE FROM GEORGIA

Although the centers of actuarial activity in the early and middle nineteenth century were, in succession, Philadelphia, Boston, and New York, in one respect all of these met their match in the work of a resident of the town of Athens, Georgia. An actuary in that remote outpost—Professor Charles F. McCay—undertook, with remarkable success, to enlighten the insurance business in general, and the Georgia legislature in particular, about the fundamentals of life company financial condition.

McCay started modestly in 1848 with an article in *The Merchants' Magazine and Commercial Review* entitled "Life Insurance With Reference to Premiums, etc., of Life Insurance Companies." He followed in 1850 with a piece in the same trade paper, "The Mortality of Baltimore: With Reference to the Principles of Life Insurance." Then in 1856 he presented a paper, "On the Laws of Human Mortality," to the American Association for the Advancement of Science. And he made himself well and favorably known in British as well as American actuarial circles in 1860–1861 with a ten-part series in the same *Merchants' Magazine,* entitled "Valuation of Life Insurance Policies," beginning with a clear description of the Massachusetts controversy over the International Life's condition, and continuing with essays on mortality rates, interest rates, and expense assumptions suitable for life company premiums and reserves.

McCay's life story is set forth in a 1983 biography by William Porter Kellam, *Episodes in the Life of Charles F. McCay—Academic, Actuary, Author and Businessman*, a copy of which is in the Society of Actuaries library, as is also a set of copies obtained from Mr. Kellam of McCay's published articles on actuarial subjects. In 1864, Professor McCay moved to Baltimore where he became the first actuary of the Maryland Insurance Department and continued his writings. His death, at age 79, was in 1889, a few weeks before the Actuarial Society of America came into being.

Legislative campaigns pursued in Georgia during McCay's residency there testify to his admiration for what Elizur Wright had accomplished in Massachusetts. Biographer Kellam relates (p. 58) that McCay campaigned successfully to achieve passage of a state law setting insurance company solvency standards, but failed to prevent that law from being repealed at the very next session, and failed also to accomplish his own appointment as insurance commissioner. He did have the satisfaction, within less than five years, of seeing a bill containing some of his proposals enacted in March 1864.

Kellam also tells us (p. 72) that McCay applied the example set by the Presbyterian Ministers Fund in Philadelphia to the needs of Southern clergy:

> In 1870, he recommended to the General Assembly of the [Presbyterian] Church that a relief fund be established for ministers of the Presbyterian Church, South, which would in case of their illness or death provide help to their families. . . . [This] was founded on January 1, 1872, with McCay serving as actuary and treasurer.

That enterprise remained small because the number of clergy covered totalled only 131, and no new members were admitted after 1880; perhaps the Presbyterian Ministers Fund was the instrument used for subsequent entrants. The points of greatest actuarial interest are two: McCay reported (1) that insurance was being provided at about half the cost of commercial company coverage and (2) that the mortality of this group was below normal.

In 1873, McCay was accorded the distinction of being invited by Mutual Life of New York to make a critical review of the manuscript of that company's official history. Mutual Life's actuary, William H. C. Bartlett, whose actuarial career had begun only two years previously after his retirement from professorship at West Point, asked President Frederick S. Winston's permission to have the text examined by "a person whose eminent mathematical attainments, intimate acquaintance with vital statistics, and practical knowledge of Life Insurance, would detect whatever of error in principle or inaccuracy of deduction it might contain." This high responsibility evidently was discharged to the full satisfaction of McCay's client company.

McCay, like many actuaries before and since, was immensely impressed by the potency of compound interest over long periods. Kellam writes of a plan (p. 79 et seq.) that McCay proposed to the University of Georgia in 1879, which, long after the deaths of McCay, the donor, and that generation of University Trustees, would neatly and usefully demonstrate the validity of the relationship:

$$\$7,000 \; (1+i)^n = \$ 1,000,000$$

where $n = 100$, and $i = .050871$ nearly.

McCay presented the University Trustees with a Deed of Trust calling for an immediate gift by him of \$7,000 in the form of bonds guaranteed by the Georgia Railroad. Their coupon rate was 8%; McCay's ingenious device for ensuring that the value of n would be about 100 was to stipulate that neither principal nor interest could be withdrawn until twenty-one years after the last death among about eighty second-generation progeny of (a) McCay himself, (b) twelve of his brothers and sisters, and (c) his friend John J. Gresham. By setting the earnings goal at just over 5% per annum, McCay was prudently allowing for some future decline in the prevailing yield and some capital losses.

This plan, reported in the Athens newspapers, created something of a sensation, but the Trustees accepted the gift in July 1880, blissfully unaware that future trustees would be quite unable to keep track of so many survivors.

When in February 1972 those in charge declared themselves incapable of saying just when the last survivor might have died and the court accordingly permitted the deferment period to end, the outcome seemed disappointing to some, but was in fact a tribute to McCay's forecasting. The fund, standing then at \$548,626.49, would have reached the million-dollar mark by 1980 if the administrators had been able to earn only 7.8% yield thereon, not at all difficult in that high-yield period of the 1970s.

1861. ELIZUR WRIGHT'S SECOND MAJOR REFORM—SURRENDER VALUES

As one writer put it, Elizur Wright moved promptly from having made life insurance safe to making it fair. In 1861 the Massachusetts legislature, on his recommendation, became the first jurisdiction to require withdrawal values. The operative provision of its Act was (*R.A.I.A.* 28, 275):

> the net value of the policy, when the premium comes due and is not paid, shall be ascertained, according to the "Combined Experience," or "Actuaries" rate of mortality, with interest at four per centum per annum. After deducting from such net value any indebtedness to the company . . . , four-fifths of what remains shall be considered as a net single premium of temporary insurance, and the term for which it will insure shall be determined according to the age . . . at the time

of the lapse of premium, and the assumptions of mortality and interest aforesaid.

If the death . . . occur[s] within the term of temporary insurance . . . the company shall have the right to deduct from the amount insured in the policy the amount at six percent. per annum of the premiums that had been foreborne at the time of death.

Wright evidently considered one-fifth of the value at time of lapse to be a reasonable surrender charge (later actuarial thinking recognized this amount as too small in early policy years and much too large at high policy durations), and Wright has been credited with devising the expression *surrender charge* to describe it.

Clinton O. Shepherd wrote in 1939 (*R.A.I.A.* 28, 281), "This act, too, must be judged against the abuses of the times." He quotes an 1869 comment by D. P. Fackler, "Its passage was a death blow to an old system of injustice and confiscation."

Shepherd stated further that there is clear evidence in the actions of three outstanding companies (New England Mutual, State Mutual, and Massachusetts Mutual) that the Act was not gracefully received. They attempted unsuccessfully to circumvent it by inserting in policy application forms an agreement whereby, for dubious considerations, the insured were induced to waive the protection of the Act's provisions.

Guaranteed values payable in cash, which in modern times have been credited to, and as often blamed upon, Elizur Wright, were not required, in fact, until long after he had been ousted from his post as Massachusetts Commissioner.

Fifty years later, in 1911, Henry Moir presented a paper (*T.A.S.A.* 12, 175) entitled "Liberality of Modern Policies." Some of that paper and most of the resulting discussion related to scales of surrender values. By that time Mutual Benefit Life had long been guaranteeing higher values in early policy years than did other major companies; that company's actuary, Edward E. Rhodes, stepped forward to rebut Moir's contention that his guaranteed values were dangerously large. Rhodes said, first, that his company had proved in the 1907 panic following the Armstrong Investigation (discussed in Chapter III) that it could afford to pay the values in its policies and, second, that "there are life insurance companies which are strong, and there are those which are weak. It is the business of the weak to become strong and not to emulate the strong while they are still weak. They can become strong only by husbanding their resources."

This remark was vigorously challenged by consulting actuary Miles M. Dawson (*T.A.S.A.* 13, 115):

It is neither proper in my judgment, nor is it even feasible, for the smaller companies of the country to wait until they have become old and prosperous before they offer policies as desirable in all respects as those of the older companies. The only consequence, if they fail to do so, is that their policies must be sold either under actuarial misrepresentation or by concealment of the fact that they are not as good as the policies offered by the other companies.

In fact, the companies that came to the fore, especially in the U.S. Midwest, in the aftermath of the Armstrong Investigation did follow generally Rhodes' rather than Dawson's theory. They sold nonparticipating policies, keeping their premiums below those of the mutual companies and guaranteeing relatively low cash values.

Dawson also made an interesting remark about Elizur Wright:

> In [this] country the most liberal surrender values were for many years offered by a small company, a very small company in those days, up in Vermont, on the recommendation of Elizur Wright; and, had Mr. Wright never become Commissioner of Massachusetts and never imposed upon any companies by force a system of surrender values, but had confined himself to recommending it to other companies as well as to the company which I have mentioned and which became one of his clients, it is not improbable that we would have been much further along that road at a much earlier date than proved to be the case.

Moir, in his author's review, did not choose to comment on this remarkable observation.

1861. THE AMERICAN EXPERIENCE TABLE

The historically interesting features of the durable American Experience Table are these:

- It was improperly named, since it represented the experience of only one company, the Mutual Life, and even that rather casually. Sheppard Homans, its constructor, had been unsuccessful in getting contributions of mortality data from other companies.
- Its famous terminal age, ninety-six, was described by Homans (*T.A.S.A.* 1, 33) as no more than "a happy accident, or a happy thought."
- The actuary, Solomon A. Joffe, who made the most thorough later study of how it was constructed (*T.A.S.A.* 12, 253) was to be the first Fellow in North America to survive beyond his ninety-sixth birthday.
- Abandonment of the American Experience Table as the valuation standard was a convoluted and unheroic episode in actuarial history.
- That table's widespread use as the mortality basis for life income settlement options in United States policy forms persisted for a quarter of a century until 1935.

1862. THE CONTRIBUTION PLAN OF SURPLUS DISTRIBUTION

In 1861, Sheppard Homans travelled to England seeking advice on how to improve Mutual Life's method of distributing its surplus, an operation performed quinquennially. The distributions in 1848, 1853, and 1858 had all been flat percentages of premiums—52, 33 1/3, and 40%, respectively. Homans, and perhaps Charles Gill before him, recognized the unfairness of this; Homans returned from England with the expressed intention of developing a plan that would recognize "that the true share of any policyholder in a given amount of surplus is in the proportion which the excess of his payments over and above the actual cost of insurance (as determined by experience) bears to the total contributions to this surplus."

David Parks Fackler, who since 1859 had been Homans' assistant, described what transpired in his first paper to the Actuarial Society, "An Account of the various

Dividend Systems adopted by American Life Insurance Companies up to 1889 . . . ,"
T.A.S.A. 1, Pt. 2, 3. A provisional system, suggested by British actuary Charles Jellicoe,
which would produce dividends proportionate to the excess of gross premiums over
corresponding premiums calculated by company experience mortality and 6 1/2%
interest, was first studied. In his paper Fackler stated that "very early in 1862 objections
were urged against it," which probably means that he himself raised those objections.

The result was the unveiling of the three-factor method that has become so widely
used on this continent that some actuaries have come to regard it as the only acceptable
system.

Who—Homans or Fackler—was the discoverer of the contribution method?
Homans, in his 1863 paper to the Institute of Actuaries (*JIA* 11, quoted by Percy C. H.
Papps, *T.A.S.A.* 11, 53), showed himself more than ready to give his young assistant a
share of the credit:

> It gives me pleasure to say, in conclusion, that whatever credit may attach to the
> origination and successful application of an entirely new method of dividing
> surplus, should justly be shared by my young assistant, Mr. David Parks Fack-
> ler. Mr. F. has also devised an independent original formula for the same pur-
> pose, which, starting from hypotheses substantially the same, produces results
> nearly identical with the method now described—the one confirming the other.
> I am in hopes that he will make his very ingenious formula the subject of a paper.

**Sheppard Homans (1831–1898) (left) and David Parks Fackler (1842–1924), influential nineteenth-century
actuaries and co-founders of the Actuarial Society of America.**

Fackler, discussing Papps' paper (*T.A.S.A.* 11, 190), began by expressing his earnest wish to avoid seeming to claim more than he was entitled to in the absence (by death in 1898) of a man upon whose reputation he might appear to infringe, and went on to quote a passage from his above-mentioned paper (op. cit., p.9):

> When it is considered that this entirely new and very intricate system was then applied to the division of three million dollars of surplus, all practical men can appreciate the responsibility assumed by the Actuary [Homans] who recommended, and also by the President [Frederick S. Winston] and Trustees who had the intelligence to understand and the courage to adopt it; all of them should receive the credit to which their action entitled them.

Fackler then (in his 1909 discussion) mentioned a descriptive pamphlet published by the Mutual Life in 1863 which illustrated the difference between that company's original percentage plan of distribution and the Jellicoe method and the contribution plan, and described his own difficulties in convincing Homans to abandon the Jellicoe method, remarking that as soon as Homans saw and accepted the new principles suggested, the way was clear. This seems tantamount to saying that he, Fackler, devised the contribution method; in fact, the anonymous writer of Fackler's obituary in 1924 (*T.A.S.A.* 25, 372) said of him:

> In 1862, when he was 21 years of age, he proposed the method of apportioning surplus to policyholders which is substantially that now in general use among American life insurance companies.

In January 1865, probably after he had decided to leave Mutual Life to become a consulting actuary, Fackler wrote a short note to President Winston asking for "some reward" (which apparently he got to the tune of $750) for his work on the origination and successful application of the contribution method. He sent with that request a letter written by Homans a few days earlier acknowledging the credit due Fackler, couched in very much the same terms as in Homans' 1863 paper but going one handsome step further by saying:

> Indeed the principle upon which that dividend was based as well as some of the most important elements of the main formula were first suggested by you.

If any further proof of Homans' magnanimity toward a former junior of his were needed, it is shown by the action of the Actuarial Society's Council at its meeting of October 24, 1890 (Homans being in the chair and Fackler absent) in deciding that a page in the *Transactions* (Vol. 1, Pt. 3, 4) with the heading "History of the Dividend Systems in the United States" should print Homans' above-mentioned letter to Fackler of January 4, 1865.

The verdict seems clear: Fackler was the discoverer of the contribution method. And this was at his age twenty-one, the youngest age at which the Actuarial Society for many years would confer Associateship—four years below the youngest age for Fellowship.

The actuarial profession in North America almost immediately developed a loyalty to the contribution plan which Henry H. Jackson in 1932 (*T.A.S.A.* 33, 123) said "assumed a patriotic aspect maintained with religious fervor." Jackson accused some actuaries of thinking, "To be sure, mutual life insurance in a crude form was first practiced elsewhere, but in our bigger and better country we will teach those Britishers how to conduct the institution with mathematical precision and moral perfection." Be that as it may, as early as 1869 (*JIA* 15, 48), the *Journal*'s editorial view was to admit the system's advantages but still to differ from its admirers as to its absolute perfection and as to the need for its universal employment. Editor Thomas B. Sprague went on:

> We can pardon, readily enough, the enthusiasm of Mr. [Lucius] McAdam, who asserts that the contribution plan "affords strict mathematical justice to all," and that "it is easily understood,—more comprehensible than the percentage system [i.e., the British reversionary bonus approach], which is inexplicable,"—that being merely the excess of zeal. We can forgive, whilst taking leave to doubt, the assertion of Mr. Homans, that, in addition to being simple and easily explained, "it is popular with agents and policyholders, and, what is of more importance, is acknowledged, almost universally, to be just and equitable,"—that being but the natural partiality of a parent for his own offspring. But when Mr. [Charles F.] McCay links the word "honest" to "just," and appeals to one's "moral sense" to support his view that "the percentage plan is unjust, and monstrously so," being "systematic robbery on a gigantic scale involving millions upon millions every year," whilst "the contribution plan is just,— perfectly just";—and when, above and beyond all this, the Commissioner [of Massachusetts] himself casts aside all judicial gravity, and, with the airs, adopts the language of stump oratory, permitting himself to say of the percentage plan, that, in dealing with the money of the insured, it "is like the hospitality of the famous old robber of Attica, who, if the legs of his unwilling guests were too long for his bed, lopped them off, and stretched them to the requisite length if they were too short";—we think it is time to protest. Such language is not scientific, nor philosophical, nor true. Is it likely to be convincing?

This difference of view across the Atlantic waters was given another airing more than sixty years later when our Joseph B. Maclean presented a paper to the Institute (*JIA* 62, 243) in which he did, in Henry H. Jackson's words, "all that is humanly possible to break down the invincible British prejudice to the contribution formula." This is not to say that Maclean succeeded, but happily, rhetoric in the 1930s had become milder than in the 1860s.

1866. THE FIRST WOMAN ACTUARY

Lucy Jane Wright, one of Elizur's large family, had learned actuarial craft for at least eight years as her father's assistant at home and in the Massachusetts Insurance Department when in 1866 the Union Mutual Life, at that time a Boston company, appointed her its actuary. For the honor of being the first woman to be given such responsibility, there was in those days no competition from Great Britain, because women were not eligible for membership in the Institute of Actuaries, or in the Faculty, until 1919.

Lucy Wright (1842-1867) was by all reports a capable practitioner with a most pleasing personality. Without ever going to college—Henry H. Jackson in 1940 (*R.A.I.A.* 29, 104) roundly criticized Elizur Wright for having neglected his children's higher education although himself a Yale graduate—Miss Wright had mastered college-level mathematics by age fifteen. Her duties at Union Mutual began on May 2, 1866, and, sad to report, lasted a mere seven months. Laid low by tuberculosis, she died on May 26, 1867. Her obsequies were fully and sentimentally reported in the insurance press.

1866-1867. TWO TRIES FOR AN ACTUARIAL ORGANIZATION

In Hartford in 1866, a move was started, not so much by actuaries themselves as by their company presidents, to form a body to be called the National Actuaries Institute. The controlling purpose was to develop uniformity in valuation of policies beyond the jurisdictional limits of a single state. Elizur Wright, who had recently been forced out of his post as Massachusetts Commissioner, was keynote speaker, and possibly was being considered to head the new body. He himself seems to have been instrumental in broadening the objective from that of a conclave of actuaries to a company association. The body that emerged in 1868 was named the Chamber of Life Insurance; its staff head was a competent actuary and lawyer, Charlton T. Lewis, who at various times had been a mathematics and classics

AND WALL STREET REVIEW.   337

Lucy Jane Wright,
LATE ACTUARY OF THE UNION MUTUAL LIFE INSURANCE COMPANY.

As there is nothing more beautiful than a life of genuine and extensive usefulness, it is natural to repine at its brevity, even when it reaches old age, but when it terminates in youth, before its bright promise is half fulfilled, the heart sinks with dismay, and the dealings of Divine Providence with man appear to us a dark and forbidding mystery.

Few lives have been at once so pure, lovely and useful as that of Lucy Jane Wright, daughter of the great actuary, Elizur Wright, and yet it faded away even in the hour of its fresh and fragrant blossoming. She was born in Dorchestar, Mass., Jan. 1, 1842, and died at Milford, Mass., May 26, 1867. Notwithstanding the brevity of her earthly existence, the earnest purpose which she seems to have cherished almost from her cradle, to make her life sublime, was accomplished, and as such it will be esteemed in the memory of all who knew her. What the world owes to her, it may never know, but those who understand the subject best, affirm that in the past, the present, and the future, the alleviation of the widow's sad cares by the safe and prompt reception of the little fund secured to her by her departed husband's forethought through a Life Insurance policy, is as attributable to this fair, young, but indefatigable actuary, as to any other, however great or eminent. And her spirit now, looking down on the good done, receives its exceeding great reward for years of incessant toil.

To Lucy Jane Wright work was worship. She entered thoughtfully into the plans of infinite life, and threw her whole energy into her own part, because the entire work fully enlisted her sympathy. As early as her fifteenth year, she had made herself familiar with the mathematical studies pursued in our colleges, and subsequently acquired great proficiency in their application to practical arts, especially civil and mechanical engineering. The drawings still existing which she made on these subjects, would be envied by many a practical man. These exercises were, however, only a preliminary schooling, to prepare her for the great work she was destined to perform. She was afterwards, for

eight years, her father's principal assistant in the Insurance Commissioners' office, on the valuation of Life Insurance Policies, and to her enthusiasm and indomitable perseverance, it is largely, if not wholly due, that the Massachusetts Insurance Reports of that period contained, from year to year, the fully analyzed and combined mortuary experience of all the companies doing business in that State. In the spring of 1866 she accepted the laborious and responsible post of Actuary of the Union Mutual Life Insurance Company of Maine, which has its principal office in Boston, and a business extending to all parts of the country. The ardor with which she entered into the duties of this office, and the zeal with which she labored to perfect new methods of securing equity among the members, tended doubtless to shorten her earthly career by rendering her incautious, and throwing her off her guard against the rigors of our winter season. A severe cold, contracted in December, compelled her to reluctantly desist from her work before the close of January, and confined her, for a month or more, to her chamber, as an invalid, in Boston. By the first of April she had recovered strength to walk, and at that date accompanied the family to Medford, in the hope of being able soon to resume the duties of her office. But an attack of bleeding at the lungs prostrated her again upon a bed of sickness, from which she only rose temporarily to glance through the window at the green fields she loved. Enduring bravely that intense suffering inflicted by an unrelenting disease fastened upon one vital organ, while the rest of the system, including the brain, remains in a healthy condition, she knew no fear of death, and felt no desire for prolonged life except for the purpose of carrying out her plans for making it a blessing for those she loved. No repining or impatient word escaped her lips; indeed, throughout her life, she never uttered one that was not redolent of the atmosphere and halo of love and truth that seemed always to surround her cheery and fervent spirit.

Though so long and laboriously devoted to what may seem a man's specialty, the thoughts of this accomplished young lady were none the less at home in any part of any of the kingdoms of nature. To a scientific zest for all phenomena, she added an artist's appreciation and a

poet's love of the beautiful. In early years, among the processes of her self-education, was included the dramatic art, in which she manifested a remarkable conception of character and great powers of personation, which those who witnessed her performances will not soon forget. She was a fixed star in the little domestic theatre which for many years sweetened life under her father's roof. And if it had also fallen in her way to give written expression to the feelings enkindled in her mind by human society and natural objects, so extraordinary were her powers of observation and so felicitous her aptitude for composition either in prose or verse, that she could hardly have failed to endear herself to many readers, or to have won a glorious name for herself in the temple of literary fame; but, influenced by a sense of duty, she devoted herself to the real instead of the ideal, and chose, instead of wandering in the pleasant realms of fancy, to employ her surprising intensity of action in lessening and lightening the ills, and in promoting and increasing the happiness of actual, every-day life.

Although Lucy Jane Wright has been removed to another and higher sphere, her spirit, the example she has set her sex and our own, and the good she has accomplished, survive among us, and we trust and believe that they will neither die nor cease to bear fruit throughout time and eternity. Such lives as hers are indeed immortal on earth as well as in heaven, for their profound sympathies are in harmony with both. She was truly poetical but equally practical, and her fervent love of the beautiful proved an incentive instead of a hindrance to her usefulness. When we consider how young, delicate, and sensitive she was, and what an expansive, potent, real, massive, enduring work she performed, we are filled with enthusiastic admiration of so noble a model, and a holy desire is kindled in our hearts to emulate the example set by one who possessed

"Reason firm, the temperate will,
Endurance, foresight, strength and skill;
A perfect woman, nobly planned,
To warn, to comfort, and command,
And yet a spirit, still and bright,
With something of an angel light."

A tribute to Lucy Jane Wright in the June 1867 issue of the *Insurance Monitor and Wall Street Review*. (Courtesy of Library, College of Insurance, New York, N.Y.)

professor, U.S. Deputy Commissioner of Internal Revenue, managing editor of a New York City newspaper, and counsel of Mutual Life. He was elected, in 1890, a member of the Actuarial Society.

It was intended that the Chamber have an Actuarial Board; William A. Hutcheson, reminiscing at the Actuarial Society's 1939 meeting (*T.A.S.A.* 40, 117), said that Elizur Wright was mentioned favorably as the Chamber's possible actuary, it being suggested that Sheppard Homans of the Mutual Life and Amzi Dodd of the Mutual Benefit Life be associated with Mr. Wright. The Chamber, however, collapsed in 1877, chiefly because the mighty Mutual Life decided to withdraw its support.

Three years before its demise, the Chamber undertook what Hutcheson described as its chief work of permanent value, an intercompany mortality study to which thirty companies contributed data. Planning for this long postponed enterprise brought together in New York on November 19, 1874, seven actuaries including Fackler, Homans, and Emory McClintock (then actuary of Northwestern Mutual, and thus bringing the U.S. Midwest into what was otherwise largely a New York effort); the subsequent letter of invitation was signed also by Howell W. St. John of Hartford.

The Chamber's unhappy history demonstrated the hazards of attempting to bring life company managements together in an era of intense individualism. One of the issues that destroyed the Chamber was that of state versus federal supervision.

In New York in 1867, a much more clearly defined and intense effort to organize an actuarial body was mounted. Fackler, who was part of it, curiously played it down in his 1909 reminiscences (*T.A.S.A.* 11, 11):

> A desire for an actuarial association was felt for over twenty years before it was gratified, and several abortive attempts were made. The first of these, I believe, was about the year 1868 when several actuaries of New York City met together one evening at the house of Mr. Sheppard Homans to consider the formation of some sort of club or society, and we had a very pleasant meeting, but without result.

Doubtless, there was a meeting at Homans' residence, but the historical record is far from supporting the impression that Fackler gave of the brevity and the informality of this attempt. *The Insurance Monitor and Wall Street Review* of November 1867 reported as follows under the headline "An American Institute of Actuaries":

> The first meeting, having in view the formation of an American Institute of Actuaries was held on the 7th of November, at 2 o'clock in the Board Room of the Mutual Life Insurance Company. Although it was informal it was well attended and conducted with spirit, perfect harmony, and good feeling. Messrs. [Elizur] Wright, [Sheppard] Homans, [David Parks] Fackler, [William H.] Beers [actuary of New York Life], [George W.] Phillips [actuary of Equitable Society], [William A.] Brewer [actuary of Washington Life of New York], [A. W.] Kellogg [Northwestern Mutual], [Lucius] McAdam [actuary of a short-lived New York company called Guardian Mutual, and many years later the first president of the real American Institute of Actuaries], and [John F.] Entz [New York consulting actuary] were present, and, in the discussion to which the object of the meeting gave rise, the gentlemen exchanged their views freely as to

measures best calculated to promote the advancement of actuarial science and efficiency. It was generally conceded that it was expedient to form a union or association of American actuaries, composed of men of integrity, experience, and ability, acting independently, both as respects individual companies and combinations of companies, and wholly devoted to the discussion of actuarial questions, to the acquisition, cultivation and extension of knowledge relative to the subject, and to the increase and elucidation of the data upon which the science itself and the immense monetary interests involved primarily depend. In harmony with these conclusions, it was unanimously

Resolved, That an Association of Actuaries is desirable, and

Resolved, That a committee of five be appointed with power to call a meeting at some future day.

The gentlemen on this committee were Sheppard Homans, Elizur Wright, D. P. Fackler, W. H. Beers, and George W. Phillips.

When this committee has drafted a resolution, a meeting of the actuaries will be called, and proceedings be taken to insure the incorporation of the projected institute by charter. Mr. [Amzi] Dodd [mathematician of Mutual Benefit Life] and other distinguished actuaries, whose sympathies are entirely in accord with the movement, were unavoidably absent on the occasion of its inauguration, but there is no doubt that it will gather strength at every step of its progress, and eventually include among its promoters all the eminent names in the profession it is designed to elevate and render the Institute of Actuaries an honour to our country.

It may reasonably be supposed that this report, expressing objectives as to the nature and composition of the actuarial body essentially identical with those that were adopted more than two decades later, was issued by the five-man committee. Certainly the roster of those who either attended the meeting or expressed support for its purpose gave solid reason for expecting that positive action would soon follow. The next public report in the same journal the following month (December 1867) was nearly as optimistic. Its text, this time under the headline "The Association of Actuaries," was in these words:

Considering that attempts to do too much at once frequently result in total failure, our actuaries, desirous of organizing a corporation that will necessarily include among the most eminent members of the fraternity, many entertaining diverse interests and views on the most vital and important subjects connected with their science, which can only be reconciled and harmonized by free and friendly discussion, the friends of the movement are proceeding with exemplary prudence and caution. Pursuant to a call of the Committee, previously appointed, a meeting of actuaries was held at the office of the Mutual Life Insurance Company on Wednesday, the 11th instant, at 4 o'clock P.M., attended by the following gentlemen: Messrs. Wright, Homans, Entz, [Nicholas G.] De Groot, [actuary of United States Life], Beers, [William J.] Coffin [actuary of Home Life], [Samuel N.] Stebbins [actuary of Manhattan Life], [Levi W.] Meech [mathematician of Charter Oak Life of Hartford], Phillips, Brewer, Fackler, [William] Sheffler [consulting actuary in Hartford] and McAdam. After a letter from Mr. Dodd had been read, expressing the regret he felt that circumstances prevented his attendance, Mr. Homans presented the Report of the Committee, which was finally adopted. It represented the inexpediency of organizing a formal association of actuaries at the present time, and it was accordingly decided to form a society to be entitled "The Association of Actuaries," of which the object should be to hold periodical meetings for the discussion and elucidation of important subjects connected with Life Insurance. For its next meeting, which will take place in January, the question,—"What is the proper method of valuation for State purposes?"—was proposed for discussion.

If the design of this association is carried out with earnestness and fidelity, it will be productive of incalculable good to the interests of Life Insurance, for the more the subject is ventilated and expounded by impartial and scientific discussion relating both to its theory and practice, the better understood, and more popular the institution will become.

Then something went wrong. Perhaps the project foundered on the rocks of divided wishes about its leadership. Twice after the Actuarial Society had come into being, Fackler made public statements about this—first in his presidential address of 1891, again in reminiscences of 1909 already mentioned—using nearly identical wordings. The following comes from his 1909 remarks (*T.A.S.A.* 11, 12):

Those who could properly be called actuaries in those days considered that the proper time had hardly arrived to found a society satisfactorily. There were too many men officially or popularly entitled actuaries who were not actuaries in any proper sense of the word; we could hardly form a society without including them, and possibly would have to give some of them important positions, so rather than have an association which would not be a proper exponent of the actuarial profession we preferred to have nothing at all.

In 1939 (*T.A.S.A.* 40, 119) Society Past-President William A. Hutcheson suggested that Fackler's targets in his comments were men employed by some of the assessment and cooperative associations that sprang up in the late nineteenth century, but this seems untenable because, first, the heydays of those bodies came later than 1867, and second, Fackler in 1909 (but not in 1891) named three who "could not properly be entitled actuaries": Elizur Wright, Professor W. H. C. Bartlett, and William H. Beers, the last two of these being actuaries of Mutual Life and New York Life. There was intense bitterness between Fackler's close friend Homans and Professor Bartlett, but this seems to date from later than 1867. Also, it was well known that Mr. Beers delegated mathematical duties to others, so the force of the comment seems to have been directed at Elizur Wright. Yet, even this seems difficult to reconcile with the wording of the editorial in the January/February 1868 issue of *The Insurance Times*, headlined "An Institute of Actuaries":

The best insurance school is a well managed insurance company. There is no adequate substitute for its practical teachings. The indispensable details and routine of the business are best learned in the office of such an institution. Mere theory can no more make a thorough insurance officer than it can enable a man to fly. . . . But the institution of insurance suffers, not only from the sudden and unmerited promotion of incompetent persons to its most responsible positions, but equally from the readiness with which many in its subordinate capacities subside into habits of lifeless routine and drudgery. ... [This diatribe against unnamed persons in high places continues here at length.]

The efforts made to remedy this defect, which is a negative evil of the most destructive kind, are comparatively feeble. For many years the subject of insurance has been shrouded in mystery, and the public has understood it about as clearly as it does the art of legerdemain. Last year an endeavor was made to drag it to the light, and submit its most essential principles to the alembic of free discussion. ... Among other gratifying features of this incipient reformation, we were flattered with the prospect of having an actuarial institute; but this has faded somewhat, and has as yet only assumed a rather dim and unsettled formation. Those engaged in the movement seemed to have concluded that we require less than was asked for, and that it was inexpedient at present to establish a formal legalized society of actuaries. The reverse is, however, the truth. We want more than was at first contemplated. We want an actuarial college or school in which actuarial science can be thoroughly and advantageously cultivated by proficients, and in which officers and clerks, practically familiar with its rudiments, can complete their study of it and fit themselves to fulfil the most difficult and important duties of their calling.

It is not the great men in the actuarial profession who are indifferent or averse to the formation of so beneficial an institution as this would prove, for they are above any selfish or venal desire to monopolize the arcana of their science. They are on the contrary, ready and anxious to impart their knowledge to others for the general good. But there are men painfully conscious that an institute of this character, conducted with earnestness and practical wisdom, would diffuse so much light and learning on every subject connected with life insurance, as to belittle their too limited attainments, and it is, therefore, no wonder that they are reluctant to assist in erecting a standard that would prove too high for their intellectual stature.

What can we make of this? It gives no suggestion that the qualified actuaries "preferred to have nothing at all," but appears to say that highly placed men were powerful and malicious enough to sabotage an organizational effort that was widely supported. The meaning of this editorial remains a mystery.

Fackler, in 1909, mentioned in passing a couple of other trivial moves, apparently by non-actuaries, to arouse interest in an actuarial body, both to no practical effect. The only other clue to any activity between 1868 and 1889 lies in a single handwritten paper which has turned up among Fackler's personal papers, marked "Memorandum of Constitution for an Actuarial Society (jotted down about 1878 –/1/80)." This sets forth four draft Articles in terms not markedly different from those of the draft Constitution laid before the delegates in 1889. Of greatest interest is draft Article III, describing who would be eligible for membership:

Persons of good repute, versed [next words indecipherable except that one of them is "practical"] in the calculations upon which Life Insurance is founded and conducted may become elected active members. [Then some words added and seemingly crossed out]. But no one shall be eligible who shall have knowingly signed or circulated any false business statement.

Other persons of good standing in the Life Insurance business or having a purely theoretical knowledge thereof may be elected honorary members.

Persons of good (moral) character whose present practical acquaintance with Life Insurance is not sufficient to entitle them to active membership may become such by passing an examination in the rudimentary calculations of probabilities & insurance and then—after a year or more spent in practical actuarial work— solve some difficult problems or prepare an elaborate essay on a topic of insurance interest.

No information has surfaced on an organizational move occurring at the time this draft was written (surely by Fackler himself). It does show the writer's dedication to high standards of conduct and to some sort of examination system as an admission requirement for inexperienced applicants.

1867. THE TONTINE DIVIDEND SYSTEM

The three large New York companies were entering, in the 1860s, the race for volume of business that was the prime cause of the 1905 Armstrong Investigation. One of these three, the Equitable Society, being the most recently organized and therefore likely to lose, came up with the bright idea of a tontine dividend distribution period. It would divide the dividend fund among the surviving and persisting policyholders in the year when the premiums paid, which had accumulated at 10% interest, had become as large as the face amount. Buyers could thus be told that the beneficiaries of those who died would lose nothing because their yield on the premiums paid was usually greater than 10%. Those who kept their policies in force could count upon earning more than 10% interest not, it is true, on the premiums, but on the annual dividends they would otherwise have received.

The system was soon changed to provide for a fixed number of years, usually twenty, as the deferment period; the revised plan was called a deferred dividend rather than a tontine system. But for the following four principal reasons, the system gave rise to major policyholder disappointment with emerging results:

1. The state authorities exercised no supervision over these funds.

2. Market investment yields obtainable by the companies were in a long period of almost steady decline.

3. The race for volume made the era one of sharply rising expenses and therefore one of declining dividends.

4. The growth of the dividend funds was greatly reduced because surrender values paid on terminating policies were increasing sharply by both legal and competitive requirements.

New York, in 1906, required that dividends be declared annually, and other states followed suit. But the less-than-estimated results on these policies contributed to the public disfavor of level premium life insurance. The system throughout its currency was highly controversial among the actuaries.

1870–1879. LIFE COMPANY FAILURES GIVE RISE TO ASSESSMENT COMPANIES

In October 1933, at the depths of what we now rightly call the Great Depression, Actuarial Society President John S. Thompson developed his topic "Life Insurance in Crisis" (*T.A.S.A.* 34, 187) by first describing prior cataclysms. His first selection, the panic of 1873, he identified as having its roots in the enormous cost of the Civil War but fostered by excessive railway building, credit inflation, huge capital investments in farms and mining ventures, and currency fluctuations. The number of U.S. life insurance companies, which had vaulted from 38 to 127 during the 1860s, fell to 61 during the decade of the 1870s, 91 failures far outweighing 25 new launchings.

Many of those ninety-one that fell by the wayside were young companies that never achieved stability, but several major companies perished, among them the Guardian Mutual of New York (Lucius McAdam, actuary). Two important companies that struggled through the 1870s but merely postponed failure into the next decade were the Knickerbocker Life of New York and the Charter Oak Life of Hartford (Levi W. Meech, actuary). Factors other than the bad economic conditions included excessive proportions of premium notes in the assets and increased stringency of reserve requirements under state laws.

A third group of companies, which met neither a quick death in the 1870s nor a slower one into the 1880s, teetered on the edge but came back from the precipice. At the Actuarial Society's inaugural meeting in 1889, George B. Woodward, speaking of his own company, said in *T.A.S.A.* 1, Pt. 1, 46, that:

> no company in the United States that I know of ever went through such trying times as the John Hancock did in 1874 and 1875, when it was only the turning of your hand, so to speak, whether the company would go into a receiver's hands or not, and, in consequence of the troubles we went through, we lost within two years, I think, between thirty and forty per cent. of our premium-paying policies.

The Massachusetts companies enjoyed a far better solvency performance in the 1870s than did the companies of other states, partly because Elizur Wright had required them to establish net level premium reserves at least several years earlier than commissioners in other states did.

A major result of public awareness of the bad failure record was a tremendous boost to fraternal societies and assessment companies that were similar to each other in one particular respect: each invited the life insurance buyer, in the jargon of those days, "to keep your reserve in your pocket." The rise of the fraternals and their conversion in due course to the legal reserve system is discussed in Chapter III. It needs to be understood that by no means all the assessment companies conducted their affairs as "pass the hat" outfits; the organizers of some of them were well aware of the basic hazard of their method and used much ingenuity in seeking a modus operandi that would assure them a degree of stability. *JIA* 26 (1887) has a thorough analysis by the eminent H. W. Manly, FIA, entitled "On the American Tontine and Mutual Assessment Schemes." That author's reason for examining the matter was that one of these societies had recently embarked on an "invasion" of England.

Edmund M. McConney, in a 1968 historical essay now in Society of Actuaries archives, described an assessment company organized in Iowa in 1879, which serves as an example. McConney wrote: "Censuses of that era [showed that] the death rate of the population was usually less than ten per thousand and it was assumed that in a benefit society the death rate would also be about the same or better with some selection of members."

The source of that figure is not clear; the national death rate shown by the 1870 census was nearer to twenty than to ten per thousand. McConney may have been speaking of some figures peculiar to Iowa when it was heavily populated by young adults and did not have yet a relatively large number of very young children. That assessment company had the wit to establish a contribution scale of $1.00 for each year of age at entry, e.g., for a 30-year-old, a $30.00 payment. Likewise, the company's quarterly call to each surviving member for his share of that quarter's death losses was not a flat payment but was proportionate to the amount of his deposit. A fund, called in due course the Emergency Reserve Fund, was built from members' forfeited deposits and all interest earnings from every source, to be called upon only if the death benefits in a year exceeded ten per thousand, i.e., 1%, of the company's insurance in force.

That company exercised close control over its expenses, and made an effort to restrict its solicitations to officers and other employees of banks so as to control its mortality experience. The result of these and other well-planned measures was that in thirty-five years of operation, no withdrawal ever had to be made from the Emergency Reserve Fund.

How much longer this might have continued cannot be known because, by the second decade of the twentieth century, there was strong agitation for state laws, in Iowa and elsewhere, requiring assessment companies to transfer to the level premium system. The company fought strenuously to forestall such legislation, even to the point of urging its agents to engage in lobbying. But that delaying tactic failed, and that assessment company was forced to become the respectable and highly successful Bankers Life Company.

MILESTONES IN SUPERVISION: 1868—CANADA; 1871—UNITED STATES

Canada. Shortly before the British North America Act came into force in Canada on July 1, 1867, establishing that country as the self-governing Dominion of Canada within the British Empire, life insurance was officially countenanced under the provisions of an 1865 act making it lawful "for any person to insure his life for the whole term thereof, or for any definite period, for the benefit of his wife and children." A federal insurance department was formed on August 1, 1868. At that time there existed just a single Canadian life company, the Canada Life Assurance Company, but there were several branches of British companies doing business, and there were also six U.S. companies authorized to issue life policies—four Hartford companies (Aetna, Phoenix Mutual, Travelers, and Connecticut Mutual), one New York company (New York Life), and one in Boston (Union Mutual).

As already noted, Professor John B. Cherriman became the first Superintendent of Insurance in 1875. Kenneth R. MacGregor stated in 1954, "From the outset, the government was very anxious that it should have a staff of fully qualified actuaries in its service"; Alfred K. Blackadar (1852–1940), who joined the Department of Insurance in 1877, was elected a Fellow of the Actuarial Society of America in April 1890. Blackadar, in 1894, earned Fellowship in the Institute of Actuaries by examination, causing Gerald H. Ryan, FIA, to describe him (*JIA* 32, 40) as "the first colonist . . . to pass the whole of [these] examinations."

The number of Canadian life companies under Dominion supervision increased substantially in the 1870s. These companies enjoyed stability in marked contrast to that of the United States companies in the same era, nearly all of them being active today, this doubtless a tribute in part to the excellence of the supervision. Important expansion and definition of the Canadian insurance law became effective in 1886, as described in *JIA* 27, 459.

United States. In May 1871, an essential first step toward making state supervision of insurance workable at all was taken at an assembly in New York City of the State Insurance Commissioners, members of their actuarial and other staffs, and invited guests. This led to the formation of the National Convention of Insurance Commissioners (NCIC), now the National Association of Insurance Commissioners (NAIC). Among the speakers were Elizur Wright, no longer an insurance department official, and John F. Entz, a New York consulting actuary, then aged seventy-four but full of ideas for reform. A major report was that of the Committee on Rate of Interest, Rate of Mortality, Valuations, etc., the following being excerpts from the report's summary:

> We respectfully recommend that this convention approve the American experience table of mortality and four and a half per cent interest per annum as the data now proper to be designated by law in each of the states, as the basis for calculating net premiums and net values of life insurance policies. . . .

> Instead of attempting to introduce uniformity in the designations of the present great variety of policies, we urgently advise the companies and the policyholders to greatly reduce the present number of different kinds of policies.

> We recommend the acceptance by each state department of the valuations made by any other state department, (in which the companies were incorporated,) when properly performed on sound and recognized principles and legal basis as above . . . .

> Your committee desire that it be understood we do not ask that this convention shall recommend that the legislatures of the respective states pass any laws abrogating the terms of existing legal contracts for insurance. We have had in view the proper future control of this business . . . .

Two insurance department actuaries active at that time, John S. Paterson of New York who had joined that department in 1867 and William S. Smith of Massachusetts since 1877 but with prior service in Kentucky, shared with Alfred K. Blackadar in April 1890 the honor of being the first insurance regulators to be elected Fellows of the Actuarial Society. William D. Whiting, actuary of the Maine Department, had similarly been elected in October 1889, but he was also a New York City consulting actuary and probably qualified by that route.

1872. FUROR OVER MUTUAL LIFE PROPOSAL TO REDUCE PREMIUMS

For a few weeks in November and December 1872, there was an uproar of major proportions when Mutual Life informed its policyholders that its Trustees had resolved upon a major reduction in its premium scale. *The Insurance Times* called it "one of the most interesting events that have ever occurred in connection with life insurance" and devoted twenty-two full pages to airing it. When the Equitable Society began to issue tontine policies in 1867, Mutual Life had felt obliged to follow suit, but President Winston was unenthusiastic and withdrew the system in favor of reducing premiums to a level that alarmed the company's competitors. The announcement stated that differences in dividends would maintain equity with present policyholders but that any of them wishing to take advantage of the new rates might surrender their policies in exchange for new ones, even at slight gain to the holder if the policies were five years old or less.

The correspondence that followed brought much of the actuarial profession into the fray. Sheppard Homans, who had recently resigned from Mutual Life* to become a consulting actuary, expressed strong objection on the grounds that the planned reduction was too large to be safe; a long list of company presidents and other officers addressed an enquiry to Elizur Wright, Sheppard Homans, and D. Parks Fackler, to which those gentlemen replied by strongly denouncing the idea itself and actuary W. H. C. Bartlett's language supporting it. Nicholas G. De Groot wrote supporting Mutual Life, and then twelve other actuaries, whose names we list here because they constitute a substantial part of the profession as it existed in New York at the time, sided with Wright, Homans, and Fackler:

G. W. Phillips	H. Cillis	R. L. Case, Jr.
J. H. Nitchie	W. G. Morgan	Henry F. Homes
S. N. Stebbins	Lucius McAdam	Henry W. Smith
William D. Whiting	Israel C. Pierson	Edward H. Sewell

Nine of the fifteen who joined together on this occasion were to join together again seventeen years later as charter members of the Actuarial Society.

Mutual Life bowed to the pressure of its industry critics supported by numerous trade paper editorials, and to a policyholder protest signed by scores of people giving addresses largely in New York's Wall Street area, announcing the following Board resolution:

> *Resolved,* That while the past experience of the company demonstrates its ability to carry out the plan of reduced premiums, according to the method recently adopted, without injury to any policy-holder in this company, but with benefit to all, yet, in compliance with the request of the memorialists above mentioned and the very respectable body of insurance companies above represented, they

---

*In May 1929, Actuarial Society President James D. Craig described Homans' departure in these words (*T.A.S.A.* 30, 2): "It is a matter of record that one illustrious founder of this Society actually refused to sign his company's statement, maintaining that discrepancies existed, and as a result was dismissed for insubordination."

direct that the proposed reduction of rates be not carried into effect until the further action of the board.

Using verbiage not untypical of the era, *The Insurance Times* commented: "Long accustomed to the arbitrary control of his own company, he [Winston] was astonished, and his courage failed him when he found the policy-holders had mustered courage enough to speak up in their behalf. The moment they showed some pluck, his bravery, like the valor of Bob Acres, 'oozed out from his fingers' ends.' He has taken all back, and will now do anything to save his place."

Looking back on this episode more than a century later, two things seem evident. First, that premium reduction need not have imperilled the company or the equities among its policyholders. Second, though so many policyholders rallied around, the struggle was really between the company and its competitors. Let us give the actuaries the benefit of the doubt and assume that they really believed the proposal unduly rash.

1881. THE THIRTY AMERICAN OFFICES TABLE

We come now to the first cooperative statistical work undertaken by North American actuaries—one that started well but finished disappointingly.

The committee in charge of this project retained Levi W. Meech (1845–1912), an actuary with experience in such matters. He had constructed the first life table from U.S. census data and had been actuary of the Charter Oak Life for several years. The company response to the committee's invitation to contribute data was quite remarkable; enrollment of thirty companies holds up well in comparison, for example, to the number of charter members (38) of the Actuarial Society sixteen years later.

The anniversary in 1874 was the closing point for exposures, and the committee must at first have been delighted to be in possession of cards covering more than 1,000,000 lives and 46,000 deaths; the American Experience Table data had to be constructed from a mere 2,900 deaths, and Mutual Benefit's experience that was published while this new work was being planned covered only 3,900 deaths.

But Meech, who was doing the calculating work from his home in Norwich, Connecticut, was forced to give the committee the bad news that the mean duration of the policies was only 4.36 years, a severe blow because the objective was to construct an aggregate table, the type with which actuaries of that era were comfortable. (The next intercompany study, in 1915, abandoned aggregate in favor of select and ultimate tables.) Some major contributors must have been unwilling to search their policy records for years far back, not surprising in view of the troubled times through which they were struggling.

A workable solution might have been for the committee to instruct Meech to construct three tables: one showing the experience in the first two policy years; one for the third to fifth policy years; then an ultimate table for years six and over. But instead, the committee chose a procedure that was to cost the project the support of the actuaries who had contributed their data.

The decision was to enlarge the exposure artificially by retaining the lives that would otherwise have gone out as "existing" by the device of assuming that those lives would experience exactly the same death and lapse rates as the study showed had been experienced by the genuine residue. Each age-at-issue group was tabulated by policy duration and given additional weight in this manner, making the final aggregate mortality at each attained age heavier than the undoctored figures would have shown. This weighting process, named the "final series method," must have immensely complicated the clerical work; it delayed issuance of the report until seven years after the closing date for the statistics.

The final aggregate table never was put to practical use, either for premium calculations or to supplant the American Experience Table as the statutory valuation standard. Probably the latter would not have occurred anyway because by then Homans' table was deeply imbedded in state laws.

1885. DEATH OF ELIZUR WRIGHT

Elizur Wright died in Medford, Massachusetts, on November 22, 1885 at age 81, having been active in life insurance affairs for nearly forty years. After his few years of prominence in state regulation, he had been greatly in demand as a consulting actuary, speaker and writer.

A brief obituary printed in *JIA* 25, 367, identified him as a prominent figure in American life assurance circles, attributed to him the introduction of the principle of state supervision, and remarked strangely that in his early manhood he had written many works upon life assurance of considerable value and merit.

His characteristics and influence have never been completely forgotten. Three examples down the years will suffice.

In 1923 (*T.A.S.A.* 24, 324) Rainard B. Robbins wrote:

> The institution of life insurance in this country has been extremely fortunate in the clear vision, the tireless energy, the uncompromising stubbornness and the bulldog tenacity of Elizur Wright . . . .

Nobody who discussed Robbins' paper challenged this assessment.

An appraisal representative of a different school of actuarial opinion was that of Henry H. Jackson in 1940 (*R.A.I.A.* 29, 103). Jackson labelled Wright the most contradictory figure in the whole history of American life insurance, pilloried him for his inconsistencies and, ridiculing the designation "Father of American Life Insurance" that had been applied to Wright by the insurance press, argued that any of the following titles might be more to the point:

> Father of Extended Insurance
>
> Father of Dictatorial Legislation for Life Insurance
>
> Father of All State Insurance Commissioners.

Jackson then concluded:

> After all, perhaps we had better abandon all these attempts at foisting miscellaneous paternity on Elizur Wright. On the whole, he does not require it. He was himself the father in the flesh, by the wife of his bosom, of eighteen children of his own.

This drew a dissenting statement by Clinton O. Shepherd (*R.A.I.A.* 29, 119):

> I think we must give Wright credit for a very substantial amount of constructive work. I do not give him credit for having invented a perfect system, but, on the other hand, I do not feel inclined to blame him too seriously for what seem to be relatively minor faults in the system which he did initiate.

Marking the centennial of Wright's death a commemorative session was held at the fall 1985 Society of Actuaries meeting, which can be found in *RSA* 11, 2399.

OUR PROFESSION IN 1888

James D. Craig, reminiscing at the Actuarial Society's fortieth anniversary observance (*T.A.S.A.* 30, 2), put the case in these words:

> The years preceding 1889 had been subject to such trying vicissitudes from the financial, agency and actuarial aspects that there was a tendency for secretiveness and distrust. Mutual confidence had not as yet become sufficiently general to render such a gathering [as an actuarial society] possible.

In addition to the specific "vicissitudes" described in this chapter, the practicing actuaries of 1888 had to worry about the continual fall in the interest rate which had been going on since 1869 and would continue until the turn of the century. In 1882 the Connecticut Mutual, of which Daniel H. Wells was then the young actuary, was the first company to respond to that hazard. Connecticut Mutual reduced its interest rate for reserves on new policies from 4 to 3%. This was considered excessively conservative and damaging to its competitive position, but others followed suit. The prevailing mortality trend was mildly favorable, but the failure of the Thirty American offices study to make this fact clear deprived actuaries of a means of lessening the impact of the interest rate decline on premiums.

The excesses committed in some companies' efforts to be number one in size were continuing unchecked; thoughtful actuaries foresaw that these would lead to great trouble.

The most careful count that can be made a century later of the number of actuaries on this continent in 1888 places the total at eighty-seven; certainly the full total was less than one hundred. Of those eighty-seven, thirty-eight would in a few months become charter members of the Actuarial Society; another thirty-three, then in junior posts, would become Fellows during the rest of the nineteenth century; eleven never joined on account of either having retired, moved into general management positions or been rejected under the Actuarial Society's rules; four became charter Fellows of the American Institute in 1909; and one (McCay) died in March 1889. Seventy-seven of these actuaries were in the United States, ten in Canada.

The number of life companies in the United States at the end of 1888 had risen from its low point, fifty-five in 1882, to sixty. Canada had twelve life insurance companies. These figures are for domestic companies only.

APPENDIX TO CHAPTER II

Papers by North American Actuaries in Volumes Earlier Than 1889 of the
Journal of the Institute of Actuaries

(These *JIA*s also contain many reports, comments on reports, reprints from U.S. trade journals, reviews, and observations on conditions in North America.)

Vol. & Page

1, 357	Charles Gill: "On the Determination of Surplus"
3, 289	Harvey G. P. Tuckett: "Opinions on Modes of Valuation"
3, 300	Charles Gill: "Rates of Mortality in the United States and California, as shown by the experience of the Mutual Life Insurance Company of New York, from 1 February 1843, to 1 February 1851."
9, 235	Sheppard Homans: "Remarks in Connection with the Report of the Committee on Vital Statistics made to the American Life Underwriters' Convention"
11, 121	Sheppard Homans: "On the Equitable Distribution of Surplus"
15, 410	Levi W. Meech: "Extract from Letter to W. M. Makeham as to the Graduation of the American Life Table: Males"
16, 355	Elizur Wright: "On Net-Premium Valuations with Reference to the American Insurance Law"
16, 384	John B. Cherriman: "On the American Ten-Year Non-Forfeiture Policies"
17, 56	Seth C. Chandler: "On the Law of the Ages at which Life Insurances Are Effective"
17, 161	Seth C. Chandler: "On the Construction of a Graduated Table of Mortality from a Limited Experience"
17, 301	Emory McClintock: "On the American Ten-Year Non-Forfeiture Policies"
18, 242	Emory McClintock: "On the Computation of Annuities on Makeham's Hypothesis"
19, 28	Walter S. Nichols: "On the Law of American Life, as Deduced from the Experience of the Mutual Benefit Life Insurance Company of New Jersey, Analysed and Adjusted by Gompertz's Law"
21, 295	John B. Cherriman: "Who First Introduced the Symbol (d_x)?"
21, 298	John B. Cherriman: "Formula for Paid-up Policy $(1 - P_x/P_{x+n})$"
21, 299	John B. Cherriman: "On the Value of an Annuity in Which a Final Payment Is Made at the End of the Term During Which the Life Fails"

Vol. & Page

22, 24   Charles F. McCay: "On the Adjustment of Mortality Tables with Reference to the Weight of Observations"

22, 134   Thomas B. Macaulay: "Retirants in the Eighth Year"

23, 62   Thomas B. Macaulay: "Relation between the Height and Weight of Men"

24, 173   Charles J. Harvey: "On a Formula for Returning to the Assured Their Contributions to the Surplus, Compared by Numerical Examples with the Results Shown by Some of the Methods in Use"

24, 296   Charles J. Harvey: "On an Average Premium"

Chapter III.

1889–1918:
THE FIRST FOUR BODIES

Speak of me as I am; nothing extenuate,
Nor set down aught in malice.

—Othello V, ii

THE DECISION TO LAUNCH A PROFESSIONAL BODY

Although opinions among the leading North American actuaries in 1889 differed— moderately on questions such as the extent of their organization's formality, and for a time intensely on the desirability of entrance by examination—unanimity on one basic matter reigned: ours was then and must continue to be a profession. In his 1909 reminiscences on the twentieth anniversary of the Society (*T.A.S.A.* 11, 28), Clayton C. Hall said:

> It is well in an organization like this to remember that the admission of a member and his value are determined solely by his character and his professional qualifications; by nothing else. I dwell upon this point because in discussions during recent years I have sometimes heard a member speak of himself and be referred to by others as representing such and such a company. Now no one in this Society can or ought to represent any company. . . . When this Society was formed there was much competition among some companies in the rush for business, a competition which at times took the form of bitter rivalry. It was a matter of surprise in some quarters that the actuaries could come together in frank conference as professional men and students, without a vestige of that feeling. And I believe that the example was not without its beneficial effect, beyond the limits of our own membership.

> But if [the] intention and purpose that this Society should be strictly a professional association should be lost sight of, and the idea gain ground and prevail that it is an association of the representatives of insurance corporations, then the usefulness of the Actuarial Society of America will be ended.

Only by initiative within the general New York area could a lasting organization be established, because, as shown by the locations of the thirty-eight charter members, that area had become the center of gravity:

New York and Newark	13
New England	10
Philadelphia, Baltimore, Richmond	6
Ontario and Quebec	4
Midwestern United States	4
California	1
	38

David Parks Fackler, at the same 1909 meeting (*T.A.S.A.* 11, 12), recounted the negotiations that led to success twenty-one years after the previous effort had collapsed:

> In the latter part of [the] year—1888—an old friend of Sheppard Homans called on him and urged that circumstances had changed so as to favor the formation of such a society as we desired, and it was decided to make the effort early in the following year. In February, 1889, Mr. St. John of Hartford, in a call at [my] office, said: "Why can we not have an actuarial society?" and Mr. McClintock stated that Mr. Hall had asked him the same question about that time, so with five of the oldest actuaries thus favorable it was clear that the time for action had arrived.

The latter part of 1888 coincided with W. H. C. Bartlett's retirement, at age eighty-four, from the position of actuary of Mutual Life; Elizur Wright had died in 1885; in 1885 also, Rufus W. Weeks was appointed actuary of New York Life. Thus, the trio who Fackler said (Chapter II) "were not actuaries in any proper sense of the word" had gone from the scene.

Although the quintet—Fackler (the "old friend"), Homans, St. John, McClintock, and Hall—share credit for getting the organizational ball rolling, the guiding hand throughout was clearly Fackler's. This was mainly because of his extraordinary leadership qualities, and also because his status as a consulting actuary kept the move from being identified with any company. In concert with Homans and McClintock he prepared the original list of actuaries deemed worthy, by dint of experience and personal integrity, to be invited to the organizational meeting; that penciled list still exists and appears to show that thirty-nine letters were dispatched, thirty-three to United States and six to Canadian actuaries. Oddly, it seems that in a few cases, the actuary's name being unknown, the letter was addressed to "The Actuary"; if so, no harm was done because letters addressed that way were generally not answered.

The circular letter of March 7, 1889, set forth the plan in these words (*T.A.S.A.* 1, Pt. 1, 3):

> *Dear Sir:* For some time past many American actuaries have desired opportunities to meet socially and discuss the various questions that present themselves from time to time, believing that such intercourse, while both pleasant and profitable to themselves would also advance the general interests of Life Insurance.

> How to bring it about has been the only difficulty.

> Five of the oldest members of the profession have lately concluded that it may now be practical to inaugurate an informal association, with meetings once or twice a year, and without attempting to say who should be eligible as members, it has been thought well to limit the preliminary call to those persons now actually serving as the Actuaries, or the Consulting Actuaries, of companies and making such life insurance work their primary business, as this gives a definite rule which can be followed without appearing to slight anyone, and it would otherwise be impossible to draw the line anywhere. When the gentlemen so invited meet, they can decide who shall be eligible to membership.

> It has been thought well that a preliminary meeting should be held in New York city in April, in a building apart from any Life Insurance Company, and that this (to further avoid any appearance of being in the interest of any particular company) should be sent by the undersigned.

Please state at your earliest convenience whether this plan commends itself to you, and if it does, which days in April would suit your convenience. Thus far all favor the proposition.

Yours, very truly,

(Signed) D. P. FACKLER

20 NASSAU STREET

So anxious were these founders to limit the membership to chief actuaries that they did not send letters to any of several eminent retired actuaries of the time. At the organizational meeting an opinion that it would be well to bring them in was expressed, but nothing was ever done about this.

On March 22, 1889, only fifteen days later, Fackler was in a position to send another circular letter, this one headed "AMERICAN ACTUARIAL ASSOCIATION," reporting the names and company affiliations of thirty-four actuaries who had expressed themselves in favor of the proposed association. April 25, 1889, was Fackler's choice; he remarked that New York hotels would be crowded soon after with celebrants of the centenary of George Washington's inauguration.

The meeting was set for the Astor House, starting with lunch, then "a private preliminary business meeting and appointment of committees to consider permanent organization, membership, etc." Dinner was to be at 6:30 P.M., "when other insurance men and reporters [could] be present." It was decided to have a stenographer at all sessions, giving future generations the benefit of the verbatim report in the first volume of the *Transactions*.

Fackler's second letter concluded thus (*T.A.S.A.* 1, Pt. 1,5):

By the next morning all will have had time for full reflection on the proposed basis of association, and a private business meeting of an hour or so, beginning at 10:30, will probably suffice for completing the organization.

Succeeding meetings may not need to last over a day, but it would seem wise to devote full time to the foundation of the Association.

Essays on any points of interest will be welcomed by the Association, and those who may be able to prepare such essays are requested to inform the secretary or chairman of the meeting, so that proper opportunity may be provided for their presentation.

The New York city members of the Association tender the freedom of their offices to those from other cities, and will bear the expenses of the entertainments and meetings as above.

Please state whether you may be expected.

Very respectfully,

(Signed) D. P. FACKLER

20 NASSAU STREET, NEW YORK, MARCH 22, 1889

The organizers' confidence that an organization would be formed prevailed in subsequent planning. On April 5, 1889, Fackler obtained written acceptance from Messrs. Homans and McClintock to head a "Reception Committee" for the Actuarial

Convention; they enlisted Weeks, Pierson, and Fackler himself to complete that group. The order of business was carefully designed, and menus printed for excellent lunch and dinner on April 25. The only material change from the original design was that "other insurance men" were not invited to the celebration dinner.

THE EVENT OF APRIL 25–26, 1889

Twenty-eight actuaries attended the inaugural meeting; some others sent their regrets. The only major life company of the time whose actuary was not identified as having at least expressed himself in favor of organizing was the Canada Life, then of Hamilton, Ontario. Sixty years later, Arthur Hunter, closing the proceedings at the Actuarial Society's final meeting (*T.A.S.A.* 50, 142), said:

> When the organization was first suggested there was considerable opposition on the part of several competitive companies who did not realize that the publication of their experience by a professional group would be of benefit to all. . . .
> A few years later, however, one of the companies which had not favored the formation of the Society had a change of heart, its President stating that the results of all actuarial investigations which would benefit the life insurance business should be made public. That broad-minded attitude was largely due to the reputation that the members of our Society had established for their zeal towards the best interests of the insurance world, keeping in mind their loyalty to their own companies.

Knowing that Alexander G. Ramsay, President of Canada Life, joined the Actuarial Society in 1893 and that actuaries of that company have given distinguished service to our profession ever since, we conclude that Ramsay was the one to whom Hunter referred.

Of the twenty-seven actuaries—Asa Wing arrived later from Philadelphia—who doubtless eyed the assembly pensively at the sumptuous opening luncheon, thirteen would later be officers of the Actuarial Society, and all but five would serve on the Council. Fackler would have the longest continuous Council service (thirty-six years until his death in October 1924); the young Thomas B. Macaulay would have the longest total service, forty-seven years between 1893 and his death in early 1942. Because of the constitutional privilege, adopted in 1891, giving ex-presidents life memberships on the Council, charter members still had majority voting power as late as 1909. That amendment had not originated with the Council but by petition of James M. Lee, almost certainly as a compliment to outgoing president, Sheppard Homans. It remained in effect until 1925 when Council membership for future past presidents became limited to ten years. When this limitation had its effect in 1936, the number (12) of ex-presidents on the Council equalled the number of elected members, excluding officers.

After the lunch, Fackler, putting the committee's plan into operation, moved that Homans be appointed Chairman and requested Israel C. Pierson to act as Secretary. Fackler than briefly narrated the events of the past months and voiced the hope "that our proceedings here will tend to develop something that will be of advantage, and not vanish in the air like some previous insurance organizations we have heard of." Pierson then suggested that each man present, except Fackler, respond in alphabetical order to the central question. This placed the onus of speaking first upon Jesse J. Barker of Philadelphia, who demonstrated true actuarial caution by just repeating the idea in Fackler's invitation letter that the new body be social in character.

William McCabe of Toronto was first to offer a detailed modus operandi, thus (*T.A.S.A.* 1, Pt. 1,11):

> I would fall in with the views expressed by Mr. Hall, that the organization should be a professional one, and I think the more closely we follow the organization either of the Actuaries of Scotland or of the Actuaries of Great Britain, the more successful our organization is likely to be. ... [I]t would be well to have an official journal in which important papers which may be read, may appear, after being properly scrutinized by the editing committee of the association.

McClintock brought up the question of classification of members, which was to be unsettled for several years (*T.A.S.A.* 1, Pt. 1, 12):

> As to the membership, we would all be connected with life insurance companies, but the membership ought not to be confined entirely to official actuaries of companies, I think. On the other hand, membership outside of the list of official actuaries should be a matter of scrutiny. There should be a committee appointed to examine any names which are proposed for membership, and to report on them, and after that report the name should be voted on by the Association, with whatever rules may be thought best in regard to the number of votes which should exclude. The classes of persons to be admitted ought to include others connected with insurance companies who have given some sign of devoting their lives to actuarial work. ... Then, of course, there are gentlemen altogether outside of companies who might very properly be admitted into such a professional organization as this would be. ...
>
> I think that while in the future we may look forward to having an institute, or something equivalent to it, which should hold strict examinations, which should in some way afford actuarial education to young men, and which should therefore be modeled perhaps in the future somewhat on the line of the Institute of Actuaries. I think to start with, it would be better to have only one class of members, and to leave the idea of a second class of members for further development, as a matter of evolution. ...
>
> As for a journal, or more properly speaking, an official publication of some sort, I won't undertake to say what the title ought to be. There is no question that we ought to have it. We cannot expect to do anything successfully without it.

In general, the discussion, skillfully led by the organizers, moved ahead smoothly in the planned direction, key questions being who should be admitted and what should be the structure of officers and the governing body. Finally, after some sentiment had been shown in favor of an odd number of members on that board, two committees were created, i.e., (1) a drafting committee of seven (Fackler, McCabe, McClintock, Miller, Wright, Wells, and Homans) to recommend a Constitution, and (2) a nominating committee of six (Barker, Hall, Weeks, Woodward, Ireland, and Smith) to propose six officers, namely, a President, 1st Vice-President, 2d Vice-President, Recording

Secretary, Corresponding Secretary, and Treasurer, and five Council members, making eleven in all.

Another matter left unsettled overnight was the organization's name. McClintock had expressed himself content with the name on the invitation letter, American Actuarial Association, though he remarked that the initials would come better if "Society" were substituted for "Association," and Wells had suggested making it "The Association of American Actuaries"; the Canadians had refrained from openly objecting to this but, as Macaulay mentioned in a letter printed in *JIA* 29, 544, three years later, "in deference to the Canadian members, and in order to emphasize the International idea, it was baptized the 'Actuarial Society of America', the noun 'America' not being limited to the United States, as the adjective generally is." McCabe doubtless brought this up at the drafting committee meeting.

The two committees did not report back until 10:30 A.M. the next day. Meanwhile the cordial atmosphere at the first day's adjournment was undoubtedly more than maintained by the carefully planned dinner; its menu and toasts are reproduced herewith.

Fackler served as toast-master. The speeches in response to the three toasts, and also the general discussion arising from prepared talks by several actuaries in response to Fackler's written invitation, are printed verbatim in Volume 1, Pt. 1, pages 31–51 of the journal, originally called *Papers and Transactions*.

To the first toast, "The Time-Tried System of Life Insurance," Homans replied by relating how he devised the American Experience Table; later in the evening he said about that table, "[T]he experience of every company so far as I know ... proves conclusively that [it], if a guess, was a most happy one. It was not a guess; it was an inspiration." W. C. Wright, the second speaker, remarked, with the work of his illustrious father, Elizur, in mind, that "one feather which at least the Massachusetts companies can claim, [is] that, excepting some experiments in the assessment line, no Massachusetts company has ever failed."

No hint was given by either Homans or Wright that the "time-tried system" they were toasting was in such bad odor with the American public that the total ordinary life insurance then in force in the United States ($3.6 billion) was only slightly greater than the total assessment insurance in force ($3.3 billion). The reputation of level premium insurance was destined to remain impaired until after abuses by some major life companies had been squelched by legislation arising from the 1905 Armstrong Investigation.

In the course of his remarks, Homans seems to have anticipated the concepts of "the valuation actuary" and "dynamic solvency" that actuaries of the 1980s regard as modern developments. Said Homans:

> [p. 31] As to being correct in practice, that would involve, of course, the collection of a premium margin sufficient to guard against adverse contingencies. ...

> [p. 34] A Company may be deficient in the net legal reserve, and yet be on the sure road to prosperity. On the other hand, a company may show a full net reserve and yet have unmistakable signs and evidences of decay.

The three members of the Institute of Actuaries in the gathering all spoke to the second toast acclaiming that forty-year-old institution. McClintock admitted that he

(Above) Menu at Inaugural Dinner of Actuarial Society of America, April 1889.
(Below) Three of the pioneers—left to right, Emory McClintock, Israel C. Pierson, William McCabe.

had never seen the Institute but hoped to do so (and indeed later did, probably several times). Macaulay spoke feelingly about the contrast between Great Britain and America on how well our profession is known over there and how poorly here. McCabe added his sentiments extemporaneously.

H. W. St. John, the appointed responder, was absent by illness. Instead, Miller and Hall spoke prophetically on "The Actuarial Profession In America."

Much having been said during the evening about mortality studies and the need for more of them, H. W. Smith pointedly urged that actuaries pay close attention to the trend in the interest rate.

The following morning, the Committee on Organization presented its draft of the Constitution, a copy of which draft exists today among Fackler's papers kept in the Society's library. Several changes were suggested and accepted. Key provisions on Membership, Elections, and Resolutions, emerged as follows:

ART. III. Membership. The membership of the society shall consist of the subscribers and of such other persons, connected with actuarial pursuits, as shall be duly elected. . . .

ART. VII. Election of officers and council. The officers and members of the council shall be elected by ballot, at the annual meeting for the term of one year. The president and vice-presidents shall not be eligible for the same office for more than three consecutive years. . . .

ART. IX. Election of members. All candidates for membership shall be nominated to the council by at least two members. The name of any candidate which shall be voted against by two members of the council shall be considered as withdrawn. . . . Candidates recommended by the council shall be balloted for by the members at the next meeting. Any candidate receiving three-fourths of the vote cast shall be declared elected. . . .

ART. XII. No resolution expressive of opinion shall be entertained at any meeting.

The Committee on Nominations not unexpectedly proposed Sheppard Homans for President and David Parks Fackler for 1st Vice-President. The entire recommended slate of eleven was unanimously elected.

The twenty-eight founding fathers must have felt pleased with the good work they had done, and to recognize themselves as that many charter members. And probably they were content that six others who had been invited but did not attend, were also in that category. But the record fails to show why an additional four—J. A. De Boer of Montpelier, R. P. Field of Philadelphia, J. H. Nitchie of Chicago, and E. B. Smith of Richmond—were later added, bringing the total to thirty-eight. There is no record that the Council ever approved these additions, although the Council did resolve at its June 1889 meeting that "the opportunity to sign the Constitution as 'Charter Members' should close at the time of the meeting of the Society in October." Presumably these four invitations were issued on the responsibility of Fackler and the others on the April Reception Committee. Table III.1 gives data on all the charter members.

The years 1889–1890 proved to be fruitful in the births of life insurance organizations. The Actuarial Society's founding was followed in quick succession by those of the Association of Life Insurance Medical Directors (1889) and the National Association of Life Underwriters (1890). An organization intimately related to ours (not least because its second president was Emory McClintock) was the American Mathematical Society (1889).

At the Council meeting on October 3, 1889, consideration was given to ten nominees, seven of whom the Council accepted, to be recommended for election that same day. One of the three whom the Council did not recommend was Henry S. Vail, a forty-two-year-old Chicago consulting actuary. He, twenty years later, would take the

Table III.1

CHARTER MEMBERS OF ACTUARIAL SOCIETY OF AMERICA, 1889

Member	Age in 1889	Years in Insurance Work	Inaugural Meeting Invited	Inaugural Meeting Attended	Company and Location
J. J. Barker	40	19	Yes	Yes	Penn Mutual Life, Philadelphia
H. Cillis	41	21	Yes	Yes	Germania (later Guardian), New York
J. M. Craig	41	24	Yes	No	Metropolitan Life, New York
J. A. De Boer	28	0*	No	No	National Life, Montpelier
G. Ellis	46	15	Yes	Yes	Travelers, Hartford
D. P. Fackler	48	30	Yes	Yes	Consulting actuary, New York
R. P. Field	39	5	No	No	Presbyterian Ministers Fund, Philadelphia
W. O. Gould	61	14	Yes	No	Pacific Mutual Life, San Francisco
C. C. Hall	42	21	Yes	Yes	Maryland Life, Baltimore
W. Hendry	55	19	Yes	Yes	Ontario Mutual (later Mutual Life), Waterloo
J. M. Holcombe	41	20	Yes	No	Phoenix Mutual Life, Hartford
S. Homans	58	34	Yes	Yes	Provident Savings Life, New York
O. B. Ireland	49	19	Yes	No	Massachusetts Mutual, Springfield
J. M. Lee	45	15	Yes	Yes	Berkshire Life, Pittsfield
C. A. Loveland	48	19	Yes	No	Northwestern Mutual Life, Milwaukee
J. B. Lunger	34	9	Yes	Yes	Prudential Insurance, Newark
T. B. Macaulay	29	12	Yes	Yes	Sun Life Assurance, Montreal
W. C. Macdonald	33	9	Yes	Yes	Confederation Life, Toronto
E. P. Marshall	44	20	Yes	Yes	Union Central Life, Cincinnati
W. A. Marshall	42	23	Yes	Yes	Home Life, New York
W. McCabe	54	18	Yes	Yes	North American Life Assurance, Toronto
E. McClintock	49	21	Yes	Yes	Mutual Life, New York
B. J. Miller	40	22	Yes	Yes	Mutual Benefit Life, Newark
J. H. Nitchie	38	19	No	No	National Life of the U.S.A., Chicago
G. W. Phillips	62	30	Yes	Yes	Equitable Life Assurance Society, New York
I. C. Pierson	46	23	Yes	Yes	Washington Life, New York
G. W. Sanders	44	14	Yes	Yes	Michigan Mutual Life, Detroit
E. B. Smith	56	23	No	No	Life of Virginia, Richmond
H. W. Smith	53	n.a.	Yes	Yes	American Life, Philadelphia
H. W. St. John	55	22	Yes	No	Aetna Life, Hartford
W. T. Standen	37	3	Yes	Yes	United States Life, New York
W. E. Starr	77	41	Yes	Yes	State Mutual Life, Worcester
S. N. Stebbins	70	29	Yes	Yes	Manhattan Life, New York
R. W. Weeks	43	22	Yes	Yes	New York Life, New York
D. H. Wells	44	15	Yes	Yes	Connecticut Mutual Life, Hartford
A. S. Wing	39	22	Yes	Yes	Provident Life & Trust (later Provident Mutual), Philadelphia
G. B. Woodward	37	20	Yes	Yes	John Hancock Mutual, Boston
W. C. Wright	43	23	Yes	Yes	New England Mutual, Boston
Median Age & Experience	**44 yrs.**	**20 yrs.**			

* The circumstances were that the original invitation was accepted by Actuary Osman D. Clark, and when he vacated in favor of Joseph A. De Boer during 1889 it presumably was considered satisfactory to accept the new incumbent.

initiative to launch the American Institute of Actuaries; history might have been different if that candidate had been accepted in 1889.

The Council's minutes of May 1895 contain the cryptic sentence:

> It was voted to confer with Mr. Levi W. Meech of Bridgeport, Conn. with reference to membership.

Minutes of subsequent meetings are silent on what transpired. Meech was then seventy-four years old, was well known for his mortality table of 1881 (Chapter II) and had just published a 1,000-page volume, the product of twenty years of planning and labor, *New Calculation Tables For Multiplication and Division* (Chapter IX). It seems that he would have been the ideal person to have been inducted into membership and then persuaded to write an account of the profession's pre-1889 era for the *Transactions*.

A later Council decision unfortunate in its effects was the rejection in March 1903 of Abb Landis (1856–1927) for membership, not in the Actuarial Society itself but merely in the International Congress. The influence of Abb Landis in the strengthening of actuarial underpinnings of fraternal benefit societies was immense even before 1903, and it would have been well to have cultivated his friendship and to have worked with him.

THE *TRANSACTIONS* AND *YEARBOOK*

Each of the first six volumes of the *Transactions*—the name was shortened by omitting *Papers and* in 1901—covered two years, i.e., four meetings. Volume 7, covered three years, Volume 8, just one year, then the two-year system was resumed until the permanent annual volume system became effective with Volume 12 in 1911.

Editorship was originally a responsibility of the secretary, thus being in the care of Israel C. Pierson (1889 to 1899) and then John Tatlock (1899 to 1905). At that point the editor's duties were separated from those of the secretary, and the editor became an officer; only six men (in succession) held that post between 1905 and the 1949 merger.

The last piece of Council business for 1899 (October 19) was a decision to print separately from the *Transactions* "a full list of members and associates once a year (with titles and addresses)." The first of these, constituting a *Year Book*, but not so named until 1927, appeared as of October 1, 1900. It was called informally "the pamphlet."

From the beginning strenuous efforts were made to develop a flow of papers and to establish quality standards, the Council itself serving as the committee on papers. At the October 1889 meeting, three papers were presented, Fackler having the honor of being the Society's first author. At the April 1890 meeting there were eight papers, all short. Papers at the next three meetings averaged four per meeting. The practice was for the president to appoint two members to contribute formal discussions of every paper that was more than an actuarial note; from this sprang the long continued understanding that senior members should speak first.

In April 1891 (*T.A.S.A.* 2, 111) Fackler contributed $250 in prizes for "the best essays regarding legislative interference with impaired life insurance companies" written by any person (not necessarily a member) having at least five years' experience in life insurance. Explaining his choice of topic, Fackler, then the Society's 1st Vice-President, wrote:

An actuary at work in 1897; Charles G. Reiter with his assistant and his calculator. (Courtesy of Metropolitan Life Insurance Co., New York, N.Y.)

> At the last meeting of the society it appeared to be generally admitted that the unwise and hasty legislation of several States concerning impairment, constitutes one of the greatest latent dangers to the cause of life insurance; and it seems clear that [now]—when no company appears in jeopardy—is the right time to correct the errors of the past and prepare sound laws for the future. . . .

> On reflection the writer has thought that the best way to induce thorough and practical consideration of the subject would be to offer prizes for essays thereupon . . . [t]he decision to be made by a committee of five members of the society to be appointed by the president next fall.

In January 1892, the committee reported (*T.A.S.A.* 2, 329) to Fackler, by then the president, that the essay, which proved to have been submitted by a Society member, Archibald A. Welch, was entitled to the $150 first prize and that no other essay was worthy of the second prize. The committee expressed surprise "that the liberal prizes offered did not lead to a sharper competition."

Welch's paper (*T.A.S.A.* 2, 330) identified the laws of New York, Massachusetts, and Connecticut as culprits in that they:

> throw into the hands of receivers all companies whose assets fall below a certain percentage of their liabilities, and provide that these assets shall then be divided among all claimants according to a certain arbitrary, technical rule. The injustice this system works to all impaired risks has served as a powerful text against the present system of governmental control. . . . Inasmuch as life insurance contracts are so different from and so much more complex than other ordinary business contracts, some system of control is advisable, [so] that the interests of all policy-holders may be equally conserved.

Oddly, Welch's paper giving his prescription for remedying this bad legislation was not discussed by the members. It was, however, soon followed by H. W. St. John's paper on the same subject at the First International Congress of Actuaries in 1895 (reprinted in *T.A.S.A.* 4, 240).

Actuarial concern about the need for legislative reform in this area had been sharpened by the inequitable treatment of policyholders in the 1888 insolvency of the Charter Oak Life Insurance Company of Hartford, apparently the largest of the many life companies that failed in North America in the nineteenth century.

In May 1900, Fackler was back with another offer—a prize for a paper written by an Associate. Not until 1904 was it won by Arthur Hunter. Fackler immediately renewed the prize, again for Associates, by then a rapidly growing group. There were three winners in the ensuing eight years, after which time the donorship was taken over by the Society.

Many years later, in 1937 (*R.A.I.A.* 26, 45), Fergus J. McDiarmid presented an analysis (by subject) of 591 papers presented to the Actuarial Society and the American Institute showing that only eight papers (1 1/3%) had dealt with investment problems and the rate of interest. There had been two such papers in 1899, one of these having earned its author, Charlton T. Lewis, lasting fame for predicting that the prevailing United States interest rate, which had moved steadily downward through the second half of the nineteenth century, was about to turn upward.

The volumes of the *Transactions* were indeed valuable, but they were by no means encyclopedic. Fackler, in a notice to members during his presidency, pointed out that many remarks in discussions and even long verbal exchanges on burning subjects were being omitted at speakers' requests. Furthermore, except for the 1889 dinner, the practice was not to print after-dinner speeches and comments, which, Fackler maintained, were in many respects the highlights of the meetings.

THE COUNCIL, 1889–1909

Table III.2 lists the Actuarial Society Council members through that body's first two decades, ending with those elected in May 1909. It shows that the heavy original proportion of New York actuaries on the Council declined as the years went by. The upward trend in total Council membership was caused by the granting of life memberships to ex-presidents and by a May 1905 increase in the number of elected members from six to nine.

THE ACTUARIAL SOCIETY'S MOTTO

In June 1891 the Council decided to solicit member suggestions for a Society motto. The response was remarkable; twenty-four were submitted, some members offering more than one. A ballot listing all these suggestions was then distributed, requesting each member to select the five that he considered appropriate finalists. Preferences were to be marked showing the order of choice. Oddly, not only was the eventual winning quotation from Ruskin's "The Stones of Venice" the last one on the ballot but also a printing error caused the members to be voting on wording that started with "The mark" rather than "The work" of science.

At the Spring 1892 meeting, the Secretary reported the following five as the leading vote-getters:

"The work of science is to substitute facts for appearances,
and demonstrations for impressions."—*Ruskin.*   35 votes

"Truth, our aim; the time to come, our care."   28 votes

"By calculation you will find the truth." (given also in
Greek)   17 votes

"Experience is the only prophecy of wise men."
—*Lamartine*   17 votes

"I have but one lamp by which my feet are guided, and that is
the lamp of experience. I know of no way of judging of the future but by the past."—*Henry*   15 votes

The question may be worthy of contemplation whether a different counting method—we are not told how preferences were weighted—or the absence of rival submissions on the themes of truth and experience, might have resulted in the feet of future generations of actuaries being guided by one or other of the runner-up mottoes. One is also struck by the similarity between the first runner-up and the motto that the Canadian Institute of Actuaries chose for itself in 1965—"Nobis Cura Futuri." (See discussion in Chapter VI.)

No responder gave the saintly William of Ockham his chance to be our profession's spiritual father by submitting his "Entia non sunt multiplicanda praeter necessitatem," a relevant translation of which is "What can be done with fewer assumptions is done in vain with more." One wonders to what extent a different motto would have produced a profession with different attitudes and restraints.

ENROLLMENT OF OVERSEAS MEMBERS

Between April 1890 and October 1898 there was an extraordinary influx of new Actuarial Society members from overseas countries, the result of a deliberate Council policy to extend such invitations. It began quietly with the election of two New Zealanders in 1890, followed by an Australian in 1891, and a second Australian in 1892 along with two English actuaries.

At least one new overseas member was elected every year until 1898. The years 1893 (seven entrants), 1895 (eight) and 1898 (ten) were specially noteworthy in this respect, the last two of these years being International Congress years that gave unusually good opportunities for extending personal invitations. By the fall of 1898, thirty-seven in all had been enrolled.

Several of these members were leading actuaries in their own countries, but few ever contributed a paper or attended a meeting in North America. Outstanding exceptions were (1) Gerald H. Ryan, FIA, then editor of the *Journal of the Institute of Actuaries,* who came to the New York meeting in October 1894 and presented a paper to the Institute four months later that included a section, "Some Observations on Insurance Matters in Canada and the United States," (2) George King, FIA, one of whose many claims to fame had been authorship of the Institute's Life Contingencies textbook in 1887, who honored our 1911 Hartford meeting with his presence, and (3)

Table III.2
ACTUARIAL SOCIETY OF AMERICA
CHART OF COUNCIL MEMBERS, 1889–1909

Election Year

	1889	1890	1891	1892	1893	1894	1895	1896	1897	1898	1899	1900	1901	1902	1903	1904	1905	1906	1907	1908	1909
S. Homans, New York	P	P	L	L	L	L	L	L	D												
D. P. Fackler, New York	V	V	P	P	L	L	L	L	L	L	L	L	L	L	L	L	L	L	L	L	L
H. W. St. John, Hartford	V	V	V		P	P	V	V	V	V	V	V	L	L	L	L	L	L	L	L	L
I. C. Pierson, New York	S	S	S	S	S	S	S	S	S	V	V	V	V	V	P	P	L	L	L	D	
W. T. Standen, New York	S																				
B. J. Miller, Newark	T	T	T	V	V	V	V	P	P	L	L	L	L	D							
O. B. Ireland, Springfield	M	M	M	T	T	T	T	V	V	V	V	V	P	P	L	L	L	L	L	L	L
W. McCabe, Toronto	M	M	M	M	M	M	V	V	V												
G. W. Phillips, New York	M	M	M	M	M	M	V	V													
H. W. Smith, Philadelphia	M	M	M	M																	
E. McClintock, New York	M	M	V	V	V	V	P	P	L	L	L	L	L	L	L	L	L	L	L	L	L
R. W. Weeks, New York		S	M	M	M	M	M	M													
C. C. Hall, Baltimore			M	M	M	M	M						M	M	V	V	E	E	E	E	
D. H. Wells, Hartford			M	M	M	M	M		M	V	V	M	M		V						
G. B. Woodward, Boston				M	M	M	M														
A. S. Wing, Philadelphia				M	M	M	M														
T. B. Macaulay, Montreal					M	M	M	M	M	M	P	P	L	L	L	L	L	L	L	L	L
C. A. Loveland, Milwaukee						M	M	M	M	M		M	M	M	M	M					
J. J. Barker, Philadelphia							M	M	M												
W. C. Wright, Boston							M	M	M	M											
W. E. Starr, Worcester								M	M	M											
J. Tatlock, New York									T	T	S	S	S	S	S		M	M			
J. B. Lunger, Newark									M	M	M	T	M	M	M	M					
E. P. Marshall, Cincinnati										M	M										
J. M. Lee, Pittsfield											M	M	M								

LEGEND

P = President
V = Vice President
S = Secretary
T = Treasurer
E = Editor, *The Transactions*
M = Elected Member
L = Life Member
D = Died during that Council Year

Table III.2—Continued
ACTUARIAL SOCIETY OF AMERICA
CHART OF COUNCIL MEMBERS, 1889–1909

Election Year

	1889	1890	1891	1892	1893	1894	1895	1896	1897	1898	1899	1900	1901	1902	1903	1904	1905	1906	1907	1908	1909
W. C. Macdonald, Toronto																M	M	M	M	M	M
J. M. Craig, New York																M	M	M	M	M	M
W. S. Nichols, Newark											M	M	M	M	M	M	M	M	M	M	M
J. G. Van Cise, New York											M			M	M	M		M			
J. K. Gore, Newark												M	M	M	M	M	V	V	V	P	P
A. A. Welch, Hartford												M	T	T	T	T	T	V	V	V	V
F. Sanderson, Toronto													M		M	M	M	M	M	M	M
S. N. Ogden, Newark															M	M	M	M	M	M	M
D. G. Alsop, Philadelphia															M	M	M	M	T	T	T
W. S. Smith, Boston															M	M	M				
A. Hunter, New York																	S	S	S	S	S
J. A. De Boer, Montpelier																	M	M	M	M	M
R. Henderson, New York																M	M	M	M	M	M
W. A. Marshall, New York																M	M	M	M	M	M
H. Moir, New York																	M	M	M	V	V
W. A. Hutcheson, New York																M	M	M	M	M	M
E. J. Sartelle, Worcester																		M	M		
F. H. Johnston, Newark																		M	M	M	M
P. C. H. Papps, Newark																		M	M	M	M
W. M. Strong, New York																				E	M
T. Bradshaw, Toronto																					M
Total Council Membership	11	11	12	12	13	13	14	14	15	15	15	16	17	17	17	21	22	22	22	23	22

LEGEND
P = President   E = Editor, The *Transactions*
V = Vice President   M = Elected Member
S = Secretary   L = Life Member
T = Treasurer   D = Died during that Council Year

Charles D. Higham, FIA, who took continuing keen interest in North American actuarial matters and bequeathed books to the Society library.

Mr. (later Sir Gerald) Ryan, in his "Observations," was generally complimentary, but expressed surprise at the high lapse and surrender rates experienced by companies in the United States and the practice of guaranteeing substantial surrender values. He commented also on the huge, beautiful home offices in New York, particularly the headquarters building of Metropolitan Life that he said "vies with the famous Paris opera house in the richness and beauty of its hall."

DOMESTIC GROWTH, 1890–1898

During the years in which the Actuarial Society was electing thirty-seven overseas members, the number of new Canadian and United States members was only slightly larger, forty members, most added before 1894. In 1890 six insurance department actuaries were elected, and membership was awarded as a compliment to the Philadelphia insurance historian and editor, J. A. Fowler; the rest in 1890 were mainly assistant actuaries in companies already represented. One interesting enrollment in 1891 was Samuel E. Stilwell of Philadelphia; the Society's rule that members must be engaged in home office work was applied so strictly that he had to resign in October 1894 by reason of having become a general agent. He returned in 1903.

Emory McClintock became so discouraged with the outlook for future membership growth that in his presidential address of October 1897 he said that he had been dissuading young men of education and promise from the thought of entering our profession. McClintock attributed the declining employment prospects for actuaries to the statutory requirement in both Canada and the United States for immediate accumulation of net level premium reserves. In fact, McClintock's assessment was, as he admitted it might have been, unduly pessimistic; very soon after he spoke, the number of companies began a solid and sustained increase, mostly in midwestern and southern states where modified valuation methods were permitted. Also, the institution in 1896 of an examination system in the Actuarial Society began to produce a flow of Associates and, after the turn of the century, Fellows. The first Fellow by examination was John Francis Roche in 1900.

CLASSIFICATION OF MEMBERS

Almost immediately after the inauguration in 1889, Fackler had started work on a system of membership grades; among his personal papers we find correspondence on this subject with Clayton C. Hall, Howell W. St. John, and Edward B. Smith. By September 1891 Fackler felt ready to discuss the subject in his presidential address, whereupon Homans moved that the subject be referred to the Council for special consideration and report. McClintock seconded this motion, which was then carried without recorded opposition.

At the March 1892 Council meeting the proposals that developed were, in summary:

    I. To establish two grades of membership;

    II. That an examination be required for admission to either grade;

III. That no one be admitted otherwise excepting by the unanimous vote of the Council and Society.

At the April 1892 Society meeting, formal notice was given of a proposed constitutional amendment (*T.A.S.A.* 2, 354) to provide for a new class of members to be called Associates.

The recommended requirements were that the applicant be twenty-one years of age, pursuing actuarial studies and looking forward to future membership; that he be nominated by at least two members of the Society; that his nomination be approved by the Council with not more than one negative vote; and that he pay such fee and pass such preliminary examination as may be prescribed by the Council.

A key point was that the persons passing these tests would not be Society members. They would be permitted to be present, without participation, at Society meetings and to receive its publications, but in those days the word "member" meant what since 1905 has been called Fellow.

A companion recommendation was offered, changing the requirements for membership (ibid.):

> Any Associate twenty-five years of age shall be admitted as a member on passing such final examination as may be prescribed by the Council as a test of professional attainments. Otherwise, no one shall be admitted as a member unless by the unanimous recommendation of the Council, followed by a unanimous ballot of the Society.

The limitation to ages twenty-five or above, which must have seemed quite natural to the members at the time, proved to be an administrative nuisance as well as an annoyance to many whose admissions had to be postponed on that account. A constitutional amendment reducing the minimum age from twenty-five to twenty-one reached the floor at the October 1902 Society meeting (*T.A.S.A.* 7, 381) but failed to receive the needed two-thirds vote. Any age limitation was completely abandoned by unanimous vote in October 1937.

The Council seems not to have feared that the proposal for an examination system might fail, but at the October 1892 meeting something went seriously wrong. The constitutional amendment, supported enthusiastically by President Fackler, was accorded an affirmative vote, but then a move for reconsideration surfaced. A motion by Homans that consideration be postponed until April 1893 was adopted, but subsequently the Council, sensing major opposition, withdrew the proposal indefinitely. The possibility of offering it again was discussed at a Council meeting on July 6, 1894, but was unanimously voted down. Not until the Society meeting of October 1895 was the question revived.

In his musings at the Society's Twenty-fifth Anniversary Dinner, May 21, 1914, recorded in a special pamphlet (kept in the Society library) not incorporated into the *T.A.S.A.*, D. P. Fackler said that, at the October 1892 meeting, "the Society voted to amend the constitution . . . to require examinations, but before adjournment some timid members moved a reconsideration of the vote." This suggests that the opposition arose from fears that an examination system might cause young people to look elsewhere for their careers.

At that 1895 meeting at which the revived constitutional change was given formal notice, the president, Emory McClintock, said (*T.A.S.A.* 4, 269):

> It is said that some of those members of this Society who in 1892 opposed the examination of candidates as a requisite for membership, with the formation of a secondary class of members, called "associates," expecting, but not yet able, to pass such final examination, are now of a different mind.

The 1892 amendment was then, after four years delay, adopted at the April 1896 meeting. For the next nine years, the two membership classes were "Members" and "Associates," the designation of the former being changed by amendment in October 1905 to "Fellows." A new Article V was then added to the bylaws authorizing use of the respective initials F.A.S. and A.A.S.

The other classification proposal that had been mooted in 1889—that the scope of the Actuarial Society be broadened by admitting some who were not actuaries—never came up again for Society consideration; the Council, at its July 1894 meeting, dropped that idea.

After the examination system had become well established, it became more and more difficult for the Council to gain the Fellows' approval of specific recommendations for elections other than by examination. Three actuaries (one of them E. E. Rhodes, quickly to become a leader in the profession) were voted into Fellowship without examination in 1906, and one in 1910, in addition to the (honorary) Fellowship conferred that year upon the distinguished British actuary, George J. Lidstone.

When yet another Fellowship candidate had been accepted upon Council nomination in May 1911, the president began to receive letters questioning that whole procedure. He therefore gave an extended explanation the following October (*T.A.S.A.* 12, 352), amounting to a spirited defense of the practice in the past (stating that "a number of them whose membership would add to the dignity and to the strength of the Society would necessarily be left out unless some special concessions were made") followed by at least a hint that the need no longer existed.

Nevertheless, four Council nominations were made in 1916 (*T.A.S.A.* 17, 388). Three actuaries were accepted as Fellows and one was rejected. The Council thereupon ceased to attempt to use this route to Fellowship except for a single case, that of Percy H. Evans in 1927. At that time E. E. Rhodes himself was president of the Actuarial Society; Evans had been president of the American Institute and at age 53 could hardly be expected to sit for examinations. Rhodes took it upon himself to mail a personal appeal to 213 Fellows and, on March 31, 1927, had the embarrassing duty of notifying Evans that 16 responders up to then had been opposed. Evans then gave up hope. Details of this incident are in an article, "Three Strikes on Percy H. Evans," by Mary G. Frankel (*The Actuary,* December 1982).

INTERNATIONAL CONGRESSES

The *Members' Handbook* of the Institute of Actuaries tells us that the structure of the International Congresses conducted by the International Actuarial Association (IAA) came into being in the following way (p. G/17):

> [F]riendship ... arose between Belgian, French and English actuaries in con-
> nexion with negotiations for publishing a translation into French of George
> King's textbook on Life Contingencies.
>
> Two Belgian actuaries, Messrs. A. Begault and L. Mahillon [both of whom were
> early overseas members of the Actuarial Society] were leaders in the initiative to
> hold an international meeting of actuaries. ...
>
> With the support of the Institute of Actuaries and the French Institute, the first
> Congress met in Brussels in September 1895.
>
> The International Actuarial Association headquartered in Brussels serves to
> provide continuity in arrangements, made by the respective host countries, for
> successive Congresses.

In the Appendixes to this and Chapters IV through VI are lists of papers by North American authors published for the Congresses of the eras described in these chapters. A problem down through the years has been actuaries' unawareness of past Congress papers on particular subjects. The Institute of Actuaries first tackled that problem on behalf of all interested actuaries by publishing an index to the *Transactions* of the first ten Congresses, in 1936, and has repeated that fine service to our profession by creating, for publication by the IAA, an index of the eleven Congresses between 1937 and 1980. It is to be hoped that before long actuaries will enjoy computer-guided access to the host of revealing Congress papers written by our colleagues around the world.

The First Congress (1895) is described in detail in Emory McClintock's presidential address (*T.A.S.A.* 4, 258); just four United States actuaries (McClintock, Pierson, St. John, and Homans) and one Canadian (Macaulay) were present. Language was a difficulty, as McClintock remarked (p. 262):

> The discussions were always in French, unfamiliar to the immense majority of
> the actuaries invited to take part. Sometimes the same remarks would be given
> in two languages, one of them French; and on one or two days a member of the
> Congress assisted his friends who spoke English only by repeating a brief
> abstract of some of their points in French. It was a situation in which broken
> French was better than none, and which therefore afforded much useful practice
> to those to whom that elegant language is not native.

One of the major subjects—indeed the perceived need that had made the idea of a Congress so widely attractive—was the necessity for a universal actuarial notation. This proved difficult to achieve even though it was the consensus that the English notation, developed by David Jones in 1843 and used in George King's textbook published in 1887, was necessary for English-speaking actuaries and for actuaries using an 1894 translation of that book. A useful resolution was adopted, but when American and other speakers pointed out that some additional symbols were needed, the subject was kept open. In fact, a comprehensive solution was not reached until after World War II.

Those present desired this to be just the first of a regular series of Congresses, which was what happened. The Second Congress met in London in 1898, serving also as a celebration of the fiftieth anniversary of the Institute of Actuaries. At that meeting, Walter S. Nichols, speaking in place of Sheppard Homans, who had died that year, presented a paper, "The Limitations of the System of Net Valuations" (reprinted in *T.A.S.A.* 5, 195), which is as good a summary of late nineteenth century thinking on that controversial topic as can be found in our literature. At the meeting's conclusion a French actuary recommended that the date of the Third Congress be changed from 1901 to 1900 so that the visitors could also attend the Paris International Exposition. McClintock then said that the Actuarial Society of America had wished to invite the actuaries to New York in 1901 and hoped that the Fourth Congress might be held in New York in 1903, an invitation that was promptly accepted.

The Fourth International Congress in New York, August 31–September 5, 1903, *Transactions* (*TICA*) for which were later published in two volumes of 1,112 and 253 pages, respectively, seems to have been an unqualified success under the leadership of Israel C. Pierson. A description of its program and a commentary by John Tatlock were printed in the *Transactions of the Actuarial Society of America* comprising Volume 7, No. 30 (specially assigned for this purpose), pages 501–540. There was not to be another Congress in North America until 1957.

On Monday September 7, 1903, the delegates and accompanying persons travelled by steamer to Albany, stopping en route at West Point. From Albany many continued by special train to Toronto and Montreal, enjoying the hospitality of actuaries and other insurance company officers in those cities.

The Council of the Actuarial Society had provided Pierson with a temporary clerical staff of one, Miss Frances Straut, to assist him with Congress preparation and with his duties as president of that Congress, duties heaped on top of his existing responsibility as president of the Actuarial Society itself. Miss Straut stayed on afterwards, as this Society's first employee, for more than forty years until her death in 1945 shortly before she was due to retire.

Three more Congresses were held before a fifteen-year interruption, from 1912 to 1927, caused by World War I and the subsequent period of personal hostilities and estrangement. This hiatus almost resulted in formation of another international actuarial body embracing only the English-speaking countries.

THE FIRST ELECTED WOMEN MEMBERS

Miss Emma Warren Cushman (1847–1923) entered the Massachusetts Insurance Department in 1875 as a clerk under the tutelage of William S. Smith, its actuary and Deputy Insurance Commissioner who had been elected a member of the Actuarial Society in April 1890. When, in 1894, he became Actuary of John Hancock Mutual, Miss Cushman succeeded him as the Actuary of the Insurance Department. It was thus natural that she be elected a Member of the Society; this was done with no evidence of hesitation or controversy about bringing a woman into this heretofore all male environment. It was well known that the Institute of Actuaries barred women from membership, a practice that continued until 1919 (coincidentally, the year that two ladies, Grace A. Martin of Waterloo, Ontario, and Estella C. King of New York earned their Associateships by examination in the Society). In the Casualty Actuarial Society, Emma C. Maycrink and Dorothy Rolph had been admitted as Fellows in 1915; that same year Henricka Beach qualified as an Associate of the American Institute of Actuaries. In

The first woman Fellow:
Emma Warren Cushman, 1895.

The first Fellow by examination:
John Francis Roche, 1900.

1916, three women, Helen E. Brown, Ethel M. Heath, and Frances D. Partridge, were elected charter members of the Fraternal Actuarial Association.

In the case of Miss Cushman, it must have been obvious that those male bastions, the Actuarial Society dinners (to which members' wives were not invited), would be affected in character and even in location by a lady's inclusion. But any such fears proved groundless; Miss Cushman did not attend a single Society meeting during the entire first eighteen years of her membership. One wonders whether an agreement with her to that end had been quietly reached.

After her retirement from the Insurance Department in 1917, Miss Cushman joined the actuarial staff of the John Hancock, continuing there until her sudden death in 1923.

MORTALITY STUDIES

Notwithstanding the hopes for early action on an intercompany mortality study expressed at the Actuarial Society's inaugural meeting in 1889, none emerged until 1903. In April 1892, Daniel H. Wells, acting as a committee of one appointed by the Council, presented a report on "Suggestions Regarding the Investigation of the Mortality Experience of Life Insurance Companies" (*T.A.S.A.* 2, 395), in which he bewailed the secrets hidden by studying only data "from which have been eliminated nearly all those already tainted by disease" and how little was known about "the exact conditions which affect the mortality rate, and the degree to which they affect it." His emphasis was less upon the value of such knowledge in improving risk selection within a company than upon the danger that variations might render premiums and reserves that were safe for one company to be hazardous for others. He mentioned many circumstances reflecting such differences, including policy type and size, residence, heredity, occupation, withdrawals, height and weight, use of alcohol, and smoking habits.

Wells' remarkable analysis was distributed to the members and discussed, but the Council made no pronouncement on what action was indicated. All was quiet on the mortality study front for another eight years, when McClintock presented a paper (*T.A.S.A.* 6, 373) essentially supporting Wells' views and leading to a blueprint in 1901 for a study that bore the title "Specialized Mortality Investigation." By that time the objectives clearly included risk selection. Thirty-four life companies contributed data going back in some cases as far as 1870. A table derived from English population and life insurance experience was designed as a yardstick to measure standard mortality amongst healthy lives. There were ninety-eight special classes of risks. Much was learned, even though the value of the results for underwriting purposes was limited by major differences in company practices that existed during that lengthy exposure period.

Actuaries at the Actuarial Society Meeting in Pittsfield, Massachusetts, October 1896. Name key is available from SOA archives.

In 1902 David Parks Fackler presented a paper to the Institute of Actuaries (*JIA* 37, 1) describing the purpose, scope, and procedure of the Specialized Mortality Investigation. Almost half of that fifteen-page paper was devoted to describing, with illustrations, the punch-card system and machines for punching and sorting the three million cards used in that investigation. This was not a Hollerith system (see Chapter IX) but one personally devised and constructed by John K. Gore, F.A.S., then Actuary of the Prudential.

By 1909 the Actuarial Society was ready to join with the Association of Life Insurance Medical Directors of America (ALIMDA) in the first of many cooperative projects, this one called the "Medico-Actuarial Mortality Investigation" (MAMI), the experience of which covered about 93% of all policies issued by all life companies in the United States and Canada since 1885. This immense work, published in five volumes in 1912–1914, was the progenitor of future investigations; one of its triumphs was a set of tables showing mortality ratings for build. An examination of its findings is printed in *T.A.S.A.* 15, page 62, and discussed on page 417.

TABLE I
STANDARD RATES OF MORTALITY PER 1000 (M. A. TABLE)

USED TO OBTAIN EXPECTED DEATHS

Policy Year	AGES AT ENTRY							Policy Year
	15-19	20-24	25-29	30-34	35-39	40-44	45-49	
1	3.1	3.3	3.5	3.7	4.1	4.7	6.4	1
2	4.3	4.5	4.6	4.8	5.2	6.4	8.8	2
3	4.5	4.6	4.7	4.9	5.4	6.9	9.5	3
4	4.6	4.7	4.8	5.0	5.7	7.5	10.4	4
5	4.6	4.8	4.9	5.2	5.9	8.0	11.3	5
6	4.7	4.8	4.9	5.3	6.2	8.5	12.2	6
7	4.7	4.9	5.0	5.4	6.6	9.1	13.2	7
8	4.7	4.9	5.0	5.5	7.0	9.8	14.3	8
9	4.8	4.9	5.1	5.7	7.5	10.6	15.4	9
10	4.8	4.9	5.2	5.9	8.0	11.5	16.7	10
11	4.8	5.0	5.3	6.2	8.5	12.5	18.1	11
12	4.9	5.0	5.4	6.6	9.1	13.5	19.6	12
13	4.9	5.1	5.5	7.0	9.8	14.6	21.4	13
14	4.9	5.2	5.7	7.5	10.6	15.8	23.4	14
15	4.9	5.3	5.9	8.0	11.5	17.1	25.7	15
16	5.0	5.4	6.2	8.5	12.5	18.5	28.3	16
17	5.0	5.5	6.6	9.1	13.5	20.1	31.2	17
18	5.1	5.6	7.0	9.8	14.6	21.9	34.4	18
19	5.2	5.8	7.5	10.6	15.8	24.0	37.9	19
20	5.3	6.1	8.0	11.5	17.1	26.4	41.7	20
21	5.4	6.4	8.5	12.5	18.5	29.1	45.8	21
22	5.5	6.8	9.1	13.5	20.1	32.1	50.3	22
23	5.7	7.3	9.8	14.6	21.9	35.4	55.1	23
24	5.9	7.8	10.6	15.8	24.0	39.0	60.2	24

Policy Year	AGES AT ENTRY							Policy Year
	50-53	54-56	57-59	60-62	63-65	66-68	69-70	
1	9.1	12.2	16.0	20.5	26.0	30.0	35.0	1
2	12.5	15.8	20.4	27.5	36.0	47.0	57.8	2
3	13.8	18.3	24.0	32.1	42.9	56.6	69.7	3
4	15.0	20.1	26.4	35.4	47.1	61.7	75.5	4
5	16.3	21.9	29.1	39.0	51.6	66.8	81.8	5
6	17.5	24.0	32.1	42.9	56.6	72.3	88.4	6
7	19.0	26.4	35.4	47.1	61.7	78.3	95.7	7
8	20.6	29.1	39.0	51.6	66.8	84.8	103.7	8
9	22.5	32.1	42.9	56.6	72.3	91.9	112.4	9
10	24.7	35.4	47.1	61.7	78.3	99.5	121.8	10
11	27.2	39.0	51.6	66.8	84.8	107.9	131.9	11
12	30.0	42.9	56.6	72.3	91.9	116.9	142.9	12
13	33.1	47.1	61.7	78.3	99.5	126.6	154.8	13
14	36.5	51.6	66.8	84.8	107.9	137.2	167.5	14
15	40.2	56.6	72.3	91.9	116.9	148.6	181.3	15
16	44.2	61.7	78.3	99.5	126.6	160.9		16
17	48.5	66.8	84.8	107.9	137.2	174.1		17
18	53.1	72.3	91.9	116.9	148.6	188.4		18
19	58.1	78.3	99.5	126.6	160.9	203.7		19
20	63.2	84.8	107.9	137.2	174.1	220.1		20
21	68.5	91.9	116.9	148.6	188.4	237.7		21
22	74.1	99.5	126.6	160.9	203.7	256.5		22
23	80.3	107.9	137.2	174.1	220.1			23
24	86.9	116.9	148.6	188.4	237.7			24

27

The Select Mortality Table used as the yardstick for the Medico-Actuarial Mortality Investigation, 1912.
(Vol. III—Effect of Occupation as Mortality, p.27. Compiled and published by the Association of Life Insurance Medical Directors and the Actuarial Society of America, New York, 1913.)

In 1911 the National Convention of Insurance Commissioners or NCIC (now the NAIC) asked the Actuarial Society to undertake construction of a mortality table reflecting recent experience among insured lives. The NCIC made no direct suggestion that the purpose go beyond that of discovering the size of the divergence in mortality from that of the American Experience Table, then nearly a half-century old. Initially, the Society Council demurred; its committee that looked into this matter pointed out, from its awareness of the MAMI experience, that a modern table might show death rates ranging from 40% of American Experience at young ages to 90% at older ages, and emphasized the potentially awkward fact that aggregate reserves by such a table would be higher, not lower, than those by the venerable existing standard. Postponement of this project, said the committee, "would be in no wise detrimental to the interests of policyholders." The Council assured the NCIC that it would take up this work when clear of its existing commitments, provided a sufficient number of companies proved willing to contribute their experience and to defray the necessary expenses.

There the matter rested until 1915 when the NCIC renewed its request. The Society Council commissioned for its Spring Meeting a paper by Henry Moir, "Should We Prepare a New Mortality Table?" (*T.A.S.A.* 16, 8), which was discussed at that same meeting; the Council then recommended that a new mortality table or tables be prepared under the Society's direction. That recommendation was adopted, and thus the American-Canadian Mortality Investigation, giving experience of 59 companies during the years 1900 to 1915 on policies issued from 1843 to 1914, was launched. The NCIC, however, performed a service to our profession by bringing the American Institute of Actuaries into the picture, making this the first occasion for cooperation between that young body and the Actuarial Society. The report was published in 1918.

THE ARMSTRONG INVESTIGATION, 1905

That American actuaries knew the race among several large life insurance companies for volume meant troubles ahead is obvious from several forecasts and hints. In his presidential address of April 1892 (*T.A.S.A.* 2, 356), D. P. Fackler said:

> The pressure on [field] managers from without, on the part of agents, and the temptations from within, through their own ambition, make it very unlikely that any voluntary limitation or cessation of competition will be permanent.

> For fifteen years past it has been urged that the State should impose some more or less direct limitation on the growth of companies, and lately the retiring manager of one of the giants publicly gave in [sic] his adherence to that doctrine. . . .

> [B]efore long we may have to discuss whether there is a point beyond which growth in a life insurance company ceases to be of advantage to its policyholders, and also whether a company's assets may become too vast and widely scattered to be properly supervised, either by its own officers or by State Insurance Departments.

A year later, Fackler was more direct (*T.A.S.A.* 3, 165):

Life insurance in this New World has grown with such marvelous rapidity that it is not strange some tares have grown up with the wheat; let us hope and work to the best of our ability that the tares may be exterminated before a revolutionary spirit is aroused that will tear up some wheat along with the tares.

Many have cherished great hopes that our organization may be the means of bringing about some beneficent changes. The need of some reforms is universally conceded and is known to us more fully, probably, than to any others—we alone fully understand how much expense the premiums were made to bear and how much has been forced upon them, and we should do our best, as far as opportunity allows, to make the truth known and appreciated by all who are responsible for the present state of affairs.

In an address to the Society, published in a separate booklet, at its banquet in Philadelphia in October 1893, charter member W. T. Standen said:

If any of us have uttered a protest against the increasing cost of business, the higher court (i.e., within our company) has set our protest aside, and we must patiently and cheerfully await the vindication that the future may hold in store for us. ... I do not think that we have so very long to wait for the vindication that I believe is sure (sooner or later) to come.

In May 1899, then President B. J. Miller undertook to point out some dangers and difficulties that life companies would soon be obliged to meet (*T.A.S.A.* 6, 108):

[T]he payment of large commissions on first premiums and the occasional practice of offering bonuses and prizes to agents securing an unusual amount of business, has encouraged the pernicious practice of rebating, and resulted in too high a ratio of lapses among young policies.

Little can be found in the Council and Society meeting minutes of 1905–1906 about New York State's Armstrong Investigation, but its effects were, of course, pervasive. It happened that the Society president at the time was Rufus W. Weeks, actuary of the New York Life, one of the three companies most deeply implicated, the other two being Mutual Life of New York and the Equitable Society. In his presidential address of October 1905, Weeks, in an oblique reference to the Investigation, remarked (*T.A.S.A.* 9, 206):

There is no established and solvent company in the land, whatever its sins of omission or commission may have been, but is entitled to ten-fold more admiration than condemnation.

The consulting actuary to the Armstrong Investigation Committee, Miles Menander Dawson (1863–1942), was a man who had only just, in 1904, qualified by examination as an Actuarial Society member. His reputation as an actuary, however, went much farther back in time. In 1895 he had come to New York City from the Midwest, where he had been with Northwestern Mutual (McClintock's former company), to practice as a consulting actuary. He was an Associate of the Institute of Actuaries and had written several books. In one, *Practical Lessons in Actuarial Science* (first edition 1898), he acknowledged substantial assistance from such members as R. W. Weeks, E. McClintock, J. Tatlock, W. A. Marshall, and W. D. Whiting. He was to be one of the leaders of thought in the Actuarial Society, the American Institute, the

Miles Menander Dawson, consulting actuary
of the Armstrong Investigating Committee,
New York, 1905. (Courtesy of State
Historical Society of Wisconsin.)

Casualty Actuarial Society, and the Fraternal Actuarial Association. Although his was
not an inquisitorial mind, he was influential in patterning the remedial legislation of
1906, and apparently was courteous and helpful to the group of actuaries who, as will
be described, came to appeal legislative remedies that they considered harsh or unsuitable.

The list of witnesses before the Committee included many actuaries. In order of
their appearance (on the official list) they were:

D. H. Wells	J. Fuhrer	M. M. Dawson
E. McClintock	J. G. Van Cise	M. W. Torrey
E. E. Rhodes	J. K. Gore	R. W. Weeks
G. D. Eldridge	J. M. Craig	W. A. Marshall
H. Moir	J. Tatlock	

Society President Weeks, in his next address in May 1906 (at which meeting he
would become the only one of that body's thirty presidents to decline reelection for the
traditional second term) said (*T.A.S.A.* 9, 277) that the Society, although not itself
officially involved, had created the friendships and the mutual respect that resulted in
valuable behind-the-scenes work by a group of its members, without which the ultimate
remedial legislation would have been much worse than it was.

As Weeks explained, one member, William A. Marshall, had taken the initiative
by inviting twenty-six Society members to a conference on the legislation just proposed.
Those actuaries found themselves of one mind on which of the proposals ought to be
appealed and appointed eight of their number to confer with the Armstrong Committee.
That working group consisted of A. A. Welch (chairman), Arthur Hunter (secretary),
J. J. Barker, J. K. Gore, Henry Moir, E. E. Rhodes, E. J. Sartelle, and M. W. Torrey.

These spokesmen conferred with the Armstrong Committee in both New York City and Albany, testified in public, and had two of their number, Welch and Rhodes, appear before the Committee in private session. Many of their suggestions were accepted, fully or partially; only one of their cardinal criticisms, namely, their objection to the complete prohibition of the deferred dividend system, was disallowed.

Three of the many postscripts to all this were:

> We life insurance men feel somewhat as if we had been through an earthquake . . . [R. W. Weeks, *T.A.S.A.* 9, 279].

* * *

> It is a matter of just pride that in all these investigations no member of this Society has been charged with anything worse than not knowing so much as some of our critics give us credit for knowing. To that charge some of us are ready to plead guilty. [Daniel H. Wells, October 1906, ibid., p. 378].

* * *

> Ten years ago this business of life insurance was the first of the so-called "big interests" to come under direct public criticism. It was purged by a fire such as no other business had ever been subjected to, and during that cleansing process, ideals for action were enunciated, and, to the slight degree possible, were written on statute books, which have so molded the practice of our business that to-day it is the cleanest, most honestly conducted business in the country. . . . In that purging fire the actuaries walked unscathed and with reputations untouched. Not alone had the mathematical principles and legal requirements been followed, but the moral code of common justice had not been broken. . . .

> To-day the Actuarial Society of America enjoys a reputation which places a greater responsibility on us actuaries than has ever rested upon us before. For in the olden days the actuary was merely the adviser of the executives of the company; to-day he is himself an executive [and] must bear the responsibilities both of the executive and of the scientific adviser. . . .

> And with this new power comes new temptations to bend our judgment, insidious calls to lower the standards which we have upheld in the past, specious arguments why our own fair standards should not be set up in the new fields that have come within our sphere of command. Place, power, and recognition by others of our success are corroding influences against which we Fellows and Associates of this Society must battle hard if ten years from now our Society is to bear as clean a character as it does to-day. . . . [A. A. Welch, May 1917, *T.A.S.A.* 19, 168].

The Armstrong Investigation's effects were to spread to other states, notably Wisconsin, and even into Canada where a Royal Commission with broad powers was set up. As V. R. Smith of Toronto said to the Centenary Assembly of the Institute of Actuaries in 1948, abuses, though none substantial in character, were uncovered and were dealt with in the Insurance Act of the Dominion of Canada in 1910. The changes that Smith described are listed in Volume III, page 100 of the Assembly *Proceedings*.

Of the Armstrong Investigating Committee's sixteen items of "Remedial Legislation" promulgated on February 22, 1906, the following were of major concern to actuaries, especially numbers 8 and 12:

    5. Limitation of new business.
    8. Limitation of expenses.
    9. Valuation of policies.
  11. Surrender values.
  12. Ascertainment and distribution of surplus.
  14. Forms of policies.

The actuary of every life company licensed to do business in New York became, more directly than ever, involved in budgetary matters because of his expertise in evaluating the statutes governing both acquisition expense and total expense. The original measuring rod for acquisition cost bore the clear stamp of Miles M. Dawson's thinking, being the sum of the premium loadings and certain assumed present values of select mortality gains calculated on the American Experience Table at 3 1/2% interest.

This formula worked well for twenty years. When changed conditions demanded its revision, the Superintendent of Insurance appointed five Fellows of the Actuarial Society to draft suitable amendments to what was then Section 97 of the New York Insurance Law. A landmark paper, "Section 97—New York Law, Revision of 1929" (*T.A.S.A.* 30, 109) by that group's chairman, M. Albert Linton, shows how well that difficult assignment was carried out. The other four actuaries were E. E. Cammack, Robert Henderson, Arthur Hunter, and E. B. Morris.

COMPLAINTS AND DISCIPLINE

In retrospect it seems strange that in an era when the Actuarial Society had fewer than one hundred Fellows (not counting the honorary overseas members), almost all of whom knew each other well, and about eighty Associates, mainly staff assistants to those Fellows, it should have been accepted as desirable that the Constitution contain a new Article entitled "Expulsion or Suspension of Members." But the Council did offer such an amendment in October 1906, and it was adopted in May 1907.

Neither the Council minutes nor those of the meetings give any clue to the genesis of this provision. It may have been prompted by some facet of the Armstrong Investigation or by knowledge that the legal profession was preparing a code of ethics; almost certainly it did not stem from any alleged unethical conduct within the Society itself.

That Article's provisions were very much in the modern form, calling for the Council to hear, in confidence, written complaints by a Fellow against any other Fellow or Associate for professional misconduct, to obtain the answer in writing, to permit appearance personally and by counsel, and for the Council, if it should so decide, to make recommendations to the Society, and for the Society to take such action as it should see fit, including expulsion or suspension by at least a two-thirds vote.

PRELIMINARY TERM VALUATION

It seems necessary to understand, as clearly as we now can, just what was the attitude of influential Actuarial Society members towards modified systems of valuation as 1909, a critical year in our profession's history, approached.

Several modifications designed to cushion the impact of acquisition costs were known, from the original plan by the European actuary August Zillmer in 1863 to Dawson's "select and ultimate" plan described in his 1903 paper, "A New Valuation Formula" (*T.A.S.A.* 7, 418), which had to be presented by Emory McClintock because Dawson, an Associate, lacked the privilege to read it personally.

As there is little record of discussion close to 1909, we must rely on remarks made later, specifically in the early 1920s. They testify that modified systems were theoretically respectable provided they did not go to the extreme of permitting the entire excess of an endowment or limited-payment life premium over the corresponding term premium to be omitted from the reserve.

In May 1920, A. A. Welch, in his paper "Preliminary Term Valuation" (*T.A.S.A.* 21, 125), wrote:

> [B]ecause so many men and women are now flitting from one intellectual or spiritual roost to another through what may seem to onlookers as loose and not-followed-through reasoning, I do desire to explain to [my] professional friends . . . the reasons why I believe that some form of preliminary term valuation, instead of the old net premium valuation, is not only safe but under present conditions for many reasons desirable.

In discussing that paper (p. 504), Henry Moir held that it was unfair to equate modified systems with extravagance, saying that in his view the extravagance originated in the older and wealthier companies; those companies effectively set the market price for business, and the younger companies could compete only by resorting to preliminary term systems. In his discussion (p. 506), Dawson said that at the time of the Armstrong Investigation:

> several companies, nearly a score, . . . were then valuing on the "ordinary life" preliminary term plan. Most of these, but not all, were my clients. I had introduced this method . . . in the United States about 1898.

In his 1924 first edition of what quickly became the leading textbook *Life Insurance,* Joseph B. Maclean wrote (p. 110):

> A company which has only recently commenced business and which has not had time to accumulate a large surplus fund could not possibly carry on business if it were required to set aside the full net premium reserve from the first year on every policy. New companies do not, in fact, carry such reserves.

Welch, however, in his 1920 paper (p. 125) stated the practical condition that existed eleven and more years earlier:

> It is but natural that one who has always been connected with long established old line life insurance companies in the east, where the full net premium valuation has been accepted as the standard for conservative underwriting, should think of any standard of valuation which requires less reserves than the full net

premium valuation as one to be looked upon with suspicion. He might also feel that he was still further fortified in this conviction when he remembers the attempts of certain companies early in this century to adopt a preliminary term valuation on certain forms of policies for the sole purpose of granting exorbitant commissions to agents. With such experiences, therefore, it is not strange that an eastern actuary should at first have looked askance on any attempt to secure the adoption of the preliminary term method of valuation.

Although the Council minutes warrant the conclusion that no actuaries of young companies in the U.S. midwestern cities were refused entry to Actuarial Society examinations, those actuaries may have justifiably felt that, even if they did qualify by examination, they would still be considered inferior because of the valuation systems of their companies.

An amusing exchange between two New York actuaries many years later (1946) seems to show that these attitudes persisted (*T.A.S.A.* 47, 345 and 359):

> J. B. Maclean: According to such information as I have, the number of companies which will change from a net level premium reserve system to the Commissioners' Reserve Valuation method is so small that it may, with something to spare, be counted on the fingers of one paw of that animal known to crossword puzzle addicts as the two-toed sloth.

> Owen C. Lincoln: Perhaps some may feel that Mr. Maclean's juxtaposing of the word "sloth" should, with more justice, have occurred with respect to those companies proposing to continue to use the net level premium valuation method.

In fact, Maclean's zoology was mildly at fault. The ai is three-toed.

FOUNDING OF THE AMERICAN INSTITUTE OF ACTUARIES—VIEWED FROM THE ACTUARIAL SOCIETY

Neither the 1909 Council minutes nor the *Transactions* contain any direct announcement, reference, or expression of good wishes related to the launching of a new actuarial body in Chicago that June. But at the October 1909 Council meeting, Arthur Hunter asked the privilege of saying a few words about the possible broadening of "the influence and usefulness of the Society." It seems fair to suppose that Hunter's meditations had been in response to the genesis of a potentially competing institution.

After Hunter had offered several suggestions, the Council responded by appointing a seven-member committee to consider them and other possibilities. The committee was asked to report promptly, which it did on December 9, 1909, with a series of recommendations, most of which were accepted by the Society members. The four of greatest consequence were these:

1. That the Constitution be amended so that Associates, even though they still might not be permitted to present their own papers, might answer questions from the floor and close the discussions thereon.

2. That an Educational Committee be formed to assist students and Associates in preparing for Society examinations.

3. That auxiliary or educational meetings be held in both eastern and western locations.

4. That St. Louis be considered as a site for the Fall 1910 Society meeting.

The first two of these steps were taken; the third was not. The St. Louis meeting did not materialize, but the Society met in Cincinnati, where the attendance was rather small. In October 1914 the meeting was in Milwaukee, but after that, the Society did not again abandon its customary eastern haunts until returning to Cincinnati in 1921.

There were, among the Society Fellows of 1909, several midwesterners, hardly any of whom joined the American Institute. But one Society charter member, Joseph H. Nitchie, established himself as also a charter member of the American Institute. A Chicagoan, he knew, of course, that the organizing move was afoot, but probably he doubted that the Society leaders would make any offers to forestall the launching of the new body, if indeed there were any they could make.

Cooperation in the American-Canadian Mortality Investigation was the first mild unifying influence. A major action to break the ice occurred in June 1916 when Arthur Hunter, then Society President, paid a formal visit to the American Institute's annual meeting. In remarks at the thirty-fifth anniversary meeting of the American Institute (*R.A.I.A.* 33, 17), O. J. Arnold gave an amusing description of that event:

> I think Arthur Hunter probably came out here just to size up the situation and find out for himself what it was that was making the Institute click. . . .
>
> [T]hat was probably the first time any dignity was added to the meetings of the Institute. I met and visited with Mr. Hunter . . . in the lobby of the La Salle Hotel that morning. . . . As the time approached for the first session to convene, I suggested, "Well, we'd better go up. Won't you come up?"
>
> He intimated to me in a few well-chosen words that it might be better for the meeting to convene and at some appropriate time a committee be appointed to escort him to the meeting. He was right, of course, but that was quite foreign to our usual procedure.
>
> A committee was appointed and conducted him to the meeting. He was very gracious and was most enthusiastically received. . . .
>
> It was a source of a great deal of satisfaction to all of us to have his "pontifical blessing." We felt reassured that we were traveling along the right road.

By May 1921 (*T.A.S.A.* 22, 294) rapprochement went further. George Graham, then president of the American Institute, spoke by invitation at the Society meeting dinner (as also did A. H. Mowbray, president of the Casualty Actuarial Society). In the fall of 1924, the Actuarial Society and American Institute had their first joint meeting at French Lick, Indiana.

By 1929, the proportion of all Fellows of both these bodies who were Fellows of the American Institute but not of the Actuarial Society was well past its peak, as Table III.3 shows.

Table III.3

RATIOS OF AMERICAN INSTITUTE FELLOWS TO TOTAL FELLOWS OF ACTUARIAL SOCIETY AND AMERICAN INSTITUTE AT SELECTED DATES

Year	(1) Total Fellows of Either or Both Bodies*	(2) Fellows of the American Institute Only	(3) Ratio of (2) to (1)
End of 1909	176	41	.232
End of 1919	231	66	.286
End of 1929	360	86	.239
End of 1939	471	73	.155
June 3, 1949	642	30	.047

*Duplications removed.

HOW THE AMERICAN INSTITUTE OF ACTUARIES WAS FOUNDED

By no means should the actuaries who organized the American Institute be pictured as strangers to the easterners of the Actuarial Society. I. S. Homans was Sheppard Homans' son. A. G. Hann's father was an actuary in the Equitable Society, New York. Six (H. W. Buttolph, H. W. Cochnower, J. M. Emery, J. W. Glover, I. S. Homans and Lucius McAdam) had attended the New York International Congress in 1903. Joseph Howard Nitchie was employed in a small New York insurance company before he moved west. W. H. Gould and Buttolph, Cochnower, Emery, Homans, V. M. Kime and J. A. McKellar were Associates of the Society. J. A. McKellar, R. M. Webb, F. S. Withington and P. L. Woolston would all have been remembered as fairly recent actuarial department employees of companies in New York, Philadelphia, or Montreal. Thus, the Actuarial Society leaders could easily size up the qualifications of more than one-third of the American Institute's founders.

Henry Sherman Vail (1847–1919), the Chicago consulting actuary and famed life insurance salesman who took the initiative to call an organizational meeting on May 12, 1909, was proud to be recognized as a great-grandson of Roger Sherman, one of the drafters of the U.S. Declaration of Independence. The mix of organizers was quite different from that of the actuaries who had assembled in New York twenty years earlier to launch the Actuarial Society; this time there were a dozen consulting actuaries among the forty-two, and four college mathematics professors. Not surprisingly, there was something of a contest between the company actuaries and those in the consulting field for the upper hand in organizational decisions; to the extent this occurred, the company men won.

Attendance at the May 1909 gathering totalled fourteen. The two major accomplishments were:

1. Agreement on the aims of the American Institute of Actuaries —a name that Henry S. Vail had suggested—expressed in the following clear terms (*R.A.I.A.* 1, 5):

   It is desired that [the] Institute shall be such a one as to command the respect and esteem of those engaged in the business of insurance and to merit an exchange

1909]   7

CONSTITUTION.

NAME.

Art. 1. This organization shall be called "AMERICAN INSTITUTE OF ACTUARIES."

OBJECT.

Art. II. The object of the American Institute of Actuaries is to advance the Science of Insurance Mathematics by associating together persons of like interests for the presentation and discussion of papers and for the consideration of such other matters as may properly come before the Institute.

MEMBERSHIP.

Art. III. The membership of the Institute shall be composed of three classes, Fellows, Associates, and Contributing members.

OFFICERS.

Art. IV. The Officers shall consist of a President, a Vice-President, a Secretary, a Treasurer and a Librarian.

GOVERNORS.

Art. V. The Board of Governors shall consist of the Officers, the ex-Presidents, and six other Fellows chosen as follows: Upon adoption of this constitution, six Governors shall be elected; two for three years, two for two years, and two for one year, and annually thereafter two shall be elected for three years. The Board of Governors shall have power to fill all vacancies occuring by death or resignation of Officers or Governors.

DUTIES OF OFFICERS AND GOVERNORS.

Art. VI. The duties of the officers shall be such as usually appertain to their respective offices. The duties of

Some provisions of the original constitution of the American Institute of Actuaries, June 1909.

of courtesies with older and well recognized Institutes and Societies of Actuaries. . . . In furtherance of these ideas it is deemed of the utmost importance that the Charter Membership of the proposed Institute be selected with the utmost care.

2. Appointment of a committee of five—three company actuaries (O. J. Arnold, Lucius McAdam, J. C. Seitz) and two consulting actuaries (H. W. Buttolph and H. S. Vail)—with sweeping powers to determine who should be invited to be charter Fellows (Table III.4), and Associates and to propose the officers and the members of the Board of Governors.

Between then and June 15, 1909, when the American Institute was formally launched, the one difficulty was to find a president. If Vail was invited, he declined. The committee, even though it had gone so far as to approach an actuary outside Chicago who was not even on their list of charter members, was forced to report on June 15, 1909, that the post remained open. (Their quarry had been Edward E. Hardcastle, a

Table III.4

CHARTER FELLOWS OF AMERICAN INSTITUTE OF ACTUARIES, 1909

Fellow	Age in 1909	Years in Insurance Work	Actuarial Society Status	Company and Location
L. A. Anderson	39	3		Insurance Department, Madison, Wisconsin
T. W. Appleby	35	4		Central Life of Illinois, Ottawa, Illinois
O. J. Arnold	36	12		Illinois Life, Chicago
W. F. Barnard	49	9		Consulting actuary, Syracuse, New York
S. Barnett	59	35		Consulting actuary, Atlanta
C. H. Beckett	33	n.a.		Consulting actuary, Lafayette, Indiana
H. W. Buttolph	39	16	A.A.S.	Consulting actuary, Indianapolis
D. F. Campbell	42	12		Math professor, Armour Institute, Chicago
C. B. Carr	44	19		American Central Life, Indianapolis
E. R. Carter	32	9		National Life of U.S.A., Chicago
H. W. Cochnower	31	10	A.A.S.	Guarantee Life, Houston
H. R. Corbett	45	9		Consulting actuary, H.S. Vail, Chicago
F. A. Draper	46	20		Consulting actuary, Pierre, South Dakota
J. M. Emery	54	17	A.A.S.	Des Moines Life, Iowa
W. A. Fricke	52	14		Great Northern Life, Wausau, Wisconsin
J. W. Glover	41	14		Math professor, University of Michigan, Ann Arbor
W. H. Gould	30	6	A.A.S.	Volunteer State Life, Chattanooga
F. J. Haight	32	7		Anchor Life, Indianapolis
A. G. Hann	30	4		Pacific Mutual Life, Los Angeles
J. E. Higdon	43	3		State Life, Indianapolis
I. S. Homans	34	11	A.A.S.	Commonwealth Life, Louisville
E. W. Hyde	66	9		Columbia Life, Cincinnati
V. M. Kime	24	3	A.A.S.	Missouri State Life, St. Louis
L. McAdam	64	42		United States Annuity & Life, Chicago
J. A. McKellar	41	9	A.A.S.	Des Moines Life, Iowa
M. McNeill	54	21		Math professor, Lake Forest College, Lake Forest, Illinois
J. H. Nitchie	58	39	F.A.S.	Consulting actuary, Chicago
B. R. Nueske	67	20		Missouri State Life, St. Louis
R. K. Orr	30	n.a.		Northern Assurance Company, Detroit
J. B. Reynolds	38	12		Kansas City Life, Missouri
H. L. Rietz	34	6		Math professor, University of Illinois, Urbana, Illinois
J. C. Seitz	31	6		Security Life, Chicago
B. J. Stookey	34	11		Illinois Life, Chicago
C. M. Vail	28	7		Consulting actuary, H.S.Vail, Chicago
H. S. Vail	62	41		Consulting actuary, Chicago
G. A. Van Der Sluis	61	n.a.		St. Louis National Life, Missouri
R. M. Webb	34	12		Kansas City Life, Missouri
B. A. Welstead	n.a.	n.a.		Michigan Mutual Life, Detroit
R. M. Wilbur	53	n.a.		Consulting actuary, Denver
F. S. Withington	50	31		Consulting actuary, Des Moines
P. L. Woolston	35	12		Consulting actuary, Denver
W. S. Wynn	59	23		State Life, Indianapolis
Median Age & Experience	**40 yrs.**	**12 yrs.**		

Note—There were also twenty-two Charter Associates.

New Zealander who had come to America about 1898, had qualified as a Fellow of the Actuarial Society in 1902, and was actuary of Union Central Life of Cincinnati.) Lucius McAdam, by far the dean of the organizing group in experience and nearly so in age at 64, was prevailed upon to accept the presidency, but was not a vigorous leader. He may have insisted on serving for just a single year; the subsequent tradition of the American Institute, as of the Actuarial Society, was for its president to serve two one-year terms.

The first slate of officers was:

President:	Lucius McAdam
Vice-President:	Henry W. Buttolph
Secretary:	Jacob C. Seitz
Treasurer:	Henry S. Vail
Librarian:	Edwin R. Carter

In addition to having Fellows and Associates from the outset, the American Institute's Constitution provided for a third important class, namely, Contributing Members. A legal reserve life insurance company applying for such status and elected by a majority vote of the Board of Governors could send any nominee of its choice to attend an American Institute meeting and to join in the discussions. It may be noted also that an Associate could participate in discussions at a time when Associates of the Actuarial Society did not have that privilege.

Perhaps encouraged by, and certainly helped by, its original corps of mathematics professors among its Fellows, the American Institute introduced examinations for Associateship, in 1910, and for Fellowship soon after.

An American Institute entrance requirement that the Actuarial Society never had was "that no applicant for admission as Associate be admitted to examination in Section B [of the Associateship syllabus] until he has had such practical experience as in the judgment of the Board entitles him thereto." This proviso seems to have been taken seriously, but the acceptable experience level apparently was not severe.

The American Institute's seal contained the words *Experto Crede*. At least some of its Fellows considered this less than a full-fledged motto and agitated for some time that an inspirational sentence be selected. At least one critic denounced it as bombastic, meaning virtually "We are the experts; follow us." In 1921, concern was laid to rest by a letter (*R.A.I.A.* 10, 365) from the Head of the Department of Latin, University of Chicago, giving the reassuring message that the words were a legitimate variant of expressions in both Virgil and Ovid with the gentle meaning, "Trust one who has had experience." Lucius McAdam, the proposer of that motto, who had died in 1913, would have been pleased.

Table III.5 shows the numbers of Fellows and Associates of the American Institute during that body's first ten years. Growth in Fellows was from an original forty-two to ninety-one Fellows on December 31, 1918. By way of comparison, the growth of the Actuarial Society in its first decade was from thirty-eight to seventy-three, not counting its honorary overseas members. So, recognizing that the American Institute could and did enroll Fellows of the Actuarial Society to make up its complement, it is fair to say that the early growth rates of the two bodies were similar.

Table III.5

FELLOWS AND ASSOCIATES OF AMERICAN INSTITUTE OF ACTUARIES, 1909–1918

Year	Admitted	Died	Withdrew	From Associate to Fellow	Roster at End of Year
A. Fellows					
1909	42				42
1910	1	1			42
1911	2				44
1912	1	1			44
1913	9	2			51
1914	11				62
1915	9				71
1916	10	1			80
1917	2	1			81
1918	13	3			91
	100	**9**	**0**		**91**
B. Associates					
1909	22				22
1910			1		21
1911	2				23
1912	1	1	2		21
1913	4		2		23
1914	6			3	26
1915	7			2	31
1916	6		3	2	32
1917	3		1		34
1918	2			1	35
	53	**1**	**9**	**8**	**35**

Of the fifty-eight Fellows of these first ten years of the American Institute other than charter Fellows, only three emerged from that body's own examination system, the first to do so being Carl E. Herfurth in 1914. But of the remaining fifty-five, twenty-two were Fellows of the Actuarial Society and another four were Fellows of the Faculty of Actuaries.

SCOTTISH INFLUENCE IN PRE-MERGER DAYS

When the Faculty of Actuaries was celebrating its fiftieth anniversary in Scotland in 1906, a cablegram arrived from New York bearing congratulations to their "Alma Mater" from seven of its Fellows: L. M. Cathles, J. B. Gibb, Arthur Hunter, W. A. Hutcheson, Henry Moir, G. R. Webster and William Young. Four of these would later be elected presidents of the Actuarial Society or American Institute. Andrew R. Davidson relates this cablegram episode on page 92 of his centenary book, *The Faculty of Actuaries in Scotland: 1856–1956*; elsewhere in the book (p. 61) Davidson mentions "a definition of the word 'actuary' due to an unidentified 'prominent citizen of the United States of America' " towards the beginning of this century:

> "A Scotsman with some mathematics and a strong business sense!"

Joseph B. Maclean, himself an FFA who came to America in 1911, remarked in reviewing Davidson's book (*TSA* 9, 109):

> Some thirty or forty years ago [i.e., c. 1922] it was popularly supposed that the majority of the leading American actuaries were Scotsmen. That was very far from being the case. The founders of the Actuarial Society in 1889 and most of the leading actuaries of that and succeeding generations in the Western Hemisphere were Americans or Canadians. Nevertheless, the number of Scottish actuaries who came to the United States and Canada about the turn of the century, and for some time thereafter, was substantial and some of them played a not inconsiderable part in the development of the profession on this continent. In speaking of this, Mr. Davidson remarks that "during the first twenty-five years of the Society's history there was only one fellow of the Institute resident in the United States" (*i.e.,* of English origin). The debt which the profession in America owes to Great Britain is, therefore, predominantly to Scotland and to the Faculty.

In reaching that conclusion, Mr. Maclean, who may or may not be the one who dubbed the period "The Era of Scottish Dominance," may be regarded as less than completely unbiased. Be that as it may, that the small band of FFAs who migrated to North America, qualifying as Fellows of the Actuarial Society after arrival, exerted an extraordinarily large influence here, is true beyond any shadow of doubt.

The two actuaries mainly responsible for this migration were that pair of renowned Scotsmen, Arthur Hunter and Henry Moir. Hunter was born in 1869, Moir in 1871. Hunter came to New York in 1893, Moir not until 1901, but both qualified in 1903 as Fellows of the Actuarial Society. Both regularly journeyed to their native heath in search of men of promise; both were successful in those forays. The most detailed discussion of all this may be found in Charles W. V. Meares' 1985 reminiscences, *Looking Back: A Memoir of New York Life,* in which that author described Hunter as "a one-man employment agency for young Scottish actuaries who wished to emigrate," and added:

> As soon as [these young actuaries] successfully completed their examinations in Scotland, they would write to Hunter to let him know of their availability. He, meanwhile, would receive inquiries from life insurance companies all over the United States and Canada asking to be put on his list for the next lot of candidates. . . . It paid off in many ways, not only for the employers and the young men, but for Hunter as well. During the years [after 1923] I knew him, he had a grateful protégé in practically every large life insurance company in the country.

Meares went on to tell the story of one of the outstanding such immigrants, Edmund B. Whittaker (who, in fact, was born in England, but of distinguished Scottish parentage and brought up in Scotland). He crossed the Atlantic in 1926, spent three years at New York Life where he was the despair of Arthur Hunter, then made his name at Prudential. Meares credited Whittaker "with putting the Pru into the position to

Arthur Hunter (left) and Henry Moir: The two famous Scottish recruiters of a generation of Scottish actuaries in North America.

forge ahead of the Met in the race for the number one spot, by hiring some of the finest actuarial and administrative talent in [this] country."

It was Moir, not Hunter, who did our profession the great favor of recruiting Andrew C. Webster, FFA, from Aberdeen in 1929. Webster may be said to have been the last of the leaders of our profession to come from the Moir/Hunter employment enterprise; he became president of the Society of Actuaries in 1963.

Of the four actuaries whom the Faculty of Actuaries honored prior to 1980 by electing them overseas Vice-Presidents, Joseph B. Maclean was the first (1954–1958), Andrew C. Webster was the third (1964–1967), and George T. Westwater of Canada was the fourth (1975–1979).

LEGAL NOTES AND BOOK REVIEWS, 1910

In *T.A.S.A.* 12, 335, the first of a long series of accounts of court cases that were to give generations of actuaries enlightenment about the workings and the pitfalls of the North American legal system in insurance and tax cases made its appearance. Wendell M. Strong, then editor of the *Transactions* and a member of the New York Bar, added the compiling of these Notes to his editorial duties. "Legal Notes" (that name gratefully copied from the same department started by the Institute in 1907) continued to be his responsibility until 1927 and again from 1935 until shortly before his seventieth birthday in 1941. From then on, the Actuarial Society, and after it the Society of Actuaries, had the benefit of the services of a Hartford insurance company lawyer, Buist M. Anderson, who furnished the "Legal Notes" until 1964 when that section of the *Transactions* was discontinued (see *TSA* 16, 466).

At the Actuarial Society's meeting in October 1910, it was announced that "a Review Committee has been appointed to look up all publications of interest to Actuaries and to insert a brief notice of them in the *Transactions*." "Notices" indeed they were initially, but their scope soon broadened. In 1921 the change was officially recognized by changing the title to "Book Reviews and Notices." This section of the *Transactions* for many years granted an opportunity, used by many, for actuaries to keep informed on business and philosophical works outside the narrow range of strictly actuarial topics as well as within that range. A segment of the review space, which in its heyday ran to dozens of pages, was a listing of papers in other actuarial journals in and outside North America.

INFLUX OF CANADIAN ACTUARIES

At the Actuarial Society's inauguration there were four Canadian actuaries; consequently, the proportion of Canadians among the charter members was 4/38, that is, about 10%, very similar to the proportion of Canadians in the total North American population.

But this ratio promptly began to increase markedly. The ratios, for Fellows only, but including Fellows of both the Actuarial Society and the American Institute (with duplications removed) averaged in successive eras up to 1945 as shown in Table III.6.

Table III.6

PERCENTAGES OF CANADIAN FELLOWS TO (UNITED STATES + CANADIAN) FELLOWS, 1889–1945

Year	Percentage
1889–1905	12.7%
1905–1915	19.6
1915–1925	27.7
1925–1935	33.6
1935–1945	36.6

These figures are taken from a not-yet-published mortality study using the respective exposures during the stated periods. The word "Canadian" means a Fellow who was born in Canada or, if an immigrant from overseas, who began his or her North American actuarial career in Canada. Of course, many of these Canadians moved to the United States, usually early in their careers.

The phenomenon, lasting for twenty years, of more than one-third of the Fellows on this continent being products of a country blessed with only one-tenth the population of the United States, was attributable to a combination of two causes. First, Canada's life insurance companies were few but comparatively large and well established; they tended to employ corps of actuarial students larger than they could absorb at senior levels. Second, the Canadian universities were effective in educating young people in mathematics and, in the early cases of the University of Toronto and the University of Manitoba, in organizing strong actuarial science courses.

ACTUARIAL SOCIETY INCORPORATION STUDY, 1911

At the Actuarial Society's Council meeting of March 29, 1910, at the suggestion of Secretary Arthur Hunter, a committee of two United States Council members (W. S. Nichols and O. B. Ireland) and one Canadian (T. B. Macaulay) was appointed "to consider the advisability of incorporating the Society in the United States and in Canada."

The committee's first report, on February 8, 1911, resulted in a vote expressing "the sense of the Council that the Society be incorporated if a satisfactory method could be found." The text of the committee's next report, on March 24, 1911, suggests that the committee still favored incorporation, but the Council as a whole had cooled somewhat. The difficulty seemed to be that incorporation in the District of Columbia (not, of course, conferring national charter status although perhaps giving the flavor of such) would be much less confining than would incorporation in New York, but might require annual meetings to be held in Washington rather than in New York, the traditional venue.

At the Council meeting on May 19, 1911, it was decided "to lay the question on the table." That same day, the Council reported to the Society as follows (*T.A.S.A.* 12, 149):

> The question of incorporation has been thoroughly considered by the Council for more than a year. It has been decided not to take any action at the present time, owing to the many difficulties in the way.

There the matter rested for seven years. On May 17, 1918, the then Council, containing at most two members directly familiar with the prior discussions, appointed a committee of five, consisting of two members from the United States, two from Canada and the president, to consider the same question. But the steam had completely evaporated; the new committee did not report until forced to do so during a 1922 Council drive to dispose of inactive committees, then recommended adversely, and was discharged.

Perhaps the Canadians had reservations about their status in the event of the Society acquiring a United States charter. At the outset there had been talk of seeking double incorporation (separately in each country), but the original committee disliked that, calling it analogous to an individual claiming citizenship in two states or countries. It was true that double incorporation had been undertaken by companies whose activities required them to own real estate in more than one country.

GROUP LIFE INSURANCE ENTERS THE SCENE, 1911

William J. Graham (1877–1963), a 1902 Fellow of the Actuarial Society, was as stated in his obituary (*TSA* 15, 221) "frequently referred to as the 'Father of Group Insurance,' for he played a key part in the 1911 discussions with the Montgomery Ward Company that led to the first of the modern forms of group insurance." Graham thus created a controversial form of coverage feared by many life companies and fraternal associations for the damage it might do to their activities. In 1913 the American Life Convention (ALC), the company association largely of life insurance firms in the Midwest, West and South, adopted the following resolution as stated in *The American Life Convention: A Study in the History of Life Insurance* by R. Carlyle Buley (p. 417):

> RESOLVED, that the issuance of group insurance by a legal reserve life insurance company without individual medical examinations is a menace to legal reserve life insurance, a discrimination against regularly examined policyholders, is unfair in principle and dangerous in practice.

This resolution was not rescinded until four years later; meanwhile, there were many efforts to persuade individual state legislatures either to outlaw group insurance or to cripple it with strictures.

A jocular 1909 remark (*T.A.S.A.* 11, 123) was made by Metropolitan Life's President John R. Hegeman, in welcoming the Actuarial Society members to that company's home office:

> Away back in the early days, when Mr. [J. M.] Craig had an occasional leisure moment, he used to come into my office and descant on the subtleties of the business. Among other things he would refer to a certain H^M table. As I look around upon this body of well-nourished, well-groomed gentlemen, bearing, too, all the outward and visible signs of inward and spiritual grace, I can say that you certainly belong to the Healthy Male class (laughter); and when the legislatures permit the Metropolitan to get its Group Insurance under way I trust the first body of men to come in as a group will be the Actuarial Society of America, and I am sure it would be entirely safe for us to take you without medical examinations. (Applause.)

It seems from this that William J. Graham may have fathered group insurance while he was on Metropolitan Life's actuarial staff, between 1902 and 1905. By 1911 he was with the Equitable Society.

Mr. Hegeman's judgment about the health and longevity of actuaries was confirmed years later by John R. Larus (*T.A.S.A.* 39, 26); the male Fellows of the Actuarial Society between their 1905 and 1915 anniversaries experienced a mortality ratio of 62% of the American Men Ultimate table—17 deaths compared with 27.5 expected deaths.

INTRODUCTION TO PENSION MATHEMATICS, 1914

In October 1914, the Council of the Actuarial Society responded to a request of the New York City Pension Commission by appointing three of the Society's Officers—Robert Henderson, William A. Hutcheson, and Henry Moir—to advise that Commission.

In that era, few actuaries had much personal experience with pensions, and the papers available to help students cope with the customarily single question on pensions in the final Fellowship examination consisted mainly of readings in British actuarial journals. A paper, "A Staff Pension Fund," by Dwight A. Walker appeared in the *Transactions* in 1915 (*T.A.S.A.* 16, 109); in his preamble, Walker mentioned the shortage of material in the *Transactions,* listing the three existing papers and adding:

> As pension funds are quite a live topic at the present time it would seem to be not amiss to offer ... the results of some calculations recently made in connection with a pension fund for the employees of one of the large railroads of America.

He then proceeded to give the derivations of the probabilities and discount factors he had worked up and the formulas for their use—indeed a useful pattern for practicing actuaries as well as students. In his author's reply to the two complimentary discussions of his paper (*T.A.S.A.* 16, 394), Walker described what an actuary might be up against:

> I have made calculations in connection with three or four such schemes within the last year or two, and I have found ... that the amount of the contributions necessary to provide benefits was very much underestimated. As a matter of fact, most pension schemes are commenced without actuarial advice and it is only after a number of years that the managers of the schemes begin to scent trouble ahead.

He explained that the fund described in his paper was one for which actuarial enlightenment required the benefits to be materially reduced and the contributions increased.

Those three Actuarial Society leaders—Henderson, Hutcheson, and Moir—by undertaking to guide the New York Pension Commission, were brought into touch with a youthful trailblazer in the public pension forest, George B. Buck (1891–1961). Buck was not, and never became, an Actuarial Society member; he was a charter Fellow of the Casualty Actuarial Society and became a 1917 Fellow of the American Institute other than by examination. His 1976 biographer, Margaret Allen Burt (*George B. Buck Consulting Actuaries Inc.: The First 45 Years,* p. 14), described the state of affairs in these words:

> The nine pension funds of the city were in chaotic condition at that time [1913]. Pension legislation had been developed largely on the initiative of employees; those groups with the strongest political backing had the most liberal benefits. ... Several of the funds, notably that of the teachers, were fast reaching the time when all reserves would be exhausted.

Burt went on to say that Buck's appointment as actuary, coming from recognition of his work for the New York City Police Fund, offered him a wonderful opportunity, calling into play his ability for organization, his ingenuity and his imagination. She mentions (p. 16) a thorough analysis of municipal pensions in a paper that Buck presented to the Casualty Actuarial Society in May 1916 (*PCAS* 2, 370).

W. A. Hutcheson, who served as chairman of the Advisory Committee, reported to the Actuarial Society in October 1917 (*T.A.S.A.* 18, 354) the results of the advisory work. The benefits promised had an aggregate value of $215 million, of which only $9 million was covered by prospective contributions and another $4 million by funds on hand. Hutcheson's report continues:

> [T]he city is confronted with a very heavy burden for its present employees. ...
> The Commission is now engaged upon the preparation of a plan to cover new entrants with a view of providing a sound method of financing the funds in so far as they refer to new entrants. ...
>
> Mayor Mitchel ... took occasion to write to [our] Committee expressing his appreciation of its services and hoping that the Committee might continue in its

Twelve charter members of the Casualty Actuarial Society photographed in 1939. (Left to right)
Standing: Winfield W. Greene, William N. Magoun, Gustav F. Michelbacher, Frank R. Mullaney,
Albert W. Whitney, Lee J. Wolfe; Seated: Lewis A. Nicholas, Everett S. Fallow, Benedict D. Flynn,
Leon S. Senior, William J. Graham and Charles Hughes.

advisory capacity until the Commission has had an opportunity to complete its
entire work of reorganizing the systems. The Committee felt that its services
might be of great value to the city and gladly agreed to the Mayor's suggestion.

Hutcheson paid tribute to George Buck (p. 357) for "his thorough grasp of the
various points which came up from time to time, and his ingenuity in making use of the
data." Testimony to New York City's appreciation of his services may be found in the
length (42 years) of his tenure as consulting actuary there.

The report did not discuss the theory that a governmental pension plan might
justifiably, in respect to the employer's share of the cost, adopt a modified reserve basis
that recognizes the perpetual existence of both the entity and the plan. This controversial
idea had been debated, however, in June 1917 at a meeting of the American Institute of
Actuaries (*R.A.I.A.* 6, 84).

THE CASUALTY ACTUARIAL (AND STATISTICAL) SOCIETY
(OF AMERICA), 1914

On November 7, 1914 in New York City, the third actuarial body in North
America—to become the Casualty Actuarial Society in 1921—came into being.

The state of affairs early in the twentieth century in companies writing insurance
other than life was quite different from that prevailing in the life insurance business.
The life company actuaries could and did complain that too often company management ignored their recommendations, but at least they knew that their expertise was

recognized as necessary; the tasks of compiling, graduating and using mortality tables, of placing a value upon liabilities arising from contracts making promises far into the future, and of ascertaining and distributing surplus were well understood to be beyond the capabilities of those who had not mastered the actuarial textbooks.

But in companies offering fire, marine, and property and liability coverages under one-year or even three-year contracts, owners' largest fears were about catastrophes such as the Chicago fire of 1871 or the loss of a ship at sea. The calculation of premiums, somewhere in the middle between an art and a science, was a secondary problem that under any approaching normal conditions could be rectified as time went on; skepticism that people called actuaries could improve upon the age-old system seemed justified. It was for this reason that as late as the 1950s the size of the Society of Actuaries, to say nothing of the pay scales of its members, was far above that of the Casualty Actuarial Society.

But by 1910 many states and some provinces in North America were adopting laws placing responsibility upon employers for at least on-the-job injuries to their workers. The old English doctrine that workers, knowing the risks in mines and factories, were accepting those risks by working there, had become obsolete even in Britain herself in the 1890s and was fading away on this side of the Atlantic. The answer to the employers' liability problem was workmen's compensation insurance, a new coverage seen to be in the actuarial realm. This type of insurance, followed soon by major growth in other new forms—automobile and public liability coverages—with long time-spreads of liabilities, brought actuaries in the non-life field into their own.

There arose at the same time an interesting problem of terminology. The expression "casualty insurance" did not cover all existing non-life types but, in the late nineteenth century, described only certain forms in which accidents were the cause of losses. State laws specified the kinds of insurance that casualty insurers, as opposed to fire and marine insurance companies, could write. This presumably posed a problem in deciding upon a name for the new actuarial body.

In the years 1912–1914, a few Actuarial Society members had undertaken to bring the complexities of workmen's compensation insurance to the attention of the life company actuaries through papers as follows:

- May 1912, W. Arthur Watt: "Workmen's Compensation Benefits," *T.A.S.A.* 13, 54.

- October 1912, Albert H. Mowbray: "A Suggestion for the Use of Statistics Based Upon European Experience with Workmen's Compensation in Arriving at Premium Rates for Insurance Covering This Risk in the United States," *T.A.S.A.* 13, 221.

- October 1913, Albert W. Whitney: "Schedules in Workmen's Compensation," *T.A.S.A.* 14, 308.

- May 1914, Albert H. Mowbray: "Criteria for Testing the Adequacy of Rates for Workmen's Compensation Insurance," *T.A.S.A.* 15, 89.

- October 1914, Harwood E. Ryan: "A Method of Determining Pure Premiums for Workmen's Compensation Insurance," *T.A.S.A.* 15, 364.

All of these writers, except Watt, and three of the members who discussed their papers (B. D. Flynn, M. M. Dawson, and C. S. Forbes) became charter members of the new body.

In countries elsewhere in the world it had been found satisfactory to envelop life and non-life actuaries into a single organization. Might this have been done in North America?

The answer probably is no, mainly because except in a few places—Hartford and New York in particular—actuaries in life companies would have no need to keep abreast of non-life techniques and developments, and vice versa. But it seems that an effort to explore the feasibility of developing within either the Actuarial Society or the American Institute study courses and forums in non-life actuarial subjects and in the theory and practice of a new branch clearly on the horizon, social insurance, ought to have been made. To have already three actuarial bodies within a tiny profession suggests inordinate satisfaction with its own status quo on the part of the Actuarial Society.

The founders of the new body did not envision it as exclusively for actuaries. The original name given it was the Casualty Actuarial and Statistical Society of America (CASSA), open to statisticians and actuaries; in fact, in the roster of charter members, which was extraordinarily large (97) because invitations were issued with little or no selection among responders, actuaries were outnumbered by statisticians and others to the tune of two-to-one. The commitment among the actuaries, however, more than made up for the smallness of their numbers; most of the early presidents were actuaries; many of the enrolled statisticians were not seen at meetings; and in 1921 no difficulty was experienced in shortening the name to the Casualty Actuarial Society (CAS).

Dudley M. Pruitt described the organizational steps in the CAS journal, *Proceedings of the Casualty Actuarial Society* (*PCAS* 51, 148):

> On May 28, 1914 a group of men, meeting as the Statistical Committee of the Workmen's Compensation Service Bureau, decided that what they needed . . . was a professional society. . . . On July 27 our organizing committee addressed a call to such persons as might be interested in joining. . . . The organization meeting was held at the City Club of New York on November 7. . . . [O]ur charter members [forty of them in attendance] adopted a constitution and by-laws and elected officers and a council [of five officers and four other council members] and listened to the presentation of three papers.

The first Council consisted of Isaac M. Rubinow, President; Benedict D. Flynn and Albert H. Mowbray, Vice-Presidents; Claude E. Scattergood, Secretary-Treasurer; Winfield W. Greene, Librarian-Editor; James D. Craig, Robert K. Orr, Frederick L. Hoffman, and Albert W. Whitney, Members.

The timing of this enterprise was excellent. As Flynn said ten years later (*PCAS* 11, 26):

> [T]he casualty insurance business and more particularly the liability branch was endeavoring to pass from a condition of haphazard to one of orderly rate-making procedure. Compensation insurance was in its infancy and there was very little information available upon which to base scientific rates. . . . This was true . . . even more so in the case of the various forms of public liability insurance and the indemnity lines.

The prime mover in launching CASSA was the man who was elected its first president, Isaac Max Rubinow, M.D., Ph.D. (1875–1936). He had come to New York from his native Russia in 1893 with his parents and brothers, fleeing the persecution of the Jews in the reign of Czar Alexander III. He was a socialist, but of the evolutionary rather than revolutionary mode; he believed that the United States would mature into a cooperative, more than a capitalist, society and devoted his life to hastening that development. His experience practicing medicine in New York City's ghettos intensified his yearning for governmental care of the needy, leading to his 1913 opus *Social Insurance* in which he developed the theme with clarity, expertise, and certainly timeliness. F. W. Kilbourne's analysis of the contrast between Rubinow's optimistic views and the caution felt by his successor CAS president, J. D. Craig, appears in *RSA* 12, No. 4A, 2218-22. That the original CAS constitution defined its field as both casualty and social insurance was undoubtedly the result of Rubinow's persuasiveness as well as of the respect in which he was held. It seems to have created a defensive attitude towards the new body by the Council of the Actuarial Society, in the form of a resolution adopted at its October 20, 1916, meeting: "That in the opinion of the Council, the members of the Actuarial Society should be prepared to advise official bodies on all questions affecting Social Insurance." This message was communicated to the Society members in the closing section (*T.A.S.A.* 17, 210) of Arthur Hunter's presidential address, "Social Insurance."

As Kilbourne explained (p. 2219), Dr. Rubinow in 1916, addressing the CAS, asked himself, "What is social insurance?", and after rejecting the suggestion from another CAS member that "social insurance is insurance at the other fellow's expense," went on to say, "I prefer to define social insurance as insurance of the masses established through organized society for the purpose of combatting destitution." Actuarial Society President Arthur Hunter, speaking on social insurance later in 1916 (*T.A.S.A.* 17, 195) said that as Dr. Rubinow could not define it satisfactorily he (Hunter) would merely state that "Social Insurance is an endeavor to give a measure of social justice through the assumption by the community of the burden of the loss which the individual sustains through accident, death, sickness, invalidity, unemployment and old age." These two definitions are not widely different; the debate, which was to continue in our actuarial journals at least until social security had been established in the United States two decades later, became more and more concerned with structures and limits rather than with broad concepts of social justice.

In 1934 (*PCAS* 21, 133), Rubinow reminisced thus:

> It would have been interesting to recall the early conflicts, friendly as they were, between the accountants, the statisticians and the actuaries—if there were any actuaries in the field at the time—as to whose influence should predominate in the new organization. . . . I have not altogether forgotten the sharp conflicts and sometimes bitter feelings centering around the term "social insurance" and its proponents in this country in years gone by. Perhaps if it had not been for that unhappy antagonism I might still be actively in the field.

It need not be assumed that those sharp conflicts were within the Society, though there must have been wide variation in opinions among its members. Dr. Rubinow's remark was made less than a year before President Franklin D. Roosevelt signed the Social Security Act into law and less than two years before Mr. Roosevelt, on learning that Rubinow was terminally ill, sent him a copy of Rubinow's own last book, *The Quest for Security* (1934), inscribed:

> For the Author—Dr. I. M. Rubinow,
>
> This reversal of the usual process is because of the interest I have had in reading your book.
>
> Franklin D. Roosevelt

Isaac Max Rubinow died on September 1, 1936. He is still, more than half a century later, renowned for his work on social security. A thorough account of his career is printed in "Isaac Max Rubinow: Pioneering Specialist in Social Insurance" by J. Lee Kreader (*Social Service Review* 50, 402).

Issac Max Rubinow (1875-1936): social insurance pioneer and first president of the Casualty Actuarial Society.

Abb Landis, renowned leader in fraternal actuarial development. In 1917 he became the second president of the Fraternal Actuarial Association.

As shown in Table III.7, seventeen of the CAS charter Fellows were Fellows of the Actuarial Society, four were Fellows of the American Institute, and ten were Associates of the Actuarial Society or American Institute, five later becoming Fellows.

There were no Canadian actuaries among the charter Fellows; Thomas Bradshaw, F.A.S., was the first Canadian to break that ice in May 1915. In those days it was extremely rare for an actuary in Canada to be doing non-life work, that business being transacted by British and United States insurance companies.

Table III.7

EIGHTY CHARTER FELLOWS OF THE CASUALTY ACTUARIAL SOCIETY*

Fellow	Age in 1914	Membership	Company and Location
W. M. Amerine	n.a.		Georgia Casualty Company, Macon, Georgia
R. Benjamin	30		Fidelity & Deposit Company, Baltimore
S. B. Black	26		American Association for Labor Legislation, New York
W. Breiby	30	A.A.S.	Fackler & Fackler Consulting Actuary, New York
G. B. Buck	23		Consulting actuary, New York
W. A. Budlong	42		Commercial Travelers Mutual Accident, Utica, New York
E. E. Cammack	33	F.A.S.	Aetna Life, Hartford
R. V. Carpenter	39	F.A.S.	Metropolitan Life, New York
R. H. Cole	42	F.A.S.	Connecticut General Life Insurance Company, Hartford
C. T. Conway	33		Massachusetts Employees Insurance Association, Boston
J. A. Copeland	31	A.A.I.A.	Consulting actuary, Atlanta
W. G. Cowles	57		Travelers Insurance Company, Hartford
J. D. Craig	36	F.A.S.	Metropolitan Life, New York
J. M. Craig	66	F.A.S.	Metropolitan Life, New York
A. B. Dawson	32		M. M. Dawson Consulting Actuary, New York
M. M. Dawson	51	F.A.S.	Consulting actuary, New York
E. H. Dearth	55		Workmen's Compensation Mutual Insurance Company, Detroit
E. C. De Kay	41		New York State Insurance Department, New York
E. H. Downey	35		Industrial Commission, Madison, Wisconsin
L. I. Dublin	32		Metropolitan Life, New York
L. D. Egbert	n.a.		Fidelity & Casualty Company, New York
S. R. Epsteen	36	F.A.I.A.	Colorado State Insurance Department, Denver
D. P. Fackler	73	F.A.S.	Consulting actuary, New York
E. B. Fackler	35	F.A.S.	Consulting actuary, New York
E. S. Fallow	29		Travelers Insurance Company, Hartford
H. Farrer	34		Hartford Accident & Indemnity Company, Hartford
B. D. Flynn	34	F.A.S.	Travelers Insurance Company, Hartford
C. S. Forbes	35	A.A.S.	Casualty Company of America, New York
C. H. Franklin	42		Frankfort General Insurance Company, New York
H. Furze	62		Globe Indemnity Company, New York
T. E. Gaty	53		Fidelity & Casualty Company, New York
E. S. Goodwin	32		Travelers Insurance Company, Hartford
W. H. Gould	35	F.A.I.A.	Froggatt, Morrison & Company, New York
W. J. Graham	37	F.A.S.	Equitable Life Insurance Society, New York
W. W. Greene	27		New York State Workmen's Compensation Commission, New York
R. C. L. Hamilton	50		Hartford Accident & Indemnity Company, Hartford
H. P. Hammond	38	A.A.S.	Connecticut State Insurance Department, Hartford
C. M. Hansen	n.a.		Workmen's Compensation Service Bureau, New York
R. J. Hillas	56		Fidelity & Casualty Company, New York

*Excluding seventeen who withdrew in the first five years.

Table III.7—Continued

EIGHTY CHARTER FELLOWS OF THE CASUALTY ACTUARIAL SOCIETY*

Fellow	Age in 1914	Membership	Company and Location
F. L. Hoffman	49		Prudential Insurance Company of America, Newark
C. Hughes	67	F.A.I.A.	New York State Insurance Department, New York
B. A. Hunt	44		Aetna Life Insurance Company, Hartford
A. Hunter	45	F.A.S.	New York Life Insurance Company, New York
W. I. King	34	A.A.S.	Columbian National Life Insurance Company, Boston
E. W. Kopf	26		Metropolitan Life, New York
J. R. Leal	29		Copeland Consulting Actuary, Atlanta
W. Leslie	24	A.A.S.	State Compensation Insurance Fund, San Francisco
D. G. Luckett	n.a.		United States Casualty Company, New York
W. N. Magoun	38		Massachusetts State Insurance Department, Boston
G. F. Michelbacher	24		State Compensation Insurance Fund, San Francisco
D. W. Miller	25		Prudential Casualty Company, Indianapolis
S. Milligan	27	A.A.S.	Metropolitan Life, New York
J. F. Mitchell	37		Maryland Casualty Company, Baltimore
H. Moir	43	F.A.S.	Home Life Insurance Company, New York
G. D. Moore	31		Royal Indemnity Company, New York
J. Morrison	n.a.		Royal Indemnity Company, New York
A. H. Mowbray	33	F.A.S.	Massachusetts Employees Insurance Association, Boston
F. R. Mullaney	26		Fidelity & Casualty Company, New York
L. A. Nicholas	40		Fidelity & Casualty Company, New York
E. Olifiers	28	A.A.S.	M. M. Dawson Consulting Actuary, New York
R. K. Orr	35	F.A.I.A.	State Accident Fund, Lansing, Michigan
S. L. Otis	45		Workmen's Compensation Service Bureau, New York
J. J. Pallay	n.a.		London Guarantee & Accident Company, Chicago
E. B. Phelps	51		American Underwriter, New York
C. G. Reiter	53	F.A.S.	Metropolitan Life, New York
C. H. Remington	38		Aetna Life Insurance Company, Hartford
I. M. Rubinow	39		Ocean Accident & Guarantee Corporation, New York
H. E. Ryan	32	A.A.S.	New York State Insurance Department, New York
A. F. Saxton	45		New York State Insurance Department, New York
E. Scheitlin	29		Globe Indemnity Company, New York
L. S. Senior	41		Compensation Inspection Rating Board, New York
J. W. Smiley	n.a.		Public Service Commission, Charleston, West Virginia
R. J. Sullivan	35		Travelers Insurance Company, Hartford
J. S. Thompson	30	F.A.S.	Mutual Life Insurance Company, New York
J. L. Train	31		Utica Mutual Compensation Insurance Group, Utica, New York
A. W. Whitney	44	A.A.S.	Workmen's Compensation Service Bureau, New York
L. J. Wolfe	32		Consulting actuary, New York
S. H. Wolfe	40		Consulting actuary, New York
J. H. Woodward	32	F.A.S.	New York State Workmen's Compensation Commission, New York
W. Young	39	F.A.S.	New York Life Insurance Company, New York
Median Age	**35**		

*Excluding seventeen who withdrew in the first five years.

An examination system was established during the Society's early months, though few sat for examinations until several years later. Even to the end of the 1920s the numbers of new Fellows by election rivalled those qualifying by examination. In early years an applicant could obtain waiver of Associateship examinations by submitting an acceptable paper for publication in the *Proceedings*.

The *Proceedings of the Casualty Actuarial Society* was a high-quality journal from the outset, and the veteran actuaries must have been gratified to be free from the necessity for having their papers published elsewhere. Longley-Cook in 1964 (*PCAS* 51, 140) itemized the papers written in other journals before 1914, indeed an impressive list. American authors listed include Miles M. Dawson, Albert H. Mowbray, Isaac M. Rubinow, Harwood E. Ryan, Joseph H. Woodward, Winfield W. Greene, William Leslie, Benedict D. Flynn, and Walter S. Nichols.

Progress towards mutual respect and cooperation among the leaders of the casualty and life actuarial bodies was painfully slow. In 1963, the Casualty Actuarial Society and the Society of Actuaries held, not a joint meeting, but meetings in the same city at adjoining times, invitations being issued for actuaries of each to attend the other's meetings. The first joint meeting took place in April 1978.

In a 1943 essay entitled "Something About Actuaries" (*Fragments,* p. 263), the paramount actuarial historian, Henry H. Jackson, nominated Benjamin Franklin as Patron Saint of actuaries in recognition of the endorsements that Franklin gave to the merits of insurance and his study of its mathematical principles. Inasmuch as Jackson's cited examples were in casualty insurance, specifically advocating crop insurance, we may conclude that Franklin would have bestowed his blessing upon the founding of the Casualty Actuarial Society.

Table III.8 shows the changes in the roster of CAS Fellows from November 7, 1914 to the end of 1918. There were no charter Associates, but forty-four qualified in that category in the years 1915 to 1918.

Table III.8

**CHANGES IN THE ROSTER OF FELLOWS
OF THE CASUALTY ACTUARIAL SOCIETY,
NOVEMBER 7, 1914 TO DECEMBER 31, 1918**

Year	New Fellows	Died	Withdrew	Fellows, December 31
1914	97			97
1915	40	2	1	134
1916	11		5	140
1917	6		2	144
1918	5	1	3	145
Total	159	3	11	145

WORLD WAR I

(Note: Examples of uses of the mathematical talents of actuaries in this and other wars appear in Chapter X, "The Profession in Wartime.")

Actuarial observers were well aware for many years that a major war impended. The most striking early forecast was uttered by Walter S. Nichols in October 1899 (*T.A.S.A.* 6, 176):

> Europe is an armed camp in which the tension is constantly growing. The exploitation of Asia and Africa, with their spheres of influence calling for delimitations, may be but the prelude to a more Titanic war than [the actuarial writer] De Morgan dreamed of. . . .

Between August 4, 1914, and April 6, 1917, Americans called the conflict "the European War," while Canadians were calling it "The War." At the Actuarial Society meeting in October 1914, President James M. Craig said (*T.A.S.A.* 15, 227):

> Since our last meeting the black cloud of war has fallen over a goodly portion of the earth. . . .

> While the scene of the war is in distant lands, its effects are world wide. Modern civilization is so complex and the relations between peoples of all nations are so interlocked that the immediate, if indirect effects of the war extend throughout the length and breadth of the peaceful neutral nations. . . .

> Looking at the war from a purely actuarial standpoint and judging wholly from newspaper accounts, it would seem as if the records of previous wars would not serve as a criterion for the cost of insurance in this conflict.

The earliest presentation of data was in an October 1915 paper (*T.A.S.A.* 16, 297) by John S. Thompson, then of Mutual Life of New York. It contained three sections:

1. Particulars of war clauses used by American companies in past wars, and by British and other European (but not Canadian) companies in the present one.

2. War claims reported thus far to Mutual Life, which then had $200 million of insurance in force in foreign countries. Those claims amounted to $400,000, of which $58,000 had arisen from the torpedoing of the "Lusitania."

3. Experiences of British companies, to the extent determinable from an assortment of published reports. The author concluded that an extra premium for military or naval service of five percent per annum would probably be adequate in any of the warring countries, an assessment disputed by those who, with the benefit of another six months of data, discussed Thompson's paper. Those discussions were given in May 1916, before the carnage of the Battle of the Somme (July–November 1916) gave a new, even more hideous, perspective to the conflict.

One of those discussions, by Arthur B. Wood of Sun Life of Canada, was recognized to be of such value that the actuaries present voted that it be published as a paper (*T.A.S.A.* 17, 49).

At the Actuarial Society meeting of May 1917, a cable was read from the Actuaries Club of London, hailing with joy the entrance of the United States into the struggle for justice and freedom among the nations. An appropriate response was dispatched.

President Arthur Hunter made extended informal remarks (which the members voted be printed in *T.A.S.A.* 18, 1), saying that, "each one of us must consider the whole situation and endeavor to decide to what extent the United States is justified in entering the war, and whether he is not in duty bound to devote his energies in assisting her in every way." Hunter then gave a ringing personal endorsement to President Wilson's message to Congress, saying that the President's words were surely the "voice of the people" and were hoped to be "the voice of God." Hunter then enunciated no fewer than six lines of conduct to be followed in order to do the right thing ourselves and to influence others toward similar thinking.

At the Council meeting of October 1917, there was evidence of sentiments that in retrospect seem almost of panic. Notice of proposed amendments to both the constitution and bylaws had already been sent to the Fellows, giving blanket power to the Council to waive or change any provisions of those documents without previous notice, provided that not more than three Council members voted negatively and that the Society at its next regular session approved with not more than ten negative votes. The Council had second thoughts about this sweeping pair of measures and proceeded to limit such power to provisions regarding payment of dues.

At the American Institute meeting in June 1918, its President Albert G. Portch devoted much of his address to the war clause situation, mentioning first that a standard provision had been recommended in 1916 by the ALC, but only one company had had the courage to adopt it. Then in April 1917, in the general rush to adopt war clauses, uniformity had been given scant consideration. Later in 1917 the NAIC had prepared a model war clause similar to that of the ALC, but it too was only partially successful in achieving uniformity. Portch's conclusions were (1) that war clauses being used by U.S. companies were far removed from uniformity; (2) that there was a tendency towards "the ultimate war clause" (limiting company liability to the policy reserve, and granting no extra-premium option); and (3) that the extra-premium war clause had proved to give the companies inadequate protection.

At the Actuarial Society meeting in May 1919, receipt of fraternal greetings and congratulations on the conclusion of the war from the Institute of Actuaries was noted, and a reciprocating message was sent expressing the resolve that "the spirit of comradeship and mutual helpfulness ... will ... be even stronger in the future, uniting us more firmly than ever as members of a great profession engaged in the service of mankind." (*T.A.S.A.* 20, 248.)

In 1920 (*R.A.I.A.* 9, 77), there appears a review of "War with Germany," a statistical summary by Leonard P. Ayres, Chief of the Statistics branch of the United States General Staff, containing significant statements:

> (1) The death rate of American soldiers and sailors from battle and disease during the period of hostilities was 2 per cent. (2) The battle losses were twice as numerous as deaths from disease. (3) The death rate from disease was lower and the death rate from battle was higher than in any other American war. (4) That for every man killed in battle, six were wounded, and five out of every six men sent to hospitals on account of wounds, were returned to duty. ... (6) The infantry and machine-gun units were the severest sufferers showing a death rate of 80.5 per 1,000 among officers and 51.7 among men. The air service came next with a death rate of 33.3 per 1,000 among officers and 1.6 among men.

DEATH OF EMORY McCLINTOCK, 1916

On July 10, 1916, Emory McClintock, characterized, we are told, by those who knew him best as "the most forceful actuary America has seen," died at his home at Bay Head, New Jersey. Nowhere in the *Transactions* can be found a more extensive obituary than that accorded him at the Actuarial Society's October 1916 meeting (*T.A.S.A.* 17, 373). The formal memorial was read by William A. Hutcheson, who had succeeded McClintock as Actuary of Mutual Life of New York at the latter's retirement in 1911. Four other Fellows followed with their reminiscences and their appreciations of his mathematical strength and his influence upon the Society's development and reputation, the total of all these comprising nine pages in the printed record. Hutcheson remarked that because of a certain modesty, almost amounting to bashfulness, McClintock was thought by many to be cold.

McClintock was born in 1840, the son of a Methodist Episcopal clergyman and theologian, attended Yale for one year and graduated from Columbia College, New York City, in 1859. From then to 1868 when he was appointed actuary of the newly formed Asbury Life of New York, he held several posts in America and abroad, including four years as vice-consul of the United States in Bradford, England. In 1871 he began eighteen years as actuary of the Northwestern Mutual Life, coming to New York to become actuary of the Mutual Life just before the Actuarial Society was organized in 1889. In 1874 the Institute of Actuaries elected him a Fellow.

He was considered one of America's leading mathematicians, serving as president of the American Mathematical Society from 1890 to 1894. Printed in the same volume of the *Transactions* as his obituary is a paper (*T.A.S.A.* 17, 290) by Walter S. Nichols, "Dr. Emory McClintock as a Great Creative Mathematician. —The Calculus of Enlargement." Nichols went so far as to say:

> The work of Dr. McClintock ... was ... a broad generalization but directed specially to mathematics in its quantitative relations and created a new branch of mathematical science comparable with the creation of the calculus by Newton and Leibnitz or analytical geometry by Descartes.

McClintock's mathematical prowess was described further in the discussion of Nichols' paper (*T.A.S.A.* 18, 170). Regrettably, his reputation was somewhat sullied by *The New York Times* in the obituary printed in its issue of July 12, 1916. *The Times* obituary writer had erred in the direction of portraying McClintock as, if not one of the culprits, at least a supporter of the practices within his company that precipitated the Armstrong Investigation. Miles M. Dawson undertook to set the record straight in a letter to the editor printed in *The Times* of July 19. That letter speaks revealingly of the man and the times in which he lived (Copyright ©1916 by The New York Times Company. Reprinted by permission.):

> I had hoped that the two misconceptions contained in [your] obituary had had their day and been obliterated.
>
> Mr. McClintock had lived a virtually cloistered life up to the time when, by the resignation of leading executive officers of the Mutual Life Insurance Company as the result of the [Armstrong] investigation ... he was suddenly forced into

the position of Vice President, with virtually entire charge of the insurance, as distinguished from the financial, management of the company. He was then 65 years of age and easily first of all the actuaries of the world in reputation and standing, but utterly unaccustomed to intercourse and to responsibilities of executive management. In the latter capacity he proved fully equal to the responsibilities which devolved upon him, as was shown by the prompt adoption of the reforms called for by the investigation and the legislation which followed. ...

Immediately upon his return [from a visit to Great Britain] he found an active campaign for the election of Trustees of the company progressing with unusual virulence. Though unaccustomed to being interviewed, he consented to make a statement which ... was interpreted to mean that Mr. McClintock was fully cognizant of and connected with [the prior] corruption, whereas nothing could have been further from the truth.

These two misconceptions, undoubtedly together with his other responsibilities and his age, had much to do with his breakdown, but they ought not to be referred to at this time as if any reflection upon his character was involved. ...

As one who acted in the capacity of actuary to the New York Legislative Commission ... , it is not improper for me to say what is well known to all actuaries and insurance men, that most of the important reforms ... as a result of the investigation were based upon the testimony of Mr. McClintock before the commission, which is justly regarded by all as the most valuable portion of the entire eight books of testimony and exhibits.

New York, July 16, 1916.   MILES M. DAWSON

FRATERNAL ACTUARIAL ASSOCIATION, 1916

The Fraternal Actuarial Association was organized in Cleveland on August 22, 1916. With its work done, it was dissolved in Pittsburgh on September 22, 1980.

An actuarial history of fraternal insurance in the United States had been written by a Canadian actuary, Sidney H. Pipe (*R.A.I.A.* 16, 29), covering the years up to the mid-1920s. The last officers of the Fraternal Actuarial Association (Bartley L. Munson, President) commissioned Vernon W. Roelofs, Ph.D., a retired history professor, to write a history of the Association's sixty-four years, which is incorporated in the final volume (1977–1980) of that Association's *Proceedings*.

The early growth of insurance through fraternal societies in the United States was attributable in part to the public mistrust of life insurance companies when so many of them failed in the last quarter of the nineteenth century and when the largest life companies were shown, in the years up to 1905, to have committed extravagances in their race for volume. The fraternal societies originally used the assessment system, which could not survive permanently even though its drawbacks were less pronounced in the fraternals (where insurance was not the sole inducement for joining or for persisting) than in the commercial assessment companies.

The major problem faced by the fraternals, once their farsighted leaders had seen the necessity for converting to the legal reserve system, was that the state regulatory system had no Elizur Wright to demand that the leaders of the fraternals act swiftly and decisively. Most states had no insurance laws to which the fraternals were subject; those societies had to make the transition themselves, which they were successful in accomplishing though it took many years and a succession of steps.

The eight actuaries who initially provided the leadership and influence necessary for the task were the following, listed in order of the year when each first became intimately acquainted with fraternal life insurance and its problems:

Year Entered Fraternal Work	Actuary
1886	George D. Eldridge (1848–1926)
1887	Abb Landis (1856–1927)
1897	Frederick A. Draper (1863–1944)
1898	Charles W. Iliff (1867–1924)
1900	Sidney H. Pipe (1877–1940)
1903	William F. Barnard (1860–1943)
1903	Miles M. Dawson (1863–1942)
1906	Lewis A. Anderson (1870–1927)

All of these became members of the Fraternal Actuarial Association either at its founding or subsequently, and all except Eldridge, Landis, and Iliff were Fellows of the Actuarial Society or the American Institute of Actuaries.

Before founding of the Fraternal Actuarial Association, the forum for fraternal actuaries as well as other officials was the National Fraternal Congress (NFC), the organization of fraternal societies. The NFC in 1897 accepted the concept of a reserve system and set about having a mortality table constructed upon which either level or step-rate net premiums would be calculated. The construction of the National Fraternal Congress Table of Mortality is rather amusingly described in Pipe's paper (*R.A.I.A.* 16, 32), though in fact the process was no more empirical than Homans employed to produce the American Experience Table, and the use of a mix of existing tables followed the procedure embraced by New England Mutual in its early years. The key point is that the NFC Table mortality rates removed much of the overstatement of the q_x values known to exist in the American Experience Table at the young ages, and worked satisfactorily with the help of the secular improvement in insured life mortality that occurred in the early twentieth century.

Pipe's paper describes a series of legislative proposals during the next several years—the "Force" Bill (1900), the Mobile Bill (1910), and the New York Conference Bill (1912). The last named constituted an important new stage in the progress toward actuarial soundness but, like its predecessors, did not require adoption of adequate reserves in fraternal society balance sheets. It required only reporting to insurance departments and the public the amounts of such reserves, thus setting goals of adequacy for the indefinite future.

Pipe says that "the fraternals riveted the fetters of this Bill firmly upon themselves, and have been struggling for more freedom of action ever since"; the principal "fetter" was a self-imposed separation of the expense loading from the mortality element in the premium, which in effect established an expense limitation difficult to meet. Reviews of two important books about this, by Abb Landis and Walter Basye, are printed in

T.A.S.A. 12, 144 and *T.A.S.A.* 21, 298. When the Fraternal Actuarial Association was formed in 1916, the fraternals still had a long way to go. As late as 1924, Joseph B. Maclean in the first edition of his authoritative text, *Life Insurance,* wrote, with perhaps undue severity (p. 290):

> There are at the present time about 100 assessment associations and over 500 fraternal orders offering life insurance protection to their members at low cost. The majority of these societies are unfortunately on an unsound financial basis. . . .

> The life insurance business of some of the fraternal orders is on a sound basis, adequate premiums being charged and adequate reserves maintained. The number which are in this position, however, is insignificant, although it includes some of the largest and most important fraternal orders in the country.

The thirty-five charter members of the Fraternal Actuarial Association (in their "Active" category, later called Fellows) are listed in Table III.9. Its first officers were George D. Eldridge, President; Abb Landis, Vice-President; Wendell P. Coler, Secretary; Sidney H. Pipe, Treasurer; and F. M. Speakman, Librarian.

The existence of the new actuarial body was recognized by Arthur Hunter in his presidential address to the Actuarial Society in May 1918, thus (*T.A.S.A.* 19, 10):

> We have recently seen the organization of a society of actuaries whose work is principally connected with fraternal orders. The members of the Fraternal Actuarial Society [*sic*] have difficult problems to solve, especially in connection with the marked changes in the management and plans of the orders. Valuations must generally be made under the Mobile Valuation Law or the New York Conference Bill Law, although failure to meet such valuations does not necessarily involve a receivership. Under the former, several years are allowed in which to comply, and under the latter the percentage of solvency need only be maintained in succeeding triennial valuations. Some orders are issuing ordinary life and limited payment policies with paid-up and extended insurance values and premium loans, and have an agency force which is paid a fee for each new member obtained, or occasionally a percentage commission on the premium. In fact, some of the fraternal orders have much of the authority granted to the regular companies, with the privilege of being practically free from taxation; the members, however, are subject to assessment under ordinary life and limited payment life policies if the reserve for the class is not equal, for example, to the American 3 1/2 per cent. An anomaly sometimes exists of an order which on the bulk of its business on the older plans is not solvent enough to carry the reserve under the Mobile or other valuation law, but on its newer plans guarantees paid-up and extended insurance values, these groups being separately classified.

Apart from a single experiment, in June 1924, with a pair of three-hour, wide-ranging tests, no examination system was ever introduced by the Fraternal Actuarial Association, although in 1920 an educational qualification for admission had been authorized. In 1930 it was proposed that the Actuarial Society be approached with a view to the Association adopting the first four examinations of the Society and

Table III.9

CHARTER MEMBERS OF THE FRATERNAL ACTUARIAL ASSOCIATION

Member	Age in 1916	Membership*	Company and Location
C. L. Alford	19		Landis Consulting Actuary, Nashville
S. E. Allison	33	F.A.I.A.	Pan-American Life, New Orleans
L. A. Anderson	46	F.A.I.A.	Wisconsin State Insurance Department, Madison
W. F. Barnard	56	F.A.I.A.	Consulting actuary, Syracuse, New York
D. A. Baxter	25	ACAS	Michigan State Insurance Department, Lansing
H. E. Brown	24		Women's Benefit Association, Port Huron, Michigan
J. D. Buchanan	25	A.A.S.	Rhode Island State Insurance Department, Providence
E. B. Burns	n.a.		Masons' Annuity Society, Atlanta
W. P. Coler	25	A.A.I.A.	National Union Assurance Society, Toledo
A. B. Dawson	34	FCAS	M. M. Dawson Consulting Actuary, New York
M. M. Dawson	53	F.A.S.	Consulting actuary, New York
G. D. Eldridge	68		Consulting actuary, Boston
J. W. Glover	48	F.A.I.A.	University of Michigan, Ann Arbor
W. H. Gould	37	F.A.I.A.	Consulting actuary, New York
M. Gunn	24		Consulting actuary, Indianapolis
F. J. Haight	39	F.A.I.A.	Consulting actuary, Indianapolis
E. M. Heath	n.a.		Ladies of the Maccabees, Port Huron, Michigan
J. P. M. Hjorth	n.a.		Masonic Mutual Life Association, Washington, D.C.
G. A. Huggins	35		Consulting actuary, Philadelphia
C. W. Iliff	49		Supreme Tribe of Ben Hur, Crawfordsville, Indiana
E. Jaqua	n.a.		Insurance Department, Jefferson City, Missouri
W. B. Kieft	56		Court of Honor Society, Springfield, Illinois
A. Landis	60	FCAS	Consulting actuary, Nashville
J. R. Leal	31	FCAS	Office of State Treasurer, Tallahassee, Florida
T. J. McComb	n.a.		Consulting actuary, Oklahoma City
F. D. Partridge	45		Women's Benefit Association, Port Huron, Michigan
F. M. Phillippi	n.a.		Life & Casualty Insurance, Nashville
W. N. Phillips	n.a.		Modern Woodmen of America, Rock Island, Illinois
S. H. Pipe	39	F.A.S.	Independent Order of Foresters, Toronto
A. M. Siegk	n.a.		Insurance Department, Baltimore
F. M. Speakman	34		Consulting actuary, Philadelphia
L. W. Squier	n.a.		Consulting actuary, Philadelphia
R. D. Taylor	48		Consulting actuary, Cedar Rapids
P. B. Twitchell	34		Consulting actuary, Denver
S. H. Wolfe	42	FCAS	Consulting actuary, New York
Median Age	**38**		

*Membership at the time in other actuarial bodies.

American Institute (these then being joint) as its admission criterion, but this was not pursued.

The Association never had an office or a paid staff. Its complete dependence upon work done and records kept by current officers and members may explain the disappearance of records that such a body would be expected to have saved.

The Association did have a library, which at its dissolution was placed in the library of the Aid Association for Lutherans.

THE INFLUENZA PANDEMIC, 1918

An account of the catastrophic pestilence that made its first appearance on the eastern seaboard of North America, especially the port of Boston, in the first week of September 1918 and moved relentlessly westward through the next two months belongs in an actuarial history for two reasons: first, because it provided a severe test of the safety margins upon which the stability of life insurance depends, and second, because of its long-term influence upon actuarial thinking about reserves and surplus.

The epidemic, said to have been the most destructive since the Black Death of the fourteenth century, was analyzed in a 1919 paper by James D. Craig and Louis I. Dublin "The Influenza Epidemic of 1918" (*T.A.S.A.* 20, 134) and in two British reports reviewed in 1921 (*T.A.S.A.* 22, 541). Craig and Dublin gave data on the experience of the Metropolitan Life, showing the differences by age and sex and by class of business. Its consequences were also examined in a 1919 paper with the unenlightening title, "Things To Be Considered" by Douglas H. Rose (*T.A.S.A.* 20, 72), in which Rose maintained that the life companies ought to build their surplus funds rapidly by substantially decreasing their dividend payments.

Rose tabulated the ratios of actual to expected mortality (by the American Experience Table) from the gain and loss exhibits of thirty-one life companies for which the desired figures could readily be obtained (none being industrial insurance companies), showing the following results:

	1913–1917	1918
Average ratio of actual to expected mortality (combined results for all 31 companies)	63.6%	98.1%
Company with highest ratio for 1918	32.9	126.6
Company with lowest ratio for 1918	57.7	78.1
Company having largest increase over its own experience in 1913–1917	32.9	126.6
Company having the smallest increase over its own experience in 1913–1917	64.5	78.2

That author's next step was to convert the excess mortality for each company (i.e., over its own 1913–1917 mortality) into dollars and to compare that amount with the total of the same company's surplus and contingency reserve on December 31, 1917. Rose found that in each of nine companies the excess mortality was less than 20% of their surplus; in twelve companies it was between 20 and 40%; and in ten it was over 40%. Apparently in no case was the excess as much as 60% of the existing surplus. The excess mortality arose, of course, from war as well as influenza mortality, but the latter was generally by far the heavier component. Analyses of experience of Canadian policyholders showed an entirely different relationship—see R. D. Baldwin's paper, *T.A.S.A.* 39, 297.

Actuaries naturally were obsessed by the possibility of a recurrence of the pestilence. This question figured in the debates (Chapter IV) of the 1920s about adoption of the American Men Table as successor to the American Experience Table as the valuation standard in the United States.

On October 15–16, 1918, two Fellows and one Associate of the Actuarial Society died. The two Fellows, Virgil M. Kime of Hartford and Albert G. Portch of Springfield, Illinois, are recorded as having died from influenza, the latter in Montreal where he had gone to attend the Society meeting there. The Associate, Oscar F. Johnson of New York City, was taken ill as he prepared to attend that same Montreal meeting; the cause of his death was given as pneumonia. The ages of these three were, respectively, 32, 36, and 35.

The fall meeting of the American Institute, scheduled for November 7–8, 1918, in St. Louis was cancelled because of the epidemic.

OUR PROFESSION IN 1918

Towards the end of the third decade of our profession's organized existence on this continent, the rosters of the four bodies showed the following numbers of members at the Fellowship or other senior level:

Fellows of the Actuarial Society of America   156 (including 19
                                                           overseas members)

Fellows of the American Institute of Actuaries   88

Fellows of the Casualty Actuarial Society   145

Active Members of Fraternal Actuarial Association   35

The total of these would be meaningless because of a considerable overlap; in fact, one actuary, Miles Menander Dawson, was on every one of these four lists. When duplications and overseas members are removed, the number of actuaries on this continent becomes 352, compared with 69 at the end of 1888.

Table III.10 gives details of the members of Actuarial Society Fellows and Associates at five-year intervals 1889–1918. For year-by-year figures on Fellows, see the statistical section of James R. Herman's "Actuaries—Past, Present and Future," *T.A.S.A.* 50, 67. From Table III.10.B it can be seen that the relative numerical strength of the dwindling corps of charter Fellows remained substantial until qualifiers by examination began to proliferate after 1903. The practice of granting Fellowships to eminent members of overseas actuarial bodies practically ceased after 1898 except for a few conferments on the occasion of the Fourth International Congress at New York in 1903.

Three examination systems, differing in content and rigor, were in effect. University courses in actuarial science were few, the senior one being at Toronto, the runner-up at Michigan.

Associates were not classified as Society members, but rather as students, until 1905. The waivers of Associateship examinations were in general restricted to persons who had passed equivalent examinations in the Institute or Faculty of Actuaries before coming to North America.

Rapport between individual actuaries had made tremendous strides, but mutual respect and cooperation among the organizations themselves was yet far

Table III.10

FELLOWS AND ASSOCIATES OF ACTUARIAL SOCIETY OF AMERICA, 1889–1918

	April 1889 Charter Fellows	Elected on Council Nomination	Qualified by Exam	Overseas (Honorary)	Total
A. New Fellows					
1889–1893	38	41		13	92
1894–1898		6		24	30
1899–1903		1	18	4	23
1904–1908		3	20		23
1909–1913		2	22	2	26
1914–1918		2	38		40
Total	38	55	98	43	234
B. Roster of Fellows at End of Each Period					
End of 1893	36	40		13	89
End of 1898	32	41		33	106
End of 1903	29	39	18	36	122
End of 1908	26	39	38	28	13
End of 1913	25	36	60	26	147
End of 1918	14	29	94	19	156

	New Associates by Exam	By Waiver	Transferred to Fellow	Died	Withdrew	Roster at End of Year
C. Associates						
1896–1898	7	1				8
1899–1903	31	10	18	1	1	29
1904–1908	69	8	21			85
1909–1913	42	16	23	1	1	118
1914–1918	50	6	40	5	4	125
Total	199	41	102	7	6	125

below a desirable level. One evidence of members' devotion to the objectives of their organizations is seen in the excellent record of papers giving individual company mortality and disability experience, the secrecy of pre-1889 days having vanished.

The insurance industry's prestige in the public eye had made substantial recovery from its lowly status at the turn of the century.

Group life insurance had become a companion to individual policies. Disability benefits, whether in health insurance policies or attached to life policies, were well received by the public but labored under the twin handicaps of inadequate supporting statistics and underwriting naivete. Warnings about insufficiency of annuity premiums were being uttered but not heeded.

The Actuarial Society had enthusiastically celebrated in turn its tenth, twentieth, and twenty-fifth anniversaries. For the first of these, Secretary I. C. Pierson had written a historical piece (*T.A.S.A.* 6, 117). At the twentieth and twenty-fifth anniversaries several charter members gave their recollections; at the latter the survivors were becoming prolix, the transcript of after dinner addresses requiring a commemorative booklet of forty printed pages.

The only actuarial club in being was the Actuaries Club established 1907 in Toronto.

The oldest living member of our profession in 1918 was Howell W. St. John of Hartford, born in 1834. One charter member, William E. Starr of Worcester, Massachusetts, had passed his ninetieth birthday in March 1902, an achievement recognized at a party hosted by his Society colleagues who presented him with a silver cup. Starr died in January 1903 while en route to his company's annual meeting. Several actuaries had established professional reputations that, seventy years later, still mark them as extraordinary in stature and influence. It seems fair to name some of these, in order of birthdate:

Emory McClintock (1840–1916)	Arthur Hunter (1869–1964)
David Parks Fackler (1841–1924)	Albert W. Whitney (1870–1943)
Walter S. Nichols (1841–1921)	Isaac M. Rubinow (1875–1936)
Abb Landis (1856–1927)	Henry L. Rietz (1875–1943)
Thomas B. Macaulay (1860–1942)	Albert H. Mowbray (1881–1949)
Miles M. Dawson (1863–1942)	Gustav F. Michelbacher (1890–1974)

It is fitting to close this account of the era in which our profession in North America began to seek a place among the learned professions, by drawing attention to an extraordinary 1899 paper, "The Actuary's Place in Science," by philosopher-actuary Walter S. Nichols (*T.A.S.A.* 6, 37). In it Nichols undertook, with a host of specific comments on other professions, to show that the doctrine of chance, which we espouse, can and should be extended to them all. His theme was that what was first perceived as truth has proved at best an approximation to truth and has had to be modified in the light of later discoveries. He summed up thus:

> Gentlemen of the Actuarial Society, when all the observations of science have been gathered, . . . it must remain for minds that are disciplined in the logic of our profession to view the finished work and say how far the builders have realized their own boast that trust is the goal which they have won.

APPENDIX TO CHAPTER III

Papers by North American Actuaries
at the First through Seventh International Congresses of Actuaries

FIRST CONGRESS 1895, BRUSSELS

Fackler, D. P. (U.S.) "Decreasing rates of interest in connection with annuities and insurances." I, p. 96.

Macaulay, T. B. (Canada) "On the intervention of the legislature to permit or assume the supervision of life assurance companies." I, p. 392.

Pierson, I. C. (U.S.) "The necessity of a universal notation." I, p. 58.

St. John, H. W. (U.S.) "On the intervention of the legislature to permit or assume the supervision of the operations of life insurance companies." I, p. 372.

SECOND CONGRESS 1898, LONDON

Nichols, W. S. (U.S.) "The limitations of the system of net valuations." II, p. 161. (Reprinted in *T.A.S.A.* 5, 195.)

THIRD CONGRESS 1900, PARIS

McAdam, L. (U.S.) "A new method of valuation where the first year's premium is to be regarded as the premium for a one year term insurance." III, p. 620.

McClintock, E. (U.S.) "On special investigations for the comparison of death losses by occupations or otherwise." III, p. 428.

McClintock, E. (U.S.) "On the valuation of the negotiable securities included in the assets of a company." III, p. 502.

FOURTH CONGRESS 1903, NEW YORK

Blackadar, A. K. (Canada) "On the growth in Canada of life insurance, assessment insurance, friendly societies, accident insurance, employers' liability insurance, health insurance, pure endowment business, annuity business, old age pensions, and other operations requiring actuarial advice." IV, Vol. I, p. 604.

Dawson, M. M. (U.S.) "Valuation, in actions for damages for negligence, of human life, destroyed or impaired." IV, Vol. I, p. 929.

DeBoer, J. A. (U.S.) "On instruction given in universities and colleges on actuarial subjects." IV, Vol. I, p. 763.

Fackler, D. P. (U.S.) "Report for the United States of America on the growth and progress of institutions and conditions requiring actuarial advice." IV, Vol. I, p. 708.

Goldman, L. (Canada) "Existing legislation for the protection of wives and children as life insurance beneficiaries against the claims of creditors." IV, Vol. I, p. 808.

Gore, J. K. (U.S.) "On the improvement in longevity in the United States during the nineteenth century." IV, Vol. I, p. 30.

Hann, R. G. (U.S.) "War mortality in the United States." IV, Vol. I, p. 80.

Hunter, A. (U.S.) "Mortality among non-Caucasian races." IV, Vol. I, p. 133.

Lewis, C. T. (U.S.) "Laws protecting life insurance against creditors." IV, Vol. I, p. 873.

Messenger, H. J. (U.S.) "Health insurance in the United States." IV, Vol. I, p. 495.

Moir, H. (U.S.) "Relationship of initial expenses and selection to valuation." IV, Vol. I, p. 954.

Sanderson, F. (Canada) "On the instruction given in Canadian universities on actuarial subjects." IV, Vol. I, p. 720.

FIFTH CONGRESS 1906, BERLIN

Dawson, M. M. (U.S.) "Formation of a mortality table for valuation purposes." V, Vol. II, p. 209.

Gore, J. H. (U.S.) "Instruction given in colleges and universities on actuarial subjects." V, Vol. II, p. 425.

Hann, R. G. (U.S.) "Loss experience of paid-up insurance in the Equitable Life Assurance Society of the United States, from 1859 to 1899." V, Vol. II, p. 227.

Hoffman, F. L. (U.S.) "Principles and elements of industrial insurance." V, Vol. I, p. 131.

Hunter, A. (U.S.) "Mortality experience among annuitants resident in the United States of America and Canada." V, Vol. I, p. 431.

Ogden, S. V. (U.S.) "Taxation of life insurance companies in the United States." V, Vol. I, p. 751.

Sheppard, H. N. (U.S.) "On the method of calculating the expected death-losses during the calendar year from the books of a life insurance company." V, Vol. II, p. 219.

SIXTH CONGRESS 1909, VIENNA

Dawson, M. M. (U.S.) "Is it possible to demonstrate mathematically the measure of profitable expenditure for new business in life insurance?" VI, Vol. II, p. 821.

Hoffman, F. L. (U.S.) "Economic and political considerations of state insurance in the United States, 1860–1908." VI, Vol. I, part 2, p. 1105.

Hunter, A. (U.S.) "Treatment of "under-average" lives — Suitable plans for their insurance." VI, Vol. I, part 2, p. 1349.

Messenger, H. J. (U.S.) "Is it desirable to divide 'under average' lives for the purpose of assurance into special classes according to their distinguishing features and if so in what way should they be classified?" VI, Vol. I, part 2, p. 1363.

Moir, H. (U.S.) "Forfeiture regulations in America." VI, Vol. II, p. 185.

Rose, D. H. (U.S.) "Investments of insurance companies, with special reference to modern developments." VI, Vol. I, part 1, p. 403.

Whitney, A. W. (U.S.) "The actuarial theory of fire insurance rates as depending upon the ratio of insurance to sound value hence a determination of the rates for use with a coinsurance clause." VI, Vol. II, p. 395.

SEVENTH CONGRESS 1912, AMSTERDAM

Dawson, M. M. (U.S.) "Governmental methods of providing old age pensions." VII, Vol. I, p. 207.

Hoffman, F. L. (U.S.) "American public pension systems and civil service retirement plans." VII, Vol. I, p. 237.

Hunter, A. (U.S.) "Improvement in mortality in the tropics." VII, Vol. II, p. 165.

Hunter R. G. (U.S.) "American methods of loading premiums." VII, Vol. I, p. 723.

Chapter IV.

1919–1948:
FAT YEARS AND
LEAN YEARS

Conservative, n. A statesman who is enamored of existing evils, as distinguished from the Liberal, who wishes to replace them with others.
—Ambrose G. Bierce (1842–1914), The Devil's Dictionary (1911)

If, as 1919 dawned, a modern Joseph amongst us had seen the three decades ahead in his dream, he might have prepared our profession for ten fat years marred by our own hesitations and mistakes, followed by ten years of severe leanness throughout which actuaries generally rose to the challenges, followed in their turn by ten years of war's devastation and subsequent partial recovery.

CHANGING ATTITUDES AND DIRECTIONS

In 1918 (*T.A.S.A.* 19, 1) Actuarial Society President Arthur Hunter perceived that the Society had already passed through two phases and was well embarked upon a third.

Its first phase he saw as that of a professional club, engaged in developing the actuarial knowledge of its members. Main objectives were to weld the fledgling body together, to remove (outside) suspicion of its motives, to extend members' horizons beyond the immediate interests of their own companies, and to develop an effective working relationship among actuaries. This era, in his view, lasted a mere seven years until the educational system was approved in 1896, but looking back, one sees elements of a private club extending well beyond that date. Strict limits, of which Hunter disapproved, on who were permitted even to sit for the examinations, continued for some years. Acceptable applicants were limited to those employed in actuarial departments of life companies considered to be in good standing.

Furthermore, within memories of actuaries now living, as well described by J. Gordon Beatty in his privately distributed *Reminiscences of an Old Soldier and Actuary* (1977), "youngsters treated the actuarial 'greats' with respect approaching awe. They sat at the front, we at the back. When they had said their pieces, unless we were called on to speak we usually took it for granted that that was all there was to be said." And the constitutional provision for life memberships of past-presidents on the Council prolonged the influence of senior actuaries in the Society's affairs. Hunter himself was a Council member continuously from 1904 until the Society merged with the American Institute in 1949, a few days before his eightieth birthday.

Hunter identified the Society's second phase as that of a scientific association, taking seriously its responsibilities to the world around it. He saw this as characterized by members' willingness to pool mortality statistics for the general good (although indeed this had been done as far back as 1875) as well as by adoption of a system for anonymous submission of papers for the *Transactions* in place of the original plan that gave Council members, but nobody else, the absolute right to have their papers printed.

In the third phase there emerged, said Hunter (p. 2), "a scientific and public society, seeing clearly its duty to educate actuaries and also its obligations to the insurance world, the community and the government." A later proposal along this line by Society President William A. Hutcheson in 1922 (*T.A.S.A.* 23, 1) was for our profession to shoulder the task of exposing the statistical errors and fallacies that we encounter in our daily life (this idea, however, failed to take root). In November of that same year, American Institute President Lawrence M. Cathles exhorted actuaries (*R.A.I.A.* 11, Pt. 2, 1) to investigate whether authorities in their local communities might be ignorantly obligating future generations to exorbitant costs of police and fire department pensions.

CLINGING TO THE AMERICAN EXPERIENCE TABLE

Having after some hesitation (see Chapter III) accepted the insurance commissioners' request that a mortality table reflecting modern life company experience be constructed, actuaries in the United States were faced immediately after World War I with the decision whether or not to recommend use of the American Men Table for determining policy reserves. Henry Moir's May 1915 paper on the question of constructing a table which had in effect been blessed by the Council of the Actuarial Society had at one point gone well into the question of the table's use (*T.A.S.A.* 16, 16):

> When public confidence is lost in any of our practices life insurance will immediately suffer. Our business is peculiarly sensitive, and all that we do should be open, above-board, and should invite the most rigid inquiry on the part of the intelligent public. Although we cannot explain our science in its more intricate detail, we should be able to make an intelligent man understand its guiding principles, and should meet and satisfy intelligent suggestions from the outside. There have been prominent statements in the press, made by well known writers in recent years, which indicate a lack of confidence in the American Experience Table. It is our duty to restore confidence in the basis of our calculations or change the basis.

By historical accident the question of recommending adoption of the American Men Table for valuation came up just at the time (May 1919) when the staggering effect of the influenza epidemic a few months earlier dominated and distorted actuarial perspective. The Council, as in 1915, arranged for the topic to be introduced by a formal paper, this time by Arthur Hunter (*T.A.S.A.* 20, 23), "Should the 'American Men' Mortality Table (A.M.) Be the Basis for Premiums and Reserves?" Much of Hunter's theme dwelt upon the hazard of using the new table (with 4 1/2% interest and realistic loadings for expenses and contingencies) to develop a scale of nonparticipating premiums, a theme which in retrospect seems less than appropriate coming from the actuary of a large mutual company. The following are samples of the author's phraseology (p. 25):

> [W]e cannot safely assume any lower future mortality than that represented by the A. M. Select Table, and some companies would not and should not be willing to assume even so low a mortality. . . .

> [I]t should be distinctly understood that *I would not approve* [emphasis added] of such a high rate of interest [as 4 1/2%] in the calculation of [nonparticipating] premiums.

In concluding his paper, Hunter summed up thus (p. 40):

> It is too early as yet to attempt to give positive answers in few words to the questions which were raised by the title of this paper. Too short a time has elapsed since the results of the A. M. Table have been published; the influenza epidemic is too recent and the warfare conditions are too strongly in our minds to enable us to see clearly whether or not the new table should come into general use.

Discussions of the paper took place on the day it was read, instead of being postponed in accordance with custom until the next meeting. It was then voted that it be discussed also at the next meeting; that second discussion apparently was informal and therefore by the practice of those days was not printed. In the immediate discussion the first stock company actuary to speak, Edward B. Morris of the Travelers, said (p. 46):

> The question naturally arises as to what will be the effect of the new table upon the non-participating rates. I think I can safely answer, very little, for the reason that the probable results under the new investigation have been long known and have been long discounted.

Morris also made the point, although not as emphatically as its importance warrants, that provision for excess mortality from wars and epidemics belongs in the margin set aside for contingencies, not in the underlying mortality assumption.

In both the paper and the discussion, legitimate points were made that adoption of the new table (for reserves and nonforfeiture values) would result in substantially longer extended insurance periods and would require change in the New York expense limitation law. No speaker specifically mentioned that a move to lower premiums at the younger ages would dilute an existing competitive advantage currently enjoyed by the mutual companies over some of the stock companies.

The gist of the discussion was not resoundingly against adoption of the new table for reserves, but Hunter in his reply thereto said (p. 69), "I do not at the present time believe in the adoption of the new table for the basis of premiums, reserves and surrender values," which doubtless reflected the majority conclusion of the Council. If that conclusion was communicated to the NCIC, it must have been done informally as the Council minutes report no such message. Perhaps the Council agreed that the prudent course was to say nothing.

For the next six years the subject remained dormant. In September 1925 William M. Corcoran, actuary of the Connecticut Insurance Department and a new Associate of the Actuarial Society, presented a paper at the NCIC meeting, "Should the American Men Mortality Table Be Made Permissive As A Legal Valuation Standard?" The views he expressed were, in summary, these (NCIC 56th *Proceedings*, p. 190):

The Actuarial Society meeting in Richmond, Virginia, October 1920: The first held in a southern state. Name key is available from SOA archives.

First—The American Experience Table is obsolete, it is entirely out of line with current experience, and the continued use of it as required by law works a distinct injustice to policyholders.

Second—The American Men Ultimate Table is a safe standard, it is the most accurate measure of present day mortality which we have, and companies should be permitted to use it for reserves as well as for premiums if they so desire.

Under the circumstances, I believe it would be extremely desirable for this Convention through an appropriate committee to investigate the desirability of making the proposed change in the valuation basis and if such change is found to be desirable, to determine the modifications necessary in existing statutory requirements to put the same into effect.

This led to appointment of a committee consisting of Corcoran himself, the actuaries of the New York and Illinois Departments, and also J. D. Craig (Actuarial Society) and George Graham (American Institute) to advise the NCIC. And this, in turn, led to appointment of an Actuarial Society committee to advise J. D. Craig; possibly also the American Institute's Standing Committee on Statutory Valuation made itself available to George Graham. The outcome was that the Corcoran Committee reported favorably, but the NCIC, by the wide margin of 28 to 4, rejected the recommendation.

Thus, it was left to each individual state to decide whether or not to permit companies to value any or all of their new policies on the American Men Table. Several states soon did so; by 1931 as Ronald G. Stagg reported to the American Institute (*R.A.I.A.* 20, 299), permission had been granted in some midwestern and southern states and also in New York and Connecticut.

The upshot: because of reactionary thinking by some actuaries and confused thinking by others, many long years were still to elapse before the American Experience Table with all its obstacles to public satisfaction with life insurance would cease to be the valuation standard for newly issued policies.

Meanwhile, the regulatory authority in Canada, the Dominion Department of Insurance, proceeded in 1927 to reach a solution entirely different from any even considered in the United States, one which—half a century earlier than in the United States—gave clear recognition to the appropriate responsibility of the company's actuary. As A. D. Watson (*T.A.S.A.* 28, 241) described the new policy valuation provisions:

> [S]omething approaching real responsibility is placed upon the actuary of a company . . . . [T]here must be appended to the exhibit [of reserves] a certificate by the actuary to the effect that the reserves are not less than the reserves required by the Act, "and in addition that in his opinion the reserves make a good and sufficient provision for all unmatured obligations of the company guaranteed under the terms of its policies." Therefore, an actuary cannot properly take refuge in the minimum reserve provisions of the Act.

The Canadian authorities protected the public from the risk of this responsibility being placed in the hands of unqualified persons by requiring that the certifying actuary be a Fellow of one of the then four recognized actuarial bodies within the life insurance field in North America and Great Britain.

That 1927 law removed all prescriptions of either bases or methods that actuaries must use and placed the Superintendent of Insurance in possession of information helpful in determining whether the reserve being maintained was adequate. The existing requirement for deficiency reserves was abolished; only the maximum valuation interest assumption (3 1/2% for insurance, 4% for annuities) was prescribed.

MORTALITY AND RELATED STUDIES

Cooperation in statistical work between ALIMDA and the Actuarial Society had begun in October 1909 when the two bodies organized a joint committee to undertake the Medico-Actuarial Mortality Investigation and was cemented in 1916 when congratulations on a worthy result were exchanged (*T.A.S.A.* 17, 159).

In 1916 also, Oscar H. Rogers, M.D., and Arthur Hunter, both of New York Life, suggested in their paper "The Need in Medical Selection of Standards by which to Measure Border-Line Risks" (*T.A.S.A.* 17, 281) that the two organizations develop standards by which to measure the value of lives for insurance, i.e., a classification system that would lead to uniform ratings of borderline risks. The committee to undertake this was originally called the Joint Committee on Standards; in 1923 it was renamed the Joint Committee on Mortality.

The Joint Committee produced the following three reports:

1918   "Standard Mortality Ratios Incident to Variations in Height and Weight"

1920   "Functional Heart Murmurs and Intermittent Albuminuria"

1921   "The Influence of Family History on Mortality"

These confirmed the feasibility of the project and the value of the committee's findings. Other such explorations followed, and beginning in 1925 with the *Blood Pressure Study,* followed in 1929 by the *Joint Occupation Study* (and its companion volume, *Occupational Mortality Ratings*) and then the *Medical Impairment Study* published in 1931 (though dated 1929) followed by its supplement on ratings, the Joint Committee undertook to furnish annual reports of insured life mortality.

The first of the Joint Committee's annual reports was published in 1934 (*T.A.S.A.* 35, 353), giving the experience of fourteen companies on standard medically examined issues of 1925 to 1932 exposed to policy anniversaries in 1933. The mortality was measured by the Basic Table 1920–1926 (one of two basic tables that had been constructed for the *Joint Occupation Study*) and showed in total a disappointing 111.9% ratio to that table. The data were used to construct a new "Basic Table 1925–'32" to be used for measurement in forthcoming studies.

These annual reports continued without a break as long as the Actuarial Society existed and into the era of the Society of Actuaries. More basic tables were constructed from time to time; they comprise a valuable record of insured life mortality during successive eras.

The Joint Committee promptly added a companion series of annual studies, viz., "Mortality on Policies for Large Amounts," a "large amount" in those Depression days being defined as an application for $50,000 or more. These studies, of course, were prompted by fear of serious adverse selection by applicants for large-amount policies. This series was abandoned in 1943 because of the strictures of wartime conditions and was not resumed after the war. As can be seen from R. D. Murphy's 1937 paper on the subject "Mortality and Underwriting for Large Amounts" (*T.A.S.A.* 38, 489), the fears were not without justification.

Other studies made by the Joint Committee were of mortality under annuities and settlement options and mortality of juveniles.

In a 1918 paper with Edward B. Morris, "Joint Mortality Experience of the Aetna Life and Travelers Insurance Companies on Group Policies" (*T.A.S.A.* 19, 29), Edmund E. Cammack of Hartford gave the first of what proved to be a long and valuable series of studies of mortality under group life contracts, at first on business of just two companies, later expanded to six. These were not under the direction of the Actuarial Society until much later (1942) when the Committee on Investigations of Mortality Experience under Group Life Insurance was appointed to carry on this work. In a 1927 paper "Mortality Tables Constructed Upon the Experience Under Group Policies" (*T.A.S.A.* 28, 247), Cammack published two group life insurance mortality tables constructed from his data. One of these covered Clerical, the other All Other Non-Hazardous Industries. As a general rule, however, group life mortality continued to be measured in terms of American Men Ultimate Table for the reason that the minimum first year premium permitted by New York State was a function of that table.

Studies of intercompany mortality of annuitants before the Joint Committee on Mortality took responsibility for this work in 1936 were the following:

1. [Emory] McClintock's Annuity Tables, published 1899 (*T.A.S.A.* 6, 13).

2. American Annuitants Mortality Tables, published by Arthur Hunter in 1920 (*T.A.S.A.* 21, 157).

3. United States Annuitants 1918–1927, published by Robert Henderson in 1928 (*T.A.S.A.* 29, 297) and in 1929 (*T.A.S.A.* 30, 237).

4. Combined Annuity Table (for group annuities), published by James D. Craig in his discussion of a paper by E. E. Cammack (*T.A.S.A.* 29, 120).

The era (especially the early part thereof) reviewed in this chapter may well be described as the heyday of submissions to the *Transactions* of individual company mortality studies. In the six years 1919 to 1925 inclusive, there were no fewer than forty of these printed, on many topics from general mortality to those of individual types such as abstainers, specific countries, various substandard classes and policy plans. These provided enlightenment for both risk selection and premium determination.

NON-MEDICAL INSURANCE

In 1921 several Canadian companies embarked upon non-medical underwriting of $1,000 policies, a practice that had been successful for years in Britain. The Canadian entry had been precipitated by physician shortages in rural areas and perhaps even more so by agitations within some medical associations, even to the point of obtaining pledges from their members to charge at least $10 for each insurance examination regardless of policy amount. The attitudes of some United States actuaries to this experiment were distinctly negative; furthermore, non-medical insurance had been made illegal in some states, usually dating from attempts years earlier by life companies and agents' groups to prevent group life insurance from being written. Nevertheless, United States companies were substantially into the non-medical field themselves less than five years after their unfriendly comments, and the original non-medical amount limit soon began to escalate.

COMPETITIVE PROBLEMS WITH PRICING AND PRODUCT DESIGN

At this stage, our profession's escutcheon was blotted in three separate ways, casting some doubt upon the degree of influence achieved by our professional bodies in fostering sound practices and competitive restraint. All three were instances of a failure that American Institute President Percy H. Evans aptly described as "a departure from an old principle that in the case of benefits of unknown or uncertain value we should begin with a redundant premium and reduce it as experience permits" (*R.A.I.A.* 15, 4).

The most serious of these mistakes occurred in the fields of disability income benefits, those attached to life policies and the noncancellable type issued separately. The history of these is so complex as to require a separate chapter on "Income Disability Benefits" (Chapter VIII). The other mistakes involved annuities and group life insurance, respectively.

The errors in pricing single-premium annuities were astounding because qualified actuaries knew that heavy losses had been suffered from annuities in Europe in bygone days, and the subject had been thoroughly discussed in papers and mortality studies as far back as the earliest days of the Actuarial Society. A summing-up of the entire debacle appears in Wilmer A. Jenkins' 1950 paper published in the *Proceedings* of the Centenary Assembly of the Institute of Actuaries (Vol. II, 254), "The Problem of Annuity Premium Rates in the United States."

Many years later, William C. McCarter in his paper "A New Mortality Table and a Graded Rate System for the Life Income Settlement Options" (*TSA* 8, 127) diagnosed the problem as arising not so much from disregard of sound actuarial principles as from grossly underestimating both the public desire for annuities and the extent of the adverse selection that might be exercised. In part, the losses stemmed from the tardinesss of actuaries, accustomed since 1900 to rising interest rates, to adapt to fifteen years of precipitately falling rates through the Depression and World War II eras. The most effective solution would have been a switch to participating annuities, an idea suggested by David Parks Fackler in 1914 (*T.A.S.A.* 15, 40).

In Great Britain a fundamental annuity pricing development, the use of forecast tables, had been described in the Institute publication by W. P. Elderton and H. J. P. Oakley, *The Mortality of Annuitants, 1900–1920*; that feature was described in the book's 1924 review (*T.A.S.A.* 25, 356) as unquestionably appropriate provided it could be satisfactorily carried out. Evidently this reviewer failed to foresee the attitude of Henry Moir, who made this curious statement in 1927 in an oral discussion (*T.A.S.A.* 28, 285):

> I am strongly against this projecting of mortality into the future. . . . I think there is no theory that can be more dangerous to our profession. . . . [T]his theory . . . if it be applied to Annuities, might equally well and properly be applied to insurance. . . . [T]he official acceptance of any such national fortune-telling by a scientific body is dangerous and objectionable.

Canadian actuary Charles D. Rutherford, whose paper Moir was discussing, politely stated his disagreement with these notions, and there is no reason to believe that they were espoused by many others. But since the large scale issuance of life annuities in North America dates from 1931, it is discouraging to note that as late as 1930 (*R.A.I.A.* 19, 97) a topic for informal discussion was: "Should McClintock's Tables [reflecting experience on annuities issued before 1892] be . . . superseded . . . as a basis for the valuation of annuities?" R. A. Hohaus (p. 99) stated that it should indeed be superseded, but its retention did not lack defenders.

Nearly every major United States company granted life income settlement options calculated on the American Experience Table with 3% interest on policies issued well into the 1930s. Some actuaries seem to have believed that consistency with the basis used for the insurance benefit was necessary, while others mistakenly assumed that the option would rarely be used. A warning about the consequences was sounded in 1921 by Robertson G. Hunter (*R.A.I.A.* 10, 138), and the general question of beneficiary mortality had been explored twice at Actuarial Society meetings, viz., in Herbert N. Sheppard's 1912 paper (*T.A.S.A.* 13, 8) and in Maximilian R. Hollenberg's 1926 paper (*T.A.S.A.* 27, 7).

In the case of group life insurance, the debacle arose from an out-and-out rate war on this almost instantly popular form of coverage. Effective action to curb competitive rate-cutting proved impossible even though many actuaries thoroughly understood that trouble lay ahead. In a 1926 discussion on premium rates and surrender values, Franklin B. Mead (*R.A.I.A.* 15, 208) said that "finally the group companies, their actuaries and executives and agency men, had to call in one of the commissioners [New York] to save them from themselves."

New York took care of the matter by establishing a minimum first-year premium, called the T-rate, subject in renewal years to experience rating, at exactly the same level that actuaries of several pioneer stock companies had adopted in 1919. Several other states followed suit. The T-rate remained in effect until experience showed in 1950 that it could safely be lowered.

SUBSTANDARD UNDERWRITING

At the 1927 International Congress in London, that keen observer James S. Elston identified the success in placing substandard life selection and pricing on a scientific basis as the second among five outstanding achievements by American actuaries during the past fifteen years (the first achievement in his estimation being growth of casualty actuarial science). The most influential actuaries in the field of impaired risks were Arthur Hunter in New York and Franklin B. Mead in Fort Wayne. It was said that Hunter regarded Mead as of the genus "whipper-snapper," which was far from true and which the latter keenly resented.

Franklin B. Mead (1875–1933) was directly instrumental in catapulting the Lincoln National Life into a premier position in an underwriting activity that was rightly considered daring. His papers on that subject, as on others, were clearly written and gave enlightening historical backgrounds. For example, his pioneering 1922 paper on impaired risks, "Substandard Insurance: Its Evolution and a Review of Some of its Principles" (*R.A.I.A.* 11, 158), explored theory and practice back to that in England in 1762 and forays in North America as early as 1887 in the Sun Life of Canada. Another

Franklin B. Mead (left) of Fort Wayne, Indiana, and John G. Parker of Toronto, Ontario: Two actuarial leaders of the post-World War I era.

excellent survey was his 1927 International Congress paper listed in the appendix to this chapter; in it Mead mentioned (p. 178) the peculiar stigma attached to writing "under-average business" which caused some major United States life companies to limit their scope to standard issues long after the technical barriers to writing substandard business had been overcome.

Mead, the invited keynote speaker at the Spring 1931 inaugural meeting of the Home Office Life Underwriters Association (HOLUA), suggested to his audience that the development of life underwriting in the United States might be divided into three eras:

1. The pre-1904 Era, before New York Life began classifying substandard risks by its numerical method and before the statistical results of the Specialized Mortality Investigation were published, Mead called the dark age of selection when underwriting "was based largely on impressions and prejudices rather than upon the result of statistical analysis."

2. The years 1904 to 1920 Mead recognized as a period of considerable progress, but he castigated those who had failed to embrace the wisdom of the numerical system and who had been generally slow to apply imaginative solutions to risk selection.

3. About the years 1921 and 1931 Mead had such mixed feelings that he dubbed them "years of advancement and decay." He approved of the more widespread use of substandard underwriting but considered too many companies had been pushed by competition rather than by desire to spread the benefits of life insurance.

Ten years earlier (*T.A.S.A.* 22, 367) Mead had reported that his own company, after only a single decade of substandard underwriting, was declining only 2% of applicants. Nevertheless, some actuaries of major companies, even though by then persuaded to accept substandard applicants, were enriching the reinsurers by setting their retention limits on such policies at needlessly low levels.

The first detailed description by Hunter of the practical procedures of the numerical system had appeared in his 1911 "Selection of Risks from the Actuarial Standpoint" (*T.A.S.A.* 12, 1). Those discussing that paper displayed at least a modicum of skepticism.

Charles F. B. Richardson in 1941 (*R.A.I.A.* 30, 122) analyzed the major patterns of substandard mortality curves and methods of applying ratings and determining cash values, and urged further exploration of the whole subject.

By way of contrast between rating procedures in life and non-life insurance, the 1925 reviewer (*T.A.S.A.* 26, 223) of a book by Albert W. Whitney, FCAS, F.A.S, commented:

> Workmen's compensation insurance in the United States, although only twelve years old, has produced a rating system probably more complicated than that of any other form of insurance.

THE LIBRARY OF THE ACTUARIAL SOCIETY

The Actuarial Society never seemed quite sure whether or not a well-equipped library was a necessity if its members were to lay justifiable claim to being in the category of learned persons. The Society intermittently voted funds for acquiring books and accepted book bequests with gratitude, notably in 1899 the library of William D. Whiting and in 1936 three hundred books from the library of London actuary, Charles D. Higham, FIA. Also, the 1912–1913 Society president, William C. Macdonald, twice made $100 gifts to purchase books. But low prestige of the Society library function probably caused other book bequests to go elsewhere, particularly to university libraries.

In general, library development fought a losing battle because of limitations in both staff and space. Unlike the American Institute, which counted a Librarian among its officers, the Actuarial Society had no Fellow distinctly charged with supervising and defending the library function during its first thirty years; a Library Committee was, however, established in 1919.

That committee reported formally in 1922, first with a reminder that a temporary Library Committee, in 1914, had viewed the library as "primarily for loaning by mail works of importance in the actuarial field to those not having recourse in their own or their company's library to such works." The 1922 committee's chairman, Wendell M. Strong, recommended that no broader purpose be considered until the Society had permanent and much more adequate quarters.

In February 1932 the Council referred to the Library Committee a suggestion by a nonmember that it might be advisable to consolidate the library with that of the Insurance Society of New York. Negotiations took place, but on the committee's recommendation, the proposal was dropped in October 1932. In September 1941 the Council received word that Metropolitan Life had just dedicated in its home office the Craig Memorial Library in tribute to James M. Craig (1848–1922) and his son James D. Craig (1878–1940), both of whom had been presidents of the Actuarial Society. In fact, space in the home office, which had long before been the elder Craig's office, was already a memorial library and study room for the Actuarial Division; this was a move to a larger area. This new library contained 7,000 books at dedication time and was and remained important to the actuarial profession; the Actuarial Society frequently used the room for committee meetings.

FIRST JOINT MEETING OF ACTUARIAL SOCIETY AND AMERICAN INSTITUTE, 1924

It was the Actuarial Society that took the initiative, at its Council meeting of May 1923, to open broadened relations with the American Institute by means of a joint meeting. Negotiations led to French Lick Springs Hotel, French Lick, Indiana, as the site, and to a program extending over three days in November 1924. The meeting minutes (*T.A.S.A.* 25, 376–80) show the structure thus:

Thursday, November 6th, Actuarial Society only, 10 a.m. to noon. Afternoon free.

Friday, November 7th, All-day Joint Sessions, consisting of a morning session chaired by Society President Arthur B. Wood at which papers by members of both bodies were presented, and an afternoon session chaired by American Institute President Percy H. Evans devoted almost entirely to Informal Discussion. . . .

Saturday, November 8th, American Institute only, 10:15 a.m. to noon, devoted mainly to business matters.

This was a propitious first step toward merger, especially as the possibility of a joint examining board was publicly discussed.

Five years were to pass before the second joint meeting (Toronto, 1929), and four more until the third (Chicago, 1933). It was then agreed to schedule joint meetings at regular intervals, which turned out to be alternate years.

On the lighter side, a satirical essay "Excerpts from Diary of a Young Actuary" (*The Actuary,* February 1970) by Oswald Jacoby (1902–1984) made this joint meeting famous beyond its time. The article, digested in our Chapter XIV, gives a historically accurate account of how things were in days when most actuaries knew each other and many were together in overnight pullmans to and from the meetings.

DEATH OF DAVID PARKS FACKLER, 1924

David Parks Fackler, the most influential actuary in North America in the days when an organization of actuaries was being thought about and through the early years of the Actuarial Society, died on October 30, 1924 at age eighty-three. Active to the end, his last personally delivered discussion is printed in the same volume (*T.A.S.A.* 25) as his obituary. His actuarial career had extended from thirty years before the Society's founding until beyond its thirty-fifth anniversary.

By courtesy of Thomas L. Bakos, the Society archives contain a 1903 nine-page pamphlet of Fackler's personal reminiscences of his first few years after he entered the profession as an eighteen-year-old graduate of City College of New York. He wrote of times when the entire office force of his employer, Mutual Life of New York, numbered only about fourteen; when the Civil War broke out, the daily issue of policies plummeted from six policies to four.

Fackler's period of service as a consulting actuary after he left Mutual Life at his age twenty-four embraced fifty-nine years. The leadership of the firm was continued by his actuary son, Edward B. Fackler, until 1950, two years before the latter's death.

Frank L. Griffin, Jr., in his 1979 book *"Wyco." The Building of a Professional Actuarial and Consulting Organization: The Wyatt Company*, devoted its third chapter to Wyco's acquisition (its first) of Fackler & Company, undertaken at E. B. Fackler's urgent request. Griffin mentioned a special part of the physical acquisitions (p.56):

> Mr. Fackler had an extensive library accumulated over many years of actuarial work; some of these books were extremely valuable. As there was no good way to evaluate them, it was finally agreed that Wyco would buy them at a fixed price "per yard," possibly the first time such a valuation method had been used!

Actuaries of recent vintage generally acquired familiarity with the name Fackler by studying the Fackler valuation functions ("u's and k's") in C. Wallace Jordan's *Life Contingencies*. This short self-checking method of calculating reserves was published by Fackler in a trade paper long before the Actuarial Society existed.

TENTH ANNIVERSARY OF THE CASUALTY ACTUARIAL SOCIETY, 1924

The progress made by the Casualty Actuarial Society under the guidance of each of its governing bodies during its first decade is of exceptional historical interest because of the circumstances that attended its founding—the bringing together of two professional groups (the actuaries and statisticians) and the absence of selection standards in its initial enrollment.

The backgrounds and actuarial credentials of the six men whom the members chose to succeed Isaac M. Rubinow in the CAS presidency tell much of the story:

- James D. Craig, 38, elected 1916 to two one-year terms, was a 1905 Fellow by examination of the Actuarial Society. He had been assistant actuary of Metropolitan Life since 1909; he and his actuary father, James M. Craig, had taken close interest in the affairs of the CAS ever since the idea of such a body had surfaced.

- Joseph H. Woodward, 36, elected 1918, was a 1907 Fellow by examination of the Actuarial Society. After brief experience at Travelers, he had been in state insurance departments in Connecticut and New York. In 1914 he became chief actuary of the New York State Industrial Commission.

- Benedict D. Flynn, 39, elected 1919, was a 1906 Fellow by examination of the Actuarial Society. Employed at the Travelers since 1898, he had been involved with casualty insurance since its formative days.

- Albert H. Mowbray, 39, elected 1920 to two terms, was a 1910 Fellow by examination of the Actuarial Society. After basic actuarial training at Pacific Mutual Life, he served in the insurance departments of North Carolina and California, then as actuary of the New York State Industrial Commission.

- Harwood E. Ryan, 40, elected 1922, was a 1907 Associate by examination of the Actuarial Society. He had served as actuary of two small life companies in succession, then for two periods in the New York Insurance Department separated by a position as assistant actuary at Travelers.

- William Leslie, 33, elected 1923, was a 1913 Associate by examination of the Actuarial Society. He had been actuary of Reliance Life of Pittsburgh, then secretary and actuary of the California State Compensation Insurance Fund, actuary in the New York Insurance Department and a consulting actuary in San Francisco.

All, thus, had passed actuarial examinations. Among them there was a variety of insurance experience, including a good deal in insurance supervision. They led the CAS to substantial growth in its first decade. Table IV.1 (a continuation of Table III.8 of Chapter III) shows what happened after 1918.

The number of Associates grew from twenty-five in May 1918 to eighty-seven in November 1924.

The number of withdrawals (twenty-eight) among Fellows during the decade was a bit high; twenty-five of these, however, were charter Fellows who probably found themselves much less interested in CAS affairs than they had thought they might be.

There was much more than just growth in the accomplishments of the Society's early years. Not only was fine work done in the field of workmen's compensation insurance, but also in the statistical theory of credibility, covered in our Chapter XIII. Scope for broadened exploration was found in the rapidly growing field of automobile

Table IV.1

**CHANGES IN THE ROSTER OF FELLOWS
OF THE CASUALTY ACTUARIAL SOCIETY,
CALENDAR YEARS 1919 TO 1924**

Calendar Year	New Fellows	Died	Withdrew	Fellows, December 31
1914–1918	159	3	11	145
1919	9		6	148
1920	7	2	2	151
1921	10	5		156
1922	6	2	3	157
1923	3		5	155
1924	6	2	1	158
Total	**200**	**14**	**28**	**158**

insurance; the first formal paper on that topic appeared in 1918, Gustav F. Michelbacher's "Casualty Insurance for Automobile Owners" (*PCAS* 5, 213).

In the development of workmen's compensation experience-rating plans for individual risks, claim frequency came to be penalized more heavily than severity; indeed, successive layers of claims received increasingly greater discounts for rating purposes. The larger the risk, based on size of payroll, the more heavily its own rather than industry experience determined its rating. Variations of this concept came to be used in rating large automobile fleet risks and large commercial liability risks. These are just examples of growing sophistication in rating systems adopted before 1948.

Whatever the views of the existing actuarial bodies about what the stature of the CAS may have been, the CAS itself had already before the end of its first decade made an attempt at establishing a working relationship with one of them. Dudley M. Pruitt in 1964 (*PCAS* 51, 173) related that in 1919 the CAS asked the American Institute to consider a joint meeting in May 1920, but received no reply. This is surprising since the American Institute itself was at that stage in its history seeking recognition within the professional family. Its 1919–1920 Board minutes fail to show that the invitation ever reached it officially.

TENTH ANNIVERSARY OF FRATERNAL ACTUARIAL ASSOCIATION, 1926

The membership of the Fraternal Actuarial Association in its "active" category, which had started with a roster of thirty-five (two-thirds of whom were consulting actuaries or insurance department officials), had grown to sixty-three by the end of 1925. This was to be its high-water mark until after World War II. The struggle of fraternal societies to achieve financial conditions of assured stability was well under way by the tenth birthday of the Fraternal Actuarial Association but still had much toil ahead.

In his discussion of Sidney H. Pipe's paper "Modern History of Fraternal Insurance" in November 1927, Joseph H. Woodward described the vitality of the fraternal system as astonishing and went on to say (*R.A.I.A.* 16, 260):

> The membership of fraternal societies as a whole is today about the same as it was twenty years ago. The strength of the fraternal position, however, has enormously increased. Nearly all of the important societies have readjusted on a sound actuarial basis. . . . This heroic reform, effected at the cost of so much effort and loss of membership, has in its turn led to an entirely new set of problems.

In the paper itself, Pipe described (*R.A.I.A.* 16, 52) group insurance as "probably the greatest blow ever received by fraternal societies," adding an observation that in retrospect seems hard to credit:

> If the fraternals had opposed group insurance with their full power at its inception, and had continued unremitting war against it, it is unlikely that the plan could have become a serious factor in competition. Their opposition has been spasmodic and half-hearted. In course of time they came to the conclusion that in self-defense they should enter the group-insurance field. A bill was drawn up granting them this power [but] . . . [t]he idea of presenting [it] to the legislatures was discouraged by [the insurance commissioners], and the fraternals have so far been content to accept this decision.

The nine presidents of the Fraternal Actuarial Association who succeeded George D. Eldridge were:

- Abb Landis, 61, elected 1917. Rejected for Actuarial Society membership, he never applied to the American Institute where surely he would have been welcomed, but he did become a charter Fellow of the Casualty Actuarial Society.

- Sidney H. Pipe, 41, elected 1918. One of three Canadian presidents during FAA history. He was a 1909 Fellow by examination of the Actuarial Society.

- Charles W. Iliff, 52, elected 1919, of Crawfordsville, Indiana. He had earned his spurs in fraternal actuarial work long before the FAA was founded.

- F. M. Speakman, 38, elected 1920, of Philadelphia.

- Wendell P. Coler, 30, elected 1921. He was a 1914 Associate of the American Institute of Actuaries.

- W. N. Phillips, elected 1922. He was actuary of Modern Woodmen of America, Rock Island, Illinois.

- Edward B. Fackler, 44, elected 1923. He was a 1906 Fellow of the Actuarial Society and a charter Fellow of the Casualty Actuarial Society. He served two terms as president.

- Robert D. Taylor, 57, elected 1925. Like his predecessor, he served two terms. He was a consulting actuary of Cedar Rapids, Iowa.

INTERNATIONAL MEETINGS

International Congresses, of which there had been seven between 1895 (Brussels) and 1912 (Amsterdam), were slow to restart after interruption by the First World War. By October 1923 the Actuarial Society was in so much doubt about the Congresses' future that the Council appointed a committee to consider whether Society members should even be asked to continue paying dues to the Congress organization in Belgium.

That committee, having communicated with the Institute and the Faculty, recommended against doing so, but the Council settled on a compromise, i.e., to solicit those who were already Congress members but not the others.

In 1926, when the British bodies were getting ready to act as hosts in the following year, the general secretary of the Congress asked the Congress representatives in North America whether there would be any objection to resuming pre-war relations with actuaries in Germany and Austria. The American actuaries took some time to consider this but eventually transmitted assurances of no objection.

Some North American actuaries, discouraged by the past cumbersome procedures in furnishing translations among the three official Congress languages and aware of agitation to increase that number to five, urged that the English-speaking countries have their own meetings. The British actuaries gave no support to this idea.

The Eighth Congress, of a splendor, cordiality, and efficiency easily sufficient to dispose of lingering doubts, assembled in London and Edinburgh, in June 1927. Accounts by no fewer than ten North American delegates (*T.A.S.A.* 28, 299) in "Impressions of the Eighth International Congress" competed in registering enthusiasm; the only puzzlement was expressed by John R. Larus:

> When the itinerary for the [Edinburgh] trip was announced, I was somewhat surprised to find that my wife was to stop . . . at the McKenzie Hotel and I at the Robinson. It was only as we approached our destination and were drawing lots for possession of the tooth paste that we discovered that the hotel was the McKenzie-Robinson and that [the organizers'] system was thereby entirely vindicated.

Succeeding Congresses were held in 1930 (Stockholm), in 1934 (Rome), and in 1937 (Paris). The 1934 Congress was to have convened in Canada, but a change was made to Rome because of justifiable fears that attendance by European actuaries at the depth of the Depression would be disappointingly small. The selection for 1940 was Lucerne; World War II killed that plan, but the many papers that had been submitted were published under the designation "Twelfth International Congress." Not until 1951 did the Thirteenth Congress assemble in the Netherlands.

During the hiatus, two excellent international meetings were held: the first in New York in October 1938, the other in London in June 1948. The New York meeting was a Joint Meeting of the Actuarial Society and American Institute attended by twenty-seven British actuaries. Discussions and speeches were permanently recorded in a special supplement to the 1938 *Transactions*. Total attendance, excluding accompanying persons, was 425, the largest actuarial gathering on this continent up to that time. The formal banquet, in the Ballroom of the Waldorf-Astoria Hotel, was a glittering event. One of its memorable features was a musical composition, "The Actuarial March" by orchestra leader Aldo Ricci, played that evening. The score has survived and may yet stir the hearts of a future actuarial generation.

The Centenary Assembly in London on June 21–25, 1948, marking the hundredth anniversary of the mother of all actuarial institutions, the Institute of Actuaries, was fully worthy of the occasion. The events and hospitality were extraordinary, especially in view of two handicaps faced by the host country: less than four years earlier their headquarters, Staple Inn Hall, had been completely destroyed by a flying bomb, and Britain's struggle to recover from the material shortages and disruptions of World War II was far from complete.

Important contributions to actuarial thought on five major topics are recorded in the three volumes of the Assembly *Proceedings*. American winners of the twenty-five guinea prizes for papers judged best in each division were: M. Albert Linton, "Social Insurance in the United States since 1935," and Alva J. McAndless and Fergus J. McDiarmid, "Investments of Life Insurance Companies of the United States."

Impressions of the meeting by the respective presidents of the Actuarial Society and American Institute, Horace R. Bassford and J. Gordon Beatty, are printed in *T.A.S.A.* 49, 277. North America was represented by fifty-one delegates who brought with them £2,250 and a silver pitcher as gifts from their members towards furnishing the yet to be rebuilt Institute headquarters.

PENSIONS

Metropolitan Life had issued the first group annuity contract in 1921, and tax-exemption of employer contributions to United States pension plans had made its welcome appearance in 1926. But private pension plans were not expanding rapidly in the prosperous 1920s and were severely inhibited by the adverse economic conditions of the following decade. Apart from the papers cited on this topic in our Chapter III and several valuable papers by Professor Henry L. Rietz, American actuarial literature on the subject was sparse.

This last condition began to change in 1927 when two papers by American actuaries were presented to the Eighth International Congress in London and published in that meeting's *Transactions* (first volume).

In one of these, George B. Buck (p. 358), "Pension and Retirement Systems in the United States of America," expressed the view that the history of such systems embraced two periods—the period of unsound pension legislation up to about 1912, followed by a period of awakening to the necessity for recognizing the accrued liabilities implicit in these systems and accumulating the assets to provide promised benefits. The author worried that many employers were slow to awaken, simply because industrial corporations were growing so rapidly that pension rolls were decreasing as proportions of active payrolls, causing company officers to suppose that their employees' average age might be counted upon to continue becoming younger through the years. Buck made the following observation about the employee withdrawal benefits (p. 369):

> [A] question which always seems to draw considerable discussion is whether the employee should receive his contributions with interest . . . in the event of withdrawal. To the actuary decision on this question usually depends on whether the employer is willing to pay a contribution sufficient to provide pensions for the employees and in addition to pay a contribution sufficient to provide for those who withdraw from service. Because of the extremely high turnover rate, in some services a provision for a benefit to an employee who withdraws of value equal to his own accumulated contributions would increase the contribution rate of the employer over 2,000 per cent. whereas in other services [this] provision . . . would

increase the employer's rate not over 20 per cent. so that there is a practical consideration that enters into the discussion as well as theoretical arguments.

In the other 1927 Congress paper (p. 183), "Social Insurance in the United States," author Reinhard A. Hohaus pondered the future as he described government plans and compulsory and voluntary schemes of employers and employees. Under the heading "Pensions," he said (p. 190):

> As to indemnity for old age, industry in the United States seemed to be progressing by the "trial and error" method which is a rather long and by no means necessarily effective process. . . . One life insurance company advises the use of individual policies. Another urges group contracts as the most satisfactory solution. Still another company recommends the purchase of annuities when the employee is retired with the cost charged against operating expenses for the current year or against a reserve built up in previous years. A fourth company suggests that the employer provide for the liabilities on his active force on a pension fund basis, and that the necessary reserves for the accruing liabilities be built up by turning the funds over each year to the insurance company. This insurance company offers to do the necessary actuarial work, credit to the funds the interest earned thereon, and when an employee is actually retired it will transfer the necessary premium for the retirement annuity from the reserve fund to the annuity account.

> In similar manner some consulting actuaries recommend the reinsurance and administration of the retirement plan by a life insurance company, while others advocate either self-insurance by the employer or the establishment of a separate insurance corporation for the employees of that particular employer. . . .

> [I]t is difficult to forecast with accuracy the particular pension method which will eventually come into general use. However, the situation is not as discouraging as may seem at first glance. The superannuation problem is being discussed widely and studied seriously by representatives of every group involved. Employers and, to a limited extent, employees are beginning to learn the fundamental principles underlying a sound solution, and the present situation may be described as one in which employers are fearful of the dangers of an unsound pension program and hence are searching for the proper remedy before taking any action.

> Further encouragement may be had from the increasing tendency of business men in America to view the problem of the superannuation of employees as primarily one of business—in the sense that a retirement plan is necessary for the maintenance of the efficiency of the personnel—and not as a problem of welfare or charity.

Hohaus maintained (p. 192) that "experience to date seems to indicate that Social Insurance can best be effected in the United States through private organizations."

In the same year, 1927, Henry R. Corbett presented to the American Institute a paper, "The Liabilities of Pension Funds" (*R.A.I.A.* 16, 9), putting forward a thesis (clearly unacceptable to most actuaries who discussed his paper) that pension fund contributions, instead of being designed to be level, should be kept relatively low while covered employees are young and increased when, as retirement age approaches, the need for such contributions will have become more obvious to the employer.

A review in 1933 (*T.A.S.A.* 34, 117) by Canadian actuary Andrew D. Watson of two books on pension systems suggests strongly that consensus on what constituted actuarial soundness continued to be elusive. Watson, commenting severely on the prevailing tendency by insurance companies to rely on patterns established by their competitors, remarked (p. 120):

> So far as *experience* of this type of plan goes, as a Chinaman is said to have shrewdly remarked of Christianity in comparison with his own much older religion, "it has not yet had a fair trial."

Testing time for actuaries in the pension field arrived in the 1940s, first with the exemption enjoyed by pension contributions from the World War II limits on wage and salary increases, then with the 1949 U. S. Supreme Court ruling requiring employers to bargain on pensions and the Steel Industry Fact-Finding Board ruling that obliged employers to provide pension and other welfare benefits. Figures by the American Council of Life Insurance (ACLI) show that the numbers of persons covered by major pension and retirement programs in the United States, estimated at 4.3 million in 1940, jumped to 10.3 million in 1950 and to 23 million in 1960.

A development during this era that eventually proved troublesome for life companies and their actuaries was the use of individual policies to fund pension benefits for employees of small firms. If small firms had always remained small and if employee turnover could have been counted upon to be moderate, these individual policy vehicles might have served the public well, but in practice the system proved cumbersome and notoriously expensive. It was difficult to persuade agents whose personal incomes would be severely diminished that pension trusts should be converted to group plans in the best interests of the buyers. Dennis N. Warters in "Group Insurance on Level Premium Plans" (*T.A.S.A.* 48, 95) described a solution using "group permanent" contracts developed in 1942; however, by the time his paper was written (1947), many large insurance companies were so deeply involved in individual policy plans that retreat was slow and painful. The advent of "combination" plans, in which low premium policies in conjunction with accumulation funds provided the insurance and retirement benefits, proved helpful though far from a panacea.

Excellent analyses of pension methods and coverage in Canada during the same era are given in Arthur Pedoe's text, *Life Insurance, Annuities & Pensions* (first ed. 1964, second ed. 1970).

AVIATION RISKS

In 1928, one year after Charles A. Lindbergh had flown a monoplane nonstop from New York to Paris within thirty-four hours, the Actuarial Society decided that its Informal Discussion of aviation questions was important enough to print (*T.A.S.A.* 29, 291) and that a Committee on Aviation Statistics should be put to work. The American Institute's earliest paper "Aviation Hazard" was presented by William F. Poorman in 1929 (*R.A.I.A.* 14, 86); casualty companies had been issuing aviation insurance since 1918. Horace R. Bassford in a paper published in *Transactions* of the Tenth International Congress in Rome in 1934, said (p. 245):

> After the initial and costly ventures by some companies into the underwriting of
> aviation risks in 1920 and 1921, the attitude of the United States life insurance
> companies became one of extreme caution. Most companies declined profes-
> sional aviators and the personnel of aviation companies. . . . By 1927, however,
> some companies attempted to grant full coverage to selected risks at extra
> premium rates and others, mostly Canadian companies, insured aviators at
> standard rates with the proviso that in event of the death from an aviation
> accident the liability . . . was limited to the reserve under the policy or to a refund
> of the premiums.

The first of many reports of the Committee on Aviation Statistics appeared in the
Transactions for 1929 (*T.A.S.A.* 30, 248); James E. Hoskins, a longtime chairman of
that Society committee, was to become a familiar figure at subsequent Society meetings,
first giving government data, then, after 1931, the results of intercompany studies also.

In *R.A.I.A.* 16, 282, James F. Little described a 1926 experiment by the Prudential to
insure aviators in the service of the United States federal government at an extra premium
of ten dollars a thousand. "Naturally," he said, "we wrote quite a number. . . . [J]ust as
another company announced they too would write them at ten dollars, we raised our rate to
twenty-five dollars. Then I noticed we did not issue any. The other company has recently
gone to twenty-five dollars."

At the Institute's Centenary Assembly (London, 1948), Hoskins presented a summary of the data on a subject upon which he had become a ranking authority.

ARTHUR PEDOE'S 1929 PAPER, "THE ACTUARIAL PROFESSION ON THE NORTH AMERICAN CONTINENT"

Pedoe submitted his paper (*T.A.S.A.* 30, 14) when he had been a Fellow of the
Actuarial Society for less than a year. He was thirty-one years old, actuary of a small
Toronto company, and had come to this continent only six years previously—yet he
strongly questioned the soundness of many Actuarial Society practices that had long
been taken for granted by senior men in his audience, such as:

- permitting Associates to write both the then two Fellowship examinations in a single
  year, encouraging, he thought, "superficial reading and mental feats quite out of
  place in a qualifying examination," and tending to "create doubts as to the standard
  required for the Fellowship qualifications";

- granting Associateship standing on completion of purely theoretical Parts that leave
  the student "totally ignorant of life insurance practice";

- inviting anyone who had passed the examinations to begin immediately serving as an
  examiner, thus failing to recognize that "examining is specialized work requiring men
  of a special type, and for which experience is essential";

- omitting from the syllabus the topics agency organization and expense analysis
  "which should be considered of fundamental importance" to the actuary;

- failing to consolidate the required reading, thus burdening the student with wading
  "through pages of reading, much of it laboriously stating some principles . . . now
  accepted as axiomatic or . . . which has been rejected or modified";

• accepting separate existence of the Actuarial Society and the American Institute when "the original motive [for the latter] has ceased to exist."

Twenty years later, James R. Herman, in his paper, "Actuaries—Past, Present and Future" (*T.A.S.A.* 50, 59), complimented Pedoe on the prophetic ability that prompted his strongly worded critique. This caused Pedoe to reminisce (ibid., p. 209) as follows:

> [I]t may be in order to recapture . . . some of the atmosphere twenty years ago or more.

> I was young, venturesome and too serious, by far. Realizing the tremendous social importance of the actuaries' work, I found difficulty in associating it with the casual lack of interest of the Actuarial Society in all things appertaining to the profession of actuary. It was a tribute to the Actuarial Society that the paper was accepted at all. I like to feel that someone [on the Committee on Papers] felt that it would be advantageous to stir the embers. . . .

> Not one senior member of the Society took part in the discussion, although it discussed the very fundamentals of its existence. Yet there were not lacking young, ardent champions. . . . The gore then shed is splattered over several pages of the *Transactions*; the victim recovered.

> Following up the determination that something should be done, I was not discouraged. I went back to Toronto and organised the Study Circles in Canada, several years before the Society decided to make such work part of its routine. . . .

> I must say that the tremendous amount of work done in recent years along the channels which I considered stagnant twenty years ago indicates a virility in actuarial circles on this continent which augurs well for the future.

Pedoe was justified in drawing attention to silence among the Society's senior members. The record indicates twenty-one seniors as presumably present—all of the Society's six current officers, five of its past presidents and ten elected Council members—among whom only John R. Larus, a newly elected Council member, and James S. Elston, a first-term Council member, spoke. If the nineteen other seniors showed displeasure by silence, several others less senior did so by their rebukes.

In discussing James E. Hoskins' "Some Fundamental Characteristics of Mutual Life Insurance," Pedoe was back in the fray again in 1931 with forthright objection to what he judged to be unnecessarily high gross premiums being charged by leading mutual companies (*T.A.S.A.* 32, 149):

> [The] backwardness of the larger participating companies in adjusting their premiums to the changing condition of a lower cost of insurance [during the 1920s] was a principal feature in aiding the development of non-participating life insurance. For, in spite of the increase of dividends allowing for this reduction in cost of insurance, the difference between participating and non-participating insurance rates, amounting to as much as 40% of [the latter], became an important factor when, through education, the needs for increasing amounts of life insurance was [sic] gradually realized by the public.

Pedoe might have gone a step further in this complaint by pointing out that unnecessarily high gross premiums also subjected the public to greater cost for its life insurance, through the additional commissions and taxes generated.

Pedoe continued for many years to present provocative papers and to challenge views with which he differed, many relating to the stature and dignity of our profession. His final discussion (*TSA* 16, 427) was also on a controversial topic—that of appropriate valuation of common stocks in life company balance sheets.

What kind of a man was this Arthur Pedoe? A 1971 observer, Donald J. Leapman, gave something of a character sketch (*TSA* 23, 51) in reviewing Pedoe's textbook already cited:

> He writes as he speaks—graphically and directly, with blacks and whites and few grays. Thus, in describing practices, he either supports or rejects categorically, with little effort to present the reader with a balanced opportunity for choice. This is to be regretted, for some of his strongly held views, definitively expressed, are certainly open to challenge. . . . To the author the long-established traditions are beyond question, so that throughout the book the past success and inevitable destiny of level annual premium guaranteed cash-value life insurance is extolled ad infinitum as a credo. Only a seer should hazard how this will date the volume for future readers. . . .
>
> In conclusion, one cannot read this book without appreciating the broad knowledge and deep conviction of its author. It is indeed a fine volume, well compiled, and must surely find its place in any library of Canadian life insurance.

Leapman's misgivings about so few "grays" in that textbook are warranted. Yet, as Pedoe's life in our profession is studied, it may be agreed that in each generation there should be a gadfly as lively, logical and resolute as he.

WOMEN FELLOWS IN OUR PROFESSION'S FIRST FORTY YEARS

A phenomenon of the second and third decades of the twentieth century was the growing frequency of appearance of women's names on Actuarial Society's pass lists. In the 1919 list for the first two Associateship parts, fourteen of the forty-two who had passed Part I and nine of the twenty-seven who had passed Part II were women. The legendary Grace A. Martin of Waterloo, Ontario, had passed both those parts *cum laude* in 1916. Few of these ladies continued to Fellowship, which may partly account for, if not justify, the then prevailing practice of paying women actuarial students less than their counterparts among the men.

The Casualty Actuarial Society and the Fraternal Actuarial Association were the earliest bodies to elect women to posts on their governing bodies. Ethel M. Heath led that parade as a 1916 Council Member of the latter.

A list of the women Fellows in all four of the actuarial bodies up to 1929 appears in Table IV.2. Eloise Koch Goodrich (1896–1980) established an interesting record by having married Clarence R. Goodrich in August 1959; both bride and groom had qualified as Fellows in the same year (1926) and the same city (St. Louis).

AMENDMENTS TO NEW YORK'S EXPENSE LIMITATION STATUTE

In April 1915 the Actuarial Society received a letter from New York Superintendent of Insurance Frank Hasbrouck outlining for discussion questions that had arisen under that state's expense limitation law imposed as one result of the Armstrong Investigation.

That letter (*T.A.S.A.* 16, 228) began by mentioning an amendment to the law that the Insurance Department had proposed to the New York Legislature "to afford relief to certain companies . . . which have mutualized, and hence become subject to the statutory expense limitation." The Superintendent was not seeking advice on that amendment—it became effective less than a month later—but was raising general questions about the workings of expense limits which had always been expressed in terms of premium loadings and of margins emerging from differences between mortality charges based on an aggregate mortality table and those based on select mortality experience.

Mutualization was then much to the fore. Prudential and Metropolitan Life had mutualized in 1915, and four other companies followed suit during the next decade: Home Life (1916), Equitable Society (1918), Provident Mutual (1922) and Guardian Life (1925). Joseph B. MacLean, in the first (1924) edition of *Life Insurance* (p. 22–23), gave his readers interesting guidance on this topic:

> Probably the best system of [life company] organization is that which provides for a temporary "guarantee capital" or guarantee fund with a provision for its redemption when the surplus funds of the company are sufficient. . . . The liability which capital stock entails upon the policyholders as a whole is, from their point of view, a drawback. As one writer has expressed it, it is necessary to employ a pilot to take a ship out of the harbor, but one does not take him along for the whole journey nor pay him a part or the whole of the profits of the voyage.

Even though friendship and respect have marked the relationships down through the years between actuaries of mutual and stock life companies, there has always been a strong difference in philosophy; Maclean's opinion is recognizable as a statement of the mutual philosophy.

Superintendent Hasbrouck's letter resulted in a paper, "Premium Loadings and Expense Limitations" (*T.A.S.A.* 16, 272) by the provocative mutual company actuary Edward E. Rhodes, in which he undertook first to define the word *loading* and then to distinguish, in the context of expense limitations, between true loading and nominal loading. This was a seven-page paper which produced thirty-four pages of discussion, almost all of it taking issue with Rhodes' views. That this proved useful to the Superintendent is unlikely since he left office before the discussion was published. It did show how careful actuaries should be in defining terms, and it pointed up the awkwardness of New York's original statute.

A constructive relationship between the New York Insurance Department and the Actuarial Society developed in December 1927 when Superintendent James A. Beha appointed a committee of five Fellows—Edmund E. Cammack, Robert Henderson, Arthur Hunter, Edward B. Morris and M. Albert Linton (chairman)—to draft amendments to the expense limitation law (then Section 97) aimed at accomplishing eight objectives sought by the Department. Linton's paper "Section 97—New York Law, Revision of 1929" (*T.A.S.A.* 30, 109) sets forth those objectives and shows that the committee worked speedily and acceptably with the Insurance Department's actuary, Grady H. Hipp, A.A.I.A., to devise a new expense limitation formula.

Table IV.2

**WOMEN WHO BECAME FULLY QUALIFIED MEMBERS
OF ANY OF THE FOUR ACTUARIAL BODIES BEFORE THE END OF 1929**

	Organization & Year Elected		Officer & Board Posts Held
Emma Warren Cushman	F.A.S.	1895	
Emma C. Maycrink	FCAS	1915	Council Member, 1938–41; Editor, 1944–54
Dorothy *Rolph* Holmes	FCAS	1915	
Helen E. Brown	FAA	1916	
Ethel M. Heath	FAA	1916	Council Member, 1916–17
Frances D. Partridge	FAA	1916	Council Member, 1917–20; Vice President, 1921–22
Irene Hartsuff	FAA	1916	Vice President, 1919
Olive E. Outwater	FCAS*	1919;	Editor, 1922–23;
	FAA	1925	Council Member, 1924–26
Estella *Fisher* King	F.A.S.*	1921	
Helen J. Williams	F.A.I.A.*	1923	
Angela C. Darkow	FCAS*	1924	
Dorothy *Jamison* Fish	F.A.I.A.	1925;	
	F.A.S.*	1928	
Annie *Mather* Motheral	F.A.S.*	1925	
Lucile M. Albright	F.A.S.*	1926	
Esther Johnson	F.A.S.*	1926	
Eloise *Koch* Goodrich	F.A.I.A.*	1926	
Helen L. Clark	F.A.I.A.*	1927	Board Member, 1950–53; Society of Actuaries
Evelyn M. Davis	FCAS*	1927	
Marian R. Albright	F.A.S.*	1928	

* Denotes Fellowship by examination.
Note—In the case of name changes during those members' professional lives, the names in italics were those appearing in early membership lists.

On February 1, 1928, the committee, having held five meetings of its own and having conducted two conferences with company people, submitted a unanimous report. About the field viewpoint on all this, Linton said (p. 111):

> There was some opposition from the representatives . . . of the New York State Life Underwriters Association [who] feared that the new provisions might adversely affect the agents' compensation and be generally disturbing to the business. . . .

> With the turn of the year . . . Hon. Albert Conway became Superintendent. . . . He was successful in allaying the fears of the underwriters and on January 31, 1929, at a special meeting called in Albany they formally withdrew opposition.

Linton pointed with justifiable pride to a later public hearing at which no one appeared in opposition to the proposal as it then stood. It became law in April 1929 and, although by its nature subject to repeated criticism from home office and field people, achieved its purpose until inflation in the 1940s made fresh changes necessary. The later history is covered in two major papers of 1948 and 1956, respectively:

- Daniel J. Lyons, "Expense Limitations in Section 213" (*T.A.S.A.* 49, 27)

- Allen L. Mayerson, "A New Look at the New York Expense Limitation Law" (*TSA* 8, 258)

DEPRESSION STRIKES, OCTOBER 1929

James D. Craig was an able actuary whose misfortune it was to serve as Actuarial Society president just when the "fat years" were about to end spectacularly. The vision conveyed in his October 1928 address (*T.A.S.A.* 29, 208) was uncomfortably close to Herbert Hoover's "permanent plateau of prosperity." "Is there any reason," Craig asked, "to suppose that the growth of industry, population and national income will not all continue to increase at approximately the same rates during the next decade as in the last? . . . Will not the life insurance companies through the initiative and co-operation of their Actuaries make life insurance more and more appealing to the population . . . ?"

At the fall 1929 joint meeting in Toronto of the Actuarial Society and American Institute, Craig pointed out, just three weeks before "Black Friday" at the New York Stock Exchange, that the first hundred billion dollars of United States life insurance in force had been passed and that the second was expected to be reached about 1940. As it turned out, life insurance in force dropped back to the one hundred billion dollar level and below, rising again to one hundred billion in 1936 and reaching two hundred billion in 1948.

To suppose that the values of common stocks immediately "crashed" in the debacle that marked the Depression's start would, however, be a mistake. The table of values of common stock prices at successive year-ends displayed in 1970 by Herbert W. Hickman, (*TSA* 22, 197) calculated from Standard and Poor's Index (1871 = 1.00), shows the trend for 1927–1933, taking dividends into account, thus:

End of 1927	50.56
End of 1928	68.90
End of 1929	65.61
End of 1930	50.21
End of 1931	30.00
End of 1932	27.07
End of 1933	40.54

Small investors who had paid in full for their stocks and cashed them in late 1929 would generally have emerged with only minor losses on purchases made in late 1928 and even with gains on earlier purchases; it was speculators who had borrowed heavily to acquire their holdings who were trapped. The large declines occurred in 1930 and 1931, not 1929. Of course, the luxury of withdrawing from the stock market was denied the large corporate buyers—a prominent case being the Sun Life of Canada, which had 50% of its assets in common stocks in October 1929. These corporations could not dump shares without destroying their residual values. The Sun Life, whose president at the time was Actuarial Society charter member Thomas B. Macaulay, had to take advantage of special valuations legislated by the Canadian government to preserve the company from bankruptcy with the

The Edgewater Beach Hotel, Chicago: A favorite actuarial gathering place. (Courtesy of Chicago Historical Society.)

help of a program of severe retrenchment. In fact, the stock market rebounded in 1936, slumped again in 1937 and picked up sharply during World War II.

The Depression years put our profession through severe tests in many ways. Actuaries had to face the effects of losses and declining yields on mortgage and bond investments that had seemed admirably safe. The volume of policy loans and surrenders caused bitter second thoughts about competitively inspired levels of surrender values. Some actuaries placed their own positions in jeopardy by declining to be involved in schemes to conceal internal financial weaknesses. Dividend scales were reduced after they had been maintained perhaps too long in the vain hope that the worst had passed. There was justifiable concern that mortality levels would rise as a result of adverse selection on surrenders and lapses, as well as from suicides, affecting especially the experience on large policies.

In 1951 Society of Actuaries President Valentine Howell described the way things were (*TSA* 3, 287):

> My first recollection starts with those gray days in 1932–1933 ... [when] Ed (Paddlefoot) Duffield, then President of the Prudential, asked a young actuary and a young investment man to figure out, on the basis of the then current rates of loan and surrender of policies, how long there was going to be any Prudential. We came back with an answer. I think it was to the effect that the Prudential had an expected after-lifetime of 4 years and 37 weeks. Mr. Duffield looked at the

calculation thoughtfully and sealed it up in an envelope. He put it in his safe. So far as I know, it was never afterward seen by human eye.

A general survey of conditions, as the Depression intensified, can be found in President Wendell M. Strong's address to the Actuarial Society in May 1931 (*T.A.S.A.* 32, 1). He did end on a brighter note, pointing out that the public, grown distrustful of its own ability to invest, was turning to the life companies as institutions to be relied upon. At that same meeting, the eminent Henry Moir presented a paper on "Unemployment Relief," whose closing paragraph expressed a viewpoint typical of that held by senior actuaries of the era (p. 109):

> History proves that the peasant and the artisan of today enjoy more satisfaction in life, more physical comfort, more variety in pleasure than the knight and the prince of a thousand years ago. . . . We are always willing to welcome the piping times of prosperity and must of necessity endure those of less abundance which follow prosperity as the night must follow the day. It is desirable to relieve economic crises as far as possible and as quickly as possible but we have always to be careful that in destroying one evil we do not give birth to another. We cannot dispense with habits of forethought and thrift—nor can we escape all unhappiness in life. It is part of the Creator's plan to develop the character of man who is allowed to suffer want, sickness, pain, and even sin, so that his qualities may be tested, so that he may learn to suffer, to resist, and withal maintain his faith.

Attacks upon elements of life policy structure—particularly upon the level premium system, the policy loan interest rate and even policy loans themselves, and upon continued use of the American Experience Table—were a source of distress to actuaries during the 1930s. The prominent critics, however, concentrated their fire on allegations easily rebuttable by well-informed persons. In 1937, M. Albert Linton undertook to clear the air with his book, *Life Insurance Speaks for Itself*. That book's reviewer, Alexander T. Maclean (*T.A.S.A.* 38, 618), even though recognizing its worth as a reference book for agents, was distinctly dubious about its prospects for educating the insuring public.

A conspicuous abundance of the Depression years was that of candidates sitting for Part I (College Algebra) of the actuarial examinations, and a luxury available to the examiners was to fail most of them. As Table IV.3 shows, the extraordinary sameness of the numbers of passing candidates could hardly fail to cause a few of them and their professors to suppose that that number had been fixed in advance.

Even though economic conditions were not the sole influencing factor—the creation of more university actuarial courses was another—it may reasonably be inferred that shortage of other employment turned many young mathematicians' eyes toward an actuarial career. There were also applications from not-so-young engineers who had become unemployed and were seeking a new career.

Since the number of students passing Part I was close to the 100-mark in each year from 1929 to 1934, and since on the average a new Fellow might be expected to emerge about six years after Part I had been passed, it is of interest to see that the average number of new Fellows in the years 1935 to 1940 was seventeen. The inference is that about one-sixth of the Part I passers reached the end of the examination trail.

Table IV.3

**PERCENTAGES OF CANDIDATES WHO PASSED THE JOINT
ACTUARIAL SOCIETY/AMERICAN INSTITUTE EXAMINATIONS
IN COLLEGE ALGEBRA, 1929 TO 1934**

Year	Candidates	Passers	Percentage Passing
1929	462	100	22%
1930	472	101	21
1931	521	107	21
1932	596	101	17
1933	661	81	12
1934	625	123	20

Source: Results of Examinations, *R.A.I.A.* 18–23.

The question has occasionally been raised whether the plentifulness of actuarial students in those days may have caused some company actuaries to include racial or religious preference among their selection criteria. It appears to be true that one professor of actuarial science was routinely warning his Jewish students that they might encounter difficulty in this respect, and it would be rash to ignore testimony that those warnings had some justification. But it is comforting to be told by one actuary that he entered our profession because he judged it to be relatively free of anti-Semitism and to observe that he was just one of many Jewish actuaries who qualified during the 1930s and have indeed been ornaments to our profession. Certainly the situation resembled not at all that of the early nineteenth century in England where, as shown in an exhibit at the 1948 Centenary Assembly of the Institute (*Proceedings*, Vol. I, 167), Benjamin Gompertz was refused the actuaryship of a large company on account of his religion.

Notable papers on Depression problems and outlook appear in the 1932 and 1933 volumes of the *Record* and the *Transactions*. American Institute President Franklin B. Mead (whose sudden death in November 1933 was a sad loss at the height of his powers) devoted his three presidential addresses to exploring basic technical aspects of the worldwide economic difficulties. In November 1932, Mead advised against the gloomy belief that the fabric of society was seriously threatened. In April 1933 his principal theme was inflation; in October 1933 he presented charts depicting the relative intensities of economic decline in several countries.

The Actuarial Society's 1932 *Transactions* offered its members two papers by leaders in our profession, the first conveying a message of supreme confidence, the second sounding a dire warning about possible disaster in a future depression.

Henry H. Jackson's paper, "The Wisdom of Mutual Life Insurance" (*T.A.S.A.* 33, 116), won for its author a $100 prize that had been offered almost six years earlier by then President Edward E. Rhodes for the best paper on the basic principles of mutual life insurance. Jackson had been inspired by the teaching of Dr. Walter B. Cannon (see *T.A.S.A.* 33, 145, note 2) that the human body is in so perfect a state of equilibrium that any disturbance of one element promptly brings into play compensating forces tending to restore that equilibrium; Jackson undertook to show an analogous tendency enjoyed by mutual life insurance. His exploration brought his listeners into touch with the doctrine of evolution as well as with the philosophical writings of Samuel Johnson, James Truslow Adams, Thomas R. Malthus (whose essay on population Jackson thought should be required reading for every actuarial student) and early actuaries Edmond Halley, James Dodson, Augustus De Morgan, Cornelius Walford, John Finlaison, Benjamin Gompertz, Elizur Wright and Sheppard Homans.

The stock company actuaries, who in those days did not occupy many of the seats of power in our profession—for example, only seven of them were on the Actuarial Society's twenty-nine-man Council of 1932—found themselves with a champion to fight back on their behalf. Ward Van Buren Hart of Hartford contributed a discussion of Jackson's paper marked by such gentle but effective repartee that he was invited to re-present it at the next Actuaries Club of Hartford meeting. Here are excerpts (p. 431):

> One does not need to read far in Mr. Jackson's paper to appreciate that he is steeped in the lore of the Victorian era. It is small wonder then that he finds in ... Mutual life insurance an example of two theories dear to the heart of the Victorian philosopher—the laissez-faire theory of political economy and the doctrine of evolution. ...
>
> We are usually prone to think of man as standing on a lofty pinnacle gazing back on ... his climb from the lowly estate of the amoeba. But, as the apt rejoinder has been made, if you could ask the amoeba how he felt about it, he might have quite a different idea! Is it heresy to ask ourselves the same question concerning Mutual life insurance? ...
>
> [The] process of evolution, ... far from being a continuous advance, frequently leads into blind alleys. ... One species of lung-fish, known to the African natives as "Kamongo," persists to this day [because in the dry season] ... it burrowed into the mud. It became so constituted that it could live in the mud six months of the year, but for it, evolution ... became most emphatically a blind alley, and for twenty million years it has remained a mud-dweller. It is to be hoped that the lung-fish of Mutual life insurance does not permanently wallow in the mire of excessive cash values, over-optimistic dividend estimates, and naive disability underwriting.

Jackson, able not just to take a joke but to join in it, responded with some delightful doggerel, or as he described it "fisherel," which has made page 452 of *T.A.S.A.* 33 a joy to read.

The theme of M. Albert Linton's "Panics and Cash Values" (*T.A.S.A.* 33, 365) was that the life companies were fortunate that, in the Depression, the policies on their books had on average been in force for only a few years, thus setting a manageable limit on the amounts of cash and loan values that had to be paid. The question was, Would the companies be so fortunate in the next Depression, or would they have been wise enough to have invested a sufficient proportion of their assets in relatively liquid securities so that the inevitably heavy demand for cash could be met? Linton looked both backward into history and forward by methods of projection to make his point about the risk of disaster, and he advised against taking comfort from six-month deferment clauses because these would merely postpone the problem, not ease it.

This paper was presented and discussed in October 1932. In early March 1933, before the Actuarial Society's next meeting, President Franklin D. Roosevelt closed all banks that had not already been closed by state authorities during the three preceding weeks; the majority judged to be in sound condition were permitted to re-open four days later. State authorities took action to protect against runs on surrender values and policy loans by permitting such payments only for specified purposes—payment of premiums, mortgage obligations, hospital, medical and funeral expenses, payrolls and avoidance of policyholder penalties on existing commitments.

At the Actuarial Society's May 1933 meeting, the so-called bank holiday and the state-imposed "moratorium" on cash withdrawals (an expression which some actuaries disliked because the stricture was imposed upon, not requested, by the companies) was explored in two ways. First, Society President John S. Thompson discussed it in his address. He began by drawing a parallel with the aftermath of the Armstrong Investigation just a quarter-century earlier, finishing with these words (*T.A.S.A.* 34, 7):

> We are confident that . . . our political and financial leaders will not so far ignore the plain teachings of experience as to embark upon any scheme of inflation or devaluation, controlled or otherwise, which has been demonstrated to have so profound an effect upon those equities, such as life insurance reserves and savings bank deposits, which represent the savings of the thrifty members of the commonwealth.

John M. Laird then presented a clear although hastily written paper, "The Moratorium on Cash Withdrawals" describing the events of the preceding three months (*T.A.S.A.* 34, 55). This paper was not immediately discussed (probably no advance circulation had been possible), but the entire program for informal discussion explored Depression matters. The first item was the moratorium, including the following subsection (d) (*T.A.S.A.* 34, 147):

> Would the general situation be improved by federal control of life insurance? To what extent is the substitution of federal for state control possible?

Then the program was arranged to take up financial and investment questions, the desirability of changes in surrender charges, mortality experience on both annuities and insurance, new business, lapses, and the possible need to restrict single premium business and lump-sum advance payments of premiums.

Laird's paper on the moratorium sketched the events leading up to the federal action to close the banks. This had started on February 14, 1933, with the closing of all banks in Michigan by the authorities there, producing a domino effect that Laird described as "a striking demonstration of the way in which the interests of various financial institutions are interwoven." By early March, bank closings had swept through a dozen states, each such action increasing the strain not just on banks elsewhere but on insurance companies which, said Laird, "should not have been expected to take on a substantial part of the normal activities of building and loan associations, saving banks, trust companies, and especially commercial banks." Even before President Roosevelt acted, the Executive Committee of the NCIC was conferring with insurance company management, and three states (Indiana, Michigan and Ohio) had introduced emergency legislation designed to give the insurance commissioner dictatorial powers.

During the national bank holiday, it was evident, said Laird, "that when the banks opened, the companies would have to draw heavily on their bank balances or possibly sell Government and other high-grade bonds in order to catch up with the accumulated demands." The insurance commissioners recognized that their first obligation was to protect those policyholders who were interested in the primary purpose of life insurance, namely, the death benefit, maturing endowments, annuities, and disability claims.

New York took the initiative on March 9, 1933, by limiting cash withdrawals to $100 per policyholder payable only on evidence of extreme need, and made this applicable to the entire business of companies operating in that state. Several other commissioners followed that lead, but some made no rulings while a few openly proclaimed that they would insist that policyholders in their states receive full value regardless of regulations elsewhere. This jurisdictional conflict may explain why the actuaries were meditating on federal control of life insurance.

Laird's paper closed with emphasis upon the special responsibility of actuaries to reconcile the banking and insurance functions of life insurance and to guarantee that in any future period of economic readjustment there would be a satisfactory relation between funds available and cash withdrawals.

By the time Laird's paper came up for discussion at the joint Actuarial Society and American Institute meeting on October 18, 1933, the situation had improved considerably. Restrictions were being relaxed in June 1933; most had been entirely removed by September. It was time to decide what lessons ought to have been learned. Although consensus on solutions was not sought, the issues clearly were the size and quick availability of cash values and the mix of life company investments. All of these matters came up again when the Guertin Committee was put to work in 1937.

In 1938, Charles F. B. Richardson devoted a section of his paper "Guaranteed Cash Surrender Values Under Modern Conditions" (*T.A.S.A.* 39, 237) to the problem of meeting abnormal cash demands. This paper summarizes nine suggestions that had been offered, ranging from guaranteeing only part of the value and paying the appropriate remainder as a surrender dividend, to various ways of paying cash values in installments. Richardson then remarked (p. 257):

> In my view any attempt to introduce into our legislation or our practice restrictions which would prevent the insured from obtaining the full guaranteed surrender or loan value in cash at any time except in the most extreme emergency would work an incalculable amount of harm to the life insurance business. Rather should we put our house in order, guaranteeing values on such a basis as will protect the continuing policyholders from losses caused by those who surrender, and so arranging our finances that we may reasonably expect to meet peak demands for cash. In the case of a panic such as we had in 1933, there is much support (e.g. F. B. Mead, *R.A.I.A.*, 22, 9) for the view that the governors and insurance commissioners should have emergency powers.

It may reasonably be argued that the banks were weaker than the life insurance companies, but confidence expressed by some that the insurance companies without help from the authorities could have taken care of the demands that bank failures imposed upon them seems unwarranted. A number of life companies did fail during the Depression—notably the Missouri State Life, Peoria Life, National Life of the United States and Pacific Mutual Life. All of these except the last named failed because of frozen or poor quality investments rather than poor product design, but many more would have failed had there been no moratorium, no help from the Reconstruction Finance Corporation, and no provision for orderly writing-down of asset values to realistic levels. One anomaly of that era was that, while actuaries were emphasizing death benefits as the primary purpose of life insurance, field forces were selling many thousands of policies primarily as savings plans.

THE UNITED STATES SOCIAL SECURITY ACT, 1935

Old-Age Benefits

The possibility that social insurance might come to this continent from Europe had been worrying champions of private enterprise for many years before President Franklin D. Roosevelt made social security part of his legislative program in 1933. As already mentioned, Isaac M. Rubinow, first president of the Casualty Actuarial Society, had placed the subject in the forefront of actuarial discussion in 1914. Actuaries tended to approach the issue with a conviction that pensions, like wages, in a free enterprise economy should be governed by the marketplace rather than by legislation. The expression *social insurance* aroused fears that it might be a step toward bolshevism. Closer to home, the actuaries' nightmare was that government pensions would be followed by government insurance, spelling the narrowing, even the demise, of private insurance.

As the minutes of the Actuarial Society meeting of May 1917 recorded (*T.A.S.A.* 18, 194): "The Chairman [President Arthur Hunter] called upon Mr. [Rufus W.] Weeks to speak to the Society and Mr. Weeks made the address printed on page 8." That address, entitled "The Coming Expansion of the Social Principle Underlying Insurance," was a remarkable presentation whose reception by the members it would be interesting to know. The following excerpts give the flavor of Weeks' prophecy:

> In most cases a prophecy presents itself to the prophet in the form of positive assertion, and can be most easily and most faithfully passed on in the same form, leaving it to each hearer to accept or reject in whole or in part, not, however, according to his fancy, but according to what after honest effort he deems to be the data of the case. . . .

> It is suggested, then, that the tremendous events and the incalculable changes into which these hasty years have hurled us [this was the first Society meeting after the United States had declared war on Germany] mark the early stages of a world-mutation which is to evolve rapidly into a new species of human society. The main line of this transformation will be an immense extension of the social-economic principle which is the creative motive of insurance. That principle is *mutual guarantee* . . . .

> The institution of insurance starts from the principle of mutual guarantee against calamity, but insurance touches only subsidiary forms of calamity, such as untimely death, fire, shipwreck. It does not cover the great economic causes

of suffering and degradation. These have to do with production and distribution—the two all-embracing processes which mean good or evil to us all.

Weeks developed his theme by specifying the weaknesses he perceived in the production and distribution systems in a private enterprise economy; the failures of the distribution system in his view were that they did not apply to all people, nor to all forms of calamity, and that in any event they were not adequate. He predicted that society would take care of these and other shortcomings through a new use of its most powerful organ, government. The closing sentence of this three-page message was:

> Only our commercial individualist obsession has blinded our eyes to this simple, most precious of truths, and now our eyes are being opened by force, never to be closed again.

This presentation apparently was on the program by arrangement between Messrs. Weeks and Hunter, since the Council minutes contain no authorization for it. It must have given at least some members food for thought; no counterpart for it appears elsewhere in the *Transactions*. Most other remarks about social insurance in actuarial journals were much different in tone. For example, Henry Moir in his 1920 presidential address on "State and National Enterprise" (*T.A.S.A.* 21, 9) said:

> It is undoubted that the pensioning of old employees in a corporation or municipality, or State or Nation, is an act tending to promote and improve efficiency; but activities of this nature should be confined to the employees of each individual section. Pension funds, on a scientific basis, may be formed for all permanent salaried employees without taking much from the spirit of independence—indeed the good accomplished probably far outweighs the ill, but general legislation covering the entire nation may be seriously questioned. ...
> The granting of such benefits nationally is an attractive but visionary theory leading further along the road towards Socialism, invading the rights of individuals and, if brought about, will doubtless be accomplished through the making of promises which cannot materialize.

At the same meeting Charles D. Rutherford of Montreal said that the Canadian Parliament had just passed an act providing for payment of old-age pensions under certain circumstances; his complaint was that no actuary's advice had been sought. Dennis N. Warters warned that there were various groups ceaselessly working in the interests of social insurance to be handled by the state itself and enumerated four areas of such activity, including Massachusetts where interviews in 1923 of a sample of the population aged sixty-five and over had revealed that over one-third had incomes below $300 per year. Warters feared that any system of state old-age pensions would be very expensive for taxpayers, even though the acts so far introduced provided pensions sufficient only to bring the persons' total income up to about $1.00 per day.

James D. Craig, in his 1929 presidential address (*T.A.S.A.* 30, 5), speaking of the same Massachusetts survey that Warters had described, advocated that state old-age benefits should be in the form of medical and other special care rather than exclusively cash payments.

In 1932 Rainard B. Robbins, reviewing Hugh H. Wolfenden's book, *The Real Meaning of Social Insurance,* said that Wolfenden had presented clearly "the most generally accepted point of view of the opponents of social insurance" in the opening sentence of his chapter summarizing that group's arguments against state benefits, which read (*T.A.S.A.* 33, 263):

> All forms of social insurance are largely incompatible with the spirit of individual freedom, responsibility, and initiative which is so largely characteristic of North America.

On June 7, 1934—just three weeks before President Roosevelt created his Committee on Economic Security to prepare legislation—American Institute President Thomas A. Phillips warned (*R.A.I.A.* 23, 2):

> A broad government program embracing unemployment insurance, health insurance, old-age and widows' pensions, and perhaps including shorter hours and more jobs, if successfully administered, might eliminate most of the need for life insurance. A growing number of persons in private and public life are advocating all or part of such a program.

> We with the knowledge and experience bred of more than a century of insurance, are positive that unemployment insurance will not work out in practice, and we are likewise dubious of the practical working of old-age pensions—at least, in the light of present circumstances and conditions. That is not to say, however, that at some future time a majority may not wish to try these things.

Looking back across the years, we may agree that actuaries were justified in questioning the feasibility of social security, and we may sympathize with those who feared that it might destroy the life insurance business. But it is hard to feel comfortable about the stand taken by those who urged complete reliance upon individual initiative, after nearly five years of economic disaster with no solution in sight and with accumulated savings decimated to provide current food and shelter.

President Roosevelt's 1934 Committee on Economic Security was assisted by a four-man Actuarial Advisory Committee: James W. Glover, M. Albert Linton, Albert H. Mowbray and Henry L. Rietz.

At the Actuarial Society's 1934 fall meeting, the first topic of informal discussion (*T.A.S.A.* 35, 448) was the pending social insurance program in the United States. One

M. Albert Linton (left) and Robert J. Myers: They left their imprints on the United States Social Security System.

subtopic, on which regrettably no record of the expressed views exist, asked about the relative merits of a reserve fund and a pay-as-you-go method of financing a general social insurance program.

One nonactuarial observer of the American scene said that in those days critics of national old-age pensions in the business community were awed into near silence by the imaginatively coined expression *social security*. It is likely that even more potent discouragement from all-out opposition came from the widespread public interest aroused by the "Townsend Plan," calling for a pension of $200 a month, to be financed by a national 2% sales tax (recognized by competent estimators as insufficient for the purpose), payable to every citizen aged sixty or older, retired or not, on condition that the $200 be spent in the United States within a month after being received. Two hundred dollars was a princely sum in those times; the national average wage was about $90 a month. A modified version of this, requiring retirement to qualify, did reach the House of Representatives but was voted down.

At the Actuarial Society meeting that convened three weeks after the Social Security Act had become law in August 1935, two Fellows who had served as advisors in its planning, Otto C. Richter and W. Rulon Williamson, outlined the legislation in a formal paper "The Social Security Act of 1935 and the Work of the Committee on Economic Security" (*T.A.S.A.* 36, 299). The plan described there never did go fully into effect; it was revised in 1939 before monthly benefits began to be paid, after having served as the basis for major, sometimes heated, actuarial discussions for several years. The three top-ranking interrelated questions were:

(a) Does a compulsory national old-age benefit system require accumulation of reserves comparable in nature to those required of a life insurance company on its level premium policies?

(b) Should such a system be directly financed entirely by workers and their employers?

(c) Should those who retire in the system's early years receive benefits greater than those that could be provided by contributions made by themselves and on their behalf?

Richter and Williamson reported that the federal authorities desired a plan that would answer all these three questions in the affirmative, but expressed the strong opinion that no plan meeting all these desiderata would prove to be manageable. These two actuaries introduced their hearers and readers to the notorious "$47 billion fund in 1980," that being the estimated (and in fact understated) fund that would accumulate under the original provisions of the act. Its size was attention-fixing, being larger than the existing federal debt. Ironically, long after the idea of a fund built on the life insurance company reserve concept had faded from practical consideration, the Old-Age & Survivors Insurance (OASI) Trust Fund peaked for the time being at nearly $38 billion in 1974. But this was in 1974 dollars, a modest fraction of the then United States national debt.

The Richter-Williamson 1935 paper closed with this summing-up (p. 348):

> The scientific approach to social security is difficult, but only through the painstaking method of inquiry, of complete analysis, of unending study,

attitudes with which actuaries ought to be familiar, can any mature wisdom arrive. It is too early for definiteness, for certitude. It is time for the adoption of the discipline of research.

In the years that followed, leaders in illuminating, and often hotly debating, these large questions were M. Albert Linton, Hugh H. Wolfenden, Reinhard A. Hohaus, Rainard B. Robbins, Robert J. Myers, Andrew D. Watson, Benjamin T. Holmes, and (later) George E. Immerwahr. A truly historic occasion of such debate was the October 1937 Actuarial Society meeting at Swampscott, Massachusetts, at which two papers on social security financing by Watson and Hohaus, persuasive men with vastly differing views, were on the program for discussion. The published account takes up fifty-four pages of *T.A.S.A.* 38 (pp. 532–86); the members raised vociferous objection when the chairman attempted to cut off that discussion in order to proceed to other business, and their wishes prevailed.

Excellent summaries of events and viewpoints of that era are to be found in four places: (i) the special supplement Report of the October 1938 Joint Meeting, already mentioned, with British guests, (ii) the section on Social Insurance Superannuation Schemes in Volume III of the *Proceedings* of the Centenary Assembly of the Institute of Actuaries, 1948, (iii) a 1935 paper by Clarence W. Hobbs, "Social Insurance and the Constitution" presented to the Casualty Actuarial Society (*PCAS* 22, 32), and (iv) Section III, "Social Insurance" of Dudley M. Pruitt's "The First Fifty Years" of the Casualty Actuarial Society (*PCAS* 51, 152).

Hohaus in November 1939 (*R.A.I.A.* 28, 225) described the events that led from the original skepticism about the financing arrangement to the passage in August 1939 of the legislation that revised the benefit objective in the direction of "social adequacy" and the financing system in the direction of a contingency reserve concept. Hohaus mentioned (p. 225) that two actuaries were members of the 1937 Advisory Council on Social Security whose recommendations led to the remedial 1939 legislation; those two were M. Albert Linton and Albert H. Mowbray.

The first of a long succession of informative papers by Robert J. Myers on amendments to social security legislation was presented in June 1939 (*R.A.I.A.* 28, 22). A paper by Rainard B. Robbins in the same volume (p. 246) told about other government plans.

The implications of the advent of social security for our profession were immense. One result was greatly increased recognition in Washington and elsewhere that there was an actuarial technology and there were people called actuaries trained to perform it. Also it added significantly to the study material that students had to cover to qualify as actuaries.

Both Richter and Williamson were invited to join the staff of the Social Security Board after their service as advisors. Richter, the more practical of the two, declined; Williamson accepted, moving from assistant actuary at the Travelers to chief actuary of the Social Security Administration, where he stayed until 1947. It is said that his strong philosophical interests, easily recognized in his actuarial discussions, interfered with his giving quite the specific help that was needed at that pioneering stage.

In 1942, a paper by Jarvis Farley and Roger Billings, "An Approach to a Philosophy of Social Insurance" (*PCAS* 29, 29), presented to the Casualty Actuarial

Society, explored the purpose, possibilities and limitations of social insurance and even the appropriateness of such a system in contrast to possible alternatives.

The scope of the Farley/Billings approach may be gathered from these excerpts:

> If the American people want a broad program of social insurance they will most assuredly have it, but in deciding how much social insurance they want they must recognize that it may not be a question of having social insurance in addition to other things which they want. . . .

> The fundamental issue . . . is whether insurance . . . should be compulsory . . . . A second issue is whether the conduct of the insurance is a proper matter for government administration or whether it should be handled by private enterprise. A third question involves jurisdiction; . . . how should the responsibility for the program be divided between the federal government and the state governments.

A 1975 paper by Robert J. Myers, "Forty Years of Actuarial Responsibilities in the United States Social Security Program" (*TSA* 27, 155), lists fifty-one who were employed by the Social Security Administration or its predecessors and twenty-four who served on or worked for the various advisory councils and committees during those four decades. Myers concluded (p. 163):

> It is essential that actuaries continue these efforts, so that this program, which is of such great social and economic importance, will continue to operate on a sound financial basis and will serve the country well in providing a basic floor of economic security protection.

Unemployment Benefits

In the 1920s and 1930s, considerable space in all three actuarial journals (*PCAS, R.A.I.A., T.A.S.A.*) was given to papers on unemployment insurance.

The Casualty Actuarial Society began first by printing the 1922 address of a visitor, Leo Wolman of the New School for Social Research, "Unemployment Insurance" (*PCAS* 9, 86), about which Dudley M. Pruitt remarked dryly (*PCAS* 51, 153), "The record does not give the reaction to this of the various insurance executives."

In 1923, James D. Craig, prominent in both the Actuarial Society and the Casualty Actuarial Society, chose the former for presenting his major paper on the same subject. The reason apparently was that Herbert Hoover, then Secretary of Commerce, had suggested that Craig's company, Metropolitan Life, itself enter that field (*T.A.S.A.* 24, 168):

> Unemployment insurance in the hands of a great institution built as yours is, is not socialism. Insurance in the hands of the Government is the encroachment of bureaucracy into the daily life of our people. . . .

> [H]ere remains the one great field in which insurance can be employed scientifically . . . and in which you can provide one of the greatest safeguards to our social stability.

Craig's paper in the main was historical, descriptive and statistical, but he did quote what the *Economic Review* had remarked about the reception given to Hoover's proposal (p. 185):

> It is certainly a striking fact that the first reaction on the minds of the administration officers of the Metropolitan Life Insurance Company to Mr. Hoover's suggestion was not that it was so out of harmony with the true function of the

company as to be inherently impossible for realization, but rather that it was quite in line with the proper development of the company's work.

Craig did not contest the accuracy of this appraisal of management thinking in his company; he just quoted the magazine writer's final word:

> It may be that a way can be found to avoid these [unemployment] evils, but the task is one of almost inconceivable magnitude.

To which remark Craig responded:

> It is, if unemployment insurance is to be conducted on the compulsory plans of Europe.

Craig then brought his text to its end with a general comment to the effect that the problem boils down to distinguishing effectively between workers laid off on account of lack of work and those who voluntarily quit.

Actuarial journals between 1923 and passage of the Social Security Act in 1935 provided two more contributions to the question. In 1931 (*PCAS* 27, 161) Thomas F. Tarbell, in his presidential address entitled "Unemployment And Insurance," catalogued in scholarly fashion existing American papers, major influences upon the unemployment experience, and a compulsory savings plan that he thought worthy of consideration. Tarbell was not optimistic about insurance possibilities. Nor was Gilbert W. Fitzhugh in 1933 (*T.A.S.A.* 34, 227); his paper "Unemployment Reserves" advocated avoidance of any insurance contract promising definite payments on the occurrence of defined contingencies, in favor of a system of building funds to be drawn upon to the extent they might prove sufficient. This was written at a time when the national unemployment rate was daunting; it had jumped from 6% of the work force in 1929 to 40% in 1933.

Two years later President Roosevelt made that phase of actuarial discussion obsolete by having an unemployment compensation system enacted under which the federal government in effect forced the states to legislate benefits according to a national pattern by confronting employers of eight or more persons with a choice between paying taxes to Washington or into a state plan acceptable to Washington. The next paper, by Reinhard A. Hohaus and nonactuary Fred S. Jahn in 1940 (*T.A.S.A.* 41, 440), concerned itself with appraisal of results and suggestions for amending the legislation at a time when the war in Europe had reduced the unemployment level in the United States to a point at which many believed that the accumulated unemployment funds were excessive.

DEPRESSION DAYS IN CANADA

Actuaries in Canada were free, except to the considerable extent that their companies operated in the United States, of the problems that the large cracks in the United States banking system inflicted upon their colleagues south of the border. The relatively compact Canadian banking network, described by John G. Parker (*T.A.S.A.* 35, 233), stood firm throughout the economic distress which in general was comparable in scope and severity in the two countries.

As already recounted, Canada's largest life insurance company, the Sun Life, was in greatly straitened circumstances because of the concentration of its assets in common stocks. The state of affairs is described in that company's 1971 centenary book, *The Century of the Sun* by Joseph Schull, depicting the decline by 1933 of the company's published surplus to one-tenth of its 1929 amount and then its successful struggle to regain prosperity. Nevertheless, Schull writes (p. 65) of Alistair M. Campbell (F.A.S. 1932), speaking in 1967 as Sun Life's president, stoutly defending the direction though not the extent of Thomas B. Macaulay's investments in common stocks, saying that in the longer term those investments had enhanced the fortunes of the company. A review by L. Blake Fewster of Macaulay's long actuarial career may be found in the *Record* (*RSA* 12, 2208).

Canadian life insurance had an enviable record of life company stability through the troubled years. Only one company, Western Empire Life, failed (because of defaults by farm mortgagors). In the interests of preserving the industry's proud record that no policyholder had ever lost a dollar by failure by a Canadian life company, Western Empire's obligations were voluntarily assumed by a consortium of eleven large companies. As it turned out, the ultimate revival of farm prosperity enabled the consortium to avoid losing any money from this guarantee.

THE CANADIAN ASSOCIATION OF ACTUARIES

Arthur Pedoe, in his 1935 paper "The Actuary in Canada" (*R.A.I.A.* 24, 189), began by drawing attention to the extraordinarily high proportion of Fellows of the Actuarial Society and American Institute who were Canadians. His comment was:

> One-quarter of the actuaries on this continent with fellowship qualifications are resident in Canada. Considering the continuous trek to the south since the beginning of this century of actuaries educated and trained in Canada, the development of life insurance on this continent must have been influenced very substantially by Canadian actuaries.

In fact, five of the ten Actuarial Society presidents between 1922 and 1940 were Canadians—three of them elected after having settled in the United States—and in the same era one-third of the new Fellows were Canadians. The explanation for this ratio occurring in a country with only one-tenth of the United States population comes partly from the successes of two university actuarial courses, those of the University of Toronto dating back to the early years of our profession's organized existence and of the University of Manitoba beginning in the 1920s. The second contributing cause was that Canada had several substantial life companies that built large staffs of actuaries and actuarial students.

Pedoe's paper gave also a full description of the study circles operated in Toronto and Montreal under the auspices of the Toronto Actuaries Club and then covered a 1935 recommendation to the Toronto Club by the Winnipeg Actuaries Club that the two bodies form a Canadian Association of Actuaries. Winnipeg's idea was that there should be a body authorized to speak for actuaries in Canada and that morale among Canadian actuaries would be enhanced if they were members of such a concern. The Toronto Club members were, said Pedoe, almost unanimously against such a move, partly on the grounds that creation of yet another actuarial body on this continent might add to overlapping of activities and duplication of effort. The proposal was dropped for the time being, but soon came up again. As J. Gordon Beatty reported in 1948 (*R.A.I.A.* 37, 5):

> During recent years there has developed a very definite feeling of concern that the influence of this [Toronto] Actuaries' Club was not nearly so great as formerly. It appeared to be largely deteriorating into a social club ... [and] it was contended that, unless the club went further than this and acted as the champion in Canada of actuarial principles, it was not serving its full purpose.
>
> Fearing that the name itself—Actuaries' Club—might be misleading in this connection, it was changed, albeit with considerable regret on the part of many members, to Canadian Association of Actuaries. At the same time, steps were taken to establish the association more as a forum for the enunciation of sound principles than for the discussion of company practices and procedures.

Thus the Canadian Association of Actuaries, open to all practicing actuaries in Canada, came officially into being in October 1946. Its membership by 1947, the earliest date for which a figure seems to be available, was 198. By 1951 (*TSA* 3, 252) its membership of 278 included "practically every active or retired Fellow or Associate residing in Canada, together with a group of actuaries in the United States who were formerly employed in Canada and have retained their connection with the Association."

The Canadian Association of Actuaries served as a helpful steppingstone toward formation of the much more formal body, the Canadian Institute of Actuaries, in 1965.

ADOPTION OF MODERN VALUATION AND NONFORFEITURE STANDARDS

The effort in the United States to dethrone the American Experience Table, and to make changes in laws governing policy reserves and surrender values that the Depression had shown to be needed, achieved success in 1948. It had started in 1911, and the final assault began in 1937 when George A. Bowles, then president of the NAIC, appointed a committee of seven—five insurance department actuaries and one representative each of the Actuarial Society and American Institute—to seek modernization of state valuation laws.

This time our profession was better able to arrive at consensus. More actuaries understood the true relation, direct and indirect, of the valuation mortality table to company soundness, and the Actuarial Society's work in compiling mortality studies and constructing "Basic Tables" contributed to confidence about prevailing mortality levels and trends.

The succession of significant steps over a decade that resulted in resolution of the tangle of conflicting statutes governing minimum levels of reserves and nonforfeiture benefits may be summarized thus:

August 1937	NAIC appointment of the first Guertin committee, named after its chairman Alfred N. Guertin (1900–1981), Actuary of the New Jersey Insurance Department.
December 1937	First public statement by the committee, setting forth its understanding of its duties. The committee's name was the Committee to Study the Need for a New Mortality Table and Related Topics.

| June 1939 | Issuance of that Committee's report. |
| 1938–1940 | Publication and discussion of four papers that explored subjects germane to the issues: |

> Charles F. B. Richardson, "Guaranteed Cash Surrender Values under Modern Conditions" (*T.A.S.A.* 39, 237)
> Clinton O. Shepherd, "The Legal Reserve System in the United States" (*R.A.I.A.* 28, 269)
> James E. Hoskins, "Asset Shares and Their Relation to Non-Forfeiture Values" (*T.A.S.A.* 40, 379)
> Bruce E. Shepherd, "Natural Reserves" (*T.A.S.A.* 41, 463)

Early 1940	NAIC appointment of the second Guertin committee, named the Committee to Study Non-Forfeiture Benefits and Related Matters.
September 1941	Issuance of that Committee's report.
June 1942	Release of the final report by a committee of commissioners.
January 1948	Effective date of new laws in jurisdictions that had adopted them. War conditions had caused postponement from 1944.

RECOMMENDATIONS OF THE FIRST GUERTIN COMMITTEE, JUNE 1939

Instead of recommending a particular mortality table to replace the American Experience Table, the first Guertin committee proposed that legislation permit use of any table approved by an insurance commissioner of a particular state provided the table met specifications set forth in the committee's submitted Model Bill, such specifications to cover the breadth and general suitability of the experience underlying such table. The American Experience and American Men Ultimate Tables were to be recognized as complying with those specifications. Permission could be

Alfred N. Guertin (left), modernizer of policy reserve and nonforfeiture regulation. (Courtesy of International Insurance Society, Inc., Tuscaloosa, Ala.) Horace R. Bassford as *Life* magazine portrayed him, 1947. (Herb Gehr, *Life* Magazine, © 1947 Time Inc.)

granted for calculating insurance nonforfeiture benefits on special tables with mortality rates up to 130% of those by the table used to calculate cash surrender values.

Existing requirements for deficiency reserves (equal to present values of the amounts by which gross premiums were less than valuation net premiums) were under fire as illogical and contrary to policyholders' interests; Clinton O. Shepherd (*R.A.I.A.* 28, 309) said that the system, in existence since 1887, constituted minimum rate regulation in an inadequate form. The committee went no further than to introduce one element of logic into the deficiency reserve calculation by proposing that a reserve be required if the gross premium was less than 105% of the net premium plus 5% of the ordinary life net premium; it was also suggested that the reserve be calculated on the statutory minimum, not the company's own, reserve basis.

For its illustrative calculations, the committee constructed a mortality table that it named "Table Z," designed to be representative of modern insured life ultimate mortality. This table was derived largely from the Actuarial Society's "Basic Table 1920–1934"; it ran to age 103 and showed ratios to the American Experience mortality rates as low as 28.6% at age 20, 46.1% at age 40, and never, even at advanced ages, as high as 90%.

Considered today, the failure to call for abandonment of the American Experience Table and the committee's bizarre provision granting commissioners the privilege of choosing valuation tables of their own preference seem timid and inappropriate. But the general tenor of the committee's conclusions was far from feeble. Perhaps its members felt constricted because they were not themselves commissioners; they showed full appreciation of the need for reform and the direction in which it should be sought.

Conspicuous, though, by its absence from both this report and the subsequent discussions within our profession was any interest in placing major responsibility upon each company's actuary to certify that reserves in the balance sheet made adequate provision for future obligations. That such a measure had been adopted in Canada more than ten years earlier went unheeded.

In the 1939 discussion at the American Institute, Sherman C. Kattell emerges as apparently the first actuary to propose the use of a valuation mortality table with specially added safety margins. He said (*R.A.I.A.* 28, 420):

> I think that a modern table, if adopted, should have some safety factors. I think it should not be a table which represents the actual mortality, [nor] that it should be as low as [Table Z].

THE WORK OF THE SECOND GUERTIN COMMITTEE

Although the second Guertin committee did not produce the final report on reform of nonforfeiture benefits—it reported to the commissioners who then compiled the final recommendations—history rightly accords to Guertin and his colleagues credit for the resulting epic pieces of state legislation dealing with reserve standards and minimum values for withdrawing policyholders.

The four operations taken to accomplish the objectives were (1) constructing the Commissioners 1941 Standard Ordinary (CSO) Mortality Table and its companion Commissioners Standard Industrial (CSI) Table for industrial policies, (2) developing the nonforfeiture law defining the minimum cash surrender benefit as the difference between the present value of the insurance benefit and the present value of "adjusted premiums," (thus abolishing the flat "surrender charge," as unsuitable in its name as in its illogical pattern), (3) loosening the historical linkage between valuation reserves and cash values and (4) introducing the Commissioners Reserve Valuation Method (CRVM), an appropriate single successor to the large existing family of preliminary term methods.

THE 1941 CSO TABLE

John S. Thompson, who with Charles A. Taylor had represented the Actuarial Society and American Institute on both Guertin committees, formally introduced the Commissioners 1941 Standard Ordinary Mortality Table to our profession in September 1941. It was the first major table to contain its own built-in margins for adverse fluctuations and contingencies. The underlying experience was that produced by the Actuarial Society's studies for the years 1930–1940 (*T.A.S.A.* 42, 325), and the margin was fixed at five percent of the reciprocal of the expectation of life at each age. This margin increased in amount but generally decreased as a ratio to the experience mortality rate as the age progressed; its appeal lay in its close resemblance to the textbook criterion for identity on whole life policies of reserves by two mortality tables. The final 1941 CSO Table appears in *T.A.S.A.* 42, 329.

Table IV.4 compares the values of $1,000q_x$ by the venerable American Experience Table, by the 1930–1940 experience, and by the 1941 CSO Table.

Table IV.4
VALUES OF $1,000\ q_x$ ON THREE MORTALITY TABLES

	Age					
	15	30	45	60	75	90
By American Experience	7.63	8.43	11.16	26.69	94.37	454.54
By 1930–40 experience	1.30	2.22	6.24	23.69	81.05	265.23
By 1941 CSO	2.15	3.56	8.61	26.59	88.64	280.99

With benefit of hindsight it appears that actuaries, when introducing the unfamiliar concept of a mortality table containing extra safety margins, would have done well to have conveyed clearly to all concerned that it did not show actual mortality rates to be expected in a group of standard insured lives. Failure to explain this caused numerous misunderstandings; one example will suffice. An agent of impeccable ethical standards painstakingly prepared an exhibit showing an employer that, if he were to insure all his executives and their deaths were to follow the CSO "experience," the result would yield him a handsome return on the premiums he would pay. When asked why the agent thought this was possible, recognizing that the insuring company has some expenses to be covered, he quite seriously attributed the result to "the magic of life insurance."

The task of setting the American Experience Table aside had been long and arduous. Those who supported that work must have been thoroughly convinced that it had been worthwhile when they saw the July 1947 issue of *Life* magazine containing an article about Metropolitan Life. Its chief actuary H. R. Bassford (then, as it happened, president of the

Actuarial Society) was pictured against a background chart showing smaller and smaller groups of survivors as ages progressed. *Life's* lively caption described the chart as "showing Americans marching to the grave" and added (pp.81–82):

> Knowing much more about this life span than John Doe does, Metropolitan's chief actuary, Horace R. Bassford ... decides how much money Doe must pay in premiums so that Metropolitan will be able (a) to pay Doe's widow when he dies and (b) to make a tidy profit by investing Doe's money in the meantime. ... [D]espite the fact that the life span of the average American has been steadily increasing since the company was founded, Metropolitan, like other insurance companies, still computes premiums with the aid of mortality tables compiled in 1868. This is a highly profitable practice.

THE STANDARD VALUATION LAW

Not every state had adopted its version of the model valuation law by the target date, January 1948, but for the majority of states that had done so, the law rang the death knell for the American Experience Table in respect of subsequently issued policies. The new statute, however, continued the requirement for deficiency reserves whenever gross premiums were less than corresponding net premiums on the valuation table being used by the company; commissioners were adamant despite arguments and pleas of leading actuaries and company associations.

The new law did accomplish one of its objectives, that of divorcing the mortality and interest bases of reserves and nonforfeiture benefits, but relatively little use was made of this provision by the companies.

The CRVM replaced the Illinois Standard and other modified valuation systems.

The full story of the work done and views expressed may be found in two volumes printed by the Actuarial Society and American Institute:

- *Report of the Committee to Study the Need for a New Mortality Table and Related Topics* (Early 1940), 202 pages.

- *Reports and Statements on Non-Forfeiture Benefits and Related Matters* (September 1942), 289 pages.

In the first of these volumes, the Committee made a point (p. 114) about provision for extra mortality from wars and epidemics that had been unclear to actuaries two decades earlier:

> The Committee is of the opinion that ... the operating margins likely to arise in a single year cannot be depended upon to meet such contingencies, and that adequate surplus funds must be accumulated out of premium income over periods of years to provide for them.

While the planning and debate about the mortality table and about modified reserve methods and nonforfeiture patterns were proceeding, the interest rates that companies were earning on their investments were steadily falling to levels unprecedented in North American actuarial history. The average yield, after deducting investment expenses, on invested assets of United States life insurance companies had dropped below 5% early in the Depression; when Commissioner Bowles appointed his committee in 1937, the yield was below 3 3/4%, and in 1944 when companies were getting ready to comply with the new laws the yield was less than 3 1/4%. The low point (2.88%) was reached in 1947; actuaries of course did not foresee that the yield would then rise steadily for nearly the next forty years. Hence, decisions involving the mortality assumption had to be combined with decisions on how far to go in reducing valuation and nonforfeiture interest rates.

A table in Elgin G. Fassel's 1944 paper, "Reserve Basis" (*T.A.S.A.* 45, 278), shows the distribution of reserve bases used for new policies by the twenty-five largest companies measured by volume of ordinary business, for the years 1897 to 1944. The most widely used reserve interest rate changed from 4% to 3 1/2% in 1901, and to 3% in 1907. In 1942 rates below 3% began to make their appearance, and by the time changes to the 1941 CSO Table had been completed, the most commonly used valuation rate was 2 1/2%, a few mutual companies adopting rates even lower than that. There was also some agitation for strengthening reserve interest rates on existing business, an advocate of this being Alfred N. Guertin himself in "The Strengthening of Reserves" (*T.A.S.A.* 45, 297). Only a few companies took major steps in this direction.

The change from the American Experience Table to a modern table had taken thirty-seven years to accomplish. Only eight years were to ensue before that subject had to be faced again.

ACTUARIAL STUDIES OF AGENCY QUESTIONS

A pioneer study of agency finance was M. Albert Linton's 1924 paper, "Returns Under Agency Contracts" (*R.A.I.A.* 13, 283), in which the "Linton A" and "Linton B" persistency tables were introduced. The "A" Table provided for a 10% voluntary termination rate at the end of the first policy year graded down to a flat 2% rate at the fifteenth year; the "B" rates were double the "A" rates at all durations. Linton considered the "A" scale "very fair in many agencies," and the "B" scale an example of adverse lapse experience.

Linton's work on revision of the New York expense limit law in the late 1920s was the next step toward establishing him as a leading authority on actuarial aspects of agency problems. After that, he became active in field compensation studies sponsored by the Life Insurance Sales Research Bureau and was joined in this work by the authors of the following major papers:

- Wilmer A. Jenkins, "Indices of Cost and Value as an Aid to Agency Management," (*R.A.I.A.* 22, 274)

- Edmund M. McConney and Richard C. Guest, "Some Basic Principles and Mathematical Tables Related to Agents' Compensation," (*T.A.S.A.* 43, 287) and "An Actuarial Study of Agency Compensation," (*T.A.S.A.* 46, 315)

- Charles F. B. Richardson, "Some Actuarial Observations on Agency Management Problems," (*TSA* 1, 131)

Towards the end of this era some companies were employing actuaries in their agency departments to give full-time attention to agency analyses and to help in marketing studies.

WORLD WAR II

This book contains a separate chapter, applicable to both World Wars, entitled "The Profession in Wartime." Hence this chronological section refers only to the effect of casualties in the Second World War upon insurance coverages and costs and to wartime disruptions in the normal activities of the North American actuarial organizations.

A 1948 paper, "War Mortality Among Life Insurance Policyholders in the United States," by Horace R. Bassford in the *Proceedings* of the Centenary Assembly of the Institute of Actuaries (Vol. II, p. 97), describes practices in the assumption of war risks by the life companies, summarizes death losses in the United States armed forces, and gives the general war mortality experience among policyholders. The following were some of Bassford's conclusions (p. 310):

> [T]he mortality rate among ordinary and industrial policyholders in the armed forces averaged over 10 per 1,000 during the war period. This is about 3 1/2 times the death-rate shown by the Commissioners' Standard Ordinary table for the average age of the personnel of the armed forces and more than four times the corresponding death-rate which might have been assumed for dividend purposes. This shows that insurance at standard premium rates could not properly have been offered to persons in or about to enter the armed forces. . . . [Since] the death-rate . . . varied over a very wide range from that in administrative assignments in the United States to that in combat infantry or aviation[,] . . . [i]t was not feasible to charge an average extra premium rate to all military risks. . . .

> Many companies attempted to give full coverage to various military risks upon payment of substantial extra premiums, but experience soon showed that these extra premiums had to be very high and in practice few people were either able or willing to pay for them. . . . The case for war clauses has sometimes been obscured by the fallacious argument that existing policyholders should bear the cost of war claims among those who apply for insurance, when war is imminent, as a matter of patriotism. . . . [But] the real purpose of war clauses is to prevent an undue number of persons from taking out large amounts of insurance when war is imminent and thus to deal fairly between new and existing policyholders.

During the period September 1939 to December 1941 when Canada was at war but the United States had not reached that stage, the normal operations of actuarial bodies headquartered in the latter country were not severely confined except to the extent that time for studies and committee work became restricted. In 1942 the organizations maintained their meeting schedules, but in 1943 meetings were reduced from two to one, and in 1944 no meetings were held at all. The Actuarial Society and American Institute members had a grand reunion in Atlantic City, New Jersey, in November 1945.

The October 1942 Actuarial Society meeting was held in Toronto under the presidency of Joseph B. Maclean. The story told in Canada is that Maclean, having decided that he should brush up on Canadian history, obtained from Canada's John G. Parker a book for that purpose. When Maclean tried to pay for it, Parker admitted that it had cost him only ten cents. It was the Ontario government's subsidized public school text, which nicely filled Maclean's need.

ANNIVERSARIES

The Casualty Actuarial Society celebrated its twentieth and twenty-fifth anniversaries in November 1934 and 1939, and the Actuarial Society its fiftieth anniversary in 1939. These events were occasions for appraisal, sentiment and forecast, as also was the thirty-fifth anniversary of the American Institute in 1944.

The events at the Casualty Actuarial Society's Twentieth Anniversary Celebration and Dinner on November 22, 1934, are fully documented in a 46-page booklet marking that occasion. Its first item was a letter from the Society's first president, Isaac M. Rubinow, saying in part (p. 2):

> I have no doubt in my own mind that it was because of the C.A.S. that casualty insurance has become so very much more scientific in this country than it had been, for instance, in England, and the value of the work of these twenty years, the value of the twenty volumes of publications accrued, not only to the insurance carriers, but what is very much more important, to the American people, for scientific insurance means insurance on a basis equitable to the insured as well as the insurer and useful to the people at large. . . .

The guest speaker, *Journal of Commerce* Editor Jules I. Bogen, assigned blame for the Depression thus (p. 4):

> After [World War I], we should have had a protracted depression in order to correct the dislocations caused by the conflict. We should have had a deflation of credit, a decline in prices and a readjustment of the relative status of wartime and peacetime industries. But the world at large sought to escape the necessity for such a necessarily painful readjustment. Central banks of the leading nations co-operated to expand credit anew, to encourage creation of additional indebtedness, to maintain purchasing power, business activity and prices. As a result, a post-war boom developed during the decade of the twenties, which not only delayed the inevitable economic and financial readjustment, but made it far more severe when it came.

Thomas O. Carlson, "The Younger Generation" viewed the prospect ahead of members of the casualty actuarial profession in encouraging terms (p. 9):

> It is paradoxically true that a fall in insurance stock brings a rise in actuarial stock—unless, of course, the insurance stock falls below the elastic point. The role of the actuary unfortunately is too frequently that of a doctor and too infrequently that of a counselor. This statement is no reflection upon any of our insurance executives. When a person is well he scoffs at medical advice. That is human nature. When he is ill the doctor is called, and it is also human nature that the doctor is often blamed if immediate cure is not effected. . . .

> There is good reason to believe that the current afflictions will leave behind them memories of more than ordinary vividness. If so, the casualty actuary should come more and more to fill the role of permanent health officer rather than of a sick-bed physician. Many companies are awakening to a realization that they need some one in the home office who is familiar with the actuarial side of insurance, some one who can explain what the rating organizations are trying to accomplish. . . , some one who can interpret the company's own

statistics, some one who can aid in treating those individual risk problems which are technically involved. ... I do not mean to forecast any bull market in actuaries. ... But ... when the financial lid is loosened a bit there will be more demand than in the past for actuarial services.

Carlson also dwelt upon "the tremendous underdevelopment of the potential casualty insurance field," mentioning as one of many examples that "it has been conservatively estimated that scarcely one-fourth of the automobiles are insured despite financial responsibility legislation."

Gustav F. Michelbacher (p. 28) spoke of the absence of data that had been available to the charter members:

> There were no statistical facts available except some fragmentary employers' liability data and a few European statistics not suitable for rate-making; the technicians called upon to wrestle with the early problems in this field possessed no personal experience with such problems ... .
>
> The period of experimentation is largely over. If the depression had not intervened, it probably would definitely have closed before now.
>
> The future will see greater complexity in the technical phases of our business, particularly in the field of rate-making, where more accurate rates for individual risks will be demanded.

The evening closed with enactment of a playlet by Clarence W. Hobbs entitled "The Quest For Wisdom" (ibid., p. 31).

Not stressed in this celebration was a subject that would challenge actuaries in days ahead—that of finding reliable methods of reserving for unpaid installments of already incurred claims. But it would have been an oracle indeed who could foresee the impact of inflation a generation ahead on that already troublesome problem.

Five years later, CAS President Francis S. Perryman said in his address "The First Twenty-Five Years" (*PCAS* 26, 5):

> The casualty insurance business has exemplified [an] urge for rapid progress, and to say that the Casualty Actuarial Society has reflected this is an understatement. I would rather put it that the Society has fostered and promoted a lot of this forward-looking activity. ... [O]ur efforts have been spotty in the sense that some branches of insurance have received far more attention than others; certainly compensation insurance has received from us much more attention than any other kind of insurance and other forms of social insurance have in many ways been sadly neglected. ...
>
> The Society should try to avoid the over-emphasis of some parts of its field and the neglect of others, and the way to do this is to bring within its membership all of the workers in the various parts of its field, and to place the running of the Society on the broadest possible cross-section of its membership. ...
>
> [T]he principles of the actuarial science that we have set out to establish should be built on a sound basis, and, above all, ... we should have developed and trained a body of actuaries capable of applying these scientific principles to whatever changes this country finds it desirable to make. What these changes may be is not for me to discuss here, although it does seem that they must tend towards the simplification and extension of insurance. I cannot believe that social insurance will not be considerably extended in scope with the passing of the years, and further I cannot avoid the belief that some of the forms of

insurance will be considerably simplified. . . . [T]he point is, whether our Society, that is to say our members, are capable of dealing with whatever changes are coming. I think the answer is undoubtedly "yes," and that implies that our Society's work has not been unsuccessful.

The Actuarial Society's Golden Anniversary in New York in May 1939 was attended by the president of the Institute of Actuaries, Colonel H. J. P. Oakley, who presented the Society with a beautifully bound set of seventy-four volumes of the *Journal of the Institute of Actuaries,* which may still be viewed in its own bookcase at Society of Actuaries headquarters. Colonel Oakley was elected an Honorary Fellow of the Society. The Faculty of Actuaries, through an American FFA, Lawrence M. Cathles, presented an inscribed gavel, also now in the present Society's display area.

William A. Hutcheson, F.A.S. 1902, delivered a paper (*T.A.S.A.* 40, 103), "Some Sidelights on Actuaries and Their Organizations," reciting British as well as American actuarial history. By pre-arrangement, that paper was discussed by Robert W. Huntington, F.A.S. 1894, by Colonel Oakley, and, on behalf of the younger generation, by Wendell A. Milliman, F.A.S. 1934. Milliman remarked, in part (p. 130):

> Mr. Hutcheson's paper will inspire many of our members to read or reread the early volumes of the *Transactions* . . . . In the process we younger members will again be reminded to look to the performances of the past as a guide to the future. We will look with respect, but we will examine critically, and we will examine the failures along with the successes. Perhaps, the more valuable lessons are to be found in these failures for they have served to more clearly outline the limits within which insurance involving life contingencies may be soundly conducted. The expansion of the science of selection of life insurance risks . . . has indicated a continually expanding field of sound endeavor, and the tragic mistakes of non-cancellable, long term, disability income insurance have marked with danger signals other broad fields of possible insurance. . . .

> We honor the founders of this organization, we recognize the difficulty of the pioneer work which they did, we appreciate the heritage they have given us, and at the same time we are more deeply grateful for the high caliber of the men who are now leading the Society,—the men who will, at the 100th anniversary of the Society, be made to live again, as Mr. Hutcheson has at this time made our founders live again.

It is noteworthy that although the numbers of Fellows of the Actuarial Society and the American Institute (combined, with duplications removed) showed continuous growth during the Depression—the figure was 362 at the end of 1929 and 472 at the end of 1939—the number of consulting actuaries among those Fellows was not holding its own. Victor R. Smith in his presidential address (*R.A.I.A.* 27, 5) showed that the consulting actuaries among the Actuarial Society Fellows declined from 17 in 1927 to 10 in 1937, while in the American Institute that number declined slightly, from 19 to 18. These falls in numbers did not mean that the consulting actuaries were a declining population, but rather that fewer of them considered it necessary to qualify by the examinations.

At the thirty-fifth anniversary of the American Institute in 1944, President Alva J. McAndless remarked with surprise that that body's twenty-fifth anniversary had passed without much comment. The celebration in 1944 consisted mainly of a paper "Comments on the Early History of the Institute" (*R.A.I.A.* 33, 12) by Oswald J. Arnold, an influential charter member who, depending perhaps a bit too heavily on his memory—he had been given very little time for preparation—recounted some of the events at the founding of the American Institute.

McAndless mentioned, for apparently the first time to the American Institute members, discussions about unifying the Actuarial Society and the American Institute, remarking (p. 12):

> If we do not give consideration to the proposal for merging, I am fearful that we will be blinding ourselves to the realities of the opportunity which exists. . . .
>
> The advantages which would accrue from a unified organization seem to outweigh any of the arguments which have been advanced against a merging of the bodies.

McAndless' attitude seems at variance with that of his successor, President Elgin G. Fassel, who said in June 1946 (*R.A.I.A.* 35, 1):

> There is at this time some sentiment in favor of meeting jointly with the Society in the fall of each year. If the actuarial meetings were thus reduced to three a year, with many overlapping activities of the two bodies eliminated as now by the co-operation of joint committees, it would seem that the advantages sought by the proponents of merger would be largely met. The opinion is held by some that two [*sic*] actuarial bodies in America are not too many.

MOVING TOWARD MERGER

The major documentation of the successive steps that resulted, on June 3, 1949, in creation of the Society of Actuaries as successor to the Actuarial Society of America and the American Institute of Actuaries is set forth in two papers and the discussion of one of them:

Before the Event

• Wilmer A. Jenkins, "On the Proposed Merger of the Society and the Institute," *T.A.S.A.* 45, 188. Three written discussions of Jenkins' paper are printed in *T.A.S.A.* 46, 69. These were contributed at a time when wartime conditions prevented meetings from being held, so there was no opportunity for oral discussion.

After the Event

• Reinhard A. Hohaus, "The Origin of the Society of Actuaries," *TSA* 1, 10. Regrettably in the historical view, this paper was never discussed.

Merger, in Jenkins' paper, was, perhaps for reasons of courtesy, postulated in somewhat tentative terms, various partial solutions receiving consideration as alternatives. A pair of sentences (p. 16) in the Hohaus paper convey the realities of the situation:

> [In 1939] both bodies amended their Constitutions to waive any part or parts of the Fellowship examinations passed in the other body (such reciprocal waiver was already in effect for Associateship parts). With that step taken eventual

merger became inevitable, especially in view of the great increase in duplication of Fellows in both bodies as brought out in James R. Herman's paper presented at the final meeting of the Actuarial Society.

Data from Table A-3 (in our Table IV.5) of Herman's paper, "Actuaries—Past Present and Future" (*T.A.S.A.* 50, 70), showed the rapidly growing overlap of Fellows in 1939 and later.

Voting privileges held in the American Institute by Fellows who were already Fellows of the Actuarial Society simply swamped those of the original Fellows of the American Institute, the reverse of course not being the case. When the Actuarial Society and the American Institute met in Quebec City in October 1947, it would have been futile to carry out the voting on merger in separate sessions of the respective bodies because, to the tune of 90%, the voters were the same people!

Table IV.5

NUMBERS OF FELLOWS OF ACTUARIAL SOCIETY OF AMERICA AND AMERICAN INSTITUTE OF ACTUARIES ON SELECTED DATES

End of	F.A.S. Only	F.A.I.A. Only	Fellows of Both	Total
1938	253	91	117	461
1939	211	73	187	471
1940	164	54	270	488
. . .	. . .	. . .	. . .	. . .
1943	150	44	328	522
. . .	. . .	. . .	. . .	. . .
1946	131	35	415	581
. . .	. . .	. . .	. . .	. . .
June 3, 1949	98	30	514	642

Hohaus' paper was precise about particulars and as complete as politeness to the. few dissidents permitted. He refrained from mentioning the successive founderings of merger proposals on the rocks of opposition by sentimental diehards on both sides.

The solution at Quebec City was to call for an informal single vote by all Fellows and Associates on the issue—the first time the views of Associates had been invited on any large question:

> Are you in favor of merger subject to satisfactory solution of the problems of regional meetings and Contributing Members?

When the 303 ballots gave 269 (89%) voting "Yes," 23 voting "No," and 11 declaring themselves "Undecided," the journey to merger was practically at its goal.

Three meetings of members were scheduled for 1948:

Annual Meeting of the American Institute   April 29–30 in Chicago
Annual Meeting of the Actuarial Society   May 13–14 in New York City
Joint Meeting of Both Bodies   October 27–29 in French Lick, Indiana

Before the first of those annual meetings convened, the members of both bodies were sent "Recommendations on Open Questions re Merger" dated March 23, 1948;

The last Board of Governors of the American Institute of Actuaries at the Edgewater Beach Hotel, Chicago, June 1949. Name key is available from SOA archives.

this is printed as Exhibit A of the Hohaus paper (*TSA* 1, 36). Its major sections were:

1. Number, Time, Place, and Nature of Meetings

2. Time and Manner of Elections

3. Privileges for Institute Contributing Members

4. Approval of Papers

The first and third of these dealt with the two issues on which opportunity for further consideration had been promised in the text of the 1947 informal ballot. The proposal on meetings was that the annual meeting be in the fall of each year and that there be two spring meetings in places different from each other and different from the place of the annual meeting. The proposal on American Institute contributing members was that those companies would have the right to send at least one representative to each meeting during the first fifteen years of the new organization.

There was also the matter of the name of the new body. Since the American Institute met first in 1948, its members had the first shot at choosing between "Society of Actuaries" and "Actuarial Society" (omitting the words "of America" from the latter); the former was preferred by the rather close vote of 112 to 82. When the Actuarial Society met two weeks later, its members avoided the contretemps of reaching a contrary conclusion on name by voting, 351 to 38, for "Society of Actuaries."

The fall meeting in 1948 was again preceded by a letter to members and contributing members, "Procedure for Merger of the Society and Institute," sending them a proposed detailed procedure and tentative constitution and bylaws. Notice was also given that the Fellows at French Lick would be asked to decide whether past presidents of the Actuarial Society and American Institute would or would not be eligible to become president of the Society of Actuaries.

At French Lick the vote on this question, perhaps more important personally to the surviving presidents of the two bodies than to the success of the new organization, was tantalizingly close. Those persons were eliminated from consideration by a margin of only six votes, 115 to 109.

The concluding event on October 28, 1948, was the selection by ballot of the Officers and Elected Members of the Board of Governors of the Society of Actuaries. The vote for President was open—no nominations were made by the Nominating Committee or from the floor. For the other officers and the Board Members, slates listing about twice as many names as there were positions to be filled were furnished by the Nominating Committee; for these posts nominations from the floor were invited.

The constitution of the Society of Actuaries, printed in that body's first *Year Book* (1950, p. 100), carried forward (without recorded discussion of its continued rationale) the famous "No resolution expressive of opinion shall be entertained at any meeting" clause that had been considered essential to the survival of the Actuarial Society in 1889.

OUR PROFESSION IN 1948

The thirty years embraced in this chapter were years in which much was undertaken, learned, and endured. Our profession had entered this era with 352 members identified as fully qualified; it emerged with 811, classified thus:

Table IV.6

NUMBERS OF FULLY QUALIFIED MEMBERS BY THE RESPECTIVE STANDARDS OF THE FOUR ACTUARIAL BODIES ON DECEMBER 31, 1948

Membership in	Casualty Actuarial Society (CAS)	Fraternal Actuarial Association (FAA)	Actuarial Society and American Institute (A.S.A.; A.I.A.)	Total (excluding duplications)
One of these only	115	47	598	760
CAS & (A.S.A.;A.I.A.)	32		32	32
FAA & (A.S.A.;A.I.A.)		13	13	13
CAS & FAA	2	2		2
All these bodies	4	4	4	4
Total	**153**	**66**	**647**	**811**

Social insurance was now a major subject of actuarial attention; pensions had just settled into their era of development; and the merger of the Actuarial Society and American Institute, although skillfully managed, was about to have side effects.

APPENDIX TO CHAPTER IV

Papers by North American Actuaries
at the Eighth through Twelfth International Congresses of Actuaries

EIGHTH CONGRESS 1927, LONDON

Buck, G. B. (U.S.) "Pension and retirement systems in the United States of America." VIII, Vol. I, p. 358.

Cammack, E. E. (U.S.) "Group life insurance in the United States." VIII, Vol. I, p. 125.

Carpenter, R. V. (U.S.) "Industrial insurance in the United States and Canada." VIII, Vol. I, p. 62.

Craig, J. D. (U.S.) "Welfare activities for policyholders of life insurance companies in the United States and Canada." VIII, Vol. II, p. 351.

Elston, J. S. (U.S.) "Actuarial science in America since the last International Congress of Actuaries." VIII, Vol. II, p. 323.

Gore, J. K. (U.S.) "Death-rates among lives insured under industrial policies." VIII, Vol. I, p. 75.

Graham, W. J. (U.S.) "The development of group insurance." VIII, Vol. I, p. 136.

Henderson, R. (U.S.) "Practical points in the insurance of sub-standard lives." VIII, Vol. II, p. 161.

Hoffman, F. L. (U.S.) "Industrial insurance in the United States." VIII, Vol. I, p. 79.

Hohaus, R. A. (U.S.) "Social insurance in the United States." VIII, Vol. II, p. 183.

Hunter, A. (U.S.) "Disability benefits under life insurance contracts in the United States and Canada." VIII, Vol. II, p. 83.

Hutcheson, W. A. and Rhodes, E. E. (U.S.) "Life insurance agency systems in the United States." VIII, Vol. II, p. 333.

Laird, J. M. and Cathles, L. M. (U.S.) "Risk premium method of reinsurance." VIII, Vol. II, p. 234.

Mead, F. B. (U.S.) "The progress and development of under-average or sub-standard insurance in America." VIII, Vol. II, p. 177.

Moir, H. (U.S.) "Mortality trend in America: Its influence on the insurance of under-average lives." VIII, Vol. II, p. 168.

Mowbray, A. H. (U.S.) "Experience rating of risks for workmen's compensation insurance in the United States." VIII, Vol. I, p. 324.

Roeber, W. F. (U.S.) "Workmen's compensation rate-making in the United States." VIII, Vol. I, p. 313.

Strong, W. M. (U.S.) "Optional modes of settlement of life insurance policies." VIII, Vol. II, p. 364.

NINTH CONGRESS 1930, STOCKHOLM

Bowerman, W. G. (U.S.) "Contribution of dividends." IX, Vol. I, p. 78.

Dunlap, E. O. (U.S.) "Practical aspects of superannuation and old age disability protection." IX, Vol. III, p. 319.

Elston, J. S. (U.S.) "Is it possible to organize life insurance without participation in the surplus in such a way as to be equally, or even more advantageous, to the policyholder than the method with participation?" IX, Vol. I, p. 361.

Geddes, G. W. (Canada) "Is it possible to organize life insurance without participation in the surplus in such a way as to be equally, or even more advantageous, to the policyholder than the method with participation?" IX, Vol. I, p. 375.

Graham, W. J. (U.S.) "Old age pension and disablement allowance schemes, private and social, in the United States." IX, Vol. III, p. 329.

Hoffman, F. L. (U.S.) "Aviation hazards in their relation to life assurance." IX, Vol. III, p. 515.

Hunter, A. (U.S.) "Tuberculosis—A review." IX, Vol. II, p. 489.

Jackson, H. H. (U.S.) "Fashions in life insurance in the United States." IX, Vol. II, p. 89.

Laird, J. M. (U.S.) "Accident and sickness insurance in the United States of America." IX, Vol. III, p. 95.

Moir, H. (U.S.) "Relative merits to policyholders of participating and non-participating insurance." IX, Vol. I, p. 386.

Phillips, J. T. (U.S.) "Technical methods in disability insurance." IX, Vol. III, p. 112.

Rhodes, E. E. (U.S.) "Relative popularity of whole life and endowment policies." IX, Vol. II, p. 104.

Rietz, H. L. (U.S.) "On the risk problem from a mathematical point of view." IX, Vol. II, p. 294.

TENTH CONGRESS 1934, ROME

Bassford, H. R. (U.S.) "The aviation risk in the United States from the point of view of mortality and disability of passengers." X, Vol. V, p. 244.

Craig, J. D. (U.S.) "The actuarial aspect of unemployment insurance." X, Vol. I, p. 169.

Ferguson, C. C. (Canada) "Depreciation in investment values and profit scales." X, Vol. III, p. 20.

Graham, W. J. (U.S.) "Group insurance." X, Vol. I, p. 596.

Gundy, H. F. and Campbell, A. M. (Canada) "Disability insurance in Canada." X, Vol. I, p. 220.

Hoskins, J. E. (U.S.) "Aviation mortality statistics in the United States and underwriting of aviation pilots." X, Vol. V, p. 260.

Hunter, A. (U.S.) "Disability benefits. Recent developments in the United States of America." X, Vol. I, p. 416.

Leslie, W. (U.S.) "The determination of the premiums and reserves for assurances against accident and civil liability." X, Vol. III, p. 487.

Linton, M. A. (U.S.) "Cash and loan values in periods of severe depression." X, Vol. III, p. 234.

Mabon, J. B. (Canada) "Suicides in Canada." X, Vol. IV, p. 407.

Moir, H. (U.S.) "American business and unemployment insurance." X, Vol. I, p. 191.

Pedoe, A. (Canada) "Disability benefits in connection with life insurance." X, Vol. I, p. 274.

Reid, E. E. (Canada) "Health service. An outline of what has been done by Canadian companies in the interest of public health movements." X, Vol. V, p. 9.

Richardson, C. F. B. (Canada) "Aviation risks." X, Vol. V, p. 155.

Rietz, H. L. (U.S.) "Some remarks on the notations in the domains of financial operations, and of sickness and disability insurance." X, Vol. III, p. 367.

Shannon, S. (Canada) "Select tables and aggregate tables. Possibility of reduction of the period of selection." X, Vol. II, p. 120.

Smith, V. R. (Canada) "Life insurance without medical examination in Canada. A review of its inauguration, development and present status." X, Vol. IV, p. 287.

Thompson, J. S. (U.S.) "Select and ultimate mortality." X, Vol. II, p. 252.

Williamson, W. R. (U.S.) "A few statistical problems of group life insurance." X, Vol. I, p. 618.

Wolfenden, H. H. (Canada) "Special considerations affecting the question of unemployment insurance in Canada." X, Vol. I, p. 64.

Wood, W. A. P. (Canada) "Group insurance in Canada." X, Vol. IV, p. 325.

ELEVENTH CONGRESS 1937, PARIS

Craig, J. D. (U.S.) "The effect of variations in the rate of interest on life insurance in the United States." XI, Vol. I, p. 119.

Flynn, B. D. (U.S.) "Accident insurance." XI, Vol. II, p. 3.

Hoskins, J. E. (U.S.) "Aviation risks in life and accident insurance in the United States." XI, Vol. I, p. 57.

Hunter, A. (U.S.) "Statistical research regarding risks on under-average lives." XI, Vol. III, p. 143.

Laird, J. M. and Cathles, L. M. (U.S.) "Survey of reinsurance in life insurance in the United States." XI, Vol. I, p. 447.

Little, J. F. (U.S.) "Relations between group insurance, employers' provident institutions and national insurance." XI, Vol. II, p. 247.

Murphy, R. D. (U.S.) "Methods employed in statistical research for risks on under-average lives." XI, Vol. III, p. 163.

Parker, J. G. (Canada) "A survey of reinsurance of life insurance in Canada." XI, Vol. I, p. 477.

Pedoe, A. (Canada) "Fire insurance rates in Canada." XI, Vol. II, p. 471.

Pipe, S. H. (U.S.) "Accident insurance." XI, Vol. II, p. 39.

Smith, V. R. (Canada) "Interest and life insurance. A review of the Canadian situation." XI, Vol. I, p. 353.

Thompson, J. S. (U.S.) "Factors determining the price of long-term loans." XI, Vol. III, p. 397.

Thompson, S. M. (Canada) "Factors determining the price of long-term loans." XI, Vol. III, p. 415.

Williamson, J. D. (Canada) "Statistical and actuarial survey of aviation risks for life insurance." XI, Vol. I, p. 85.

Williamson, W. R. (U.S.) "Unemployment compensation features of the Social Security Act of 1935." XI, Vol. III, p. 55.

Wolfenden, H. H. (Canada) "The problem of unemployment." XI, Vol. III, p. 69.

TWELFTH CONGRESS 1940, (PLANNED FOR) LUCERNE*

Bassford, H. R. (U.S.) "The basis and technique of personal accident and sickness insurance." XII, Vol. II, p. 417.

Boschan, P. (U.S.) "Some considerations concerning probability in actuarial science and the foundation of the Extended Life Table." XII, Vol. I, p. 159.

Crowe, E. W. (Canada) "War risk." XII, Vol. III, p. 131.

Graham, W. J. (U.S.) "The development of sickness and hospitalization plans, private and social in the United States." XII, Vol. II, p. 435.

Hunter, A. (U.S.) "Recent experience on persons with medical impairments." XII, Vol. III, p. 459.

Lukacs, E. (U.S.) "Theory of mean risk founded on theory of probability." XII, Vol. I, p. 171.

*Because of World War II, this Congress was not held. Papers prepared for the Congress were published in this volume, however.

MacCharles, F. D. (Canada) "Investment practices of Canadian life insurance companies." XII, Vol. I, p. 569.

Neumann, E. M. (U.S.) "Values granted upon withdrawal or cessation of premium payments." XII, Vol. II, p. 111.

Shannon, S. (Canada) "Some assumptions and hypotheses underlying actuarial calculations." XII, Vol. I, p. 137.

Stephenson, H. R. (Canada) "Surrender values of Canadian life insurance companies." XII, Vol. II, p. 59.

Stowe, H. J. (Canada) "Withdrawals in life insurance." XII, Vol. III, p. 31.

Williamson, W. R. (U.S.) "Disability insurance—Individual, group and social." XII, Vol. II, p. 459.

Chapter V.

1949–1964: EXPANSION AND FRESH DIRECTIONS

"In the present improved state of the science of life assurances, it is not sufficient . . . to follow old customs, and calculations, drawn from a less perfect experience than we now have now the means of obtaining."
—*Benjamin Gompertz (1820), quoted by Henry H. Jackson (R.A.I.A. 30, 431)*

As was typical in the second half of the twentieth century, the pace of change steadily accelerated for the actuarial profession. Actuaries found themselves coping with a spectrum of developments ranging from organization of professional bodies to formation of certification procedures and standards of conduct new to their experience. Even the structure of actuarial activities was being transformed. Whereas in 1939, 87% of Fellows and Associates of the Society of Actuaries' two predecessor bodies were employed by life companies, by 1964 this figure had dropped to 78% and, because of the growth of consulting actuarial firms, would move down even more sharply in the years ahead.

In his closing address at the final (May 1949) meeting of the Actuarial Society, President Horace R. Bassford (*T.A.S.A.* 50, 7) had stressed the fitness of actuaries to deal with problems in industry and government that involved setting up and administration of insurance and annuity benefits and appraisal of long-range programs of expenditures, concluding thus:

> The birth of the Society of Actuaries may well mark the threshold of a new era for the actuarial profession.

EARLY DAYS OF THE SOCIETY OF ACTUARIES

The Society of Actuaries came officially into existence as an incorporated body in the State of Illinois on June 3, 1949. Its first Board of Governors had been elected in October 1948 and had held its first meeting on January 7, 1949. The nominees for Officers, other than the president, had been selected to give close to pro rata geographical representation. The original slate of Officers follows:

President	Edmund M. McConney	
Vice-President	Benjamin T. Holmes	Canada
Vice-President	Walter Klem	Eastern U.S.
Vice-President	Ronald G. Stagg	Central U.S.
Vice-President	Clarence H. Tookey	Western U.S.
Secretary-Treasurer	Henry F. Rood	Central U.S.
Editor	John R. Larus	Eastern U.S.

Horace R. Bassford and J. Gordon Beatty, the final presidents of the predecessor bodies, served two-year terms on the new Board, and there were eighteen Elected Board Members, six of whom served one-year terms, six two-year terms, and six three-year terms.

Of the total twenty-seven Board members, only one, Wendell A. Milliman, was a consulting actuary, but this was close to that group's pro rata share. The initial 642 Fellows included only forty consulting actuaries; furthermore, among the 427 original Associates, only thirty-one were employed in actuarial consulting firms.

The Nominating Committee had made no nominations for President, but it was widely known that the two most favored candidates were Reinhard A. Hohaus and Edmund M. McConney. Hohaus having been made ineligible by a close vote on October 27, 1948 (*T.A.S.A.* 49, 583) that excluded from consideration any president of either of the prior bodies, McConney (1891–1977) was elected on the first ballot. This was a most happy choice. Whether measured by his diplomatic ability, prestige, wit, location outside the large eastern establishment (Iowa), his Canadian background but current United States residence, or his readiness to work hard for the new Society, McConney possessed attributes eminently acceptable to his constituents.

A significant constitutional change that had been adopted at the above-mentioned session in October 1948 was that of a one-term limit upon its presidents; both the prior bodies operated with provision for two possible one-year terms, and almost all presidents of both had served two terms. The one-term limit had the advantage of spreading the honor but was a considerable handicap to incoming presidents who, until the welcome creation of the President-Elect position in 1959, were forced to take up the duties with no advance warning and to step aside soon after they had become fully experienced.

In what amounted to emulation of a toast at the inaugural dinner of the Actuarial Society sixty years earlier, the Society of Actuaries paid tribute to the Institute of Actuaries. The sentiment was voiced by the Society's ranking orator, Henry H. Jackson, at a November 1949 dinner, probably of the Senior Actuaries Club at which the Institute's president, Sir George Maddex, was the honored guest. Jackson closed his address thus:

> It is not possible to sum up in a few words the debt which The Actuarial Society
> of America, the American Institute of Actuaries, and, through them, the

**Edmund M. McConney (1891–1977),
first President of the Society of Actuaries.**

Society of Actuaries must owe to their great exemplar. Our debt to our exemplar is one we can not pay ''in any coin of any realm on any reckoning day.'' But so long as Great Britain and this continent are inhabited by those who love the English speech and are devoted to the free way of life, that debt can never be forgotten by multitudinous beneficiaries. It is in recognition of that debt and with the devotion inspired by gratitude that you and I tonight, in the presence of distinguished guests from overseas, can pledge now

THE INSTITUTE OF ACTUARIES!

The full text of that address is printed in *Fragments,* published in 1950 by Jackson's company, National Life Insurance Company (Vermont). Sir George presented to the new society (*TSA* 1, 659) on behalf of the Institute a gavel, a striker, and a case made from timber taken from the ruins of Staple Inn Hall, which had been destroyed by a flying bomb in August 1944. The bronze of the striker plate was from a bell of a London church destroyed in another bombing. At the Society meeting in March 1950 this compliment and sixty years of friendship were acknowledged by unanimous enrollment of Sir George Maddex as an honorary Society Fellow without examination and with waiver of dues.

In attendance also at that 1949 inaugural meeting were representatives of several other actuarial bodies, bearing welcome gifts and good wishes.

The election to membership of Sir George Maddex was followed, in 1956, by that of Kenneth K. Weatherhead, FFA, this latter in recognition of the centenary of the Faculty of Actuaries being celebrated in Edinburgh that year.

ORGANIZATION MEETING - FIRST BOARD OF GOVERNORS - SOCIETY OF ACTUARIES - JANUARY 7, 1949

The first Board of Governors of the Society of Actuaries, 1949–1950. Name key is available from SOA archives.

INFLUX OF FELLOWS OF THE INSTITUTE AND FACULTY OF ACTUARIES

One of the earliest acts of the first Board of the Society of Actuaries was to announce, at the Society's meeting in November 1949 (*TSA* 1, 660), that membership at the Associateship level was available to Fellows (by examination) of the Institute of Actuaries or the Faculty of Actuaries. This was not a departure from past practice; for many years the Actuarial Society had waived Associateship examinations for these actuaries, and in its early days the American Institute had granted Fellowship status to those who had moved to the United States. What was different was that the 1949 announcement constituted an invitation to Fellows of those British societies to acquire Society of Actuaries membership even though they had no intention of emigrating to America.

The response was gratifying. In 1950 alone, nineteen actuaries were accepted into this form of membership, and the average number of subsequent entrants was a steady five per year. By 1964 the number of overseas Associates had jumped from twelve to ninety-nine; all were highly valued members, and at least a few took advantage of opportunities to attend meetings.

The Casualty Actuarial Society took no such lenient view. A Fellow of the Institute of Actuaries who came to the United States in November 1949 and found employment in a casualty company leading to CAS presidency twelve years later was faced with the formidable task of passing all eight examinations after a thirteen-year absence from the examination room. By no means, however, did this signal lack of CAS respect for the Institute's standards; the point was that Institute and Faculty of Actuaries Fellows coming to North America were unlikely to be experienced in applying actuarial principles to non-life insurance.

Gifts to the new society from actuarial bodies in London, Amsterdam and Madrid, November 1949.

FORMATION OF THE CONFERENCE OF ACTUARIES IN PUBLIC PRACTICE (CAPP), 1950

Six consulting actuaries met at lunch in Chicago in the fall of 1949 to discuss the need for a consulting actuarial organization. James Luther Mims (1889–1973) of Fort Worth, Texas, a consulting actuary of more than twenty-five years experience, had suggested that they meet; the other five were Chicago consulting actuaries: Edward D. Brown, Jr., Harley N. Bruce, Donald F. Campbell, Jr., Chase S. Conover and Harry S. Tressel. Mims had been a member since 1923 of the Fraternal Actuarial Association; at one time he had been actuary of the Texas Insurance Department. Campbell, not a member of an actuarial body, was a 1930 graduate of Professor Henry L. Rietz's actuarial course at the University of Iowa. He had learned the practical side of actuarial work from his father, a charter Fellow of the American Institute with long consulting actuarial experience, particularly in public employee pension systems and in assisting fraternal societies to convert from the assessment to the legal reserve system. Brown had earned Associateship by examination in the American Institute in 1929.

Events moved rapidly. On January 6, 1950, the first meeting of seven incorporators— Mims was absent but John A. Copeland of Atlanta and Robert D. Taylor of Cedar Rapids, Iowa, as well as the original five Chicagoans, were present—had in hand a Certificate of Incorporation dated December 10, 1949, and proceeded to decide upon the bylaws.

There was no reason for animosity towards the new body on the part of either the Society of Actuaries or the Casualty Actuarial Society since neither of them was active in serving the special needs of consulting actuaries. But the Conference leaders were at pains to build a friendly and cooperative relationship from the outset. In this, Brown, being a Society of Actuaries member, had a primary role; he informally discussed the new body's plan with Reinhard A. Hohaus at the Society of Actuaries meeting in November 1949 and, in describing the plans of the Conference by invitation at the Society meeting of May 1951, expressed the matter in part as follows (*PCAPP* 1, 29):

> In January, 1950 the Conference of Actuaries in Public Practice came into being. It has long been recognized by some of us in the consulting field that there was need for an organization for the purpose of considering the problems of the consulting actuary. Neither the old Society or Institute nor the present Society of Actuaries devote any special attention to the consulting field. This statement is not made in any critical vein, since the basic objects and purposes of the Society cover the general field of actuarial science while the problems of the consulting actuary are generally peculiar to the field of public practice.

> The basic purposes of the Conference are to have an organization through which consulting actuaries may meet to discuss their problems, to establish certain standards of qualification in the consulting field, to develop certain ethical standards to be observed in public actuarial practice, to cooperate in every possible way with the Society of Actuaries and local actuaries' clubs, and to educate the public to the value of actuarial service. . . .

> Membership in the Conference is divided into three classes: Members, Associates and Affiliates. In order to qualify as a Member, the applicant must be actively engaged in consulting practice in a proprietary capacity and have not less than fifteen years of actuarial experience. Associate members must be engaged in actuarial practice but not necessarily in the consulting field and must have not less than five years of actuarial experience. Affiliate members include anyone interested in the Conference and its aims and are not necessarily engaged in actuarial work. . . .

> We would like to have it distinctly understood that at no time was there any thought of any conflict between this organization and the Society of Actuaries or any other actuarial organization. . . . We realize fully the magnitude of the debt which we owe to the Society for its unending efforts in the advancement of actuarial science.

The Conference *Proceedings* (*PCAPP*), Vol. 1, also called *Year Book* 1951, lists, on pages 9 through 13, seventy-seven charter members, but it needs to be understood that this listing was made before those people had been classified into the two categories of Members and Associates (there were initially no Affiliates). When that classification had been made (as shown in *PCAPP* 2, vi–xi), forty-three were given the senior status of Member; these are listed in Table V.1.

The first general meeting of Conference members was held in Chicago on October 3, 1950. This was an evening meeting at the then mecca of insurance people, the Edgewater Beach Hotel, beginning with a banquet attended by forty-four members of

Table V.1

OFFICERS, OTHER BOARD MEMBERS, AND NON-BOARD SENIOR CHARTER MEMBERS OF THE CONFERENCE OF ACTUARIES IN PUBLIC PRACTICE, 1950

Officers

Harry S. Tressel	President	Chicago, Illinois
Edward D. Brown, Jr., ASA	Vice President	Chicago, Illinois
Harley N. Bruce	Secretary	Chicago, Illinois
Donald F. Campbell, Jr.	Treasurer	Chicago, Illinois
Joseph Froggatt, Jr., FCAS	Editor	Los Angeles, California

Other Board Members

Clarence L. Alford	Nashville, Tennessee
Chase S. Conover	Chicago, Illinois
John A. Copeland, Sr., FCAS, ASA	Atlanta, Georgia
Frank E. Gerry	Springdale, Connecticut
James L. Mims	Fort Worth, Texas
Frank M. Speakman	Philadelphia, Pennsylvania
R. D. Taylor	Cedar Rapids, Iowa

Others

Louis Arbeit	New York, New York
John H. Baird	Cleveland, Ohio
Walter J. Barr	Oklahoma City, Oklahoma
Henry E. Belden	Los Angeles, California
Alvin Borchardt	Detroit, Michigan
Maurice F. Brennan	Chicago, Illinois
J. Huell Briscoe	Chicago, Illinois
John A. Copeland, Jr.	Atlanta, Georgia
L. C. Cortwright	Springfield, Illinois
Donald B. Dahn	Indianapolis, Indiana
Frank H. Davis	Indianapolis, Indiana
E. I. Evans	Columbus, Ohio
Clyde L. Ferguson	Charleston, West Virginia
Richard Fondiller, FSA, FCAS	New York, New York
A. G. Gabriel	Detroit, Michigan
Miles B. Gammill	Dallas, Texas
William E. Groves	New Orleans, Louisiana
Arthur M. Haight	Omaha, Nebraska
Scott Harris, ACAS	New York, New York
Robert Merriman	Scranton, Pennsylvania
Earl Nicholson	New York, New York
Thomas M. Oberhaus, FCAS	New York, New York
John S. Rudd, Jr.	Austin, Texas
Charles A. Sloan	San Francisco, California
Charles F. Smith	New York, New York
Harmon R. Taylor	Cedar Rapids, Iowa
Paul A. Turner, FCAS	Los Angeles, California
George Van Fleet	Austin, Texas
Lindsay M. Webster	Philadelphia, Pennsylvania
Max J. Werkenthin	Austin, Texas
Clayton Williams	Philadelphia, Pennsylvania

Note—The designations of memberships in other bodies are those in effect when the Conference was organized.

the Conference and a number of guests. Special tributes were paid to two actuaries, James L. Mims, for his initiative in the founder's role, and R. D. Taylor, whose place in the affections of the gathering was similar to that of William E. Starr in the Actuarial Society half a century earlier. Taylor "stated that he was approaching his eighty-third birthday, that he had devoted a business lifetime to the consulting profession and . . . that the firm which he founded [in Iowa] over half a century ago, now had three generations of Taylors concurrently serving. . . ." He thereupon resigned from the Board, the vacancy being filled by Harmon R. Taylor, his son. R. D. Taylor died in 1952, severing this link with early days of actuarial consulting firms.

Another significant bond between the Conference and our profession's formative era was that the consulting firm represented by founding member Frank E. Gerry was originally established by the distinguished actuary Miles M. Dawson when he came to New York City from Chicago in 1895.

Volume 1 of the Conference *Proceedings* contains a section (p. 31) entitled "Organization of the Conference of Actuaries in Public Practice." Its text, thoughtfully written by Harley N. Bruce, went far beyond the scope suggested by the title (p. 33):

> Much higher public recognition of the independent actuary is claimed for Europe than for America. This is a matter which the Conference might explore and if it be found that there are European fields, other than insurance offices, in which the actuary successfully serves, similar American fields can be cultivated by Conference endeavor. . . .
>
> Some critical minds regard the term, consulting actuary, as bordering on the presumptuous and tending toward self elevation. No greater misconstruction could be placed upon the intent of a term. The consulting actuary soon learns that, like the general practitioner in the medical profession, his vocation is characterized by ceaseless hours of strenuous endeavor; he must be a generalist like his counterpart the country doctor. . . .
>
> It is not a Conference design to interfere with any actuary now in public practice who is striving sincerely to conduct his business above reproach, even though there is question of his right by reasonable standards of experience and training to employ the title of actuary. . . .
>
> A noticeable tendency has been observed for a few men of questionable qualifications to enter the unregulated field of public practice by mere self-appointment. . . . Some of these men should voluntarily discontinue use of the term actuary in their firm titles and substitute a term which would indicate the sales promotional aspects of their undertakings.

Substantial growth was achieved during the first decade of the Conference's life. The number in its senior category, Members, rose from forty-three to ninety-three. Ten of the original Members had gone (seven of them by death), and sixty had entered, either by joining or by promotion from the Associate ranks. Fully one-third of these sixty were Fellows of the Society of Actuaries or the Casualty Actuarial Society.

The total roster in 1960 was 322 (93 Members, 165 Associates, and 64 Affiliates). The Conference presidents who succeeded Harry S. Tressel during that decade were all from the original membership, viz.:

1952–53	Edward D. Brown, Jr., Chicago
1954–55	Harley N. Bruce, Chicago
1956–57	Donald F. Campbell, Jr., Chicago
1958	Arthur M. Haight, Omaha (died 1959)
1959–60	Harmon R. Taylor, Cedar Rapids

By 1960, the meeting pattern that was to serve the members and visitors effectively in the future had become well-established. For example, the program of the eleventh annual meeting at Chicago in October 1960 was:

Insurance
Forum: Problems of Insurers
Life Insurance Company Taxation Aspects of Phase III (Paper)
Payment of Reserve as Additional Death-Benefit Contract (Paper)

Pensions
Forum: Problems of Pension Funds
Some Implications of Pension-Fund Growth (Paper)
The Dilemma of Compulsory Retirement (Paper)
Cost Calculations for Pension Funds Subject to Adjustment for Inflation (Paper)

Social Security
Federal Tax Treatment of Pension and Other Employee-Benefit Plans (Paper)
Some Social Security Problems (Paper)

General
Problems in Life-Estate Valuations (Paper)
Actuaricks, by Harry M. Sarason (Book Review)
The Aims of Education (Paper)
Committee Reports, Treasurer's Report and Other Business

APPREHENSIONS OF THE NUCLEAR ERA

At the American Institute meeting in June 1946, two actuaries (Walter A. Merriam and Arthur Pedoe) expressed grave concern about the atomic bomb threat. Merriam (*R.A.I.A.* 35, 135) considered the hazard beyond the power of the companies to deal with; Pedoe urged that the life companies adopt the long-continued property insurance practice of excluding the war hazard. But when the atomic bomb ceased in 1949 to be an American monopoly and when the next year a conflict of unforeseeable proportions was mounted in Korea, actuaries had to ponder the hazards that might follow.

A discussion topic at the Society of Actuaries March 1951 meeting was (*TSA* 3, 82):

> What plans should be considered by the life insurance companies for mitigating the catastrophe hazard with respect to policyholders in the event of a major war?

> [Ray] D. Murphy [p. 87] ... gave some background.... Shortly after the outbreak in Korea, the Life Insurance Association [of America] and the American Life Convention formed a ... Joint Committee on War Problems. One of a number of problems which came before it was whether or not any assistance should be sought from the Federal Government by reinsurance or otherwise of our liabilities in the event of very severe losses from bombing. The

discussion ... was unanimous and quite emphatic that [such] assistance ... should not be sought.

It was thought, however, that consideration should be given to a plan for sharing the load of that danger and a subcommittee was set up on pooling of risk. ...

The idea of pooling is fast maturing as something which can reasonably be considered. A possibility would be for three pools to be established, one for ordinary life insurance, one for group insurance, and one for industrial insurance. Entrance into them would be purely voluntary by any company and the purpose would merely be to smooth out the burden in the event of a catastrophe. The losses (less, perhaps, the gains from annuities) would be distributed among the companies that had entered the pool in proportion to the net risk of those companies nation-wide. ... The life companies in this country have about 4 billion dollars in surplus and have very large margins coming in from all their ordinary sources so that a very substantial degree of catastrophe could be met ...within their financial means. ...

[The liability] must be handled to the limits of our financial power and if the devastation goes beyond that nobody can predict what would happen in the whole economic field in this country.

Two other actuaries discussed this matter, one of them outlining a plan used by a company to microfilm its critical records.

The Reading Room of the rebuilt Staple Inn Hall, London, September 1955. Its furnishings are tributes from actuaries of North America.

By the next meeting (May 1951) the assigned question had become (ibid., p. 233):

> In the event of warfare *on this continent,* would the hazard of such a magnitude be bearable (a) by individual companies, (b) by the industry with suitable pooling of risks?

The discussion ran the gamut from descriptions of plans for record preservation to prophecies that the risk, as specified, could not be covered by the companies. At this point, the subject was dropped—presumably because no cooperative solution commanded industry support.

LIFE COMPANY INVESTMENTS

By the early 1950s investment yields were steadily improving from the depth reached in 1947. Several items in the *Transactions* reflect gradually changing views.

In a November 1950 Forum on Interest and Investments (*TSA* 2, 435), Fergus J. McDiarmid pointed out that current investment philosophy had been formulated during the century of relatively stable purchasing power preceding World War I. He described the outlook as rather clearly for further deterioration in the purchasing power of money, giving the opinion that most of us would jump at a chance to settle for a steady decline of 1% a year in purchasing power of the dollar.

McDiarmid then made a remarkable prediction. His exact words are lost because in those days the Society was experimenting with third-person digests of informal discussions; the printed attribution was (p. 436):

> The argument that life insurance contracts are payable in dollars, and so investments payable as to principal and interest at a fixed rate in dollars are entirely satisfactory to back them, may satisfy accountants and even some actuaries. However, except where premiums are largely used to pay for current protection, it is likely to have only minor appeal to policyholders who are concerned with the real purchasing power of life insurance proceeds for themselves in their old age or for their dependents. [McDiarmid] felt that the time has come for reconsideration of investment in equities as the only way of doing for policyholders something which ought to be done.

All of the eleven discussions that morning, particularly one by Geoffrey N. Calvert pointing out that provision for investment of pension fund money in common and preferred stocks was becoming normal procedure, give valuable indications of then current actuarial thinking; regrettably the digest records no comments on McDiarmid's opinion about the future of level premium life insurance. Reginald C. Barnsley drew attention to a remark made about common stocks by Wendell M. Strong in June 1929 (*R.A.I.A.* 18, 117):

> We have heard a great deal recently about the advisability of companies investing in common stocks. It is very significant to me that this comes after there has been a tremendous appreciation in the price of common stocks. We heard nothing about the advisability of such investments in the latter part of 1920 and 1921 when there was such a depression in prices that a reasonably intelligent diversified selection was almost sure to give a profit. Then common stocks were worth investing in. Whether or not they are today, I do not know; do you?

When the subject of equities came up at the Society of Actuaries meeting in October 1962, the presentation was by four distinguished panelists exploring "The Economic Outlook" (*TSA* 14, D470). One of them presented a chart (p. D497) of the Dow-Jones Industrial (DJI) Averages since 1897 with his own trend-line justifying (present author's interpretation) the long-range assumption of an annual growth of about 4 1/4%. Since its value at the time was about 600, that growth rate maintained to 1988 would have resulted in a DJI value of about 1,800. All of those presentations (one by a Canadian) are of interest in the light of subsequent events.

In November 1951 (*TSA* 3, 605), William M. Rae discussed the cyclic theory of interest rates, which holds that they rise for a period of about twenty-seven years, then decrease for an equal period but to a lower level than before.

At the Society's 1953 annual meeting, the distinguished British actuary Frank M. Redington (*TSA* 5, 359) turned American actuarial attention for the first time to the problems of mismatching of assets and liabilities.

THE 1958 COMMISSIONERS STANDARD ORDINARY MORTALITY TABLE

Less than a decade after the 1941 CSO Table had become the mandatory valuation standard in the United States, it was time to tackle that painful subject again. The companies writing nonparticipating policies were once more seeking relief from the barrier to justifiable reductions in gross premiums imposed by the flawed state requirement for deficiency reserves. After several efforts to substitute a more rational deficiency reserve system (or to remove the necessity for such reserves by persuading states to follow New York's lead in banning premium scales that were inadequate on reasonable underlying assumptions) had proved unsuccessful, it became clearly necessary to produce a successor to the 1941 CSO Table with its excessively high mortality rates.

In 1956 the Society's Board of Governors decided to cooperate with the NAIC in constructing a new table that the Board cautiously specified "might be used by companies on a permissive basis." A Society Committee, chaired again by Alfred N. Guertin and this time with Henry F. Rood as vice-chairman, proceeded, with extraordinary dispatch attributable largely to employing modern electronic equipment, to produce a recommended new table. The table, given the temporary name "X_{17}," consisted again of mortality rates arbitrarily increased over an experience table, in this case over ultimate mortality rates derived from the Society's intercompany studies of insured life mortality in the years 1950 to 1954.

Rood described the committee's task (*TSA* 8, 509) as:

> to provide a mortality table for valuation that would be safe for all companies ... to use for policies issued at standard premium rates. This would include companies with strict underwriting rules and those with liberal underwriting rules, those operating nationwide and those ... [in] small areas, those issuing a large proportion to females and those selling almost entirely to males, those issuing primarily to business and professional men and those covering semi-industrial or other special occupational groups, such as military or aviation risks. With this decision made, the Committee had undertaken to adjust the mortality rates upward to

cover for each age group the deviation from the average that might reasonably be expected for these various types of companies.

Nowhere in the discussion of this wide-ranging blueprint did anybody question the propriety, in the public interest, of introducing a margin large enough to take care of every company in the United States, regardless of how inefficient that company's underwriting or operations might be.

The proffered X_{17} Table immediately became controversial. Actuaries of small stock companies preferred no change at all rather than for major companies to adopt, as loss leaders or otherwise, premium scales lower than they could match. Even actuaries of some mutual companies sought margins stiffer than those proposed, in the interests of desired dividend slopes by duration. And some challenged the committee's decision to keep the mortality rates from materially exceeding those of the latest population table, U.S. White Males 1949–1951.

In response to these objections, the X_{17} Table was discarded, to be replaced by a table named the 1958 CSO Table (*TSA* 10, 696), employing higher mortality rates at most ages. Table V.2 gives a comparison.

Table V.2

VALUES OF $1,000 q_x$ BY FOUR MORTALITY TABLES AT DECENNIAL AGES

	Age					
Table	**20**	**30**	**40**	**50**	**60**	**70**
1941 CSO Table	2.43	3.56	6.18	12.32	26.59	59.30
1950–1954 Experience	0.84	1.08	2.36	6.71	17.56	43.30
Discarded Table X_{17}	1.46	1.82	3.30	7.84	20.20	49.79
1958 CSO Table	1.79	2.13	3.53	8.32	20.34	49.79

After the smoke had cleared and the NAIC had decided that the new table was to be mandatory, not permissive, the Society's Board of Governors rendered the opinion that in future the Society should limit its share of such work to constructing experience tables, leaving the thankless task of selecting safety margins to technical (i.e., doubtless, actuarial) subcommittees of industry advisory committees that the NAIC would appoint. The Board minutes of June 5, 1958, say that this decision was reached "at dinner with a number of senior actuaries." In March 1959 this approach was made applicable to construction of a modern valuation table for industrial insurance.

The pros and cons of deficiency reserves, the possible alternatives if they were to be abandoned, and their nature as long as they continued to be a statutory requirement were debated by several actuaries at the Society's March 1957 meeting (*TSA* 9, 212). Two of those expressing their views were in the regulatory field: W. Harold Bittel of New Jersey and Richard Humphrys of Canada.

BEGINNING OF A PRODUCT REVOLUTION

Life insurance coverages, which had previously changed slowly and moderately except at chaotic times such as the aftermath of the Armstrong Investigation, entered the modern era of rapid change in the early 1950s. Malvin E. Davis devoted much of his 1957 presidential address (*TSA* 9, 320) to cataloguing them:

Cost Differential by Size of Policy

Terminal Dividends

Premium Rates Differing by Sex

Salary Savings Plans

Pre-authorized Check Plans

Split-Dollar Plans

The Family Life Insurance Policy

Group Permanent and Group Life with Paid-up Plans

Accident and Sickness Insurance Written by Life Companies

Fergus J. McDiarmid in 1958 (*TSA* 10, 576) presented a paper, "Inflation and Life Insurance," which is historically important both for the views that the author expressed and the controversy they sparked. Eleven years later, Charles B. Baughmann (*TSA* 21, 379) expressed sorrow that McDiarmid's analysis had received almost no support and noted the changed attitudes that time had wrought.

A highly criticized product, introduced by two companies in 1956 and copied by others, was a whole life policy containing cash values equal to the full level premium reserve in all policy years including the first. This was primarily for use in the so-called Bank Loan Plan; it brought in large volumes of business from buyers in high income tax brackets and created major problems and high lapse rates in some companies. It was eventually subjected to limits on tax deductibility imposed by the U.S. Treasury Department.

In 1956, Melvin L. Gold (*TSA* 8, 320) drew attention to European discussion of a policy whose face amount would increase each year by, say, 3% in anticipation of inflation. This plan was later introduced on this continent (see John M. Bragg and David A. Stonecipher, "Life Insurance Based on the Consumer Price Index," *TSA* 22, 333).

M. Albert Linton (*TSA* 7, 535), in perhaps the longest book review in the *Transactions*, examined the two-volume 1,700-page *A Study of Saving in the United States* by Raymond W. Goldsmith, which had been financed by the life insurance business. Linton's comment was, "[W]e can hardly fail to wonder what practical use will be made of the results."

A soul-searching 1960 discussion of the competition with other media for the public's savings dollar produced a comment by Harold R. Lawson (*TSA* 12, 722) to the effect that:

> One of the things that inhibits the life insurance business as a medium for the savings of the public is the fact that it is tied to fixed income investments. Not everyone is prepared to invest all his money in fixed income investments. Some people are going to save some of their money in common stocks and that means that they can't do it directly through life insurance.

Lawson went on to describe how his (Canadian) company had "improved on the mutual fund idea ... by making available with their [companion] mutual fund a variable annuity ... [but] not selling the variable annuity through their life agents."

ACCIDENT AND HEALTH INSURANCE

The severe financial problems that life and casualty companies shared in the disability income field before and during the Depression are described in Chapter VIII of this book. Despite those discouragements, desire to make federal coverage unnecessary prevented the matter from being neglected after World War II. The largest life companies, aware of how much their widespread field forces could do to spread voluntary benefits, felt particularly responsible for getting the actuarial obstacles overcome. No fewer than three texts on health insurance were published by the Society of Actuaries during its first twenty years.

In June 1952 at a Forum on Individual Health and Accident Insurance, John H. Miller's presentation was reported (in the third person) thus (*TSA* 4, 392):

> The individual health and accident business is an area which the actuarial profession has largely neglected. Since the 1945 examinations, the subject has not appeared on the [Society of Actuaries] syllabus .... The Casualty Actuarial Society gives it a rather light treatment in its examinations. Many actuarial papers ... were presented in the twenties and thirties. Through 1940, the *Proceedings* of the Casualty Actuarial Society record 17 papers, the [American] Institute one, and the Society seven. Since 1940 only three papers have appeared, each dealing with the specialized subject of reserves for noncancelable policies. The actuary who wishes to acquaint himself with the problems of this business finds the literature somewhat limited, with most of the published material predating the important developments of the last decade.

> He will, however, find ...that this is a very interesting field for research. As compared with life insurance, where it requires a large body of exposures and a considerable period of time to develop significant results, health and accident as a subject for experimentation and research, like the guinea pig, produces quick results.

In 1954 (*TSA* 6, 350) James T. Phillips presented a paper, "Some Considerations in the Development of an Individual Accident and Sickness Program," after his company, New York Life, had been in that field for just over two years. He pointed out that eighteen of about forty-two companies with a billion dollars or more of ordinary life insurance in force were by then writing Individual Health and Accident Insurance, nine of these having started since 1950; in an Appendix (p. 374) he gave particulars of the policies and commission practices of fourteen of these.

In discussing his company's choice of coverages to be offered, Phillips said (p. 351):

> The first decision which confronted us was whether to issue the noncancelable or the "commercial" form .... In choosing the commercial form, whereby the company has reserved the right to reunderwrite policies, we were influenced by the fact that over 90% of the total Individual A & S business was issued on this basis.

But in looking to the future, Phillips said (p. 370):

> The use of this [right to reunderwrite] even if used sparingly may cause policyholder dissatisfaction and could detract from the good will and reputation for fair dealing which life insurance companies have earned for themselves.

> The obvious alternative ... noncancelable insurance ... is not without its problems. The major consideration is the problem of adequately controlling the business so as to avoid large financial losses. ...

> In attempting to develop an A & S program which meets the needs of the insuring public and yet can be satisfactorily controlled, the best answer ... might lie somewhere between the commercial and noncancelable approaches. ...

> [An] approach, used by the Prudential on hospital expense policies, [involves] relinquishing the right to refuse renewal for any reason, but retaining the right to increase premiums for an entire class of policyholders. ...

> When the scale of rates for a whole class is increased because of unfavorable claim experience the reaction should not be unduly unfavorable. ...[By] making needed increases soon enough after the need for an increase develops, increases could be kept small and thus there would be less resentment and fewer lapses by the better risks.

This soon became a widely used system known as "guaranteed renewable," greatly reducing the quantity of business issued with the right of cancellation.

In 1956 John H. Miller had reduced the gap in literature that he had deplored four years earlier by writing a text, *Accident and Sickness Insurance Provided Through Individual Policies*. Revisions to keep abreast of developments were made in 1963 and 1968 by Edwin L. Bartleson under the title, *Health Insurance Provided Through Individual Policies*.

INCREASING THE SUPPLY OF ACTUARIES

At the very first Society of Actuaries meeting in 1949 (*TSA* 1, 575), a program item for Informal Discussion was:

> Is the current rate at which actuarial students are entering the profession sufficient to meet the probable future demand for actuaries?

This failed to produce much grass-roots opinion, but did invite consideration of a matter that received considerable attention during the 1950s. In his October 1953 address (*TSA* 5, 234), President John R. Larus gave figures on numbers of members (Fellows and Associates combined with duplications in the prior bodies removed), at twenty-year intervals starting in 1893. Table V.3 is an elaboration of that part of Larus' table giving compound annual growth rates over ten-year intervals.

An illuminating table of occupations by President Walter Klem two years later (*TSA* 7, 341) is given in digested form here along with figures for 1964 and 1983 (see Table V.4). This shows that consulting actuarial firms, small users of Society members before World War II, began to be an important employment factor numerically in and after the 1950s.

A Committee to Review Membership Requirements reported in 1959 (*TSA* 11, 146) its estimate (by the questionnaire method) of immediate membership needs and, as best

Table V.3

**NUMBERS OF FELLOWS AND ASSOCIATES OF SOCIETY OF ACTUARIES
AND ITS PREDECESSORS AT TEN-YEAR INTERVALS, 1893–1983**

Year	Number of Members	Compound Annual Growth Rate
1893	78	—
1903	152	6.9%
1913	327	8.0
1923	440	3.0
1933	702	4.8
1943	866	2.1
1953	1,346	4.5
1963	2,309	5.5
1973	5,045	8.1
1983	8,927	5.9

Table V.4

**FELLOWS AND ASSOCIATES OF SOCIETY OF ACTUARIES
AND ITS PREDECESSORS BY TYPE OF EMPLOYMENT ON SELECTED DATES**

Employment	1909	1939	1955	1964	1983
Life insurance companies	187	679	1,156	1,660	4,434
Consulting practice	25	37	159	344	2,826
Other	35	65	93	129	529
Subtotal	**247**	**781**	**1,408**	**2,133**	**7,789**
Retired	2	34	100	196	727
Resident abroad	36	22	66	69	411
Total membership	**285**	**837**	**1,574**	**2,398**	**8,927**

such an estimate might be made, future needs in 1963 and 1968. The essence of these findings was: (1) that the profession on this continent was 450 members short of reported immediate needs; (2) that, admitting the impossibility of producing so many more actuaries immediately, an annual compound growth rate of 14% would be required to catch up with demand within five years; and (3) that if catching up were to be achieved within ten years, the corresponding growth rate would have to be 6 1/2%.

Several steps were soon undertaken to make the opportunities of this profession better known to students and to make the examination requirements more palatable. The steps to familiarize young people with what an actuary is and does were made the responsibility of a Public Relations Committee, first appointed in 1956. That committee and a committee of the Casualty Actuarial Society entered into cooperation with the Mathematical Association of America in sponsoring its annual mathematics contest, produced descriptive pamphlets, and in 1964 designed an Actuarial Aptitude Test for use by guidance counselors and employers of actuarial students. Eighteen years later the Society, to keep up with changes in legal requirements, had to issue the following warning about the test's use (*The Actuary,* October 1982):

We remind employers that the Actuarial Aptitude Test has not been validated for employment discrimination purposes, and should not be used in making employment decisions such as hiring, promotion, or changes of position.

	NUMBER OF MEMBERS BY FIELD OF ACTIVITY									
	ACTUAL MEMBERSHIP				ESTIMATED MEMBERSHIP NEEDED (INCL. PRESENT STAFF)†					
FIELD	In 1956*		In 1958		Immediately		In 1963		In 1968	
	Fel-lows	As-soc.	Fel-lows	As-soc.	Fel-lows	As-soc.	Fel-lows	As-soc.	Fel-lows	As-soc.
180 Life Companies employing members of Society and replying to questionnaire 1958	727	544	753	482	883	604	1,184	948	1,523	1,332
Consulting Actuaries..	83	83	78	86	97	115	151	196	197	270
National Government.	5	8	5	8	31	21	46	32	63	38
State, Provincial and Local Government and Dominion of Canada...........	12	12	14	14	20	31	29	48	34	57
236 Life Companies which do *not* employ members of Society, replying to questionnaire 1958........	0	0	0	0	13	25	58	120	160	254
Subtotal.........	827	647	850	590	1,044	796	1,468	1,344	1,977	1,951
Retired............	44	19	45‡	20‡	45	20	80	35	121	54
Miscellaneous........	19	18	21‡	19‡	21	19	36	35	54	54
Nonquestioned Companies, no replies, etc..............	§	§	62‡	136‡	74	178	104	303	140	444
Total Members.....	890	684	978	765	1,184	1,013	1,688	1,717	2,292	2,503

* 1956 numbers from another survey.
† Numbers through subtotals are from questionnaires; the rest are estimated.
‡ Estimated distribution of number needed to balance to total number of members.
§ Included above.

The shortage of actuaries as depicted in March 1959.

PENSIONS

Intense pioneering work in pensions by actuaries in the consulting field and in life companies was demanded by vast expansion of pension plan opportunities, sparked in the first instance by employers' freedom during World War II to grant pension credits in lieu of heavily controlled pay increases, and in the second by a United States court decision of 1949 (*Inland Steel Company* vs. *United Steelworkers of America*) making pensions an item of required bargaining and thus turning unions from antagonism to its exact opposite, a potent force in pension plan development. Soon after came the next major influence—the rise of conglomerate and multinational companies—confronting actuaries with problems of mergers and acquisitions and requiring them to master the details of employee benefit practices in other countries.

Actuaries met these challenges by finding ingenious solutions and notably by enunciating principles and methods for general use within the profession. One difficulty in adequately cataloguing these developments is that many relevant papers were published in journals other than those of the Society or the Conference.

The earliest actuarial paper of this era, "Pensions—1949" by Dorrance C. Bronson (*TSA* 1, 219), began by reviewing the past, comparing the Actuarial Society's readings for students in 1910, 1918, 1923, 1935 and 1948. It had not been until 1935 that references of authors here had begun to outnumber those in British journals, and even in 1948, "Group Annuities" by Reinhard A. Hohaus written in 1929 (*R.A.I.A.* 18, 51) was the one major North American contribution to student enlightenment. Bronson remarked that funded pension plans along rather modern lines existed in Great Britain as far back as the middle of the nineteenth century.

After identifying the State, the Insurance Company, the Trust Fund, the Union Welfare Fund and the Bureau of Internal Revenue as the five main vehicles, institutions or influences upon old-age pension benefits in the United States, Bronson concluded (p. 241):

> [F]or each . . . the pot is boiling vigorously. Or is it a pressure-cooker without a safety valve? How long can the steam continue to generate without dangerous consequences, under a spreading system of low-geared funding on the one hand or the problems of enormous reserve accumulations on the other?

Bronson's paper showed clearly the growing pains being experienced in the pension field—not least in its babel of technical terms. As incentive toward uniformity of pension language, he composed a glossary. Some who discussed the paper applauded this effort, but many years were to pass before authoritative actions in the direction of standardization were taken. A discussion by Samuel Eckler described the Canadian pension scene, and one by Sir George Maddex, FIA, touched on the history of pensions in Britain.

Another classic 1949 paper on pensions was "A New Mortality Basis for Annuities," by Wilmer A. Jenkins and Edward A. Lew (*TSA* 1, 369). It introduced actuaries on this continent to the concept of forecast annuity tables based on direct estimates of future mortality decline rather than on the crude device of setting back the ages in existing tables. It also presented the Annuity Table for 1949, a greatly needed successor to the 1937 Standard Annuity Table, constructed from data in the annuitant mortality reports of the Joint Mortality Committee (of the Actuarial Society and American Institute) by adjusting for subsequent mortality improvement.

The next major contribution to pension literature in the *Transactions* came in 1952 (*TSA* 4, 17), "Fundamentals of Pension Funding" by Charles L. Trowbridge. He introduced his theme thus:

> The funding methods commonly used in the pension field are perhaps fairly well understood by the actuaries who use them, but the actuarial literature on this subject is extremely sparse. The classic British papers on pensions devote themselves largely to the techniques of valuing complicated benefits. They put little

or no emphasis on the possible variations in funding method, relying almost entirely on what is essentially individual level premium funding. Perhaps the best description of the various methods will be found in the "Bulletin on Section 23(p)" put out by the U.S. Treasury Department. Even this is only a very sketchy and superficial treatment, and the beginner in the pension field pretty much has to dig the ideas out for himself. This paper attempts, in some measure, to get at least the fundamentals of pension funding into actuarial literature.

Trowbridge undertook to classify the range of funding methods into six classes, from Class I (pay-as-you-go) at the one extreme, to Class VI (the theoretical ultimate in heavy funding) at the other.

The paper was discussed, generally in complimentary terms, by a diverse group composed of two consulting actuaries (Clark T. Foster and Frank L. Griffin, Jr.), one in academia (Cecil J. Nesbitt), one in government (George E. Immerwahr), three in life companies (Robert F. Link, Chalmers L. Weaver and William M. Rae) and two of our profession's leading philosophers (W. Rulon Williamson and Hilary L. Seal). Trowbridge expressed complete agreement with Link's remark that his paper had "barely scratched the surface of a great body of potential scientific knowledge of various funding methods."

Also in 1952 the Pension Research Council of the Wharton School of Finance and Commerce, at the University of Pennsylvania was organized by Ben McGiveran, a leading writer of insured pension plans, to study the field of private pensions. Leading actuaries in the pension field were prominent from the outset in the work of the Council.

The Council's first publication, *Fundamentals of Private Pensions* by its Research Director Dan M. McGill, emerged in 1955 (and by 1988 had reached its sixth edition). Morgan H. Alvord, the first edition's reviewer (*TSA* 7, 554), credited the author with having courageously faced many controversial areas in the field, and said that the book's tables and appendixes "enable those without actuarial training to understand the mystery of [pension cost] calculations without very much study."

Bronson followed up in 1957 with a book published by the Council, *Concepts of Actuarial Soundness in Pension Plans*. That book's reviewer, Wendell A. Milliman, complimented the author on having conveyed the elusiveness of "actuarial soundness," summing up as follows (*TSA* 10, 122):

> Surely if the phrase "actuarial soundness" has so many meanings and facets, and at the same time there is reason to expect eventual legislative action on the subject, this is a matter which each actuary should study. A good place to start is with Mr. Bronson's scholarly and philosophical study.

Meanwhile, the Teachers Insurance and Annuity Association (TIAA) had launched its running-mate, the College Retirement Equities Fund (CREF), described by Robert M. Duncan in 1952 (*TSA* 4, 317). This plan gave participants the choice of having up to one-half of their total employee and employer contributions invested in equities through CREF, the balance going into fixed-dollar annuities in TIAA. Benefit accumulations were expressed in pension units rather than in dollars.

Geoffrey N. Calvert, in an article, "Cost-of-Living Pension Plan" (*Harvard Business Review,* September-October 1954), established himself as a pioneer advocate of automatic benefit adjustments for inflation in conjunction with substantial investment in equities, subject to prudent ceilings on such benefit increases and to flexibility of investment policy. The system had been developed in conference with executives of National Airlines, whose resulting plan was, in Calvert's words (p. 104):

> a plan which (a) would expressly provide benefits geared to the cost of living and payable until death, (b) would fund the resulting liabilities partly in equities (subject to proper investment management), and (c) would provide such actuarial safeguards as are necessary to protect the employer against the twin dangers of overcommitment in the event of catastrophic losses in the fund or a "blow-off" inflation.

"Blow-off" inflation was destined to strike, not once but twice, two decades later.

Naturally, in the discussions of variable annuity plans (in which benefits were stated in terms of units rather than dollars treating common stock investments as hedges against inflation) the question at issue was whether or not the stability of common stock investments was adequate to protect employer and employee interests. Duncan in his 1952 paper, and later Herbert W. Hickman in 1970 (*TSA* 22, 191), furnished ample historical data for retrospective analysis of this question. Calvert had begun, as far back as October 1948 in the *Journal of Commerce,* "Interest and Mortality Factors in Pension Financing," to stress to corporate officers and pension plan designers the importance of achieving optimum yields on pension fund assets in the face of rising pension costs caused by declining annuitant mortality. In 1952 he issued a pamphlet on the pros and cons of profit-sharing plans, which had been little used until then, and followed in 1955 with two pamphlets, "The Role of the Actuary in Variable Pension Planning" and "The Rise of Split Funding As a Method of Providing Retirement Benefits."

The philosophical question of actuarial soundness came up in a different connection in a 1954 paper by Abraham M. Niessen, "Measure of Actuarial Soundness in a Pension Plan of the Railroad Retirement Type" (*TSA* 6, 26). But much of this debate was offstage; Niessen said (p. 31):

> At a special forum of the American Statistical Association held in December 1952 in Chicago, three prominent members of this Society (D. C. Bronson, G. B. Buck, and R. M. Peterson) were invited to present their views on actuarial soundness in pension plans. The opinions expressed ranged from the very strict requirement (Bronson) that upon termination of the plan assets should match liabilities based on past service (with an acknowledged amortization period for initial unfunded liabilities) to the very liberal criterion (Buck) that the present and contingent liabilities of the plan be balanced by the amount of present and contingent assets, both actuarially computed as of the valuation date.

In a footnote Niessen expanded substantially on this description of Buck's views, and then continued:

> Mr. Peterson thought that actuarial soundness cannot be defined in a manner applicable to all pension plans, but must be related to the pension plan's objectives and consequent liabilities. One of the most interesting features of the discussion was the lack of agreement among the speakers on such a fundamental actuarial concept.

In November 1959, Dennis N. Warters and William M. Rae presented a highly controversial paper, "The Risks in Equity Investment for Pension Funds" (*TSA* 11, 920). Among the authors' conclusions were these (p. 943):

> Even under so-called optimum conditions, [a pension fund] can involve liquidation of assets. Actual experience will fluctuate widely on both sides of any assumed averages. . . .

> The employer and the employees have conflicting interests particularly in regard to common stock investment. . . .

> A deeper analysis of the surface record of common stocks shows they do not meet the day-to-day living requirements of the pension fund without possible liquidation at unfavorable times.

Critics who discussed this paper made the following observations:

> [Frank L. Griffin, Jr., p. 946] The paper looks to me like an attempt to counter incomplete statements on one side of an issue with incomplete statements on the other.

> [Wilmer A. Jenkins, p. 951] I think it important . . . that it be stated that with minor exceptions a well-designed variable annuity fund does not lead to the operational problems mentioned by the authors. . . .

> I think we must agree that over a long period of past decades there have been substantial increases in both the level of consumer prices and the level of stock market values, and that we have no proof that these increases will not continue in the future, with intermissions, and perhaps accelerate.

> [Cyril J. Woods, p. 952] I must compliment the authors on their industry. . . .

> They have demonstrated conclusively a fact that, hitherto, was merely obvious—that in certain circumstances the outgo of a pension fund may exceed its income.

> [Geoffrey N. Calvert, p. 953] The authors of this paper have produced many figures and arguments, but have completely failed to establish a case against the use of common stocks in a pension fund. . . .

> For our own part, we are not impressed, and are hopeful that the actuarial profession will not regard this paper as providing a valid argument against the use of equities, within proper limits, in pension funds.

Five months earlier, Calvert had told a conference of municipal finance officers that 43% of corporate pension fund money had been invested in equities.

> [Fergus J. McDiarmid, p. 954] The possible need for liquidation of assets sometime in the future is one reason among many why pension funds should probably be invested in substantial part in fixed dollar investments with a reasonable staggering of maturities. However, I do not see how this in itself rules out the investing of another substantial part of these funds in equities.

Authors Warters and Rae in their response to all this pointed out that they had concerned themselves with (p. 970) "what to many, particularly at this time, is the unpopular side of the question. . . . Yet we would all agree that it is important that the actuary be in a position to point out both the popular and unpopular side of the question." Their closing observation was this (p. 974):

> Let us take to heart the lessons to be learned ... from John Law's experiments with credit in France between 1716 and 1720, from the history of our own Continental currency between 1775 and 1780, from the greenbacks of our Civil War, from the great German inflations which culminated in 1923 and 1948, and from the very recent inflation in France and other European countries. It would seem that the only answer is to have the courage to be guided by past experience and travel the hard road, not believing we have some new magic answer.

All in all, this paper (with its discussion) is one of many testaments to the virtue of having important questions explored in formal papers, responses to which can be the results of considered thought. The decline of such papers in modern times in favor of informal discussions seems to be one of our profession's moves in the wrong direction.

In 1962 the concern among actuaries about the urgent necessity for ensuring that sound actuarial advice will be given to employers and that the interests of the employees will not be treated as of secondary importance was coming to the forefront. In October 1962 (*TSA* 14, 586) the Society of Actuaries began acting upon a recommendation of its Committee on Professional Status that the actuarial bodies jointly attempt to establish some type of official accreditation in the field of private pension and other employee benefit plans. Professor McGill had just published for the Pension Research Council *Fulfilling Pension Expectations,* of which Allen L. Mayerson in his review said (*TSA* 14, 543):

> One statement of considerable interest to this Society is: "There is widespread agreement that some form of public control is needed with respect to those persons who guide the actuarial destiny of pension plans." Professor McGill explores licensing of actuaries, or certification of actuaries by a state or federal agency, as a solution, but prefers instead the accreditation of actuaries by "each governmental agency whose responsibilities include the collection and evaluation of actuarial data." He suggests that Internal Revenue Service, the Department of Labor, or the Department of Health, Education, and Welfare develop standards for the accreditation of actuaries and that these standards (though he does not say how this is to be accomplished) be accepted by all other federal and state agencies. This procedure would allow persons not accredited as actuaries to continue to practice as such in areas where such accreditation is not necessary.

Perhaps the airing of this question about who should be permitted to perform such consulting work was as much responsible as was the creation of the American Academy of Actuaries for the launching of the American Society of Pension Actuaries (ASPA) in Texas four years later (discussed in Chapter VI).

A recommended step in refinement of, as well as emphasis upon, one element in the determination of pension plan funding was proposed by William F. Marples in 1962 (*TSA* 14, 1) with his paper, "Salary Scales." Marples encouraged actuaries to improve techniques in the construction of salary scales as a means of allowing for the effects of inflation. Calvert, in the discussion, reminded readers that inflation affects the asset as well as the liability side of the pension fund balance sheet, the former at least partially offsetting the latter; hence, the need to give full recognition to inflation in salary scales was, in Calvert's view, not as pressing as Marples' analysis purported to show.

In October 1963 (*TSA* 15, D269) four authorities on the implications of these large questions in the United States (John K. Dyer, Jr., Dan M. McGill, Ray M. Peterson and Frank L. Griffin, Jr.) and a Canadian expert (Kenneth R. MacGregor) formed a panel to enlighten Society members on the "Security of Private Pension Expectations." Dyer, Peterson and Griffin were all members of the Society committee to study pension plan problems that had been given responsibility for pursuing the October 1962 accreditation recommendation. These panelists were convinced that prompt and substantial remedial action would be necessary if severe government regulation were to have any chance of being moderated. Peterson said (p. D280):

> In considering possible areas of improvement, the actuary engaged in pension work may well measure his performance by a set of standards . . . that I will call the "Seven C's of Competence" . . . [i.e.,] (1) complete client communication; (2) courage of convictions; (3) compatibility of cost components; (4) conscientious carrier comparisons; (5) candid cost comparisons; (6) collateral cost cautiousness; and (7) constructive citizenship.

Later in the session, Peterson described pejoratives that he had originally considered listing as the other side of the coin, under the title of the "seven sorry sins."

Griffin, discussing the role of the consulting actuary, emphasized the actuary's dual responsibility to employers and employees, and added (p. D285):

> An element of judgment on the part of both the employer and his actuary obviously is required. This is what makes the educational role of the actuary so important. Most consulting actuaries whom I know are doing a commendable job here as well as in the exercise of judgment and imagination. . . .

> It is apparent that I take strong issue with views on protecting pension expectations which suffer from the wearing of blinders against the larger picture. I feel it is time we gave as much attention to protecting the employer's continued operation expectations.

McGill identified several major threats to sound actuarial guidance: the lack of legal recognition of the actuarial profession, the absence of any formal means of enforcing actuarial responsibility, the intense competition among life insurance companies and banks for pension plan assets, and the limited role played by actuaries in the design of many plans.

In 1963 Charles L. Trowbridge published a sequel to his 1952 paper, his new title being "The Unfunded Present Value Family of Pension Funding Methods" (*TSA* 15, 151). He had succeeded in linking funding methods into a "family" by employing a parameter (k) which, he said "can be set at any point within a range [thus determining] just where the particular member of the family falls within [a general] classification." One of the many who discussed this paper, Dorrance C. Bronson (p. 181), called it an "elegant development of how to fund—not from the gamut of alpha to omega but, say from gamma to rho," and then directed attention to the new environment which "could narrow, or even pinpoint, the choice within the laissez faire of the Trowbridgean scale." The non-actuarial influences Bronson had in mind were a recently published IRS

Revenue Ruling (63-11) and the ideas being expressed by the accounting profession. Bronson warned also of the limitations threatened by disclosure legislation in states and in one Canadian province, and by federal law in the United States, the Welfare and Pension Plans Disclosure Act of 1958. This Act had led to formation of an Advisory Council, two of whose members, Charles A. Siegfried and Joseph Musher, described their experiences in a 1970 panel discussion (*TSA* 22, D504 and D514).

In October 1964 (*PCAPP* 14, 119) the Conference of Actuaries in Public Practice held a discussion forum, "Government Regulation of Private Pensions—Present and Future," the participants being John K. Dyer, Jr., John Ireland (a Canadian guest), Dan M. McGill, Frank L. Griffin, Jr., Meyer Melnikoff, and an official of an oil company. McGill, regrettably, gave his contribution off the record.

The literature of this era contains a number of references to individual policy pension trusts. Bronson, in his 1949 paper already cited, intimated that the trend was away from the use of individual policies in large corporate plans. That trend was in fact less pronounced than the best interests of the actuarial profession demanded. Too many of such plans continued in effect until they had grown to substantial size and the employers relying upon them were belatedly advised of their inefficiency by other employers or consultants. Group permanent contracts, described by Dennis N. Warters in 1947 (*T.A.S.A.* 48, 95) had most of the characteristics of individual policies but were relatively economical. A comparative analysis of the individual policy and group permanent products was given by J. Henry Smith in his discussion of Warter's paper (ibid., p. 297).

SOCIAL SECURITY

Discussions of social insurance in the 1949–1964 era were distinctly milder than in either the prior or following days. The Social Security Administration's Chief Actuary, Robert J. Myers, presented lucid explanations of Social Security Act amendments passed in every even-numbered year between 1950 and 1960, also in 1961; W. Rulon Williamson in 1960 described these changes as "depending on the Fabian principle of gradualism enunciated in Great Britain in the course of her descent from personal self-sufficiency into the welfare state" (*TSA* 12, 100).

The major dissertation was Ray M. Peterson's 1959 paper "Misconceptions and Missing Perceptions of Our Social Security System (Actuarial Anesthesia)" (*TSA* 11, 812). That author's stated purpose was to help actuaries make clear to the public the limitations of the figures furnished in reports by actuaries of the Social Security Administration and the United States Railroad Retirement Board. Said Peterson:

> Actuaries should be the first to warn that actuarial balance [of contributions and benefits], while a *necessary* condition, is not a *sufficient* condition. The work of the actuary must not become a soothing agent that unduly quiets a legitimate concern as to the truly successful operation of programs established by one generation which will have powerful effects upon future generations.

Peterson mentioned an interesting remark, by President Franklin D. Roosevelt, to explain why he had supported the contributory principle (p. 813):

We put those payroll contributions there so as to give the contributors a legal, moral, and political right to collect their pensions and their unemployment benefits. With those taxes in there, no damn politician can ever scrap my social security program.

Peterson proceeded, in his forty-page paper, to explore the social security financing method, alarming symptoms of trouble and growth, dangers in the political influences, widespread misunderstandings of how social security was intended to accomplish its purpose, the mystery of why benefits were made tax-exempt, and his reasons for believing that a study of greater breadth and depth than that of the recent Advisory Council on Social Security Financing was sorely needed.

In the same volume (*TSA* 11, 286) Peterson also reviewed the 1959 report of that Advisory Council, two members of which, Carl H. Fischer and Reinhard A. Hohaus, were Fellows of the Society of Actuaries.

The discussions of Peterson's paper took up more pages than even the paper itself, and the author then needed twenty-five pages to respond. The whole text makes instructive and fascinating reading, particularly in the light of subsequent events.

A companion paper on the Canadian situation by Laurence E. Coward, "Pension and Welfare Plans in Canada—History and Trends" (*TSA* 10, 174) and its discussion, are also historically valuable. In 1960 and 1961 (*TSA* 12 and 13), actuaries were beginning to worry also about state and national health coverage for the aged. Medicare lay a few years ahead.

INTERNATIONAL CONGRESSES

Five Congresses were held in the 1950s and early 1960s—one of them (1957) in North America.

The first postwar Congress convened in 1951 at Scheveningen, a city in the Netherlands on the North Sea. It seems to have been little noticed by actuaries on this side of the Atlantic, perhaps because they had become unaccustomed to these events since the Paris Congress of 1937. Nine papers by Canadian and United States authors were presented at that Congress.

The 1954 Congress in Madrid was rated a huge success, stimulating the North American delegates to propose that the next Congress be held on their continent. In Boston on October 19, 1954, the Society of Actuaries Board voted to join with the United States and Canadian officers of the Congress in extending an invitation to hold the Fifteenth Congress in New York City in October 1957. That invitation was accepted by the Europeans and confirmed soon afterwards.

Planning for the event, which seems to have been done by the Society of Actuaries without seeking participation by the other North American bodies, involved cancelling the customary three-day Society meeting scheduled for November 1957 and substituting a one-day affair on October 14, to be followed by the Congress on the next four days. The locale in New York City was the Commodore Hotel next to Grand Central Station.

The Society's Executive Committee supervised the operation and appointed a Congress Program Committee chaired by James T. Phillips. Electronic data processing was chosen as a major program topic, to be explored on the first half-day, followed by an Electronics Seminar during the last two days.

The estimated financial requirement was $80,000, most of which was subscribed by a few large life companies.

Among the notable events was the formation at that Congress of a new section of the International Actuarial Association for the promotion of mathematical research in non-life insurance. This was named ASTIN (Actuarial Studies in Non-Life Insurance).

Unfortunately, on the Friday before the Congress was to begin, Society President Malvin E. Davis suffered a heart attack. This placed unexpected responsibilities upon Walter Klem and Henry F. Rood, who shared the duties of presiding over business and social events.

On the Saturday after the Congress, the visiting actuaries and accompanying persons went to Washington, D.C. (where they were greeted by President Eisenhower), then to Niagara Falls and Toronto.

A session at the Society's April 1958 meeting (*TSA* 10, 63) was devoted to general discussion of what had been learned from the experience, one conclusion being that the Congress size was becoming so large as perhaps to require a future limit on attendance.

In June 1960, attendance at the Brussels Congress was even larger than that in New York, consisting of 1,100 actuaries, 10% of whom were from North America. This Congress is fully described by Benjamin T. Holmes (*TSA* 12, 738).

A description of the 1964 Congress, held in London and Edinburgh, is printed in *TSA* 16, 459. This Congress originated the system of National Reports on subjects selected in advance, which have proved to be gold mines of information on actuarial practices around the world. The subject of the 1964 National Reports was "The Development of the Actuarial Profession," that report for the United States being written by Walter Klem, and for Canada by Ernest W. Crowe, Benjamin T. Holmes and J. Edward Morrison.

PROFESSIONAL CONDUCT

The original Constitution of the Society of Actuaries contained a provision for expulsion or suspension of members quite similar to that which had apparently served the Actuarial Society satisfactorily for many years. But in 1954 a serious complaint against a Fellow revealed shortcomings in the Board's legal powers. Hence, in October 1954, a Committee on Professional Conduct headed by Wilmer A. Jenkins was appointed to explore the matter thoroughly. A report to the May 1957 Society meeting (*TSA* 9, 302), which was itself a revision of a version discussed at the Society's March 1957 meeting, described the nature of the problems uncovered and gave some ideas for constitutional amendments and a set of Guides to Professional Conduct.

Before that report emerged, two presidents—Walter Klem in 1955 and William M. Anderson in 1956—had devoted their addresses to that subject.

Klem described the rules of conduct and of practice in professions far back into history, not neglecting the Hippocratic Oath of the fifth century B.C. Klem gave five considerations (*TSA* 7, 333) tending to support the need for guidelines, even though recognizing that these could not by themselves suffice unless members were fully imbued with determination to protect the profession's repute. These five were (i) that other major professions have found them necessary; (ii) that the actuary's employer and client, and the public generally, are entitled to every safeguard available; (iii) that as our profession has grown, we have inevitably lost the benefits of what in the past had amounted to an apprenticeship system of training new actuaries; (iv) that the rapidly growing proportion of self-employed members has created difficulties not formerly encountered; and (v) that temptations to influence decisions in the interests of personal gain have been multiplied by the expansion in the employee benefit field.

President William M. Anderson (*TSA* 8, 243) pointed out the inapplicability, to a small profession whose members' activities run far across political boundaries, of a state or provincial system of licensing such as has worked satisfactorily for doctors and lawyers whose activities are generally conducted within a single jurisdiction.

In later discussion of these matters, a member, J. A. Greenwood (*TSA* 10, 707), drew attention to an 1856 letter by the eminent British actuary Augustus De Morgan, proposing that each person practicing as a doctor declare his qualifications in a published register, with the consequence, declared De Morgan, that:

> every man who practices would be obliged to tell the whole world what his claim is, and would run a great risk if he dared to tell his patient in private anything different from what he had told the whole world.

The 1957 report of the Jenkins committee mentioned that in its early discussion and in those at local clubs there was much doubt whether publication of guides was a good idea. The committee found itself unable to make a recommendation without first seeing what a set of guides would look like, and therefore had a subcommittee consisting of a consultant (Dorrance C. Bronson) and a company actuary (Henry F. Rood) prepare a first draft. The more the committee studied and revised these drafts, the more its members became convinced that a set of guides for the Society was necessary.

From the outset difficulties were recognized in writing guidelines that would apply to the obviously different circumstances and constraints of actuaries employed in insurance companies and those dealing directly with clients in consulting capacities.

The first edition of the Society of Actuaries Guides to Professional Conduct was approved by its Board of Governors in December 1957 and issued in pamphlet form in 1958. At an informal discussion of the need for clarifying or modifying them in October 1958 (*TSA* 10, 655), only two actuaries are recorded as having spoken. Both of these (G. Frank Waites and Geoffrey N. Calvert) were consultants, the group most affected.

The Casualty Actuarial Society and the Fraternal Actuarial Association in 1959, and the Conference of Actuaries in Public Practice a year later, adopted Guides to Professional Conduct similar in general approach to those of the Society of Actuaries.

One legal difficulty, which apparently had existed unnoticed for half a century, was that although the constitutions of the Society and its predecessor bodies had purported to confer on their governing bodies certain disciplinary powers, nowhere was there a statement that the purposes of these bodies included responsibility to promote high standards of professional conduct. This omission was remedied in 1957.

LEADERS IN INCOME TAX FORMULATION

The pioneer actuarial advisor to the United States government in life company income tax development was Edward E. Rhodes in the negotiations leading to the Revenue Act of 1921. His successor in this work was Alva J. McAndless, who produced the formula for use in the Revenue Act of 1942.

Prior to passage of the Revenue Act of 1959, the services of five actuaries, who became jocularly known as "the five wise men"—George H. Davis, Alfred N. Guertin, Richard C. Guest, Norman M. Hughes and Henry F. Rood—were loaned to the Treasury Department to advise and work on possible approaches. The resulting legislation included an allocation system called the Menge Formula after its inventor Walter O. Menge. Another actuary prominent in this work was Bruce E. Shepherd, actuary and later executive head of the Life Insurance Association of America. Rood described this work and its fruits in a 1962 paper, "Life Insurance Company Income-Tax Act of 1959 as Viewed in 1962" (*PCAPP* 12, 237).

The leading analysis of the consequences of the 1959 Act was John C. Fraser's "Mathematical Analysis of Phase 1 and Phase 2 of 'The Life Insurance Company Income Tax Act of 1959'" (*TSA* 14, 51). This paper became famous for its thorough coverage of the concept of marginality.

MORTALITY STUDIES

Two items of fresh research into old subjects were brought to actuaries' attention in the early 1950s.

In 1952 (*TSA* 4, 350), Wilmer A. Jenkins referred briefly to the destruction, by Arthur Pedoe in a prize-winning paper presented to the Institute of Actuaries Centenary Assembly of 1948 (*Proceedings*, Vol. II, 28), of the long-held theory that a decrease in mortality at the younger ages necessarily produces a corresponding increase at the older ages by reason of the survival of weaker lives. Pedoe's findings were discussed, generally with approval, by actuaries of other countries as recorded in the Assembly's Vol. I, 83. One of the speakers in that discussion was E. William Phillips, FIA, whose paper "A Basic Curve of Deaths" in 1954 (briefly noted in *TSA* 7, 175) won for him the Institute of Actuaries gold medal in 1964.

In November 1950 (*TSA* 2, 178), Society of Actuaries President Edmund M. McConney ventured a forecast about mortality of older people:

> The death rate at the older ages had shown practically no improvement in the last one hundred years. . . .
>
> We are now, however, on the threshold of great advances in the betterment of the death rates at the older ages.

Another expert observer, Mortimer Spiegelman, expressed compatible views in 1951 (*TSA* 3, 337). And that same volume summarizes experience at all ages of social security insured lives and primary beneficiaries ("Mortality Experience under the Old-Age and Survivors Insurance System" by Louis O. Shudde, *TSA* 3, 201).

TSA 2, Part 2 contains, beginning on page 76, a remarkable paper by Walter G. Bowerman, "Annuity Mortality," of which that author said in his reply to discussion (p. 423):

> What I did was in accordance with the modern scientific method of drawing a little circle and spending one's time within that circle.

One of that paper's many achievements was to record the changes over more than a century in the value of $\log_{10} c$ as defined by Gompertz in 1825. Its original value, .04, said Bowerman, had tended downward, as shown in Table V.5, in important North American tables as the years went by.

Table V.5

VALUES OF GOMPERTZ'S CONSTANT IN SELECTED MORTALITY TABLES

1868	American Experience	.046	1920	American Annuitants	.035
1881	Thirty American Offices	.041	1928	Combined Annuity	.035
1918	Canadian Men	.040	1938	Standard Annuity	.033
1918	American Men	.034			

That author's reply to discussion explored this matter further. Many years later William H. Wetterstrand (*TSA* 33, 159) pursued this more extensively with the aid of a computer program named GOMPQ. Interested readers will find a biography of Gompertz published in *JIA* 91, 203 (1965) marking the centenary of his death and a reprint of that extraordinary actuary's original paper in *JIA* 16, 329 (1872).

In 1951 (*TSA* 3, 664) the Board of Governors announced that a 1951 Impairment Study was in preparation—it was unveiled by Committee on Mortality Chairman Leigh Cruess in 1954 (*TSA* 6, 287)—and that Society of Actuaries' studies would henceforth be printed in special "Reports Numbers" of the *Transactions*. The devotion of individual members and their companies in disseminating valuable statistics was at its peak in that era, as may readily be seen from the length and diversity of the listings under "Mortality" in the indexes to the *Transactions* (*T.A.S.A.* and *TSA*).

The first modern actuarial discussion of relative mortality of smokers and non-smokers, moderated by William J. November and addressed by three medical authorities including Dr. E. Cuyler Hammond of the American Cancer Society, took place in October 1963 (*TSA* 16, D118). But, as pointed out by Sue Ann Collins in 1980 (*TSA* 32, 215), the earliest such study was made in the second decade of the twentieth century in the Phoenix Mutual Life. The attention of actuaries had been drawn to this subject in several book reviews—in 1952, *TSA* 4, 198; in 1957, *TSA* 9, 491; and in 1958, *TSA* 10, 804.

In 1959 (*TSA* 11, 987), in a panel moderated by Alton P. Morton, Edward A. Lew gave a full report of one of the most ambitious of the mortality studies of that time, the *1959 Build and Blood Pressure Study*. Among its major findings were that existing tables of average and optimum weights were obsolete, but that average blood pressures had not changed much from those recorded a quarter-century earlier. The measuring rod for this study was the Basic Table 1935–1954.

CERTIFICATION OF ACTUARIES

In October 1958 (*TSA* 10, 319), Society of Actuaries President Henry F. Rood told the members that the question of legal recognition of qualified actuaries had been brought into sharp focus by passage of the Federal Welfare and Pension Plans Disclosure Act, designed to prevent abuses in administering such plans. He categorized three possible forms of legislation that might give such recognition: (1) requirement of an actuarial certificate signed by a qualified actuary; (2) requirement of a certificate signed by a certified actuary; and (3) requirement of a license to practice actuarial science. After analyzing the prospects and pros and cons of each of these, Rood concluded with this suggestion (p. 327):

> [I]t will not be enough to secure legal recognition of qualified actuaries. The public must be educated to appreciate that a "Certified Actuary" has passed rigorous tests and is fully qualified, at least in the field for which he is certified.
>
> Other organized groups, such as the certified public accountants, have very effective public relations programs. They not only work at the national level but use every means to influence directly those individuals who are in a position to recommend their services.
>
> The Society should follow a similar practice. We must convince bankers, employers, Government agencies, and union leaders that they should seek actuarial advice from qualified actuaries only. We must be able to help them select those who are qualified.
>
> Also, when we have chosen the course of action that seems to have the most merit, we must forcefully push in all states for statutory recognition of qualified actuaries. This will require a legislative organization as well as a public relations program.

In that same year, Reinhard A. Hohaus was appointed the first chairman of the Society of Actuaries Committee to Investigate Possible Certification and Licensing of Actuaries. The original problem, to get attention from authorities to our small, fragmented and little understood profession, demanded and received full cooperation among the five actuarial bodies.

In November 1961 (*TSA* 13, D472), Hohaus chaired a panel discussion at which William Leslie, Jr., spoke for the Casualty Actuarial Society and Edward D. Brown, Jr., for both the Conference of Actuaries in Public Practice and the Fraternal Actuarial Association, all these bodies having committees working on the question. The Canadian Association of Actuaries was also exploring the matter but was not represented because the topic here was confined to United States problems. Hohaus described the development of the cooperative work as having started at a July 1960 meeting hosted by the president of the Casualty Actuarial Society at which advice was sought from legal authority James B. Donovan of New York. Hohaus said that Donovan (p. D473):

told us that if actuaries wished to seek the benefits and privileges of professional status, it must be coupled with a willingness to accept certain additional responsibilities and limitations which cut across the assignments of a number of committees, such as Professional Conduct, Membership Requirements, Possible Certification or Licensing of Actuaries, Public Relations, and Education and Examinations. He [Donovan] recommended that the task of coordinating all the activities in regard to matters of professional status be handled by a special committee for that purpose.

That 1961 panel, speaking under the title "The Actuarial Profession," gave valuable historical descriptions of the several bodies, and demonstrated the cooperative atmosphere that the circumstances had engendered. In that spirit a Joint Committee on Organization of the Actuarial Profession was organized in February 1963 under the chairmanship of Henry F. Rood, leading directly to the founding of the American Academy of Actuaries in the United States and the Canadian Institute of Actuaries in Canada two years later.

CHALLENGES TO TRADITIONAL ACTUARIAL PREROGATIVES

Pensions

In quick succession two practices that actuaries had long regarded as safely within the profession's bailiwick were challenged by powerful outside forces.

In September 1960 the Society of Actuaries Board had appointed a Committee on Pension Fund Accounting, one of whose main purposes was to work with representatives of the accounting profession (through that profession's Accounting Principles Board) in an effort to define boundaries of responsibility between actuaries and accountants in the matter of pension plan funding. Committee members included Preston C. Bassett, Howard H. Hennington, Ralph H. Maglathlin, Otto C. Richter (succeeded by Frederick P. Sloat), Charles L. Trowbridge, and Frank L. Griffin, Jr., Chairman. The committee's duties were largely educational and to keep watchful eyes on new developments; this assignment quickly brought its members into touch with the first of the two challenges, determining the amounts of annual contributions to corporate pension plans.

Bassett described the issue thus in 1964 (*TSA* 16, 321):

Many corporations take the position that the charge for pension expense is a minor item on the income and outgo statement, and thus simplicity should be overriding. Other corporations feel that management should have some flexibility to meet changing conditions by varying contributions—pension-plan charges—from one year to the next.

But, Bassett went on to explain, accountants exercising the audit function or depending upon the information in company financial statements considered that taking advantage of such flexibility had the effect of unreasonably distorting corporate financial statements. They did not share the view that the item was minor nor presumably did the Internal Revenue Service and the Securities and Exchange Commission.

By 1964 the scope of the Griffin Committee's work had been broadened to read:

> to explore, with the Conference of Actuaries in Public Practice and the American Institute of Certified Public Accountants, the possibility of acceptable and relatively uniform standards of accounting for pension costs.

At the same time the Society had a Committee to Study Pension Plan Problems chaired by John H. Miller, whose role was:

> to study problems resulting from the growing importance of pension funds to the public welfare with particular reference to (a) the role and responsibilities of actuaries in explaining and publicizing the actuarial principles and practices necessary to insure the sound operation of pension funds in the public interest, and (b) the obligation or responsibility of the Society in respect to these problems.

The discussion of Bassett's paper made clear that large differences of opinion among actuaries in pension work had not been resolved. Dorrance C. Bronson devoted his discussion to the continuing obstacle of diverse terminology, which he called "semantical confusion thrice confounded." Oddly, he made no reference to the glossary that he had set forth fifteen years earlier.

At the same Society meeting at which Bassett's paper was discussed, there was a panel discussion moderated by Robert G. Espie on "Relationship Between Actuaries and Certified Public Accountants" (*TSA* 16, D233). This was a large question that came within the orbit of the American Academy of Actuaries after that body had solved its own organizational problems.

Financial Statements

The second challenge to long-held actuarial beliefs and procedures was also mounted by the accounting profession, but supported by stock analysts and managements of some insurance companies. Espie, speaking at the 1964 panel, described the matter as having started at least as far back as 1957 and having as its first result an Exposure Draft in November 1960 of an "Audit Guide for Fire and Casualty Companies," which had proved so controversial that by 1964 it had still not been promulgated. Espie continued (ibid., p. D235):

> The next major move occurred in the fall of 1962, when the Accounting Principles Board announced to the membership of AICPA that henceforth industries subject to governmental regulatory authorities, including ... insurance companies ..., would nevertheless have to prepare their financial statements in accordance with generally accepted accounting principles and that CPA's would not be allowed to certify to them without taking exception for deviations from these ... principles. ... [I]nsurance companies objected, since they felt that ... their statements met the requirements of the laws under which they operated, and they had not been consulted as to the validity or relevancy of the so-called generally accepted accounting principles.

Since the accounting profession had the power to deny a clean audit report to companies failing to comply with its requirements, the actuaries had to conduct negotiations delicately, which they proceeded to do over a period of years through an Academy Committee on Relations with Accountants.

Before the accounting profession entered the scene, securities analysts had become increasingly interested in life insurance stocks as the market values rose sharply in the 1950s and 1960s, in some cases to values much higher than the actuaries of those companies professed to believe they were worth.

The analysts generally were content with rule-of-thumb adjustments to statutory valuations. One commonly used adjustment was the ten-to-one rule, by which the value of ordinary and industrial life insurance in force was taken to be worth ten times the current annual earnings displayed in the company's statutory exhibit by line of business. This may have come from a 1921 paper, "Value of Business Reinsured in Bulk," by Adolph A. Rydgren in which that author wrote (*T.A.S.A.* 22, 75):

> Opinions will vary regarding the number of years' profit that may be anticipated in the purchase price of reinsured business; but probably ... no company, that appreciates the speculative elements involved, would be disposed to anticipate profits for more than ten years.

In his discussion of Rydgren's paper, Joseph B. Maclean said (*T.A.S.A.* 22, 112):

> I confess that the processes described by the author remind me of an expression used by an eminent actuary in describing some tables based on composite material, and which he referred to as a "delicate mosaic." ... It is not clear that the discounting of profits for the entire duration of the policy should be considered as speculative, nor does any reason appear for adopting any specified term of years rather than the whole duration of the policy.

Maclean, reflecting the views of other actuaries, added:

> An alternative course for estimating a very considerable part of the whole profits is provided by a form of Gross Premium valuation.

Actuaries, at least in the early part of the post-World War II years, probably were too much inclined to take a hands-off attitude to the pseudo-scientific valuation systems that were in vogue.

FRATERNAL ACTUARIAL ASSOCIATION

As the Fraternal Actuarial Association approached its fiftieth anniversary, its members could legitimately congratulate themselves upon virtually completing the uphill task of bringing insurance activities of the fraternal societies to a condition of actuarial soundness and upon immensely improving the status of its members in the societies that employed them. Walter L. Rugland in 1963 (*Proceedings of the Fraternal Actuarial Association,* Vol. 35, 10) remarked:

> [T]he fact of the matter is that the actuary was until comparatively recent years a "persona-non-grata" in the fraternal field in America. ... [p. 12] Abb Landis ... and his actuarial contemporaries knew well what their duties and responsibilities were and were capable of performing them, but unfortunately too often their advice went unheeded. ...

Rugland then quoted Henry F. Scheig, FAA's 1962 president (p. 16):

> [T]he place of the actuary in a fraternal society is better accepted today. Fraternal management seeks actuarial advice rather than resisting it. Perhaps this results in less need for us to band together in a united effort.

Fraternal insurance had become increasingly similar to mutual life insurance. Hence FAA members began to find the other actuarial bodies providing current information and new ideas they needed.

Growth of the Association had practically ceased. Its Active Membership category (later to be renamed Fellowship), which stood at 66 in 1948, had reached but 75 by 1963, and only 14 of these held full-time positions in fraternal societies, the majority being consulting actuaries.

A search was on for a suitable definition of the expression "Active Member." For almost two decades the existing definition was irrelevant, since it required candidates to "take such examinations as shall be required by the Council" or "equivalent examinations conducted by another recognized actuarial organization," yet the FAA had no examination syllabus. In 1949 the Council adopted essentially an experience requirement, and in 1958 it began calling for ten years of substantial actuarial experience (at least five in the fraternal field), and either Associateship in the Society of Actuaries or Membership in the Conference of Actuaries in Public Practice.

In 1966 the category of Fellowship replaced that of Active Membership, the requirement being Fellowship in the Society of Actuaries or Casualty Actuarial Society.

From this it may be concluded that although there was useful work yet to be done, the Fraternal Actuarial Association had more fruitful days to look back upon than to contemplate.

SOCIETY OF ACTUARIES LIBRARY MOVED TO NEW YORK, 1963

In February 1963, the lead article of *Mentor,* the undergraduate newspaper of the College of Insurance in New York City read:

ACTUARY LIBRARY RECEIVED

February 26, 1963 marked two very important occasions for The College of Insurance. On this date, the 62nd birthday of the Insurance Society of New York was celebrated, and also, equally as important, a valuable collection of insurance books was received. This collection which was presented [*sic*] to the Insurance Society by the Society of Actuaries of Chicago, combined with the existing collection of the Casualty Actuarial Society, will become one of the most comprehensive sources for life and casualty actuarial material in the world.

The Society of Actuaries (of Chicago) has concluded that in the interest of efficiency and economy, it is desirable to house its library . . . at the College of Insurance, whose professional library staff will administer this in addition to its responsibilities with the Casualty Actuarial Society.

This action was communicated to the Society of Actuaries members by a change in the instructions for book borrowing in subsequent *Yearbooks* and may have been mentioned by the Treasurer in presenting his 1963 Financial Report, which showed a surplus increase of only $11.29. At the time the total salary expense was only $28,000, few books were being borrowed, and the economics appeared to speak for themselves.

All the same, the effects of this move were not entirely favorable. The College of Insurance fulfilled its part of the bargain until the arrangement was terminated in 1980, but books not published by the Society itself were not systematically added to the collection. In fact, the collection received the minimum of care until a professional librarian post was added to the Society staff in 1986.

END OF "LEGAL NOTES," 1964

For more than half a century, actuaries had looked to the "Legal Notes" section of the *Transactions* for authoritative information on important United States court decisions affecting their work. Introduction of this department had been approved in October 1909 for a trial period by the Actuarial Society's Council and, except for a hiatus between 1928 and 1935, had been the handiwork of Wendell M. Strong, a leading actuary who was also an LL.B. Strong was overtaken by his terminal illness in 1940, whereupon the Council gratefully accepted as his successor Buist M. Anderson, a member of the Alabama, Connecticut, and United States Supreme Court Bars, and Counsel of Connecticut General Life. The Society of Actuaries elected to continue "Legal Notes" until Mr. Anderson resigned in 1964, at which time a feature that had been of great educational value and interest to generations of actuaries and students was regretfully discontinued. The Board pointed out (*TSA* 16, 466) that this material was available in other publications, but it is doubtful that as a practical matter those other publications even remotely filled the void.

ELECTION PROCEDURES, SOCIETY OF ACTUARIES

Historian Victor E. Henningsen (*TSA* 21, 604–607) has placed on record the particulars of several important changes, generally necessitated by increased size, in the duties of officers and the procedures for electing them, in the Society of Actuaries. These included creation of the office of President-Elect and separating the posts of Secretary and Treasurer, both effective in 1960; introduction of the preferential ballot in 1963; and advance distribution of ballots in 1966. It was always considered desirable to achieve balance, geographically and by occupation, on the Board—so much so that the presiding officer during the several stages of the election frequently reminded the Fellows what was needed to accomplish a distribution consistent with that of the roster of Fellows.

In the predecessor bodies the annual meetings had always been held in the respective home cities (New York and Chicago), but the Society of Actuaries held them in various cities and resort areas. There were some who believed that the choice for President—after 1959, President-Elect—depended too much on the venue. At meetings held on Canadian soil in 1951, 1955 and 1965, Canadians were elected to head the Society, but this matter became moot when voting by mail was introduced in 1971.

COMPLETING THE CASUALTY ACTUARIAL SOCIETY'S
FIRST HALF-CENTURY

The ranking philosopher among casualty actuaries in the 1950s and 1960s was Dudley M. Pruitt of Philadelphia, president of the Casualty Actuarial Society in 1957–1958. Three of his papers give general views of that Society's goals and needs in those days.

"The Seat of Wisdom" (*PCAS* 45, Pt. 2, 11), Pruitt's presidential address in November 1958, dealt first with issues of professional conduct and accreditation:

> I detect two areas of current professional concern: the one a concern for professional status, standards of acceptance and accrediting, and what to do about incompetent competition; the other a concern for professional ethics, standards of conduct and behavior, and what to do about improper practices. . . .

> Perhaps both these concerns spring in part from a shortage of supply. As our industry has grown more complex the need for qualified actuaries has increased and, in the absence of effective inhibitions, the tendency can be to supply this demand with persons unqualified by training, temperament, or moral fiber. We have a special committee, headed by past president [Norton E.] Masterson, working on the matter of standards of professional conduct.

And then, by way of pointing out how members should broaden their professional scope into the underwriting as well as the ratemaking sphere, Pruitt concluded (p. 13):

> [The company actuary] can and should be the energetic engineer devising underwriting instruments. Webster defines "actuary" as "an expert who calculates insurance risks and premiums." It seems to me that we have concentrated on the calculation of the premium and forgotten our first duty of calculating the risk. . . . It is our duty to discover and display relationships, and it is in a clear and easy reading of these relationships that the underwriter may expect to substitute scientific assurance for hunch and hope. . . .

> Our fellow actuaries in life insurance have for years been practicing what I am preaching and are now being amply rewarded for it. . . .

> Finally, when we have solved all the pressing problems of the industry, when we have substituted measurements and quantitative relationships for hunch and hope, all the while keeping our conduct free and above reproach, we shall at last have no concern for status. Eight hundred and fifty insurance managements will discover their insatiable need for us.

Pruitt, in his November 1959 presidential address, "St. Vitus's Dance" (*PCAS* 46, Pt. 2, 149), began by describing the distress within the industry attributable to severe underwriting losses in automobile and homeowners' coverages, and went on to urge improvements in the guidance that actuaries might give (pp. 153–54):

> While insurance is certainly based on the principles of pooling, it has none of the elements of charity. . . . The mathematical science underlying the insurance business . . . is the science of finding mathematical measures of hazard, of determining the bounds of reasonable probability of an occurrence, including, to the extent practicable, a quantitative differentation of such circumstances as who, where, and when. . . .

Because we are so firmly committed to the regulation of rates rather than the supervision of their administration, we find ourselves taking an unrealistic and essentially Procrustian approach to rating philosophy. We imagine that all risks can be fitted into a limited number of specific classifications, subject to exact definition, and that by the mere fact of fitting risks to a definition which describes their tangible attributes we can make them homogeneous. . . .

But let us never make the basic mistake of considering the actuary a brake on competition. . . . With his analytic training, his interest in discovering relationships, and his familiarity with the substantive data of the business, he is uniquely placed for the exercise of creative imagination. He should be the source of new ideas and of new approaches to old ones. Such talents are much in demand in a free competitive system and the freer the system the greater should be the demand.

The last of Pruitt's trio, his greatest, "The First Fifty Years" (*PCAS* 51, 148) was the centerpiece of the Society's celebration of its golden anniversary in 1964. Although he denied that it qualified as a history, it constitutes an informed view of the events, obstacles and achievements of that tumultuous half-century. Its eight sections were these:

 I. *How We Began.* This was a capsule of the events that led to the organization meeting at the City Club of New York on November 7, 1914.

 II. *The Pioneers.* This memorialized the founder, Isaac M. Rubinow and ten other charter members who later became presidents and made outstanding contributions to the Society's work.

 III. *Social Insurance.* Here it is explained that social insurance was the organization's raison d'etre and therefore the major topic of the early days but soon moved into the background as the members faced day-to-day problems in the existing and new fields of insurance. It returned to the forefront as the United States Social Security Act came over the horizon and into the law. Special reference was made to Jarvis Farley's November 1942 paper, "An Approach to a Philosophy of Social Insurance" (*PCAS* 29, 29).

 IV. *Examinations, Admissions and Membership.* (These topics are covered in our Chapter VII, "Actuarial Education.")

 V. *Meetings and Proceedings.* Pruitt's description, contrasted with those of meetings of the larger actuarial bodies, shows clearly the benefits and handicaps of the smaller compared with the larger gatherings. Pruitt said that the business meetings were "uniformly dull," but this must have been in contrast with the entertainments given by talented members which evidently outshone those achievable in the societies whose members were not as well acquainted with each other.

 VI. *The Society's Professional Contributions.* Here attention is given to the development of credibility theory (covered in our Chapter XIII, "Thinking Statistically"). References are made also to Retrospective Rating and to Remarriage Table of 1933, and the Table of Mortality for Disabled Lives in 1946. These tables for many years provided the basis for death and disability benefit calculations in workmen's compensation.

VII. *Our Life Insurance Brethren.* The early relationships with the Casualty Actuarial Society on the parts of the predecessor bodies of the Society of Actuaries, and the Society of Actuaries itself were mixed in terms of cordiality and respect. "I think it fair," remarked Pruitt, "to say that the life Societies have in the past made it clear that, much as they liked us, they could not consider us professional equals." This attitude could be attributed to the less rigorous hurdles to qualification represented by the CAS examinations of bygone days. It was not until shared problems of gaining professional recognition forced the bodies to work toward a common goal that they came to know each other well and to find fraternization natural and constructive.

VIII. *What Is a Casualty Actuary?* As if difficulties with other breeds of actuary were not troublesome enough, there were suspicions and incompatibility between actuaries and underwriters, and between the actuaries in the fire insurance and those in other non-life lines. In 1950 the CAS constitution was amended to state that its field of endeavor was "insurance, other than life insurance," replacing earlier words "casualty and social insurance." Pruitt concluded (p. 179):

> We are quite proud of our profession, though we have suffered somewhat from the sense of inferiority imposed on us by our older brothers, the life actuaries. But we have insisted that qualities are demanded of us not required of life actuaries. In comparing the two, Francis Perryman [CAS president, 1938–1939] said [*PCAS* 25, 294] "Casualty business involves less technical and mathematical work and essentially deals more with what I term 'humanities' and quicker results are looked for."

The original separation of the various actuarial bodies in the United States paralleled to some extent the mandated separation of corporate powers. Life companies were not permitted to write property or casualty insurance, nor fire companies to write general liability or other lines. In companies called multiple-line, the walls separating those lines were high. Also, the interest element in life insurance and pension calculations and its resulting involvement with investment departments had limited parallel in the casualty and property fields until high interest rates and mushroom growth of litigation in liability claims entered the scene in the 1970s. These circumstances may well have contributed to, though they would never completely excuse, the respective groups of actuaries treating one another as foreigners.

In May 1958, Laurence H. Longley-Cook had shown an unsatisfactory state of affairs and yet an inviting opportunity for the future in his short paper, "The Employment of Property and Casualty Actuaries" (*PCAS* 45, 9):

> The 1958 Year Book of the Casualty Actuarial Society reveals that there are 186 Fellows ... but this figure gives a false impression of the number of qualified actuaries actually engaged in Property and Casualty insurance. ... [A]t the end of 1957, after excluding Fellows of the Society of Actuaries, those employed by life insurance companies and those retired, 6 [CAS] Fellows were in state employment, 23 were employed by rating and advisory bureaus and 78 by Fire and Casualty

insurance companies. A further 15 Fellows were consultants or were employed in industry, as investment counselors, and in other capacities. . . .

An additional statistic which may help in this cause [of recruiting young actuaries] is that, of the Fellows . . . employed by insurance companies, who have been qualified for at least 5 years, 45% have the rank of Vice President or equivalent.

Six months later (*PCAS* 45, 12), Dudley M. Pruitt supplemented Longley-Cook's analysis:

A little research of my own brings out the fact that only 41 associates are currently employed by Fire and Casualty companies, and, allowing for organizations employing more than one actuary, we have only 43 companies or groups employing fellows or associates of our Society. . . . [W]e have about 850 fire, marine, and casualty managements. Perhaps one hundred of these have felt the constraint either to employ a member of our Society or to call some nonmember their actuary, in spite of the fact that all a company needs to do to have an actuary is to call him one. Clearly most managements have failed to see what possible use an actuary could be to them.

THE PROFESSION IN MEXICO

The Mexican Institute of Actuaries, the first such body in that country, was organized by fourteen co-founders in July 1937. Nine of these fourteen were civil or agricultural engineers, one was a certified public accountant, and the remaining four were more closely in actuarial pursuits. All were Mexicans except Alfredo Wülf, a German who in 1927 had published the first Mexican mortality table, and Frederick A. Williams, an Englishman who after brief residences in Canada and the United States had gone to Mexico in 1908 as actuary, later president, of La Nacional.

Williams, whose obituary appears in *T.A.S.A.* 39, 184, had qualified by examination as a Fellow of the Actuarial Society of America in 1909; he was unanimously elected the first president of the Mexican Institute but died in April 1938.

In 1946, the Mexican Institute started formal training of actuaries at the Mexican National University. This continued even though the Institute itself ceased its existence for about a decade beginning in the early 1950s. An account of later developments in the profession in Mexico may be found on page 278 of this book.

The following additional facts are from Mexico's National Report to the 1964 International Congress of Actuaries (p. 201):

The actuary who practises his profession in Mexico requires authorisation from the Directorate of Professions of the Ministry of Education in our country. . . .

The profession of actuary has been taught for more than 10 years at the National Autonomous University of Mexico and, as a consequence, the number of actuaries and assistant actuaries practising in insurance companies and financial institutions has increased sufficiently to satisfy the present demand for their services. The actuaries of an earlier period [possibly a reference to F. A. Williams' influence] played an active part in the establishment [at the University] of the course of professional studies.

The duties and responsibilities of actuaries in life insurance operations include full responsibility for the execution or supervision of all necessary calculations for life insurance, as well as the study of markets and the commercial viability of insurance plans. . . .

At the end of last year we founded the Mexican Association of Life Insurance Actuaries [Asociación Mexicana de Actuarios del Seguro de Vida, A.C.], whose purpose, besides grouping together all actuaries specialising in life insurance, is to promote the study of and research into actuarial techniques on all levels, as well as the establishment of relations with other similar groups. . . .

Organs of the State also employ the services of actuaries, particularly the Institution of Social Security, the pension funds for civil servants and members of the armed forces.

The role of the actuary in the organisation of pension funds is as yet rather restricted, and the organisation of pension systems, particularly of the administration trust kind, has not thrived on account of the limitations to which that kind of investment is subject in our country. This is especially true of insurance companies, for present legislation allows only established trustees and banks to receive funds in trust.

OUR PROFESSION IN 1964

The fully qualified actuaries in North America according to the respective standards of the Society of Actuaries, Casualty Actuarial Society, Fraternal Actuarial Association and Conference of Actuaries in Public Practice (duplications not removed) had increased as shown in Table V.6.

There was about to be a new pair of measures of our profession's size in North America, viz., the aggregate memberships of the American Academy of Actuaries and the Canadian Institute of Actuaries, involving only minor duplication.

The burgeoning segment of the profession was that of consulting actuary. Walter Klem, in the National Report to the 1964 International Congress, reported 426 persons in the four organizations at the end of 1962 identified as consulting actuaries; a considerable additional number applied in 1965 for membership in the Academy. The total number of consulting actuaries, including Canadians, must have been at least 600.

Table V.6

NUMBERS OF SENIOR MEMBERS OF FOUR ACTUARIAL BODIES, 1948 AND 1964

	(1) End of 1948	(2) End of 1964	(3) (2) ÷ (1) as Percentage of (1)
Society of Actuaries (Fellows)	647*	1,377	212%
Casualty Actuarial Society (Fellows)	153	213	139
Fraternal Actuarial Association ("Active")	66	75	112
Conference of Actuaries in Public Practice (Members)	—	143	n.a.

*Predecessor bodies (duplications removed).

In the National Report for the United States to the 1984 International Congress, its author William A. Halvorson characterized the years 1950–1964 as "The Post-War Business Period," as contrasted with 1965–1979, which he called "The Governmental Period," and 1980–1984 as "The World Economy Period." Halvorson chose the label for 1950–1964 to portray it as an era of emphasis on private business growth. Businesses, he said, gradually threw off their conservative "we're headed for a new depression" ways. Personal and corporate savings and investment rates were high (by United States standards). The rapid growth of private pension plans caused strong demand for actuaries skilled in pension plan design, in insurance companies as well as in consulting firms. Halvorson mentioned also the "burst of new life insurance companies, formed by anyone with an idea and access to a market place." "It was," said Halvorson, "during this period of phenomenal growth in reliance on actuaries . . . that the sense of the professionalism and public responsibility of the actuary began to emerge."

This was also a time when actuaries looked for measures of life company prosperity in terms not only of safety to policyholders but also of value to investors in life company stock. A leading contributor to the solution of this problem was James C. H. Anderson, whose 1959 paper, "Gross Premium Calculations and Profit Measurement for Nonparticipating Insurance," won for him a Society of Actuaries Triennial Prize.

In these years the profession ceased to be compact. The days when actuaries could explore problems and opportunities in an atmosphere of considerable intimacy (if not always complete harmony) were rapidly fading.

In a Jubilee Lecture to the Institute of Actuaries in London in 1986, visiting speaker Mark Weinberg characterized the century from 1862 to 1962 in Great Britain as the Golden Age of traditional life assurance. Much the same could be said for this continent.

Andrew C. Webster, in his 1964 address as president of the Society of Actuaries, said (*TSA* 16, 213):

> Two years ago marked the bicentenary of the Equitable Life Assurance Society [in London]. Our profession was born with that Society, and I sometimes wonder if we have not inherited some of the defects as well as some of the advantages of the eighteenth century; if, in short, our actuarial outlook is as modern as we would like it to be. The eighteenth century was the age of reason, the age of enlightenment, and the age of the encyclopedists. Man was quite sure that there were answers to all questions. . . . Actuarial science sometimes has a certainty about its methods more apparent than real. Possibly the time has come to take a fresh look at actuarial concepts.

Those words have a prophetic ring about them as we turn to examine the next fifteen tumultuous years.

APPENDIX TO CHAPTER V

Papers by North American Actuaries
at the Thirteenth through Seventeenth International Congresses of Actuaries

THIRTEENTH CONGRESS 1951, SCHEVENINGEN, HOLLAND

Barnsley, R.C. (Canada) "Estimating surplus." XIII, Vol. I, p. 21.

Bronson, D.C. (U.S.) "Methods of financing voluntary schemes of old age and disability pensions in the United States." XIII, Vol. I, p. 545.

Campbell, G. C. and Cody, D. D. (U.S.) "Applications of mathematical statistics to life insurance in the United States." XIII, Vol. I, p. 645.

Hansen, S. (Canada) "Methods of financing social insurance." XIII, Vol. I, p. 268.

Hohaus, R. (U.S.) "Health insurance in the United States." XIII, Vol. III, p. 224.

Linton, M.A. (U.S.) "Reserve problems under federal old-age insurance in the United States." XIII, Vol. I, p. 563.

Myers, R.J. (U.S.) "Estimates of the reserves under the old-age insurance system in the United States." XIII, Vol. I, p. 576.

Shepherd, B.E. (U.S.) "Taxation of Life Insurance in the United States." XIII, Vol. III, p. 63.

Shepherd, C. O. (U.S.) "Interim financial statements of life insurance companies in the United States." XIII, Vol. I, p. 203.

FOURTEENTH CONGRESS 1954, MADRID

Beatty, J.G. (Canada) "Actuarial problems appertaining to reinsurance and especially to life reinsurance." XIV, Vol. II, p. 407.

Davis, M.E. (U.S.) "Financial stability of life insurance companies." XIV, Vol. II, p. 478.

Gundy, H. F. (Canada) "Conditions that must subsist for a risk to be assurable." XIV, Vol. I, p. 29.

Holmes, H. (Canada) "Securing the financial stability of a life insurance institution: A Canadian view." XIV, Vol. II, p. 95.

Longley-Cook, L. H. (U.S.) "Insurable hazards." XIV, Vol. I, p. 291.

Menge, W. O. (U.S.) "Notes on modified coinsurance." XIV, Vol. II, p. 744.

Murphy, R.D. (U.S.) "The problem of maintaining the stability of life insurance companies during war." XIV, Vol. II, p. 463.

Neumann, E. M. (U.S.) "Standards of insurability under group insurance contracts." XIV, Vol. I, p. 267.

Patterson, W. D. (Canada) "Actuarial instruction in different companies." XIV, Vol. II, p. 619.

Perryman, F. S. (U.S.) "Uninsurable property risks." XIV, Vol. I, p. 99.

Spoerl, C.A. (U.S.) "The education of American actuaries." XIV, Vol. II, p. 670.

FIFTEENTH CONGRESS 1957, NEW YORK-TORONTO

Alvord, M.H. (U.S.) "Insured pension plans in the United States and Canada." XV, Vol. I, p. 187.

Cueto, M.R. (U.S.) "Development and use of electronic data processing equipment." XV, Vol. I, p. 89.

Deas, R.G. (U.S.) "The science of approximations in actuarial computations." XV, Vol. II, p. 521.

Dyer, J.K. (U.S.) "Uninsured pension plans in the United States." XV, Vol. I, p. 240.

Finelli, J.J. (U.S.) "Application of electronic data processing equipment of office operations—A report by the electronics seminar committee." XV, Vol. III, p. 5.

Finelli, J.J. (U.S.) "A report on the electronic activities of a large life insurance company." XV, Vol. I, p. 11.

Fitzhugh, G.W. (U.S.) "Employee welfare funds." XV, Vol. I, p. 205.

Gray, J.R. (Canada) "Present practices in Canada in connection with life insurance on substandard risks." XV, Vol. II, p. 11.

Greville, T.N.E. and Stickell, Edward E. (U.S.) "Use of electronic data processing equipment by the U.S. Social Security Administration." XV, Vol. I, p. 110.

Jenkins, W.A. (U.S.) "The place of variable annuities in staff pension plans." XV, Vol. I, p. 251.

Lukacs, E. (U.S.) "On condensed select tables (A study of a simplified method for the graduation and for the use of select mortality tables)." XV, Vol. II, p. 533.

Morton, A.P. (U.S.) "Classification of risks for individual life insurance—Developments in underwriting practices for selecting risks for life insurance." XV, Vol. II, p. 25.

Murch, A.D. (U.S.) "Some observations on the application of large-scale electronic computers in the Prudential." XV, Vol. I, p. 34.

Myers, R.J. (U.S.) "Effect of differing fertility and mortality trends on costs of social insurance programs providing old-age benefits." XV, Vol. II, p. 455.

Peterson, R.M. (U.S.) "The regulation of private pension plans in the United States." XV, Vol. I, p. 218.

Pettengill, D.W. (U.S.) "Group life insurance—Current practice and techniques in the United States." XV, Vol. I, p. 289.

Ritchie, J.W. (Canada) "A Canadian company's approach to the use of electronic equipment for data processing." XV, Vol. I, p. 72.

Slater, R.E. (Canada) "Program of the John Hancock Mutual Insurance Company regarding electronic equipment." XV, Vol. I, p. 55.

Slezak, L.F. (U.S.) "Development and use of electronic data processing equipment—Impact on personnel." XV, Vol. I, p. 47.

Smith, J.H. (U.S.) "Group life insurance in the United States and Canada." XV, Vol. I, p. 274.

Watson, G.N. (Canada) "Group life insurance—Current practices and techniques in Canada." XV, Vol. I, p. 303.

Webster, A.C. (U.S.) "Classification of risks for individual life insurance—Developments in underwriting practices for selecting risks for life insurance." XV, Vol. II, p. 38.

Wells, E.H. (U.S.) "Group pension plans of modular construction for small businesses." XV, Vol. I, p. 308.

Whitbread, F.G. (U.S.) "Life insurance on substandard risks in the United States of America." XV, Vol. II, p. 49.

Wolfenden, H.H. (Canada) "On mortality comparisions and some extensions of the indirect method of standardizing death rates." XV, Vol. II, p. 472.

SIXTEENTH CONGRESS 1960, BRUSSELS

Bell, J.H. (Canada) "Mortality trends in Canada." XVI, Vol. II, p. 342.

Campbell, J.A. (Canada) "Additional benefits in life policies in Canada." XVI, Vol. I, p. 96.

Green, E.A. (U.S.) "Initial and experience rating of combined coverage group policies." XVI, Vol. I, p. 112.

Levinson, L. (U.S.) "Changes in American mortality 1901–1949–1951." XVI, Vol. II, p. 420.

Lew, E.A. (U.S.) "Build and blood pressure study 1959." XVI, Vol. II, p. 468.

Lew, E.A. (U.S.) "The trend of mortality in the United States." XVI, Vol. II, p. 444.

McGuinness, J.S. (U.S.) "Uses and limits of motor merit-rate plans." XVI, Vol. II, p. 85.

Martin, D.B. (Canada) "Automobile insurance rate-making in Canada." XVI, Vol. II, p. 37.

Matthews, A.N. (U.S.) "Recent developments in private passenger automobile rate-making in the United States." XVI, Vol. II, p. 102.

Myers, R.J. (U.S.) "Actuarial analysis of pension plans under inflationary conditions." XVI, Vol. I, p. 301.

Nesbitt, C.J. and Schuette, D. R. (U.S.) "Premium and reserve components in case of additional benefits for a particular cause of death." XVI, Vol. I, p. 126.

Phelps, J. (U.S.) " A study of mortality on reinsured lives in certain Latin American countries." XVI, Vol. II, p. 401.

Winter, B.A. (U.S.) "Claim cost experience of dependents covered by family and similiar policies." XVI, Vol. I, p. 141.

SEVENTEENTH CONGRESS 1964, LONDON-EDINBURGH

Anderson, W.M. (Canada) "Design for desirable old-age spending power in Canada." XVII, Vol. III, p. 29.

Blagden, H.E. (U.S.) "Developments in the field of group annuity contracts in the United States during the past twenty years." XVII, Vol. II, p. 410.

Bronson, D.C. (U.S.) "Twenty years in the life of a United States pension plan." XVII, Vol. II, p. 428.

Carlson, T.O. (U.S.) "Observations on casualty insurance rate-making theory in the United States." XVII, Vol. III, p. 541.

Coward, L.E. (Canada) "Developments in methods of pension provision during the past twenty years." XVII, Vol. II, p. 487.

Duncan, R.M. (U.S.) "Variable annuities and other equities funding of pensions by insurers in the United States 1952–1962." XVII, Vol. III, p. 121.

Elkin, J.M. (U.S.) "Multi-employer pension plans under collective bargaining." XVII, Vol. II, p. 539.

Ellis, D.M. (Canada) "The analysis, allocation and control of expenses in life business." XVII, Vol. II, p. 61.

Groth, A.A. (U.S.) "Adjustment of pensions for inflation under trust fund plans in the United States." XVII, Vol. III, p. 155.

Kahn, P.M. (U.S.) "The application of utility theory to group experience rating." XVII, Vol. III, p. 578.

Lipton, M.F. (U.S.) "Some developments in private pension plans in the United States 1942–1962." XVII, Vol. II, p. 616.

Marples, W.F. (U.S.) "Contribution systems for pension plans." XVII, Vol. II, p. 659.

Myers, R.J. (U.S.) "The effect of dynamic economic conditions on a static-provision national pension scheme." XVII, Vol. III, p. 328.

National Reports (Canada) "The development of the actuarial profession in Canada." XVII, Vol. I, p.77.

National Reports (U.S.) "The development of the actuarial profession in the United States." XVII, Vol. I, p.276.

Phelps, J. (U.S.) "Practical aspects on non-proportional life reinsurance." XVII, Vol. III, p. 615.

Richardson, C.F.B. (U.S.) "Analysis of expenses." XVII, Vol. II, p. 260.

Rood, H.F. (U.S.) "Expense allocation by line of business." XVII, Vol. II, p. 272.

Ross, K.H. (U.S.) "Pension plans of the various religious denominations." XVII, Vol. II, p. 727.

Stearns, J.L. (U.S.) "Individual policy pension trusts." XVII, Vol. II, p. 744.

Warren, D.B. (U.S.) "Financial projections for new life insurance companies." XVII, Vol. II, p. 308.

Winter, B.A. (U.S.) "Expense units for asset shares." XVII, Vol. II, p. 327.

Wood, M.J. (U.S.) "Budgeting and expense planning." XVII, Vol. II, p. 344.

Chapter VI.

1965–1979:
A NEW PROFESSIONAL
STRUCTURE

Where there is much desire to learn, there of necessity will be much arguing, much writing, many opinions; for opinion in good men is but knowledge in the making.

—John Milton (1644)

A JOURNALIST'S VIEW OF THE PROFESSION

A two-part article in *Fortune* magazine by writer T. A. Wise (issues of December 1965, p. 154, and January 1966, p. 164) examined our profession's craft and performance under the title, "Those Uncertain Actuaries."

The contents page (p. 2) for the first article gave this summing up:

> The function of the actuary is to deal with uncertainty—to reduce to mathematical terms the probability of the occurrence of an uncertain event.... Once concerned only with life-insurance rates, [actuaries] are today busy with atomic power, auto accidents, health plans, data processing, pensions, and even labor negotiations—and there are far too few of them....

> Not subject to any government licensing, actuaries include some incompetents and phonies in their ranks. But of the 3,000-odd people who call themselves actuaries, about three-fourths are members of the actuarial organizations, which promote professional standards.

The preamble to the first article read this way:

> Social security, pension plans, and even corporate profits now hang on the figuring of this small, exclusive profession, which has come a long way from mortality tables. If they're wrong, look out!

The text (p. 154) emphasized actuaries' remoteness, and yet their "new importance ... in an age of swirling uncertainties."

Wise's interviews had been with several actuaries whose names he gave, and with officers of corporations who had dealt with consulting actuaries in the design and funding of their pension plans. One of these apparently led him astray; on the subject of "incompetents and phonies," he alleged as follows (p. 156):

The roots of this curious situation lie in a decision made in the 1920's, when actuaries first began to think of themselves as a profession with special responsibilities to the public. Some of them who were organized in actuarial societies advanced the view that a form of government accreditation, based on qualifying examinations, would enhance their status with the public and their own employers, the insurance companies. Their employers, however, concluded that there was nothing in it for *them* except a new kind of government regulation, and so they quashed the idea.

Returning to reality, Mr. Wise went on:

Not very surprisingly, the continuing redefinition of the actuary's job has got the profession entangled with several others whose work it overlaps. The biggest fights, both about jobs and about working procedures, have been with the accountants.

The second article was devoted entirely to private pension plans beginning thus:

Perhaps the most arresting fact about the actuaries these days is that they don't really know how to do their jobs. Or to state the case a bit more precisely and less invidiously, they are beset by swelling uncertainties when they tackle what may be their most critical job. This job is determining the cost, present and future, of the pension benefits that corporations have been committing themselves to pay.

There followed some horror stories of wide differences between pension cost forecasts and eventual outcomes, or between cost projections for the same plan presented by different actuaries. John K. Dyer, responding in the letters column (p. 89) of the March 1966 issue, characterized the first article as presenting "a reasonably accurate and tolerably sympathetic picture of the actuary as a professional" but pointed out seriously inaccurate comparisons in the second article's analyses. The two articles probably gave North American business leaders a clear enough view of the profession to do more good than harm. No letter of commentary from any corporation officer was printed in *Fortune*'s later columns.

TWO NATIONAL ORGANIZATIONS ARE LAUNCHED

In April 1965, Henry Root Stern, Jr., New York Superintendent of Insurance, said (*TSA* 17, 74):

[A] man could set up as an actuary in the United States today with no more legal requirement than was demanded by Roman laws of 40 B.C.

This was the state of affairs that the five existing North American actuarial bodies, by joint action, undertook to rectify by sponsoring national organizations to represent qualified actuaries of all specialties in Canada and in the United States during that same year, 1965.

The task faced by our profession's leaders in both countries was twofold: first, to devise organizational structures that would have solid legal standing in the eyes of the governmental authorities and the public; second, to establish qualifications for memberships in those bodies that would give them the needed stature and yet would be as fair as possible to the groups of actuaries with differing educational and experience backgrounds. Doing this proved to be relatively straightforward in Canada but difficult in the United States.

In Canada, the Canadian Institute of Actuaries (CIA) came into being on March 18, 1965; in the United States the date of organization of the American Academy of Actuaries (AAA) was October 25, 1965.

Canadian actuaries enjoyed a major advantage; almost all practitioners in that country were qualified by examination in at least one of the examining bodies on this continent or in the United Kingdom. In June 1964, the objectives and the new body's initial membership qualifications, described in a report by J. E. Morrison (*TSA* 16, D8), had been formally approved by the voting membership of the Canadian Association of Actuaries. Among the key points were these:

- The new organization was to achieve legal status by application to Parliament for federal incorporation, with continuity with the prior body but provision for future changes, and with no change in the existing relationship of Canadian actuaries with the Society of Actuaries and the other bodies headquartered in the United States.

- And the new organization, through its bylaws, would initially grant Fellowship to Fellows of the Society, of the Casualty Actuarial Society, and of the Institute in London and the Faculty in Edinburgh, and also, to Associates possessing at least ten years of experience of a nature approved by the new organization's governing body. This last group was known to be small in numbers, and there was no intention to extend this privilege to future Associates.

Although immensely simpler than in the United States, classification of entrants into Canada's new national organization had its own element of complexity, which the Canadians solved tidily. Determined to avoid the confusion inevitable if there were to be a Member class within a membership composed of members, they started by steering away from the word *membership* to that of *corpus*.

The initial corpus of the Canadian Institute was then made to consist of four groups: (a) Members and Fellows, (b) Other Members, (c) Students, and (d) Correspondents. Class (a) actuaries were those possessed of Fellowship in any of the four North American or United Kingdom bodies, and also those at Associateship level who had at least ten years of acceptably responsible actuarial experience. Class (b) were actuaries at the Associateship levels in those bodies who were members of the Canadian Association of Actuaries but lacked the ten-year experience qualification; they were promised later promotion to the senior grade when their experience reached ten years if they then applied for it. Class (c) were students on their way to actuarial qualification by examination. Class (d) was a courtesy category for nonresidents of Canada who asked to be on the Canadian Institute mailing list and to have the privilege of attending occasional meetings.

As E. Sydney Jackson pointed out (*TSA* 16, 464), since the purpose was to facilitate accreditation, certification, and possibly licensing of actuaries, it was considered necessary that the Class (a) be in general limited to Canadian residents, the one exception being actuaries of other countries whose responsibilities currently required them to furnish actuarial advice in Canada or to sign actuarial certificates required by Canadian regulations.

Table VI.1 shows the Canadian Institute roster in November 1965 (when enrollment was almost complete) by place of residence, with totals in June 1987 for comparison.

Table VI.1

ROSTERS OF CANADIAN INSTITUTE OF ACTUARIES, NOVEMBER 1965 AND JUNE 1987

| | November 1965 | | | June 1987 |
| | Place of Residence | | | |
	Canada	Elsewhere	Total	Total
Fellows and Members	316	0	316	1,414
Other Members	147	42	189	16
Students	8	0	8	601
Correspondents	0	37	37	55
Total	**471**	**79**	**550**	**2,086**

No difficulty was experienced in achieving federal incorporation; the Canadian Institute of Actuaries—French name Institut Canadien des Actuaires—became successor to the informal Canadian Association of Actuaries. Carmen A. Naylor, CAA's 1964–1965 president, had the honor of finishing his year as CIA's first president. On June 3, 1965, he was succeeded by Richard Humphrys. E. Sydney Jackson became President-Elect; Cecil G. White, Secretary; Ian G. Michie, Treasurer; and John T. Birkenshaw, Editor.

At the first meeting on April 6, 1965, J. Gordon Beatty greeted the new Institute thus:

> Hail to the Canadian Institute of Actuaries! I am very pleased that we are now a corporate body as this should improve ... our whole actuarial status in Canada without detracting from our close relationship with the Society of Actuaries[.]... I would be loath to see Canadian actuaries lose the intimate personal contacts with our United States contemporaries which are so valuable from business standpoints.

> The new Institute will also help to clarify our image in Continental Europe where ... many actuaries become confused and tend to look on us as "Americans".... I have the highest regard for our neighbours to the south but I am proud to be a Canadian and prefer to be recognized as such....

The only difficulty seems to have been the search for a suitable motto. On June 9, 1966, the Motto Committee Chairman reported that 300 entries had been received, 292 of which were rejected by the Committee, and the other 8 by the Council. The objective was one readily translatable from English into French or vice versa, but this was proving so difficult that a Latin motto was sought. In February 1967 the $50 prize and an inscribed plaque were awarded to Lloyd G. Rollerson, and the motto "Nobis Cura Futuri," translatable as "Our Care Is for the Future" was adopted.

Rollerson later confessed that he had submitted "mihi cura futuri," which he had found in a book entitled *Latin Family Mottos* in a Toronto bookstore. The Motto

Committee easily persuaded him to change his entry to the plural. For some time afterwards he was receiving requests for assistance made on the assumption that he was something of a Latin scholar.

In October 1967, Society of Actuaries President Harold R. Lawson, who rightly claimed by reason of Canadian birth and employment in both countries to have special interest in the Society's international character, spoke of the Canadian Institute (*TSA* 19, 163) as:

> a new factor ...which, although not directed in any way at the international nature of the Society, indirectly affects and, possibly, threatens it. ...

> The threat to our internationality arises from the fact that the Canadian Institute could decide to set up its own examination system, with the result that future candidates for membership might lose interest in trying the examinations of the Society. This development would, of course, be accentuated if the Academy of Actuaries—a national organization—were to take over the examination system now administered by the Society and, in part, by the Casualty Actuarial Society. ...

> [In favor of] separate examinations in Canada it is argued that licensing or accreditation by federal and provincial authorities in Canada might be easier to obtain if the examining body is a Canadian one. ... The Canadian Institute must also be mindful of the needs of students whose mother tongue is French. Finally, it is argued that meetings of the Society are too large and often of limited value to Canadians in their pursuit of useful knowledge. ...

> The principal argument against the establishment of a separate education and examination system by the Canadian Institute of Actuaries is the amount of work involved. ...

> It is my understanding that few, if any, [Canadians] ... would like to see a completely separate education and examination system set up in Canada. There is some opinion that the early examinations of the Society, say, up to the Associateship level, serve the purpose adequately and that a Canadian counterpart to the later examinations should be provided in Canada. It is, in fact, possible that this degree of made-in-Canada separation might become necessary if the Canadian Institute should decide to seek the licensing of actuaries. On the other hand, many Canadians still feel that the Society examinations could be modified sufficiently—possibly by optional questions—to adapt them to the needs of Canadian students.

As it turned out, Lawson's premonition that Canadian members would tend to visit Society meetings less frequently did come to pass. The examination system has been satisfactorily fitted to Canadian needs by creation of C (Canadian), U (United States), and CU (all candidates) requirements in the final two Fellowship examinations.

In the United States, the events leading to the formation of the American Academy of Actuaries are picked up here from February 1963. That was the time described in Chapter V when the actuaries who were brought informally together in Chicago by Henry F. Rood went back to their respective organizations with a proposal, readily agreed upon, that a Joint Committee on Organization of the Actuarial Profession be put to work.

A detailed account of the decisions reached, the steps taken, and the work of actuaries who played leading roles, has been placed on record in a set of Historical Notes compiled by Walter L. Rugland in June 1986 and now in the Academy's archives. Two other accounts by participants exist, viz.:

1. Remarks by Henry F. Rood in October 1974 (*TSA* 26, D408). This is just a partial text; Rood's complete prepared script is on file at the Academy and Society of Actuaries offices.

2. An address by John H. Miller to the Canadian Institute of Actuaries in November 1976. This likewise has been filed at the above two offices.

Reinhard A. Hohaus attended that February 1963 gathering but by then had become the "former chairman" of the pivotal Committee to Investigate Possible Certification or Licensing of Actuaries that he had headed since 1958. Hohaus had given his swan-song as banquet speaker at the Conference of Actuaries in Public Practice in October 1962, "Professional Status of Actuaries." He pointed out that thirty-eight years earlier, at the first joint meeting of the Actuarial Society and American Institute in November 1924 (*R.A.I.A.* 13, 396), a question for discussion had been:

> Should any steps be taken to have the word "actuary" officially defined in state laws or otherwise?

Hohaus' forecast that evening was (*PCAPP* 12, 297):

> I wish I could be optimistic and state that a program of legal and public acceptance of professional status of actuaries in all areas could be developed and made effective in the next year or two. I regret to state that I am now convinced it will take some years . . . because some basic changes will probably be required in the way in which the actuarial profession is now organized.

At that time the concept of a separate actuarial organization in the United States (the Academy) had not surfaced. Perhaps something of the kind was in Hohaus' mind, but nothing came up even four months later at the informal gathering of February 1963. But by the time of the Society of Actuaries meeting in June 1963, a topic for informal discussion under the title "New Actuarial Association" was (*TSA* 15, D131):

> Should the Society join with other actuarial organizations on the North American continent to form a new actuarial association, membership in which will form the qualifications for a "certified actuary" for accreditation by the United States government and the governments of the various states?

In his 1976 address to the Canadian Institute, John Miller explained how, but was unspecific on when, the idea of the new actuarial body was first brought up for consideration:

> The necessity of encompassing all persons who were in fact practicing as actuaries and so regarded by their employers or clients appeared, for a time, to create an impasse, since it was considered highly unlikely that actuaries who had passed the rigorous examinations of the Society of Actuaries or of the Casualty

Society would agree to anything tantamount to a merger with organizations whose membership requirements stressed experience but did not include comparable examination requirements. At this point a member of the Hohaus Committee [Miller modestly refrained from saying that he was that member] suggested the concept of a new organization which would be neither subordinate to, nor would have any authority over, any other actuarial professional organization, but which would enroll all actuaries who had been accorded membership at a specified level in other organizations unless they opted to be excluded. In addition, persons who had been practicing as actuaries but who were not members of any organization, or who were below the specified minimum level of membership, could apply for enrollment under a grandfather clause, subject to satisfying an admissions committee as to their professional competence and experience.

Thus was born the blueprint for the American Academy of Actuaries. Lost in the mists of time is the identity of the person who suggested the word *Academy*. It is recalled that one of the assisting lawyers recommended that the name have a collegiate flavor.

Each of the actuarial bodies named one member to the Joint Committee, namely, Henry F. Rood (Society of Actuaries), Chairman; Laurence H. Longley-Cook (Casualty Actuarial Society); Frank E. Gerry (Conference of Actuaries in Public Practice); and Frank J. Gadient (Fraternal Actuarial Association). George M. Bryce was the indefatigable Secretary. To facilitate parallelism and coordination between the Canadian and United States efforts, E. Sydney Jackson participated on behalf of the Canadian Association of Actuaries. The Committee was ably assisted by two staff lawyers of Metropolitan Life, Richard S. Walsh and H. Powell Yates.

Both the main committee and its several specializing subcommittees proceeded energetically. The greatest sense of urgency was naturally among consulting actuaries because of expectation of federal regulation in the pension field. Company actuaries foresaw the Academy's usefulness in pursuing negotiations with the accounting profession on pension and insurance company financial statement questions. An important early step, suggested by Hohaus, was retention of a nationally renowned legal authority, James B. Donovan, as Committee Council.

The Committee's leaders went to great pains to keep all actuaries, whether or not they were members of the existing bodies, fully informed of plans and prospects. In February 1964 an explanatory message, the full text of which forms Appendix A of Rugland's "Historical Notes," was addressed "To the Actuaries in the United States"; telephone books in public libraries were combed for names, and accounts of the message were widely published in trade journals. The topic was placed on the programs of local clubs as well as of the sponsoring organizations. A revised version (Rugland's Appendix B) was sent "To All Actuaries" in May 1964.

The founders showed themselves keenly aware that the rights not only of members of the actuarial bodies but also of nonmembers who had competently served the life insurance companies and the public demanded consideration. Thought had been given to the possibility of providing for affiliate memberships in the Society of Actuaries, but New York State officials predicted emphatically that a licensing authority would not grant special privileges to a subdivision of a profession. The Society of Actuaries people understood that any attempt to pursue accreditation on their own would be ill-advised and probably fruitless.

Initial progress with efforts to have the new body incorporated by federal charter seemed promising. Rood, Donovan, Dorrance C. Bronson, and Robert J. Myers visited Senator Thomas J. Dodd of Connecticut, who agreed to introduce the Senate bill and suggested that Representative Emmanuel Celler of New York be approached to perform the corresponding House action. By August 1964 there was good news that the Senate bill had passed and that Congressman Hale Boggs of Louisiana (a cousin of consulting actuary William E. Groves, FCA) had introduced the House measure, which had been referred to the Judiciary Committee. Regrettably, that committee's chairman, Congressman Celler, showed little sympathy, insisting on hearings but setting no date for them. This forced consideration of a state as the place of incorporation; Illinois, home state of two of the actuarial bodies, was chosen, but attempts for a federal charter were not abandoned. Bills were again introduced in the 1965 Senate and House with about the same results as in 1964. As hopes dwindled, the Joint Committee took steps in the direction of Illinois incorporation, proceeding meanwhile to establish the Academy *pro tem* as an unincorporated entity.

At short notice the organization meeting of the (unincorporated) Academy convened on October 25, 1965, off United States soil—in Montreal where the Society of Actuaries happened to be meeting. Fifty-seven actuaries (selected so as to represent as many states as possible with experienced actuaries) had agreed to serve as incorporators; thirty-three of them attended. The slate of officers, offered by the Nominating Committee which the Joint Committee had appointed, was elected unanimously as follows:

President	Henry F. Rood, FSA
President-Elect	Thomas E. Murrin, FCAS
Vice-Presidents	Frank J. Gadient, FFAA
	Laurence H. Longley-Cook, FCAS, ASA
	John H. Miller, FSA, FCAS
	H. Raymond Strong, FCA
Secretary	George M. Bryce, FSA
Treasurer	Robert E. Bruce, FCA, FFAA

Eighteen Directors, six each for three-year, two-year, and one-year terms, were elected. The Board immediately met to establish several committees, but no administrative steps were taken; it was recognized that this body would soon be dissolved in favor of an incorporated association, which was done in Illinois in April 1966. Left in President Rood's hands was location of a temporary Academy office: he placed it in space made available in the Society of Actuaries office at 208 South LaSalle Street, Chicago, Illinois.

The first presidents of the American Academy of Actuaries and the Canadian Institute of Actuaries: (L) Henry F. Rood (R) Carman A. Naylor (Courtesy of London Life Insurance Co., London, Ontario)

The initial Academy membership comprised three groups, as follows:

First, Members Automatically Enrolled. All, except six actuaries who were not members of any of the founding bodies but who had key roles in establishing the Academy, were in the top ranks—Fellows or corresponding thereto—of the four bodies. Since two of the four bodies had no examination requirements for admission and even the Society of Actuaries and the Casualty Actuarial Society had a few Fellows other than by examination, this meant that some automatically enrolled Academy members had never passed actuarial examinations. This in effect was a grandfathering arrangement.

The actuaries in this first group, all United States residents, became the only ones shown as "Enrolled 1965" in Academy *Yearbooks*. Their number was 1,427, and they may be considered the charter members. A few of those eligible declined to be enrolled.

Second, Members Enrolled Without Examination Requirements. These were Fellows by examination not resident in the United States and Associates and others within or outside the United States whom the Admissions Committee determined should be accepted after they had submitted satisfactory evidence of experience in responsible actuarial work totalling at least five years for Fellows, seven years for Associates.

Third, Members by Examination. These were practicing actuaries who were not members of any of the founding bodies, although many had passed some of the early examinations of the Society of Actuaries or Casualty Actuarial Society. They had first to be nominated by two Academy members, to give satisfactory evidence of at least seven years of experience in responsible actuarial work, and to pass special examinations set by the Academy Admissions Committee.

The result of this enrollment work confirmed that indeed many had been performing actuarial work in the United States without formal qualifications. After all initial enrollment had been completed, it was found that about one-tenth of all Academy members were in this category.

The qualifying examination administered to candidates in this third group was not rigorous but was considered adequate to weed out applicants whose experience was in sales or routine administration rather than work requiring basic actuarial knowledge. The problem, which was satisfactorily solved, was to devise tests considered fair by both the Academy founders who had become actuaries by examination and those who had not.

When the Society of Actuaries acquired its first Executive Director in 1968, the Academy arranged, throughout the incumbencies of Charles Barry H. Watson and later his successor Gary N. See, to have them serve as part-time Executive Directors of the Academy. Expansion of the Academy's national work caused all this to be changed in January 1976 when Washington, D.C., became the major site of Academy operations under the direction of its first full-time Executive Director, Stephen G. Kellison, FSA, MAAA, formerly Professor of Actuarial Science at the University of Nebraska. The first full-time employee of the Academy, dating from 1970, was Madeline M. Madden, who served the Academy faithfully until her retirement in 1987.

A major part of the Academy's initial effort was to obtain recognition by means of legislation in at least some key states, a project originally spearheaded by Andrew C. Webster as chairman of the Academy's Committee on Accreditation. One of Webster's early reports, published in the June 1967 issue of *The Actuary,* confessed that:

> To date we have not been too successful, although we have in Indiana a statute providing for the certification of Actuaries. The legislation sought parallels that of the C.P.A.'s in that it is permissive legislation requiring certification for the public practice of actuarial science. This does not forbid others from practicing actuarial science for employers, but it would prevent the noncertified actuaries from signing certain reports.

Webster went on to describe the implications of state recognition or licensing applicable to any profession, i.e., that it gives the state the right to determine who shall and who shall not be certified and what standards are to be applied. He also mentioned the prospect at the federal level of giving a then proposed pension commission the right to accredit actuaries in that field. It was clear that there was a long way to go and that vigilance would be necessary to prevent actuarial science being undertaken by unqualified persons without excessively limiting freedom of action by those who were qualified.

All of this strenuous and eventually successful work by the Canadian Institute and the American Academy in their respective spheres occurred at a time of major transition in both economic affairs and public attitudes in North America. Inflation and prevailing interest rates were showing initial surges to unprecedented levels, and "consumerism" was becoming a force in both countries.

An important change in the Academy's membership requirements was announced in that body's newsletter of February 1979 as follows:

> Ratifying the belief that all practicing actuaries who are qualified by education, training, or experience *for the functions they are performing* [emphasis added] should be recognized by the Academy, the Membership . . . has voted approval of Bylaw amendments creating a single class of membership, and establishing a three year experience requirement. The basic premise of the Academy at its founding was that its membership designation (MAAA) should be the hallmark of a qualified actuary in the United States.

A category benefiting from this was that of Enrolled Actuary, authorized by federal law to provide actuarial services in the pension field. It had previously been admitted into a junior class called Affiliates.

CONFERENCE OF ACTUARIES IN PUBLIC PRACTICE

By 1965, the fifteenth anniversary of its existence, the Conference of Actuaries in Public Practice had firmly established its role within the profession—first and foremost, that of providing timely and expert information on current events and portents to its members through papers and panel presentations at its meetings. Its *Proceedings* gave verbatim coverage to the discussions, providing a valuable permanent record of actuarial thought in insurance, pension, social security, and other professional topics.

Allied with this was intense concern about professional ethics. A 1954 paper by Frank E. Gerry "Professional Ethics for Consulting Actuaries" (*PCAPP* 4, 60) reveals how early in Conference history this thorny question was brought to the attention of members who, by reason of never having been enrolled in an actuarial organization, had previously considered this on their own rather than in discussion with their peers. Gerry quoted from an October 1952 report of the Conference's Committee on Professional Ethics; pointed out that, without a meeting of minds on the wording of a code of conduct, it would not be feasible to enforce the rules already set forth in the bylaws; mentioned the earliest paper on this subject in this continent's actuarial literature, "Duties of an Actuary from a Practical Standpoint" by Joel G. Van Cise in May 1900 (*T.A.S.A.* 6, 272); and postulated several instances of dilemmas that members might already have faced personally or heard about. In his conclusion, Gerry said:

> Certainly it seems that a great deal of study should be given before any code of ethics is approved, and the wording should be of such a nature as not to cause harm to anyone conducting a legitimate consulting practice.

In May 1964, the Conference bylaws were amended so that Members were renamed Fellows. The junior grade without voting powers continued to be Associates. The Associate category embraced insurance company actuaries having major examination qualifications but lacking experience in consulting work.

The Conference leaders had given serious consideration to instituting their own examination system but had decided to continue relying on successful consulting experience with increasing consideration by the Admissions Committee of examination qualification in other bodies. By 1965 the complement of Fellows stood at 163, more than half of whom were members of other actuarial bodies that did have examination requirements.

At the October 1966 meeting (*PCAPP* 16, 423), a session entitled "Future of the Conference" moderated by Thomas P. Bowles, Jr., presented no fewer than twelve panelists in an exhaustive analysis of that organization's operations. Most of the time was devoted to describing developments between 1950 and 1965 and appraising current effectiveness measured against original aims, making the printed account a valuable permanent record of leadership thinking at that juncture. None of the speakers expressed disappointment with past accomplishments, except that one, John Hanson (p. 442), criticized past discussions having to do with the profession's growth as insufficient in depth, and another, Samuel N. Ain (p. 448), maintained that program subjects were set in concrete so many months ahead that matters that had arisen more recently were not discussed. The panelists looking into the future were well satisfied that the scope and services being provided needed only minor improvements.

The twenty-fifth anniversary of the Conference in 1975 was briefly recognized in a historical review by charter Member Donald F. Campbell (*PCAPP* 25, 446) in which he drew attention to the solid foundation laid by the first president, Harry S. Tressel, and other early presidents and Boards of Directors.

In 1978 the educational requirements for Fellowship were raised so as to require Fellowship in at least one of the examining actuarial bodies in North America or Britain, prompting the 1981 president, William A. Ferguson, to remark (*PCAPP* 31, 452) that this educational standard, along with the experience requirement, had made the total Fellowship requirements of the Conference "the most stringent of any of the actuarial organizations." Ferguson added:

> Some would say that the Conference is on the path to becoming an "elitist" organization. It is both timely and appropriate for the Conference to determine whether this direction is the best for the long-term interests of Conference members or whether the Conference should embrace all actuaries who are authorized by law to practice publicly—or to take some intermediate position.

The Conference membership in October 1979 totalled 648, composed of 395 Fellows, 156 Associates, and 97 Members. The Affiliate (company) membership category had been abandoned in favor of an open policy of permitting guests to attend and to participate in the meetings.

AMERICAN SOCIETY OF PENSION ACTUARIES

In 1966, one year after the Academy was organized, a new body named the American Society of Pension Actuaries (ASPA) came into being in Texas with membership throughout the United States. There was a surface similarity to the founding of the Conference one year after the Society of Actuaries had been formed; in each case the organizers consisted mainly of persons who were not members of existing bodies. But ASPA's founders had immediate concern about jeopardy to their livelihoods, largely in the field of individual policy pension trusts, stemming from foreseeable United States legislation specifying qualifications for giving actuarial advice on pension plans.

The central figure in ASPA's founding was Colonel Harry T. Eidson, who (quoted in ASPA's historical note in its newsletter in 1986) concluded that "no existing group adequately represented the interests of the pension practitioner and thus there was a need for a new organization to do so."

ASPA's purposes, as originally formulated, included bringing together persons with professional or vocational interests in the design and administration of pension and other employee benefit plans; providing opportunities for members to increase their knowledge and their performance capabilities in the pension field; engaging in research, discussion and exchange of information among members; and providing information on legislation affecting the profession.

Membership categories were framed so as to attract not just persons possessing qualifications as pension actuaries, but also those engaged in administration and sales rather than actuarial work in product design or advisory functions. For the purpose of distinguishing between actuaries and non-actuaries, the founders designed a single-question test that an applicant seeking to be designated as a Fellow (FSPA) was required to certify had been answered without help. The question was:

> Assuming mortality in accordance with the 1949 annuity table male, no terminations, no expense, and 4% interest; calculate the annual deposit necessary for a male 35, to provide $10,000 in the event of death before retirement at age 65, or $100 per month for life in the event of survival to age 65.

That problem's assumptions had been chosen to preclude the applicant's use of published commutation columns presumably placing Fellowship outside the grasp of applicants possessing no knowledge of elementary mathematics of life contingencies but requiring laborious arithmetic by those with such knowledge. ASPA's membership became composed heavily of persons in membership categories other than actuarial Fellows, many having no reason to aspire to be considered actuaries. This proved to be an obstacle to reaching accommodation with the Academy and Society of Actuaries because the name chosen by the new body made it appear to be composed mainly if not entirely of actuaries.

About five years after its formation, ASPA sought help from Dr. Lloyd A. Knowler, a professor and a holder of a degree in actuarial science at the University of Iowa. Professor Knowler, working with actuarially qualified ASPA leaders, developed an educational syllabus and examination system that made ASPA Fellowship professionally respectable for those who qualified after the system was in place. ASPA has been one of the sponsoring bodies for the Enrolled Actuary examinations since their inception in 1977.

CASUALTY ACTUARIAL SOCIETY

The 1965–1979 era in the Casualty Actuarial Society was marked by a surge in its membership. The numbers of Fellows and Associates both doubled. Such rapid expansion resulted in some growing pains but was beneficial organizationally as well as in meeting company and consulting needs in the property/liability field. It was of benefit also politically; in 1978 (*Academy Newsletter,* August 1978), Academy spokesman W. James MacGinnitie, FCAS, cited growth statistics in testifying to the NAIC that there were and would continue to be enough qualified actuaries in the country to take care of newly proposed reserve certification requirements.

The era also witnessed a surge in the range and complexity of questions with which actuaries are faced. One of these was in the field of automobile liability insurance. The *Proceedings* for 1966 (*PCAS* 53, 213) furnished a short historical sketch by Paul W. Simoneau of that coverage's development since the automobile's early days. In 1969, three CAS Fellows along with an FSA employed in a multiline company enlightened life actuaries on the status of proposals that the traditional tort liability be replaced by some system resembling workers' compensation. Allen L. Mayerson, FSA, FCAS, that session's chairman, said (*TSA* 21, D311):

> Ever since the invention of the automobile, the question of who should pay whom, and how much, in the aftermath of an accident causing bodily injury or property damage has been determined by the common law principles of tort liability. ...

> Proposals to replace tort liability, in whole or in part ... have been made at frequent intervals [but] ... [n]one really attracted much public attention until the publication, in 1965, of a book entitled *Basic Protection for the Traffic Victim,* by Professors Robert Keeton of Harvard and Jeffrey O'Connell of the University of Illinois.

Mayerson and panelists John W. Wieder, FCAS, Roy R. Anderson, FSA, and Herbert E. Wittick, FCAS, explained the range of proposals that the Keeton-O'Connell idea and earlier experiments in Canada had sparked, giving appraisals and some cost estimates. Wittick said (p. D324):

> In Canada ... we have gone a long way toward solving the problems of compensating the victims of automobile accidents as well as many of the other problems of automobile insurance.

This confident assessment came from experience with a Saskatchewan plan dating back to 1946, and with modern developments in Ontario and British Columbia. Wittick continued (p. D328):

> The feeling in Canada among not only insurers but also the general public and government officials is that the combination of basic accident benefits and tort liability for excess amounts is the proper way to compensate automobile accident victims.

But attitudes in the United States were quite different from this. In 1977, the federal Department of Transportation published a report (reviewed in the CAS newsletter *The Actuarial Review*, January 1978) outlining such conclusions as appeared to be warranted despite a severe shortage of useable data, from experience under no-fault insurance in the seven years 1971–1977 in the several states that had tried this approach. These conclusions were not sufficiently compelling to persuade many other states to approve the new system.

Another of the era's questions for casualty actuaries arose from a determination by the American Institute of Certified Public Accountants (AICPA) that loss (i.e., claim) reserve calculations, traditionally the arithmetical sum of values determined for the duration of the claim, should recognize the time value of money by being discounted at some reasonable interest rate. The actuarial profession accepted this as a change too logical to be worth opposing.

In 1969, the Casualty Actuarial Society became a not-for-profit incorporated body in Illinois. This did not affect the location of its office (New York City). In 1971 the Society adopted the president-elect system, and changed the name of its governing body from Council to Board of Directors.

In 1972, Frederick W. Kilbourne, FCAS, FSA, warned the life actuaries that the whole profession would do well to pay attention to the external events occurring in the domain of any one actuarial body (*TSA* 24, D857):

> There is a marked tendency among insurance people, and perhaps notably life actuaries, to view those working on the other side of the life/casualty rift as being part of an entirely separate industry.... This view ... is not shared by the man in the street. ... He sees us all as being in the same boat, and calls it "insurance." ...
>
> Now it may seem that no-fault automobile and workmen's compensation and medical malpractice are far removed from the familiar old health insurance.... If we will ... take a critical look at what we really have to sell—reasonable protection from medical expenses and lost earnings—we will see that [these coverages] are really health insurance in disguise. Each is merely a special form of named-peril medical expense and income replacement coverage.

Matthew Rodermund, in an article, "Casualty Actuaries Face New Challenges" (*Academy Newletter,* September 1974), summarized the new events confronting the property/liability actuary in five categories. Major emphasis was on no-fault alternatives, but noted also were the residual market (formerly called "assigned risk") problem, the rating classification problem, the catastrophe reserve problem, and NAIC tests of solvency and profitability. Rodermund concluded:

> Then, of course, there are the actuaries' usual problems: among others, establishing adequate, legal reserves in a period of high inflation and establishing rates for a variety of lines and coverages, that meet statutory considerations where they apply, that meet political considerations, that meet consumer and competitive considerations, and that also produce profits.

In the *Academy Newsletter* of July 1978, the body's Executive Director, Stephen G. Kellison, remarked that the contemplated NAIC requirement for a signed statement of actuarial opinion on casualty loss reserves, on which the NAIC had sought advice from several CAS members and others, loomed as a major new public responsibility for the actuary as a professional. The first need, he said, was for the profession to exert its influence in obtaining a suitable definition of the person (the "qualified loss reserve specialist") upon whose certification the NAIC planned to rely. The draft regulation had failed to reflect the special expertise of actuaries vis-à-vis accountants; its definition of a "qualified loss reserve specialist" was a member of the Academy, the Casualty

Actuarial Society or the AICPA, or a person who has otherwise demonstrated his or her competence in such matters to the insurance commissioner's satisfaction.

Two other proposed requirements unsatisfactory to the profession were (1) that the specialist be independent of the company whose reserves he was certifying, and (2) that the signer declare his opinion that the amounts of the reserves have "a probability of at least 90% of not being rendered inadequate" (by more than a percentage that the signer would be required to specify).

The Academy, in its capacity as testifier on behalf of the profession, gave sufficient reasons opposing these requirements to be successful in having the specialist phraseology redefined as (*Newsletter,* September 1979):

> a member in good standing of the American Academy of Actuaries who meets the qualification standards of the Academy for this type of statement, or ... a person with an appropriate period of responsible experience relating to loss reserve evaluation and who has successfully completed Part 7 of Casualty Actuarial Society's examinations.

After extended discussions, NAIC adoption of the regulation was postponed.

The rating classification problem on Rodermund's list was described by William S. Gillam, FCAS, in 1978 (*RSA* 4, 28), as it affects private passenger automobile insurance:

> Although much of the controversy involves the criteria used in formal classification systems, unfair discrimination has also been charged in connection with the underwriting and marketing phases of property and casualty insurance operations, including the use of residual market mechanisms. ...
>
> The principal classification criteria in connection with which [legal] restrictions have been considered are age, sex, and marital status—generally pronounced and considered, as if they were one word—and geographical criteria....
>
> [T]here has been considerable agitation over the last few years in a number of large cities ... for doing away with ... rating difference [by territory]. In several instances, the controversy arose because the insurers had subdivided the cities for rating purposes. It was charged that the primary purpose of such subdivision was to isolate certain racial and ethnic groups....
>
> Otherwise, the concern ... is largely a reflection of the affordability issue. Experience clearly shows higher loss costs ... in urban areas where residents are generally less able to afford the higher premiums.

Gillam concluded, after discussing the statistical justification, social acceptability, and practicality of classification systems (p. 32):

> If the insurance business hopes to make its view of competition work effectively, ... it must give more attention voluntarily to social, economic, and political factors. Otherwise we risk being forced to do so by regulatory decrees or through the legislative process.

On that same 1978 occasion, a joint Casualty Actuarial Society/Society of Actuaries meeting, Richard J. Decker of the Automobile Insurance Plans Service Office

(AIPSO) discussed availability and affordability of automobile liability insurance, saying (*RSA* 4, 311):

> Automobile insurance is made "available" in this country through two marketing devices, the competitive market and the shared market. ...
>
> The *"shared"* market consists of those consumers that apply to a company for insurance, which said company believes *cannot* be included in its book of business at its filed rate level. The business is shared in two ways. Applicants . . . are divided equitably among the companies (AIP), or the experience of this pool of consumers is equitably shared (JUA & RF).

Decker described the several mechanisms identified by these symbols, pointed out that in the 1970s automobile insurance had afflicted the companies with staggering losses (even though 95% of those insured were in the competitive and only 5% in the shared market) and emphasized the dangers inherent in increasing conflicts between cost pressures and social pressures.

EXPANSION OF RESEARCH

There was not a single entry under the primary label "Research" in the cumulative index to the first ten volumes (1949–1958) of the *Transactions* of the Society of Actuaries, and only one such entry in the succeeding ten-year index. In part this was semantic; intercompany studies were listed elsewhere. In Victor E. Henningsen's thorough documentation "Society of Actuaries—Its First Twenty Years" (*TSA* 21, 591) research was discussed in the context of the 1964 appointment of a Committee on Research and its cosponsoring with the Casualty Actuarial Society of "seminars on risk theory, operations research, and similar topics on new methods of statistical analysis." Henningsen commented (p. 599):

> This committee has also organized special sessions at Society meetings on such subjects as "Mortality Measurement and Risk Theory Aspects of Mortality" and "Claim Fluctuations." These single-topic, specialized meetings extend the influence of the Society beyond the interests of those of our own members for whom these particular areas have special appeal, thereby contributing to the advancement of actuarial science.

The prime mover in broadening research within the profession in those days was Edward A. Lew, the Committee's chairman during its first eight years. One of his enterprises with major consequences, achieved just as he became chairman, was organization of a panel discussion in October 1963, "Mortality of Smokers and Nonsmokers" (*TSA* 16, D118), at which American Cancer Society speaker Dr. E. Cuyler Hammond pointed out that as early as 1859 a French physician had reported in his opening remarks that all his patients with buccal cancer were smokers, and that in 1936 a connection between cigarette smoking and lung cancer had been noted.

In 1966 the Committee on Research, jointly with the Casualty Actuarial Society and several universities, inaugurated annual research conferences. At a discussion on actuarial research, Dale E. Lamps described in graphic terms the types of research favored by persons differing strongly in views on this controversial matter (*TSA* 25, D630):

> Practical men are most interested in research which I will call "Type A" research. In terms of the dimension of technique, this is characterized by a minimum of time and effort in developing new theories and techniques; in the practicality dimension, there must be a well-defined and practical goal; in the communicability dimension, the research will be tailored to the peculiarities of the company systems and the company way of doing business, thus minimizing communicability.
>
> The opposite . . . is what I will call "Type E" research. It is characterized by heavy emphasis on development of new techniques; it is not characterized by any strong emphasis on practical results that are clearly apparent; it is publishable and communicable, even though at times many of us may find it incomprehensible.

Consideration during the early 1970s of financing and operation of an autonomous research organization was materially affected by the coexistence in the actuarial bodies of "Type A" and "Type E" opinions as well as by hesitation within the successive Boards of Governors to countenance passing control of research projects into the hands of a separate organization.

Actuaries played leading roles in the production of a 164-page "Future Outlook Study," *With An Eye to Tomorrow,* published by the Institute of Life Insurance in 1967. John H. Miller was Project Director; three of the project's eight Task Group chairmen were Norman F. Buck, Edward A. Lew and James B. Ross.

In November 1970 the Society of Actuaries Board began exploration of a proposal for establishing its own Memorial Fund to receive monies contributed in memory of deceased members, such funds to be used for such educational and research purposes as the Board might from time to time decide. Almost concurrently, a Committee on Professional Development was at work under the chairmanship of Paul A. Campbell studying ways to increase involvement of younger members in Society affairs. One of its many recommendations was aimed at broadened research; exploration was entrusted to a committee chaired by Dwight K. Bartlett III. By 1974 this had blossomed into a Joint Committee (of all six actuarial bodies) seeking solutions to four problems:

1. How to establish a foundation or fund to which both corporations and individuals could make gifts,

2. How to ensure that the actuarial profession would maintain control of the foundation or fund,

3. Whether there should be separate foundations or funds for education and research, and

4. What scope should be given to such education and/or foundations or funds.

That committee, under Bartlett's chairmanship, made recommendations that were approved in principle by the Council of Presidents in June 1975. An Actuarial Education and Research Fund (AERF) was to be established "to stimulate, promote and coordinate actuarial research and the production of educational materials," under a Board of Directors composed of two appointees of each of the six bodies. In June 1976 the AERF emerged as a not-for-profit corporation under Illinois law. Its first officers were Dwight K. Bartlett III, FSA, Chairman; M. Stanley Hughey, FCAS, Secretary; and Steven H. Newman, FCAS, Treasurer.

One of the first AERF projects was in the casualty field under the initiative of Charles C. Hewitt, Jr., resulting many years later (1984) in publication of a monograph on Loss Distributions, written by two University of Iowa professors, Robert V. Hogg and Stuart A. Klugman assisted by Charles C. Hewitt and Gary Patrick of the Casualty Actuarial Society.

An early disappointment was AERF's failure, despite substantial effort, to obtain a contract to study public employee retirement systems for the United States Department of Labor.

In 1979–1980, a major study facilitated by AERF explored the feasibility of mandating universal coverage under Social Security for the participants of state and local public employee retirement systems. This was done for the Universal Coverage Study Group of the Department of Health and Human Services.

A suggestion in the late 1970s by Charles A. Siegfried for a monograph on actuarial aspects of Social Security became an AERF project culminating in the 1987 publication of *Actuarial Projections for the Old-Age Survivors and Disability Insurance Program of Social Security in the United States of America* by George H. Andrews and John A. Beekman.

AERF funds have come from several sources: memorial gifts, responses to solicitations of members of the actuarial bodies, and funding of individual projects by insurance companies, actuarial consulting firms and the sponsoring bodies themselves. Investment income and sales of AERF publications have also helped significantly. The balance of funds on hand at the end of 1979 was $45,813.

Since 1978, AERF has administered the David Garrick Halmstad prize for the best paper on actuarial research. These annual awards are listed in the *Yearbooks* of the Society of Actuaries.

Later the Fund began assisting individuals to prepare actuarial books, monographs, and papers through an Annual Grants Competition started in 1983.

Professor Cecil J. Nesbitt, FSA, University of Michigan, became the first AERF Executive Director in 1981.

A research project unique in the annals of the profession was unveiled in October 1975 by John C. Wooddy, Chairman of the Joint Committee on Theory of Risk. It was a working computer model named SOFASIM—acronym for Society of Actuaries Simulation Model. Wooddy described it thus (*RSA* 1, 971):

> SOFASIM was built to answer questions with regard to adverse deviation in future mortality, interest, lapse and expense of stock life insurance companies. ... [T]he overall view of a life insurance company which we *attempted* to embody in the model was that of individual insureds taking out policies, paying premiums, dying and requiring death claims to be paid, surrendering and receiving cash values, with accompanying payment of ... expenses, and

investment of company funds in bonds with specific coupon rates and
terms to maturity. ...The numbers of deaths and lapses are determined
by random numbers generated by the program. Random variation in the
numbers of new policies sold was included to give a little more realism in
the simulation.

During the years following its availability, the SOFASIM model was put to
substantial practical use by interested actuaries. Discussions of its use appear in
RSA 5, 183 (1979) and in Wooddy's monograph *Adverse Deviation,* Chapter 3
(1981).

In 1957 it had been generally recognized that the educational work of the
Society of Actuaries Committee on New Recording Means and Computing Devices
had put life insurance companies and some actuaries well into the vanguard in
making use of electronic equipment. But by 1979 (*RSA* 5, 171) Henry K. Knowlton
felt obliged to say:

> In the past 20 years the actuarial profession has regressed in the use of com-
> puters, relative to the state of the art of computers. We continue creating ex-
> pected value models rather than stochastic ones. We do not use econometric
> models to drive our actuarial models. We are in the business of financial projec-
> tions yet often we make these projections in an economic vacuum!

Society of Actuaries President Edward A. Lew in 1974 had said the following about
one aspect of research (*TSA* 26, 331):

> Recent events have given force to the statement that we are living in an age of
> discontinuity. There is relatively little in actuarial literature that speaks to the
> problem of discontinuities. The best we have done is to conduct studies aimed
> to identify a number of plausible futures with the aid of more elaborate models
> and bolder conceptions of input. This type of research has recently been carried
> on by the Joint Committee on the Theory of Risk of the Society of Actuaries
> and the Casualty Actuarial Society.

That Joint Committee had been announced by the Society of Actuaries Board
in November 1971. The *Reports Numbers* of the *Transactions* continued during this
era to provide experience studies of mortality and disability in individual insurance,
individual annuity, and corresponding group domains. There was, however, increasing difficulty in maintaining the breadth of company contributions of data to
these studies. This seems odd since computers were making such tasks less onerous
and perhaps less expensive; the root of the problem may simply have been that the
increasing size of the Society of Actuaries resulted in its members becoming less
acquainted with each other than in former times and consequently less devoted to
cooperative endeavors.

A cooperative endeavor that was completed with conspicuous success was the *1979
Build and Blood Pressure Study.* It revealed marked differences in experience and in
human characteristics from its predecessor of two decades earlier.

All research done in the period here reviewed was accomplished without staff help
from Society of Actuaries headquarters except that given personally by the Executive
Directors. The staff position of Director of Research did not exist before 1980.

NEWSLETTERS

Actuarial periodicals on this continent prior to 1980 sprang up in the following order:

1964	*The Actuarial Record*
1967	*The Actuary*
1971	*The Academy Newsletter* (later *The Actuarial Update*)
1972	*ARCH* (*Actuarial Research Clearing House*)
1974	*The Actuarial Review*
1974	*Disability Newsletter*
1976	*Enrolled Actuaries' Report*

Credit for being the first to propose an informal journal belongs to a now unknown individual who raised it at a Society of Actuaries Board of Governors meeting; a minute of the Board's April 1952 meeting records that the Board decided not to try to publish a regular periodical or magazine but authorized consideration of bulletins designed to give prompt information of newsworthy and informative reports of Society meetings. At the Board's November 1952 meeting even the special bulletins idea was dropped because the committee exploring the matter concluded, presumably from informal enquiries, that there was insufficient member interest. Oddly, this consideration and rejection seem not to have been reported to the general membership, but the decision itself was unsurprising, the total membership being less than 1,200.

The matter next came up in 1960 during informal discussion of "Society Meetings and Publications" (*TSA* 12, 382–84) when Joseph W. Moran proposed a monthly magazine to contain texts of papers as soon as these appeared in galleyproof, along with various notices to members, announcements of forthcoming actuarial club meetings, reporting of members' job changes, letters to the editor, and particulars of Society committee activities.

Whether or not Moran's idea came to the Board's attention, it stimulated one Fellow, Ralph E. Edwards, to launch a monthly publication, *The Actuarial Record,* starting in January 1964. Edwards produced, at a subscription price of $6.00 per year, a well received eight-page newsletter consisting half of job changes and short articles and half of chronological indexes of papers and discussions in recent volumes of the *Transactions.*

This successful venture prompted the Society Board to appoint in succession two committees chaired in turn by Floyd T. Beasley and Ernest J. Moorhead. The second committee received Board approval to launch a newsletter that would be provided gratis to members and by annual subscription to students and others, and recruited Andrew C. Webster as editor. This newsletter, originally six pages but soon expanded to eight, was named *The Actuary.* In its first issue, March 1967, Society President Harold R. Lawson expressed confidence that it would "come to be regarded in the years ahead as one of the great traditions of our Society," and added:

> In recommending publication ... Mr. Moorhead's committee said, "... [W]e believe that the best beginning, is a modest beginning, and that the appropriate compliment to the Editor is to give him as free a hand as possible to build upon a well but not too precisely planned foundation." The Board has given the Editor this free hand and I do not know any more than any other member what he has

in mind. My only hope is that some editorial philosophy will emerge which will give to *"The Actuary"* a significance that the mere conveyance of news items would not have.

From the outset the newsletter's masthead absolved the Society of responsibility for statements made or opinions expressed; successive Boards carefully protected the journal's independence. Editor Webster set an example for his successors not only by the standards he demanded of contributors and his own humor and linguistic skill but also by remaining at his post for more than eleven years during which the number of issues exceeded one hundred. An editorial by Robert B. Mitchell in the *National Underwriter* greeted *The Actuary* under the headline "A Lighter Touch in Actuarial Fare."

Edwards, who had been a valued member of the Moorhead Committee, bowed out graciously and with expressions of approval of the editorial plan. His own publication had shown its mettle through thirty-seven issues, copies of which are shelved at Society headquarters. The format designed by Editor Webster and his Associate Editors Mortimer Spiegelman and John B. Cumming served for twenty years, through the incumbencies of Webster (1967–1978), Moorhead (1979–Sept. 1984) and C. Lambert Trowbridge (Oct. 1984–June 1987).

Volume 1, No. 1 of the *Newsletter* of the American Academy of Actuaries made its appearance in November 1971 when Robert J. Myers was Academy (and also Society of Actuaries) president. It was much more of an official organ than was *The Actuary,* announcing actions taken by the Academy and developments within that body's purview. Starting as a quarterly, its masthead showed no editor's name until a year after launching. Its early editors were Ernest J. Moorhead (Nov. 1972–Sept. 1973), Charles A. Yardley (Dec. 1973–March 1976), Robert H. Hoskins (May 1976–Nov. 1978) and M. Stanley Hughey (Feb. 1979–Oct. 1981). During the editorship of Hughey's successor, Mary H. Adams, the journal's name became *The Actuarial Update.*

The *Actuarial Research Clearing House* (*ARCH*), not exactly a newsletter but having some such characteristics, was described in October 1973 by Russell M. Collins, Jr., thus (*TSA* 25, D641):

> In order to encourage new literature and research by actuaries, the Committee [on Research] inaugurated *ARCH,* an informal research publication, in 1972. Unlike most professional journals, *ARCH* has as its primary goal the speedy dissemination of current thinking and aids to research rather than the publication of thoroughly edited and polished papers. It is intended as a means for sharing among actuaries of current research, quickly and informally. It also acts as a clearinghouse for such things as items embodied in letters between researchers, useful computer programs, and translations of appropriate material from foreign languages. To avoid typesetting and printing costs, the format is a Xeroxed reproduction of individual items with a covering index for each issue and an editorial page. . . . *ARCH* is distributed on a nonperiodical basis at such times as sufficient material has been collected for publication. . . . The service is provided to subscribers at cost. . . .

Currently there are 287 subscribers to *ARCH*, 67 of whom reside outside the United States, and the number of subscribers is growing rapidly.

The Casualty Actuarial Society, when it launched its newsletter in 1974, chose as its name *The Actuarial Review*. Throughout its entire existence it has had one editor, Matthew Rodermund, who thus holds the record for tenure among all such actuarial publications on this continent. The initial issue, before the publication had even acquired its name, stated its aims in these words:

> This is the first issue of a new quarterly publication of the Casualty Actuarial Society . . . . A newsletter of this kind has long been in the minds of members of the Board of Directors, and Past Presidents LeRoy Simon and Charles Hewitt gave the idea a shove with their presidential newsletters. Now President Paul Liscord has moved actively to formalize the publication.

> The purpose is to provide better and quicker communication between the Board of Directors and the membership. In addition to the President's regular comments [it] will contain information on the activities of the Board and its committees: information about the Syllabus and the examinations; news of the actuarial organizations affiliated with the CAS; reviews of actuarial articles, reports and books that might otherwise escape the attention of the membership; and, not least important, letters from members or friends of the CAS—questions, complaints, comments about anything in the property/ liability actuarial world that anyone wants to write about. Letters . . . will be edited only to eliminate libelous material, personal references in bad taste, and the most outrageous syntax.

The Actuarial Review has adhered to these principles and achieved its purposes. Unlike *The Actuary,* it has always been distributed free to CAS students.

In December 1974, John H. Miller, FSA, FCAS, launched the *Disability Newsletter,* announced as to furnish "international coverage of current statistics and other information bearing on disability insurance and rehabilitation of the disabled." Editor Miller described its justification and role in these words:

> Between the great depression and the end of World War II the writing of long term disability insurance was all but abandoned. Subsequently most of the major life companies and some non-life companies entered or re-entered the business. Unfortunately few guideposts exist for the administrators charged with the conduct of this business. No experience on long term disability issued through individual policies has been published since 1952, and that relates to a more restrictive definition than is being offered today. In the hope of making a modest contribution toward the sound growth of a renascent disability business, this newsletter is being introduced.

Miller, an authority in this field, quickly established the corps of subscribers needed to make this enterprise successful, and has persuaded actuaries to contribute experience data available nowhere else. His essays have provided historical as well as current information, and he has never hesitated to criticize practices that he considered inappropriate or unsound. All in all, the *Disability Newsletter* has been educational and an influence for the good.

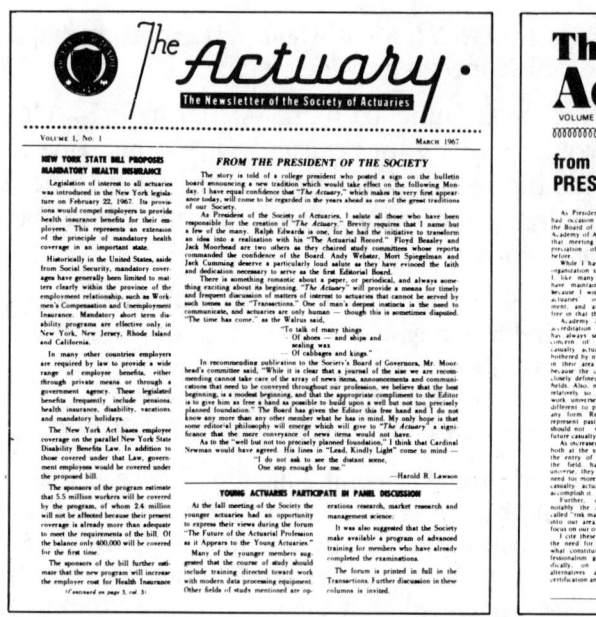

The first formal issues of the newsletters of the Society of Actuaries and the Casualty Actuarial Society.

The *Enrolled Actuaries' Report* (the apostrophe was soon dropped) was launched in July 1976, first as a supplementary insert in the *Academy Newsletter* under the care of Associate Editor Harold J. Brownlee, to specialize in meeting the informational needs of the newly created breed under United States federal legislation, Enrolled Actuaries. In January 1977 Charles E. Farr became its editor; it became a separate publication the following month. Daniel M. Arnold succeeded to the editorship in December 1979. The *Report* has been distributed gratis to all Academy members.

These seven periodicals have been immensely helpful. Important articles have been disseminated, needed information has been circulated promptly, and contributing actuaries have been shown to possess fine senses of humor. Issues have been debated; philosophies have been formulated.

But one problem remains unsolved, even though recognized when the era of newsletters began. In 1966 Rea B. Hayes put the question thus (*TSA* 18, D24):

> Have you ever had the experience of trying to look up a talk or a pet subject or of checking to see whether a possible topic for a paper or an actuarial note has ever been done? We need some kind of central service of this kind. As a suggestion, the Society with a larger staff could be of service here. It perhaps needs the co-operation of an actuary and a librarian. To index available literature [is] too much for one man or even one company.

John K. Dyer, Jr., responded by proposing that anything like a cumulative index of actuarial writings be international in scope. Two decades after the first issue of the first actuarial newsletter came off the press we need to be aware that immense storehouses of actuarial knowledge and opinion are lost to practical use unless the powers of the computer are harnessed to make the essence of them retrievable. The same difficulty applies to the Society of Actuaries *Record* started in 1975. It has excellent annual indexes but suffers severely from lack of cumulative indexes.

THE SOCIETY OF ACTUARIES PEERS INTO ITS FUTURE

In 1966, the Society of Actuaries Board of Governors appointed a Committee on the Future Course of the Society chaired by Walter Klem. This was announced as the fourth, and the one with broadest mandate, in the Society's seventeen years. The prior trio had been Committees on Organization and Procedure in 1952, 1956 and 1962.

The Klem Committee Report was issued in two parts. The first, (*TSA* 18, 332) concentrated on the issue of public expression of professional opinion. The remainder, delivered to the Board in October 1967 and considered at length in December 1967, was never printed in the *Transactions* nor discussed at a Society meeting. President Morton D. Miller devoted most of his October 1968 Address (*TSA* 20, 309) to explaining its recommendations and what was being done about them. The report did have major influence on the direction taken by the Society of Actuaries in the years immediately ahead.

Of the report's seven main topics other than the public expression matter, the largest was that of education both before and after Fellowship, described in this book's chapter on "Actuarial Education." The other six were as follows:

1. **Relationships with the other actuarial bodies.** The major question was how soon the two-year-old American Academy of Actuaries would be taking over governmental relations activities then in the hands of the four existing organizations. The committee correctly predicted that changeover would require considerable time.

2. **Consequences of membership growth and member specialization.** The committee foresaw that meeting formats and locations would have to be changed to accommodate the rapidly growing and diversifying membership. It concluded that election procedures might well continue unchanged, a verdict that was not shared by the membership a few years later.

3. **Desirable changes in the Society's internal structure.** The committee's recommendation on this topic and its important consequences related to the responsibilities in and leadership of the Society's headquarters staff are described in Chapter XI, "Administration and Finance." The proposals and subsequent action were in recognition that the days when many Fellows could be counted upon to give large amounts of their time to Society work were coming to a close.

4. **Need for additional income.** The report showed that the annual expenditure per member had increased from $35 in 1964 to $39 in 1967 (the maximum dues being $40), and offered various ideas for raising more income in the years ahead.

5. **Sharing costs of mortality and morbidity reports.** Noting that consulting actuarial firms were becoming a much larger element in both number and size, the report suggested that they be asked to take care of part of the expenses of compiling and

printing experience studies for the *Reports Numbers* of the *Transactions*, which until then were borne by insurance companies.

6. **Relations with the ALIMDA.** The report explored, at the Board's specific request, the particulars of the cooperative arrangements with the medical directors that had been working with essential smoothness for many years, and continued to do so afterwards.

PUBLIC EXPRESSION OF PROFESSIONAL OPINION

The Society of Actuaries and its predecessor bodies had lived with apparent comfort for three-quarters of a century with a constitutional ban, not against expressions of opinion, but against "resolutions expressive of opinion."

The sole purpose of this prohibition in 1889 had been to forestall the possibility that divergent views on controversial questions might tear the young Society apart. That provision seems never to have inhibited officers or committees from expressing views on behalf of themselves or the members. As examples, in 1917 (a report on New York City pension plans), in 1919 (merits of preliminary term valuation methods), and in 1927 (revision of the New York expense limitation statute) all were expressions of professional opinion; none, however, was put to a floor vote.

In 1964, Andrew C. Webster said in his presidential address (*TSA* 16, 216):

> The members of the Society may, because of their affiliations, find themselves in difficult positions, but, recognizing that we owe an obligation to our employers and to our clients, is it not possible for us to speak as members of a profession? . . . I think that a solution must be found. Perhaps too long we have hesitated to speak as actuaries on social welfare and on other subjects. . . . If we continue our silence about matters within our knowledge and our skill, some other, and possibly less capable, group is going to make itself heard. . . . I am not asking for resolutions or opinions. I am asking for facts, for critical analysis of matters financially affecting the welfare of our nations.

In 1966 at the Board's request, the Committee on the Future Course of the Society took up this question ahead of all others on their agenda. In November 1966 (*TSA* 18, 361) it was announced that the Board had approved that committee's recommendation that the Constitution be amended "to reflect current needs of the Society." The issue was whether, and to what extent, the Society, its Board of Governors or any committee should take a position on a public question relevant to our profession. After Committee Chairman Walter Klem had explained the proposal (*TSA* 18, 332), the resulting general discussion (ibid., D691) showed a wide range of member opinion.

Subsequent difficulties in reaching consensus might have been alleviated if, at that point, the portion of the proposal relating to the Society as a whole expressing an opinion had been quietly dropped. Such a provision has never been used; all opinions emanating from the Society of Actuaries have been on behalf of the Board or of a committee speaking with Board authorization.

After thorough discussions at two 1967 spring meetings (*TSA* 19, D176 and D291), an amendment that would permit public expression under controlled conditions was voted upon at the 1967 Annual Meeting. Affirmative votes were cast by a majority of those voting, but not quite by the two-thirds required for adoption.

In June 1970 the Board authorized President Ernest J. Moorhead to address a letter to all Fellows seeking a preliminary response to a new proposed amendment, which if adopted, would be operative only until the end of 1974, after which it would have to be dropped or put to a fresh vote. The wording had been revised to require that adequate reference be made in any release to the differing opinion of any substantial minority.

Responses came in from 67.4% of all Fellows. Those who favored presenting the amendment for vote by Fellows at the 1970 annual meeting totalled 86.2% of those replying (58.1% of all Fellows). At the annual meeting itself, 485 Fellows voted, of whom 390, a comfortable majority, expressed themselves in favor.

In 1974, when the time arrived for deciding whether to make the temporary measure permanent, voting by mail had become the accepted practice. Of the Fellows who responded to a mailed ballot on this issue, 91.7% favored adoption of the permanent Article X of the Constitution (*TSA* 26, 674). By that time the American Academy of Actuaries was assuming major responsibility for public statements by actuaries in the United States, and likewise the Canadian Institute in Canada. The temporary provision had been availed of three times in the 1970–1974 period—in 1971 (*TSA* 23, 680) for opinions expressed by the Joint Actuarial Committee on Financial Reporting, and twice in 1974 (*TSA* 26, 676) for reports of the Special Committee on Cost Comparison Methods and Related Issues on the matters of dividend illustrations and cost comparison methods.

Meanwhile, the Casualty Actuarial Society Fellows quietly adopted a public expression amendment of the same general tenor as that of the Society of Actuaries. Such an opinion for the CAS as a whole required "advance approval by an affirmative vote of at least ninety percent of the Fellows who vote in a mail ballot."

In 1978, the matter of public expression came up in a most unhappy context. As reported to the readers of the December 1977 issue of *The Actuary,* the Society of Actuaries and the Academy submitted a joint brief *amici curiae* to the United States Supreme Court in the *Manhart* case, a dispute about sex discrimination in a California municipal pension plan. The May 1978 and subsequent issues of *The Actuary* give details and views about the objections raised by seven Society members, partly to the contents of that brief and partly to its submission at all without the Society Board having followed the procedures constitutionally required. The Board's original view was that the brief would not be judged an expression of opinion; it had been neutral in the sense that it did not urge the court to rule either for or against the plaintiff. But Donald S. Grubbs, chairman of the drafting task force, commented (*The Actuary,* May 1978, p. 8):

> It was certainly my intention as coordinator of the task force, and I believe the intention of the task force as a whole, to present information which would give the court more understanding of the subject under consideration, but not to provide opinions. I personally believe the brief generally met that objective, and I do not agree that the brief is 'largely' actuarial opinion.
>
> Upon review, however, I can see some instances of opinion in the brief. I personally apologize for those instances. I would say that the time pressure to

produce the brief ... did not give us the opportunity to review it as carefully as any of us would have preferred.

Distressing though it was, this incident was useful in showing the hazards of error to be guarded against in making public pronouncements while Article X of the constitution remains in the form approved in 1974.

The opportunities and the demands for actuarial opinions to be expressed, and the complexities of arriving at an acceptable procedure for doing so, were set forth at the Academy's annual meeting in October 1978 (*JAAA* 4, 57).

BIRTHDAY CELEBRATIONS

In 1969 the Society of Actuaries celebrated its twentieth anniversary, and followed this in 1974 with an even more ambitious observance of completion of its first quarter-century.

The 1969 ceremony consisted of two elements. The first was a paper, "Society of Actuaries—Its First Twenty Years," written at the Program Committee's invitation by Victor E. Henningsen. Just as in the case of Reinhard A. Hohaus' similarly important "The Origin of the Society of Actuaries" twenty years earlier, no provision was made to have Henningsen's paper discussed by members—a regrettable omission. The balance of the observance was a panel presentation, "Past Is Prologue" (*TSA* 21, D551) moderated by Thomas P. Bowles, Jr., in which Henningsen and Hohaus looked at the heritage and H. Douglas Lee, Charles Barry H. Watson and Walter S. Rugland considered the outlook. The banquet address by the Society's first president, Edmund M. McConney is printed in *The Actuary*, January 1970.

Anniversary features at the 1974 New Orleans meeting were Guests, Gifts, A Book, Two Invited Papers, and Two Panel Presentations. (All references that follow are to *TSA* 26.)

The names of the many distinguished guests from overseas and from this continent are given on pages D395–96. The welcome gifts from thirteen bodies of actuaries are catalogued on D396. The commissioned book by Robert B. Mitchell, *From Actuarius to Actuary: The Growth of a Dynamic Profession in Canada and the United States*, is reviewed on page 641 and discussed by its author on page D405. The two papers exploring the profession's future appear on page 335 (with a supplementary paper on page 409) and on page 417. The panel presentations appear on page D397, "Long-Range Prospects for the Actuarial Profession."

The New Orleans celebration was organized by Morton D. Miller, his committee, and Adrienne M. Rihouey of Miller's company. Many notable exhibits and films assembled for the event were subsequently made available for use by actuarial clubs throughout the continent.

THE NEW SOUTH LIFE CASE

In October 1971, officials of a small life insurance company doing business only in South Carolina notified the insurance commissioner of that state that their actuarial consultant had discovered serious understatement of their policy reserves. The company was insolvent by a wide margin; liabilities at the end of 1972 were $25 million, and assets only $15 million according to a financial statement prepared later by a major accounting firm.

This case became an item of actuarial history in June 1973 when the South Carolina Insurance Commission asked the Academy to appoint a committee from its members to make recommendations for the Commission's use in the court case then in process.

Academy President Morton D. Miller appointed a committee composed of John M. Bragg (chairman), Delos H. Christian and Allan F. Lebourveau. That committee responded promptly and fully in a report dated August 30, 1973.

Although the life company was very small, the case had many points of high actuarial significance and educational value. Some of these were: How could so large a deficiency have remained undiscovered for, as was revealed, many years? What were the company's prospects for financial recovery, and what was the best route? What lessons about appropriate actuarial tests of policy reserve determinations did the case teach? And what pointers did it offer about professional conduct? The case attracted the attention of Dr. James L. Athearn, Professor of Insurance at the University of South Carolina, who made some pointed remarks in a November 1973 address to the Southeastern Actuaries Club about what he saw as failures by the actuarial profession to meet its responsibilities to the public. Athearn had published a case study in the university's *Business and Economic Review* of April 1973.

An editorial in *The Actuary,* June 1983, by Ernest J. Moorhead commented:

> Until recently, the [Bragg committee report] was kept confidential for reasons associated with the life company's rehabilitation. We are pleased to learn that secrecy about it is no longer necessary; now the excellent work done ten years ago by an actuarial trio ... can and should belatedly receive our profession's recognition. ...
>
> Practicing actuaries should study the committee's approach, its conclusions and the outcome. Plenty of thought should be given to whether attention to the reserve reconciliation on page 6 of the Annual Statement might have readily shown that something was seriously awry.

But by then it was too late to arouse actuarial attention to this worthy object lesson.

MINORITY RECRUITING

The word *minority* as applied to groups within the actuarial profession originally meant racial minority but later came to include also gender minority.

A recruiting effort began in 1969 in the Actuaries Club of New York as described by Peter L. Hutchings (*The Actuary,* June 1970), by David Langer and Louis Weinstein (ibid., November 1970) and by Robert J. Randall (ibid., January 1971). Randall was chairman of the first committee, which secured financial aid from several life companies in New York.

Robert J. Randall himself had become the first black Fellow of the Society of Actuaries in 1952. The first black woman Fellow was Marsha M. Bera in 1978.

The work of the earliest Subcommittee (of the Public Relations Committee of the Society of Actuaries) for Minority and Disadvantaged Recruitment was described by Herbert J. Boothroyd (*The Actuary,* October 1972). Later that subcommittee became an instrument of the Career Encouragement Committee, its name becoming the Sub-committee on Minority Recruiting.

In 1975, as a tribute to J. Henry Smith upon his retirement from the Equitable Life Assurance Society, that company established the J. Henry Smith Scholarship Fund, to be administered by the Society of Actuaries. That fund was designated for the benefit of "women and minority actuarial students," thus bringing women into future subcommittees' sphere. Another fund has been established by the CIGNA Corporation.

Activities of the original Ad Hoc Committee and the later Subcommittee during the 1970s included working with Negro colleges, furnishing lecturers and recruiters for campus visits, conducting summer institutes to help students pass the Society's first mathematical examination, and obtaining summer employment for program participants.

In 1977 the Casualty Actuarial Society joined the Society of Actuaries in this endeavor.

At least twenty Fellows and Associates have been helped to achieve these qualifications by the various Subcommittee programs and the contributed funds.

DESIGN AND PRICING OF INDIVIDUAL LIFE INSURANCE

In the late 1960s, actuaries engaged in individual life insurance were faced with grim and puzzling conditions. Many had been brought up to trust such dogma as:

- The best prescription for most buyers is a level premium whole life policy—perhaps ushered in by a few years of term insurance, and supplemented by a superimposed term rider.

- A cash value policy with annual dividends reflecting portfolio investment yields is the finest savings plan available.

- A nonparticipating policy can, because of its lower premium, compete with a participating policy in the marketplace.

- The solution to profitability problems is a low policy termination rate.

- If a policy's cash value at the end of, say, twenty years is larger than the sum of the premiums less any dividends, it is acceptable to label the difference as a profit to the policyholder.

Diverse new circumstances combined to vitiate such comfortable arguments. A leading cause was simply that mortality levels had fallen sharply while expense levels had risen to the point that lower benefit to the beneficiary was becoming noticeable even to the uninitiated. One of the first to warn about this was Nathan F. Jones in 1965 (*TSA* 17, D336):

> [W]e have, for individual insurance, a pricing structure based generally on age, plan, year of issue, and mode of premium payment, with, nowadays, some concession to size of sale. ...The result is that our pricing is generally at average cost levels for all other factors, offering sharpshooters the obvious possibilities for skimming the cream. Because of very real difficulties, they have not done much about it yet—or am I forgetting the growth of group, association group, and pseudo-group, to coin a phrase? When something is done about it, we can expect that it is at distribution cost that aim will be taken

first, where we have an almost rigid, traditional sales compensation structure, pitched, not at the average cost level, but at the highest cost level at which insurance can be sold at all.

Social security benefits had risen to levels at which the accepted need for life insurance after retirement was much less than formerly, seriously weakening the argument that level premium life insurance rather than term insurance was essential to protect against spiralling premiums. Forms of personal saving previously known to only a few (if available at all) were being aggressively marketed in competition with the once preeminent life insurance policy; in an era of rising market interest rates some of these offered access to immediate high yields in contrast to the slow rise in the savings element of a cash value policy. And consumer magazines were revealing that differences in the relative attractiveness of life insurance policies offered by different companies were much larger than the public had been led to believe.

At the Society of Actuaries Atlanta meeting on March 31, 1977, James C. H. Anderson and Ernest J. Moorhead debated the affirmative and negative sides, respectively, of:

> Resolved . . . The Life Insurance business, as transacted today, is in its terminal stages.

At that time, the annual inflation rate in the United States had just dropped (in 1976) to 5.8% from the shocking 11% of 1974 but was only two years away from the even more horrendous 11.3, 13.5, and 10.4% CPI increases of 1979, 1980 and 1981. This debate was the most candid discussion of the problem within actuarial circles since the little noticed comment by Jones a dozen years earlier.

A product metamorphosis was already well under way. John C. Fraser, Walter N. Miller, and Charles M. Sternhell had presented a trail-blazing paper eight years earlier (*TSA* 21, 343) on fixed premium variable benefit individual life insurance, a form whose essence was "that the policyholder would bear the entire investment risk" that traditionally had been taken by the insurance company. The words *Universal Life* were being used to denote an "unbundling" of the elements of a whole life policy into its term and investment segments, previously a concept widely regarded as heretical. The notorious weakness of level premium nonparticipating insurance in an era of widely fluctuating market yields was bringing onstage flexible premium nonparticipating policies. By 1979 a new breed of contracts described as "interest sensitive" was on its way into company rate books. It remained for the future to show whether these policies would be as sensitive to market interest rate changes that were on their way down as they were to such changes on their way up.

The actuarial profession in those tumultuous days did not ignore the force of consumerism, but it temporized by being content to react rather than to act. A prime example of temporizing was in the search for valid and enlightening methods of policy cost comparison.

POLICY COST COMPARISONS

As early as the mid-1950s when interest rates available on bank savings deposits were just beginning to make the time value of money significant to typical life insurance policyholders, some life companies were taking unreasonable advantage of the existing "net cost" system (that ignored interest) for determining which policies in the marketplace were among those deserving of buyer confidence. The two devices used to obscure the picture were illogical patterns of terminal dividends in published illustrations and steeply graded annual dividends. The New York Insurance Department put something of a crimp into the terminal dividend misuse, but most other departments did not follow suit.

At the Society of Actuaries October 1962 meeting (*TSA* 14, D353) a topic for informal discussion was:

> [A]re the traditional average net cost and average net payment illustrations still satisfactory? How far should companies go in assuming a rate of interest for projecting accumulations?

Leaders in the profession took no firm stand, except as representatives of their own companies, on either of these rather clear issues. That was at a time when Professor Joseph M. Belth of Indiana University was beginning to develop ideas on cost comparisons and policy replacement criteria that belonged in the actuarial sphere but that were not being explored in an intellectual atmosphere of search for truth. In 1966 Belth recommended a disclosure system, and Ernest J. Moorhead recommended a plan called the "one-thirtieth method," which was similar in concept to the interest-adjusted method that would gain currency in the following decade.

Neither Belth nor Moorhead enjoyed success in arousing actuarial discomfort with existing practices. But in 1968 a matter that looked unimportant made the whole subject explosive; Senator Philip A. Hart in Washington learned that veterans converting their servicemen's group insurance were being victimized by being sold high-priced policies without being given the opportunity to exercise intelligent choice among available products.

A few insurance commissioners, but not many, became worried about federal encroachment; some life insurance leaders thought the issue important enough to justify appointment of an industry committee chaired by Moorhead to recommend a voluntary solution, but too few took a strong stand in 1970 when the committee unanimously recommended adoption of the interest-adjusted method. The committee was discharged without industry endorsement of its proposals and without any plan for seeking some other solution. When Virginia Knauer, President Nixon's Consumer Affairs Advisor, criticized the abandonment of this search and the NAIC showed signs of seriously pursuing the matter with its own recommended method, the industry belatedly espoused the interest-adjusted method but substantially weakened the force of that espousal by countenancing a companion to the interest-adjusted index (which companion the industry committee had warned against), i.e., a "payment index." In 1974 one of the industry associations, the Institute of Life Insurance issued a booklet, "The Nature of the Whole Life Contract," branding as artificial any split of a life insurance premium into savings and pure insurance elements.

In 1973 the Society of Actuaries appointed a committee to report on whether an opinion should be expressed on any of these issues. Soon afterwards the Board authorized that committee, chaired by Bartley L. Munson, to undertake research projects requested by the NAIC. The two reports that emerged answered the questions that the NAIC had posed but neither of them resulted in any worthwhile guidance by the profession on the underlying issues.

Discussions of the two reports are in *TSA* 26: "Philosophies in the Computation and Dissemination of Dividend Illustrations" on page D597, and "Analysis of Life Insurance Cost Comparison Index Methods" on page D683.

The Society's 1975 historian, Gary Corbett, remarked about all this (*TSA* 27, 543):

> There is little question that the Society's efforts in the area of cost comparisons will be influential. With that in mind, should we have stated a preference for one method over all others? Some actuaries believe that we should have done so. It is reported that participants in the concurrent session on this topic in New Orleans [October 1974] favored stating a preference. Knowledgeable members hold opposing views on the relative superiority of the two families of methods.

The Canadian Institute of Actuaries in 1976 published a report of its committee on cost comparison expressing preference for a method akin to a Belth proposal.

Descriptions of Society of Actuaries involvement in policy cost comparison matters have been recorded by its 1974 Historian John C. Maynard (*TSA* 27, 523), and by its 1977 Historian Harold G. Ingraham, Jr. (*TSA* 29, 461). Ingraham's report describes also the work of the Society's Committee on Dividend Philosophy created in March 1976 "to study in depth the underlying actuarial principles and practical problems relating to the calculation and illustrations of dividends including related matters of philosophy."

The record of those years shows instances in which our profession might have made but did not make public expressions on major consumer questions that clearly belonged within the area of actuarial competence. An early example was in 1965 when the Huebner Foundation for Insurance Education sponsored a book by Professor Belth, *Participating Life Insurance Sold By Stock Companies,* pointing out shortcomings in treatment of policyholders, including failures by some companies even to perform the calculations necessary to determine the amounts of divisible surplus accruing on policy contracts that contained promises of policyholder participation in such profits. In 1978, doubts about actuaries' acceptance of responsibility in policy dividend distribution were at least implied in the appointment of an industry advisory committee to the NAIC on "Manipulation," the reference being to policies whose designs tended to hamper the usefulness to the public of cost comparison approaches. The Committee on Dividend Philosophy tried to deal with these problems; it issued reports in 1977, 1978, and 1979 but, after all that effort, did not emerge with recommended solutions to problems involving participating business of stock companies.

There was, however, considerable impact on the opinions professed by agents in the field, as revealed by annual surveys published jointly by the National Association of Life Underwriters and the Life Insurance Marketing and Research Association. In 1970, 42% of responding agents stated that they agreed with the proposition, "There is little difference in net cost for similar policies"; by 1978 this view was expressed by 28% of the repliers, a proportion still suggesting widespread naivete or hesitation about recognizing the existing condition.

LIFE INSURANCE COMPANY FINANCIAL STATEMENTS

This section continues (from Chapter V) the story of the profession's response to the discontent, first by stock analysts and then by accountants, with the usefulness for their purposes of the financial statements required by insurance departments in the United States and Canada.

The last shot fired by the stock analysts before the accountants took the center of the stage was in December 1969, reported by Thomas P. Bowles in *The Actuary,* April 1970. The "Final Report from the Committee on Life Insurance Earnings Adjustment" of the Association of Insurance and Financial Analysts (AIFA) began by saying that obstacles in the form of disagreements within the industry and among accountants and imperfections of available data "have precluded the Committee from devising a simple approach." The committee was also baffled by the difficulty of recomputing the policy reserve to reflect modern mortality and interest factors, and concluded that it might be sufficient to adjust only the reserve interest rate by some method of approximating what interest rate the actuary had assumed in calculating the premiums. This, the committee thought, might be combined with an amortization system for acquisition expenses. Bowles was critical of the proposal but sympathetic to the need for action, requiring, he said, "even more cooperation among all interested parties."

In 1964 (*TSA* 16, D236), William A. Dreher gave actuaries a sketch of the 50,000-member AICPA, which, he said, had two objectives of its own closely paralleling those of our profession, i.e., to unite their profession and to promote and maintain high professional and moral standards. Dreher continued (p. 237):

> One of the primary objectives of [AICPA] is to define what are known as "generally accepted accounting principles [GAAP]" for the guidance of its members. ...
>
> A generally accepted accounting principle is often a broad guide to the solution of a particular accounting problem. Frequently there is not a unique and direct solution; any of several alternatives may be satisfactory in a particular set of circumstances. Principally, the accountant regards as a generally accepted accounting principle an opinion given by the Accounting Principles Board. ...There are, however, other sources of what is "generally accepted" to which the accountant may look.

Actuaries soon discovered that CPAs were not accustomed to probability concepts in measuring assets and liabilities; having shorter time-horizons than actuaries, accountants were not naturally inclined to consider the time value of money. But they quickly embraced the concept.

Those actuaries who had not taken seriously the AICPA's 1966 entry into a study of the application of GAAP to life insurance company accounting suffered rude awakenings in late 1970 when a draft, "Audits of Life Insurance Companies," was circulated for discussion. Actuaries of mutual companies in particular found that their companies might not be exempted. Society of Actuaries President Edwin B. Lancaster, in his Address on November 8, 1971, summarized the events of the preceding twelve months thus (*TSA* 23, 200):

The Joint Actuarial Committee on Financial Reporting [of the Academy, Canadian Institute, Conference and Society] ... was formed in an atmosphere of near-crisis immediately following last year's annual meeting of the Society. Operating under the able chairmanship of Robert C. Winters, the committee prepared a remarkably detailed and complete actuarial response to [AICPA's] exposure draft of an audit guide for life insurance companies. ...

[T]his important and highly controversial matter ... will certainly present the members of the actuarial profession with some difficult challenges if it is implemented in its present form. As I see it, some of these challenges are (1) the temptation to be expedient, (2) pressure to influence the incidence of life insurance company earnings, and (3) potential fundamental disagreement with the accounting profession as to the suitability of financial presentations of life insurance companies.

The Joint Actuarial Committee's Response to the AICPA draft, issued on May 14, 1971, contained fourteen separate comments for the accounting profession's consideration. The fourteenth, advancing the committee's proposal for the actuary's role, was:

We urge that public reporting of the financial operations of life insurance companies requires much more extensive participation of qualified actuaries than the exposure draft ... recognizes. We recommend that an auditor render an unqualified opinion ... *only if* [emphasis in original] he has an opinion from a qualified actuary with respect to the actuarial items contained in them. ... [T]he scope paragraph of the auditor's report should [state] that an actuarial opinion has been obtained.

In two successive afternoons at the Society's meeting in Des Moines on June 3–4, 1971, a Seminar on Adjusted Earnings explored that subject to the tune of seventy-four pages in *TSA* 23. Robert C. Winters, moderator of the second session, expressed objection to the term *adjusted earnings* for two reasons (p. D422):

First of all, it suggests a concentration on earnings.... What we are really talking about is the financial statements of life insurance companies, not just the earnings report. Second, the term suggests that we start with numbers that are somehow improper and adjust them so as to remove those improprieties.

The first session started with an explanation by a guest accountant, J. Theodore Arenberg, of why the insurance industry was receiving so much attention. Arenberg spoke of (p. D369):

a lack of understanding as to the degree to which the accounting and reporting practices of the [insurance] industry have differed from those used by business enterprises in general. ... Their long usage and uniformity stem from regulatory influence and ... concern with respect to serving the needs of only one, albeit important, segment of society, namely, the policyholders. This ... has created a kind of tradition, or obsession, which has made it almost a sacrilege to suggest that the accounting and reporting practices followed may not adequately serve the needs of the owners, prospective owners, and possibly even management. ...

[T]he answers you get frequently are not meaningful and, in fact, can be downright misleading. ...It will be until you deal with these problems, and others, that you can enter the current accounting debate on an equal footing with other industries. Even then, you will find that there will be little progress if you point to the "other guy" as your excuse for not following sound accounting practices. . . . The establishment of accounting principles is not a matter of a popularity contest. It is a matter of fairness in reporting.

These were strong words, but actuaries had known of these shortcomings long before. A recent addition to the readings for Part 6 of the Fellowship examinations had been "An Evaluation of the Association Blank," Chapter 38 of *Life Insurance Accounting* (1969) by Joseph C. Noback, FSA, devoting seven pages to cataloguing the peculiarities and perceived inadequacies of the NAIC Statement.

At the seminar, Dale R. Gustafson defended the NAIC Statement over the GAAP system on the ground that (1) the GAAP objective may be unreachable, and (2) groups needing financial information would be wise to concentrate on assets and liabilities rather than presumed yearly gains and losses (p. D378):

It is from the thinking of [Elizur Wright] . . . that the basic concepts of statutory valuation and nonforfeiture bases and, in effect, solvency accounting developed. . . . [T]his concept can be described as taking full cognizance of the long-term nature of the life insurance contract and setting up . . . a financial reporting system that carefully and surely safeguards the policyholders' interests and the long-term financial stability of the enterprise. . . .

It has always been implicit in life insurance financial reporting that it is the balance sheet that counts. It has been generally axiomatic in actuarial and management thinking that the assignment of earnings to specific accounting periods is relatively meaningless and at best, arbitrary, and that it is present values and long-term considerations that are important in life insurance accounting. . . .

While there may already be lurking somewhere in the background genuine principles, they certainly cannot be articulated very readily from the statements that have been made recently about GAAP. It seems to me that it is more accurate to describe what has been going on as an attempt to cloak preferred practices with a mantle of respectability that they do not deserve by invoking the power of "principle." . . .

[T]he stakes in this current controversy are so high that there is a grave danger of serious damage to the life insurance enterprise unless some significant attention is given to the real principles involved.

We seem to have so many principles floating around that each individual can readily find a set to support his own personal preferences.

Robert L. Posnak, CPA, (p. D386) said (using the Statement's old name "Convention Statement"):

The plain fact is that one financial statement will never serve the needs of all users. But *one statement must, as a practical matter, be used,* [emphasis added]. . . . [In general accounting], owners and creditors are deemed to constitute the most important classes of users of financial statements, and general-purpose financial statements are oriented to the objective of serving their needs. . . .

The needs of policyholders, creditors, and employees seem to be adequately served by the Convention Statement. Management has the power to draw up financial statements for its own use in whatever form it sees fit. With respect to taxation and the life insurance industry's roles as financial intermediary and risk carrier, the general public's interest is adequately served by the Convention Statement.

The conclusion is inescapable that the audience for general-purpose financial statements of life insurance companies is much more limited than is the case with respect to commercial and industrial enterprise. Thus the traditional assumption that financial statements prepared primarily for the use of owners and creditors will also serve the needs of other users is not entirely valid simply because the needs of other users are adequately served by the Convention Statement.

Gary E. Corbett said (p. D391):

Basically, we [the Joint Actuarial Committee on Financial Reporting] do not believe that the continued existence of dual sets of GAAP and statutory statements is in the interests of the industry, of the stockholders, or of the public. We think that the existence of two sets of statements will be confusing and misleading. Our resolution of this situation is based on two assumptions: first, the statutory income statement is meaningless; second, the GAAP balance sheet could be misleading, in that it identifies as surplus those funds that must be retained for the protection of policyholders.

Corbett went on to describe a single-statement compromise plan devised by the Joint Committee. W. Harold Bittel, actuary of the New Jersey Insurance Department, also spoke strongly against GAAP and proposed two alternative approaches, both involving "a concerted attack on the appropriateness of GAAP" for life insurance statements.

The seminar's second session on June 4 began with a description by Daniel F. Case of AICPA's ideas on making the policy reserve item more realistic, and the Joint Actuarial Committee's response thereto (p. D414):

[T]he integrated approach which [first] offered itself [after study by Gary Corbett and Robert L. Posnak] was the so-called "natural reserve" method. . . . One further point of agreement at that time was that natural reserves did not always have to be at least equal to the cash surrender value. It was felt that to set an arbitrary "cash value floor" would . . . distort the pattern of adjusted earnings. Provided that suitable lapse rates are employed in the natural reserve calculation, it seems correct not to impose a cash value floor.

This concept of cash values as appropriate subjects for probabilistic treatment rather than as akin to demand deposits was in sharp contrast to actuarial and state regulatory thinking down the years. Case went on to explain that subsequent study caused actuaries to doubt the merits of the natural reserve method, which he pointed out was not identical to the natural reserve definition historically employed (p. D415):

The [Joint Actuarial Committee] has recommended to the AICPA committee that (1) the natural reserve method be considered as an acceptable method located at one end of a range of acceptable methods, the others of which would involve a later incidence of expected profit, and (2) the assumptions used ...should contain a margin of conservatism, chosen with due regard to the long-term-risk nature of the typical life insurance policy.

Samuel H. Turner then gave highlights of the 148-page Joint Committee response, mentioning that it included endorsement of a "release from risk" concept as a generalized and unifying reserve system that accomplishes a reasonable matching of revenues and costs. A paper, "Life Insurance Earnings and the Release From Risk Policy Reserve System" by Richard G. Horn, who developed that method, is printed in *TSA* 23, 391.

Charles Barry H. Watson then discussed the role of the actuary, a matter which the Academy Board had accepted responsibility for presenting through a letter to the AICPA committee signed by Academy President H. Raymond Strong. Watson said (p. D420):

It is the view of the AICPA that, for GAAP to apply, the auditor must satisfy *himself* as to the appropriateness of all aspects of the statement, including the reserve liabilities; otherwise, the auditor is not rendering a whole opinion, and implicitly not a clean one. ...

This is not to say that accountants do not recognize the importance of actuaries ... or would want to do without them. Every accountant the Joint Actuarial Committee has talked to ... has stated that he and his firm would continue to rely on actuaries. But they do not want to say [so] in the auditor's statement. ...

Watson went on to mention our profession's request that the auditor's scope paragraph state that a qualified actuary had rendered an opinion, it being recommended that for this purpose membership in the Academy be the test of qualification. Watson pointed out that the accounting profession demands that the auditor be completely independent of the company he audits, and will require the same independence of the experts he consults, thus making independence of the actuary a matter for our profession's urgent consideration.

Robert C. Winters, closing the seminar on the topic "Possible Future Developments," predicted that the NAIC would stand vigorously by the statutory balance sheet as the proper solvency test, and that it would probably sanction alternative earnings reports but might not accept the notion of a separate balance sheet. About the accountants' probable actions, Winters said (p. D423):

I think ... that we will see a published audit guide issued this year, including coverage of mutual companies, but probably not effective or required for 1971. ...[W]e have discovered a lot of common ground between the accountants and the industry representatives, and I think that there is a very good chance that we will find enough more to reach what might be termed a mutually satisfactory resolution. ...

Whereas the accounting profession is a rather diverse group, ... there is in the actuarial profession a single, closely knit group with a reasonably uniform educational standard ... whose special area of competence, is exactly the key

issue in life insurance accounting: reserving. Therefore, it seems to me unnecessary to extend into the life insurance area the kinds of rigidity ... which may be
necessary in other industries. That position, in turn, suggests that there is a
responsibility for actuaries to serve professionally ... in developing, ar-
ticulating, promulgating, and codifying the proper ways to go about preparing life insurance company earnings and other statements, and the proper
reserving bases. At the same time we should probably move somewhat more
in the direction of the self-discipline that the accountants now seek.
Presumably this would mean, for the Academy, more extensive activity in the
area of guides to professional conduct and disciplining membership; for the
Society, more work on the content of reserve systems for life statements; and,
for the Casualty Society, perhaps a parallel responsibility in connection with
the casualty blank.

A second exposure draft, renamed "Audits of Stock Life Insurance Companies"
and therefore giving mutual companies a breathing spell, emerged in 1972. It dashed
the hopes of those who at Des Moines the previous June had looked for compromise in
the form of a single balance sheet; it did bring Horn's release from risk reserve system
into primary use, and it resolved a number of other points of disagreement.

Society of Actuaries historian, John C. Maynard, reported in 1974 (*TSA* 27, 526):

> The third and definitive version of the audit guide, *Audits of Stock Life In-
> surance Companies,* was published in 1973. It became necessary to apply new
> concepts to the calculation of actuarial reserves....

> With the issue of the audit guide, actuaries found that guidance was needed with
> respect to principles, techniques, and professional conduct in the calculation of
> reserves under GAAP. ...First, [the Academy's] Professional Conduct Com-
> mittee prepared an Opinion which serves as a broad guide to the actuary and
> which requires him to consider the Recommendations of its Committee on
> Financial Reporting Principles. Second, the latter committee prepared a number
> of Recommendations and Interpretations which described the principles that
> should be followed.

The original Opinion A-6 supplemented by Recommendation 1 and Interpretations
1-A, 1-B and 1-C appeared in the Academy's 1974 *Year Book*; to these several more
Recommendations and Interpretations were added during 1974. Maynard added (p. 527):

> A few years ago [the actuary's] responsibility was confined to the determination
> of actuarial reserves for statutory statements. ...Today the actuary is required
> to determine actuarial reserves ... appropriate for taxing authorities, and ac-
> tuarial reserves ... consistent with GAAP. ...Considerable judgment is now
> needed for these tasks.

Maynard then described the corresponding state of affairs in Canada (p. 528):

> In 1973 the Canadian Institute of Chartered Accountants published its re-
> search study *Financial Reporting for Life Insurance Companies.* Many
> similarities and some differences exist between this report and the United
> States audit guide. It is significant that the research committee included one
> actuary (François J. F. Vachon) who rendered a minority opinion that was
> published separately in the report.

After considering the matter for more than a year, the Committee on Financial Reporting of the Canadian Institute of Actuaries in April, 1974, issued its report *Financial Reporting for Life Insurance Companies in Canada*. This comprehensive report investigates principles and is noteworthy for its analysis of the professional relationships between actuaries and accountants.

In May, 1974, the Committee on Life Insurance Accounting of the Canadian Life Insurance Association issued its special report *Financial Reporting for Life Insurance Companies*.

By 1978, the Academy *Year Book* contained forty-three pages of Recommendations and Interpretations on this one subject.

The necessary preoccupation with new financial statement requirements heaped upon actuaries during the rest of the decade is illustrated by the programming, shown in *RSA* Volumes 1–5 (1975–1979), of no fewer than sixteen concurrent sessions and teaching sessions on aspects of a subject that not only was broad to start with but also was complicated by the unprecedented inflationary conditions of those years. New expressions such as "valuation actuary" came into currency; a statement of actuarial opinion on reserve adequacy was introduced by the NAIC in the United States; insurance officials, accountants and actuaries in Canada undertook to find out whether the best features of statutory and GAAP approaches might be combined into a single statement; and important new entities such as the Financial Accounting Standards Board (FASB) entered the scene. And casualty and life actuaries found themselves to be comrades with essentially the same problems—Jarvis Farley, FCAS, chairman of the Academy's Committee on Financial Reporting Principles from 1972 to 1976, became as well-known and respected in the one group as in the other.

An important contribution to the work of this tumultuous period was made by the Committee on Financial Reporting Principles of the American Life Convention and Life Insurance Association of America. This committee was comprised heavily of actuaries, one of them, Henry B. Ramsey, Jr., being its chairman.

In 1980, the Academy Committee published a survey of company practices in constructing GAAP statements, which showed that comparability of results among companies was proving to be an elusive goal.

The whole GAAP exercise gave presumably valuable analytical experience to actuaries and partially freed life company executives from the discouragement of being shown that sales of even high-quality new business apparently depressed their profits.

THE ACADEMY IN THE 1970s

The Academy's first three presidents—Henry F. Rood, FSA, ACAS, Thomas E. Murrin, FCAS, and John H. Miller, FSA, FCAS—although engaged heavily in organizational details, were able to lead the new body into operational matters to the point that the fourth president, Wendell A. Milliman, FSA, FCA, in his July 1969 report to the members, could announce that the Academy had been recognized by the NAIC, by the AICPA in its Opinion No. 8, and by the Securities and Exchange Commission.

Toward the objective of accreditation at the state level, the original plan to seek legislation had not been pursued because of what Milliman described as "political and administrative complications": Indiana had become the one and only state to enact the Academy's model bill into law. Said Milliman:

> Consequently, our [accreditation] efforts at the state level are now directed toward obtaining action by insurance commissioners ... in the form of administrative orders or regulations. ... This is a problem which must be pursued with considerable discretion. ... [O]nly two states, New Jersey and Kentucky, had taken specific action.

On federal accreditation, Milliman's comment was:

> Appropriate recognition of the actuarial profession ... primarily in connection with pension plans, remains a prime objective of the Academy. To make sure that our interests are effectively represented in our nation's capital, the Committee on Accreditation has been expanded to include a Washington Sub-Committee under the chairmanship of Edwin F. Boynton ... assisted by William T. Gibb, III, ... a member of the Washington office of the Life Insurance Association of America. ...

> It seems likely that appropriate recognition ... at the federal level may result, at least in part, from legislative action. However, we wish to be certain that [this issue] ... is not confused by the public or Congress with the arguments ... on ... advisability of federal imposition of additional benefit or financial requirements upon private pension plans.

President Walter L. Rugland a year later announced having hired legislative counsel in July 1970 in the person of Richard Congleton, a retired Prudential lawyer; Congleton educated many Academy leaders in Washington mysteries until he died in office in January 1976. An obituary is printed in *JAAA* 2, 4. William D. Hager was appointed General Counsel in September 1979.

Data in the Academy's 1974 *Year Book* show that Society of Actuaries members held about two-thirds of the Academy's numerical strength, while the Casualty Actuarial Society, the Conference of Actuaries in Public Practice, and the members not attached to any existing body had about one-tenth each. The small remainder were members of the Fraternal Actuarial Association. The presidency, determined each year by the Board rather than by vote of the members, was satisfactorily rotated among the founding bodies. In eight years the Academy membership had grown to more than 3,000.

The *Journal of the American Academy of Actuaries* began publication in 1975, the first two issues, paperbound, consisting entirely of annual meeting proceedings. *JAAA* 2, 11 contains the first report of Executive Director Stephen G. Kellison, describing the multifarious activities, a major one being that concerned with the new professional category of Enrolled Actuaries. Beginning with the third volume (1977) the *Journals* were clothbound until 1984 and contained, in addition to the annual meeting proceedings, complete indexed lists of Academy-sponsored public statements and letters. In 1977 to 1979 the average number of such statements was twenty-nine.

The standard pattern for annual meetings, which always were held as adjuncts to meetings of, in turn, the constituent bodies, was, *first*, the address of the president and reports of officers and of the nominating committee chairman, and second, presentations and discussions of matters that had figured prominently in the Academy's year. The value of the *Journal* in making available these special subject summaries ought not to be overlooked.

Among the special subjects of the years 1975 to 1979 were these:

1975	Recognition of the Profession by Federal and State Governments
	Professional Conduct and Discipline
	Financial Reporting
1976	Current Issues in Accounting
	Actuarial Principles and Practices
	Enrolled Actuaries
1977	Actuarial Opinions on Casualty Loss Reserves

In 1978 and 1979 these were concurrent sessions:

1978	Financial Reporting
	Legislation Affecting Pension Plans
	Expression of Public Opinion
	Classification and Privacy
1979	Specialty Designations
	Risk Classifications

The "Classification" sessions noted in 1978 and 1979 placed on record clear descriptions of conflict between, on the one hand, social and political objectives of certain groups in the population, and, on the other, the results of applying actuarial logic in risk selection ratemaking on many insurance, annuity and pension benefits. The August 1977 report of the Academy Task Force on Risk Classification chaired by Michael J. Mahoney summed up the state of affairs thus (*JAAA* 4, 76):

> Although the original charge was on the unisex issue, it was readily apparent that the issues and restrictions on classification are spreading to all classes (e.g., race, sex, physically handicapped, age, geographic location, etc.), to all forms of insurance (e.g., life, health, annuities, automobile, etc.), and at all levels and forms of government (e.g., State and Federal—laws, regulations, guidelines and court cases).

INDEPENDENCE OF THE ACTUARY

The issue of independence arose as a side effect from the natural insistence by the actuarial profession that auditors obtain actuarial opinions on balance sheet items that are determined by actuarial processes. This brought up the question of circumstances that would disqualify an actuary from rendering an opinion by reason of conflict of interest or duress.

In 1973 the Academy president arranged to have a Joint Committee on Independence of the Actuary formed under chairmanship of Edward H. Friend "responsible for drafting a position paper and a set of guidelines on the circumstance, if any, in which organization and financial independence of the actuary are desirable to avoid what may appear to be conflict of interest in certification and other actuarial duties."

In October 1974, Friend said (TSA 26, D411):

> The main theme of the [Joint Committee's first] report may be summed up in a few words—that independence cannot be defined and, as a result, professionalism and disclosure must take the place of independence. In order for that to work, professionalism and disclosure requirements must be strengthened.

A final committee report emerged early in 1977, whereupon the Academy, the Conference and the Society of Actuaries formed committees to consider what action should be taken. At the Academy meeting in November 1977, its Secretary reported (*JAAA* 3, 4) that one of its Board actions had been:

> Adoption, with revision, of resolutions proposed by the Ad Hoc Committee on Independence, which call for drafting Guides to Professional Conduct and other actions to clarify and promote financial and organizational independence of the actuary in situations where such independence is appropriate.

Revisions of the Guides followed. One piece of the history seems to be missing, in that the Academy arranged and doubtless conducted a concurrent session on Independence of the Actuary, but the contents page of the 1979 *Journal* informed readers that its text could not be printed but would be in the 1980 *Journal*. It was not printed there.

ELECTIONS IN THE SOCIETY OF ACTUARIES

During the first twenty years of the present Society, no major changes were introduced into election procedures. Features of highest significance were (1) a completely open choice for President-Elect (President, before 1961); (2) maintenance of proportionate Board representation geographically and by type of employment; and (3) as much assurance as possible to Canadian Fellows that they would be accorded the presidency and vice-presidencies with appropriate frequency, always a source of underlying concern.

In fact, worrying about having enough Canadian presidents had not solved that problem. Archie R. McCracken remarked in 1971 (*TSA* 23, D242):

> [F]rom 1950 through 1970 . . . at twenty-one meetings, there were twenty-two presidents or presidents-elect chosen. At three out of the four meetings held in Canada the top post went to a Canadian. At the seventeen meetings held in the United States none of the eighteen people elected to the top post were from Canada.

Nine years were to pass after that before a Canadian was elected. During those years the meeting locale ceased to be significant because the election-by-mail system supplanted that of balloting at annual meetings, but the problem seemed as acute as ever. In 1979 the Committee on Elections Chairman and the Editor and Editor Emeritus of *The Actuary* agreed amongst themselves (after the first ballot results were known to the first of this trio but not to the other two) that it would be best to insert a brief notice to the voters in the correspondence columns of *The Actuary* (September 1979). That message pointed out that the last time a resident Canadian was elected to lead the Society was twenty-four years previous and added:

> Is there a risk that because of our growth in numbers (causing us as individuals to be less well acquainted with each other), or because of the election-by-mail system (removing the former influence of where the annual meeting is held), or for some other reason, we may never have the satisfaction of welcoming to the presidential chair an actuary from the extremely important and vibrant territory up north?

> When we elect a Canadian President we are not only honoring the individual but recognizing his actuarial fellow-countrymen.

The nominee from Canada was elected. Nobody but the elections chairman, since deceased, ever knew whether the message had any bearing on that result.

Appointment of a committee to study the possibility of conducting Society elections all or partly by mail was announced at the Society's November 1970 meeting. That committee chaired by Morton D. Miller produced a background memorandum, which was mailed to members and was discussed at all three 1971 spring meetings (*TSA* 23, D41, D235, and D240). A constitutional amendment at the November 1971 meeting in Toronto granting discretion to the Board either to continue the existing system or to send ballots through the mail passed easily with 433 affirmative and 75 negative votes. At its next meeting the Board decided to make the change immediately.

Thus an annual meeting event that had been in effect since 1889 and was always interesting and occasionally dramatic became just a fond memory among old-timers. Naturally the change resulted in a substantially larger number of ballots, although the

Two Millers who presided over both the Society of Actuaries and the American Academy of Actuaries: (L) Morton D. Miller, (R) John H. Miller.

ratio of votes to eligible voters has since been steadily declining as the organization grows larger. A few have urged that candidates be required to give the electorate their views on major professional current issues, but this has never been done. Substantial information about candidates' past participation in professional activities and in contributions to actuarial literature has been furnished as well as photographs of the nominees along with facts about residence and type of employment, but lack of widespread personal acquaintanceship with the candidates is an inevitable handicap (which the Institute of Actuaries in London has always avoided in one respect by having the Council rather than the Fellows choose the president).

The successive systems and practices in effect through the entire period from 1949 to and including the 1987 election have given 203 Fellows one or more terms on the Board of Governors for an average of 5.6 years each. Only two of these have served as many as twelve years in Elected Board Member posts, i.e., excluding years as officers, while another five have served nine, ten, or eleven years. The record for total Board service is shared by two past presidents: Victor E. Henningsen and Robert J. Myers, eighteen years each.

The transferable vote procedure, under which first-choice ballots cast for candidates who had to be eliminated from the running were used to help second- and later-choice nominees, was adopted for officer posts when voting by mail came into effect. It had already been used for non-officer elections since 1963.

COUNCIL OF PRESIDENTS, 1972

Surely the single most effective action to bring the North American actuarial bodies into cooperative work and mutual appreciation was the founding of the Council of Presidents, which through the initiative of Morton D. Miller held its first meeting in December 1972. Strictly informal at first and conducting its work without any structure of bylaws and other trappings, this group rather quickly became the primary medium for exchanging information and for coordinating, and later even initiating, projects affecting all bodies.

This, however, was not the first meeting of the presidents. Miller reported (*TSA* 20, 312) that they were all invited to the initial meeting in February 1968 of the Joint Committee on Review of Education and Examinations, and "all but one were able to take part in this historic occasion."

After a few experimental years, a regular schedule of quarterly Council meetings has become the rule. The minutes are distributed to the offices of the constituent bodies and to the participants who include presidents-elect as well as incumbents.

INTERNATIONAL MEETINGS

Eminently successful International Congresses, strongly supported by North American actuaries in attendance and in submissions of papers, were held in Munich in 1968, Oslo in 1972, and Tokyo in 1976. Arrangements were made for the 1980 meeting in Switzerland.

Stemming from informal gatherings of consulting actuaries at the 1960 and 1964 Congresses, a new body, the International Association of Consulting Actuaries (IACA), was established at the 1968 Congress. This new organization developed through the initiative of consulting actuaries in Great Britain, the United States, the Netherlands and Germany, its first Chairman and Secretary being Geoffrey Heywood and Maxwell Lander, both of the United Kingdom. IACA immediately adopted the practice of meeting separately from the Congresses, the first of its biennial gatherings being in Washington, D.C., and San Francisco in 1970.

Part of the North American delegation reaches Tokyo in October 1976 for the earliest International Congress ever held outside Europe or America.

TROUBLE IN THE OLD-AGE SURVIVORS AND DISABILITY INSURANCE (OASDI) SYSTEM

All actuaries and others wishing to learn about the social security system of the United States are fortunate indeed to have available to them Robert J. Myers' three comprehensive books, viz.:

- *Social Insurance and Allied Government Programs*, 1965, reviewed by George W. K. Grange (*TSA* 17, 95).

- *Social Security*, 1975, reviewed by A. Haeworth Robertson (*TSA* 28, 339).

- *Social Security,* 2nd. ed. 1981, reviewed by C. L. Trowbridge (*TSA* 33, 781).

The decade of the 1970s was by far the most turbulent for the social security system in the United States since the original debates of the late 1930s on financing principles. At the Society of Actuaries meeting on June 4, 1970, Robert J. Myers announced (*TSA* 22, D313) his resignation as Chief Actuary of the Social Security Administration, this after twenty-three years in that post, thirty-five years altogether. Myers emphasized that this move was not the result of political pressure nor of personal opposition to the administration's recent financing proposals, but of his opposition to an expansionist philosophy pursued by the Administration's two top policymakers. Their aim, he said, was complete economic security through governmental means for virtually the entire nonworking population of the United States.

Charles L. Trowbridge succeeded Myers in 1971 but resigned in 1973. Martha Derthick (*Policymaking for Social Security*, 1979, p. 394), reported, on the strength of her interview with Trowbridge, that "he found that he could not tolerate the chaos of Washington, where he was bombarded with demands that he had to meet no matter how arbitrary they seemed or what the motives behind them might be." The next incumbent, A. Haeworth Robertson, accepted the post in late 1974 and stayed until March 1978. In February 1979 he was succeeded by Dwight K. Bartlett III, who announced his resignation in the November 1981 issue of *The Actuary*. His successor was Harry C. Ballantyne.

In 1972 the Congress enacted an amendment substituting automatic benefit increases for previous ad hoc changes aimed at protecting beneficiaries from losses of purchasing power in their social security incomes. The trouble was that the chosen benefit formula was ruinously sensitive to major inflationary surges, one of which occurred the very next year. A 3.3% CPI increase for 1972 jumped to 6.2% in 1973, then to 11.0% in 1974. The difficulty was accentuated in the short range by unexpected increases in disability claims and in the long range by decline in the country's fertility rate to levels never previously experienced or even contemplated.

In 1977 (*TSA* 29, 433) Trowbridge said:

> Even before the final passage of the 1972 amendments, actuarial cost estimates on a dynamic basis were pointing up the sensitivity of these estimates to the future course of consumer prices and covered earnings. ...

> It was clear to the Social Security Administration (SSA) actuaries that this sensitivity . . . to the events over which the system had no control was an important problem, one that certainly would cause difficulty in the future. Attempts to find a better answer were started . . . even before the passage of the 1972 amendments, although little real progress was made until 1973.

But the earliest public warning of trouble ahead was that voiced by Geoffrey N. Calvert in his address "New Realistic Projections of Social Security Benefits and Taxes" to the American Pension Conference in December 1973, in which he said:

> In this address I shall be raising questions and placing information before you of the utmost importance and gravity relating to the future of the Social Security system, its benefits, its costs, its likely future impact on private benefit plans, and its ability to survive in its present form in the face of current economic and demographic trends.

This address, published in pamphlet form by Alexander and Alexander Inc., was described by Robert J. Myers (*Social Security*, 1981 ed., p. 282) as "a challenging and incisive demonstration and discussion."

Gratefully acknowledging the contributions of work and data from his associate, R. Norman Wood, FIA, and the SSA Office of the Actuary, "which provided the results of some new long-range cost projections," Calvert proceeded to point out the flaws in the formula that he repeated in a Society of Actuaries session in October 1975 (*RSA* 1, 751):

> If . . .the consumer price index were to rise at more than 55 percent of the rate of increase of the wage index, which is the situation we have now and seem likely to have in the future, then . . .the system will provide benefits more liberal and more costly than intended even though the economy would be laboring and not doing well, with real wages advancing slowly if at all.

Calvert closed his remarks to the Society of Actuaries with a specific suggestion:

> Until this great problem of the basic benefit formula is removed from the Social Security system, there can be no rational cost estimates or benefit forecasts, and the design and indeed the very existence of private pension plans . . . can only be looked at as highly tentative. We cannot assume that Congress will automatically understand this whole technical matter, or will think it is easy to make fundamental changes. . . .
>
> The actuarial profession . . . is in a natural position to assist Congress greatly in the task of deciding to act on this matter, by *expressing its opinion as a profession*. . . .
>
> The Society of Actuaries now has within its Constitution the provisions for making such an expression. [I] ask and urge the members . . .to take this step in the interests both of the Social Security system itself, and in a broader sense, of this nation.

In June 1974 the Senate Committee on Finance, impelled by a warning printed in the 1974 OASDI Trustees Report that the long-range actuarial cost estimates were showing a negative actuarial balance over the 75-year valuation period substantially outside the acceptable limit of variation, called for appointment of a panel to give that Committee an independent analysis of the problem. That panel, composed of its chairman, William C. Hsiao, three other actuaries, and two economists, responded in January 1975 with three findings (that the actuarial status of the system was unsatisfactory; that the benefit formula responded irrationally to changes in the rate of inflation; and that methodology for forecasting and analysis was inadequate) and with three recommendations for action based on those findings. The report touched on the question whether salvation was to be found by a price-indexing or a wage-indexing approach, expressing tentative preference for the former.

In March 1975 the Advisory Council on Social Security told the Congress of its opinion that a serious technical flaw in the benefit structure demanded remedy, whereupon the Congress engaged a group of consultants to recommend a specific revision of that structure. That panel was composed of three actuaries; William C. Hsiao (Project Director), James C. Hickman, and Ernest J. Moorhead, along with Peter A. Diamond, Ph.D., an economics professor. Frank L. Griffin also had been a panel member during much of its work but was not at the time of the report.

A review of the Advisory Council's report by K. Arne Eide appears in *TSA* 27, 651, and a review of the Hsiao Consultant Panel report by Charles L. Trowbridge is in *TSA* 28, 367. The latter review compared the recommendations of the two reports. The Advisory Council had opted for a solution by wage indexing, while the Consultant Panel had adhered to price indexing, thus inspiring, in Trowbridge's words, "some degree of friendly debate among actuaries and others interested in the technicalities of the OASDI benefit formula." The Society of Actuaries chose not to try for the official expression of opinion that Calvert had favored, leaving that responsibility to the Academy. The Society's hands-off decision was regrettable; the choice of indexing system was a question of great importance, and there was enough competent actuarial support on each side to warrant opening it to thorough internal discussion and an attempt at resolution. The two systems were discussed at the October 1976 meeting, Hsiao's comment there being (*RSA* 2, 902):

> The actuarial profession has an unprecedented opportunity to help shape the social security program. ...Perhaps in the future more actuaries will devote more time to social insurance and will take a crucial part in the coming discussions and debates.

Society President Robert T. Jackson voiced three "generalizations," his second and third being germane to this matter (*TSA* 29, 4):

> The second is that we have done a terrible job of persuading the public of the value of membership in our Society.

> The third . . . is that in all this recent actuarial history the role of the Society has been reactive, not initiative.

The indexing alternatives did not come up again on a Society program until October 1977 in the Moorhead and Trowbridge paper "The Unresolved OASDI Decoupling Issue" (*TSA* 29, 429) and a teaching session six months later by those two actuaries (*RSA* 4, 325). By that time, passage of the 1977 amendments in Congress had made the choice no longer unresolved; wage indexing was operative.

In the Academy, two statements on this subject were made. The first, in February 1976 (reported in the *Academy Newsletter,* March 1976), said:

> [I]t is premature for the Academy to take a position with respect to the precise formula, but we expect to do so in due course. We believe, however, that it is not too early to endorse the "uncoupling" principle recommended by the 1974–75 [Advisory] Council.

But at House hearings in July 1977, Chairman Robert F. Link of the Academy's Social Insurance Committee said (*JAAA*, 3, 124):

> Decoupling is apparently non-controversial. Everybody wants to do it. The only questions have to do with how and to some extent with initial benefit levels. Actuaries have participated in the development of the Advisory Council approach to decoupling, on which the proposals of the Administration and the American Council of Life Insurance are based. They have also participated in the work of the Panel of the Congressional Research Service, which developed an alternative approach. In early 1976, the American

Academy of Actuaries issued a position paper favoring decoupling. A copy is attached to this testimony.

Actuaries have no united position as to whether the Advisory Council approach or the Panel approach would be preferable. However, in approaching this question, it is helpful to have several points in mind.

1. There are some differences between the two approaches relating to transition arrangements, initial benefit levels, formula breakpoints, and so forth. The crucial difference is the basis for indexing the wage history—by average wages or by the CPI. ...

2. With reasonable assumptions, the standard of living for successive waves of newly retired persons will rise under either approach. Under the Advisory Council approach, it will rise as fast as it does for workers. Under the Panel approach, it will rise more slowly than it does for workers.

3. The Advisory Council approach intends to fix a scale of replacement ratios that will remain level in the future. The Panel approach expects replacement ratios to decline, leaving room for Congress to adjust the system from time to time in accordance with currently perceived benefit standards.

A Panel member can readily concede the soundness of these three statements as a capsule explanation of the differences between these approaches, but, in the light of subsequent history, may be permitted to doubt that Link's fourth point was warranted:

4. These adjustments can be technically troublesome. Trying to make sensible changes that are consistent for people who have just retired and people who are about to retire leads to benefit formulas that are complicated and messy.

In the fall of 1976, the Academy had distributed (upon request) a Social Security Speaker's Kit developed by Moorhead and Myers. Decision to offer such a kit had been announced in an article by those two actuaries, "Actuaries Urged—and Helped—To Teach on Social Security" (*Academy Newsletter*, May 1976), remarking that the need to restore shaken public confidence in the system gave actuaries an exceptional opportunity to render public service of a kind that actuaries were better equipped than any other groups of citizens to offer.

Educational items recommended by the Academy Committee, in addition to the Speaker's Kit, were the 1977 Moorhead and Trowbridge paper and an article by Donald D. Cody, "Financial Appraisal of Social Security Proposals," which appeared in special supplements to *The Actuary,* October 1977 and April 1978. Cody described these proposals in *RSA* 4, 151 also.

The 1977 amendments were confidently described in the 1978 OASDI Trustees Report as having restored the financial soundness of the cash benefit program throughout the remainder of this century and into the early years of the next one. But, as Table VI.2 shows, the condition of the OASDI trust funds departed seriously from the 1978 forecasts only two years later, and by 1981 the balance in those funds was headed for quick exhaustion.

Table VI.2

OASDI TRUST FUNDS, DECEMBER 31, 1976–1982
Estimates on Intermediate Assumptions in 1978 Trustees Report

	1976	1977	1978	1979	1980	1981	1982
In Billions of Dollars							
Estimated, 1978	—	—	30.6	28.6	27.9	35.3	46.2
Actual	41.2	35.9	31.7	30.3	26.4	24.5	12.4*
As Percentage of Disbursements of Following Year							
Estimated, 1978	—	37	28	24	21	25	n.a.
Actual	47	37	30	24	18	15	7

*Excluding another $12.4 billion borrowed.

The trouble was the inflation rate, already high in the years 1976 to 1978 at between 6 and 8% (though encouraging in contrast to the 11 and 9% of the years 1974 and 1975), jumped to 11.3% in 1979 and remained in double digits in 1980 at 13.5% and 1981 at 10.4%. The stability of the indexing formula adopted in 1977 was ruined by the quite natural failure of national wage increases to keep pace with unprecedented inflation exceeded in severity only once in United States history, i.e., between 1917 and 1920.

A bipartisan National Commission on Social Security Reform was appointed by President Reagan in December 1981 with instructions to report after the 1982 elections. Our profession earned favorable notice by the appointment and performance of Robert J. Myers as that Commission's Executive Director. After trust fund exhaustion had been averted by borrowing from the disability and hospital insurance funds, a package of remedies, including taxation of benefits for higher-income people, reduction of windfall benefits, raising of payroll tax rates and increases in normal retirement age starting in the year 2000, ensured that the burden would be shared by employers, contributors and beneficiaries.

The Academy was active in 1981 with statements (numbered 5, 11, 14, and 18 in that year's *Journal*). Statement No. 5, by the Committee on Social Insurance, mentioned (a) that if the 1977 amendments had provided benefit increases based upon the smaller of wage or price increases, short-term cash-flow problems would not now be upon us, and (b) that greater attention should have been paid to the message conveyed by the pessimistic assumptions in the 1978 Trustees Report. No. 5 was one of several statements urging that actuaries responsible for estimates be free to use their best professional judgment and expertise independent of pressures for political expediency and (successfully as it turned out) that the chief actuaries be required to issue opinions certifying the reasonableness of the actuarial assumptions they used.

Volume 33 (1981) of the *Transactions* is a veritable library of information and well-considered opinions on the social security problems of the previous decade: five papers and their discussions, one, Dwight K. Bartlett's "Measures of Actuarial Status for Social Security: Retrospect and Prospect" containing historical analysis back to the 1930s; and reviews of the 1981 Trustees Reports, of the Final Report of the

National Commission on Social Security, of A. Haeworth Robertson's *The Coming Revolution in Social Security,* and of the second edition of Robert J. Myers' *Social Security.* Reviews in prior volumes should also be mentioned: of Alicia H. Munnell's *The Future of Social Security* (*TSA* 30, 502); of Robert M. Ball's *Social Security—Today and Tomorrow* (*TSA* 30, 505); and of Martha Derthick's *Policymaking for Social Security* (*TSA* 31, 555).

DISCIPLINE

As memberships of actuarial bodies grew and fields of specialization proliferated, caseloads of the several Committees on Professional Conduct (or on Discipline) inevitably became heavier. Most complaints never reached the Board level because the alleged misconduct was minor and the offending actuary simply admitted his error and promised to mend his ways. Professional conduct was also a consideration in several unfamiliar respects, such as relationships with other professions, independence of the actuary, annual statement certifications, and new governmental requirements.

The subject turned up regularly in presidential addresses and newsletter editorials. In the May 1978 *Academy Newsletter,* Mary H. Adams and Jarvis Farley embarked upon a series entitled "Professional Conduct: What Would You Do?," each such query being followed by reporting in due course what responders felt they would have done. The first such puzzle was about a consulting actuary experienced in life company operations who was asked for help by a client on the adequacy of reserves in an affiliated casualty company, posing the question of qualifications needed to justify giving advice in specific situations. This series must have stimulated actuaries to think about professional conduct guides and opinions, which were being expanded and revised in yearbooks. A quite remarkable contributing effort in October 1977 (*RSA* 3, 767) was "The Reality of Professional Conduct"; this was a mini-drama in which Dale R. Gustafson, Daphne D. Bartlett, and W. James MacGinnitie played roles of actuaries and other executives pondering aloud their responsibilities in difficult cases that had arisen or might arise in practice. The following spring at the Casualty Society MacGinnitie starred again this time with Mavis A. Walters and Charles C. Hewitt, in a series of the same kind described in *The Actuarial Review,* July 1978.

In 1974 (*TSA* 26, D531) at a session chaired by Robert J. Myers, visiting speakers in the accounting, legal, and medical professions gave the benefit of their views and experiences with professional ethics.

A sad day for the profession came in March 1973 when headlines revealed a complex pattern of frauds committed for nearly a decade in the California head office of the Equity Funding Life Insurance Company, involving two young actuaries, both Fellows of the Society of Actuaries and Academy members. The misdeeds, creating records of fictitious policies so as to acquire money from reinsurers that were paying temptingly high allowances on first premiums remitted to them, were of a nature and gravity unparalleled in actuarial annals.

The senior of the two actuaries had presented a paper to the Conference in 1969 describing the nature and basic appeal of the company's contracts designed to enable policyholders to achieve "leverage" by earning a higher yield on mutual fund shares than that charged on their loans to pay life insurance premiums.

The fraud was the subject of much publicity, including several books, one of which, *Crime by Computer* by Donn B. Parker, devoted a 56-page chapter to it. Authors Ronald L. Soble and Robert E. Dallos of another book, *The Impossible Dream*, asserted that the younger of the two offending actuaries had rationalized the sale of fictitious insurance as no more than temporary borrowing of money without collateral.

Even though the disciplinary procedures of the Society of Actuaries had been immensely strengthened since doubts about their feasibility in such extreme cases had been expressed in 1954, the length of time until final action was taken in this case aroused concern among the members. The delay was necessitated by court proceedings having nothing to do with actuarial conduct rules. In June 1975 the Society and Academy announced that the two actuaries had been expelled from membership, the only instance of such extreme action ever found necessary in our profession's history on this continent. A session at the Conference (*PCAPP* 23, 93) delved into the details of the fraud.

In early 1977, the younger of the two expelled actuaries conferred a favor upon his former profession by agreeing to a taped interview giving, as he said, "insight as to the thought process that was involved." His revealing observations are printed in *RSA* 3, 778, as Scene 6 in the already mentioned "The Reality of Professional Conduct."

A letter from Society of Actuaries Past-President Gilbert W. Fitzhugh printed in *The Actuary,* December 1976, raised some thought-provoking questions about actuarial responsibilities:

> Why is our profession so afraid to come out with strong statements not watered down to accommodate the most timorous on such publicly demoralizing issues as the effect of inflation on actuarial reserves and the people's future, or the serious economic and moral problems involved in deferring pension costs to future generations. . . ?

> Have we forgotten that we have one of the most sacred trusts of all—making sure that promises made now are kept many years in the future, many times for beneficiaries of people no longer here to check up on us?

> Is this change in focus just an unfortunate side effect of the general decline of moral and intellectual standards in the country, or is it possibly due partly to the exponential growth in our numbers? . . .

> I'm old enough to know that there are usually more than two sides to every question, so I hope . . .these remarks [may] start a dialogue or multilogue. . . .
> It just might be healthy.

Although rather little response to this query appeared in the newsletter's columns, it is known that Fitzhugh's worries along these lines sparked some of the healthy debate that he had sought. His propositions still deserve to be pondered.

PENSIONS

The sparsity of actuarial pension literature on which Bronson, Trowbridge, and others had commented became a thing of the past in the mid-1960s as a steady flow of papers, discussions and reports began to appear. Society of Actuaries President Gilbert W. Fitzhugh set the stage in his 1966 address, (*TSA* 18, 117):

> [P]ractically all actuarial work involves the evaluation of long-term obligations. . . . Whether or not these . . . will be fulfilled is determined, perhaps more than by anything else, by the ability and integrity of the actuary. . . .

> Along with these tremendous increases in the responsibilities of actuaries, there has fortunately been a great increase in the numbers of our members. . . . While the primary job [of developing qualified new members] is naturally one for our hard-working and effective Committees on Education and Examination, there is much more to the training and education of a truly qualified actuary. . . . A great variety of qualities is developed through daily work on actuarial jobs and through the personal associations between younger and older members of the Society. In the past, when the Society was much smaller and the responsibilities of its members were more homogeneous, this development process was easier. A large part of it came about through a sort of osmosis. With our current size and heterogeneity of interests, it is more difficult. . . .

> With 35 million people having a private pension program of one form or another, we have [a] tremendous group of people . . . relying on actuaries to play well their significant role in the sound design and operation of these programs for their economic security in old age. . . .

Groundwork had already been laid for the Employee Retirement Income Security Act of 1974 (ERISA), but there was reason for doubt whether actuaries could find sufficient consensus to make any worthwhile statement to the authorities. In 1972 Blackburn H. Hazlehurst described the state of affairs (*TSA* 24, D48):

> In 1965 the Committee to Study Pension Plan Problems of the Society put in hand a project that was intended to result in a book [about actuarial principles and practices for pensions plans]. . . . Several versions of this book were drafted. *To date, each draft of this book has been tabled.* It is extremely difficult for actuaries to agree on detailed discussions of acceptable and, by implication, unacceptable working procedures. . . .

> Indeed, the credibility and viability of the entire private pension industry is being questioned. . . . Among the complaints leveled at the private pension system is the suggestion that pension "promises" go unfulfilled for many if not most of those who are covered by pension plans at one time or another and that the funding and investment of pension assets may reflect the business needs of the plan sponsor more than the retirement needs of the plan members.

> Beyond this, the business community occasionally has its attention drawn to the fact that differing actuarial reviews of the same set of circumstances may produce widely differing cost conclusions, casting doubt upon the validity and usefulness of any actuarial report.

Hazlehurst mentioned also that "anyone can call himself an actuary, and a variety of people do," and "some firms are prepared to . . . [use] virtually any assumption they are requested to use—usually performing a 'computer' rather than an 'actuarial' service."

Canadian actuary F. Eugene Smith said that it is too late to sit back and say (ibid., p. D58):

> "We are qualified actuaries, so you must accept what we say about pension plans without question.". . . Pension legislation in Canada may be at a turning point. I believe that we have to move, and move fast, or run the serious risk of being put in a legislative straitjacket that will convert us from pension actuaries to pension mathematicians.

Solution to the vexing obstacle of diversity of pension actuaries' language was still years away. As late as 1975, Donald S. Grubbs was repeating the theme (*TSA* 27, 657):

> Actuarial terminology presents problems because there is no uniformity in the terms used within the profession.

The following year (*TSA* 28, 327), the Society of Actuaries Committee on Pensions issued a report containing a recommended glossary but admitted that its contents arose from compromises that would not completely satisfy anyone. It was not until July 1981 that a Joint Committee (of the Academy, ASPA, the Conference, and the Society) issued a pamphlet optimistically described as a final report. Nevertheless, in 1985, Arthur W. Anderson, author of *Pension Mathematics for Actuaries,* a book commissioned by the profession, felt it necessary to say in his introductory chapter that there continued to be "some differences between real-life actuarial usage and the recommendations of the Joint Committee."

Pension trail-blazing was being accomplished by authors of several books and papers, notably the following:

1965   "Measuring the Investment Yield of Pension Funds," R. Norman Wood, pamphlet by Alexander and Alexander, Inc.

1965   "It's Time to Tell the Story to Employees" by Geoffrey N. Calvert, first of a series of Alexander and Alexander pamphlets on Calvert's work in this field.

1966   "Concepts of Adequacy in Pension Plan Funding," Frank L. Griffin, Jr., *TSA* 18, 46.

1969   Griffin and Trowbridge, *Status of Funding under Private Pension Plans,* a Pension Research Council study reviewed by Preston C. Bassett and A. Charles Howell, *TSA* 21, 629.

1970   "Private Pension Plan Performance, Vesting, and the Coverage Dilemma" Griffin, *PCAPP* 20, 1.

1972   "Progressive Approach to Pension Funding," Preston C. Bassett, *Harvard Business Review,* Nov.-Dec. 1972, 52.

Turning back now to the discussions between actuaries and accountants on pension matters—Frank L. Griffin's six-page review in 1965 (*TSA* 17, 575) of Ernest L. Hicks' *Accounting for the Cost of Pension Plans* (AICPA's Accounting Research Study No. 8) consisted of four segments, viz., Background, Scope of the Published Study, Summary of Conclusions and Recommendations, and Comments (by Griffin himself and others). The result was a useful statement of the accounting profession's first considered views and some reactions thereto.

Under Background, Griffin said:

> Publication of Accounting Research Study No. 8 brings to a conclusion nearly
> five years of information-gathering, discussion, drafting, and editing by the
> [AICPA] research staff.... The Project Advisory Committee appointed to
> consult with the director and his staff consisted, at one time or another, of one
> partner from each of four major accounting firms [Hicks being one of these],
> four representatives of industrial organizations, and three professional men
> (including two members of the Society of Actuaries—B. Russell Thomas, F.S.A.
> and Sylvester J. Huse, A.S.A.). ...

> [The Society's] Committee to Study Pension Accounting [chaired by Grif-
> fin] ... reviewed three preliminary drafts of the accountants' study and
> made a number of suggestions through its individual members as well as
> in the form of a committee draft of "actuarial guidelines." Two mem-
> bers ... Frederick P. Sloat and Charles L. Trowbridge, were singled out
> in [Hicks'] credits.

In summarizing the report's contents, Griffin said (p. 576):

> The one recommendation ... fundamental to all the others is that pension costs
> should be accounted for on the accrual basis rather than the cash basis, which
> has been generally followed in the past. ... [I]f the employer selects a 30-year
> amortization period, the accounting charge will be normal cost and 30-year
> amortization, even though the employer contributes more or less than this
> amount.

Griffin then listed and briefly commented on ten conclusions of the study having
a bearing upon the amount of the accounting charge to be made or specifying balance
sheet and disclosure requirements, and summed up (p. 580):

> Notwithstanding a number of valid criticisms of this study, the author has done
> a creditable job on a difficult research project.

That review also drew attention to dissenting opinions by Thomas and W. A.
Walker published with the study, and other criticisms by actuaries John Hanson and
Howard H. Hennington.

The very first (March 1967) issue of *The Actuary* reported on a session of the
American Pension Conference on what had become Accounting Principles Board
(APB) Opinion No. 8 of the AICPA (issued in 1966), the main discussion being a
dialogue between Sloat and Hicks.

Particulars and initial attitudes by actuaries to APB No. 8 are set forth in *TSA*
19, D68, D240, and D572. That document proved influential, one consequence
being a 1966 request by the Society of Actuaries Board of Governors that its Committee to Study Pension Problems develop what amounted to a guide for actuaries
to accepted principles and practices in valuation of pension liabilities. John K. Dyer,
in 1972 opened a discussion (*TSA* 24, D45) on that issue, explaining that committee
opinions were divided on the contents of such a guide, and even on whether one was
desirable. A possible advantage, he said, might be reduction of encroachment by the
accounting and other professions and by the IRS into decision-making areas properly

belonging to the actuaries. His view was that actuarial practices of at least borderline validity were still disturbingly prevalent.

As the Academy acquired strength and influence, its committees and the joint committees that it organized steadily took over more of the work of advising the drafters of the clearly impending federal legislation. In 1974 the Society of Actuaries hosted a session on "Accepted Actuarial Practices for Pension Plans" (*TSA* 26, D743) at which committee leaders George B. Swick, Dyer, Thomas P. Bleakney, Hennington, M. David R. Brown, and Bassett described the problems and the substantial progress that had been made. The already mentioned 1969 Griffin and Trowbridge study had given encouraging evidence that most of the major plans then existing were more substantially funded than had been widely supposed. But diversity was still the rule. Edwin F. Boynton said in October 1973 (*TSA* 25, D483) that there were many recognized funding methods in common use, all of these strongly endorsed by one or more actuaries as the proper way of doing things. He reported:

> The accounting profession, after probably ten or more years of study, attempted to answer these questions in the exposure draft of "Audits of Pension Funds," issued last spring. The proposals in the guide were objected to so strongly by both the business and the actuarial communities that the guide has been withdrawn at least temporarily and the project turned over to the Financial Accounting Standards Board.

Passage of ERISA in September 1974 made some issues obsolete and turned discussion mostly to themes of compliance and accreditation. But the need for communication between the actuarial and accounting professions and respect for each other's responsibilities continued, and was met by establishing a Committee on Relations within each profession to meet jointly at regular intervals. The Academy's 1974 *Year Book* described the functions of these committees thus (p. 11):

> Task forces will operate under the aegis of each profession's committee, as needed, to work on particular questions. However, this [Joint] Committee initiates dialogue at an early stage of any situation involving both professions and provides means for anyone in either profession to seek an answer to a question involving expertise of the other profession.

This mechanism and the good sense within both professions resolved many difficulties of prior years and enabled their leaders to know and appreciate each other as never before. Prominent among actuaries who had laid the foundation for all this were Bassett, Calvert, Griffin, and Frederick P. Sloat. The last named was particularly able to help inasmuch as he was employed by a leading accounting firm.

Among ERISA's provisions of high significance to our profession were the unprecedented fiduciary responsibilities placed on the shoulders of consultants, regulations in matters of eligibility, vesting, funding, actuarial reports, plan termination insurance through the Pension Benefit Guaranty Corporation (PBGC), and qualification standards for Enrolled Actuaries.

The governing authority on Enrolled Actuary qualifications was the Joint Board (of the IRS and Department of Labor) for the Enrollment of Actuaries. Its Executive Director from the outset has been Leslie S. Shapiro who quickly became known for his grasp of educational needs and his attention to actuaries' views. The Board's original Advisory Committee included three actuaries: Rowland E. Cross, Donald S. Grubbs, and Ellis W. Scott.

In May 1975, the Joint Board listed a proposed regulation on eligibility and other enrollment requirements setting standards of education and organizational affiliation that in our profession's view were seriously flawed. Only specified college degrees were called for, and membership in ASPA was to be on a par with that in the Academy, the Conference or the Society. The Academy's response, reported to its members in the *Academy Newsletter* of June 1975, urged that enrollment be established in such a fashion that the Joint Board and the public could be assured that any Enrolled Actuary had met at least a minimal level of actuarial competence. The only way to achieve this, said the Academy, was to rely upon the examination of the Joint Board as a uniform standard of minimum required actuarial knowledge, adding this proposal:

> We recommend, therefore, that the Joint Board, after establishing the degree of difficulty of its examination, waive such examination for persons who have already passed a series of examinations which are at least of the level of difficulty of the Joint Board exam.

In due course, essentially these recommendations were adopted, one consequence being that the enrollment examinations became parts of the Society of Actuaries curriculum. ASPA was made a joint sponsor of those examinations, and the Society of Actuaries and ASPA learned how to cooperate in that work.

Views of federal regulation, before ERISA's passage but after it was obvious that federal legislation was inevitable, may be found in *TSA* 24, D21. One of many descriptions of ERISA's provisions was circulated in a November 1974 special edition of *The Actuary*. There followed a long series of explanations and discussions of the Act's unfolding regulations and other guidelines, in *RSA, PCAPP,* and the Academy's *Newsletter, Enrolled Actuaries Reports* and *Journal*.

Envelopment of Enrolled Actuaries into Academy membership was accomplished in a series of steps. First, in January 1976, those Enrolled Actuaries who were not otherwise members were accorded Affiliate status, subject to acceptance of their applications by the Academy. Three years later that distinction between Affiliates and Members was dropped. Subsequently, the basic educational requirement was defined as Associateship in the Casualty Actuarial Society or Society of Actuaries or status as an Enrolled Actuary. The letter "e" was used to identify Enrolled Actuaries in *Yearbook* listings until "E.A." was adopted in 1985.

In the companion field of public employee pension systems, discussions in 1971 (*TSA* 23, D465) and 1972 (*TSA* 24, D167) had shown that actuaries were worried about chronic underfunding, although sympathetic with problems peculiar to the genre. Nevertheless, there was acute embarrassment in early 1974 when, as Gary Corbett later summarized it (*TSA* 27, 540):

> [T]he assistant city manager of Sacramento, California, wrote letters to the Academy and the Society, in which he questioned the seemingly irreconcilable differences in actuarial assumptions used by different actuarial firms with respect to the funding of the city's retirement system. ....

After an investigation under the auspices of both the Academy and the Society, certain funding questions including some in reference to the effects of inflation, were referred to the Academy Committee on Principles and Practices in Connection with Pension Plans. In a draft Recommendation this committee determined that the probable effects of inflation should be considered in actuarial statements. . . . [This] controversy is an example of the pressures on the actuarial profession to move toward making more explicit its technical principles and practices, even if the result is a lessening of desirable flexibility.

In 1972, a primer for legislators and others outside the actuarial profession, *Retirement Systems for Public Employees* by Thomas P. Bleakney, had been published. This was reviewed by J. Darrison Sillesky (*TSA* 25, 199).

A major study of pension mathematics, *Introduction to the Dynamics of Pension Funding*, by three actuarial science professors, Newton L. Bowers, Jr., James C. Hickman, and Cecil J. Nesbitt, was published in 1976 (*TSA* 28, 177). The authors considered, and those who discussed the paper concurred, that it laid a foundation for the mathematical exploration of pension funding under conditions of growth arising from inflation or other causes. Also in 1976, a new textbook, *The Theory and Practice of Pension Funding* by C. L. Trowbridge and C. E. Farr, was published under Society of Actuaries sponsorship for its course of reading. A review by Paul H. Jackson is in *TSA* 29, 482.

Nevertheless, outgoing Academy President Edwin F. Boynton gave a discouraging summing-up in October 1978 (*JAAA* 4, 12):

> The problem of the development of [standards of practice for pension plans] has been compounded by a number of factors, including not only the well-known independent spirit typical of most consulting pension actuaries, who all believe that they have the right answers, but a number of [others], some of which were beyond our control.

Other factors that Boynton mentioned were the pervasive character of ERISA, the negotiations with accountants, and the new conditions imposed by high inflation rates. Later in that meeting (ibid., pp. 34–56), four panelists outlined current and prospective legislative developments affecting pension plans. One of these speakers, Thomas C. Woodruff, Executive Director of the President's Commission on Pension Policy, which was just starting work to define a national retirement income policy and to institute public discussion and debate about federal legislation under consideration, reported on its program. Lawrence M. Franklin, Policy Analysis Officer of the PBGC, the entity created by ERISA in 1974 to give pension plan participants some assurance that their vested benefits would be protected in event of plan termination, reported on that body's activities and problems.

At the close of the decade, one of substantial accomplishments in increasing actuaries' abilities to cope with complex pension problems never previously anticipated, much still remained to be done. A Supreme Court decision (the *Manhart* case concerning discrimination against women, to which the Academy and Society had contributed a brief) had posed new questions. A President's Commission on Pension Policy, which

Preston C. Bassett served part-time as staff actuary, was conducting a review of retirement and disability programs, both private and public, aimed at developing a national retirement policy. And the profession was actively in the field of education and enlightenment of Enrolled Actuaries by examinations, seminars and the regular bulletin, *Enrolled Actuaries Report.*

ATTEMPT AT CONSOLIDATION OF ACTUARIAL BODIES

An unsuccessful effort to streamline our profession in North America began through the Council of Presidents in 1975, when a report of its Joint Committee on Organizational Coordination proposed that the then six actuarial bodies be reduced to three: one international body and two national bodies (one each for Canada and the United States).

By early 1976 the number of such proposals had jumped all the way to four, descriptions of which were printed in *The Actuary* of May 1976 and *The Actuarial Review* of October 1976. These and other reports as well as discussions at actuarial clubs aroused much debate and many letters to editors. The Society of Actuaries Board then appointed a Board subcommittee called the Actuarial Restructuring Committee (ARC) to study the subject. ARC, chaired by John C. Wooddy, agreed that restructuring was urgently needed but considered none of the existing proposals sufficiently flexible. Thus a fifth plan, the ARC proposal, was up for consideration; the Board appointed a steering committee chaired by Julius Vogel to work with the other actuarial bodies in a search for an acceptable compromise. None being forthcoming, the Vogel committee was authorized in September 1977 to discuss merger of the Society of Actuaries with the Conference and the Fraternal Actuarial Association.

No plan ever aroused sufficient membership enthusiasm to warrant putting it to a vote. An article in *The Actuary* (December 1976) by Donald A. Rholl, "Actuaries Are Not For the Birds" neatly satirized the confusion caused by such a host of proposals.

Vogel, in his October 1980 presidential address to the Society of Actuaries, expressed his view of the, by then, moribund effort (*TSA* 32, 4):

> It seems to me that the missions of our various organizations are, in the aggregate, to facilitate the following activities:
>
> 1.   The education of new actuaries.
>
> 2.   The continuing education of existing actuaries.
>
> 3.   Research in matters of actuarial interest.
>
> 4.   The making of statements to the public and to government agencies. . . .
>
> 5.   The establishing of appropriate standards of professional conduct.
>
> 6.   Social interchanges among actuaries.
>
> These seem rather straightforward objectives, and it is hard to see why it requires so many overlapping organizations to accomplish them. Now I . . . appreciate that unification of the actuarial professions by merger or voluntary dissolution of the various organizations is a very unlikely near-term or middle-term prospect.

FAREWELL TO THE FRATERNAL ACTUARIAL ASSOCIATION

At this juncture, one of the six North American actuarial bodies, the Fraternal Actuarial Association, proceeded with voluntary dissolution. Its demise had no direct connection with the general attempt at consolidation but had been foreshadowed for many years. The FAA's large tasks from its founding days in 1916 had been to bring fraternal societies to a condition of actuarial soundness, and to provide services to fraternal actuaries that were not available through the other actuarial bodies. Once the conversions of fraternal societies to the level premium reserve system or some modification thereof had been achieved and Fellowship in the Society of Actuaries or the Casualty Actuarial Society had become, in 1967, a prerequisite for FAA Fellowship, the need for that actuarial body had obviously declined. The question, which stirred up a brouhaha in the final two years of FAA's existence, was what professional status might be made available to FAA Fellows of pre-1967 days who were still active but were not members of other bodies.

In 1978, an informal proposal that the FAA merge with the Society of Actuaries seemed to have rallied some support. A plan surfaced to admit retired FAA Fellows and all FAA Associates into the Society of Actuaries as Associates.

This plan caused the Society Board some difficulty. It was brought up at Board meetings in October 1978, January 1979, and May 1979, resulting in a ratifying constitutional amendment being submitted to the Society Fellows in June 1979. The vote was reminiscent of the responses by Fellows to recommendations in the early twentieth century that Fellowships be granted other than by examination; the 1979 ballot produced a much larger response (nearly 80%) than even the fall elections did. The proposal was soundly rejected despite considerable promotion by Society leaders.

The Fraternal Actuarial Association thereupon proceeded with its own dissolution, which became effective September 30, 1980. Its small band of members were entitled to feel proud of what they and their forebears had accomplished. A history of the Association written by Dr. Vernon W. Roelofs with the assistance of the Association's last president, Bartley L. Munson, and other officers and past officers, is printed in the last volume, 1977–1980, of the Association's *Proceedings*.

FIRST JOINT MEETING OF THE CASUALTY ACTUARIAL SOCIETY AND SOCIETY OF ACTUARIES, 1978

After having existed together for sixty-four years and having gradually become accustomed to working jointly on numerous projects, including examinations since 1963, the Casualty Actuarial Society and Society of Actuaries held their first joint meeting in New York City in April 1978. Long before then, discussions at Society of Actuaries meetings had begun to embrace topics outside the life and pension fields. Among these were:

1958   Affiliation of small life companies with fire and casualty companies (*TSA* 10, 303).

1958   Entry of casualty interests into the life insurance field (*TSA* 10, 686).

1961   Description of CAS structure and activities (*TSA* 13, D474).

1972   Impact on life actuaries of no-fault, workmen's compensation, and malpractice insurances (*TSA* 24, D857).

1973   Effect of no-fault auto insurance on health insurance (*TSA* 25, D37).

1978   Claim reserves for property and casualty insurance (*RSA* 4, 221).

1978   Actuarial certifications and opinions rendered (*RSA* 4, 241).

Also since 1971, the *Academy Newsletter* had helped to bring problems of one body to the attention of members of other bodies. An example, in the September 1974 issue, was an article by Matthew Rodermund, "Casualty Actuaries Face New Challenges." Another was a March 1979 editorial labelled "Attention Life and Pension Actuaries" that opened with:

> If you have not been following the problems which casualty actuaries are having with the proposed NAIC statement of opinion on property-liability claim reserves, you are making a mistake.

LIFE INSURANCE RESERVES AND NONFORFEITURE VALUES

At a Society of Actuaries session in May 1972 (*TSA* 24, D281), panelists explored the virtues and defects of the Guertin laws of the 1940s, expressing strong consensus that the time had come for them to be completely reviewed. In October 1973 the Society Board appointed a Committee on Nonforfeiture Values and Reserves to study this broad subject. Subsequently it was recognized that the questions of valuation and of minimum surrender benefits might better be examined separately. Two committees therefore came into being, the one pursuing policy reserve and surplus matters being initially chaired by Robert N. Houser (succeeded in 1977 by Charles L. Trowbridge), while the committee to explore surrender values was chaired by Henry C. Unruh (succeeded in 1976 by Ardian C. Gill). Both committees realized that their reports would be given to the NAIC, in which body John O. Montgomery, a Society Fellow, had come to the forefront as an authority determined to develop modern laws for recommendation to the states.

COMMITTEE WORK ON STATUTORY MINIMUM
NONFORFEITURE BENEFITS

The Unruh Committee Report in October 1975 (*TSA* 27, 549) undertook to express its views on the fundamentals and the technical features of nonforfeiture benefits. Recognizing that "equity, like beauty, is in the eye of the beholder," it began by setting forth the divergent views of the five groups concerned: terminating and continuing policyholders, the insurance company, the agent, and the regulator. The committee made few specific recommendations but did say (p. 565):

> We think it undesirable that minimum nonforfeiture values be set at such a high level . . . that they significantly alter [field] compensation practices or adversely influence the cost to continuing policyholders to any great extent. . . . While the adjusted premium method of the Standard Nonforfeiture Law has a number of

defects, it has worked very well over the several decades it has been in use. In the absence of compelling reasons to change to another method, our committee's conclusion was to suggest keeping fundamentally [that] method ... and to concentrate on improving it.

Having endorsed the method, the committee turned its attention to the interest, mortality, and expense factors to be employed. It tested the effects of a "Modern CSO" table that it developed from recent mortality experience and fortified with margins by the same formula as had been used to construct the 1958 CSO table. The interest rate in these tests was 4% with a range of possible expense rates.

The committee also explored the long sought goal of reducing or removing the policy-by-policy linkage between valuation reserves and cash values. The case for substituting an aggregate requirement was set forth cogently in a committee paper by John R. Gardner, printed in the November 1976 issue of *The Actuary.*

The committee report was reviewed by Linda B. Emory (*The Actuary,* March 1976) and by William H. Bowman (*TSA* 28, 343) and was extensively discussed at spring meetings that year (*RSA* 2, 329 and 707). Charles F. B. Richardson (ibid., p. 338) described the initial reactions of the NAIC committee to which the report had been sent. In the matter of the interest rate, Richardson expressed the thought, new to many, that minimum values, if they could be divorced from policy reserve assumptions, should be based on rates perhaps even as high as 5 or 6%. For guidance on the appropriate expense formula, the NAIC in due course turned to Richardson who was a member of its committee; his exploration and recommendation are contained in a paper, "Expense Formulas for Minimum Nonforfeiture Values," (*TSA* 29, 209). The formula that he found would fit the facts of his expense study "rather well" was remarkably simple: 125% of the 1958 CSO 3 1/2% net level premium plus $10 per $1,000. In one material respect, Richardson's view on minimum values expressed in that paper differed from that which had shaped the Guertin laws (p. 211):

> The consumer movement has become a powerful force in many sectors of private business, and neither the life insurance industry nor the regulators can safely ignore it. Today it does not seem politically feasible to base minimum values on expense factors that would accommodate the expense rates incurred by marginal or high-cost companies, as was the objective of the formulas in the Guertin laws.

In framing amendments to the Standard Nonforfeiture Law in 1976, the NAIC Committee accepted Richardson's expense formula and adhered closely to the Society committee's ideas. Those amendments are summarized in *RSA* 6, 185.

A committee headed by Charles A. Ormsby was appointed to develop a suitable successor to the 1958 CSO Table. The result of its work became the 1980 CSO Table, described in a July 1979 committee report printed in *TSA* 33, 617. Comparison of mortality rates over the eleven decades that separated the fifth from the first valuation table for ordinary life insurance in the United States is given in Table VI.3 for its historical interest.

Table VI.3

MORTALITY RATES PER 1,000
BY AMERICAN EXPERIENCE AND 1980 CSO TABLES

Table	Age				
	20	35	50	65	80
1868 (American Experience)	7.80	8.95	13.78	40.13	144.47
1980 CSO, Males	1.90	2.11	6.71	25.42	98.84
1980 CSO, Females	1.05	1.65	4.96	14.59	65.99

For the first time in the checkered history of valuation mortality tables, a professional actuarial recommendation was adopted by the actuaries without internal dissension and was accepted by the NAIC precisely as presented.

CHANGES IN STATUTORY VALUATION REQUIREMENTS

Introduction of new valuation laws was much more difficult and time-consuming than in the case of surrender values, mainly for the following three reasons: (1) the hazardous effects of the surge in inflation demanded that any change in statutory reserves be accompanied by company and regulatory consideration of appropriate levels of surplus and contingency reserves; (2) the range of products had become much broader than ever before, affecting even the degree of risk assumed by the company and the insured, respectively; and (3) the perennial problem of staffing insurance departments with qualified actuaries to administer the laws was far from having been solved. Two comments at a 1975 panel discussion, "Life Insurance Assets and Liabilities and Their Difference" (*RSA* 1, 398), testify to the problems and the turmoil:

> [Charles F. B. Richardson] I make a plea for a practical, realistic approach . . . and a strong effort to reach solutions, both to the nonforfeiture value and valuation problems, that can be properly administered by the very limited supply of technical personnel available in the state insurance departments. These problems demand broad, practical solutions rather than theoretical and idealistic approaches. In any event, one cannot legislate wise management.

> [John C. Wooddy] To pick an extreme example [of the circumstances we face today], if, tomorrow, market interest rates should go to 30% and stay there for a few years, a large proportion of the life insurance companies in this country would go bankrupt. . . .

> "Immunization" is fine under circumstances when it works . . . but, if cash flow cannot be forecast, then "immunization" may turn out to have been a trap.

The steps along the trail towards (a) a reserve system adapted to conditions of unprecedented inflationary surges and (b) phasing out rule-of-thumb surplus formulas (such as an arbitrary fixed percentage of assets) in favor of attempts at scientific solutions, can be traced through the Society of Actuaries volumes as follows:

1975   Two panel sessions on statutory and GAAP valuations and cash-flow hazards, in which guests from the United Kingdom contributed information on European experience (*RSA* 1, 139 and 375).

1975   The first broad discussion of risks of "adverse deviations," i.e., fluctuations, economic or internal, that might pose a threat to solvency (*RSA* 1, 887). Some of our actuarial forebears would have been puzzled by an introductory remark by moderator Edward A. Lew: "We must be careful not to freeze an excessive portion of [total] funds in reserves," and by Richardson's warning: "The fundamental fact is that, when you are in trouble, you need, not statutory reserves, but surplus in one form or another."

1976   A sequel to the previous year's sessions, this time under the label, "Solvency Standards for Life Companies in the United States, Canada, and the United Kingdom" (*RSA* 2, 179). The last of that session's four topics was, "Taking action when events presage possible insolvency."

1976   A session mainly on the nonforfeiture topic, which, however, included the first public remarks by Robert N. Houser on the work of his committee on valuation (*RSA* 2, 329).

1977   A session labelled "Surplus Needs of Life Insurance Companies," at which Charles L. Trowbridge made a brief preliminary statement saying that the committee's general purpose was "to develop a complete and consistent theory for the *entire* balance sheet of an *insurance enterprise* [his emphasis]" (*RSA* 3, 943).

1978   A multipurpose session, "Actuarial Certifications and Opinions Rendered"(*RSA* 4, 24), dealing with financial statements of casualty and life companies and also pension funds. Kenneth T. Clark informed United States actuaries of the introduction in Canada of the position of "valuation actuary." Details of the valuation actuary concept were given later that year at sessions entitled "New Actuarial Standards for Insurance Company Reporting in Canada" (*RSA* 4, 547 and 713).

1978   Two sessions, "Current Developments in Financial Reporting," including the topic, among many, of pending NAIC recommendations for fundamental changes in statutory reporting by both life and casualty insurers (*RSA* 4, 535 and 727).

1979   Text of a Discussion Draft, regarded also as a preliminary report of the Committee on Valuation and Related Problems (*RSA* 5, 256), and discussion of it (ibid., p. 241). Chairman Trowbridge again identified the project's aim, remarking that "the practical world of solvency regulation cannot build upon a solid base of consistent theory unless and until such theory is developed." He proceeded to identify risks to solvency labelled C_1, C_2 and C_3, and the corresponding contingency reserves designed to cope with those hazards, viz.,

         C_1—Contingency Reserve for Asset Depreciation

         C_2—Contingency Reserve for Pricing Inadequacy

         C_3—Contingency Reserve for Interest Rate Change

Research into these had been started, but much work and education lay ahead.

1979 "Proposed—A 'Dynamic' Valuation Interest Rate" (*RSA* 5, 917), a session designed to inform interested actuaries about a proposal that an ACLI subcommittee had been working on, intended to modify the Standard Valuation Law. Moderator Yuan Chang, chairman of that subcommittee, said: "The proposed modifications involve a revolutionary change in the approach to the prescription of the statutory maximum valuation interest rates," pointing out that the subcommittee had no choice in the current economic turmoil but to move speedily, and thus lacked the luxury to indulge in theoretical pursuits. He explained that the concept involved "automating the future prescription of statutory maximum valuation interest rates by making such rates a function of the trends in the financial market." The specific plan was to tie the maximum valuation rate to Moody's Average of Yields on Seasoned Aa Utility Bonds averaged over specified recent periods.

This plan was indeed developed and adopted promptly. A brief description of the outcome appears in articles by John O. Montgomery (*The Actuary,* Nov.- Dec. 1981 and Jan. 1982).

THE FIRST WOMAN PRESIDENT

In November 1977, the Casualty Actuarial Society laid the groundwork for a record-setting step when its members chose Ruth E. Salzmann as its president-elect. When she took office as president of that Society in November 1978, she was the first woman ever to head an actuarial body in North America. And she missed by only a month being first in the world; a section of the International Actuarial Association, ASTIN, had named Giovanna Ferrara of Italy as its chairman in October 1978. Salzmann's election, however, occurred eleven months earlier than Ferrara's.

Salzmann had qualified as a Fellow of the Casualty Actuarial Society in 1947 and had been elected to the CAS Council in 1967 and to vice president in 1976. She had contributed extensive committee service and numerous papers and panel presentations at meetings of the Society. The next woman to head an actuarial body was Barbara J. Lautzenheiser, who became president-elect of the Society of Actuaries in 1981 and president of that body in 1982–1983.

OUR PROFESSION IN 1979

This chapter is a logbook of a journey through troubled waters which actuaries had not been brought up to expect. Sudden change became the rule, lack of preparedness the major difficulty. Actuaries became too busy for adequate reflection. Some espoused a rite called futurism, expecting it to provide protection against at least some surprises.

Several experienced observers commented on the events and on what they revealed about the profession. Arthur Pedoe remarked in 1966 (*PCAPP* 16, 472):

> Actuarial work is an "art" not a "science."...The approximate nature of the actuary's calculations, the margin of error that he insists upon and does not excuse, his insistence that there may be more than one ... answer to a problem, are all the reverse of the academic mind, which expects the precision of the multiplication table. ...The actuary is a veritable "Doubting Thomas."

Fergus J. McDiarmid in the December 1979 issue of *The Actuary* reflected that, for inflation, his forecasts of 1958 had worked out much too well, while for common stock performance they had proved quite reliable in the first ten years but poor in the second ten. He predicted that stocks would do better in the 1980s than in the 1970s.

It was too early to see how well John M. Bragg's predictions about the future of the profession (e.g., *TSA* 26, 355) would pan out, but he remarked (ibid., p. 349):

> It seems to this author that there has been a trend in recent years toward activities which are not designed to provide service to the public and are not in the long-term interests of the profession.

He cited excessive preoccupation with profits, thousands of hours given to calculations of adjusted earnings, which "have not succeeded in bringing about uniformity and have not clarified the position of life stocks for investors," the rash of mergers and acquisitions of stock companies, and the unhappy historical "first" for the profession—actuaries accused of falsifying financial information.

William A. Halvorson in 1978 said (*TSA* 30, 4):

> [O]ur publics do not understand how the actuarial profession can defend differences of opinions by qualified actuaries that produce cost estimates differing by as much as 50 percent, or even 10 percent. Our credibility is strained beyond belief by statements that both actuaries might be right.

Some actuaries were beginning to demand definitions of standards of actuarial practice, while others despaired of defining these in a manner that would be helpful rather than just bureaucratic.

The public's awareness of the actuarial profession was growing fast but was not always accompanied by deference towards its practitioners. A perception of narrowness in actuarial training threatened to bring the actuaries of 1979 back to being considered, as they had been a century earlier, "mere mathematicians." Effect of specialization had reached the stage at which more and more large insurance companies had no officer bearing the title "chief actuary."

Improvement in usability and capacity of electronic machinery was transforming actuarial duties at junior and senior levels, and was altering the relationship of demand for actuaries to supply.

The state of actuarial research was accorded a mixture of compliment and censure by speakers in a 1978 session, "Actuarial Research—A Credit to the Profession?" (*RSA* 4, 951).

In the Casualty Actuarial Society, striking growth in membership, in prestige and in influence lay just ahead. Wide fluctuations of the underwriting cycle in most liability lines in the 1970s, together with a sharp increase in inflation, promised to create new actuarial problems. Reserving and rating uncertainties in the long-tail liability lines became so pressing that companies that had not thought they needed actuaries were scrambling to hire them or to contract with actuarial consulting firms. Naturally, the numbers of casualty actuaries in companies as well as in the consulting business mushroomed.

The growth of the CAS itself demanded more efficient management of that Society's affairs, which was to be effected in 1983.

Casualty reinsurance, formerly almost exclusively the realm of underwriters, had started to demand actuarial attention in the 1960s and by 1979 was a major subject for discussion.

In the lengthening list of joint projects by casualty and life actuaries, their assistance to the NAIC Blanks Committee in devising its so-called IRIS (Insurance Regulatory and Information System) ratios by which relatively quick tentative evaluation of a company's financial condition became possible, warrants mention.

Also in 1979 the CAS embarked upon its Discussion Paper program in which a major theme for each spring meeting was to be announced well in advance and papers on that subject invited. Those papers were not to be edited and were inexpensively copied and paperbound for distribution before the meeting. A cash prize was granted to the author of each year's best paper.

At an October 1979 Society of Actuaries session, "North American Actuarial Organizations" (*RSA* 5, 759), Mexican Actuarial Association President Jorge Susan Vallez reported that the Association had grown from fifteen members at its 1962 founding to more than two hundred, but even this was a mere one-third of Mexico's actuaries—so many emerging from actuarial training at Mexican National University were being drawn into the computer, statistical, and operations research fields. But the profession would grow rapidly. Casualty and property insurance was gaining recognition as an area for work by Mexican actuaries.

John T. Birkenshaw, speaking for the Canadian Institute of Actuaries, analyzed the relations between Francophone and Anglophone actuaries and between consulting and company actuaries:

> It is no secret that some 20 years ago . . . [F]rancophones were pushing hard to form their own separate group. . . . I believe Quebec actuaries [have come] to recognize the value of having a solid organization behind them. . . .
>
> Similarly, consulting actuaries presented a case for a separate forum. . . .
>
> [But the] Canadian Institute has had a fair degree of success in keeping the interest of all actuaries together and . . . this gives us a great deal of credibility in the eyes of the public.

Looking ahead after eighteen decades of actuarial practice on this continent during which the profession had grown from one lone actuary to more than 7,000, Julius Vogel, the last Society of Actuaries president of the 1970s, said (*TSA* 32, 4):

> As actuaries we have a key role in assuring the long-term survival of our companies, and we should remember . . . that in the long run what is best for the public is what is best for the companies; otherwise, the companies will not survive.

APPENDIX TO CHAPTER VI

Papers by North American Actuaries
at the Eighteenth through Twentieth International Congresses of Actuaries

EIGHTEENTH CONGRESS 1968, MUNICH

Attwood, J. A. (U.S.) "The current range and funding of insurance group pension contracts." XVIII, Vol. II, p. 1.

Bassett, P. C. (U.S.) "Bases of calculation and funding requirements for private non-insured retirement, disability and dependents' benefits within the United States." XVIII, Vol. I, p. 581.

Clarke, E. E. (Canada) "Canada pension plans." XVIII, Vol. I, p. 613.

Collins, R. M., Jr., and Hill, J. S. (U.S.) "Simulation models for life insurance." XVIII, Vol. II, p. 851.

Coward, L. E. (Canada) "Funding of employee pension plans." XVIII, Vol. I, p. 629.

Griffin, F. L., Jr. (U.S.) "Funding versus accounting under private pension plans in the United States." XVIII, Vol. II, p. 69.

Gundy, H. F. (Canada) "Mortality experiences in Canada." XVIII, Vol. I, p. 285.

Jackson, P. H. and Hamilton, J. A. (U.S.) "The valuation of the equity assets of pension funds." XVIII, Vol. II, p. 127.

Kahn, P. M. (U.S.) "A survey of some recent developments in credibility theory and experience rating from the Bayesian viewpoint." XVIII, Vol. II, p. 473.

Kormes, M. (U.S.) "Testing the adequacy of mortality and remarriage rates for widows, and permanent total disabilities under the 'West Virginia Workmen's Compensation Act.' " XVIII, Vol. I, p. 363.

Kraegel, W. A. (U.S.) "The actuary and data processing—1957 to 1967. A dynamic decade." XVIII, Vol. II, p. 915.

Lew, E. A. (U.S.) "An updated mortality basis for immediate annuities." XVIII, Vol. I, p. 377.

Longley-Cook, L. H. (U.S.) "Statistics and ratemaking for commercial fire insurance." XVIII, Vol. II, p. 511.

McGuinness, J. S. (U.S.) "Considerations in rating large-area structures for fire insurance." XVIII, Vol. II, p. 535.

Minor, E. H. (U.S.) "Comments on U.S. sickness insurance and bases of premiums therefore." XVIII, Vol. II, p. 561.

Morton, A. P. and Schmidt, W. H. (U.S.) "Trends in mortality among insured lives in the United States." XVIII, Vol. I, p. 449.

Muller, N. (Mexico) "A quantitative foundation of managing decision." XVIII, Vol. II, p. 975.

Myer, G. G. (Canada) "The interdependence of funding and investment in life assurance and pension funds in Canada." XVIII, Vol. II, p. 181.

Myers, R. J. (U.S.) "The actuarial bases of the United States national pension system: Cost assumptions and financing bases." XVIII, Vol. I, p. 833.

National Reports (Canada) "The present methods of participation in profits and distribution of profits in life, annuity, sickness and automobile insurance in Canada." XVIII, Vol. I, p.103.

National Reports (U.S.) "United States of America report on present methods of participation in profits." XVIII, Vol. I, p.243.

Rosser, H. (U.S.) "Interpolation by computer." XVIII, Vol. II, p. 1013.

Seal, H. L. (U.S.) "The use of multiple regression in risk classification based on proportionate losses." XVIII, Vol. II, p. 659.

Sternhell, C. M. (U.S.) "Calculation of gross annual premiums for participating non-cancellable monthly income disability policies." XVIII, Vol. II, p. 675.

Weaver, A. G. (U.S.) "Funding and investment during inflation." XVIII, Vol. II, p. 299.

NINETEENTH CONGRESS 1972, OSLO

Bitzer, J. F. (U.S.) "Uniform company pension plan objectives for international use; adaptation required by social insurance." XIX, Vol. III, p. 335.

Bragg, J. M. (U.S.) "Life insurance with guarantees against inflation." XIX, Vol. I, p. 341.

Cannon, G. E. and Timpe, R. E. (U.S.) "Methods of forecasting the development of an insurance company during the next ten years." XIX, Vol. II, p. 39.

Collins, R. M., Jr. (U.S.) "A non-proportional (spread-loss) reinsurance pool." XIX, Vol. IV, p. 633.

Cooper, S. H. (Canada) "Equity linked life insurance with variable premiums." XIX, Vol. I, p. 353.

Di Paolo, F. P. and Myer, G. G. (Canada) "A method of forecasting expense rates for corporate planning projections." XIX, Vol. II, p. 237.

Friend, E. H. (U.S.) "The coordination of survivor benefits between private pension/insurance plans and U.S. Social Security." XIX, Vol. III, p. 397.

Greeley, C. (U.S.) "The life insurance product in an inflationary economy." XIX, Vol. I, p. 433.

Hazlehurst, B. H. (U.S.) "Extending the rate of private pensions as a supplement to Social Security in the U.S.A." XIX, Vol. II, p. 415.

Jacobson, R. I. (U.S.) "Projection of life insurance business under various conditions and with various product strategies." XIX, Vol. III, p. 123.

Lawson, H. R. and Galloway, C. T. P. (Canada) "Variable annuities utilizing an outside investment fund." XIX, Vol. I, p. 509.

Miller, J. H. (U.S.) "Actuarial treatment of the risk process in disability insurance." XIX, Vol. IV, p. 667.

Murphy, T. B. (U.S.) "Forecasting for the seventies." XIX, Vol. II, p. 199.

Myers, R. J. (U.S.) "The role of private pension schemes." XIX, Vol. III, p. 505.

National Reports (Canada) "The governmental control and supervision of the private insurance industry in Canada." XIX, Vol. I, p. 67.

National Reports (U.S.) "The governmental control and supervision of the private insurance industry in the United States of America." XIX, Vol. I, p. 301.

Roffey, A. E. and Weaver, A. R. (Canada) "The planned development of an insurance company." XIX, Vol. II, p. 251.

Roy, J. (Canada) "L'assurance-vie et l'assurance retraite liées à des investissements--une étude des contrats émis au Canada durant la décennie 1960–1970." XIX, Vol. I, p. 575.

Sibigtroth, J. C. (U.S.) "The New York Life approach to variable life insurance." XIX, Vol. I, p. 583.

Thomas, B. R. (U.S.) "Correlation of private pension plan benefits with United States Social Security." XIX, Vol. III, p. 563.

Trowbridge, C. L. (U.S.) "A non-proportional (stop-loss) reinsurance pool." XIX, Vol. IV, p. 705.

Walker, H. (U.S.) "Some reflections on the development of variable life insurance in the United States." XIX, Vol. I, p. 653.

TWENTIETH CONGRESS 1976, TOKYO

Bragg, J. M. (U.S.) "Mortality differences and trends in the United States of America, taking account of color, sex, and socio-economic status." XX, Vol. II, p. 391.

Di Paolo, F. P. (Canada) "The pricing of ordinary life insurance under severe competitive conditions." XX, Vol. I, p. 87.

Givens, H., Jr., and Miller, M. D. (U.S.) "Determination of adequate income benefits levels in the United States of America." XX, Vol. III, p. 107.

Halmstad, D. G. (U.S.) "Exact numerical procedures in discrete risk theory." XX, Vol. IV, p. 557.

Hazlehurst, B. H. (U.S.) "Inflation and retirement: U.S.A." XX, Vol. III, p. 151.

Hennington, H. H. (U.S.) "Problems of maintaining purchasing power of pension benefits." XX, Vol. III, p. 161.

Jackson, P. H. and Fellers, W. W. (U.S.) "Mortality rates under noninsured pension plans in the United States of America." XX, Vol. II, p. 443.

Khury, C. K. (U.S.) "Actuarial balance in the operation of a property and casualty insurer." XX, Vol. IV, p. 585.

Kilbourne, F. W. (U.S.) "Premium rate-making for non-life insurance lines." XX, Vol. I, p. 147.

McGuinness, J. S. (U.S.) "Catastrophe concepts for retentions, reserving, and ratemaking." XX, Vol. IV, p. 607.

Mereu, J.A. (Canada) "A projection system for ordinary life business." XX, Vol. IV, p. 619.

Myers, R. J. (U.S.) "Financing problems of social insurance schemes covering small industrial categories—a case history." XX, Vol. III, p. 253.

National Reports (Canada) "The diversification of insurance products in recent years and anticipated future development." XX, Vol. I, p. 55.

National Reports (U.S.) "The diversification of insurance products in recent years and anticipated future development in the United States." XX, Vol. I, p. 351.

Nesbitt, C. J. and Gerber, H. U. (U.S.) "Actuarial aspects of survival studies of cystic fibrosis patients." XX, Vol. II, p. 625.

Parsons, R. D. (U.S.) "Some thoughts on protecting the real value of pensions in an inflationary environment." XX, Vol. III, p. 267.

Seltzer, F. (U.S.) "International and United States regional mortality comparisons—Cardiovascular diseases and malignant neoplasms." XX, Vol. II, p. 665.

Smith, C. (U.S.) "Trends in the mortality of individually insured lives in the United States of America since 1900." XX, Vol. II, p. 717.

Trowbridge, C.L. (U.S.) "Adjustment of private pension and insurance plans in the United States of America to social security—and to inflation." XX, Vol. III, p. 359.

Vanderhoof, I. T. (U.S.) "Inflation, expenses, interest rates and benefits." XX, Vol. I, p. 315.

Veit, K. P. (U.S.) "The use of systems dynamics simulation models for corporate long range strategic planning." XX, Vol. IV, p. 801.

Chapter VII.

ACTUARIAL EDUCATION

There is no royal road to geometry.

—Euclid, fl. 300 B.C.

ORIGINAL TEXTBOOKS

To actuarial students of bygone days, the famous textbook authors were Hall and Knight, Todhunter, and George King, applicable to algebra, compound interest and life contingencies, respectively. All these textbooks emanated from Great Britain and date back to the nineteenth century. Their full titles were:

Higher Algebra, H. S. Hall and S. R. Knight, earliest edition before 1891.

Interest, including Annuities-certain, Ralph Todhunter, new edition 1901 (but this was just a revision of an 1882 text of the same title by William Sutton, which had been the Institute's Text-book, Part I).

Life Contingencies, including Annuities and Assurances, George King, first edition 1887. (This was the Institute of Actuaries' Text-book, Part II.)

But this revered trio of books was not the earliest group of texts in their subjects. There were of course many algebra authors before Hall and Knight; compound interest certainly was not a new subject; and several authors before King produced texts on life contingencies.

At the Jubilee Dinner of the Institute of Actuaries in May 1898 (*TICA* 2, 880) its president, Thomas E. Young, identified the 1843 two-volume work by David Jones, *Value of Annuities and Reversionary Payments,* as "the first Students' Text-book of our science"; much more recently, M. E. Ogborn (*JIA* 82, 242) offered several nominations.

Ogborn recognized Richard Price's *Observations on Reversionary Payments,* which went through seven editions from 1771 to 1812, as the first major work on actuarial science, in general, and went on to mention William Morgan's *The Doctrine of Annuities and Assurances on Lives and Survivorships* published in 1779, Francis Baily's *Doctrine* (2 vols. 1812–1813), and Joshua Milne's *Treatise* (2 vols. 1815). Actuaries in North America, beginning with Jacob Shoemaker, must have studied these texts, at least until David Jones' work came on the scene employing the notation that in due course became official throughout our profession.

In a letter read to the Actuarial Society in May 1909, charter member Joseph H. Nitchie reported the difficulties that must have plagued many before the Institute's official texts appeared in the 1880s (*T.A.S.A.* 11, 48):

I have frequently regretted that in my own preparation there was not the spur and discipline of a system such as this Society has adopted in its requirements for admission. When I began [in the 1870s] the study of rudiments, such requirements and anything like adequate direction were lacking so far as I was aware; I was left to pick my way through Jones and Chisholm as best I could with no suggestions covering special preparation for more advanced study.

Which "Chisholm" Nitchie had in mind is not clear; probably it was a D. Chisholm whose work on probability was published in 1852.

Robert Henderson devoted his May 1923 presidential address to the Actuarial Society (*T.A.S.A.* 24, 1) to "a few of the men whose names are most prominently connected with the early history of our science." Books by several of them were probably available for study by early North American actuaries.

The only organization in North America known to have given examinations on probability and life contingencies before the first Actuarial Society examination in 1897 was the University of Toronto. A nine-question examination of 1885 is illustrated herewith. The examiner, Alfred K. Blackadar (F.A.S. 1890), was not a member of that university's faculty; he was employed in the Dominion Department of Insurance in Ottawa, and qualified by examination as an FIA in 1894.

EDUCATION AND EXAMINATIONS BY ACTUARIAL BODIES, 1897–1928

Actuarial Society of America. The first Examination Committee, appointed at the Council meeting of October 8, 1896, consisted of the Society's President Emory McClintock along with David Parks Fackler, William McCabe, Frederick W. Frankland and Joseph A. De Boer. This imposing group outnumbered the candidates who sat in the fall of 1897; those who passed and thus were enrolled as Associates were Charles H. Angell, Samuel S. Hall and Douglas H. Rose; one candidate, Alva C. Washburne, had the unhappy distinction of being the first ever to fail a Society examination—he persevered, qualifying as an Associate in 1900.

At first the examinations for Associateship and for Membership (renamed Fellowship in 1905) were single-session tests of about twenty questions each, but these were quickly found inadequate to cover the wide subject range; in 1904 the Associateship examination was divided into two Sections, A and B, and in 1907 the same treatment was applied to Fellowship. Those Sections could be passed at one time or in separate years, but no credit was granted for Section B unless Section A had been passed.

The earliest Fellow by examination was John Francis Roche in 1900. Two qualified in 1901—Samuel S. Hall and William R. Hitchins, the latter being the first Canadian to do so.

Examination centers were provided to suit the convenience of two or more candidates. On one occasion the University of Michigan was refused an Ann Arbor center because it produced only one candidate.

The Associateship (but not the Fellowship) examinations were waived for Associates and Fellows of the Institute or Faculty of Actuaries. In 1903 the Council decided that this waiver would not apply if those British examinations had been taken while the candidate was resident in North America. Presumably the purpose was to encourage Canadians to support the Society examinations, but the immediate effect was exactly the opposite.

University of Toronto.

ANNUAL EXAMINATIONS : 1885.

CANDIDATES FOR B.A.

THEORY OF PROBABILITY.

HONORS.

Examiner: A. K. BLACKADAR, M.A.

1. If the odds are n to m against an event, how do you express the chance of the event happening?

Prove that the probability of throwing a number n with p dice is the coefficient of x^n in the expansion of $x^p(1-x^6)^p(1-x)^{-p}$, divided by 6^p.

2. If p and q be the respective chances of two independent events, shew that the chance that both will happen is pq.

Seven alphabets represented by 7 sets of 26 tickets each are thrown into a box. What is the probability that if 7 tickets are drawn in succession and placed in the order of their appearance on the table, they will spell the word "Toronto"?

3. What is the probability that out of five individuals of a given age x, two at least will die in one year?

Find the probabilities, that of two lives x and y, (1) both will not survive n years, (2) x will die in the nth year, y surviving.

4. Find the expression for the value (a_{xy}) of an annuity payable during the joint continuance of two lives aged x and y.

Shew that the value of an annuity on a life x, not entered on until after the death of the survivor of y and z is $a_x + a_{xyz} - a_{xy} - a_{xz}$.

5. Find an expression for the present value of (or, single premium for,) an assurance of 1 payable at the end of the year in which a person aged x dies.

If A_x and A_{x+1} represent the single premium for the ordinary whole life assurance at ages x and $x+1$ respectively, shew that the probability that x will die in a year $= \dfrac{v - A_x}{v(1 - A_{x+1})}$.

6. A and B are playing with 2 dice, each having staked \$10, the highest throw to win. A has thrown 6. What is B's expectation?

7. Explain what is meant by inverse probability.

If an observed event may have arisen from any one of several different causes, all of which are *a priori* equally probable, shew how to find the probability that the event is the consequence of a certain specified cause.

There are 5 candidates at an examination, A solves on an average 2 problems out of every 3; B, 3 out of 5; C, 2 out of 9; D, 1 out of 6; E, 3 out of 10. A certain problem is found to be solved on the papers of two candidates only, find the probability that the papers belong to A and B.

8. Out of $m + n$ trials it is found that the most probable combination is that an event will happen m times and fail n times. When m and n are large numbers, shew that the probability that in $m + n$ trials the event will happen exactly m times is $\sqrt{\dfrac{m+n}{2\,mn\pi}}$ approximately.

For example, shew that in 12,000 throws with a die the probability that there will be thrown exactly 2,000 aces is ·0098 nearly.

9. If a straight line be divided at random into three parts, shew that the chance (1) that a triangle of any kind can be formed with the three parts is $\frac{1}{4}$. (2) That an acute angled triangle can be formed with the three parts is $3 \log 2 - 2$.

Find the chance that two lines will intersect within a circle, one of them being drawn at random through the centre, and the other drawn at random through any random point within the circle.

The 1885 examination paper in Theory of Probability at University of Toronto. Sharp-eyed observers will notice an error in Question 5. (Courtesy of University of Toronto Library)

Canadian students, who constituted the majority of candidates because of intense actuarial activity at the University of Toronto, boycotted the Society examinations, with the interesting result that the total number of first-time candidates in 1905 was only 15 but jumped to 73 in 1906 (after this issue had been settled by an informal waiver).

It is hard to assess the severity of gradings in those early days because surviving records show only how many candidates had been authorized to sit, not how many actually turned up at the centers. Over the period 1897 to 1908 it appears that the Associateship successes were about half the authorizations. In the Fellowship tests of the same period, 63 new Fellows emerged from certainly fewer than 125 Associates, so the passing ratio must have exceeded 50%. In some cases these successes were achieved on second or later attempts.

The earliest year for which full records of examination results have survived is 1908. In that year the Associateship examinations consisted of two parts as shown in Table VII.1.

Table VII.1

1908 ASSOCIATESHIP EXAMINATION SUBJECTS

Part A	Part B
Arithmetic	Life Contingencies
Algebra	Valuation
Geometry	Insurance Contracts
Probability	Life Insurance History
Finite Differences	Mortality Tables
Compound Interest	

The wide variety of subjects about which candidates were required to display their mastery in each of these parts caused these examinations to be severe tests. Beginning in 1910, the number of parts was increased from two to four; in 1930 it was further subdivided into eight parts.

Table VII.2 contains the 1908 examination results.

Table VII.2

1908 ASSOCIATESHIP EXAMINATION RESULTS

For Candidates Sitting for One Part Only

Number of Candidates (Part A)	Number of Candidates (Part B)	Number Who Passed Part A	Number Who Passed Part B
26	12	3	4

For Candidates Sitting for Both Parts

Number of Candidates	Number Who Passed Both	Number Who Passed A Only	Number Who Passed B Only
19	6	4	0

The 1908 Fellowship parts consisted of Sections A and B embracing the subjects shown in Table VII.3.

Table VII.3

1908 FELLOWSHIP EXAMINATION SUBJECTS

Section A	Section B
Construction and Graduation of Mortality Tables	Expense Assessment
	Surplus Distribution
Advanced Life Contingencies	Policy Changes and Surrenders
Gross Premiums	Life Insurance Bookkeeping
Valuation of Life Company Liabilities and Assets	Annual Statements
	Investments
Substandard Business	Banking and Finance
Pension Funds	Life Insurance Laws

In 1910, an ominous sentence that was to confront generations of nervous candidates made its first appearance on examination papers:

> Candidates are expected to show a reasonable knowledge of each subject in the syllabus.

Its proposer (Percy C. H. Papps, at the Council meeting of May 1909) had suggested a modifying clause, "but it is understood that the examiners shall have considerable latitude in interpreting this requirement." The Council agreed with this but decided not to print this subordinate clause in the syllabus or in the Instructions to Candidates on the examination papers. The entire provision, however, seems rarely to have been the cause of any candidate being denied a passing grade.

In 1911 the practice of printing examination papers (*T.A.S.A.* 12, 151) and results (p. 353) in the *Transactions* came into effect. The American Institute had printed its first examination paper in 1910 (*R.A.I.A.* 1, 28). Two years earlier Henry Moir had suggested the desirability of giving public credit to students who passed examinations with distinction; the first cum laude designation was awarded in 1914.

In 1909 the topic of Pensions had been added to the syllabus. In 1915, three other new subjects—Selection of Risks, Branches of Insurance Other Than Life, and Current Topics—made their appearance. The next addition was Statistics in 1926. In 1939, Social Insurance became a recognized separate subject; it had already been a requirement as one of the current topics of several prior years. Throughout the entire period, there continued to be heavy emphasis on the mathematics of Graduation of Mortality Tables; in retrospect this seems to have been disproportionate to the subject's importance to most practicing actuaries.

The combined effects of increasing examination scope and swelling enrollments placed heavy strains upon the Examination Committees. In April 1907 the Council received a letter from Examination Committee Chairman Wendell M. Strong (cosigned by Council Secretary Arthur Hunter) drawing attention to the large and increasing volume of work, and proposing that three examiners be appointed for the Associateship and three for the Fellowship examinations and that the maximum period of committee service be three years. Strong said that the time he had spent on examination work was "pretty nearly equal to the total office hours for a month." Those changes were made, but only four years later, it was necessary to expand the committee again by creating the post of General Chairman supported by four Part Chairmen. At best, these structural changes kept the volume of work manageable; in those days as well as later, the devotion and endurance of the committee members have been beyond praise.

The early Associateship pass lists for 1919 and years shortly after that are notable for the substantial numbers of women among the successful candidates. For example, in 1919 (*T.A.S.A.* 20, 270) and 1920 (*T.A.S.A.* 21, 324), the results were as shown in Table VII.4.

Several presidents expressed concern about examination and education matters in their formal addresses. William A. Hutcheson in October 1920 (*T.A.S.A.* 21, 328) said:

I cannot but feel ... that the great purpose of the Society now is to help in the education of young actuaries. ...

[T]he student ... must cut himself off for a considerable period from many of the pleasures of social intercourse. The self-denial and effort necessary in these years of study is compensated, luckily, by an upbuilding of character. ...

The average time taken [in the ten years ending in 1919] for the 85 members to become Associates was three and one-third years from date of enrolment, for the 63 Associates to become Fellows it was four and one-quarter years from date of becoming Associates, and for the 34 to become successively Associates and Fellows it was slightly more than six years from date of enrollment. ...

[I]n these days of universal unrest, loafing and pleasure seeking, it is evident that the temptations not to work are great and that the effort which the student must make nowadays is greater than we older members had to put forth in our day. ... I would like to remind those with whom I am sympathizing, however, that the increased difficulties they have in preparing for the examinations are offset by greatly increased facilities of study.

Table VII.4
NUMBERS AND PERCENTAGES OF WOMEN WHO PASSED ASSOCIATESHIP EXAMINATIONS IN 1919 AND 1920

Year	Total Men and Women Who Passed	Women Who Passed	Women's Percentage
1919	69	23	33%
1920	17	2	12%
Total	**86**	**25**	**29%**

That paper contains the earliest published survey of numbers of years required to complete the Associateship and Fellowship examinations.

Hutcheson went on to offer help in one syllabus subject, History of Life Insurance, by sketching the evolution of life insurance from A.D. 136 in Rome up to the establishment of the branch office system by the Scottish Widows Fund in the 1860s. This account comprised thirty pages of the *Transactions*.

The following spring (*T.A.S.A.* 22, 1) Hutcheson was in a position to say:

What I had to say [last October] regarding the average time taken [to complete the examinations] was not without results. First, at our Dinner, and then at our Council meeting, the matter was commented on, and resulted in a committee being appointed last October ... to look into the whole question of our examinations. ... [It was decided] to define more clearly the scope intended to be covered in the subjects [described in the early examination syllabus]. These recommendations are set forth in the circular of February 28, 1921, entitled "Associateship Examinations—Parts I and II," and this year's examination papers will doubtless reflect these recommendations.

In October 1925 (*T.A.S.A.* 26, 265) President Arthur B. Wood expressed keen disappointment about the large proportion of failures in the early examinations and offered a possible remedy:

> Our present procedure seems to be deficient in that no definite standard has been adopted to determine in advance the fitness of the applicant. . . .

> We might with advantage consider whether the time has not arrived for the establishment of a definite matriculation standard of a purely mathematical character, the supervision of which might appropriately be placed under the Committee on Admissions. . . . My idea would be to substitute for Part 1 a matriculation examination of a reasonably high standard, its scope being at least as broad as that of Part 1. To relieve our own [Examination Committee] members, the services of outside examiners might be employed to perform the entire work of preparing the questions, drafting the papers and examining and marking the answers of the candidates. . . .

> For some years a paid examiner has been employed to read and mark the papers for Part 1 but the work of preparing the questions, drafting the papers, and also of reviewing doubtful cases, devolves upon the Committee. . . . Considerable relief would be afforded and the work of the Committee would, I believe, be more effectively carried out.

This idea for a precursor of the much later Actuarial Aptitude Test was not adopted.

In October 1926 (*T.A.S.A.* 27, 253) President Edward E. Rhodes mentioned that justice had been tempered with mercy in that year's early examinations, saying:

> There were 286 candidates for Part I and 169 candidates for Part II. Only 36 and 16 candidates, respectively, were considered by the Examining Committee as clearly entitled to pass.

> Desiring to exercise the utmost possible liberality, the papers of the remaining candidates were reviewed a second time with the result that 13 more were passed for Part I and 14 more were passed for Part II. This action resulted in passing altogether 17% of the candidates for Part I and 18% of the candidates for Part II.

The American Institute of Actuaries. After its founding in 1909, the American Institute gave impetus to the Actuarial Society's efforts to make its entrance requirements as attractive to young mathematicians as was consistent with maintaining standards. The new body, even though from the outset aspiring to become the Actuarial Society's equal in prestige, was willing to offer Fellowships to established actuaries whose examination progress in the Society had stalled at the Associateship level. In the years 1913–1916, eight Society Associates— Sinclair E. Allison, Henry W. Allstrom, Isaac Davenport, Charles Hughes, William O. Morris, George B. Pattison, Thomas A. Phillips and James H. Washburn— were granted American Institute Fellowships; also in 1913 two Fellows of the Faculty of Actuaries practicing in the United States who earlier had obtained Society Associateships by waiver, joined the American Institute as Fellows. Both of these— George Graham in 1920 and Lawrence M. Cathles in 1922—were in due course elected presidents of the American Institute.

The syllabus created by the American Institute for its students was greatly influenced by that of the Actuarial Society, but the examination grading was less stringent. Students were attracted to writing both sets of examinations because failure in one organization might be countered by a passing grade in the other. Listed in *T.A.S.A.* 50, 212, are the names of thirty-five (affectionately called "two-timers" by Reinhard A. Hohaus who was one of them) who passed separate and distinct examinations in each body from the first Associateship part to the last Fellowship part.

Statistics on growth of numbers of Associates in the early years of the Actuarial Society and American Institute are not readily available because Schedules of Membership were not published until 1915 by the Society, and until 1924 by the American Institute. Table VII.5 gives information in condensed form for the missing periods.

Table VII.5
ROSTERS OF ASSOCIATES OF ACTUARIAL SOCIETY OF AMERICA AND AMERICAN INSTITUTE OF ACTUARIES FOR SELECTED PERIODS, 1897–1923

| Period | Associates Enrolled | | Associates Removed from Roster | | | Roster at End of Period |
	By Exam	By Waiver	By Admission As Fellows	By Death	By Withdrawal	
(A) Associates of the Actuarial Society, 1897–1914						
1897–1899	18	7	1		1	23
1901–1904	25	5	19	1		33
1905–1909	76	8	25			92
1910–1914	33	17	23	1	2	116
	152	37	68	2	3	116
(B) Associates of the American Institute, 1909–1923						
1909		22(charter)			22	
1910–1914	10	3	3	1	5	26
1915–1919	15	13	6		4	44
1920–1923	21	12	6		4	67
	46	50	15	1	13	67

Corresponding figures for Fellows in these years were likewise not published, but in their case this gap was filled by James R. Herman in 1949 ("Actuaries— Past, Present and Future" *T.A.S.A* 50, 67–70).

The Casualty Actuarial Society. Founded in November 1914, the CAS had established its examination system by March 29, 1915. By the end of 1928, 132 new Fellows (other than the 97 charter Fellows) had been inducted, but only one-third of these qualified by examination, the other two-thirds entering by election.

Dudley M. Pruitt summarized the sequence of events in 1964 (*PCAS* 51, 156):

> Joseph H. Woodward . . . was the first chairman of the Committee on Examinations. . . . [The] first syllabus was ambitious, that for Associateship being in four parts, each part having four sections. . . . Part I covered elementary algebra, plane trigonometry, analytical geometry and . . . bookkeeping. Part II covered

advanced algebra, . . . calculus, finite differences, and probabilities. Part III included compound interest and annuities certain, statistics, life annuities and assurances, and . . . economics. Lastly Part IV included the practical side of the business: practical problems in statistics, policy forms and underwriting practice in casualty insurance, practical problems in insurance accounting and statistics, and insurance law.

[In the two-part Fellowship examinations] Part I covered calculation of premiums and reserves, inspection of risks, and the adjustment and settlement of claims, investments of insurance companies, and an all-encompassing section called "current problems." It is a clear indication of the bent of mind of our founders that the whole of Part II, one half of the entire Fellowship examination, was devoted to Social Insurance or its relatives, covering the principles and history of Social Insurance, compilation and use of census or other government statistics, systems of invalidity, old age and unemployment insurance, and the calculation of premiums for and valuation of pension funds.

Since Woodward was a 1907 Fellow by examination of the Actuarial Society and had served on its examination committee, it is not surprising that this pattern differed from the Actuarial Society only to the extent indicated by the occupational differences between casualty and life insurance actuaries. Pruitt's account goes on (p. 157):

Although the syllabus was most ambitious in its requirements for Associateship, it was immediately evident that the practical situation at the time made [it] unworkable. Announcement was, therefore, made that only Part IV, that part covering the practical side of the business, would be required and given for enrollment as Associate in 1915 and that only Parts III and IV would be required and given in 1916 and 1917. . . . This waiving of Parts I and II was later extended to 1919 and again to 1920. . . .

On May 2 and 3, 1917, again the abridged Associateship examinations were given and for the first time a full set of Fellowship examinations. . . . The honor of being the first Fellows of the Society to achieve that status by examination went to A. H. Brockway and Robert J. McManus. . . .

[In 1921] the whole question of examinations was reviewed . . . . Apparently some statisticians [the Society had been organized as an actuarial and statistical body] had been a bit restive and were asking for more than equal treatment. The committee determined, however, that the difference between the actuary and the statistician "was mainly a slight difference in point of view" and that there should be no distinction in examination requirements between the two groups. The committee felt that there was some virtue in pursuing an easier examination policy . . . with the conscious expectation of tightening up as we grew stronger, citing the example of the Actuarial Society of America as a worthy precedent. Then the committee discussed the distinction between Fellow and Associate, expressing the opinion that the Associateship should be more than merely a step toward the Fellowship, and should "be an evidence of certain qualifications which might justify an executive of a casualty company entrusting certain work definitely to those who had so passed Associate examinations."

The committee then proposed a radical change in the syllabus which abridged the Associateship portion materially, retaining generally the elementary mathematics and the practical insurance problems of the old Part IV though adding the word "simple" in front of "practical problems." The more advanced mathematics, statistics, and life contingencies were transferred to the Fellowship portion and Social Insurance which had been the main thrust of a full half of the old Fellowship examination was reduced to two words in one section which read: "advanced practical problems in compilation and use of statistics relating to casualty (including social) insurance problems." . . . Our syllabus had finally become practical indeed.

But this did not last for long. On November 17, 1925, the Council adopted a second complete revision of the syllabus, which concentrated *all* the mathematics sections into the Associateship and *all* the "practical problems" of the insurance business into the Fellowship. Gone was the concept that a casualty company executive might entrust certain work to Associates. Henceforth Associates might gain all the needed know-how from college textbooks.

One reason why so high a proportion became Fellows other than by examination was that there were two such possibilities, called by Pruitt the "invitation route" and the "paper route." The former was by vote of the Fellows, just as in the two life bodies. The latter involved substitution of a thesis, i.e., a worthy paper to be published in the *Proceedings*. Pruitt explained the inherent difficulties (p. 162):

> The Society was . . . embarrassed . . . when a candidate, usually of some moment in the business . . . produced with evidence of hard labor, an unacceptable paper. For many years the Society needed both members and papers rather urgently, or so we felt, and the "paper route" served its day. [It] was closed in 1962 . . . .

TUITION AND TEXTBOOKS

The beginning of the never-ending search for ways to help students reach Fellowship was a remarkable paper, "Some Suggestions Regarding the Education of Actuarial Students and the Future Activities of the Society" presented to the Actuarial Society by Arthur Hunter in May 1905. This was at a time when the examination system was less than ten years old, and Hunter had been a Fellow for only two years (although he was age thirty-six and had been a Fellow of the Faculty of Actuaries since 1893). Hunter wrote (*T.A.S.A.* 9, 26):

> We have taken the first steps towards requiring a high degree of technical and practical education from the new members by insisting upon their passing examinations, but we have made no plans looking towards the assistance of the students.

Hunter's suggestions, supported and amplified by Walter S. Nichols (ibid., 185), were many and wide ranging, including the following:

1. Inculcating a habit of study, recognizing that "the atmosphere of New York or any other large city is not conducive to persistent study, and . . . there is considerable overtime work done in the offices during the winter, which makes inroads into . . . evening time."

2. Impressing, especially upon university graduates, awareness that the mathematical knowledge they already possess is not sufficient to pass the actuarial examinations.

3. Providing the books that contain the information students must have on the examination subjects.

4. Enabling students to gain the office experience needed to appreciate practical problems.

5. Adding to the syllabus subjects not already included that actuaries would need in their professional work.

6. Reconsidering the need for the existing minimum ages: age 21 for associateship, age 25 for full membership.

7. Arranging meetings monthly in New York City, from November to March inclusive, at which lectures on several subjects would be given. These lectures would then be published as the "Text-Book of the Actuarial Society of America" and would be the continuation on practical lines of the Institute of Actuaries' Text-Book, Parts I and II.

One of Hunter's arguments in favor of bringing students rapidly through the examinations emanated from a remark he attributed to a Professor William James of Harvard, to the effect that "most men begin to be old fogies at the age of twenty-five." James' thesis had been (p. 30):

> It is true that a grown-up adult keeps gaining well into middle life a great knowledge of details, and a great acquaintance with individual cases connected with his profession or business life. In this sense, his conceptions increase during a very long period; for his knowledge grows more extensive and minute. But the larger categories of conception, the sorts of thing, and wider classes of relation between things of which we take cognizance, are all got into the mind at a comparatively youthful date. Few men ever do acquaint themselves with the principles of a new science after even twenty-five.

Whether or not one welcomes Hunter's support of Professor James' discouraging theory, it is clear that Hunter's paper opened the door to many helpful devices later adopted. One important reason why they were adopted is that Hunter had just been elected to the Council where he promoted his ideas. The only one that failed to gain prompt acceptance was removal of minimum entry age limits; that change was not made until 1937.

At its December 1909 meeting, the Council created an Educational Committee "to assist students and Associates in preparing for the examinations." That committee began by publishing a pamphlet outlining a recommended course of study. It was ready in time to be shown to the members at the 1910 fall meeting (*T.A.S.A.* 11, 573).

The immense project that Hunter advocated was to publish a shelf of North American literature on actuarial practice. In fact, there were two significant books already in existence before 1905; three more had been produced before Hunter's dream came true. These five works were:

The Principles and Practice of Life Insurance, first written in 1872 by Nathan Willey (1831–1874), a New York City consulting actuary and journalist. By 1906 it had reached its seventh edition, the work having been carried on by two Actuarial Society members, Henry W. Smith and John Tatlock.

Practical Lessons in Actuarial Science, by Miles M. Dawson, first edition 1898, enlarged to two volumes in 1905. This work in its final form embraced compound interest, probability, mortality tables and their graduation, life contingencies and surplus distribution.

Notes for Use In Preparation for the Fellowship Examination of the Actuarial Society of America, by Henry Moir and Miles M. Dawson, issued in 1906. This 222-page book never was printed, but copies were made to be lent to Fellowship candidates. A copy of this rare and interesting precursor of modern study notes was presented to the Society of Actuaries Library by the Actuaries Club of New York in 1956.

Actuarial Society Examinations, in 1905, a reprint in book form by *The American Underwriter* of questions and solutions that had originally appeared in the columns of that journal. Bound into that same volume was an essay on the fundamental principles of probability by Robert Henderson, who had earned his Fellowship in 1902 and was on the road to becoming a ranking authority on actuarial science.

Problems and Solutions, 1915–1919, published in 1921 by the Actuarial Society. It covered Associateship examinations only; it seems that similar study material on examinations of other years was distributed also, but this was the only volume of its kind.

Hunter in 1905 had in mind a single text covering actuarial subjects beyond compound interest and life contingencies (for which he was wisely content to rely upon the Institute of Actuaries' Text-books, Part I and II). But the ground to be covered was much too large; furthermore, students' convenience was better suited by publishing a separate book for each subject. Thus emerged over a long span of years a series of Actuarial Studies, listed here in order of appearance:

1919   *Sources and Characteristics of the Principal Mortality Tables: Actuarial Studies, No. 1.* Principal contributor for the first edition was Henry Moir; for the second in 1932, James S. Elston.

1919   *Graduation of Mortality and Other Tables: Actuarial Studies, No. 4.* Principal contributor for both the first edition and also the second (1938) edition (given a new title, *Mathematical Theory of Graduation*) was Robert Henderson.

1920   *Total Permanent Disability Benefits in Relation to Life Insurance: Actuarial Studies, No. 5.* Principal contributor for the first edition was Arthur Hunter; for the second edition (1932) labelled *Disability Benefits in Life Insurance Policies,* there were two principal contributors, Arthur Hunter and James T. Phillips, and also four associate contributors. The preface to the first edition stated that a draft had been completed six years earlier but fortunately had been withheld from publication during a period of great liberalization and expansion of disability benefits. Ironically it was those liberalizations that proved so financially disastrous to the companies that when the second edition, four times the size of the first, was published, many American life companies were announcing that they would cease to offer the disability income benefit.

1922 *Construction of Mortality Tables from the Records of Insured Lives:—Actuarial Studies, No. 2.* Principal contributors were Ray D. Murphy and Percy C. H. Papps. The reviewer of this book (*T.A.S.A.* 23, 468) predicted that students would welcome it because exposed-to-risk formulas had "been a bugbear to many."

1925 *Population Statistics and Their Compilation: Actuarial Studies, No. 3.* Principal contributor was Hugh H. Wolfenden. In this book's preface it was explained that Miles M. Dawson and John S. Thompson had long ago undertaken this project, but that "it was not found possible at the time to publish the results of their labors." There are grounds for suspecting that the difficulty was Wolfenden's vigorous objections to the Dawson/Thompson manuscript.

Publication of Wolfenden's text on population statistics seems to have completed the entire original project except for a volume on valuation of policy liabilities that was in the planning stage at the Council meeting of April 1924 but never was published. In 1937 the Actuarial Society published *Distribution of Surplus* written by Joseph B. Maclean, Edward W. Marshall being Supplementary Contributor. The book was labelled *Actuarial Studies, No. 6* but seems not to have been planned as part of the original series.

In 1946, a monograph by Morton D. Miller, *Elements of Graduation,* was published jointly by the Actuarial Society and the American Institute. This, together with a section of Hugh H. Wolfenden's 1942 work, *The Fundamental Principles of Mathematical Statistics,* eased to some extent grave difficulties encountered by students in understanding portions of Robert Henderson's mathematics in his 1938 graduation text.

Texts by CAS authors in the same era were:

1925 *Workmen's Compensation* by Gustav F. Michelbacher, co-authored by T.M. Nial of the National Bureau of Casualty Underwriters.

1928 *Casualty Insurance* by Clarence A. Kulp, co-authored by John W. Hall, a professor at the then Georgia State College.

1930 *Casualty Insurance Principles* by Michelbacher.

Also used in education was a 1933 *American Remarriage Table* to which the principal contributors were Paul Dorweiler, Ralph M. Marshall and William F. Roeber (*PCAS* 19, 279). This study was carried forward by Robert J. Myers in 1949 (*PCAS* 36, 73).

The possibility of paying tutors to coach students was considered by the Actuarial Society's Educational Committee in 1911, but the difficulties of recruiting good tutors and of bringing the students together caused the idea to be abandoned. Prospects for arranging tuition by correspondence also were considered poor. In 1920 (*R.A.I.A.* 10, 291), the American Institute undertook to devote time during its meetings to student instruction, but that idea was soon dropped.

Fellowship lectures in New York City began to be offered in 1919 (*T.A.S.A.* 19, 4). These attracted students from near and far even though subsequent reports on their usefulness were not universally favorable. Their reputation, however, was sufficiently positive to keep the series operating until the Council in November 1945 approved their discontinuance "due to substantial development in panel work." John M. Laird in his May 1941 presidential address mentioned the lectures and study or discussion sessions available and added a comment that may have displeased candidates unable to receive those benefits (*T.A.S.A.* 42, 5):

> Naturally, a single student in a remote city must largely work out his own salvation, but this may be a blessing in disguise as it forces him to develop self-reliance, initiative and originality. Furthermore, he may have a better opportunity to concentrate and, if in a small company, can more readily get a perspective on all phases of its operations and perhaps on the life insurance business.
>
> If the candidate is married, his wife can help a great deal by cooperating in adjusting their family life in such a way as to leave time for study. . . .
>
> On our first two examinations about 15% to 20% of the candidates are successful on each part tried. On later examinations the ratio varies from about 25% to 35%. This seems low, but many candidates prepare for one part and take a flier at another. . . .
>
> Roughly, out of ten candidates who started our examination program twelve years ago, one is now an Associate and one a Fellow. . . .
>
> Among those who finally achieve Fellowship, the average time required to pass the nine examinations is ten years, or about one each year. Perhaps because some start our examinations while still at college, the average age at time of becoming a Fellow is thirty.

Illustrated here is a surviving announcement, for the year 1922, of the New York Lectures.

SCHEDULE OF LECTURES FOR FELLOWSHIP EXAMINATIONS OF
THE ACTUARIAL SOCIETY OF AMERICA
1922
TO BE HELD IN THE OFFICE OF THE SOCIETY, 256 BROADWAY, NEW YORK CITY

EXAMINATION Part	Section	SUBJECT (Short Title Only)	LECTURER	DATE	DAY	TIME
I	4	Office Premiums	J. R. Larus, Jr.	May 10	Wednesday	9.30—12.00 A.M.
	2	Sources and Characteristics of Mortality and Disability Tables	P. C. H. Papps	May 10	Wednesday	2.00— 3.15 P.M.
	6	Changes in or Surrender of Policies	F. H. Johnston	May 10	Wednesday	3.15— 4.30 P.M.
	1	Construction of Mortality Tables	H. H. Wolfenden	May 11	Thursday	9.30—12.00 A.M.
		Graduation of Mortality Tables	H. H. Wolfenden	May 11	Thursday	2.00— 4.30 P.M.
	3	Selection of Risks	Arthur Hunter	May 12	Friday	9.30—12.00 A.M.
	5	Valuation of Company Liabilities	Henry Moir	May 12	Friday	2.00— 4.30 P.M.
II	5	Insurance Law	W. M. Strong	May 13	Saturday	9.30—12.00 A.M.
	6	Pension Funds	D. A. Walker	May 13	Saturday	2.00— 4.30 P.M.
	2	Life Insurance Accounts	J. D. Craig	May 15	Monday	9.30—12.00 A.M.
	1	Analysis and Distribution of Surplus	W. A. Hutcheson	May 15	Monday	2.00— 4.30 P.M.
	4	Elements of Banking and Finance	J. S. Thompson	May 16	Tuesday	9.30—12.00 A.M.
	3	Theory and Practice of Investing Company Funds	S. W. Baldwin	May 16	Tuesday	2.00— 4.30 P.M.
	7-9	Industrial Insurance	R. V. Carpenter	May 17	Wednesday	9.30—10.45 A.M.
		Workmen's Compensation and Liability Insurance	S. B. Perkins	May 17	Wednesday	10.45—12.00 A.M.
		Accident and Sickness Insurance	S. Milligan	May 17	Wednesday	2.00— 3.15 P.M.
		Group Life and Disability Insurance	W. I. King	May 17	Wednesday	3.15— 4.30 P.M.

To Candidates for the Fellowship Examinations, 1922:   April 17, 1922.

The Educational Committee of the Society has arranged the annual lecture course again this year, as indicated in the foregoing schedule. It is hoped that the maximum number of candidates will avail themselves of the privilege of attending these lectures, as we believe they will be of much value in clearing up difficulties that may remain after the preparatory home study. The lectures under Part I and Part II are open to Fellowship candidates who may be planning to present themselves for one examination only. It is suggested that candidates for Part I make a special effort to attend the lecture on Industrial Insurance, as questions on this subject have sometimes appeared in the Part I examination.

It will be much appreciated if those who are planning to attend the lectures will notify the Secretary of the Actuarial Society, 256 Broadway, New York City, just as soon as possible, stating what lectures they plan to attend. *You are encouraged to send in advance to the lecturers any specific questions that you would like to have answered.*

The Educational Committee

John M. Laird   James F. Little   Edward W. Marshall   Herbert R. Stephenson
M. Albert Linton, *Chairman*

The topics and speakers at the New York lectures in 1922.

The pioneer in securing regular guidance and material for candidates in their studies was Arthur Pedoe. After urging in 1929 (*T.A.S.A.* 30, 17) that local actuarial clubs make student education one of their activities until the actuarial organizations could assume that responsibility, Pedoe and Benjamin T. Holmes organized study circles in Toronto in a thoughtfully planned fashion described in 1935 (*R.A.I.A.* 24, 194).

An essential element of that study circle system was furnishing, to those students who participated wholeheartedly in the prescribed regimen, a mimeographed set of readings. Pedoe wrote (ibid., p. 195):

> A series of notes is now available, prepared over the course of years and based on experience, dealing with the difficulties encountered by the students in their reading of certain parts of the construction of tables and the mathematical sections of certain papers on graduation. Nothing in the nature of summaries for examination purposes is attempted, and these notes are only of value to students who follow the set reading conscientiously.

That Toronto Actuaries Club material was later incorporated into the "Panel Notes" issued from New York and became the inspiration and pattern for the study notes that have become a staple of student education.

EARLY UNIVERSITY COURSES IN ACTUARIAL SCIENCE

Practically every university course on actuarial subjects in North America arose from the pioneering enthusiasm of some mathematics professor inspired by recognizing that few careers other than teaching or actuarial science could give livelihoods to mathematicians.

The first such professor seems to have been John B. Cherriman (1833–1908), a graduate of Cambridge University who came to Canada in 1850 to join the mathematics faculty at the University of Toronto. Cherriman left the University in 1875, the same year that he was elected a Fellow of the Institute of Actuaries; he was succeeded by Alfred Baker (1848–1932) with whom Michael A. Mackenzie (1866–1949) became associated in 1904. Professors Baker and Mackenzie achieved such extraordinary success in attracting students and preparing them for actuarial careers that the University of Toronto became not only the earliest, but continued for many years as the leading, provider of actuarial talent on this continent. Mackenzie in particular extended the course into life contingencies subjects and encouraged company actuaries in Canada and the United States to offer positions to his graduates. Others who assisted Professor Mackenzie and continued the work after his retirement in 1936 were Samuel Beatty, Irvine R. Pounder, Norris E. Sheppard and Donald C. Baillie.

The University of Michigan's first connection with the actuarial profession was in 1859 through Professor John Emory Clark who was later to serve (1875–1877) as consulting actuary to the newly formed Prudential Insurance Company. Professor James W. Glover (1868–1941) started the actuarial course there in 1902 and remained with that program until 1937. He was assisted in his last decade by Walter O. Menge;

several distinguished actuaries, including Thomas N. E. Greville, Cecil J. Nesbitt, Carl H. Fischer, Allen L. Mayerson and Donald A. Jones, built on the foundation that Professor Glover laid.

Actuarial courses being formed in North America early in the twentieth century were described in three papers delivered at the Fourth (New York 1903) and Fifth (Berlin 1906) International Congresses by authors as follows:

Congress	Country	Author
Fourth	Canada	Frank Sanderson
Fourth	U.S.	Joseph A. De Boer
Fifth	U.S.	J. Howard Gore

Professor Gore reported that three universities—Yale, California and New York—were building courses in actuarial subjects, but in fact the next major developments were elsewhere.

Actuarial science courses have been offered continually at the University of Iowa since 1913; their beginnings, however, go back as far as 1902 when a course, "The Mathematical Theory of Insurance," was conducted by Dr. Westfall. By 1917 Professor John F. Reilly was teaching three actuarial classes. In 1918 he was joined by the famous Professor Henry L. Reitz, firmly establishing Iowa as the continent's third major producer of actuarial talent. In 1939 Professor Lloyd A. Knowler joined the faculty to become instrumental in developing courses. Since then actuarial educators have included Byron J. Cosby, James C. Hickman, Stuart A. Klugman and Richard Ziock.

Professor Albert H. Mowbray (1881–1949), an authority in both casualty and life actuarial fields, was appointed Professor of Insurance at the University of California in 1923, making Professor Gore's 1903 prediction come true two decades later. Mowbray served there until his death.

During World War I, Professor Lloyd A. H. Warren (1879–1949) set his sights upon an actuarial course at the University of Manitoba. He was eventually successful in building the continent's fourth major source of actuaries. His tenure was followed by that of Lee F. S. Ritcey in 1949 and by Ernest R. Vogt and Hendrik J. Boom in 1958.

Trinity College in Hartford, Connecticut, although never establishing an actuarial program in the usual sense, has earned its niche in actuarial history through the distinctions of its graduates, first of whom in 1906 was Everett S. Fallow, who eight years later became a charter member of the Casualty Actuarial Society. Horace R. Bassford came to the profession from the class of 1910, Henry S. Beers and Sydney D. Pinney (CAS president in 1940) from the class of 1918, and Alfred N. Guertin from the class of 1922. In all, five Trinity alumni have been CAS presidents. Marjorie VanEenam Butcher, an Associate and daughter of an Associate of the Society of Actuaries, has taught mathematics at Trinity College since 1956 and has helped and encouraged many young men and women to pursue actuarial careers.

THE BEGINNINGS OF JOINTLY ADMINISTERED EXAMINATIONS, 1928

In May 1927 the Actuarial Society and American Institute announced that negotiations on possible joint examinations were under way. Credit for first public advocacy of this eminently sensible way to economize on the work of the respective examination committees belongs to the American Institute in 1924 remarks by Percy H. Evans and Percy C. H. Papps (*R.A.I.A.* 13, 199 and 396). It seems clear that the smaller of the two bodies had to be first to speak on this delicate matter; if the Actuarial Society had been the proposer, opposition by American Institute leaders who feared losing their independence would surely have scuttled any plan. As Reinhard A. Hohaus pointed out in 1949 ("The Origin of the Society of Actuaries," *TSA* 1, 12), this, although not the first instance of cooperation between the two entities, was the first joint action of the "more intimate sort," its need having arisen "not only out of the virtual identity of the educational ground to be covered, but also out of the growing common membership of the two bodies."

This step must have been applauded by the twelve-member Examination Committee of the American Institute, which in 1927 was composed of eight Fellows of the Actuarial Society and only four solely from the American Institute.

Wisely, the immediate objective was set at combining only the basic mathematics subjects—algebra, trigonometry and calculus—which became joint in 1929. The only minor hitch in the negotiations seems to have been that the Actuarial Society people wanted to continue examining candidates on arithmetic; hence the 1929 examination had just the following single arithmetic question before that subject disappeared in 1930:

> Divide the least common multiple of 3,354 and 2,331 by the greatest common
> divisor of 2,849 and 3,367, and then divide the quotient by the excess of 3.428571
> over 1.270.

In 1931, joint examinations for the rest of the Associateship parts were explored, this being accomplished in 1932. The much more difficult task of reconciling differences in standards, subjects and courses of reading on the Fellowship parts was accomplished in time to have these administered jointly in 1938.

In 1939 each body announced that Fellows by examination in the other body need only apply in order to be admitted to its Fellowship. This privilege was quickly used by many, and thus a giant step was taken, making merger inevitable ten years later.

During the 1930s, misgivings arose whether the Associateship examinations were sufficient to justify public confidence in actuarial advice given by persons lacking more than Associateship credentials. It was clear that few members of the public were able to appreciate the distinction between a Fellow and an Associate, and it was observed that the numbers of practicing actuaries who had ceased writing examinations upon reaching Associateship were expanding faster than were the numbers of Fellows. By 1938 the Actuarial Society roster showed an exact balance, 371 Fellows and 371 Associates, while in the American Institute the Associates outnumbered the Fellows by 306 to 208. Some may have regretted the Society's failure in 1909 to adopt Emory McClintock's proposal (*T.A.S.A.* 11, 25) that:

> Associates ... [be] listed ... as "Associates, Temporary," ... so that they should retire automatically after five (or perhaps seven) years ... .

The major Associateship subjects had long been composed of Mathematics, Theory of Probabilities, Compound Interest and Life Contingencies, while the Fellowship examinations were in two main segments as follows:

Fellowship Part I	Fellowship Part II
Mortality and Disability Tables	Distribution of Surplus
Graduation	Life Insurance Accounts
Selection of Risks	Investments, Banking and Finance
Gross Premiums	Insurance Law
Valuation of Liabilities	Pension Funds
Nonforfeiture Values	Non-Life and Current Topics

The Actuarial Society Council minutes of March 1934 show the following, without elaboration on what brought this up or what charge the committee was given:

> On motion the President was directed to appoint a Committee to report on the scope and nature of the examinations.

This committee, later to become a Joint Committee with the American Institute, was to be kept at work for four years under three chairmen, James E. Hoskins, succeeded by Henry Moir, and upon Moir's sudden death in June 1937, by John G. Parker.

In March 1935 the Council approved in principle a sweeping committee proposal that all the subjects listed under Fellowship Part I be required for Associateship qualification. But when the matter came up for final decision in February 1938 as part of the plan for making all examinations joint with the American Institute, the Council voted to move only the first three of those Part I subjects to the Associateship syllabus. Nevertheless, the effect on the numbers of Associates in the first several years of the new arrangement was considerable as the figures in Table VII.6 show.

Table VII.6
NEW ASSOCIATES OF
ACTUARIAL SOCIETY OF AMERICA
BY EXAMINATION, 1937–1941

Year	Number of New Associates
1937	35
1938	32
1939	9
1940	28
1941	21

NEW DIRECTIONS, 1939–1948

Actuarial Society and American Institute. In a 1949 paper ("The Actuarial Examinations" *TSA* 1, 42), Charles A. Spoerl described the considerable change in the pattern of actuarial education that had been made during the 1940s. Those responsible for these recommendations had available to them four important papers on the subject, viz.:

"The Education of the Actuary," Arthur Pedoe (*T.A.S.A.* 40, 50), 1939.

"A Technique For Facing the Actuarial Examinations," Harry M. Sarason (*R.A.I.A.* 30, 462), 1941.

"Selection and Training of Actuarial Students," Edmund B. Whittaker (*R.A.I.A.* 31, 455), 1942.

"Proposals for a Revision of the Educational System of the Actuarial Society of America and the American Institute of Actuaries 1939," Benjamin T. Holmes and James Hunter (in the Society of Actuaries archives), 1940.

Pedoe, always the archenemy of complacency, espoused the principle of education stated in the eighteenth century by a tutor of Robert Malthus, Gilbert Wakefield (op.cit., p. 54):

> The greatest service of tuition to any youth is to teach him the exercise of his own powers, to conduct him to the limits of knowledge by that gradual process in which he sees and secures his own way, and rejoices in a consciousness of his own faculties and his own proficiency.

(Left to right) Four happy actuarial students, Gathings Stewart, Samuel P. Adams, John Phelps and new Fellow Margaret Walker, receiving exam-passing recognition from Lincoln National Life President Alva J. McAndless in 1939. (Courtesy of Lincoln National Life Insurance Company, Fort Wayne, Ind.)

Pedoe cited statistics of the percentages of candidates who passed the Fellowship examinations which, read in conjunction with those given on page 66 of Spoerl's 1949 paper, give these figures for every year from 1926 to 1949 with the exception of 1938. Pedoe offered many specific criticisms and suggestions about the examinations, the course of reading and the texts as well as the roles of the New York lectures and the several existing study groups. He passed along also an idea by James E. Hoskins (p. 56):

> [T]here is a need for a text of actuarial readings covering thoughts and ideas of permanent value in the early volumes of the *Transactions*. . . . There are similar matters outside the *Transactions* and not readily available to students which might be re-discovered in this way. It is a task which two or three of our Fellows would enjoy and it would make us their permanent debtors.

This suggestion was not picked up then or later.

Two historically important comments in the discussions of Pedoe's paper were:

> [Charles F. B. Richardson, p. 468] The time is fast approaching when we shall have to recognize three distinct classes of actuarial students: (1) Those employed by life insurance companies, (2) Those employed by the Government in connection with Social Insurance, etc., (3) Students working with consulting actuaries, who expect to engage in that line of work. It might be well worth while considering whether, in the future, we should not cater to these different types by giving in the later Fellowship examinations an opportunity to specialize in certain subjects. . . .

> [Henry H. Jackson, p. 469] Some of [the qualifications required of an actuary] have been well indicated today . . . but I think so far one word has been left out which is of the utmost significance in our profession. True, actuaries must be men of ability; they must be men of character; above all, they must be men of courage. Possibly courage may be insufficiently stimulated if all available knowledge of the subject is predigested before it is fed to the candidate.

Sarason's homespun, or as he called them "Dutch-uncle," tips to students on how to study effectively, how to review, how to write the examinations, how to repeat, and even when to quit, produced thirty-five pages of discussion, most from actuaries who praised his ideas but expected others to be shocked or disapproving. Two contributors, Arthur Pedoe and Arthur A. Windecker, gave historically valuable analyses of the periods required to reach Fellowship or Associateship. Pedoe for example showed that forty-eight university graduates needed 8.6 years on average while seven others required 10.1 years.

Whittaker's contribution gave a candid description of the successes and failures in the Prudential's program of building its actuarial staff over the preceding twelve years. He said that by trial and error the company had hit upon a selection method that was practically foolproof; in his reply to the discussion he mentioned (*R.A.I.A.* 32, 214) that "out of seventeen new Fellows of the Society and Institute for the year 1943, six were Prudential employees at the time they wrote the final examinations."

Whittaker also aroused interest in the possibility of devising an effective test for forecasting the success of prospective actuaries with the actuarial examinations; Prudential, he remarked, had found a particular Life Office Management Association

(LOMA) Clerical Aptitude Test surprisingly predictive. Prudential's experience also showed the value of acquiring a capable instructor for the early examinations. Finally, Whittaker contributed several suggestions for modifying the examinations so as to reduce the length of time required for qualification.

Holmes and Hunter undertook to outline proposals for educational activity sponsored officially by the Society and Institute that (a) would be available equally to all students, and (b) would not descend to "spoon-feeding" them. Their proposal was that the New York lectures be discontinued and a young Fellow be employed (on the understanding that he would remain at least five years) to prepare and distribute appropriate study material, and to issue quizzes to which students would be invited to submit short essays for his marking and comments. The scope of this would be limited to the last Associateship and all the Fellowship examinations. The service was to be financed by student fees estimated at $50.00 per part.

With this wealth of suggestions and many other ideas of its own, a Joint Special Committee on the Education and Training of Actuaries chaired by Henry S. Beers went to work early in 1943, continuing for three years until evolving into a permanent Advisory Committee to the Education and Examination Committee.

Joseph B. Maclean in his presidential address to the Actuarial Society in October 1942 (*T.A.S.A.* 43, 223) commended the Joint Educational Committee upon having made available "to students everywhere the valuable notes which formerly were accessible only to those in a few large centers," and went on to emphasize the necessity for (1) reducing the time required to attain Fellowship and (2) increasing the prospect for ultimate success of the average candidate who had passed the first examination. Maclean said (p. 232):

> [P]art of the solution lies in a reduction both in the range of subjects included in the syllabus and in the volume of the prescribed reading. More emphasis might well be placed on those fundamental and practical matters which should be familiar to every actuary and less on subjects which are either only indirectly connected with the usual functions of an actuary or of interest chiefly to the specialist.

The development of recommendations brought to the fore two actuaries (Beers and Charles A. Spoerl) in the same company (Aetna) who gave immensely of their time and talent to that work. Both were brilliant mathematicians; this was a source of concern to some who would have preferred the fate of students to be in the hands of people more easily able from their own experience to appreciate the difficulties of the run of the candidates. Joseph B. Maclean in his May 1945 presidential address (printed in *T.A.S.A.* 46, 1, but never personally delivered because wartime conditions prevented a meeting being held) described the Beers Committee recommendations as in some respects revolutionary.

Spoerl's paper in *TSA* 1 is a document of extraordinary historical value, because it covered an epochal change in examination procedure and described the dilemmas that afflicted the redesigners and the uncertainty they felt in several instances about the validity of their own conclusions.

A new expression, *preliminary examinations,* came into actuarial terminology, denoting those designed for completion while candidates were still in college. To get these used it was necessary for the first time in our history to bow to college practices rather than to follow patterns that actuaries had long considered preferable. One of the most revolutionary innovations was adoption of multiple-choice questions, about which Spoerl said (p. 46–48):

> [When] this suggestion first reared its ugly head, the reactions of the committee members ran the full scale from consternation and horror to the feeling that at last we were "getting somewhere." ... I am convinced that the only thing responsible for so remarkable a change was the access of knowledge that came with our study of the theory of setting examinations. ...
>
> The salient point is that, while the old type of examination purports to test the candidate's ability to organize his material as well as his grasp of details of technique, it too often does no such thing, particularly if the questions are as difficult as ours have been. ...
>
> Moreover, the element of subjectivity is bound to creep in. My own work in supervising the marking of the old examinations amply demonstrated this, but never to the extent dramatized on a problem in Probability, on which the first marker gave one candidate full marks while the second gave him zero.

The wording of that question, in the 1945 Part 3, was:

> Prove that, if a die is thrown 4 times, the odds are in favor of a five turning up at least once. Answer the objection that this result is inconsistent with the fact that, on the average, 6 throws are required to turn up a five.

Significant reaction, especially by students, to the changes in examinations by 1946 is set forth in November 1946 discussions by Harold E. Dow, Donald D. Cody and Cecil J. Nesbitt (*R.A.I.A.* 35, 412–15).

The essence of Spoerl's spirited advocacy of multiple-choice questions was that they permitted replacing a comparatively small number of somewhat complicated problems by a large number of questions, each designed to test one definite point.

The committee's work had brought it into touch with the examining body that in 1947 became the Educational Testing Service (ETS). On that organization's advice a Language Aptitude Examination, considered appropriate because (*TSA* 1, 45) "a large part of the actuary's work deals with words, exact shades of meaning [and] interpretation," was introduced as an experiment. Support for it was never more than half-hearted; it was decided to limit its use to "weeding out illiterates." The test was shortened from three hours to one hour in 1950 and dropped entirely in 1960.

Spoerl emphasized the urgent need to influence mathematics professors so that at the very least they would stop warning their students away from taking actuarial examinations.

The remainder of Spoerl's paper described revisions made or still being considered in the later Associateship and Fellowship examinations and changes in the structure and operations of the Education and Examination Committee. Those who discussed this landmark paper were generally respectful of the efforts made although divided about their efficacy.

All this restructuring was, as the summary (in Table VII.7) by three-year periods shows, rather slow to generate a major increase in the numbers of new Fellows.

Table VII.7

**NUMBERS OF NEW FELLOWS OF
SOCIETY OF ACTUARIES AND
ITS PREDECESSOR BODIES, 1946–1963**

1946–1948	120	1955–1957	148
1949–1951	130	1958–1960	184
1952–1954	121	1961–1963	216

Actuaries were hesitant to take advantage of what college professors could teach about techniques in education. Whittaker was particularly emphatic on one approach that he considered unfruitful (*TSA* 1, 86):

> Some suggestion has been made in Mr. Spoerl's paper that we talk to college professors on subjects of technical interest. I cannot imagine anything more useless than getting a dozen college professors down to New York for a seminar on osculatory interpolation. They would leave town with even less idea of what an actuary does than they have now and we would never get any practical actuaries.

In 1975, Charles L. Trowbridge spoke on the same theme in his presidential address (*TSA* 27, 1):

> Perhaps we do not so readily recognize ... that actuaries are in a very unusual relationship to the academic world. In contrast to medicine and law, we put little or no emphasis on academic degrees, and we have no university-connected actuarial schools giving the equivalent of M.D. or J.D. degrees. ... We have a distant or hands-off relationship with academia, and what must be viewed as a go-it-alone approach.

Casualty Actuarial Society. This was an era in which the numbers of candidates sitting for the CAS examinations were small, a condition that was shortly to change dramatically. Pruitt, in his 1964 paper (*PCAS* 51, 159), mentioned a few revisions in syllabus content having been made in 1941, and used the expression "de-mathing" (of the examinations in 1948 and 1955) to describe the elimination of all mathematical sections except Statistics, Probability, and Elementary Life Insurance Mathematics. Pruitt said (p. 160):

> The expressed theory ... was that examining a candidate in basic mathematics was unnecessary, since a good working knowledge was implicit in the sections devoted to applied mathematics. Although this theory was probably sound enough, the candidates did not understand it that way, and proceeded to demonstrate, by their wretched showing in the remaining sections, that they, along with some vocal elements in our membership, thought we were letting down the bars.

DEVELOPMENTS 1949–1962

The era centered in the 1950s is notable for (1) establishment of new university courses, (2) the publishing of several important texts as well as large expansion of study notes, and (3) debate about syllabus changes that had been instituted upon recommendations of the Beers Committee and changes still felt to be needed to stimulate a greater flow of aspirants to the profession.

Ten college courses in actuarial science, following in the footsteps of the pioneers mentioned earlier in this chapter but introducing a variety of innovative approaches, have been prominent among those that came into being in the thirty years following World War II. The names of actuaries on the faculties of those courses up to 1979 are placed on record here; descriptions of their systems are preserved in the Society of Actuaries archives.

1946 Drake University. Floyd S. Harper and Eli A. Zubay joined the faculty in 1947, Donald R. Schuette did so in 1959, Warren R. Adams in 1967 and Newton L. Bowers in 1969.

1948 University of Wisconsin-Madison. Robert E. Larson introduced the modern actuarial program. William S. Bicknell joined the faculty in 1956, Donald R. Schuette in 1965 and James C. Hickman in 1970. The original connection with the profession had been made in 1903 when Wisconsin's Professor Balthaser H. Meyer, described as "Lecturer on Actuarial Subjects," accepted Emory McClintock's personal invitation to membership in the Fourth International Congress.

1951 Université Laval. This was to become a highly successful program in the interests of the French-speaking actuarial students of Canada. The original lecturers were Jean-Paul Picard and Claude Castonguay. Gaston Paradis in 1962 became the first permanent professor and has remained in charge of the program. Professor André Premont joined the faculty in 1967.

1957 Nebraska. The founders of this course were the Nebraska Actuaries Club and that state's insurance industry. Robert E. Larson, who brought the course into being, was followed successively by Stephen G. Kellison in 1966 and Cecil D. Bykerk in 1975. Loren V. Petersen joined the staff in 1976 and Warren R. Luckner in 1977.

1958 Georgia State University. Under the leadership of Dr. Kenneth Black, Jr., a center for actuarial education was established under direction of Professors Floyd S. Harper and Eli A. Zubay. From the outset, strong encouragement, technical advice and financial support were furnished by the Southeastern Actuaries Club. Professor John E. Brown joined the faculty in 1968, and Professor Robert W. Batten became program head in 1972.

1958 University of Texas. The history of this university's training of actuaries, which began in 1912, is well-covered in Lloyd K. and Annie N. Friedman's 1988 book *On The Trail of Actuaries In Texas 1844–1964*. On the initiative of the Actuaries

Club of the Southwest and the Texas Life Convention, Byron J. Cosby developed the modern course in 1958. He was followed by Eugene Wisdom in 1968.

1963   Northeastern University. This was a special type of "work and study" program in which the student worked full time for parts of the year at a life company that subscribed to the program, and studied full time at other parts of the year, an arrangement excellently suited to an era when the demand for actuarial students substantially outran the supply. The details were skillfully worked out by retired actuary Harold A. Garabedian under the aegis of the Actuaries Club of Boston. The course continued successfully until 1981 under the direction throughout of the school's Dean and Director, Geoffrey Crofts. A description by Crofts and Richard L. London is printed in *The Actuary* November 1982.

1964   University of Waterloo. This program has become one of the most ambitious and wide-ranging as can be found anywhere. University of Waterloo, which came into existence in 1957, began to offer tuition in actuarial science early in the 1960s and brought in Peter L. J. Ryall as its first full-time actuarial faculty member in 1964. He was followed by Michael Bennett in 1968 and by Robert L. Brown in 1971. Associated with them have been Frank G. Reynolds (1971), Allan Brender (1975), William H. Aitken (1976), and Harry H. Panjer (1980).

1970   Ball State University. This course has been conducted by John A. Beekman, with colleagues Richard G. Driskill (1970), William H. Wetterstrand (1976), and Beda Chan (1979).

1974   Pennsylvania State University. This course has been led by Arnold F. Shapiro assisted, for topics in early actuarial examinations, by instructors in that university's mathematics and statistics departments.

Major textbooks published by the Society of Actuaries in these years were:

Life Contingencies, by C. Wallace Jordan, 1952.

Population Statistics and Their Compilation, (2nd. ed.) by Hugh H. Wolfenden, 1954.

Introduction to Demography, by Mortimer Spiegelman, 1955.

Accident and Sickness Insurance Provided Through Individual Policies, John H. Miller, Principal Contributor, 1956.

Selection of Risks, by Pearce Shepherd and Andrew C. Webster, 1957.

Measurement of Mortality, by Harry Gershenson, 1961.

The Casualty Actuarial Society's Gustav F. Michelbacher authored a text, *Multiple Line Insurance*, in 1957.

At Society of Actuaries meetings between 1955 and 1958 there were three discussions of education and examination issues.

In 1955 (*TSA* 7, 286) actuaries were invited to discuss whether the right type of person was being attracted to the profession; what changes in the syllabus should be made; whether it would be well to list, but not examine on, advanced reading in specialized fields; whether examination standards were appropriate; and what might be done to induce more colleges to provide actuarial instruction. One speaker contributed an extension for the years 1950–1954 of the examination success ratio statistics that had been given by Charles A. Spoerl in 1949. Another described the major reductions in syllabus references accomplished in the past decade. Another remarked that the ratio of actuaries (Fellows and Associates) to the population in the United States was only one-fifth of that in Great Britain and only one-third of that in Canada.

Descriptions were given in 1957 (*TSA* 9, 95) of high school mathematics contests, particularly the Society's sponsorship of the continent-wide competition conducted by the Mathematical Association of America. There was complaint about the small number of qualified actuaries yielded thus far from among winners of the Society's prizes that had been awarded since 1947.

At the 1958 session (*TSA* 10, 671), the Education and Examination Committee reported that the average time from first examination to Fellowship had declined to eight years from eleven years a decade earlier, and that recent changes in examination rules would make it theoretically possible for the examinations to be completed in three years. By 1983, however (*The Actuary,* April 1984, p. 5), the results among 211 candidates showed a 7.5-year median and an 8.27-year mean qualification period.

COOPERATION IN EDUCATIONAL REQUIREMENTS, STARTING IN 1963

The days when any one actuarial body could make decisions on educational and examination matters by itself were coming to an end in the early 1960s.

The first step in the direction of cooperation was taken in 1963 when the Society of Actuaries and the Casualty Actuarial Society joined in sponsoring the examination in General Mathematics, an arrangement that ought to have been started much earlier. Thoughts about extending this to later examinations began being voiced soon after, but action had to await resolution of questions about differences in standards and syllabuses. In 1961, Laurence H. Longley-Cook, FCAS, had looked into this question of standards and had concluded (*TSA* 13, D475):

> Examinations of the CAS are similar in length to those of the Society of Actuaries . . . . The Casualty Actuarial Society general mathematics examination paper is rather easier than the Society of Actuaries paper, but the passing mark is higher, so that the difference between the two is more apparent than real. . . .
>
> CAS students need only have a rudimentary knowledge of life contingencies, but are required to have a considerable knowledge of ratemaking techniques in casualty and property lines. . . .
>
> The standards of the Casualty Actuarial Society examination were lower at some periods in the past than they are now, and fellows of the Society of Actuaries should not judge the present casualty actuarial examination on these standards. . . .
>
> Work in the more difficult areas of credibility theory requires a very high standard of mathematics, higher than is required in any life actuarial work, but to ask every student to be able to carry out such advanced theoretical research would be quite impractical, and the Casualty Actuarial Society has always tried to attract and develop a rounded individual rather than the back room expert.

A change introduced by the Society of Actuaries in 1963 responded to the steadily increasing specialization of actuaries and was a factor in reducing the quantity of readings. Candidates in the later Fellowship parts were required to choose between two alternatives—the "I" examinations on individual policy subjects and the "E" examinations on employee benefit topics. Of the five Fellowship parts, the first three were classified as "Basic" involving no such choice, and the last two as "Specialized" with "I" and "E" segments.

Next came a warming attitude toward multiple-choice questions. In March 1964 the ETS presented an eleven-page report to the Education and Examination Committee pointing out persuasively how much more of the load the ETS could assume if "objective" (i.e., multiple choice) questions could be used more extensively.

By 1968 the Academy was feeling pressure to remove a barrier that was preventing it from developing the comprehensive entrance examination for Academy membership that its bylaws required to be in effect by January 1970. This barrier was the difference in opinion between the two founding bodies, which had examination systems, and the other two, the Conference of Actuaries in Public Practice and the Fraternal Actuarial Association, which had no such systems. A Joint Committee for Review of Education and Examination composed of three representatives from each of the six constituent bodies and chaired by H. Raymond Strong, FCA, began meeting in February 1968 to settle these questions, and soon began talking about a new concept called the "Alternate Route." (A few purists decried the adjective *alternate* rather than *alternative,* but by that time, the expression was imbedded in actuarial terminology.)

In November 1969, Wendell A. Milliman, then president of the Academy as well as the Society of Actuaries, explained the concept and the need for considering it in these words (*TSA* 21, 337):

> [F]or the Academy to accept the examinations given by the Society of Actuaries and the Casualty Actuarial Society as though they were its own . . . did create a problem for the other sponsoring organizations . . . . This problem results from the understanding, in connection with the creation of the Academy, that these other organizations would also establish examination requirements at the time that the examination route becomes the only route to membership in the Academy. . . .
>
> Out of this background has developed consideration of the possibility of establishing an "alternate route" for qualifying for membership in some or all of our several actuarial organizations. Essentially, this proposal would recognize that the present examinations . . . are geared to a self-study educational process. The concept of the alternate route is that somewhat different examinations might be more appropriate for prospective actuaries who have taken courses in specified areas of basic actuarial knowledge from qualified collegiate institutions. In its original form the alternate route proposal would have recognized an individual who had acquired a Master's degree in actuarial science from an "accredited institution" as having obtained such an education. It was proposed that such an individual should be able, by passing a comprehensive examination covering the appropriate subjects, to receive credit in the Academy for the equivalent of the first five examinations of the Society of Actuaries or the Casualty Actuarial Society. . . .

> It should be emphasized that . . . much work must be done before a satisfactory plan can be worked out; indeed, before all the problems involved will be known. . . .
>
> How important such an alternate route might be in the near future in terms of numbers qualifying for membership in any one of these bodies is debatable. This is not necessarily, however, the best test of its value to the profession. Many of us believe that it is high time that more positive steps be taken by our profession to encourage broader participation by collegiate institutions in the academic training of actuaries. A program such as the alternate route may well be one of the most effective ways of giving that encouragement.

This idea was intermittently debated through the next half-dozen years, but the majority of Fellows were just as adamantly opposed as their forebears were more than half a century earlier when the Council of the Actuarial Society attempted to have Fellowship granted to a few worthy persons by shortcutting the established examination process. Gary Corbett, the 1975 Society of Actuaries historian, said (*TSA* 27, 535):

> "Keeping up the standards" is of great importance to all members of the Society—seemingly more so after one has attained F.S.A. status. This concern with standards is the main reason why the proposal for an alternate route to Associateship has been gestating so long.

Two years later (*TSA* 29, 469), the 1977 historian, Harold G. Ingraham, reported that the Advisory Committee on Education and Examinations had reversed its previous decision to support, in principle, an alternate route to full Associateship by means of a comprehensive examination. That reversal gave the quietus to what at one time had seemed a promising possibility.

At least one other seminal idea blossomed in the late 1960s from the discussions of the aforementioned Joint Committee for Review. In December 1968, John H. Miller laid before that committee a three-page essay he had written entitled "A Generalized Approach to Actuarial Mathematics." He introduced this topic as follows:

> Traditionally the teaching of actuarial practice in life insurance and pension work has proceeded from a study of mortality tables to commutation functions, and then the application of the latter to specific plans of life insurance or annuities. . . . The property-casualty actuarial trainee follows a somewhat parallel course.
>
> By this process the student learns a number of specific applications of principles which are basic to all lines of insurance and pensions without being shown the common trunk from which the separate branches stem. It is suggested that we should instead present to the student a universal concept and then lead him from the general to the particular. This method, it is believed, is a sounder technique of teaching and a more interesting approach to learning since it would give the elementary course of study more apparent relevance to an actuarial career.

Developing that theme, Miller defined the element $q^{(k)}$, the probability of occurrence of a risk, and k, the cost to the insurer when the insured risk occurs. He recognized this cost as, especially in the casualty field, contingent on developments that might require years to liquidate, and he mentioned that "it is usually assumed that any investment income from reserved funds is more than offset by upward price trends which affect the ultimate cost." Here Miller was taking a position on a subject (discounting of loss reserves) that was destined to be much to the fore in the years ahead. This point, however, was not essential to Miller's theme.

Miller's thinking was a harbinger of the new approach to the teaching of actuarial mathematics that was to be adopted in 1982 in advance releases from the textbook, *Actuarial Mathematics* by Newton L. Bowers, Hans U. Gerber, James C. Hickman, Donald A. Jones and Cecil J. Nesbitt.

Textbooks written by actuaries that became available to students in the 1970s included:

- Stephen G. Kellison, *The Theory of Interest,* 1970

- Barnet N. Berin, *The Fundamentals of Pension Mathematics,* 1971

- Thomas P. Bleakney, *Retirement Systems for Public Employees,* 1972

- Stephen G. Kellison, *Fundamentals of Numerical Analysis,* 1974

- Charles L. Trowbridge and Charles E. Farr, *The Theory and Practice of Pension Funding,* 1976

- Robert W. Batten, *Mortality Table Construction,* 1977

Several key changes in actuarial education had their beginnings in the 1970s. Among them were the following:

1. Effective in January 1973 the examinations administered by the Society of Actuaries came under joint sponsorship with the Academy, the Canadian Institute, the Casualty Actuarial Society (which was already involved), the Conference and the Fraternal Actuarial Association. The announcement (Society of Actuaries 1973 *Year Book*, p. 264) made the following general statement about the implications of this:

   > Successful completion of certain of the examinations . . . is accepted by these [other] organizations as meeting a portion of their qualifications for membership . . . .

2. In 1977, Part 9 began to consist of Part 9A for all candidates, followed by separate Parts 9B and 9C for Canadian and United States candidates, respectively. Parts B and C covered Accounting, Law, Taxation and Advanced Social Insurance, and the Canadian sections became requirements of the Canadian Institute for Fellowship in that body.

3. In 1979, a new major subject, Operations Research, was added to the Associateship syllabus; candidates were told that the emphasis was primarily on problem-solving and only secondarily on theoretical considerations. As far back as 1956, Society of Actuaries President William M. Anderson had advocated this (*TSA* 8, 246):

   > I believe it is highly important for us to realize that within recent years a whole new science and profession somewhat akin to ours has been developing with astonishing rapidity. I refer to what is known as Operations Research or Management Science. While many of its fields of activity are far removed from

ours, it is surprising to realize that a large part of the work involves reliance on mathematical techniques which are either those with which we are now familiar or others involving no greater degree of difficulty. A number of parts of Operations Research involve the quantification of management problems by means of mathematical models and the application of specialized mathematical techniques in order to determine the best solution . . . as related to management objectives. A particularly important aspect is that, with problems of any degree of complexity, access to electronic machines is imperative if the methods of solution are to be practical.

My review of the development of this new science has led me to the conclusion that we, as actuaries, should be giving it active and continuing attention. . . .

[W]e can expect that familiarity with Operations Research methods will make actuaries interested in and valuable to lines of business which are now outside our field. This might occur first within firms of consulting actuaries but it could lead to substantial demands for actuaries by other businesses. . . . Quite evidently, the glamour and potential of Operations Research has made itself felt in the colleges today . . . .

Victor E. Henningsen in his 1965 presidential address reminded the Society of Actuaries of Anderson's remarks just quoted, and said (*TSA* 17, 231):

What has occurred in the intervening years? The subject has been before the Society on several occasions. But have actuaries given [it] "active and continuing attention"? With all due respect to our Society Committee on Research, and those individuals who have presented papers or discussions, it seems fair to state that our members have not taken hold of this new tool to the extent that might have been expected. . . . [We] might well sponsor a seminar or seminars . . . as [we] once did in meetings devoted wholly to the feasibility of [electronic data processing] for life insurance companies.

4. In 1979, both the Associateship Part 4 and the Fellowship Part 7 were modified to include examinations to meet the educational requirements for enrollment to perform actuarial services under ERISA in the United States.

THE RAPPAPORT/PLUMLEY PAPER, 1975

In their paper, "The Education of the Actuary in the Future" (*TSA* 27, 441), Anna Maria Rappaport and Peter W. Plumley began by summarizing the history of actuarial education in the Society of Actuaries, i.e., since 1949, with emphasis upon the major differences between the syllabus of 1963 and that about to be introduced in 1976.

With respect to the Fellowship syllabus, the authors stated (p. 444):

The general design for the new Fellowship examination syllabus was first proposed by Charles B. H. Watson in August, 1970. . . . [H]e proposed a system of four Fellowship examinations: Part A, "Assumption of the Risk" (types of coverage, underwriting the risk, the agency system); Part B, "Paying for the Risk" (gross premiums, valuation, and reinsurance); Part C, "Maintaining the Risk" (dividends and experience-rating, analysis of expense and other experience, nonforfeiture values, changes, and investment of assets); and Part D,

"The World Outside" (law, taxation, annual statement, and social insurance). The revised system of Fellowship examinations closely follows his original recommendation. . . .

Since the present examinations included too much memorization of detail and too little concentration on principles, one of the major purposes of the restructuring was to improve the content of the course of reading . . . .

The authors went on to describe the essence of the new Associateship examinations (already in effect) and then set forth the merits of joint sponsorship of the examination system by all the North American actuarial bodies, including the ones without an examination system of their own, remarking (p. 448):

The trend is toward closer cooperation . . . . There is little doubt that in the future the several . . . organizations will have an increasing voice in the education of actuaries.

After philosophizing on the purposes of actuarial education and on the external factors that made curriculum changes necessary, Rappaport and Plumley turned their readers' attention to the future (p. 461):

As an important step in meeting this challenge [posed by external influences], the authors suggest a major addition to the program of study available to actuaries.

Their proposal was that the two-phase (Associateship and Fellowship) system that had been in effect since 1896 be broadened to a three-phase system (p. 465):

[The new third phase] would be similar to that which leads to a Ph.D. degree, in that it would be characterized by independent study, a less rigid syllabus, more original work on the part of a student, and a thesis requirement as well as examinations. . . . [It] is not intended to replace the current Fellowship studies and would not be required for attainment of Fellowship.

The new course of study would be available to either Associates or Fellows who might wish to specialize in any of the areas covered. These areas . . . would not be product line-oriented but instead would be designed to prepare the actuary for working in one or more of the emerging disciplines for which the actuarial studies at the Associateship level would be useful.

This happened to be one of the earliest papers whose discussions appear partly in the *TSA* and partly in the just introduced new publication, the *RSA*—in this instance in *RSA* 1, 781. In effect this became the modern equivalent of the traditional mixture of written and oral discussions, but with, it seems, one disadvantage, that readers of *TSA* have been given no clue to the existence of additional discussion in another volume. The production schedule for the *Transactions* appears to permit this to be solved by an editor's note in *TSA* directing readers to the discussions elsewhere.

STEPS TOWARD LINKAGES

In the closing years of the 1970s, leaders in actuarial education became firmly committed to achieving linkages:
(a) of the mathematics of casualty insurance, life insurance and pensions; and
(b) of risk theory with contingency theory.

A joint meeting of the Casualty Actuarial Society and the Society of Actuaries in April 1978, and specifically a concurrent session, "Education for an Expanding Actuarial Profession" (*RSA* 4, 255), was the occasion for preparing members to view old subjects in new ways.

James C. Hickman, FSA, ACAS, said (p. 256):

> Broad social, economic and demographic trends, far beyond our ability to control or even shape, have reduced the relevance of some classical actuarial models. Inflation at the rate experienced in most of the decade makes one question whether life contingency models with fixed interest rates and fixed benefits are sensible. The same force has made time series analysis of claims experience necessary to keep property and casualty insurance premiums from losing the race with inflation. The rollercoaster path followed by the U.S. fertility rate since 1945 makes one wonder if it is worthwhile to study stationary population theories. . . .
>
> Whether we like it or not, the areas for growth in actuarial employment may come in non-traditional fields such as unemployment insurance, the management of self insurance systems for large corporations, risk management for HMOs [Health Maintenance Organizations], the organization and management of catastrophic pools, and the development of equitable systems for intergenerational transfers of income to supplement funded private pensions. . . .
>
> The key to [an] adaptive response is to create a unified, rather than a specialized, education program . . . .

Kevin M. Ryan, FCAS, said (p. 258):

> In some areas casualty insurance technical activities have often been considered accounting in nature, although cloaked in actuarial terminology. I believe the routine handling of questions of risk and the inability of the non-professional actuary, who performed that function without necessarily pretending to be an actuary, is the major cause of the problem currently facing the casualty insurance industry. . . . We have been taught that the loss reserves are tested and evaluated by using actuarial formulas. Until recently, I would suggest that what had been used was accounting principles. Accounting principles are not necessarily in contention with actuarial principles, but they do not provide a sufficient basis for an actuarial evaluation of reserves. The soundness of reserves depends a great deal on how much professional actuarial expertise is utilized in their development, especially in the long-term liability line. . . . It is absolutely necessary to develop reserves by utilizing the same considerations as those used in developing rates.

Charles C. Hewitt, FCAS, said (p. 265):

> [U]ntil several years ago, the role of the casualty actuary had evolved into pricing (including securing approval from rating authorities), product design and loss reserving.
>
> However, the casualty actuary of today is beginning to find himself in a new role—that of a technician floating on the crest of the new waves of social, economic and environmental change that are filling out the nineteen-seventies.

Hewitt's belief was that actuaries as a group should be preparing themselves to make greater contributions in fields such as:

- Long-range financial planning

- Planning for nontraditional product lines

- Asset and liability valuation

- Rate regulation in periods of rapid change

- Limitations in coverage availability and affordability.

He foresaw also that recertification, already demanded in some branches of the medical profession, might some day become a requirement for actuaries.

Events moved rapidly in the direction these and other actuaries had portrayed. In the following year, October 1979, the discussions at the Society of Actuaries meeting included two sessions heralding new approaches, viz.:

- "Proposed—A 'Dynamic' Valuation Interest Rate (*RSA* 5, 917), which the moderator Yuan Chang introduced as a revolutionary change in the approach to the prescription of the statutory maximum valuation interest rates for individual life insurance.

- "Current Professional Topics" (*RSA* 5, 1189) in which panelist James J. Murphy spoke, as one of seven goals, of making the study of actuarial science relevant to the practice of actuarial science. Linking risk theory with basic contingency theory was to be undertaken in a new textbook that would replace the series of life contingencies texts that had begun in England in 1843, and since 1950 had been C. Wallace Jordan's *Life Contingencies.*

CONTINUING EDUCATION

Agitation, by no means limited to this profession, for assurance that practitioners would keep themselves adequately informed about new developments throughout their careers, led to consideration of how this might best be accomplished. The 1967 Report of the Committee on the Future Course of the Society of Actuaries (Walter Klem, chairman) contained the following observation:

> Our Committee feels that special interest seminars, research activities, committee studies of newly-developing fields of interest to the actuary, greater specialization in regular meetings, and so on, will become increasingly important.

The Klem Committee recommendations included appointment of a Committee on Continuing Education; the Board followed that advice in 1968, placing Charles L. Trowbridge initially in charge. The Trowbridge Committee made its recommendations to the Board in the fall of 1969. These were distributed to the members early in 1970, leading to panel discussions at both 1970 spring meetings (*TSA* 22, D271 and D315).

Under direction of each of Trowbridge's several successors, the continuing education function soon was organized by type of activity. By 1975, the then general chairman, William H. Schmidt (*RSA* 1, 789), spoke of eight principal committees on Computer

Science, Economics and Finance, Health Insurance, Life and Health Corporate Affairs, Life Insurance and Annuities, Retirement Plans, Research, and Social Insurance.

Schmidt reported that each committee was working closely with the Program Committee to assist in planning topics, concurrent sessions, workshops and teaching sessions. He said that one spring meeting was specializing in a continuing education topic, and he pointed approvingly to the active role of the Committee on Research which had carried on continuing education work long before 1970, specifically by teaming up with a university or another professional society in conducting seminars on specific topics.

Production of literature, further research and sponsorship of seminars were mentioned by Schmidt as goals yet to be reached. In 1978 the Society of Actuaries embarked upon regular seminars, the groundwork for which had been prepared by Plumley and Director of Education Warren R. Adams. These seminars have amply demonstrated their worth and their attractiveness to many members, and in general have been self-supporting through their registration fees.

Preston C. Bassett surveyed actuarial education within the Society of Actuaries and its predecessor bodies in his 1985 presidential address (*TSA* 37, 1). Bassett stressed the difficulties that our predecessors faced and their success in adapting to changing conditions; he then gave his prescription for changes still needed. Bassett's successor, Richard S. Robertson, gave to his address the title, "The Sad State of Actuarial Education in the United States" (*TSA* 38, 1); his theme was the shortage of university instructors who are fully qualified members of the profession, and the consequent impracticality of bringing the universities more fully into the education system by some appropriate variant of the "alternate route."

AT THE TWENTY-FIRST CONGRESS: "THE TRAINING OF THE ACTUARY"

"The Training of the Actuary" was the assigned subject for the national reports segment of the 1980 International Congress of Actuaries in Switzerland. Thus there exists, in the "N" volume of the *Transactions* of that Congress, a 283-page account of the aspirations and procedures in twenty-seven countries for the education of actuaries at the end of the 1970s.

The report for Canada appears on pages 147–64 and that for the United States on pages 257–74 of that volume.

There are also several discussions of this subject in the same meeting's "S" volume. A summary of the individual country reports, in French only, is printed on pages 37–42.

TREND OF STUDENT POPULATION IN THE LATE 1970s

As Linden N. Cole showed (*The Actuary*, June 1982, p. 1), the number of students passing Part 1 (General Mathematics) of the Society of Actuaries/Casualty Actuarial Society examinations, which had its historic peak in 1976, began a downtrend for several years after that. Cole's figures for 1976 to 1981, extended to 1988, are displayed in Table VII.8.

Table VII.8

**NUMBERS OF STUDENTS WHO PASSED
THE GENERAL MATHEMATICS EXAMINATION, 1976–1988**

1976	1,654	1983	1,512
1977	1,526	1984	1,620
1978	1,523	1985	2,121
1979	1,285	1986	2,590
1980	1,249	1987	2,693
1981	1,225	1988	3,329
1982	1,337		

These figures exclude students who obtained credit for the General Mathematics Examination by passing the Graduate Record Examination.

These figures constitute the base from which future Fellows of both bodies must come. Planners within the profession should be kept aware of their trend.

Chapter VIII.

INCOME DISABILITY BENEFITS

"To collect under life insurance, you must die; under accident insurance, you must have an accident; under health insurance, you must have a policy."
—*John M. Laird quoting B. A. Page, Ninth TICA, III, 95.*

This chapter portrays the difficulties that actuaries encountered in gradually learning what forms of disability income benefit might be offered safely, and how to price, underwrite and administer them in the face of interference from market forces and particularly competitive pressures.

ADVANCE WARNINGS

Long before actuaries moved into the treacherous field of lifetime disability incomes—those first provided in life insurance policies in 1915, and noncancellable disability contracts in 1918—there was testimony that health insurance was a trap for the inexperienced and the unwary.

At the New York International Congress in 1903, Hiram J. Messenger described some health insurance experiments in the United States before 1850, and then quoted an 1852 comment by actuary and journalist Harvey G. Tuckett (*Proceedings,* Vol. 1, 498):

> In no department of the science of insurance have greater mistakes occurred than in that of health. Parties entered upon the speculation, one taking another's printed rates as a guide, deducting ten, fifteen, or twenty per cent., as fancy dictated or the greater number of policies could be obtained. ... The mischief which has been done is not irretrievable, if the proper calculations are placed before the public.

Messenger then classified the 1850–1903 era into two distinct periods, a long one ending in 1897, and a short one, 1898–1903. He considered the first as characterized throughout by failures, attributing them to insurance men who had no conception of the necessity for contingent liability reserves, whose companies lacked sufficient financial backing, and whose statistics came perforce from the English friendly societies. Yet Messenger was optimistic that lessons had been learned (ibid., p. 516):

> It may be that some of the difficulties connected with health insurance are insurmountable, but the real solution of the problem would be of such great value to the whole country that it is to be hoped before many years have passed,

319

inasmuch as some progress has been made, and the question is now in more competent hands, it will be ... eventually placed upon a basis that will be reasonable to the insured, fairly profitable to the company, and permanent in its nature.

EARLY WARNINGS

Three actuaries—William C. Johnson, FCAS in 1918, Arthur Hunter, F.A.S., FCAS in 1920, and Edmund E. Cammack, F.A.S., FCAS in 1921—pronounced warnings that were heeded by some actuaries but not by others.

Johnson, in the words of John H. Miller in his *Disability Newsletter* (No. 34, August 1982):

> sensed the high risk in payment [of claims under noncancellable disability policies] for the duration of disability [throughout lifetime] and conceived the idea of an aggregate limitation on the period of compensable disability. ...

> [T]he insurers writing policies with benefit period limitations or aggregate indemnity provisions, enjoyed generally favorable experience.

Hunter's warning in 1920 was less clear. As author of the first edition of the Actuarial Society's *Actuarial Studies, No. 5, Total Permanent Disability Benefits in Relation to Life Insurance,* he tried to answer the question whether his own 1911 tables were to be regarded as safe and conservative for premiums and reserves. He began (p. 57) by invoking statements by several actuaries at a Wisconsin hearing in 1917 that "judging from the experience of their companies, the tables ... were safe and conservative." Hunter then qualified this by reminding readers "that the disability benefits granted [in 1920] are much more liberal than those granted by the Fraternal Orders, on which experience [Hunter's] tables are constructed." He might have added that fraternals were much better equipped than insurance companies were to appraise the merits of disability claims and to benefit from the loyalty of their members (definable as "I will not cheat my brothers").

Cammack, in his 1921 paper (*PCAS* 7, 270), said:

> An examination of the rates being charged for non-cancellable Health insurance by companies now transacting it discloses most astonishing differences of opinion. ...

> American companies, for the most part, are charging the same rate for all ages at entry. This course can be justified only if it can be shown that sickness rates do not increase with age, and this we know is not so.

Cammack also criticized the American companies for charging premiums much lower than those of British companies, although the British had much more experience than the Americans and the American policies were more liberal in their terms, particularly in paying lifetime benefits while the British benefit payments ceased at age 65.

Food for thought by company actuaries was provided in 1923 by Joseph H. Woodward, F.A.S., FCAS, in his paper, "Fraternal Sickness Insurance" (*PFAA* 6, 82); his advice to the fraternal actuaries was that even though their rates might appear to be yielding satisfactory results, they would ultimately prove to have been too low as the average age of the membership increased.

The *Transactions* of the 1920s contain two rather extraordinary references to the problems of income disability benefits.

In his October 1921 address (*T.A.S.A.* 22, 318), Actuarial Society President William A. Hutcheson, while speaking enthusiastically about the inherent possibilities in disability coverage, said:

> Statistics as to death rates are more or less accurate, so that we can apply the theory of probabilities to life contingencies, but, on the other hand, we have much to learn regarding disablement rates, and doubt may even exist as to the applicability of actuarial science to accident and sickness insurance.

Nevertheless, less than a year later, Hutcheson's own company, Mutual Life of New York, was one of two (the other being New York Life) that began offering an extreme form of lifetime benefit under which an initial monthly income of $10 per thousand would increase after five years of disability to $15, and after the next five years to $20.

In an encyclopedic paper, "The Development of Life Insurance in the United States During the Last Ten Years," presented to the Actuarial Society in October 1926 for the particular instruction of students, James S. Elston summed up that era in these words (*T.A.S.A.* 27, 378):

> A critical reader not somewhat acquainted with life insurance might suggest that only the bright side of the picture has been painted. But there seems to be no very dark side, at least discernible now. ... Many companies may be saddled with an immense amount of insurance in force with inadequate disability rates, but their total premium rates are probably sufficient, in most cases much more than sufficient.

REPORT OF COMMITTEE ON DISABILITY EXPERIENCE, 1926

Hunter's Disability Tables of 1911 (*T.A.S.A.* 12, 66) remained by default the accepted standard for fifteen critical years during which benefit provisions were being liberalized in two ways: by the contractual terms and by the influence of court decisions. At the Actuarial Society meeting in May 1924, after informal discussion of some pointed questions (*T.A.S.A.* 25, 168) about possible "progressive tendency towards an increased rate of disability ... as the policyholders become better informed on the subject," and about the influence of the 90-day clause upon premium adequacy, a resolution was passed calling for a committee to consider conducting an intercompany investigation (p. 169) "to determine, if possible, the suitability of Hunter's Disability Table."

That committee, chaired by Hunter himself, produced for publication in 1926 a *Report of Committee on Disability Experience*. Data had been collected from twenty-nine companies on several types of benefits, but much of the data were never published; the profession's attention became concentrated on a segment of what was published called "Class 3," this being the experience on policies providing for $10 per thousand of monthly income (with premium waiver) issued by companies whose rates of disability were in the middle and upper range among the contributors. The report was supplemented by papers written by actuaries of, respectively, Metropolitan, Aetna and New York Life.:

"Disability Benefits. A Practical Application of the Disability Committee's Report."
    James D. Craig (*T.A.S.A.* 27, 39).
"The 'Ninety Day' Disability Experience," Henry S. Beers (ibid., 279).
"Disabled Life Reserves." Walter G. Bowerman (ibid., 293).
A clear picture of the court decisions on disability benefits during the era may be found in Chapter XI, "Legal Decisions" of the second (1932) edition of *Actuarial Studies, No. 5. Disability Benefits in Life Insurance Policies* by Arthur Hunter and James T. Phillips.

Differences between the values in Hunter's Tables and the Class 3 results were large. Data in Table VIII.1, a variant of tables published in Joseph B. Maclean's *Life Insurance* (6th ed., 1945, p. 340), show the contrasts. The Class 3 disability rates were many times those of Hunter's; claim values were much smaller than Hunter's because the 90-day clause resulted in many recoveries from disability. The net effect of these was a major excess of Class 3 cost over Hunter's.

Table VIII.1

COMPARATIVE VALUES OF DISABILITY FUNCTIONS IN
HUNTER'S TABLES (1911) AND IN CLASS 3 EXPERIENCE (1926)

	Age			
	20	30	40	50
A. Rate of Disability per 10,000				
Hunter's Table	5	6	8	17
Class 3	44	41	47	76
B. Value, at Time of Disability, of $10 Monthly, at 3% Interest				
Hunter's Table	$ 623	$955	$966	$876
Class 3	246	356	431	449
C. Net Annual Premium for $10 Monthly, at 3% Interest, Coverage to Age 60				
Hunter's Table	$ .80	$1.07	$1.48	$2.20
Class 3*	1.99	2.51	3.30	4.48

*In 1926 it had been supposed that these net premiums would prove to be considerably too low because the policies studied were all at very low policy durations. The 1952 Society of Actuaries Disability Study (*TSA 1952 Reports,* p. 70) showed this supposition to be correct.

The Committee Report of 1926 contained a lengthy Section D (p. 36) entitled "WARNING," the gist of which was that (a) because of the short experience, variety of policy provisions and diversity of company practices, the Committee had "hesitated greatly" about publishing net premiums derived from the data but decided to do so in response to many requests, (b) opinions of the committee members differed as to what the future courses of these rates would be, and (c) any actuary would be in a position after studying the report "to determine what disability rates his company should charge for any particular form." In view of the size of the problem, it is arguable that the committee itself should have gone further than this with specific suggestions.

ACTIONS TAKEN TO CURB DISABILITY LOSSES, 1927 TO 1930

In the aftermath of publication of the 1926 Committee Report, actuaries in the United States were faced with three distinct problems: (1) what disability clauses to incorporate in new policies, (2) what premiums to charge, and (3) whether to strengthen reserves on existing business. Two potential influences on their decisions lay in the unknown future—the Depression of the 1930s and the advent of social security in 1935.

There had been a steady succession of benefit extensions in the 1920s, the major ones being:

1920   Payment of the monthly income (of 1% of the policy face amount) was to begin one month after proof of totality and permanence.

1921   Continuous total disability of ninety days duration was to be presumed permanent until the contrary appeared.

1922   Various plans surfaced for substituting the original level payments by payments increasing with disability duration, up to, in some cases, double the starting amount. Some plans provided 2% from the outset.

1922   One company announced a "professional men's clause," priced at an extra premium of twenty cents per thousand, defining total disability as "inability to perform the duties of his own occupation."

1926   Payment of the monthly income was made retroactive to the onset of the total disability.

It was difficult for companies to take unilateral action in scaling benefits down; in 1928 Edward B. Morris (*PCAS* 15, 9) published a survey of the clauses of the fifty largest companies offering disability coverage, finding little trend to conservatism.

Early in 1928 the New York Superintendent of Insurance appointed a committee of five actuaries chaired by James D. Craig to consider standard provisions. In December 1928 a resolution favoring uniform disability clauses was adopted by the NCIC, resulting in appointment of a committee of five insurance department actuaries chaired by Grady H. Hipp. These two committees working together agreed upon the following pattern of provisions (*T.A.S.A.* 30, 260):

Prescribed	7 Provisions
Permitted	8 Provisions
Prohibited	7 Provisions

These recommendations, which the NCIC approved in September 1929 to be effective January 1930, along with a recommendation that reserves be put on an adequate basis, did more to prevent future experiments in competitive liberalization than they did in the direction of stepping back. It had been suggested that no benefits be paid until the end of six months of disability, but a period of not less than four months (nor more than one year) was prescribed. The report of the two committees said that in some respects their recommendations represented a compromise between opposing points of view. This one, for example, was a compromise between companies which did not desire any fixed period and those which continued to support a three-month waiting period with retroactive payments.

By 1932 nineteen states had put these recommendations into effect; fourteen others favored them although having no authority to enforce them.

The second (1932) edition of *Actuarial Studies No. 5* said about premium scales (p. 7):

> When it was evident in 1929 that the basis for premiums should be more conservative, a number of consultations were held by the actuaries of several companies to exchange experiences and to determine what would be a reasonable basis on which to calculate new premiums. ... It was then decided to employ Class (3) as the basis of premiums with a suitable loading .... All the large companies and many others throughout the country adopted that basis or something approaching thereto.

A description of the range of company actions taken up to 1929 is given in Arthur Hunter's paper of that year (*T.A.S.A.* 30, 386). At the Actuarial Society's meeting of October 9–11, 1929—about three weeks before the stock market crash heralded the years of heavy unemployment—the bases planned by the companies for disability premiums under the new standard provision were informally discussed (*T.A.S.A.* 30, 495). There was a surprising air of optimism among the speakers that premiums for income disability could safely be based upon Class 3 experience loaded 15% and fifty cents per thousand. The only considerable note of caution was by Franklin B. Mead (p. 498):

> [A]ccording to a well established principle of casualty insurance, if the premium charge is increased the claim rate will likewise increase. ... I, therefore, wish particularly to call attention to the fact that with increased rates we will also have increased necessity for more careful underwriting. ...
>
> Each and every case should be viewed as a matter of casualty underwriting apart from life underwriting. It is quite probable that our adverse experience in the past has been largely due to the fact that we did not look at each case from these two viewpoints.

THE FLIGHT FROM INCOME DISABILITY COVERAGE, 1932

The effect of the Great Depression was to deepen the company losses; disability benefits became in reality combinations of disability, unemployment and retirement benefits. The extent of losses suffered by the companies never became completely known but were large—in the hundreds of millions of dollars. By 1931, among thirty major United States companies, ten decided to stop issuing the income benefit (Maclean, op. cit., p. 359); these ten also increased premiums on the waiver benefit to 150% of Class 3 net premiums substantially loaded, and lengthened the waiting period to six months. The other twenty companies raised premiums for the income benefit to 165% of Class 3, reduced the monthly income per thousand from $10 to $5, extended the waiting period to six months, reduced the terminal age for coverage from sixty to fifty-five, and ceased offering the income benefit to women. There was reluctance to be the first company among the ten to discontinue offering the benefit;

Metropolitan Life and Travelers took the plunge in late 1931, and the others promptly followed suit.

New York Life was a leader among the companies that decided to take a further step to trim their losses, i.e., to pay smaller dividends on policies containing income disability coverage at inadequate premiums than on policies without such coverage. The final decision in the company's favor after a long court battle ending in 1936 is covered in Legal Notes, *T.A.S.A.* 38, 167.

The companies that continued to offer income disability took steps to avoid featuring the benefit. Hunter reported an instance to the Rome Congress of 1934 (*TICA* X, Vol. I, p. 418):

> One company which issued 60% of its policies with income benefits prior to 1932 granted less than 15% in that year while another which ceased to issue any literature on the subject for the use of its agents and did not publish the rates for the income disability benefits among the regular premium rates found that its new business on the income form dropped from 65% in 1930 to 1% in 1933.

Subsequent experience on the income benefits issued in the tumultuous years 1918 to 1930 by seven companies was revealed as part of the 1952 Report of the Society of Actuaries Committee. Table VIII.2 contains a short excerpt comparing actual results with those expected by Class 3 factors.

Table VIII.2

DISABILITY CLAIM RATES AND DISABILITY ANNUITY VALUES IN 1930 AND LATER YEARS MEASURED BY 1926 CLASS 3 YARDSTICKS

A. Ratios of Actual Disability Claims by Amount to Expected by Class 3 Rates

	90-Day Clause Non-Retroactive	90-Day Clause Retroactive
During 1930–1935	147%	197%
During 1935–1939	135	168
During 1939–1946	n.a.	n.a.
During 1946–1950	102	124

B. Comparison of Disability Annuities of $10 Monthly at Decennial Ages

Age	Actual by 1952 Study for 90-Day Clause Non-Retroactive	Expected by Class 3	Ratio Actual/Expected
27	$ 403	$ 331	1.22
37	476	408	1.17
47	554	450	1.23
57	662	416	1.59

Source: *1952 TSA Reports,* pp. 96 and 125.

THE PACIFIC MUTUAL LIFE CASE

The Pacific Mutual Life, founded in 1868 and not a mutual company but with a block of participating business, had pioneered noncancellable disability insurance policies in 1918 at a flat premium of $2 for a $10 monthly benefit, issued for a maximum of $1,000 per month with coverage continuing to age 66. From time to time the company had increased premiums moderately on subsequent new issues, and in due course had also reduced the coverage termination age to 61, then to 60 and in 1932 to 55. But the steps taken were utterly inadequate; conditions, particularly unemployment, worsened the situation to the point of bankrupting the company by 1935.

In that year, working in cooperation with insurance departments of several states which were conducting a triennial examination, the company undertook vigorous rehabilitation measures. A new Pacific Mutual Life was created to reinsure all the life and accident and health business on the books; disability benefits were reduced, by 80% in the case of the original $2 premium block, scaled down to 10% for recently issued policies; and a plan was designed to mutualize the company effective when restoration of full benefits had been accomplished. This required consent of at least 10% of the holders of participating life policies, which was obtained in 1946.

A committee to determine the appropriate price to be paid to stockholders of the old company for mutualization, composed of an investment banker and three eminent actuaries (Alva J. McAndless, Ray D. Murphy and Horace R. Bassford), was then appointed. This committee, assisted by Joseph A. Christman as actuary for the project, studied the matter for three years and then announced a plan so well constructed that it withstood repeated legal challenges, the final one in the United States Supreme Court.

The committee estimated that the company's financial condition would be sufficiently strong to permit mutualization by 1973, a pardonably conservative assessment in view of the uncertainty in 1950 of post-war economic conditions; in fact, wise management accomplished the task by 1958.

Credit for vision, technical competence and determination in their contributions to a project that ended so successfully belongs also to several actuaries not already named: William Breiby, Louis Garfin, Alfred N. Guertin, Carl E. Herfurth, F. Edward Huston and Albert H. Mowbray. It is unfortunate that, after it was all over, none of the actuaries involved described this remarkable and instructive affair in a formal paper for the enlightenment of future generations of actuaries.

MUTUAL BENEFIT LIFE, A NOTABLE CONTRAST

Edward E. Rhodes' company, Mutual Benefit, chose a path entirely its own. That company during the chaotic early 1920s had stayed out of the disability field completely, not issuing even the waiver benefit. In 1929 it entered that field with a new approach in which Rhodes had great confidence; consequently he objected strenuously to some of the standard provisions adopted in 1930 as well as to the many company decisions to abandon the disability income benefit in 1931.

His company's solution is described in his paper to the Institute of Actuaries in January 1932, "Is Disability Insurance Practicable?" (*JIA* 63, 115). Rhodes answered

Yes to the question posed by his title, subject to six provisos, all critical of the flaws in the American company experiments. These provisos were (p. 131):

1. The policy contract must be framed throughout as a contract of indemnity [against lost, rather than desired, income].

2. The contingency insured against must be the occurrence of a pecuniary loss as the result of disease or accident. Mere incapacity to earn income through injury or disease is not sufficient.

3. The standards of selection must be those which apply to health and accident underwriting.

4. Claims should be allowed or disallowed in accordance with the terms of the contract and without regard to the effect which disallowance would have upon the life business of the company. After a claim has been allowed there must be constant watchfulness to see that payments are not continued beyond the date of recovery.

5. A prompt presentation of claims should be required by the terms of the contract.

6. ... [I]n a very real sense I regard [the matter of premium rates] as the least troublesome phase of the matter. I am convinced that any table of rates which a conservative actuary is likely to adopt will suffice if the other conditions to which I have referred are observed.

The actuaries at Staple Inn Hall who discussed the paper expressed more than a tinge of skepticism, to which Rhodes, who quite recently had been honored by election to Fellowship of the Institute, replied with courtesy but no yielding. It would be interesting to know how Rhodes' approach worked, especially through the depths of the Depression, but no account appears in the *Transactions*. The author did show in his paper (p. 128) that up to September 1931, disability insurance had been issued in connection with about 8% of the volume of life insurance, and a surplus of $103,000 had accumulated from $278,000 of premiums.

THE EXPERIENCE IN CANADA

The experience by Canadian life companies on their Canadian business issued up to 1932 had characteristics like the experience in the United States but was less drastically adverse because benefit liberalizations had been adopted more slowly, the retroactive benefit had never been adopted, and the Canadian courts were not inclined to construe the contracts more liberally than the companies intended.

The history of disability benefits in Canadian life insurance policies up to 1958 appears in a paper by James A. Campbell presented to the 1960 International Congress of Actuaries. Campbell wrote (*TICA* 16, 101):

In 1932 all but one of the United States companies doing business in Canada ceased to issue income disability and six of the largest Canadian companies adopted the same course. ...

However, a number of Canadian companies were reluctant to give up a benefit which their experience had shown was of inestimable value to policyholders faced with the disaster of total disability. These companies had only small amounts of business in force in the United States .... So far they had not suffered losses and they were willing to make at least one more effort to save the income disability benefit. The leaders in the attempt ... worked out a new form of benefit which came into effect in the middle of 1932. ... The waiting period became six months, the limiting age was reduced to 55, ... income payments continued at the $10 per $1,000 rate for only fifty months, and were reduced to $5 per $1,000 for the next one hundred months. At the end of one hundred and fifty months if the life insured was still disabled the sum insured would become payable and the policy would cease to be in force.

Along with the changes in benefit went a more exacting selection procedure. ...

The continuation of income disability benefits turned out to be a successful decision. ... By 1936 the income period had been extended ... to the anniversary nearest age 65 .... The Canadian companies which abandoned income disability in the 1930's came back into the field at various times between 1947 and 1951. However the original enthusiasm for income disability has never been fully restored even by the companies which continued to issue it throughout and no company has anything like the proportion of its business with income disability that it had in 1931.

Campbell's paper quotes the experience of two companies in post-World War II years on their income disability business, showing in each case a claim rate within that expected and a disability termination rate comfortably above that expected.

HOW THE NONCANCELLABLE CONTRACTS FARED

The companies, which had issued noncancellable disability policies separate from life insurance and had reached for relatively safe ground by ceasing to offer lifetime benefits, did not experience woes on the scale of those of the life companies offering the benefit in connection with life insurance. Table VIII.3 is a condensed version of a table given by John H. Miller to the Casualty Actuarial Society in 1935, in his paper, "History and Present Status of Noncancellable Accident and Health Insurance" (*PCAS* 21, 238).

Table VIII.3

NUMBERS OF COMPANIES THAT HAD ENTERED, WITHDRAWN, AND REMAINED ACTIVE IN THE NONCANCELLABLE DISABILITY FIELD BY ENDS OF YEARS 1919, 1924, 1929 AND 1934

To End of Year	Number of Companies That Had:		Companies Currently Active	Companies Currently Offering:	
	Entered	Withdrawn		Lifetime	Aggregate Limit
1919	5	0	5	5	1
1924	19	4	15	13	3
1929	26	9	17	11	11
1934	30	13	17	6	15

In the Financial Experience section of his paper (p. 246), Miller focussed upon the contrast between underwriting results of nine companies that had written the life indemnity form and the experience of four companies that had written principally the aggregate form. These groups together embraced more than 85% of all ordinary noncancellable business in the United States. Miller quoted both unadjusted loss ratios (omitted in Table VIII.4) and loss ratios approximately adjusted to remove the effect of an overstatement attributable to the method employed.

Table VIII.4

NET PREMIUMS AND ADJUSTED LOSS RATIOS ON NONCANCELLABLE DISABILITY POLICIES OF THIRTEEN SELECTED COMPANIES, 1925, 1928, 1932, 1933 AND 1934

Year	Net Premiums Written		Adjusted Loss Ratio	
	Nine "Life Indemnity" Companies	Four "Aggregate Indemnity" Companies	Life Indemnity	Aggregate Indemnity
1925	$5,439,000	$6,286,000	109%	69%
1928	6,959,000	9,520,000	82	63
1932	7,379,000	9,845,000	119	66
1933	6,772,000	8,594,000	175	61
1934	6,664,000	8,837,000	146	56

Miller's comment was that the experience under life indemnity coverage had been extremely unsatisfactory; since the expense ratio averaged over 30%, this type of insurance resulted in an underwriting loss during every year, 1925 to 1934.

Five years later, Jarvis Farley delivered "A 1940 View of Non-Cancellable Disability Insurance" to the Casualty Actuarial Society. Under the heading, The Future of Non-Can, he remarked (*PCAS* 27, 75):

> There is a wide need for the types of insurance offered by non-can companies. Men familiar with non-can believe that if the moral hazard is controlled the need can be largely satisfied. Control of the moral hazard lies in the company and its underwriting attitudes. . . . If a company has the necessary degree of self-control to keep the moral hazard in line, the dangers of the business will be found not so much in loss experience as in acts bearing directly on the business by men unfamiliar with its requirements. Legislatures and insurance departments cannot make non-can, but they can break it. . . . Such misconceptions have more than once caused government officials to make moves which were not in the best interest of either the business or the public.

And his 1940 view in general was (p. 76):

> The right arm of management is the actuary, [who] must understand the problems and the inter-relationships of the departmental experts. Mathematical formulae and theories are not nearly enough. . . . Non-can must have a sound actuarial foundation, but that foundation must be realistic and independent in

its recognition of human nature . . . . Upon such a foundation, honestly laid, can
be erected a structure which may lack something of mathematical exactness but
which promises to be both sound and socially desirable.

The troubles of the noncancellable line were not over. When the social security
system began to pay substantial disability benefits, the problem of overinsurance with
its ill effects on both the rate of claim and the tendency towards delayed recoveries
became serious. There were recurring periods of adverse experience as companies became careless or complacent in risk selection and claim administration. When the
guaranteed renewable type was introduced in the 1950s, noncancellable contracts were
regarded at first as inferior in profitability; opinions changed, however, when experience showed that companies wishing to raise premium scales on guaranteed renewable contracts faced what was considered unreasonable opposition from insurance
departments and consumer advocates.

An important influence for the good of the business was John H. Miller's *Disability
Newsletter* (DN) first published in 1974. For historical information, DN34 (August
1982) is particularly recommended; that article, "Evolution of Noncancellable," contains tributes to the work of two actuaries mentioned in this chapter: Jarvis Farley and
Edward E. Rhodes.

Chapter IX.

HOW ACTUARIES CALCULATED

Ther nys no werkman, whatsoevere he be,
That may werke wel and hastily

—Chaucer

BEFORE THE MECHANICAL CALCULATOR ERA

In one sense, actuarial history in North America had no pre-mechanical calculator era. Calculating machines had been built in Europe as early as the seventeenth century. But not until the late 1800s were calculators manufactured in quantity.

Even after desk calculators were in common use, many actuaries, disliking their noise, continued to depend upon logarithmic tables. And at least two other devices were used in actuarial departments: Tables of Quarter Squares and Multiplication Books.

Tables of Quarter Squares made use of the relationship:

$$ab = \frac{1}{4}(a+b)^2 - \frac{1}{4}(a-b)^2$$

to convert the process of multiplication into subtraction. One such table accommodates, in only fourteen 5″ by 7 1/2″ pages, multiplications of figures whose sums $(a+b)$ do not exceed 5,100; for example, in these tables $3,174 \times 1,889$ equals $6,408,492 - 412,806$, i.e., $5,995,686$. British scientist and sometime actuary, James J. Sylvester, FIA (1814–1897), who was for several years mathematics professor at Johns Hopkins University, described this approach in his 1854 paper, "On Multiplication by Aid of a Table of Single Entry" (*JIA* 4, 236).

Multiplication Books were used by actuaries well into the twentieth century—witness, for example, H. C. Plummer's 1912 paper, "On Aids to Calculation," (*JIA* 46, 193).

American actuary Levi W. Meech made a notable—although probably commercially unrewarding—entry into multiplying book design in 1894. Pictured in this chapter is Meech's 1,014-page *New Calculation Tables for Multiplication and Division*. This is by courtesy of Robert H. Taylor, FCA, this book having been in his consulting office through three generations of consulting actuaries—grandfather, father and son.

In the book's Introduction, Meech explained that he had consulted Charles Babbage and actuary Augustus De Morgan in London (certainly before 1871, the year that both those authorities died). Meech remarked:

Although reluctant to criticise calculating-machines, [De Morgan's] mature preference was decidedly in favor of calculation Tables with ledgered projecting slips. "Such an arrangement," said he, "is a book-machine where you can place your finger at once on the page and line you want." ... [A]fter the trial of many new devices and methods in the probable direction suggested by Professor De Morgan, the present book processes have been discovered.

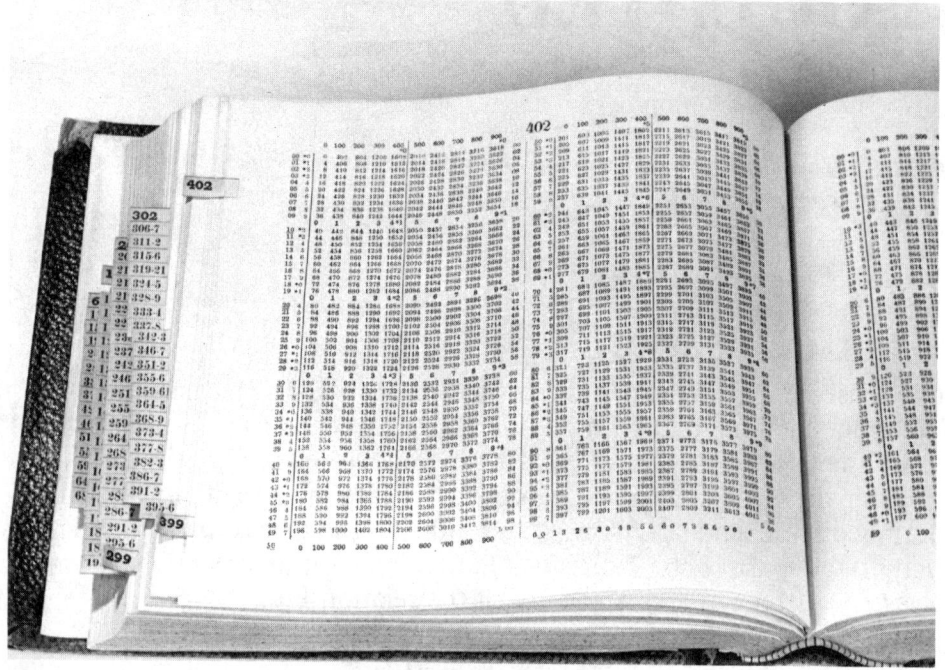

Sample page from Levi W. Meech's 1894 multiplying book.

Any notion that a multiplying book's usefulness is limited to dealing with operations on pairs of three- or four-digit numbers disappears when the following examples, among many given by Meech, are examined:

- Multiplying 37,524 by 73. Book gives answer 2,739,252.

- Multiplying 47.7121 by 7.854. Book gives answer 374.7308334.

- Multiplying 1,370,532 by 402. Book gives answer 550,953,864.

- Another example, the product of 5,489,137 and 415,817, gives the answer 2,282,476,479,929, but addition of two numbers on paper is necessary.

- Dividing 87,942,583 by 143. Book gives answer 614,983 with a remainder of 14.

- Dividing 408,759,219,805,310 by 507,461. With a modest amount of paper work, the quotient emerges as 805,498,786 with a remainder of 362,964.

To get full value from Meech's extraordinarily compact system, users had to wade through nine 10 1/2″ by 9″ pages of fairly demanding instructions.

BABBAGE, SCHEUTZ AND WRIGHT

Invention of mechanically functioning calculating machines more advanced than the abacus (described by William T. Thomson in *JIA* 4, 232) dates back at least to a calculator produced at the beginning of the seventeenth century by an assistant to the astronomer Johannes Kepler and one built by mathematician Blaise Pascal about 1642.

The life work of Charles Babbage (1792–1871) was the inspiration for subsequent calculation machine inventors even though his "Difference Engine" employing the system of finite differences never was completed. Demographer William Farr, in the introduction to his 1864 volume, *English Life Table No. 3,* said that the Babbage machine "had been so far completed as to show beyond a doubt the practicability of the conception."

Babbage's machine, Farr had said thirty years earlier, inspired Sweden's George Scheutz with such enthusiasm that he exclaimed, "I also will make a calculating machine." He and his son Edward succeeded after years of labor. Their invention, said to have had 4,320 parts, won the gold medal at the 1855 Paris Exhibition, and was brought to England where a committee of the Royal Society reported favorably on its powers. It was then purchased by a rich American named Rathbone who presented it to the Observatory in Albany, New York. A successor machine embodying several improvements was constructed in England with the help of the younger Scheutz, and performed the calculations for *English Life Table No. 3,* producing commutation tables as well as life table values.

The success of the Messrs. Scheutz encouraged a host of inventors, most of them in Europe, to construct calculating machines of increasing efficiency and declining bulk. Descriptions of several are in Cornelius Walford's *Insurance Cyclopaedia,* also in Volume 1, page 177 of the *Proceedings of the Centenary Assembly of the Institute of Actuaries* (1948).

Elizur Wright's famous Arithmeter (pronounced as in *arithmetic*) is a member of the slide rule family. Three detailed descriptions of it exist: one by its inventor himself, one by Emory McClintock printed in *The Insurance Times* of November 1872 "bearing witness to the extreme practical usefulness, in various cases of frequent occurrence, of the instrument in question," and one written in the 1930s by Gardner F. Knight, F.A.S., to accompany one of Wright's machines in an exhibit:

> [A]ddition or subtraction is mechanically performed on two concentric brass cylinders one meter in circumference and six inches high. By means of a crank, these cylinders are made to revolve about a common axis hung horizontally between brass uprights. The cylinders may be revolved in unison, or the one on the operator's left may be uncoupled and the one on the right revolved independently. A brass scale in which slides an indicator, adjustable for length, is held in position, against the cylinders, parallel to their axes.
>
> The cylinders are covered by parchment upon which a continuous spiral is drawn. This spiral is graduated at logarithmic intervals from 1000 to 9999. . . .
>
> [A]ll problems are first reduced to the form of a fraction multiplied by a factor. Thus, for multiplication, the numerator of the fraction would be taken as one

of the two original factors, and the denominator would be taken as 1. For division, the numerator would be the original dividend, the denominator the divisor, and the factor 1. Having these three elements given, the cylinders are coupled and turned until the graduation of the left cylinder, corresponding to the numerator, is opposite the brass scale. The left end of the indicator is then brought opposite this reading. Next, the cylinders are uncoupled and the right cylinder is revolved until the graduation corresponding to the denominator is opposite the scale, and the right end of the indicator is brought into coincidence with this reading, the left end being held in its former position. The cylinders are again coupled, and the second factor (which equals 1 in division) is set on the right cylinder against the scale, and the right end of the indicator, moved as a unit, is then brought into coincidence at that point. The left end of the indicator will then show, on the left cylinder, the desired product or quotient.

Walter C. Wright, Elizur's son, while New England Mutual's actuary in 1869, marketed his father's patented invention at a $600 offering price. Only fifteen or sixteen instruments were ever manufactured and sold; Walter Wright's explanation was that its English competitor, Tate's Arithmometer, was more efficient and less expensive.

Four arithmeters still exist: one at New England Mutual, one possessed by Christopher Wright, a descendent of the inventor, and the others in display cabinets at Northwestern Mutual and Society of Actuaries headquarters. This last one is marked "Instrument #14."

It (#14) had been purchased by Augustus F. Harvey, F.A.S., actuary of the Missouri Insurance Department. In 1914 his son, Julian C. Harvey, F.A.I.A., gave it to James M. Craig, then Actuarial Society president, who presented it to the Actuarial Society. From then until 1940, it was in the Society's successive offices in New York where few ever saw it and where the Society's one employee found it a burden. Metropolitan Life actuary, Horace R. Bassford, solved that problem by offering to house the artifact in the Craig Memorial Library at Metropolitan Life "until such time as the Society might provide a suitable place of its own." In 1987 it at last found its home in Society of Actuaries headquarters.

DESK CALCULATORS

The expression *desk* applied to a calculator denotes the type of instrument that might be assigned to actuarial department people for use as their needs dictated. The early ones were much too large to fit on a desk and must have been placed on a separate stand. Machines were manually operated by a crank until electric calculators gradually replaced them in the 1930s. In models requiring a turn of the crank for each unit in the multiplier, the operator learned to economize by using complements; for example, the multiplier 887 would require 23 $(8 + 8 + 7)$ turns if operated inefficiently, reducible to 6 turns if mentally recognized as $(1,000 - 113)$.

Most of the model names with which actuaries in North America were familiar are in the list of seventeen in Table IX.1, the date in parentheses showing when each came on the market. The letters NA (North America) and E (Europe) denote the continent of manufacture.

Table IX.1

DESK CALCULATORS USED BY NORTH AMERICAN ACTUARIES

NA	Allen (1927)	E	Mercedes-Euklid (1910)
E	Archimedes (1906)	E	Millionaire (1893)
NA	Baldwin (1875)	NA	Monroe (1911)
E	Brunsviga (1892)	E	Odhner (c. 1875)
NA	Ensign (1905)	E	Tate (1883)
?	Friden (?)	NA	Thacher (1881)
E	Madas (1914)	E	Thomas (1820)
NA	Marchant (1911)	E	TIM (1907)
?	Mathematon (?)		

The word *Arithmometer* does not appear in this list because, although originally identifying the Thomas machine, it became a generic term applied to products of later manufacturers.

A few actuaries used slide rules in the office. It is known that a spiral form of slide rule, much more accurate than the standard type, had adherents, mainly in England. Even the abacus was not unknown in actuarial departments, although the only recorded account found is of one used expertly by an Oriental employee.

The Actuarial Society's book for students, *Problems and Solutions, 1915–1919* gave its readers an abbreviated multiplication procedure by which one worked from the left sides of the multiplier and multiplicand. Students were advised to master it so as to save precious time in the examination room; mercifully, however, arithmetic was removed from the syllabus a few years later.

As late as 1932 (*T.A.S.A.* 33, 267), it was considered worthwhile to announce in the "Book Notices" column a text entitled *Checking Calculations*: "A description of

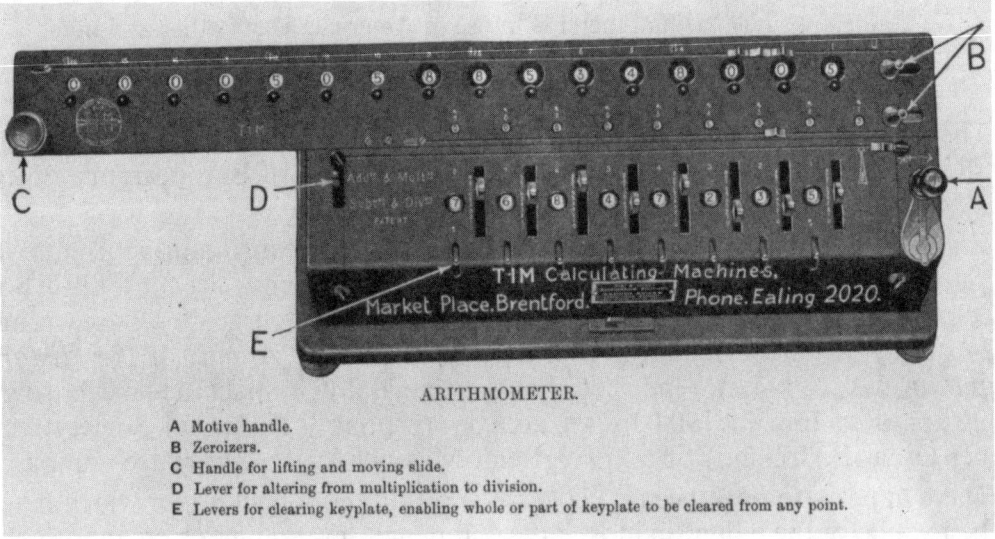

ARITHMOMETER.

A Motive handle.
B Zeroizers.
C Handle for lifting and moving slide.
D Lever for altering from multiplication to division.
E Levers for clearing keyplate, enabling whole or part of keyplate to be cleared from any point.

Arithmometer displayed in E.F. Spurgeon's *Life Contingencies* (1922) and in other British texts.

several check systems or devices, including the well-known 'Casting out nines,' for checking rapidly the accuracy of calculations."

Actuarial Society President John M. Laird reminisced in 1941 about stories he had heard about pre-calculator days (*T.A.S.A.* 42, 3):

> The older actuaries liked to recall the drudgery of their early days when there were no calculating machines. One brilliant mathematician spent his first year adding "in his head" page after page of deferred premiums. But the work was not monotonous. About every sixth item was a premium "paid in advance" and it had to be *subtracted* as his eye ran up the long column.

Several papers and discussions in the *Transactions* and the old *Record* testify to actuaries' ingenuity in problem-solving and arithmetical shortcuts. One such was Elgin G. Fassel's 1925 paper, "Cube Root by Abridged Division and by Machine" (*R.A.I.A.* 14, 35).

Among numerous descriptions of desk calculators in actuarial journals, the earliest in the *Transactions* was an 1891 paper by Max H. Peiler, "Tate's Arithmometer: An Improved Quotient Register" (*T.A.S.A.* 2, 35). This paper contains a picture of that famous machine which Peiler suggested be improved in design. In George King's Institute of Actuaries life contingencies textbook of 1887, an arithmometer was displayed; E. F. Spurgeon's successor volume showed a TIM machine, but retained verbatim the description in the old text. Spurgeon in 1922 commented (p. 358):

> The most powerful aid to calculation in the construction of actuarial tables is the Arithmometer, which is now so universally employed by actuaries that it is thought no student should experience any difficulty in seeing one in practical use before reading this chapter; a step he is strongly advised to take.

The North American reviewer of Spurgeon's book (*T.A.S.A.* 24, 248) objected strongly to this, remarking:

> We doubt if a single arithmometer is in use in America. Many other and much more powerful machines are in use and we are astonished to find that these are apparently unknown in Great Britain.

The later editions of Spurgeon in 1929 and 1932 reprinted his original statement even though many of the "more powerful machines" were of European manufacture, certainly extant in British actuarial departments.

Frank S. Baldwin of St. Louis, the earliest American manufacturer of desk calculators, credited his entry into this field to having seen a French-built Thomas (de Colmar) arithmometer in a St. Louis life company. George C. Chase, writer of a 1924 survey of desk calculators reprinted (1980) in the *Annals of the History of Computing,* Vol. 2, No. 3, remarked that the first Baldwin machine he ever saw was demonstrated to him in 1904 by an actuary (probably Actuarial Society charter member Oscar B. Ireland) of a Springfield, Massachusetts, insurance company.

There appears to have been no consensus on this continent about which machine gave best value for the dollar; in most large companies several types were in use concurrently. Testimony by actuaries now retired suggests that the Millionaire was both the sturdiest and noisiest. One of its suppliers proudly advertised that it would multiply 18,769,423 by 23,769,814 in six to seven seconds.

HOLLERITH AND GORE

The charter members of the Actuarial Society were quick to recognize the potential of the punched card system that had been invented by Herman Hollerith (1860–1929). Hollerith, while working on 1880 United States census data, realized how helpful a mechanical sorting operation would be, and picked up the idea of using punched cards from their use by Joseph Marie Jacquard (1752–1834) in his mechanized loom. Hollerith's original machine was ready in plenty of time to receive data of the 1890 census. The minutes of the Actuarial Society's Council meeting of April 15, 1890, show this item:

> The President was requested to accept the invitation of Mr. Hollerith to inspect his electric machine on Friday [i.e., April 18, 1890] afternoon.

The first-day minutes of the Society meeting of April 24–25, 1890, in New York (*T.A.S.A.* 6, 134) say:

> The President read an invitation from Mr. Herman Hollereth [*sic*] to examine his "electric tabulating machine." On motion, it was voted to accept the invitation for April 25th, at 2 P.M.

Thus it happened that thirty-five Society members became witnesses of tabulating equipment on the afternoon of the first anniversary of the Society's existence. A report of that meeting printed in the *New York Tribune* told its readers that "prospective uses of tabulating equipment were discussed."

The earliest references in the *Transactions* to uses of the Hollerith system are in 1909 papers—by Arthur Hunter (*T.A.S.A.* 11, 252) and Henry N. Kaufman (ibid., p. 276). Geoffrey D. Austrian in his 1982 biography, *Herman Hollerith: Forgotten Giant of Information Processing,* names several life companies—Mutual Benefit, New York Life, Phoenix Mutual, Prudential and Travelers—whose actuaries paid close attention to the system's possibilities. Capabilities of tabulating equipment steadily increased: first, becoming able to perform subtractions which until the 1920s had to be accomplished by adding the complement of the figure to be subtracted; then replacing the original 45-column card by one with 80 columns; eventually performing multiplications which until then had required a digiting approach described in 1934 by Wendell Milliman (*T.A.S.A.* 35, 253). Walter G. Bowerman, discussing Milliman's paper (*T.A.S.A.* 36, 77), compared the merits of IBM's automatic multiplying punch with those of digiting.

An early competitor of Hollerith equipment was the Pierce system described by Percy C. H. Papps in 1914 (*T.A.S.A.* 15, 49). James D. Craig's discussion (*T.A.S.A.* 15, 409) supported Papps' view that the Pierce system had significant advantage over the Hollerith system; Metropolitan Life hired Pierce shortly after World War I and never seems to have regretted its adherence to his devices. A later entry in the field, Powers equipment manufactured by Remington Rand, was preferred by some actuaries to the Hollerith equipment, which by then had become the IBM, system.

The first use of Hollerith cards in an Actuarial Society study was in 1909—the Medico-Actuarial Mortality Investigation (*T.A.S.A.* 11, 252 and 539). John K. Gore (1864–1943), an extraordinary innovator as well as an eminent actuary, invented his own equipment, which is reported to have worked splendidly for his company, the Prudential, for many years. A detailed description of the Gore system along with pictures of its card-punching and sorting equipment is in a 1902 paper to the Institute of Actuaries (*JIA* 37, 1) by David Parks Fackler.

The earliest Casualty Actuarial Society paper majoring on punched cards was presented by Thomas F. Tarbell in 1925 (*PCAS* 12, 215).

The following description by Prudential's Blair E. Olmstead appeared in a 1978 company memorandum:

> In 1895 Prudential installed punched card machines invented by Mr. Gore and constructed by his brother-in-law. These machines continued to be used in connection with the valuation of industrial policies into the 1930's. The basic Gore machine was a sorter which operated at an average rate of about 15,000 cards per hour. ... After sorting, the cards were counted using an International Postal machine which operated at the rate of 850 cards per minute.

It was not until 1932, said Olmstead, that Prudential went to outside manufacturers, and then only because the Gore machines were wearing out. Gore cards continued in use until the end of 1937, more than forty years after they had been introduced. Gore patented his apparatus in April 1894; the patent office documents and diagrams still exist; copies are in the Society of Actuaries archives.

Among tributes to Gore's ingenuity is the following in a 1937 letter in Prudential's files:

> For instance, his clerical staff was instructed how to riffle a convenient lift of cards evenly and count them by listening as they were snapped under the thumb. ... And [he taught his staff to use] the so-called Nicholson method. Nicholson [had observed that] there were only 165 possible combinations of three significant figures [zeroes excluded], and taught students to regard these combinations very much as a combination of letters is subconsciously regarded as a word. For example, "cat" is interpreted as a word and not a mere succession of letters: [similarly, Nicholson-system users would interpret the figures] 7,8,9 as 24 without any thought whatever of its component parts. ... [C]lerks attained a dexterity and facility in handling cards and making simple calculations that would seem in this day almost unbelievable.

Gore's obituary contains the following (*T.A.S.A.* 44, 449):

> His sense of humor, coupled with his ability to maintain a perfectly sober countenance, was unexpectedly delightful and elusive. The combination of his humor and his mathematical sense of form and structure enabled him to attain to considerable skill in the construction of humorous verse. His parody on "Danny Deaver" is a classic to most of the older members of the Society.

Sadly neither those older members nor Gore's Prudential colleagues seem to have placed that parody on the record for posterity.

John K. Gore's sorting equipment illustrated in 1902 in the *Journal of the Institute of Actuaries.*

Meanwhile, Arthur Hunter at New York Life was discovering the value of women clerks in preparing data for tabulating machines. In his 1907 "Note on an Approximate Method of Making Mortality Investigations" (*T.A.S.A.* 10, 361), he said:

The problem which presented itself was,—

1st, to determine methods of procedure which could be carried on by a force of women clerks, and did not require the services of a staff of embryo actuaries or actuarial assistants; and

2nd, to establish a division for mortality investigations in which the work would be largely automatic, and which would require the minimum of expert supervision.

In order to carry out both these ideas it was necessary to make the rules as simple as possible. . . . [T]he results have shown that women become very proficient in their work, turning out a large supply of it, and that supervision is largely confined to seeing that each clerk has a proper share of work, that no hitches arise, and that the accuracy and output of each clerk are properly determined.

Another tribute to the quality of women's work, this one in 1914 at Mutual Benefit Life, appears in *T.A.S.A.* 15, 414.

PHILLIPS, BERKELEY AND FINELLI

On January 27, 1936, E. William Phillips, FIA (1892–1968), General Manager for Great Britain of Manufacturers Life, presented to the Institute of Actuaries a paper entitled "Binary Calculation" (*JIA* 67, 187). He even displayed the essential parts of a binary calculator of his own design; it was a light-ray machine operating through an inserted array of punched holes, the digit 1 represented by a hole and the digit 0 by absence of a hole. That device was eventually lodged in the Science Museum in South Kensington, London, where it remains as a record of a worthy step toward the electronic computer.

An article, portrayed here, in the April 10, 1936 issue of *The Eastern Underwriter* in New York brought the news to actuaries in North America:

It is doubtful if any paper delivered before an actuarial body has attracted more attention in years than [Phillips'] address. . . . He explained the rudiments of a newly invented machine, the selenium photo-electric cell, which will be capable of doing an enormous amount of calculations in an almost incredibly short time. For many centuries the denary scale of notation [s.n.] has been used. . . .

Mr. Phillips would replace the figuring by ten by the figuring of eight. . . . There is really no great evolutionary discovery in this as the octonal method was used when arithmetic first came into existence. . . . In the British Museum is the Rhind papyrus [which used the octonal s.n. system], . . . a gathering together of problems in both geometry and arithmetic. . . .

The rest of that lengthy *Eastern Underwriter* article used text already published in *The Policy,* a London periodical; we revert here to Phillips' paper (op. cit.):

[This paper's] ultimate aim is to persuade the whole civilized world to abandon decimal numeration and to use octonal numeration in its place. . . . However, it seems unlikely that the whole civilized world will be persuaded to complete this change during the next twelve months, having previously declined similar invitations. Therefore the more immediate aim is the adoption of octonal numeration for scientific and business purposes, . . . the few final results for presentation to the layman being transformed into the denary scale of notation . . . by means of conversion tables, or otherwise. . . . [This] author [has been] looking . . . for the missing link [between s.n.10 and s.n.2] and he now submits that it has been discovered in s.n.8. As soon as it is thought of it becomes obvious, and it would

April 10, 1936  Page 3

E. W. Phillips' New Calculating Machine

Invention of British Actuary Attracts Attention Internationally; Based on Principles Many Centuries Old

It is doubtful if any paper delivered before an actuarial body has attracted more attention in years than the address before the Institute of Actuaries, London, by E. William Phillips, general manager of the Manufacturers Life in Great Britain, and which was already briefly discussed in the news columns of The Eastern Underwriter. He explained the rudiments of a newly invented machine, the selenium photo-electric cell which will be capable of doing an enormous amount of calculations in an almost incredibly short time. For many centuries the denary scale of notation (n.s.) has been used by mathematicians. "Denary" means containing the figure 10. That system owes its origin to the fact that there are ten digits on our two hands and people began to figure with their fingers in fives and tens. Before that, by the way, there was considerable quinary figuring—by fives.

Mr. Phillips would replace the figuring by ten by the figuring of eight; in other words, have an octonal numeration replace the denary numeration. There is really no great evolutionary discovery in this as the octonal method was used when arithmetic first came into existence, which was 5,000 years ago. In the British Museum is the Rhind papyrus, author of which was Ahmes, and it was antedated by other works of scribes. The Rhind papyrus is a gathering together of problems in both geometry and arithmetic with the answers given.

In his address before the actuaries Mr. Phillips discussed various notation scales of former centuries, including the ancient method of repeated doubling as developed by the Egyptians before 1650 B. C.

A simplified description of the new method of calculation—simple enough for actuaries, but the ordinary layman will have difficulty in grasping it, was published in London by The Policy. It follows:

We should explain that the whole purpose of the new suggestions is to lead up to mechanical calculation, Mr. Phillips appearing in the dual role of mathematician and mechanic. Obviously, in this machine age any new method of calculation is only of practical value if it leads to a mechanical process, and the fact that Mr. Phillips has designed a machine of which a large part has already been constructed is interesting from a practical point of view.

We are all so familiar with the customary methods of calculation that we perhaps do not realize just exactly what is the underlying process. It will, however, be readily agreed that a sensible man, confronted with a calculation, will carry it out in whatever form leads to the greatest convenience. For example, if we are dealing with pounds, shillings and pence, it may be convenient to convert our figures into pounds and decimals of a pound, and indeed, this is precisely what is done in every insurance office at the present time when multiplication is involved. The existing type of calculating machine requires it, but if we keep an open mind on the problem we shall realize firstly that it would be possible instead to reduce everything to pence, and secondly that it would be foolish to be hidebound to the decimal system if in a particular case a reduction to pence simplified calculation.

Counting in Eights

Our usual method of counting is by tens, but we count pence by the dozen and shillings by the score; and pounds in groups of fourteen (one stone). There is therefore nothing fundamentally heterodox in Mr. Phillips' first suggestion, which is to convert figures into a form where the counting is done in eights; not a very frightening idea when we remember that we have already 8 drams in a fluid ounce, 8 gills in a quart, 8 pints in a gallon, 8 gallons in a bushel, 8 stone in a hundredweight, and 8 furlongs in a mile. However, eight is only a stepping-stone leading to a system of calculation which can be best realized by considering a few figures. They are set out below for convenience but the reader can calculate them for himself, the process being to start with 1, to double it, then

to double the answer, then to double that and so on.

1	32	1024
2	64	2048
4	128	4096
8	256	8192
16	512	16384

Now, suppose we had a set of weights corresponding to the figures above in ounces, only one of each, only fifteen in all. We should find that we could weigh any number of ounces from 1 to 32,767 by using one or more of these fifteen weight. This point is interesting, and is in fact a well-known and well-used principle in making sets of weights. The following schedule shows, for example, which weights would be used to weigh any number of ounces from three to seven (one, two, and eight being obvious) and again from twenty to twenty-seven; the weights used being indicated

by the figure 1, the 0 indicating the weights not used.

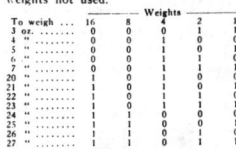

To weigh ...	16	8	4	2	1
3 oz.	0	0	0	1	1
4 "	0	0	1	0	0
5 "	0	0	1	0	1
6 "	0	0	1	1	0
7 "	0	0	1	1	1
20 "	1	0	1	0	0
21 "	1	0	1	0	1
22 "	1	0	1	1	0
23 "	1	0	1	1	1
24 "	1	1	0	0	0
25 "	1	1	0	0	1
26 "	1	1	0	1	0
27 "	1	1	0	1	1

By using 0 to show that a particular weight is not to be used we can dispense with the column headings, and indeed with the column themselves. For example, if we say we can weigh 27 ounces with the weights 11,011, our meaning will be obvious at once.

Powers of Two

Our weights are the powers of 2 that is to say, each and every one consists merely of a number of 2's multiplied together. What we have in fact discovered is that any number can be represented as the addition of powers of 2, never using more than one of any power. Ordinarily we represent numbers by powers of ten, using from 1 to 9 of each power. For example 234 means, as every schoolboy knows, 2 multiplied by ten tens, plus 3 multiplied by ten, plus 4. Suppose we had to weigh 234 ounces, the 256 ounces weight too big, the largest weight we can use being the 128; this leaves 106 ounces, so that we can use the 64, the 32 (but not the 16 because we have now only 10 ounces left), the 8 and the 2. Precisely as we write two hundred and thirty-four in the abbreviated form 234 we can indicate the weights to be used as 11,101,010. Starting from the right-hand side 0 indicates that we shall not use the 1 ounce weight,

E. WILLIAM PHILLIPS

the 1 that we shall use the 2 ounce weight, and the next 0 that we shall not use the 4 ounce weight; then the next three figures indicate that we shall use the 8 and the 32, but not the intervening 16, and the two digits on the extreme left indicate that we shall use both the 64 and the 128. Any quantity can be expressed simply by using ones and noughts. In short, just as we can turn shillings and pounds into pence, or pounds and hundredweights into ounces, so we can turn any figures into a form where we count only in pairs, and pairs of pairs, and pairs of pairs of pairs, and so on, a form where we have only two figures to deal with, namely 1 and 0. When once it is grasped that any two numbers whatever can be expressed by means of nothing else but ones and noughts, it will be realized that the process of multiplying them together in this form is a very simple one, multiplications tables being in effect abolished, since all we have to know is that $1 \times 1 = 1$.

Danger of Error Removed

We understand that Mr. Phillips has been considering for some years the ease and simplicity of calculating secured by expressing numbers by the "0 and 1" method, but was for long deterred by the exasperation and the danger of error which would result from having page after page filled with nothing by 0's and 1's. This difficulty he has now removed by making use of the simple fact that $8 = 2 \times 2 \times 2$. Figures tabulated in a system of counting by 8's instead of by 10's can be converted on sight into the "0 and 1" form by remembering only that the first seven digits are represented in that form as follows:

1...............001	5...............101
2...............010	6...............110
3...............011	7...............111
4...............100	

Simple substitution is all that is required. For example, 111 $4 + 2 + 1 = 7$. Take the case of 234 ounces al-

(Continued on Page 6)

It is the carriage of the machine which does the calculating. It is here shown at the commencement of its passage across the pins which are set up by the punched roll of paper entering the machine.

North American actuaries get foretaste of computer possibilities from *The Eastern Underwriter*, April 1936. (Courtesy of James Mann, Archivist, Metropolitan Life Insurance Co., New York, N.Y.)

be difficult to understand why it was not previously found, but that one did not know what one was looking for. S.n.8 converts into s.n.2, and the latter reconverts into s.n.8, on sight. Any clerk can master the conversion in two minutes, for he has only to commit [a short conversion table given in the text] to memory. . . .

So it is definitely part of the present submission . . . that records and factors should be kept year after year in s.n.8, every calculation except such simple ones as the mere addition of two numbers being performed in s.n.2, the conversion from 8 to 2 and back to 8 being as easy as the conversion from type to script when we copy with pen and ink from a printed book.

As reported in an article, "Ahead of His Time" (*The Actuary,* November 1980), the Sunday *Times* (of London) printed a letter in September 1965 from Phillips describing his mental processes through the years from 1913 to 1934. He wrote of 1934 that "Babbage's 1834 sleeping beauty had awakened—after the proverbial hundred years."

Although naturally not counting upon a machine being built to handle the entire conversion from s.n.10 to s.n.2 and back again, Phillips had a prophetic vision of the computer age. Few in Staple Inn Hall that evening grasped that they were being introduced to a new world of calculating efficiency and speed; one said years later that the occasion was widely regarded as a pleasurable relief from the Institute's usual deep and serious meetings. A visiting scientist in the audience felt that one problem with a Phillips machine would be to find enough work to keep it occupied; he was not the only speaker who may later have wished that his words had not been recorded. Institute President C. R. V. Coutts considered it necessary to encourage Phillips to pursue his idea "despite any cold water thrown upon it this evening."

Phillips did pursue his idea, even though severely handicapped by governmental imposition of secrecy as the value of computers in waging war became recognized. Phillips, in 1961, in *The Journal of the Institute of Actuaries Students' Society* (Vol. 16, 322), suggested that the scientist's objection that such a machine would quickly run out of work had discouraged the British Department of Scientific and Industrial Research, "and so was a major contribution to that delay which allowed our American cousins to get ten years ahead of [the British] in computer development." Phillips added:

Now we know that the commutation column, the formulae of approximate integration . . . and approximate valuation methods . . . are as dead as the dodo. . . .

Phillips' unpublished 1963 paper, now lodged in the SOA archives, entitled "A Note on the History of the Electronic Computer" reveals first, that his interest in scales of notation began during World War I when he used more than one such scale in assisting to develop anti-aircraft gunnery; second, that in 1935 his project had been offered as a gift to the British government, and that his paper's presentation had been delayed pending application for provisional patents; and, third, that he and John R. Womersley, a mathematician, having become acquainted by chance (although their offices were opposite one another in Baker Street, London) had pursued their work in tandem during 1943–1945, at which time Phillips, "satisfied that the work would proceed without any further prodding by him, and not being without other avocations, was glad to drop out.

With Womersley as the first Superintendent of the Mathematics Division of the National Physical Laboratory, ... the actual construction of ACE [Automatic Computing Engine, a pioneer British computer] commenced as soon as the war was over."

That memorandum also records that:

> Womersley went to America [in early 1945] for three months and learned, what was then a secret, that the relay type of machine based on telephone equipment was already a fact (Harvard Mark I) and he saw ENIAC which was then about half built. As both these were designed to work in s.n.10 he reminded his hosts of Phillips's 1936 advocacy of s.n.2.

ENIAC (Electronic Numerical Integrator and Calculator), the world's first electronic computer, all thirty tons of it, was dedicated at the University of Pennsylvania in February 1946.

The Council minutes of February 28, 1947, show how the Actuarial Society's first interest in computers happened:

> The President [Edward W. Marshall] referred to correspondence and conversations which he and the Secretary [Walter Klem] had had with Mr. E. C. Berkeley of the Prudential Insurance Company regarding projects for the development and construction of sequence controlled calculators for use in life insurance company problems. Following discussion, the Council authorized the President to appoint a special committee to explore the possibilities for Society participation in such projects.

Berkeley had served in the U.S. Navy during World War II. In 1945 and 1946 he was assigned to the Computer Laboratory at Harvard to assist Commander Howard H. Aiken who participated with IBM in developing the Automatic Sequence Controlled Calculator called "Mark I." After returning to Prudential, Berkeley went far beyond just notifying Actuarial Society Council of the significance to actuaries of what he saw happening; he wrote a paper, "Electronic Machinery for Handling Information and Its Uses in Insurance" (*T.A.S.A.* 48, 36), which he presented at the Society meeting on May 8, 1947, only about a year after ENIAC had become operative. That paper concluded thus (p. 52):

> We are at the threshold of a new development that will reduce materially the present clerical work going on in life insurance companies. It will tend to change some actuaries into engineers dealing with information machinery. It will transform the numerical work for many actuarial calculations, and enable all actuaries to do many things they now only dream of doing.
>
> In fact, the new machinery will put the English actuary Charles Babbage's analytical engine into the hands of actuaries—a hundred years late, but with the wings of electrons.

The three discussions of Berkeley's paper on October 1, 1947 (*T.A.S.A.* 48, 278) by William P. Barber, Edward H. Wells and Edward A. Rieder are of great interest in the light of what has since happened, perhaps especially Rieder's forecast of the flexible policy form structures that computers would some day permit.

In 1949, Berkeley published a popular book, *Giant Brains or Machines that Think*. In its Chapter 11 he offered some forecasts of what such machines might accomplish for mankind; in *The Actuary,* November 1980, he gave his views on how those predictions had worked out, and he set forth some more prophesies for years then ahead. Blair Olmstead, in the 1978 essay already mentioned, remarked about him that "everyone who knew him has a favorite Berkeley story"!

By the time of the Society's Council meeting on May 7, 1947, the Committee on New Recording Means and Computing Devices (originally called the Committee on Society Participation in Development of Calculators) had been formed. That committee's lifetime was in two phases—first in the Actuarial Society and then in its successor, the Society of Actuaries.

The groundwork was laid by the first (Actuarial Society) committee, although the members heard little about it, their meetings in 1947 and 1948 being heavily taken up by plans and decisions about merger with the American Institute. The committee chairman, Malvin E. Davis, outlined to the Council on May 7, 1947 how the study of computers might be conducted. Council minutes of May 12, 1948 contain the following item:

> Mr. M. E. Davis, Chairman, submitted a written report . . . in which he . . . stated that the Society's Committee is in the process of developing a model office set-up . . . built around the latest developments of new equipment, with a view to aiding both insurance personnel and the scientists engaged in the development of such equipment in a better understanding of: (a) the usefulness of these developments to life insurance companies and (b) the specific problems that still must be solved to make such equipment practicable for use by life insurance companies.

The work of the second (Society of Actuaries) Committee on New Recording Means and Computing Devices under its successive chairmen Malvin E. Davis and John J. Finelli resulted in two special presentations and three formal reports, as follows.

At a committee presentation to the Society members on April 25, 1952 (digested in *TSA* 4, 170), Davis said that electronic computers had become sufficiently reliable and versatile to be used effectively in day-to-day insurance work but that to use computers effectively, far-reaching changes in methods and organizations appeared necessary.

This remark was a preamble to the presentation of a "Consolidated Functions Approach," explained by William P. Barber with the aid of a functional chart (p. 171). Finelli continued this explanation, displaying several more charts, sample cards and a computer diagram. Davis concluded by emphasizing that moderately sized companies ought to be able to take advantage of these new tools. This presentation became so famous in American business circles that it was repeated to the American Management Association and elsewhere.

The first committee report, "Adaptations of Electronic Machines to Life Insurance Operations," devoted to the consolidated functions approach, was presented at a special meeting in New York City on September 25, 1952 (*TSA* 4, 422) and was further discussed in June 1953 (*TSA* 5, 190).

The second committee report, "Current Status of Magnetic Tape as a Recording and Data Processing Medium," June 1955, was presented at a Society Forum on Electronic Machines (*TSA* 7, 312).

The third report (available in the Society's library), "Application of Electronic Data Processing Equipment to Office Operations," October 1957, received its presentation not just to the Society of Actuaries but to the actuarial world as centerpiece of the Fifteenth International Congress of Actuaries in New York that month, and was published by the Society in hardbound form.

John J. Finelli's credentials include an endorsement by Phillips himself ("Finelli and Electronic Procedures," *The Review* of London, March 4, 1960):

> John Finelli, of the United States of America, shares with Prof. Dr. Engelfriet of the Netherlands the distinction of belonging to that small band of people who have been constant and unshaken in believing in the potentialities of electronic computers, working in the binary scale of numeration, ever since January, 1936. . . . Finelli [since 1948] . . . has "lived" electronic computers, "breathed, eaten and drunk," and probably "slept," electronic computers. During the last six of those twelve years he has had the supervisory responsibility for the direction and co-ordination of the magnetic tape electronic equipment of the Metropolitan Life, . . . the first use of such equipment for commercial purposes anywhere in the world.

Phillips went on to thank Finelli for having given to the Institute of Actuaries in 1960 (*JIA* 86, 326) as well as to the British Computer Society ("Development of EDP Units," *The Computer Bulletin,* 4, No. 1, June 1960) "what could be purchased only at a cost of hundreds of thousands of pounds, the fruit of that experience which has, in fact, cost his great Company millions of dollars." The generosity of the early actuarial experts in sharing their knowledge with people in North America outside the profession is also worthy of note.

Finelli contributed further to computer literature by writing the story of Metropolitan Life's UNIVAC (Universal Automatic Computer) the first of those machines ever sold, for W. D. Bell's *A Management Guide to Electronic Computers,* (McGraw-Hill 1957). UNIVAC came into the public eye on election night 1952 through its use to give rapid analyses of the emerging presidential returns.

A 1986 book by Charles J. Bashe et al., *IBM's Early Computers,* gives the insurance industry credit for being early students and users with "cautious-but-determined attitudes."

The many discussions of computer work in Volumes 6–10 of the *Transactions* show clearly that widespread use was being made of the committee reports. One example (*TSA* 8, 1) was John M. Boermeester's "Frequency Distribution of Mortality Costs," employing random-number generation to help determine the desirable magnitude of contingency reserves.

Among Canadian actuaries, interest in speedy calculation equipment began when Toronto actuary Hudson J. Stowe received a copy of Phillips' 1936 Institute paper from its author. Prompt discussions were held with Canadian representatives of the leading tabulating machine company, but war intervened. Soon after World War II, the National Research Council bought a Feranti computer, which was housed at the University of Toronto; the University was persuaded to give lectures about its operation to representatives of Toronto Life companies. The machine was used to calculate annuity premiums, using a program written by John H. Bell. In 1947, Stowe, as president of the Insurance Accounting and

Metropolitan Life Insurance Company's UNIVAC I, 1954. (Courtesy of James Mann, Archivist, Metropolitan Life Insurance Co., New York, N.Y.)

Statistical Association, arranged to have Berkeley present to that body a paper on the use of computers for underwriting.

In *The Actuary,* January 1973, after introduction of transistors in 1956 and the computer chip in 1959 had led to vast changes from the monster ENIAC, L. Timothy Giles gave the comforting news that actuaries could now program "in commonly understood notation and plain English." He concluded, "If programming becomes as easy as driving an automobile, then tomorrow's actuary had better learn where the highways go." But in 1969 (*JIA* 95, 278), the eminent British philosopher-actuary Frank M. Redington (1906–1984) expressed a different thought: "I am fearful that the computer may have the same effect on our minds as the car is having on our bodies."

One drawback of the computer boom pointed out in 1955 by Karl M. Davies (*TSA* 7, 286) was the obstacle to actuarial recruiting arising from opportunities in data processing offered to young people with mathematical leanings.

Our profession did not lack for actuaries to advise against jumping too rashly into computer solutions to all problems. The late Gordon C. Streeter was one of these; it is reported that in his 1953 warning (*TSA* 5, 195), he remarked that Aetna Life was still getting policy reserve work done quite satisfactorily by four ladies using desk calculators.

At meetings in April, May and June 1969 (*TSA* 21, D109 and D445), the Society of Actuaries held its first full-scale discussions on the topic, "Computer Models and Simulation." This was followed in 1975 by the presentation, described in Chapter VI, of the first Society model of its own, called SOFASIM.

As the 1970s ended, the era of microcomputer technology, immensely significant in actuarial work, was dawning.

NOTATION

Necessities for actuarial calculation comprise not just the machines that expedite the actuary's work but also the notation, the mathematical symbols, by which life table values, premiums and benefits are identified and understood. The early history of this subject was explored, instructively and entertainingly, by Henry H. Jackson in his 1937 paper, "Notes on Actuarial Notation Before 1800" (*R.A.I.A.* 26, 6). The founding father of modern actuarial symbols familiar to recent generations of actuaries was a London actuary, David Jones, in his landmark 1843 volumes, *Value of Annuities and Reversionary Payments*. Jones' notation was given the informal name "halo notation" because the main identifying symbol was surrounded by a nimbus of modifiers.

In 1872, the Institute of Actuaries officially approved Jones' family of symbols in time for it to be used by George King in his 1887 life contingencies textbook. Translation of that text into other languages caused European actuaries to become familiar with the notation to the point of embracing it. Accordingly at the First International Congress (1895) unanimous passage of a resolution that King himself proposed was easily achieved (p. 442):

> That the Notation of the Institute of Actuaries shall be employed in preference by the actuaries of all countries.

Israel C. Pierson, speaking for the North American actuaries, expressed complete approval. The young Actuarial Society had already threshed over the notation matter beginning at its October 1890 meeting at which the following Council-sponsored resolution was adopted (*T.A.S.A.* 1, Pt. 4, 22):

> RESOLVED, that in the presentation of papers the Symbols of the Text-Book of the Institute of Actuaries, with the additions noted below, be followed when convenient, and that in any event the use of such symbols in other senses be avoided; that the letters denoting commutation columns, according to the system of Dr. Farr, customarily followed by American actuaries, be printed in plain "full-face" type; and that otherwise there be entire liberty as regards notation.

The "additions noted below" consisted in the main of the u_x and k_x factors previously chosen for Fackler's valuation functions, which apparently were not in general use in Great Britain.

For many years after that, Actuarial Society members were routinely reminded of this resolution in an introductory page to the *Transactions*. In 1912 a set of symbols for disability benefits became part of that reminder, but this was removed in 1932 when the second edition of *Actuarial Studies, No. 5, Disability Benefits* was published.

On the international scene it remained for consensus to be reached on sets of symbols for coverages other than life insurance and annuities, particularly for pension fund work—a step that was not taken for many years. In 1939, a comprehensive recommendation was circulated in preparation for the 1940 Lucerne Congress, but the outbreak of World War II left that in limbo.

At the Actuarial Society Council meeting of November 7, 1945, it was reported that the Society's own committee on notation headed by John S. Thompson was recommending adoption of the 1939 plan. It was decided to give the committee complete authority to act; the result was a lengthy description of the recommendation in 1947 (*T.A.S.A.* 48, 166).

The Casualty Actuarial Society was likewise concerned about consensus in notation. Two major papers were published by Francis S. Perryman in 1949 (*PCAS* 36, 123) and by Jeffrey T. Lange in 1968 (*PCAS* 55, 196).

Within a few years, the advent of the computer introduced a new complication described by John M. Boermeester (*The Actuary,* December 1972):

> The computers could not digest the normal notation and since the computers are all-powerful (pace 2001!), the notation should be changed to fit the computers.

The essence of the difficulty was that computers required that all symbols be in straight lines, completely ruling out the halo system. As Boermeester reported in that same article:

> At Oslo [the 1972 Congress] there was a stimulating and even exciting meeting on the subject of the proposed new notation. Suffice it to say that there was no unanimity for the adoption of the proposed new notation and the opposition was by no means confined to the members of the establishment.

Frank P. Di Paolo, who succeeded Boermeester as chairman of the Society of Actuaries Committee on Standard Notation and Nomenclature, reported fully (*The Actuary,* March 1976) on the large number of linear notation proposals that had been placed on record as the 1976 Tokyo Congress approached, and again (*The Actuary,* April 1977) on what happened at the Congress. These were described by Frank G. Reynolds in a series of articles in *The Actuary* between June 1982 and June 1983. Agreement still lay ahead in 1979, but by this time computer technology had reached the point at which linear notation was no longer an absolute requirement.

Chapter X.

THE PROFESSION IN WARTIME

Will no one tell me what she sings?—
Perhaps the plaintive numbers flow
For old, unhappy, far-off things,
And battles long ago.

—Wordsworth, "The Solitary Reaper"

INTRODUCTION

North American actuarial literature regrettably lacks descriptive papers on the wartime experiences of actuaries and the effects of wars' events upon the profession. At least the following aspects in addition to honor rolls need to be recorded:

1. Actions by governing bodies to help authorities employ actuaries to the best advantage for war efforts.

2. Uses made of actuarial talents in prosecuting the war, and resulting benefits to the profession.

3. Wartime changes and disruptions in the actuarial bodies themselves.

4. Illustrative anecdotes of individual wartime activities.

With respect to World War II, the Institute and Faculty of Actuaries have accomplished more than the North American bodies have in covering these subjects. In Volume III of the *Proceedings of the Centenary Assembly of the Institute of Actuaries* published in 1950, an entire section is devoted to "Actuaries and Problems of War"; two of its four papers were submitted by American actuaries: "Applications of Actuarial Techniques to Some Military Problems" (p. 298) by Edward A. Lew and Frank A. Weck, and "Actuaries in the Operations Research Group, U.S. Navy" (p. 329) by Gordon D. Shellard.

The Faculty of Actuaries took a direct approach. At one of their 1947 meetings (*TFA* 18, 190) eight members described their wartime activities that involved applications of actuarial knowledge and training.

In contrast, the sole direct reference to such activities in the *Transactions* consists of digested remarks by Gordon D. Shellard, Charles M. Sternhell and Nathan F. Jones in 1958 (*TSA* 9, 90).

349

RECORDS OF MEMBERS IN MILITARY SERVICE

The respective honor rolls of the Actuarial Society and American Institute, with duplications removed, show that in World War I (*T.A.S.A.* 19, 348, and *R.A.I.A.* 7, (Pt. 1), xv) 11 Fellows, 23 Associates and 17 Students were in service —a total of 51. The corresponding World War II total (1945 *Year Book,* p. 62) was 358—57 Fellows, 68 Associates and 233 Students.

Table X.1 on page 351 lists the names of the ten members and students whose lives were lost in the military service of three wars in combat or from war-related causes.

Five of these men are memorialized by obituary notices in the *Transactions*, and two of those five—John Victor McLean and James Miles Langstaff—are honored also among the eighty-two names on the 1914–1919 War Memorial pictured in Reginald C. Simmonds' *The Institute of Actuaries 1848–1948*, facing page 172. Simmonds tells us (p. 172):

> When Staple Inn Hall was destroyed [in 1944] . . . grave fear was felt that the Memorial had been shattered beyond repair. In the event, it was recovered unbroken and substantially undamaged . . . . Now [it] rests in the 'New Hall'.

The Actuarial Society committed unhappy errors in both World Wars by failure to print certain of these obituaries. In World War I the oversight involved Robertson Macaulay Cushing who was a nephew of Thomas B. Macaulay, the sixth president of the Actuarial Society.

Cushing qualified as an Associate in 1909 and had passed one of the two Fellowship parts before leaving his company, the Sun Life of Canada, in August 1915 to serve in France. The following is an excerpt from the account of his death furnished by a present-day Sun Life official and now placed in the Society of Actuaries archives:

> [Lieutenant] Robertson Macaulay Cushing died at 12:30 a.m. on 30 April 1918. . . . In a courageous attempt to rescue one of his men, Robertson received severe wounds from an exploding shell and perished within twenty minutes.

Three of the men lost to our profession in the World Wars: (Left) Robertson Macaulay Cushing (in World War I), Jerome R. Cross and Donald H. Robb (in World War II).

Table X.1

DEATHS FROM WAR AND WAR-RELATED CAUSES
AMONG MEMBERS AND STUDENTS OF THE
NORTH AMERICAN ACTUARIAL BODIES

Name	Age	Home City	Date of Death	Memorial Notice
In the Spanish-American War				
William Lamb Daughtrey (Associate)	25	Richmond, Virginia	April 30, 1901	*T.A.S.A.* 7, 72
In World War I				
John Victor McLean (Student)	29	Montreal, Quebec	July 17, 1916	*T.A.S.A.* 17, 385
William Campbell Macdonald (Fellow)	60	Toronto, Ontario	January 21, 1917	*T.A.S.A.* 18, 186
James Miles Langstaff (Fellow)	33	Toronto, Ontario	March 1, 1917	*T.A.S.A.* 18, 191
Robertson Macaulay Cushing (Associate)	33	Montreal, Quebec	April 30, 1918	None
In World War II				
Donald Hamilton Robb (Student)	25	Toronto, Ontario	March 31, 1941	See Below
Donald J. Wiltsie (Student)	25	Springfield, Mass.	1942	See Below
Jerome R. Cross (Student)	27	Cedar Falls, Iowa	January 24, 1944	See Below
Richard Edward Dietrich (Student)	25	Bloomington, Indiana	June 6, 1944	See Below
John Henry Vanular (Associate)	30	Quebec, Quebec	May 11, 1945	*T.A.S.A.* 46, 511

Donald Hamilton Robb, who had been at the London Life Insurance Company, was a Sub-Lieutenant in the Royal Canadian Navy. He was serving on the cruiser H. M. S. *Bonaventure* when it was torpedoed and all hands were lost in the Eastern Mediterranean during convoy duty south of Crete.

Donald J. Wiltsie, who had been at Connecticut Mutual Life, joined the United States Army Air Corps as a meteorologist and went to the Pacific Island area where he lost his life in a flying accident.

Jerome R. Cross became an actuarial student at Metropolitan Life Insurance Company in June 1939 and entered the armed forces in January 1942. He was a Lieutenant in the United States Army Air Corps when he was killed during a training flight near Farmington, Louisiana. The instructor's plane, which he was piloting, collided in midair with another plane.

Richard E. Dietrich, a graduate of Indiana University highly rated in mathematics, had been an actuarial student at Aetna Life Insurance Company. He enlisted in the United States Army in May 1942. As a Second Lieutenant in the airborne artillery on D-Day, he was a member of the glider operation that preceded the troop-landing that morning. He was killed in action at Ste.-Mere-Eglise, Normandy, when his heavily loaded glider crash-landed.

None of the particulars about these four men received notice in the *Transactions*.

In World War II, the names of four actuarial students who had died in military service were announced by the Actuarial Society president in October 1945 (*T.A.S.A.* 46, 229), but the further step of printing their obituaries in the *Transactions* never was taken. Enquiries made after a lapse of more than four decades at the companies where they had been employed—the London Life, Connecticut Mutual, Metropolitan and Aetna—and in the case of Richard Dietrich, a letter from his widow, have brought to light the information about those men that is set forth in Table X.1.

COMMENDING ACTUARIAL TALENTS TO WARTIME AUTHORITIES

Presumably the Councils of the Actuarial Society in both world wars could not take action to encourage the authorities to make effective use of the special talents of actuaries until both the United States and Canada were participants, in April 1917 and December 1941, respectively.

At the Actuarial Society meeting in May 1917, President Arthur Hunter, after asking the Canadians to bear with him as he treated his subject "from the American standpoint" said (*T.A.S.A.* 18, 1):

> Having decided, . . . that our duty calls upon us to do our part in this great world war, we are naturally trying to find out in what way we can best help. . . .
>
> The natural question arises: What can I do in my professional capacity to help the government or my community? I should counsel men not to rush into work for which they are not suited, but to wait until their services can be used to advantage. . . . With the training which actuaries receive there should be many ways in which their services may be used. . . .
>
> I am very glad to say that the Council has placed the services of the Society and of its individual members at the disposal of the United States government and of the authorities of the Dominion of Canada.

A resolution was then adopted supporting the Council decision that Hunter had just mentioned. Copies of the letters sent a few days later to the Secretary of State in Washington, D.C., and to the Minister of Militia & Defence in Ottawa are printed in *T.A.S.A.* 18, 195. No responses appear in Council or Society minutes.

At the corresponding time during World War II (March 1942), the presidents of the Actuarial Society and American Institute asked W. Rulon Williamson, FAS, then chief actuary of the Social Security Administration, to explain the potential uses of actuaries to the federal authorities. Williamson's first approach was to the War Production Board; he learned that there were four offices likely to need information about persons with specialized training—the Roster of Scientific Personnel as well as two groups in the Army and one in the Navy. By September 1942, a letter from the National Defense Research Committee was relayed by the Society president to United States members and students. A second informative letter was circulated to them in June 1943 conveying information that Williamson had obtained.

Shellard's Centenary Assembly paper described the content of the September 1942 letter (op. cit., p. 329):

This letter, which quoted a letter from Dr. Philip M. Morse of the Massachusetts Institute of Technology and the National Defence Research Committee, read in part as follows: 'Recently the opportunity has arisen for the use of men with actuarial training in important and urgent War Research Projects. ... The work consists of the statistical analysis of various kinds of military data, and the drawing of conclusions upon which actions can be based. It may involve, from time to time, long hours of concentrated effort. For these reasons it is probable that men of ages between 25 and 35, without heavy family responsibilities, would be preferable. ... In addition to the requisite training in statistics, a certain amount of experience in the practical applications of statistics is valuable, and additional training or experience in physics or electronics is particularly desirable.'

Whether or not this circular letter specified that volunteers would retain civilian status is not known, but a November 1945 Navy Department letter of commendation to at least one actuary made the point:

This work has been performed by you in a civilian status, because it has been the opinion of the Navy that it could be most effectively carried out in this manner.

Special arrangements such as these created embarrassment about printing honor rolls that recognized military service but not civilian contributions to the war effort. In World War I the Actuarial Society tried to solve this problem by printing a list of members engaged in "Public and Patriotic Work" in a civilian capacity; this proved highly unsatisfactory because of failure to gather full information and to define *public and patriotic* satisfactorily.

No record relating to World War II has been found of any advisory information sent to Canadian actuaries and students. Several Canadians did find their way into wartime activities in military or civilian capacities comparable to those recorded in this chapter for the United States.

USES MADE OF ACTUARIAL SKILLS IN TWO WORLD WARS

In World War I, the most spectacular recorded case of an actuary's participation as a civilian in the war effort was that of William Macfarlane, FAS 1913 (1888–1974), set forth in *Looking Back: A Memoir of New York Life* by Charles W. V. Meares (1985). Macfarlane had enlisted in the United States Army in 1917 as a sergeant and managed to make innovations in the Office of the Surgeon General; for example, he introduced a punched card system for classifying physicians and surgeons throughout the country. While on a 24-hour pass he dropped in to visit Arthur Hunter, his peacetime boss, just when Hunter was conferring with some army generals on means for establishing what later became the National Service Life Insurance Program. On Hunter's recommendation his visitors engaged Macfarlane to develop and administer that embryo system. The snag was that Macfarlane, having come from Scotland in 1910 and still a British subject, was ineligible to be raised to officer rank; this was overcome by giving him an honorable discharge and employing him as a "dollar-a-year" civilian on loan from New York Life.

Meares relates that, since Congress was not then in session and had not appropriated funds for the approved program, Macfarlane persuaded the Army Paymaster

William Macfarlane, FSA, organizer of the United States Bureau of War Risk Insurance. (From *Looking Back: A Memoir of New York Life* by Charles W.V. Meares, 1985.)

General to issue to him personally a $5 million check as a loan for organizational expenses. From that extraordinary start, he built the Bureau of War Risk Insurance into an enterprise with 16,000 employees under his direction.

Turning to World War II, and the project made known to actuaries and students in the National Defense Research Committee's circular letter of September 1942, the following eighteen men (out of a total staff of about eighty scientists) participated:

John M. Boermeester	Howard H. Hennington	Abraham C. Olshen
Arthur W. Brown	Lambert A. Holloway	Robert R. Seeber
Donald D. Cody	Fred A. Holsten	Gordon D. Shellard
Walter L. DeVries	Nathan F. Jones	Charles M. Sternhell
Jarvis Farley	Richard J. Jones	Carl E. Thompson
Earl B. Gardner	John B. Lathrop	Ralph E. Traber

Their contribution to the war effort followed a path which had first been developed in Britain when the war was foreseen but had not yet broken out. John Plymen explained how this happened (*Centenary Assembly Proceedings*, Vol. III, 313):

> [The Operational] Research Section, known as O.R.S., was formed in 1938 to assist the Royal Air Force with the special problems involved in the operation of a chain of radar stations. ... [R]adar experts ... [acting] as liaison officers between the scientists, who developed the radar equipment, and the R.A.F. personnel who were to use this complicated apparatus ... mixed freely with all ranks of the R.A.F.: consequently the O.R.S. [civilian] staff assimilated the 'Service' point of view thoroughly and were able to represent the special requirements of the Air Force to their colleagues engaged on the design of new equipment.

At first, the work of the Research Section consisted largely of periodical visits to the radar stations.... In due course, however, the Section was consulted about all important problems. ...

Eventually, the chief officer of O.R.S. was recognized as the Scientific Adviser to Fighter Command and became a close associate of the Commander-in-Chief. In consequence, many technical problems, outside the usual radar sphere, were referred to the Section for solution. At this stage (June 1942) several actuaries joined the staff to assist with the rapidly developing statistical work.

This description of a group of scientists, including actuaries, developing a close personal relationship with the pilots who were their clients draws its importance here from the fact that in 1942 Dr. Morse who was developing ASWORG (Anti-Submarine Warfare Operations Research Group) went to England and saw this system in action. As Shellard described ASWORG's early days (op. cit., p. 330):

At any one time, approximately half the members of the Group were in the Group's central office in the Navy Department at Washington, while others were at test stations or were scattered throughout the theatres of naval warfare as close to actual operations as practicable.

Although ASWORG (later ORG, Operations Research Group, as its activities broadened from those of combatting submarines) recruited actuaries from its early days, those recruits had to prove themselves. Nathan F. Jones commented in a personal letter:

World War I had been the "chemists' war"; World War II was the "physicists' war." ... Naturally what [the ORG leaders] would have wanted was physicists...but [these] were hard to find [while actuaries and other] technically trained people [were] much more readily available. ... I actually had the impression that, *in the beginning* [those leaders] thought that actuaries might be useful as routine statistical clerks. ... I am glad to say they found that actuaries were useful far beyond that.

Prove themselves those ORG actuaries certainly did. Asked to elucidate the question, Why did actuaries star in this work?, Donald D. Cody, by letter, gave this analysis:

Why were actuaries successful [in multi-disciplinary Operations Research]? Certainly not because actuarial techniques were useful, as such.

Actuaries are accustomed to think in terms of total systems and we continuously monitor and react to changes in the systems. ... We tend to think in an orderly manner with simplified models. We have a healthy skepticism of impressions and a fetish for substituting facts. We respect other specialties. ... We live by innovation. In other words, a good actuary is a good operations research man. ...

Effective operations research is a state of mind. [An actuary is trained to nurture that state of mind even though] problems solvable by operations research approaches may not need any of the tools in the [Society of Actuaries] syllabus.

Cody pointed out that the usefulness of actuaries in this type of work might also be attributed to our profession's respect for the dictum pronounced by the fourteenth century philosopher William of Ockham, i.e., "Occam's Razor":

> Entia non sunt multiplicanda praeter necessitatem.

which may in this context be acceptably translated:

> What can be done with fewer assumptions is done in vain with more.

Shellard's paper (op. cit.) gives several examples of ORG projects, including ways to destroy the enemy's convoy-attacking submarines, advice on patterns for plane attacks on enemy merchant ships, bombardment of enemy shore positions, and protecting ships attacked by suicide planes. The wide range of problems that proved susceptible to solution by probability theory is described; there was even a study that "involved the preparation of a 'mortality' table (graduated by Makeham's formula) which showed the rates of loss of United States submarines while on war patrol according to 'combat age' " (p. 332).

Howard H. Hennington has commented in a letter:

> Some of the original work done by the actuaries in ASWORG involved absolutely [rudimentary] statistical data collection that brought forth remarkably useful results. DeVries, with [guidance from Professor Samuel S. Wilks of Princeton] set up a grid system along the Atlantic coastal waters in large squares. . . . We got aircraft flying reports and some ship reports and we summarized flying hours in each square separately by day and by night. . . . Combining that with the submarine sighting reports it became clear that at night surfaced submarines were close to shore, but the best daytime results [for attacking from the air] came from flying far offshore. [This] was very elementary but very useful information that had not previously been recognized!

After the war ended, the ORG operation was widely publicized, notably in a Navy Department press release of November 18, 1945, entitled "Civilian Group Helped Navy Solve Top Tactics Problems"; in Philip M. Morse's autobiography, *In at the Beginnings*; and in Lincoln R. Theismeyer and John E. Burchard's *Combat Scientists* (1947). This last reference specially mentions one of the actuaries (p. 114):

> The [Operations Research] Center took care of administrative details for the entire ORG and maintained an Intelligence Section for distributing technical reports and exchanging scientific information. . . . This Section was capably administered by Mr. Abraham C. Olshen, insurance examiner from the State of Oregon. His alertness and facility in negotiations with the many agencies concerned brought an increasing flow of material to ORG.

The camaraderie of its members caused ORG to live on after the war as an Operations Evaluation Group (OEG).

The paper submitted by Lew and Weck (op. cit.) to the Institute's 1948 Centenary Assembly gave illustrations of problems of a demographic nature solved by those authors during their service in the United States Army, cataloguing these under the following headings:

> Casualties and Casualty Rates
>
> Replacements [needed to maintain effective strength]
>
> Requirements for Medical Service
>
> Forecasting Personnel Structure by Grade and Age
>
> [Evaluation of Military] Retirements Benefits

The authors' conclusion, clearly supported by their illustrations, was this (p. 312):

> The topics discussed in this paper ...indicate only a few of the many types of problems in which actuarial knowledge and techniques can be applied with advantage. Some of these would not ordinarily be recognized as falling in the actuarial sphere. ... [P]ersons with actuarial training and experience have much to contribute to the solution of a wide variety of non-military as well as military problems where practical decisions have to be made from quantitative data.

The individual findings were in several cases quite different from those that the uninitiated would expect, e.g. (p. 299):

> In both the first and second world wars, diseases and non-combat injuries were responsible for the great bulk of the casualties in the United States armed forces. Even between 6 June 1944 and 'VE-day,' during which time Army hospitals in the European and Mediterranean theatres admitted more than 450,000 wounded, this number was only 35% of the total number of patients admitted for all causes.

It cannot be emphasized too strongly that many other actuaries, individually or in small groups and in civilian or military capacities, worked on mathematical problems comparable to those described in this section. Unless, even at this late date, an effort is made to assemble more particulars, much instructive information will be lost forever. At the Institute's Centenary Assembly British actuary Max Lander quoted a 1946 remark by Geoffrey N. Calvert to the Actuarial Society of Australasia (*Centenary Assembly Proceedings*, Vol. III, 291):

> [W]ould it not be a happy thought for actuarial bodies throughout the world to co-operate in pooling the experience of those who went out into the fray itself and the organization behind it, and to prepare a symposium depicting the things of professional interest which were then achieved?

Individual requests for such accounts to be included in this chapter produced responses such as the following (edited for purposes of connecting separately written portions):

> [Henry F. Rood] I worked with the Marine Corps and Bureau of Medicine in developing requirements for both men and materials. The doctors welcomed assistance but it was hard to convince a Marine that there was a better way. My best contribution [derived from my experience in calculating non-par premiums] was in getting them to use realistic factors and then add one safety factor rather than using redundant factors.

* * *

> [John A. Bevan] My first assignment was to improve the Norden bombsight which had the reputation of pickle barrel accuracy under test conditions but had an average miss of about a mile under combat conditions in Europe. ... We were told that combat pilots preferred tested weaponry and seat of the pants judgement to any new gadgets coming out of Washington. [But we learned that] General [Claire L.] Chennault, after trying unsuccessfully for some time to

bomb a critical bridge in Burma, dropped an entire stick right on the bridge when he tried the radio-controlled bombs with our modification of the Norden.

* * *

[Charles C. Hewitt] Many actuaries and actuarial students ... went into meteorology during World War II. [I was one of them—first as student, then as a teacher and lecturer on forecasting techniques, eventually as a station weather officer in North Carolina and then China.] ...

I never heard even a hint that [my work was a form of operations research], let alone that actuaries were involved. I studied and taught the subject at New York University [and] was sent to the University of Chicago for a briefing on the latest techniques.

Immediately after the War, I was offered a position as instructor in meteorology but instead went into casualty actuarial work.

* * *

[Geoffrey N. Calvert] When World War II was declared in 1939 I quickly transferred from the New Zealand Government Actuary's Department to set up a statistical division of the new National Service Department. ... One of the first tasks was to make estimates of the number of men in each category who would be found to be physically fit for overseas service, and to prepare a timetable for mobilization. In all this, my previous experience with [social security] cost projections proved invaluable. ...

I was soon coordinating the statistical systems of the Army, Navy and Air Force, and preparing overall studies of manpower strengths, resources, locations, casualty and reinforcement rates. [This brought me directly into the drafting of War Cabinet Orders.] ...

I made one tactical error [by footnoting some results obtained] by a sampling technique with a remark that the probable error was less than one-half of one percent. "Probable error! Don't bring figures here with probable errors in them!" stormed the Prime Minister. I learned my lesson.

Some of the Orders in Council that I drafted turned out to have substantial direct influences upon New Zealand's subsequent birth rate. [After the War, I estimated that measures for which I was responsible had caused 30,000 extra babies to be born.] Years later, walking down the main streets of Auckland and Wellington, I wondered which of the fine strong young people I saw were in that 30,000.

* * *

[Robert G. Espie] I was assigned temporarily to the 69th division in Mississippi. In that time I did some work in the Survey unit using triangulation to get angular direction and distance for 105mm howitzers. We first read angles, then looked up numerical values of tans [in trigonometric tables] then looked up logarithms of those values, then went through a formula process to get distances. I sent home for my high school table of direct log tan values. It made the work a lot easier. But the sergeant caught me at it and ... gave me K.P.: "It ain't the Army way!"

Other accounts come from obituaries in the actuarial journals, not, however, a surefire or an easily accessible source. Three examples follow:

[From the obituary of William Leslie, *PCAS* 49, 236] In 1946 the War Department awarded him the Certificate of Appreciation for his "patriotic services in a position of trust and responsibility for outstanding services rendered the War Department in its insurance procurement program during World War II while Chairman of the Joint Rating Committee for Comprehensive Rating Plan Covering War Projects."

[From the obituary of Joseph B. Maclean, *TSA* 22, 430] With the outbreak of war in 1914 he returned to Scotland and enlisted as a private in the Cameronians, a famous regiment of Scottish Rifles. He served with the First Battalion at Nieuwpoort, Ypres, Passchendaele, and other places on the British front. He came out of the war a captain and was awarded the Military Cross for gallantry in action. This decoration was bestowed upon him in 1919 on board the British battle cruiser H.M.S. *Renown* in New York harbor by the Prince of Wales (now the Duke of Windsor).

[From the obituary of Oswald Jacoby, *TSA* 36, 616] His knowledge of numbers made him valuable to the Navy in his assignment of breaking codes during World War II and the Korean conflict.

The direct benefits gained by the profession from the contributions of members to war efforts whether within the armed forces or as civilians may be summarized as follows:

- Recognition of what an actuary is or does, on the part of many who were at best vaguely aware of the meaning of the word *actuary*.

- Enhanced abilities by the returning actuaries attributable to their wartime experiences.

- Prompt appreciation of the potential in electronic computers.

- Less prompt but nonetheless beneficial spread of knowledge about the significance in management of the concepts of operations research.

WARTIME DISRUPTIONS OF THE PROFESSION'S ACTIVITIES

In World War I, the sum total of its effects upon Actuarial Society activities revealed by Council minutes consisted of (1) a 1916 decision not to appoint delegates to a meeting of the "Society to Enforce Peace," (2) a dues waiver arrangement applicable to members in military service and to European members, (3) exploration of a plan (apparently never implemented) to waive the final Fellowship examination for Associates in service who were certified to have prepared thoroughly for it, and (4) authorization to give examinations at any time to candidates in service.

In World War II, special examination facilities for candidates called under the United States Selective Service Act were authorized in October 1940. Provisions for suspensions and waivers of dues and for examination centers overseas were authorized in March 1942.

The likelihood of meetings being cancelled came up in May 1942; from the fall of 1942 on, the schedule of meetings was as follows:

1942   A Joint Meeting of the Actuarial Society and the American Institute was held in Toronto, October.

1943   The American Institute met in June only; the Actuarial Society met in October only.

1944   The American Institute met in June only; the Actuarial Society had intended to meet in October, and even requested special consideration by the Office of Defense Transportation (*T.A.S.A.* 45, 184), but it was denied. Elections of officers and Board members by mail ballot seem not to have been considered; terms were extended one year.

1945   A Joint Meeting of both bodies was held in Atlantic City, November.

ANECDOTES

Liberty is taken to present a few stories of actuaries in wartime. These are offered partly on their own merits and partly to illustrate what efforts to collect more of these might produce.

About the American Civil War:

Of the Actuarial Society charter members who had served in the Civil War, two records are of special historical interest:

1. James Morgan Lee (1844–1911) is reported in his obituary (*T.A.S.A.* 12, 354) to have fought on both sides—first in the Confederate Army until honorably discharged through disablement by rheumatism, then after recovery, in the Union Army from which he was honorably discharged at the close of hostilities;

2. Edward Buckey Smith (1833–1890), a lieutenant colonel in the Southern forces at the fall of Richmond, successfully transported a hoard of gold to safety at Danville.

About World War I:

In 1977, J. Gordon Beatty of Toronto wrote an amusing essay, *Reminiscences of an Old Soldier and Actuary,* and followed it with a 1982 sequel, *More Reminiscences of an Old Soldier and Actuary.* Both contain, as John C. Maynard who originally distributed them, remarked in his covering letter, "more than eighty years of [Gordon's recollections] as a Canadian World War I veteran, Canada Life man, and an Actuary with friends around the world." Copies are lodged in the Society of Actuaries archives.

About World War II:

This chapter may appropriately be closed with a first-hand account that the teller has given us permission to print:

> Christmas Day 1943. We were well within the Arctic Circle. It was dark 24 hours a day. I had been escorting convoys to Russia for over a year as the Radar officer of H.M.S. *Norfolk*, an old 10,000-ton cruiser with four twin turrets of 8-inch

guns but no protective armour except round its magazines. On these trips from our Iceland base to Murmansk we never saw our convoys until we reached port.

We had warning that the heavily armoured pocket battleship *Scharnhorst* had come out of Alten Fjord to attack the convoy. She was 26,000 tons and had nine 11-inch guns.

We spotted her on radar at 9:30 a.m. December 26th (St. Stephen's Day) and, with two other cruisers in our squadron engaged *Scharnhorst* at 10,000 yards. Norfolk's radar-controlled guns destroyed her primitive radar with our first or second salvo, but the Germans were excellent on optics and ranged on our flashing cordite.

At my post on the bridge I saw an 11-inch shell pass a few feet over our heads. A second killed all nine crew members in one of our aft turrets. The third from that salvo went through our main deck, cutting most of my radar communications and landed on some coils of rope in a hold without exploding.

Fortunately *Scharnhorst* turned and ran. At 4:40 P.M. that day she was cut off and sunk by H.M.S. *Duke of York*. The fire on our main deck took three hours to extinguish.

The British actuary who experienced this settled in Philadelphia after the war, served as President of the Casualty Actuarial Society in 1961–1962, and was active in the formative days of the American Academy of Actuaries. His name: Laurence H. Longley-Cook, FIA 1937, FCAS 1951.

Chapter XI.

ADMINISTRATION AND FINANCE

The heavy trouble, the bewildering care
That weighs us down who live and earn our bread.
                    —*William Morris, "The Earthly Paradise"*

OPERATIONS OF THE ACTUARIAL SOCIETY OF AMERICA

During its first fourteen years, the Actuarial Society operated without an office or any clerical help other than that provided gratis by its officers. In 1903 when its president, Israel C. Pierson, was faced with the extra duties of presiding over the New York International Congress, a supposedly temporary employee, Frances Straut, was hired to assist him. As it turned out, she remained on the Actuarial Society staff for more than forty years, being the one and only employee until about 1930. At the end of 1903, the Society opened its first office consisting of two rooms in the Metropolitan Life building at One Madison Avenue, New York City "as a permanent headquarters, for its office and for the reception of its library and archives" (Council minutes, December 29, 1903). The rent was $400 a year; Straut's salary was $50 per month.

The Society's landlord throughout its sixty years was always to be one of the New York City life insurance companies. These locations after four years on Madison Avenue were:

1907   New York Life, 346 Broadway

1920   Home Life, 256 Broadway

1932   Equitable Society, 393 Seventh Avenue

At some time between 1928 and 1933 the office staff was increased to two. Names of the second position incumbents were Leach, Jelliffe, Ruth Moore and, in 1943 Beatrice McIntyre. When Frances Straut died on November 3, 1945, McIntyre was placed in charge, remaining so with assistance by Helen Nelson until merger with the American Institute caused the New York office to be closed.

At its organizational meeting in 1889, the Society set its annual dues at $10 per member; at its dissolution sixty years later, the dues for Fellows were still $10. In fiscal year 1896–1897, the earliest for which figures are now known, expenses totalled $1,853 (in round numbers $18 for each of its 101 members); in 1948–1949 expenses were $25,021 ($25 for each of the then 996 members). This was a remarkable record of stability, but

363

it is arguable that a dues increase to broaden services to members and to ease the burdens suffered by examination and other committees might have been desirable.

For many years the Society felt no need to establish a retirement fund. But in 1938 recognizing that Frances Straut had passed age 55, the Council began making annual appropriations of $1,000 each for a pension to her; she died, however, before age 65. Council minutes of November 7, 1945 show authorization of a gift of $1,000 to Straut's sister who had cared for her during her final illness.

A general view of Actuarial Society finances can be seen from Table XI.1, which shows the major items of income and expense at three historical stages, viz., in fiscal years 1896–1897, 1919–1920 (the Society's midpoint), and 1948–1949 (its final year).

Table XI.1

INCOME AND EXPENSES
OF ACTUARIAL SOCIETY OF AMERICA
IN THREE SELECTED YEARS

	1896–1897	1919–1920	1948–1949
INCOME			
Members Dues	$ 960	$ 1,922	$ 8,230
Examination Fees	1,205	2,752	
Advertisements	1,180	762	2,663
Sales of Publications		1,651	10,843
Investment Income	21	716	1,665
Other Income		100	1,309
Total Income	$ 2,161	$ 6,356	$ 27,462
EXPENSES			
Printing	$ 1,293	$ 3,444	$ 10,725
General Expense	337	1,262	3,138
Education & Examinations		567	3,600
Meeting Expense	223	406	113
Salaries & Rent		2,076	7,445
Total Expenses	$ 1,853	$ 7,755	$ 25,021
NET INCOME	$ 308	$(1,399)	$ 2,441

Additional to the 1948–1949 disbursements in Table XI.1 was the Society's share of a gift of £2,000 given jointly with the American Institute, to the Institute of Actuaries to help rebuild Staple Inn Hall, which had been destroyed by a flying bomb in August 1944. The description and the Institute's gracious expression of thanks by Charles F. Wood, FIA, are recorded in *TSA* 6, 654.

The income item "Advertisements" constituted a means by which the Actuarial Society received a considerable subsidy from some insurance companies whose actuaries were Fellows. The practice was for each such company to purchase space in the paper-bound copies of the *Transactions* (omitted from the bound volumes). The space might be a page or part thereof; for example, in the paperbound issue of May 1920 there were twenty-two pages of these, taken by thirty-six sponsors.

In September 1948, the Joint Committee on Finances appointed to analyze the financial needs of the prospective Society of Actuaries recommended against future solicitations of this kind:

> It will be noted that we are recommending the elimination of company advertising . . . [so that] any money received from companies . . . will be obviously for value directly received. . . . The Society of Actuaries will be a purely professional society with which no outsider has any right to interfere by reason of giving financial support. In the long range of time this is the only safe position for such a society to be in. . . . [W]e should remember that we as students . . . benefited by [the Society's educational and examination] work and that we might consider that we are gradually paying back in our later lives for this particular debt which we owe our profession. In any event we recommend that we launch the Society of Actuaries on its career with its budget based upon this principle and we express the earnest hope that it will prove practicable in operation.

The Actuarial Society's operating deficit of $1,399 in 1919–1920, constituting 22% of income, arose from World War I inflation; this was the first experience with such a phenomenon by the profession on this continent. In the first quarter-century of the Society's existence the CPI (as later constructed, 1967 = 100) had moved only from 27 in 1889 to 30.4 in 1915, but by 1920 it had soared to 60. The chart on page xxiv, "The Trend of the United States Consumer Price Index," shows how extraordinary this was. In 1921, however, the inflation was cured; the index dropped sharply to 53.6 and remained in the low fifties until again declining in the Depression. The special committee appointed by the Actuarial Society Council in October 1920 restored a balanced budget, partly by persuading more companies to participate in the aforementioned advertisements, while raising their price to $40 for a full page, and by increasing prices of Society publications.

The accounts show no income from meeting registration fees. The Actuarial Society never charged any such fees to members; its rules prohibited nonmembers from attending its meetings unless personally invited by the president.

When the Actuarial Society ceased operations in June 1949, it had accumulated funds of $102,000 to contribute to the coffers of the Society of Actuaries.

OPERATIONS OF THE AMERICAN INSTITUTE OF ACTUARIES

After conducting its affairs for eighteen years without an office, the American Institute leased space in early 1928 at 720 North Michigan Avenue, Chicago. An office secretary, name not now known, was engaged at $110 a month. In February 1938 the office was moved to the Field Building, 135 South LaSalle Street, where it remained through the balance of the American Institute's existence.

The office secretary for a time was Lydia Webber; in 1943 she was succeeded by Margaret Hrncsjar at a starting salary of $150 a month. Hrncsjar ran the show, first by herself, later with one full-time and one part-time assistant. After the 1949 merger, she continued in the office of the Society of Actuaries as second in command to the executive secretary. She retired with thirty years service in 1973.

The organization's original dues for Fellows were $10; in 1922 when inflation had struck, those dues were increased to $15.

The American Institute never copied the Actuarial Society's system of company subsidy via advertisements; instead, it created at the outset a class of subscribers called Contributing Members. These were life insurance companies which, in return for an annual fee, were permitted to nominate persons to attend the meetings and to engage in the discussions. This was a major difference from the Actuarial Society's rigid practice of excluding nonmembers from its gatherings. Originally the dues of Contributing Members were $10 a year, but in 1922 these were raised to $25 and continued to be an important help to American Institute finances.

Table XI.2 illustrates the financial operations by displaying them at two points in American Institute history, 1923–1924 and the final year 1948–1949.

Table XI.2

INCOME AND EXPENSES
OF AMERICAN INSTITUTE OF ACTUARIES
IN TWO SELECTED YEARS

	1923–1924	1948–1949
INCOME		
Members Dues	$ 1,870	$ 10,029
Contributing Members Dues	3,000	4,300
Sales of Publications	359	6,390
Examination Fees	741	1,797
Investment Income	168	750
Total Income	$ 6,138	$ 23,266
EXPENSES		
Printing	$ 2,150	$ 9,457
General Expense	1,010	3,060
Education & Examination Expense	287	3,570
Meeting Expense	626	244
Salaries & Rent	425	6,907
Total Expenses	$ 4,498	$ 23,238
NET INCOME	**$ 1,640**	**$ 28**

Not included in these 1948–1949 disbursements was the American Institute's half-share of the aforementioned contribution to the rebuilding of Staple Inn Hall.

At the closing of its operations in June 1949, the American Institute contribution to the funds of the Society of Actuaries amounted to $73,000, indeed a worthy sum from a body younger and smaller than the Actuarial Society.

Warmest thanks are due Miss Hrncsjar for contributing to our history the following reminiscences given in her capacity as the surviving office staff member from pre-Society of Actuaries days:

I came to the American Institute in 1943 by a piece of pure good luck. My sister was secretary to Mr. Howard C. Reeder (a new Fellow that year), and learning from him that the then office girl was leaving, I told him I was considering a job change. I had no idea what the work of an actuary involved, but after things were explained to me I was very much interested.

The office consisted of a small general room, a small library, and a stockroom cluttered with books. After a few weeks I got permission from the officers to have temporary help to get things into workable shape.

My work week was Monday to Friday, 32 1/2 hours, almost unheard of in those days. A 40-hour week came into effect after the merger.

Our record-keeping equipment consisted of an Addressograph Machine, its plates tabbed with colors to distinguish Fellows, Associates and Contributing Companies.

Some of the first officers I had the pleasure of meeting were Messrs. Will MacKinnon, Gordon Beatty, Ronald Stagg, Ross Moyer and Victor Henningsen. When I had problems, I usually phoned one of the officers.

Being employed by such a distinguished institution gave me great pride and satisfaction. I was elated to be kept on at the time of the merger, and promoted to Administrative Assistant to Mr. Arthur McKinnie, the Executive Secretary—another piece of good luck that neither of the girls in the Actuarial Society office cared to move from New York to Chicago. At the time of my retirement (May 1973) the office staff had increased to fourteen individuals.

I greatly enjoyed attending the Institute and Joint Meetings. Most memorable was the formal affair launching the Society of Actuaries at the Greenbrier, White Sulphur Springs (November 1949). Mr. McConney (the first president) invited several of us to his suite after the meeting. He was a most gracious host and delighted us with his Scottish stories.

OPERATIONS OF THE CASUALTY ACTUARIAL SOCIETY

Little is on record about the administrative premises and facilities of the Casualty Actuarial Society during the many years through which its first two secretary-treasurers labored without paid help. Those officers were Claude E. Scattergood, 1914–1917, and Richard Fondiller, 1918–1952.

Dudley M. Pruitt paid special tribute in his paper "The First Fifty Years" (*PCAS* 51, 152) to Fondiller's administrative management over a thirty-five year span.

Albert Z. Skelding succeeded Fondiller in 1953, continuing in that post until 1968. During and since his term, office quarters in New York City and clerical help have been furnished by arrangement with the National Council on Compensation Insurance, of which he was assistant general manager. The first Council employee to assist with Society work was Gladys Sorensen, who retired in 1972. In 1955 another Council staff member, Edith F. Morabito, was loaned to the Society to assist Sorensen. Morabito's service continued for thirty-three years, during which she performed her duties admirably, earning promotion to executive secretary and office manager of the Society. The office between 1953 and 1957 was at 200 Fourth Avenue, New York City; it moved in 1958 to 200 East 42nd Street, and again in 1977 to One Penn Plaza on New York's 34th Street.

In 1974, by constitutional amendment, provision was made for the Secretary and Treasurer posts to be held by different people.

Table XI.3 shows condensed financial statements for 1923–1924 (the earliest one now available), 1953–1954, and 1978–1979.

Table XI.3

**INCOME AND EXPENSES
OF CASUALTY ACTUARIAL SOCIETY
IN THREE SELECTED YEARS**

	1923–1924	1953–1954	1978–1979
INCOME			
Members Dues	$ 1,970	$ 4,631	$ 43,758
Sales of Publications	1,281	1,249	19,152
Examination Fees	205	964	26,078
Investment Income	43	125	10,199
Other Income		579	(199)
Total Income	$ 3,499	$ 7,548	$ 98,988
EXPENSES			
Printing & Stationery	$ 1,961	$ 4,541	$ 49,034
General Expense	225	494	5,649
Examination Expense	211	552	3,777
Meeting Expense (Net)	49	468	7,214
Secretarial Work	360	600	45,744
Library Fund	2	45	
Total Expenses	$ 2,808	$ 6,700	$111,418
NET INCOME	$ 691	$ 848	$(12,430)

OPERATIONS OF THE FRATERNAL ACTUARIAL ASSOCIATION

Throughout the sixty-four years of its existence, the Fraternal Actuarial Association conducted its affairs on the volunteer system without any office or any direct employees. A summary of its accounts from 1922 to 1980 is printed in the final (1977–1980) volume of its *Proceedings,* "History" section, page 70. It is apparent from the several Treasurer's Reports in that volume that in its last years the Association was collecting no dues, its financial needs being filled by interest earnings and appropriations from the National Fraternal Congress.

Unneeded funds on hand at dissolution amounting to $2,687.73 were donated to the Actuarial Education and Research Fund. The final membership consisted of 54 Fellows, 59 Associates and 2 Affiliate Members.

OPERATIONS OF THE SOCIETY OF ACTUARIES

The Society of Actuaries started in 1949 with a fund of $175,000 contributed by its two predecessor bodies, a maximum dues scale (for Fellows and for Associates of five or more years standing) of $30, a new headquarters at 208 South La Salle Street,

Chicago, and a staff of four including Executive Secretary Arthur A. McKinnie. Mc-Kinnie, a high school teacher, had studied actuarial science under Professor James W. Glover at the University of Michigan, graduating in 1928.

There were two reasons why the maximum dues were set at $5 above the sum of the dues of the prior bodies. First, both those bodies were considered to be on the edge of needing more income, and second, the Executive Secretary post involved greater responsibility and therefore more pay than the previous top positions.

In fact, for the next twelve years, finances were the least of the Society's problems. The surplus—later called the "operating fund" and still later the "membership equity"—remained at more than two years' income until 1960, during which time the number of members almost doubled, from 1,069 in June 1949 to 2,004 in June 1960. The gross income per member during the 1950s remained almost steady at about $60.

Conditions began to change early in the next decade. In 1963 the maximum dues were raised to $40. In 1964 the Board of Governors took the unprecedented step of charging members a registration fee to attend meetings; subsequent Boards raised that fee from $10 in 1963 to $15 in 1964 and to $20 in 1968. But despite these and other actions to increase income, a mixture of inflation and broadened services had reduced the operating fund from its original two-and-a-half years of income to only eight months of income.

Financial problems in the 1970s erupted even more vexatiously. Income rose from $374,000 to $1,477,000; expenses rose from $391,000 to $1,638,000; membership equity in 1979 ($425,000) covered only three-and-a-half months of income. The 1974–1975 Board was faced with the necessity to raise maximum dues to $100, which it did by a split vote.

Three actuaries were in charge of the Society's administration during those tumultuous years, viz.:

1968–1972   Charles B. H. Watson

1972–1975   Gary N. See

1975–1979   Peter W. Plumley

The Society's 1949–1950 Board of Governors had considered obtaining the services of an actuary in a capacity such as Executive Director, but no consensus on this point was reached until McKinnie's retirement was in prospect. McKinnie retired in 1971 after twenty-two years of quietly efficient service and died on November 29, 1978. Appreciations of his work and character appear in *The Actuary,* January and April 1979.

By the late 1970s, it was clear that the administrative element of the executive directorship outweighed the actuarial element, making it desirable to acquire primarily administrative talent in that position and to employ actuaries in more specialized functions. Accordingly, the Board secured the services of John E. O'Connor, Jr., in May 1979 to succeed Plumley as Executive Director; an article about O'Connor, "Why He's Who He Is," is in *The Actuary*, June 1979. Warren R. Adams, FSA, who had become Director of Education in 1977, was succeeded by Linden N. Cole, FSA, in 1980. The staff had grown to twenty-one by 1977.

Charles B. H. Watson
SOA, AAA: 1969–1973

Gary N. See
SOA, AAA: 1973–1975

Peter W. Plumley
SOA, AAA: 1976–1979

Stephen G. Kellison
AAA: 1976–1988

John E. O'Connor, Jr.
SOA: 1979–Present

Colin E. Jack
CIA: 1980–1985

Six executive directors of North American actuarial bodies.

Although serious discussion about computerizing the Society files began in 1974, it was not until January 1978 that an IBM System 32 arrived in the office. It was replaced within a year by a computer with greater storage and memory capacities. In 1982, computer capabilities were further increased.

OPERATIONS OF THE CONFERENCE OF ACTUARIES IN PUBLIC PRACTICE

The minutes of the Conference's Thirteenth Annual Meeting in October 1962 summarized that body's early administrative arrangements in these words (*PCAPP* 12, 399):

> The Secretary [Robert E. Bruce] announced that an office secretary had been employed for the first time by the Conference to handle many of the clerical tasks which had heretofore been assumed by the Chicago Board members and other officers.

Up to that time and for twelve years thereafter, the quarters were in the office of Past-President Harry S. Tressel at 10 South La Salle Street, Chicago. In 1974 an arrangement was made with the Society of Actuaries to rent space in the Society's headquarters at 208 South La Salle Street, which arrangement has continued ever since at the Society's subsequent addresses.

That first office secretary of 1962 was Hazel H. Hopkins who continued as Assistant Secretary until her retirement in early 1974. Grace Cunneen who had been a part-time assistant to Hopkins since 1965 succeeded her, remaining until retirement at the end of 1980. Cunneen's successor, with the title Director of Administration, was Maryrose Sloan who served until 1985. A second full-time employee, Debra Anton, Administrative Assistant, was hired in July 1984. In 1985, when the Conference had reached a total membership of 870, Claudia M. Krueger became Director of Administration, and Rita K. Chastain became Assistant Director, replacing Anton. Chastain succeeded Krueger as Director of Administration in December 1988.

OPERATIONS OF THE CANADIAN INSTITUTE OF ACTUARIES

Because the Canadian Institute's predecessor, the Canadian Association of Actuaries, had no office or employees and the Canadian Institute's membership at the end of its first calendar year, 1965, numbered only 556 (*PCIA* 1, 98), it was natural for the new body to postpone official consideration of establishing an administrative structure. But the matter was discussed with the members at the annual meeting on June 9, 1966; Cecil G. White commented (*PCIA* 1, 185):

> The prestige of the C.I.A., and its status in the Canadian community, will depend not only on the professional competence of the members, but also on the professional way in which [its] affairs are conducted. Therefore, the Canadian Institute of Actuaries should have a proper headquarters, a good staff, attractive letterhead, a good crest, a good motto, etc. . . .

> [T]he location of the headquarters will be important for the long-term success of the organization. The C.I.A. is the national professional body to represent all actuaries in Canada—French-speaking as well as English-speaking, consultants as well as employees of insurance companies or governments. ... [W]hat could be more logical than to establish their headquarters in the city that is nearest to the "weighted" centre of all the actuaries resident in Canada [i.e.,] the national capital of Canada, a very good place to locate the headquarters of a national organization for professional actuaries.

Eight years later in 1974, White said to the Society of Actuaries (*TSA* 26, D9):

> Has the [Canadian] Institute reached the stage in its growth at which it needs its own full-time staff? Should [it] have an Executive Secretary? . . . [T]he Executive Secretary could render great assistance in arranging and staging membership meetings, in producing the *Year Book* [and] the *Proceedings*, and in expediting the work of the various committees of the Institute.

A few months later, the Canadian Institute opened its first headquarters office at 116 Albert Street in Ottawa. The office was managed by Executive Secretary Christine Burke. The membership at that time numbered 870.

In September 1980, the Canadian Institute employed one of its own past presidents, Colin E. Jack, FCIA, FSA, as its first Executive Director; Burke became Director of

Administration. The first Executive Director's Report to the members appears in *PCIA* 12, No. 3, 4 (June 1981).

OPERATIONS OF THE AMERICAN ACADEMY OF ACTUARIES

In its early years the Academy depended heavily upon the Society of Actuaries for both space and clerical help. The Society office was the Academy's mailing address. From 1965 to 1971 the Society's Executive Secretary, Arthur A. McKinnie, was also the Academy's Executive Secretary; from 1968 to 1975 the Society's Executive Directors, Charles B. H. Watson and Gary N. See, were also the Academy's Executive Directors.

The Academy reimbursed the Society annually for the agreed-upon values of the services rendered by Society staff members, including particularly those of Bernard A. Bartels in the early days. In 1970, Madeline M. Madden became the Academy's first permanent employee; she served the Academy as Membership Manager until her retirement in 1987.

The Academy opened its Washington office at 1835 K Street in January 1976 after securing the services of Stephen G. Kellison, FSA, as Executive Director. The cooperative system with the Society continued in matters such as maintenance of membership records. When the Society's computer system had come fully into operation in 1980, this arrangement became essential for economical recordkeeping because the Academy and the Society had such large proportions of their memberships in common.

By October 1979, the total staff of the Academy was seven—six in Washington, one in Chicago.

DUES SCALES OF ALL ACTUARIAL BODIES AT TEN-YEAR INTERVALS

A general picture of the dues scales of the several bodies is given in Table XI.4.

Table XI.4

**MAXIMUM DUES CHARGED
BY NORTH AMERICAN ACTUARIAL BODIES
AT TEN-YEAR INTERVALS, 1909–1979**

	1909	1919	1929	1939
Actuarial Society of America	$ 10	$ 10	$ 10	$ 10
American Institute of Actuaries	10	10	15	15
Casualty Actuarial Society	-	10	10	10
Fraternal Actuarial Association	-	5	5	5
	1949	**1959**	**1969**	**1979**
Society of Actuaries	$ 30	$ 30	$ 50	$100
Casualty Actuarial Society	20	40	50	80
Fraternal Actuarial Association	10	10	15	0
Conference of Actuaries in Public Practice	-	35 (est.)	70 (est.)	120
American Academy of Actuaries	-	-	10	75
Canadian Institute of Actuaries	-	-	30	115

Chapter XII.

ACTUARIAL CLUBS

*No man is born unto himself alone; who
lives unto himself, he lives to none.*

—Francis Quarles (17th century)

THE BRITISH EXAMPLE

The first Actuaries Club was formed in London in November 1848, four months after the Institute of Actuaries had been founded. That club's thirteen original members founded it not as a companion to the Institute but as a rival, and they remained aloof for thirty-six years—nearly as long as was required for the Actuarial Society and the American Institute to coalesce. In R. C. Simmonds' *The Institute of Actuaries 1848–1948,* the breach is explained thus (p. 6):

> When, in 1848, the first general consideration [of organizing the Institute] was given to the question in London, it became clear that there was a definite division of view upon the nature of any such combination. One section, small, compact and powerful, desired at most only an Association of Managers of Life Assurance Offices—the remainder, larger, looser and individually less weighty, wished to establish a Professional Body of Actuaries as such. . . .

> [O]ne of the fundamental considerations of [the Club's] founders was that they represented what, even in the Life Assurance world of to-day, men still call 'first-class Offices.'

Throughout those years until 1884, the actuaries in the Club concentrated on matters of office practice, while those in the Institute explored actuarial questions. When, happily, the two bodies joined under the Institute banner, the Actuaries Club continued as the most venerable among the now numerous groups that meet socially for dinner at the close of Institute sessions.

The early North American equivalent of that British social system was the dinner that used to be held regularly at the end of the first day of each Actuarial Society meeting. It performed both a social function and an occasion for informal discussion, often graced by visits from overseas actuaries.

The four earliest actuarial clubs on this side of the Atlantic were:

> The Actuaries Club (Toronto, 1907)
>
> The Actuaries Club of New York (c. 1923)
>
> The Actuaries Club of Hartford (1926)
>
> The Senior Actuaries Club (1928)

373

THE ACTUARIES CLUB

Although the word *Toronto* was never in its title, the Actuaries Club, at its founding in 1907, consisted entirely of life company actuaries in that city. In 1916 the Club began admitting actuaries in other Ontario cities and, in 1921, extended its territory into the Province of Quebec.

The following particulars are taken from an address (contained in the Canadian Association of Actuaries minutes), "The Actuaries Club (A Brief History)," presented by John G. Parker in April 1948:

> About November 1906, Mr. P. C. H. Papps . . . sent a letter to various Actuaries in Toronto suggesting the formation of an Actuaries' Club. . . . In all, the replies were favourable, so that an initial meeting was called in the Manufacturers Life [Papps' company] on January 31, 1907. . . . It was decided to hold a meeting ... on February 12th.
>
> At this meeting the Constitution was adopted, although the word "Constitution" was not used in the minutes but merely a statement was made: "the following rules and regulations were adopted." The Club was to be called "The Actuaries Club" and the object was stated to be "to promote in a social way actuarial knowledge of assurance among its members." The rules limited Club membership to Fellows or Associates of the British Institute, the Faculty and the [Actuarial] Society. An amendment was made in 1913 under which others engaged in actuarial pursuits who might be approved by a three-fourths vote of the members present could be admitted to membership. This was not a popular amendment and at a later meeting in the same year a motion was made to rescind this rule. However, the motion to rescind was lost on a vote of ten to nine.
>
> In 1925 the Constitution was again amended so that Fellows and Associates of the American Institute of Actuaries were eligible for membership.
>
> In 1931, when [J. Gordon] Beatty was President, a great deal of discussion took place in regard to a change in name of the Club, but no action on this matter was taken. [That topic was: "In view of the size and importance of the Club and also the fact that the membership is drawn from practically all parts of Canada, is it desirable to change the name to, say, 'The Canadian Institute of Actuaries'?"] . . .
>
> While the rules and regulations specified that the object of the Club was "to promote in a social way actuarial knowledge of assurance," the members of the Club were not in any way limited by this objective. At various times they undertook work of a very practical nature ... . [Parker mentioned developing a uniform card for mortality studies, making such studies, suggesting ratings for hazardous occupations, following life insurance legislation, and designing a disability benefit clause that companies used as a guide.] . . .
>
> In conclusion, I believe that the greatest advantage of the Club has been in the creation and maintenance of a strong personal friendship between the members.

When the Actuaries Club, fulfilling what amounted to a prophetic vision in 1931, changed its name and its character, first into the Canadian Association of Actuaries in 1946 and then into the Canadian Institute of Actuaries in 1965, it may have been regretfully supposed that the days of that club had reached their end. But this was not the case.

In December 1970 (*The Actuary,* February 1971) "the oldest Actuaries Club became the youngest" as the club in Toronto re-formed. There had been a Younger Actuaries Committee of the Canadian Institute of Actuaries that was sufficiently active and diverse in its projects to be established as a separate self-supporting entity, so that it appropriately took the name Actuaries Club of Toronto, devoting itself to informal discussion and social events for Canadian Institute members within daily commuting distance of that city. Its first president was Donald J. Leapman.

Experience having demonstrated that evening meetings were unwelcome to many, the new club has relied on luncheon gatherings except when assembling on the evening of a Canadian Institute meeting.

The original 1907 organization can claim a distinction not enjoyed by any other actuarial club of having its records preserved in the National Archives of its country, in Ottawa.

THE ACTUARIES CLUB OF NEW YORK

The Actuaries Club of New York (renamed in 1987 the Actuarial Society of Greater New York) has for many years been the largest club on this continent and, after Toronto, the most venerable. In terms of service to actuaries and students in the New York City and northern New Jersey area and to the profession elsewhere, it has merited high ranking. Its only failure seems to have been the lack of a recorded history; one peculiar result was that it erroneously celebrated its fiftieth anniversary in June 1982, unaware that its existence dates back to the early 1920s.

About 1923 there was a Junior Actuaries Club of New York, of which James R. Herman said in 1929 (*T.A.S.A* 30, 538):

> It was called Junior Actuaries' Club because a qualification for membership was membership in a recognized Actuarial Society for less than ten years. This limitation was made not because of any objection to the fellowship of the older members of the Society but because the purpose of the Club was to stimulate informal discussions and it was felt that the younger men would be more apt to participate in the discussions if the heads of the various companies were not present.

Bruce E. Shepherd in 1936 (*R.A.I.A.* 25, 250) delivered some remarks that seem to need what nowadays is customarily called "clarification":

> In New York we have three actuarial clubs. One of them is known as the Senior Actuaries' Club ... . The other two organizations grew out of what was originally known as the Junior Actuaries' Club of New York, which was organized somewhere around 1920. I believe the primary purposes of that club were to promote an interchange of ideas between the members, give them an opportunity to become acquainted with each other, and to ... get up and express themselves in public. ...
>
> The club proceeded along those lines for several years, after which some of the junior actuaries found that they were not quite as "junior" as they once were,

and there was a suggestion made that the membership ... be limited to those who had [been Fellows] for a specified number of years. ...

That proposition ... was voted down ... with the result that we continued on our originally established basis for several more years. During that time it appeared that less and less interest in the club was being taken by these older members. ... So a few years ago this whole matter was taken up again, and it was decided to split the club, as had been originally suggested, so that ... after [members] had held their Fellowships for seven years ... they would automatically graduate into the senior branch .... We have been operating on that basis ever since.

Shepherd seems to have been mistaken in his reference to "three actuarial clubs"; the Senior Actuaries Club, as distinct from the senior branch of the Actuaries Club of New York, was not based in New York but was the present body of that name whose activities are outlined later in this chapter.

A description of the Club's structure in 1951 is printed in *TSA* 3, 255. Club records show that a Committee to Study the Future Course of the Actuaries Club of New York existed in 1969; no references to senior or junior branches are contained in the minutes of an October 1969 meeting of a "Committee to Implement the Reorganization Report of the Actuaries Club," so it is likely that the branches were merged in that reorganization.

The Society of Actuaries in 1970 established a committee to seek ways for the Society and the actuarial clubs to cooperate in serving the profession's needs. In 1972 that committee published a "Club Profile" setting forth the eligibility requirements, activities and other data reported by thirty of the thirty-four existing clubs. Even though some large clubs failed to contribute to this report, it seems clear that the Actuaries Club of New York with 675 members was by far the largest. New York also showed an impressively wide range of activities, including scholarships for minority groups, prize awards in high school mathematics contests, an array of business and social meetings, public relations and continuing education.

At its 1982 celebration in Atlantic City, the Club was in a position to present general sessions, simultaneous sessions and workshops. It also conducted a contest for a Club motto, which in the finest tradition of such efforts within our profession resulted in every one of the entries being rejected.

MORE CLUBS APPEAR

The examples set in Toronto and New York, the growth in numbers of Associates and students, and particularly Arthur Pedoe's urging in his 1929 paper "The Actuarial Profession on the North American Continent" (*T.A.S.A.* 30, 14) stimulated organization of clubs in the principal insurance-company cities of the 1920s and 1930s. In the discussion of Pedoe's paper, Reinhard A. Hohaus said (*T.A.S.A.* 30, 519):

I concur in the author's suggestion that the Society encourage the formation of Actuarial Clubs in the various communities which are life insurance centers. ...

A satisfactory method ... might be to have a Committee appointed by the parent bodies which would act as a liaison between the various groups. ... [T]he local organizations should ... be developed ... in accord with the local conditions ... with full knowledge of the success or failure of the different plans already tried.

Other speakers mentioned clubs already established—in Hartford, Philadelphia, Indianapolis and Winnipeg.

By far the most complete surviving documents on the organizational days of this second generation of clubs are those of the Actuaries Club of Hartford. The following account taken from those papers kept in the Society of Actuaries archives may serve as generally representative of the procedures elsewhere.

THE ACTUARIES CLUB OF HARTFORD

The club formed in Hartford in 1926 has been said to have been the second club in that city, but no record of any earlier one has been found. On December 22, 1926, Edward B. Morris convened a dinner meeting to formulate the rules for this proposed body; his speaker's notes show that he pictured membership in the Actuarial Society or the American Institute as necessary and sufficient for entry, and that he thought that members of the Casualty Actuarial Society (of whom there were then no fewer than twenty-nine in Hartford not also members of the life bodies) might also be eligible. It was voted, however, not to entitle them to club membership; probably the organizers doubted that the programs could easily be arranged so as to interest casualty actuaries, or else they regarded the resulting club size—almost eighty—as uncomfortably large.

The Constitution outlined at this dinner and ratified at the first regular meeting on February 9, 1927, defined the purposes as "to promote friendships among the actuaries of Hartford and vicinity and to foster discussions of actuarial matters." (The document identified Springfield, Massachusetts, as being in the vicinity.) Some puckish organizer arranged for the Club motto to be "Logic is neither an art nor a science but a subterfuge," but this was quietly dropped after a few years.

The extent to which the Club should be considered as for the benefit of younger members came up, it being recognized that in those days senior actuaries tended to dominate discussions at Actuarial Society meetings. By way of compromise it was decided that Fellows of greater than ten years duration be honorary members, permitted however to speak at the meetings. In October 1937, it having been observed that the honorary members would soon outnumber the regular members and that the awe caused by their presence was not what it used to be, the distinction was abandoned.

There were no women among the original forty-eight members, but there was no hesitation later about admitting them to all gatherings except the annual Field Day. About 1969 the women members expressed their objection to this limitation, and the men promptly caved in. Dorothy R. Stanton of Pittsfield (which city had been defined in 1928 as "in the vicinity") qualified for club membership in April 1929 but never attended a meeting; the first woman to attend was Martina E. Doyle in December 1948.

The Club has always had just one officer, the Secretary-Treasurer, serving until his or her successor is elected. The chairman holds that post for a single meeting only. The Hartford Club may be the only one of the early organizations that has kept faithful track of the chronological identity of each meeting, that number having reached a venerable 242 in 1988.

At the May 1948 meeting, desirability of merging the Hartford and Boston Clubs into a single regional body was discussed, but the preference was just to have occasional joint meetings. The first such event was held in Worcester on April 1, 1949, and it immediately blossomed into an annual gathering. A note on the history of the Actuaries Club of Boston filed in the Society of Actuaries archives in 1989 shows that it has been in existence since March 1931.

THE SENIOR ACTUARIES CLUB

The Senior Actuaries Club was founded by some Fellows of the Actuarial Society in 1928, probably because they wished to continue the pleasant informality that had characterized discussions among the older members of that body in former times. It has had some of the attributes of a secret society—for instance, it has been understood that members will not mention that Club in, say, *Who's Who* or in their prepared obituaries—but its existence ranks among the profession's worst-kept secrets. Its Constitution requires that membership depend upon having "gained marked recognition in the actuarial profession or made an outstanding contribution to actuarial science." The overriding limitation has been numerical (for many years, forty), and use of a preferential ballot has been relied upon to resolve the issue of recognition or eminence. Membership, originally exclusive to male Fellows of the Actuarial Society, has been broadened to include Associates, members of the Casualty Actuarial Society and women. The first CAS representative was Laurence H. Longley-Cook in 1968 and the first woman, Josephine W. Beers in 1972.

Antitrust policing in the United States in 1948 raised fears about suspicion being attached to a group of leading professionals meeting under even a tattered cloak of secrecy. One large company required its actuary to withdraw, but the concern died down when the Club began keeping comprehensive minutes.

Among the Club's traditions have been the circulation of a snuff box (a 1938 gift from the Actuaries Club of London) and the presence from time to time of eminent actuarial visitors from overseas who have addressed the members.

THE REGIONAL CLUBS

Regional clubs—definable as those that draw their membership from an area already containing local clubs but performing so as not to interfere with the continued operations of those local groups—began to be a force in the 1940s. Their top-ranking purpose was continuing education; they were better equipped than were most local clubs to conduct meetings of all day or longer duration and to obtain widely known speakers. Their procedures have become not unlike those of the actuarial societies, and their success and intimacy have tended to reduce attendances at society meetings. Even after some of them became as large as the societies themselves had once been, they still took care of the social needs of their members far better than the societies could.

When the Canadian Association of Actuaries was formed in 1946, it first resembled a regional club but soon began to speak on the profession's behalf to federal and provincial authorities and confirmed its status as a national body when it became the Canadian Institute of Actuaries in 1965. The earliest regional clubs were the Pacific Coast (later the Pacific States) Actuarial Club, established in 1928 (*R.A.I.A.* 25, 253)

Senior Actuaries Club members and their overseas guests on the occasion of the Fifteenth International Congress of Actuaries, New York City, October 1957. Name key is available from the SOA archives.

379

and the Middle Atlantic Actuarial Club formed in 1934 to serve the profession in Maryland, Virginia and the District of Columbia, expanding into North Carolina in 1946.

CLUBS SERVING CASUALTY ACTUARIES

Between 1963 and 1979, four actuarial clubs for casualty actuaries were organized across the United States. In order of formation these were:

1963   Casualty Actuaries of the Mid-Atlantic Region (originally named "of Philadelphia")

1964   Midwest Actuaries Forum (centered in Illinois)

1971   Casualty Actuaries of Greater New York (originally "of New York")

1972   Southern California Casualty Actuarial Club

Since 1979, all these have continued to flourish, and four others—Casualty Actuaries of New England, Casualty Actuaries of the Northwest, Southwest Actuarial Forum, and Casualty Actuaries of the Bay Area—have been formed.

Membership in these bodies consists of Fellows and Associates; some accept CAS students, academics and other professionals, as subscribers.

RELATIONSHIPS BETWEEN ACTUARIAL SOCIETIES AND CLUBS

The Society of Actuaries, since it began listing actuarial clubs in its *Yearbooks* in 1953, has taken pains to state that the clubs have "no official connection with the Society but supplement many of its activities." The Casualty Actuarial Society on the other hand lists the clubs in the non-life field as its affiliates — possibly a distinction without a difference.

One of the first official acts of the Society of Actuaries in 1949 was to invite the officers of the then existing clubs to informal gatherings in New York and Chicago during the final meetings in those cities of its two predecessor bodies. The New York event was hosted by Society of Actuaries President Edmund M. McConney, other speakers being Henry F. Rood and Reinhard A. Hohaus. The Chicago event doubtless followed the same pattern.

McConney and Hohaus explained how the clubs might, if they wished, help the new Society to fulfill the needs of actuaries of the smaller companies, to keep young actuaries active in professional affairs, to promote a flow of formal papers on subjects in danger of being neglected, and to choose appropriate topics for the Society's programs. McConney stressed that there was no thought of attempting to bring clubs under Society control. The close cooperation existing today between the Society and the clubs dates from those meetings and has been fostered by a tradition of presidential visits to clubs that have extended such invitations.

In his November 1950 presidential address (*TSA* 2, 179), McConney described the clubs as having "an entirely different, but not contradictory, function from that of the Society." He mentioned that there were then more than fifteen clubs flourishing around the continent; subsequent *Yearbook* listings show that by 1965 the number of clubs (including the aforementioned CAS affiliates) had risen to thirty-two, and by 1980 to forty-two.

DATA FROM 1972 COMMITTEE STUDY

The "Club Profile" committee study of actuarial club activities released by the Society of Actuaries in 1972 included the following information (and a great deal more).

The total membership in the thirty reporting clubs was 4,136, the arithmetic mean being 138 and the median 89. On the one hand, the true totals were materially understated because of the four clubs that failed to report, two (Boston and Philadelphia) were large ones. On the other hand, there is a source of overstatement here in that many actuaries were members of more than one club.

The two largest clubs were New York (675) and Hartford (423); the smallest were Western Pennsylvania (8) and Little Rock (13).

In answering the committee's question, "Is the Club involved in the encouragement of actuarial courses at local colleges?" the following clubs answered affirmatively and gave the name of a college:

Name of Club	Name of College
Atlanta	Georgia State University
Des Moines	Drake University
Hartford	University of Connecticut
Indianapolis	Ball State University
Nebraska	University of Nebraska
Southwest	University of Texas
Twin Cities	University of Minnesota
Wisconsin	University of Wisconsin

Several clubs reported that they were funding fellowships or scholarships or otherwise promoting the actuarial profession at nearby educational institutions.

Chapter XIII.
THINKING STATISTICALLY

. . . and still the wonder grew,
That one small head could carry all he knew.

—Oliver Goldsmith (1770)

VIEWS ON MATHEMATICAL STATISTICS BY
NORTH AMERICAN ACTUARIES

It must first be realized that actuaries in the non-life and life fields have had different senses of urgency about bringing statistical theory into their practical work.

British actuary Robert E. Beard, in a 1978 book review, congratulated life company actuaries upon their good fortune in having, in the typical life table, a comfortably stable model from which to calculate premiums, and went on to say (*JIA* 105, 108, quoted in *The Actuary,* February, 1979):

> In [non-life] insurance many of the risks [are] unique and the concept of expectation has to be assessed in subjective terms. . . .

> For a great deal of non-life business the premium and claim expectation are linked by the subjective judgment of the underwriter. . . .

> The essential stochastic variable in life assurance is the time of payment of the event concerned and we know that in suitable circumstances this variability can be neutralized, so reducing the problem to deterministic terms. In non-life business we cannot eliminate the stochastic element, and our models must make specific allowance for it. If we attempt to use simple deterministic forms we may expect to find strange results.

William H. A. Carr in his 1967 book about the Insurance Company of North America, *Perils: Named and Unnamed,* told a story about that company's chief executive officer asking his actuary, Laurence H. Longley-Cook, in December 1953 whether he could predict the probability of two airliners colliding in mid-air (p. 342):

> Concluding [in a memorandum several days later] that the available data on airline accidents was sufficient to reach a prediction, Longley-Cook said that although there had been no mid-air collision of airliners causing fatalities or serious damage up to then, "it is possible to envisage an accident, involving the collision of two fully loaded passenger liners, where the total possible liability and property damage would be very great." . . .

> After touching briefly on the mathematical foundation for his solution, Longley-Cook stated the chances:

"Other conditions remaining equal, we may reasonably expect anything from 0
to 4 air carrier-to-air carrier collisions over the next ten years, and the possibility
of one such catastrophe involving [immense] damage is not so remote that it can
be ignored. In considering the adequacy of premium rates for air carrier business, the probability of losses on this scale should be taken into account. Further,
the protection of such an account by reinsurance ... seems essential."

Carr went on to explain that during the next seven years two such collisions
did happen—in June 1956 over the Grand Canyon and in December 1960 over
New York City.

Returning to the general topic of this chapter, "Thinking Statistically" is, as
Edward A. Lew* has put it, central to actuarial science because our discipline rests on
a body of knowledge about a variety of risks and on reasoning about them; this
knowledge comes to us largely in the form of statistics while the reasoning calls for
drawing conclusions from statistics. But recognizing and accepting this centrality come
more easily when the choice of the stochastic route is made obvious by the circumstances.

James C. Hickman has expressed the view that the sharp split between actuarial
science and statistics was a phenomenon of the twentieth century; before that almost all
actuaries considered themselves statisticians, and most of the giants of statistics were
also interested in actuarial problems. Hickman speculated that actuaries may have
become more interested in examinations than ideas, while statisticians were gaining
more satisfaction from planned experiments than from observational studies.

The respect of today's actuaries for the analytical achievements of our forebears of
three centuries ago can readily be established—or enhanced if that appreciation already
exists—by reviewing an English-language paper in the *Scandinavian Actuarial Journal,*
1987, pp. 4–18 by Anders Hald, "On the Early History of Life Insurance Mathematics."
A copy is available in the Society of Actuaries library.

Stuart Klugman has suggested that the use of mathematical statistics by the actuarial profession in North America may reasonably be classified into four areas:

1. Credibility, clearly an actuarial triumph (described later in this chapter).

2. Mortality estimation, including both the development of exposure formulas and
   certain graduation methods.

3. Risk theory, in which actuaries on this continent have built upon models developed
   by the Scandinavians.

4. Variability and error, subjects that have placed demands on the casualty actuary in
   computing loss reserves and more recently on the life insurance valuation actuary.
   The opportunity for students to develop early familiarity with this topic has been
   opened up by the publication in 1982 of advance releases from the textbook *Actuarial Mathematics* by Newton L. Bowers, Jr., Hans U. Gerber, James C. Hickman, Donald A. Jones, and Cecil J. Nesbitt.

---

* The author has gathered much of his material for this chapter through personal correspondence with several of the actuaries mentioned herein.

The Casualty Actuarial Society, in 1915, became the first North American actuarial body to include statistics on its syllabus. The Actuarial Society followed suit a decade later on the recommendation of a Council committee which stated, without recorded elaboration, that "an actuary should have at least some knowledge of statistics." Regrettably many Actuarial Society students were unclear on why they were studying the subject; the place of statistics in the kit of the practicing life actuary has proved to be controversial even into the 1970s and beyond. Robert W. Batten, challenging changes in the Society of Actuaries syllabus, said in November 1982 (*The Actuary,* March 1983) that "creation of an optional specialty exam covering advanced statistical techniques for types so inclined, would be a major step in the right direction." Michael J. Cowell, General Chairman of the Education and Examination Committee, responded in the same issue of *The Actuary,* asserting that the syllabus changes being implemented were "appropriate to the challenges that will face tomorrow's actuaries."

THE INFLUENCE OF R. A. FISHER

Reference to the work of an extraordinary British statistician, R. A. (later Sir Ronald) Fisher belongs in this account because of the influence of his book, *Statistical Methods for Research Workers,* first published in 1925. Originally controversial within the community of statisticians, it remained in print for half a century through nineteen editions. It introduced refined methods for gaining reliable information from small samples. The enlightenment it gave to interested actuaries in North America became significant after World War II.

The acquaintance of North American actuaries with developments such as Fisher's may be said to have begun when Professor Henry L. Rietz published *Mathematical Statistics,* an important American study, in 1927; this was reviewed that year by James W. Glover (*R.A.I.A.* 16, 125) and the following year by Hugh H. Wolfenden (*T.A.S.A.* 29, 139).

CREDIBILITY AND EXPERIENCE RATING

Charles C. Hewitt, Jr., FCAS, has labelled the analysis of credibility—meaning calculation of the partial recognition justifiably attributable to statistical findings from limited data—an "American idea"; he might well have called it a "CAS American idea." The Casualty Actuarial Society owes its founding to the search for actuarial principles underlying workmen's compensation insurance. Even the earliest papers in the 1912-1914 *T.A.S.A.* volumes were written by actuaries who shortly afterwards became founding members of the Casualty Actuarial Society.

Hewitt traced the mathematics of credibility thus:

> As data became available for the new [workmen's compensation] line of insurance the question was how to revise the previously established hypothetical rates to take account of this new evidence. In 1918 a group of casualty actuaries, led by Albert W. Whitney, conceived the idea of assigning weights in the linear expression:
>
> New Rate = (Credibility x Observed Rate) + [(1 - Credibility) x Old Rate]

At that time the contribution of Thomas Bayes (1702–1761), published posthumously in 1763 by the famous actuary Richard Price, had not been formally presented to the profession in North America. That analysis postulated that *a priori* probabilities could be assigned to several hypotheses, the probability of each outcome being then calculated for each hypothesis. Then, after one or more observations came to hand, the *a posteriori* probabilities could be calculated, thus conveying greater insight into the range of the true underlying probabilities.

Whitney's mathematics to determine the value of the term "Credibility" in the above-stated formula was implicitly Bayesian but limited to a specific *a priori* distribution and a specific random process. It produced the expression:

$$\text{Credibility} = \frac{\text{Number of Observations}}{\text{Number of Observations} + K}$$

where K was a positive constant to be determined from the underlying factors.

But in those days and for many years to come, mathematical statisticians as a whole—in particular, those subscribing to the Neyman-Pearson school whose influence predominated in the CAS debates—did not accept the Bayesian system of partial adjustment to new evidence; to them each hypothesis had to be either accepted or rejected on its own merits. For this reason and also because practicing actuaries were quickly faced with demands by buyers of large amounts of insurance that enjoyed better-than-average experience that their experience be given full credibility, much of the actuarial literature up to the 1960s sublimated the Bayesian approach to various devices for assigning 100% credibility (i.e., $K = 0$ in the Whitney formula) at the point at which practical competitive considerations seemed to make this necessary.

There were, however, notable exceptions. As the concept of credibility arose in group life insurance, Ralph Keffer (*T.A.S.A.* 30, 130) supported the application of Whitney's formula to that coverage, giving credit to Horace R. Bassford for having previously done so in *PCAS* 8, 307. The Bassford-Keffer method was Bayesian although not there introduced by that name. In 1940 a Bayesian approach to health insurance ratemaking was proposed in Sweden by Ova Lundborg. In 1950 Arthur L. Bailey (*PCAS* 37, 7) resurrected the mathematics of the 32-year-old Whitney paper and reaffirmed the underlying strength of the Bayesian roots of credibility theory in his influential paper, "Credibility Procedures—La Place's Generalization of Bayes' Rule and the Combination of Collateral Knowledge with Observed Data."

In the years 1960–1962, Bayesian approaches were applied to experience rating of private passenger automobile insurance by Lester Dropkin, Robert A. Bailey (Arthur L.'s son) and LeRoy J. Simon.

The renaissance of credibility via the Bayesian concept was assured by two actuaries—Hans Buhlmann in Switzerland and Allen L. Mayerson in North America. Mayerson contributed a paper, "A Bayesian View of Credibility" in 1964 (*P.C.A.S.* 51, 85) and five years later said, in his discussion of a paper by Ralph D. Maguire (*TSA* 21, 228):

> [M]ost members of the Casualty Actuarial Society, after using a semi-empirical approach to credibility for more than fifty years, are beginning to build a solid and consistent theoretical framework for credibility theory, using the statistical insights provided by the Savage de Finetti school of statistics.

In that discussion Mayerson enlightened Society of Actuaries members on work done by several actuaries mentioned above as well as by Francis S. Perryman in 1932, Laurence H. Longley-Cook in 1962, and Mayerson's colleagues Donald A. Jones and Newton L. Bowers.

In a paper, "Experience Rating and Credibility," published in a 1967 ASTIN Bulletin, Professor Buhlmann demonstrated that the K in the Whitney formula was:

$$K = \frac{\text{Variance of the Processes}}{\text{Variance of the Hypotheses}}$$

Since then the use of subjective probabilities has been increasingly accepted, at least theoretically. Many actuaries have explored the subject in the CAS *Proceedings*; Professor William S. Jewell at the University of California, Berkeley, has been prolific in research and publication, and actuaries in Europe and Australia have contributed admirably.

But practical application of the Whitney formula still lags behind the theoretical. The ideas are on record, however, and actuaries will not be the last to apply them.

OTHER APPLICATIONS OF BAYES' THEOREM

Donald C. Baillie in 1967 (*TSA* 19, 122) remarked that "actuaries are all basically Bayesian, whether they know it or not." Another of the applications to the solution of actuarial problems that justifies so sweeping a statement is that of graduation. Major coverage of graduation of mortality tables by statistical approaches is given in Hugh H. Wolfenden's 1942 volume *The Fundamental Principles of Mathematical Statistics,* Chapter XI, "An Outline of a Course in Graduation."

Also in 1967 (*TSA* 19, 66) Professors George S. Kimeldorf and Donald A. Jones presented a paper, "Bayesian Graduation." Professor Jones two years earlier (*TSA* 17, 33) had invited members' attention to the history and practice of Bayesian statistics, remarking in his conclusion (p. 54):

> I would liken statistical analysis to the black box of systems engineering (i.e., one feeds certain inputs into a black box in return for an output). The classical statistician has many black boxes, each bearing some of the labels "unbiased," "sufficient," "consistent," "efficient," "stringent," "uniformly most powerful," "asymptotically unbiased," ad infinitum. Each of his boxes has an intake hole at the top for the experimental data and an output hole at the right end. There is a warning on each box which says: "Use seriously only with k units or more of input." He would then offer you any of his boxes, counseling you that your choice should be based on the labels. The Bayesian has only one black

box—but it has three holes: an additional intake hole on the left for experience, information, and prior opinion.

I think actuaries should be among the most ardent welcomers and users of the Bayesians' one black box. In all their work and training actuaries emphasize that decisions are based on the data and judgment, but classical theories of statistics have never offered a place for, or required, a well-defined judgment factor.

Professor Jones' 1965 paper gives a bibliography (p. 56) listing twenty-three books and papers bearing upon his subject.

SOME NORTH AMERICAN LEADERS IN STATISTICAL APPROACHES TO ACTUARIAL PROBLEMS

In addition to the authors already mentioned in this chapter, the following stand out:

1937   Walter O. Menge, whose paper "A Statistical Treatment of Actuarial Functions" (*R.A.I.A.* 26, 65) tackled the practical problem of determining the amount of life insurance a company could safely retain on a single individual.

1942   Arthur L. Bailey, whom Thomas O. Carlson described at the Seventeenth International Congress (*TICA* 17, Vol. 3, 541) as "...probably the most profound contributor to casualty actuarial theory the United States has produced." Bailey's 1942 groundbreaking paper bore the title "Sampling Theory in Casualty Insurance" (*PCAS* 29, 50).

1964   Nathan F. Jones, one of whose contributions is an unpublished paper "Actuarial and Related Operations Models" prepared for the Tenth Annual and First International Meeting, Western Section, Operations Research Society of America, and dated September 14, 1964. This paper, now lodged in the archives of the Society of Actuaries, contains in an appendix a valuable list of source material, much of it by North American and British actuaries.

1964   James C. Hickman, among whose contributions was "A Statistical Approach to Premiums and Reserves in Multiple Decrement Theory" (*TSA* 16, 1).

Edward A. Lew labored for years as chairman of the Society of Actuaries Committee on Research; he was the moving spirit behind the Annual Research Conferences that started in 1966 for interested members of both the Society of Actuaries and the Casualty Actuarial Society. These meetings majored heavily on mathematical statistics, particularly, as judged by their titles, the following:

1966   Risk Theory and Multivariate Analysis

1967   Bayesian Statistics

1969   Analysis of Decisions under Uncertainty

1972   Time Series Analysis and Actuarial Applications

1974   Credibility Theory and Its Applications

1976   Multivariate Analysis

1979   Statistical Estimation

These and other authors and discussion leaders may be said to have earned the approval of British actuary W. S. B. Woolhouse, who in an 1873 paper "On the Philosophy of Statistics" (*JIA* 17, 37) had written regretfully of "the neglected logical science of statistics."

HEWITT'S STORY OF SINCLAIR LEWIS

Charles C. Hewitt, Jr., prefaced his contribution to this chapter with a story about a remark made publicly in the 1920s by author Sinclair Lewis, and the response it evoked from the pen of columnist Arthur Brisbane:

> "I do not believe there is a God," said Lewis (in substance). "If, in fact, there is one, let him strike me down here and now!"

> "Lewis, you poor misguided fool" wrote Brisbane (in substance). "You remind me of the ants who lived along the right-of-way of the Atchison, Topeka and Santa Fe Railroad. This colony of ants depended for its existence upon the crumbs thrown from the dining cars of the railroad trains as they passed by.

> "It came to pass that the ant colony fell upon hard times because—through chance—no crumbs were thrown out near its particular habitat. The situation became desperate and the colony decided to hold a meeting. It was suggested that they all pray to the president of the Atchison, Topeka and Santa Fe Railroad to send more dining cars so that crumbs would be thrown off in their area.

> "So they did pray and the following day they waited, but no crumbs were thrown off where they lived. So the ants concluded that there was no such person as the president of the Atchison, Topeka and Santa Fe Railroad."

Chapter XIV.

LAUGHING AT OURSELVES

[A] man who can't laugh and doesn't laugh—fundamentally—at himself, is not a humorist in the full sense.

—Irvin S. Cobb

Any serious material-gathering effort for a chapter on actuarial humor quickly engulfs the would-be retailer in quips, anecdotes and miscellaneous caprice. Much more than a chapter would be needed to do justice to the multitude of entertaining remarks to be found in the journals of the North American actuarial bodies.

It becomes necessary to limit this chapter's purpose to cataloguing rather than to narrating the amusing interludes that have enlivened a hundred years of meetings and twenty of newsletters. Even with this limitation, no more can be done than to record, with occasional particulars, some memorable contributions to the art of entertainment. Much of the material is quoted from personal correspondence with actuaries mentioned here.

As Matthew Rodermund, FCAS, himself a frequent contributor to the profession's light side, has remarked:

> The image of actuaries depicted on stage and screen, in books and comedy routines has been that of staid, humorless, unimaginative creatures, their minds immersed in numbers—lacking, it has been said *ad extremum,* the personality to be an accountant.
>
> But many of us humans are staid, humorless, and unimaginative. Why shouldn't some be actuaries?
>
> The truth is that color, humor, and imagination are found in actuaries as much as—dare we say, more than?—elsewhere. Those qualities have been revealed in speeches, in papers, in discussions, in hearty and uproarious unrecorded get-togethers. For some of these, alas, we must depend upon our own or somebody else's recollections.

THE LIGHT SIDE IN THE CASUALTY ACTUARIAL SOCIETY

Winfield W. Greene was a leading CAS charter member who frequently larded his speeches and papers with wit and humor. He also indulged in literary parody and wrote topical skits. Among his classics preserved in journals and archives are a fable, "The Actuary and the Grain of Truth," and a "Reinsurance Soliloquy." The latter's opening lines are:

> To cede, or not to cede; that is the question;
> Whether 'tis better in the end to suffer
> The Casualties and Claims of hazard and catastrophe
> Or take precaution 'gainst their sea of troubles
> And by reinsuring ease them?

Clarence W. Hobbs, the Society's editor from 1933 to 1943 and a versifier in his own right, frequently joined Greene in producing skits. His notable contribution, "The Lady Casualty and Her Servitors," presented at the twenty-fifth anniversary dinner in 1939 (*PCAS* 26, 168), was in thirty-three verses; the following give the flavor:

> And I fell for the tale of the blithesome dame, and I got me up behind,
> And for the ensuing sixteen years I've labored my step to mind
> In the company true of the goodly crew who labor in every season
> To try to keep the masterless jade within a rule of reason.

> For this is what my Lady said as we started on our ride:

> . . .

> "Most serious-minded men are they, yet not without sense and wit.
> They believe in truth, and they tell it, too—whenever their bosses permit.
> They believe in reason, that golden dream, and close-knit logic true.
> They even believe in their formulas—so they may believe in you."

> "Graphs and factors of many kinds, statistics and tabulations,
> Loss-ratios, rate-levels, manual rules and oodles of classifications,
> Differential equations, and interpolations, and Charlier's curves, indeed,
> These shall be to you as an open book that will put you asleep to read."

Greene, Sydney D. Pinney, Charles J. Haugh, Thomas O. Carlson, Dudley M. Pruitt, Charles C. Hewitt, Jr., and Frederick W. Kilbourne—were all CAS presidents who brought light touches to their performances. Pinney, who was blind, is remembered fondly for his 1943 presentation (*PCAS* 30, 91), asking:

> *What* is so peculiar about an actuary?

> What *is* so peculiar about an actuary?

> What is *so* peculiar about an actuary?

> What is so *peculiar* about an actuary?

> What is so peculiar about an *actuary?*

Pinney answered each question with emphasis on the key word, in, said Pruitt (*PCAS* 51, 179), "a measured speech of well over a half hour completely from memory and in the most delightful spirit."

In 1951 (*PCAS* 38, 9) Carlson opened each section (and there were many) of his paper, "Rate Regulation and the Casualty Actuary" with a pertinent quotation. Pruitt, in his review of the paper at the next meeting, responded in kind.

Hewitt wrote profound papers on profound subjects, but his presentations never seemed profound. He warmed up his audience and carried them along with appropriate anecdotes; an example appears at the end of Chapter XIII.

Kilbourne's ability to disarm his listeners and readers has won their attention to his serious ideas. He also likes to needle the profession. In *The Actuarial Review* (August 1984), deciding that actuaries needed more exposure to culture, he asserted that "the professional life of the actuary may rival television as a vast cultural wasteland" and hence introduced his colleagues to allegedly classical poetry with actuarial relevance. Two of his poems follow:

On credibility:

> Flightily, mightily
> Art, Duke of Wellington
> Bettered Napoleon
> At Waterloo;
> Proving forever his
> Superiority—
> Or was it luck? Or some
> Blend of the two?

On risk classification:

> Jiggery, pokery
> Ludwig van Beethoven,
> Brilliant composer in
> Spite of much strife:
> Where are the roots of such
> Super creativeness?
> Forged at conception, or
> Molded by life?

Rodermund, in 1959, began a series of entertainments at CAS meetings. Those diversions included skits spoofing ratemaking procedures, programs of song parodies, and take-offs on musical theater.

His first skit ("Of All Sad Words") imagined a rate hearing following an insurance commissioner's refusal to approve a *reduction* in rates. All the usual arguments were reversed. Another ("Son of Of All Sad Words"), had a large fire and casualty company petitioning a commissioner for a rate increase in all lines to recoup its investment losses.

In "How To Succeed as an Actuary," inspired by the Broadway show "How To Succeed in Business Without Really Trying," Rodermund entertained CAS members in 1973 and at the ASTIN 1977 meeting, with parodies such as:

> I am the very model of a smart insurance president;
> I'm eloquent and diligent and properly benevolent.
> . . .
> I've built enough capacity to guard against catastrophe;
> And analyzed a bond to every comma and apostrophe;
> I know the reinsurance game as if it were the alphabet;
> But I don't know why I haven't made an underwriting profit yet.

And, to the tune of "Carolina in the Morning," the underwriters chided the actuaries, singing:

> What can be as scary as an eager actuary in the morning?
> . . .
> Read the ASTIN bulletin, it gives you a chill,
> And, says the underwriter, it will
> Make you more than wary of a hairy actuary in the morning.

to which a chorus of actuaries responded:

> Who could be contriter than an errant underwriter in the morning?

In 1964 (*PCAS* 51, 126), Rodermund in "How To Tell a Pure Actuary from a Lay Actuary," gave such tests for making that distinction as the following:

> Any paper whose mathematical demonstration includes a χ^2 test is a paper written by a pure actuary. On the other hand, any paper whose mathematical demonstration is consummated by an expression in x^2 is a paper written by a lay actuary.
>
> A discussion of an actuarial problem that includes the word "stochastic" is a discussion by a pure actuary. A discussion in which the favorite descriptive term is "fantastic" is probably a discussion by a lay actuary.

His parody on E. B. White's "How to Tell a Major Poet from a Minor Poet," ended with White's own words:

> The truth is, it is fairly easy to tell the two types apart; it is only when one sets about trying to decide whether what they write is any good or not that the thing becomes complicated.

THE LIGHT SIDE IN THE ACTUARIAL SOCIETY OF AMERICA

The presumptive ancestor of all North American actuarial anecdotes was told by Israel C. Pierson at the Actuarial Society's inaugural dinner on April 25, 1889. Although macabre, its intent was serious—to buttress Pierson's warning that premiums then being charged might prove insufficient. We have slightly modified the printed text—revision in italics—to take care of ambiguity attributable either to transcription or to the lateness of the evening (*T.A.S.A.* 1, Pt. 1, 48):

> That is like the poor fellow who had lost his leg on the battle-field, and, while bleeding to death, accosted a cavalryman who was riding by, and begged him to take him on his horse to the surgeon's headquarters: the cavalryman consented to do it, put him on his horse, and said: "Grip me tight around the waist, and I will take you as fast as I can to the surgeon's headquarters"; and he went as fast as he could, but on the way a cannon ball came along and took the poor fellow's head off. When he got to headquarters *the horseman* said to the surgeon, "Here is a poor fellow I picked up on the battle-field; he has lost his leg and is bleeding to death." The surgeon looked at him and said, "Why he hasn't any head." The cavalryman turned his head to look and said, "Why, the infernal liar, he said he had only lost his leg." Moral: The expenses take the leg and blood of the premium, then the mortality decapitates what remains.

For some years after that, examples of humor in the *Transactions* were few—not because our forebears always took themselves seriously but because informal discussions and particularly after-dinner remarks were not printed. The 1943 obituary of John K. Gore, an 1896 member who was president in 1908–1909 remarked of him (*T.A.S.A.* 44, 449):

> His sense of humor, coupled with his ability to maintain a perfectly sober countenance, was unexpectedly delightful and elusive. The combination of his humor and his mathematical sense of form and structure enabled him to attain to considerable skill in the construction of humorous verse. His parody

"They've decided to expand eligibility for certifying reserves. Requirements have now been met by a number of CPAs, math professors, and two software salesmen."

"They just adopted a resolution barring actuaries from signing their own tax returns."

"I'm sorry, sir — he's not accepting calls. He's working on his reserve review."

"I only suggested that, at 14% yield, it didn't make good business sense to pay claims — and he fired me!"

Samples of cartoons in *The Actuarial Review*, poking gentle fun at the actuarial image, by Stephen L. Christiansen, FCAS.

on "Danny Deever" is a classic to most of the older members of the Society, and as a young man he contributed on several occasions to the humorous paper "Life."

That members in the early days preferred that the proceedings be lightened from time to time is indicated by recollections of the 1895 Society meeting voiced by Robert W. Huntington, who was then attending his first such meeting. In 1939 (*T.A.S.A.* 40, 124) he said:

> The First Vice President at that time was Mr. Emory McClintock, a large impressive man wearing mustache and goatee, quite formal in his manner and appearance, earnest and kindly. His knowledge was wide, his judgment excellent, his ability distinguished. I always had the feeling that he had one trait in common with the late President [Charles William] Eliot of Harvard, who,

when walking home from a meeting of a certain pundits' club with Dean [Le Baron Russell] Briggs, remarked, "That was a particularly good meeting—no humor."

By May 1927 Society President Edward E. Rhodes commented (*T.A.S.A.* 28, 1):

> [T]he control of the Society's affairs is passing to the younger members. This is as it should be, however disconcerting to some of us. . . . The situation is not one of foreboding.

It seems clear that in the 1920s the awe on the part of the younger members toward their elders was fading. Two amusing incidents, five years apart, support this conclusion.

The then twenty-one-year-old Oswald Jacoby reported about the May 1924 meeting (*The Actuary,* February 1970, "Excerpts From Diary of a Young Actuary"):

> Monday . . . Finally old enough to attend a meeting. Off to French Lick tomorrow for first joint meeting of Society and Institute. They expect almost 200 and I have orders to join in the discussion of one of the papers and get myself known.

> Might as well be hung for a sheep as a lamb so will take on Arthur Hunter and his current paper on mortality.

> Tuesday noon . . . Aboard one of two special cars from New York. . . . [H]ope we can organize a poker game.

> Tuesday midnight . . . Poker game did develop. Twenty dollars ahead at dime limit after paying for cards and refreshments; some sort of record. . . .

> Wednesday 7 P.M. . . . Good afternoon. Discovered Brown Hotel which looked like a gambling house and was. Ran my twenty to a hundred. . . . John Larus got me into a croquet game with two of the grandees, A. A. Welch and E. E. Rhodes. . . . Hope I will be as young as they are if and when I reach their age. [Welch at the time was 64, Rhodes 56—Jacoby lived to 81.] . . .

> Thursday 7 P.M. . . . Gave my discussion this morning. Instead of an Olympian blast, [Hunter's] reply was that he had arrived at the same conclusions I had some time back and was waiting for more statistics before presenting them. . . .

> Thursday 10 P.M. . . . Saw Mr. [James D.] Craig before dinner and asked permission to leave meeting early. Not only did he let me go but told me to take Monday off if I felt like it. . . . After dinner, I organized reinsurance pool of twenty actuaries who contributed a dollar each to my twenty. We proceeded en masse to Brown Hotel and after an hour of careful play we liquidated with 200% profit. . . .

> Friday on train. Certainly proud to be an actuary. They are a wonderful group of old men. . . .

The second relevant episode, at the Society's fortieth anniversary meeting (May 1929 in New York City) suggests that some senior actuaries were still inclined to stand on their dignity. After the customary dinner, some Hartford actuaries staged a skit depicting a meeting of "The Actuarial Society of Liberia." The script, believed to have been written by John R. Larus and William H. Burling, was skillfully designed to tease their elders who were present. The names of the Liberian actuaries were themselves take-offs on the targeted seniors:

Arthur Hunter	=	Art Murmur Bunter
Henry Moir	=	Hence Ever More
Thomas B. Macaulay	=	Thomas Make-All-He-Can
Robert Henderson	=	Robert Hindersome
Wendell M. Strong	=	Gosh But I'm Strong

These are the recollections of actuaries who were there; sadly, the script has not survived. The writers took advantage of Hunter's pomposity by being particularly hard on him; "Bunter" was president of the Liberian body and opened the meeting by announcing that ten papers would be presented— nine by himself, the tenth by "Hindersome."

The playlet caused a sensation; Hunter was incensed; a public apology was recommended and was given the following morning.

A story about Oswald Jacoby has come in via George B. Swick, contributed by Mr. Orton H. Hicks of Dartmouth College, participant in the incident. As told by Mr. Hicks:

> In the fall of 1941 I became a dollar-a-year man with the War Production Board. I was assigned an office in the old District of Columbia Jail. It contained an old-fashioned double desk. For a week I wondered who my "roommate" would be. He soon appeared: the fabled Oswald Jacoby!
>
> Ozzie and I became good friends, but saw little of each other socially. I had one or two chances a month to play bridge with him, and I knew well enough always to let him ask me.
>
> About seven o'clock one Monday morning as I was getting off the sleeper from New York someone behind me shouted my name. It was Ozzie, saying: "I hope you can have dinner and play bridge tonight about six at the Army Navy Club." I allowed that I could.
>
> When I reached the Club I found Ozzie already with two Vice Admirals; I am sure I had never seen anyone of that rank before. When we sat down for bridge I discovered it was a set game against the Admirals at half a cent a point—rather steep stakes in those days.
>
> About eleven o'clock the game ended with Oswald and Hicks each losing about $25. Afterward I apologized to Ozzie for letting him down and offered to pay his loss as well as mine, whereupon he slapped me on the back with great glee. "Ort, you still don't get the pitch. For six months I have been trying to get a commission in Naval Intelligence, most of that time working to set up a bridge game with the officer who was on your left, Vice Admiral Train who is in charge of Naval Intelligence. As I left Washington on Friday the Admiral's secretary phoned to say he was available for bridge tonight. All weekend I was trying to figure out who would be my ideal partner. I needed someone who knew the rudiments of the game, would be trying hard every minute, but with whom I would be sure to lose!"
>
> Ozzie was deadly serious and he was 100% right. Three weeks later he had his commission.

P.S. Years later when I told this story to a friend of Ozzie's, his response was unexpected: "Ort, it is Ozzie who owes you the $25. I can guarantee he knew exactly what undetectable mistakes to make so that your team would lose, and lose almost exactly $25. Stop blaming yourself!"

THE LIGHT SIDE IN THE AMERICAN INSTITUTE OF ACTUARIES

The *Record* of the American Institute consists heavily of informal discussions, many of them containing flashes of wit. Here are three by way of illustration.

In 1941 (*R.A.I.A.* 30, 462) Harry M. Sarason gave actuarial students many helpful hints on how to pass the examinations. In closing he gave solace to any of his readers who failed an examination three times by advising:

It is nothing to bother about if you are not suited for actuarial examination passing. ....All of us have our weak spots. The classic example is of a janitor in the school system who was fired because he couldn't write. ...He finally got into politics and became mayor of his city. Someone, on just learning of his illiteracy, exclaimed: "What would you have been if you had been able to read and write?" The answer was: "I know what I would have been, I would have been a janitor."

In November 1943, Charles A. Spoerl, discussing the fifth paper by prolific author Simon Shannon on the theory of automatic premium loan approximations, and desiring to head off the possibility that a sixth might ever be written, gave his response entirely in verse (*R.A.I.A.* 32, 431):

In his wigwam, Hiawatha
Read the words of Mr. Shannon,
Pondered long and pondered deeply,
Then he muttered certain comments.
"Why does Mr. Simon Shannon
Keep on solving this equation
Making new approximations
Always new approximations?
What is needed is a system
To distinguish 8 from 9 days,
26 from 27,
92 from 93 days
Like the one of Mr. Keffer
In the pages of *The Record*.

All these fine approximations
Do not really solve the problem,
If they make a 1-day error,
Just a little 1-day error,
Just a tiny 1-day error.
For the question is a problem
In the Theory of Numbers,
Whole and undivided numbers."

In his wigwam, Hiawatha
Put aside the Loan equation,
Closed the book, perhaps, forever.

Sadly, this unique discussion was not delivered verbally, the November 1943 meeting having been cancelled because of wartime travel restrictions. But Shannon got the last word: In his author's review he quietly set forth a sixth approximate method.

At the dissolution ceremonies of the American Institute in June 1949, Lawrence M. Cathles, describing differences in outlook between actuaries of that body and those of the Actuarial Society, said (*R.A.I.A.* 38, 121):

From the first the Institute had its own western individuality. Its meetings were sometimes rather rowdy and informal, but they were always friendly. . . .

The western actuary had to learn to talk insurance in a language which a western company officer, agent, or policyholder could understand. . . . [S]ometimes he even had to look actuarial theories straight in the face and pass them by. I confess doing that myself in an attempt to prove to my then company's biggest producer that a big case he had should stay declined. I told him it wasn't a 50-50 proposition, as he seemed to think. I explained to him that the most the company expected to make on its insurance business was about $2.00 a thousand. So, if he was right, the company might make $40 or $50 a year profit; but, if we were right, the company would have to pay the full $20,000 insurance very soon, almost certainly within ten years, so the company was betting $20,000 against $500 or less. I explained that when we gave such odds we had to be careful, and he then said: "Gosh, I never realized that. O.K."

THE LIGHT SIDE IN THE SOCIETY OF ACTUARIES

The first twenty years of the Society of Actuaries may rightly be identified as the heyday for actuarial humorists and their many admirers. Members who attended meetings regularly knew who the humorists were, and since the practice was for discussers to move forward to the front of the hall awaiting their turn, it was easy to see that an Andrew C. Webster, an Edmund M. McConney or a Harold R. Lawson—to name three among many—was about to give the audience a treat.

Regrettably, few of these gems turned up in the *Transactions*. For example, the 1958 discussions of Webster and Victor E. Henningsen on the pros and cons of the newly developed family plan recorded in *TSA* 10, D71 and D73 give no clue to the event as recollected by Samuel E. Shaw:

We watched what felt like a Gilbert and Sullivan performance with endless encores. The new product had aroused the passions of those actuaries; each man (Henningsen doubting, Webster enthusiastic) refused to give each other the last word and exchanged argument and repartee until fatigue brought a truce. They succeeded in giving the impression that the future of the industry was at stake.

Shaw recalls also the 1961 discussion of a paper by Edward A. Green in *TSA* 13, 320:

One of the first discussers gracefully acknowledged the paper's literary quality but attributed its form and scholarship to Mrs. Green who was in the audience. From then on, speaker after speaker paid homage to Mrs. Green who after recovering from her initial embarrassment appeared to be either accepting the tributes or enjoying the protracted episode as much as the audience did.

Another popular humorist was Milton J. Goldberg, one of the tallest actuaries, who had earned his reputation in premerger days for his classic discussion of B. Franklin Blair's paper, "Relations Between the Average Amount of Insurance per Policy and the Height and the Weight of the Insured" (*R.A.I.A.* 30, 197). Undoubtedly by prearrangement, Goldberg was followed immediately to the podium by William O. Morris speaking entertainingly as a representative of the undersized actuaries.

Goldberg was an actuary in his company's agency department, so many of his amusing scripts appear in journals of the Life Insurance Agency Management Association (LIAMA, now LIMRA). On the same circuit at the same time was Ernest J. Moorhead who in 1953 added the word *auktuary* to life insurance terminology in a 1953 address in the LIAMA *Proceedings* mocking the supposed concern among actuaries that they were about to be superseded by computers:

> The Auk was a queer bird with low mentality and peculiar habits, that became extinct just a century ago, in 1853. You are now looking at a specimen of another queer bird called an Auk-tuary. This species exists and multiplies in the moss and underbrush of life insurance companies, and appears to be thriving. Nevertheless, it too is doomed to disappear due to the advent of marvellous machines called High Speed Electronic Sequence-Controlled Digital Computers, or, more spectacularly, Giant Brains.

> Forty years ago the automobile first scared the horse to death, and then made him obsolete. Exactly the same thing is now happening to the Auk-tuary. The horse became useful only for wagering purposes and for producing other horses—so doubtless it is destined for the Auk-tuary.

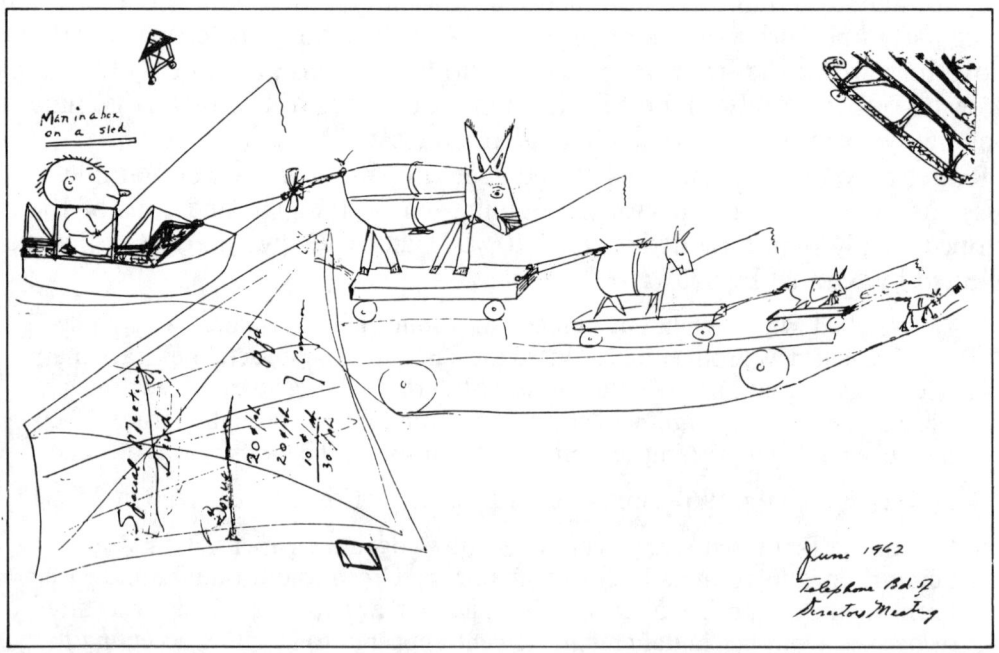

James A. Hamilton, FSA, was a talented doodler. This sample, drawn during a telephone conference of directors of the Wyatt Company in 1962, may, says Frank L. Griffin, have a hidden meaning.

It was not until *The Actuary* began publication under Webster's editorship in 1967 that a reasonably good record of instances of actuarial humor began to be preserved. The following is just a sampling of many enjoyable quips and stories accumulated from that source and others:

Two parodies of W. S. Gilbert, the first by Webster, the second by Morton A. Laird:

> As a young Scots lad I served a term
> As office boy in an insurance firm.
> I quickly became a junior clerk
> With an innate talent for avoiding work.
> At avoiding work I grew so wary
> That I qualified, son, as an Act-Uary.

* * *

> Your thought is a good one, we'll study it well,
> In Committee, Committee, Committee.
> And on every aspect will thoughtfully dwell,
> In Committee, Committee, Committee.
> If you wistfully ask why you've had no reply
> To the question you raised back in early July,
> In due course you will get an evasive reply,
> From Committee, Committee, Committee.

Some definitions of actuaries by actuaries:

> An actuary is a person who can influence people without winning friends.

* * *

> An actuary, ladies, is a man who till the end of his days can always name the date he first met you, and the date he first kissed you. A smart actuary is one who arranges for those two to be the same date.

Two more items on the popular topic of actuarial osculation:

> Girl to absentminded actuary:

> Am I the first girl you ever kissed?

> Now that you mention it, you do look familiar.

* * *

> It takes but just a moment, lad
> To give your wife a peck
> And it's mighty good insurance
> To avoid an auto wreck.
> For figures plainly show, lad
> That each time you leave the house
> You risk a tangled fender
> If you fail to kiss your spouse.

THE LIGHT SIDE IN THE CANADIAN INSTITUTE OF ACTUARIES

An encyclopedia of Canadian actuarial humor has already been compiled. The compiler was Frank P. DiPaolo; he accomplished this in November 1971 by organizing a meeting of the Younger Actuaries Section of the Canadian Institute devoted to the topic "Actuarial Feats and Foibles," and persuading Benjamin T. Holmes, George Ryrie and Arthur Pedoe to be the speakers.

The resulting script totalled forty pages—eighteen each by Holmes and Ryrie, and four by Pedoe. Pedoe, however, had already, in November 1960, addressed a life insurance meeting on the topic "Life Insurance Stories—True or False or Just Amusin'" (nine pages) and used some of that material.

The whole wide-ranging packet of forty-nine pages has found a worthy place in the archives of the Society of Actuaries. Here is given just one sample contributed by each of these actuaries:

> [Benjamin T. Holmes] Just before Christmas 1931 a letter reached my company's actuarial department from an agent in Winnipeg who had been canvassing a difficult prospect. The topic of the bases of life insurance had arisen and the agent had dilated on the mathematical wizardry of his actuaries in Toronto. "Very well," said the prospect, "I have a little problem which your mathematical wizards will no doubt find simple to answer. What are the factors of seventeen ones (i.e. 111111, etc.) in a row?"

> We replied that the problem would no doubt be easy for us to solve, but we were now in the midst of year-end work and it would be some time before we could give it our attention. As time permitted in succeeding months we spared no effort to find the answer. Machine time, books, advice from other actuaries, assistance of the University of Toronto mathematics department were utilized—all to no avail. Since no more was heard from Winnipeg, we quietly shelved the whole project in the autumn of 1932.

> Twelve years later, thumbing through a book of mathematical puzzles, imagine my excitement on reading, "The number composed of 17 ones has only two divisors 2,071,723 and 5,363,222,357"; apparently an Arabian mathematician had published them in the first half of the 13th century.

> Another three years passed, when an anonymous letter arrived, stating that the number of Malaysians was known to be 2,071,723 and the average number of hairs on the head of a Malaysian was established at 5,363,222,357, and asking, "What is your actuarial opinion of the total number of hairs in Malaysia?" We of course could not respond to that enquiry, and decided that no useful purpose would be served by forwarding our findings to Winnipeg.

* * *

> [George Ryrie: about his own entry into the profession in Toronto in 1923] While attending night school to polish off my Grade 13 mathematics, I met a chap who said he intended to become an actuary because a qualified actuary would get $10,000 a year—I was earning $10 a week so it made some impression. What impressed me more was that there was a course of study and examinations but it was essential to work for a life insurance company.

> Confederation Life had previously turned me down because I didn't know what an actuary was. Thereafter—despite my new-found facility with the word "actuary" courtesy of Webster's Dictionary— two other brilliant companies turned me down—the Canada and Manufacturers. North American

Life fortunately looked favourably on my application—but within a month I found that the chief actuary's salary at North American Life was only $7,000.

When I told my friends I wanted to become an actuary, I was met with the cynical comment, "You can either become an actuary or stay normal."

As I moved through the exams, I became the chief underwriter—not by a process of training but just overnight. Seven years in that capacity were upsetting in some ways but on later reflection, provided the most educational experience a young actuary could have had. I heard a lot about actuaries. One frustrated agent said to me about our chief actuary, "I know he's not bad enough to be put away in a mental institution but I'm darned sure if he were already in one, he wouldn't be let out."

Then I moved into a facet of agency work and more abrasion and more education. Literally, out of the frying pan into the fire. I fully appreciated the story of the five-year old daughter who was being punished by having to eat her supper alone at a small table in a corner of the dining room. She wasn't allowed to talk and nobody paid much attention to her until she was heard saying this blessing: "Thank you, Dear Lord, for preparing a table before me in the presence of mine enemies."

In these experiences as an underwriter and an agency actuary, I still had responsibility for the Actuarial Department; in our small company everybody had several jobs. But, in the Actuarial Department, we could chuckle at some of the more sophisticated humour about our profession. For instance:

> Experts in poor morbidity,
> Valuations and liquidity,
> We never can explain them without hearing bawdy yelps.
> Though we're terribly sincere,
> It seems we're somewhat queer,
> We don't have to be crazy but we know darn well it helps!

* * *

[Arthur Pedoe] The following may be the oldest story in life insurance. But someone has to hear it for the first time. Also let us not pretend we are so old that we can't chuckle again at an old chestnut.

Hubby died, and going through his papers his widow found a life insurance policy for $5,000 dated at the time of their marriage. How wonderful of him! She hurried to order a large tombstone extolling his virtues and ending with: "Rest in Peace." A claim was filed, but alas! The insurance company informed her that the policy had lapsed years ago, only one premium having been paid. It was too late to cancel the tombstone order but she had added to "Rest in Peace"— "Till We Meet Again."

The fact that the Canadian Institute from the outset staggered the United States actuaries by using the abbreviation "CIA" caused Ernest R. Vogt to suggest (*The Actuary*, March 1969) that the abbreviation "CANINACT" be used instead. Ardian Gill in response (May 1969 issue) proposed adopting the four beginning and four ending letters of the entire title, producing "CANARIES."

THE LIGHT SIDE IN THE CONFERENCE OF ACTUARIES
IN PUBLIC PRACTICE

H. Raymond Strong has contributed his "most unforgettable experience" as having occurred while he presided at CAPP's banquet at the Continental Plaza Hotel, Chicago, in 1964:

> The Program Committee had warned me that an unusual ending was planned and that I should not be alarmed, no matter how unusual it might appear.

> The program ending, of which I knew nothing, was for the after dinner speaker to be interrupted by a beautiful but very "high" lady coming up the aisle to the rostrum waving her hand and observing loudly that we had had enough of that nonsense and should get on with something more exciting. This she did to perfection, and was hustled out of the room only to reappear at another entrance and do the same thing. After about three of these interruptions, the guest speaker (as planned) threw his sheaf of papers into the air and stalked off the platform.

> The audience was expected by this time to have caught on to the joke and to be holding its sides with laughter. Not so! The speech had been so interesting, the actors so good, that not a smile was cracked; half the crowd left the room and the prevailing feeling was that the organization had been affronted. Some wanted to banish the whole program committee from the membership. Order was never restored that evening; I'm sure it will be a cold day in July before another such "unusual ending" will be undertaken.

The Conference also had its poets. One of them, David L. Hewitt in 1975, came up with an ode of sorts to ERISA (*Academy Newsletter*, Vol. 4, No. 4, September 1975):

> ERISA, while it does much good,
> 'S administrative monsterhood.
> It's too ambitious and complex,
> And has no element of sex.
> EROS, God of Love, abhorred
> ERIS, Goddess of Discord. . . .
>
> To comprehend this Act and then
>   to write the regulations,
> Cannot be done within the time.
>   It will take generations.
> The paperwork will drag us down,
>   the [X]erox belching endless.
> There won't be time to read the rules
>   the bureaucrats must send us.

THE LIGHT SIDE OF GUEST PRESENTATIONS

So many overseas guests have delighted us North Americans with the range and gentleness of their humor that it is appropriate to close with a sample from the lips of Dr. Hans Ammeter, president of the Swiss Actuarial Association (*The Actuary*, December 1971):

> To retain this day in memory and to demonstrate our special friendship to your Society, I have brought with me a small present. It is a pewter jug with a set of six matching goblets and a platter. The jug bears the inscription:

PRESENTED TO THE SOCIETY OF ACTUARIES BY SWISS ACTUARIAL ASSOCIATION 1971.

I suppose many of you may have read that some of the most fascinating traditions in Switzerland have something or other to do with eating. Nevertheless, as you can see for yourselves, this jug and the goblets have nothing to do with eating but only with drinking.

In Spring each year the guilds [of Switzerland] organize a festival to celebrate the death of the winter and the reawakening of nature. A great traditional procession finally stops at a big fire at which a bogey representing the winter is symbolically burnt. The fire, of course, produces an immense thirst. This thirst is then quenched as best one can in the cellars of the guild, where the wine is poured out of just this type jug. I have been told that on these occasions people drink slightly more than is strictly necessary to quench the thirst.

As the potential of thirst varies, there are naturally different sizes and dimensions of pewter jugs. We considered that for our American and Canadian friends a large-size jug would probably be more suitable, since the enormous tasks of the President and his Committee Members must necessarily lead to very dry throats and to a corresponding degree of thirst.

I believe this meeting must have imposed considerable burden on these gentlemen. I should straight away act as a fireman and conduct a fire drill. Let me, therefore, pour Swiss wine into these goblets here and ask you, gentlemen, to drink with me "to the Society of Actuaries and its members—and more particularly to our ladies.

"May this toast be a symbol of friendship between our countries and our Association!"

Acronyms & Abbreviations

AAA	- American Academy of Actuaries
A.A.I.A.	- Associate of the American Institute of Actuaries
A.A.S.	- Associate of the Actuarial Association of America
ACA	- Associate of the Conference of Actuaries in Public Practice
ACAS	- Associate of the Casualty Actuarial Society
ACE	- Automatic Computing Engine
ACIA	- Associate of the Canadian Institute of Actuaries
ACLI	- American Council of Life Insurance
AERF	- Actuarial Education and Research Fund
AFA	- Associate of the Faculty of Actuaries
AFAA	- Associate of the Fraternal Actuarial Association
AIA	- Associate of the Institute of Actuaries
AICPA	- American Institute of Certified Public Accountants
AIFA	- Association of Insurance and Financial Analysts
AIPSO	- Automobile Insurance Plans Service Office
ALC	- American Life Convention
ALIMDA	- Association of Life Insurance Medical Directors of America
AM	- American Men (Mortality Table)
APB	- Actuarial Principles Board
ARC	- Actuarial Restructuring Committee
ASA	- Associate of the Society of Actuaries
ASPA	- American Society of Pension Actuaries
ASTIN	- Actuarial Studies in Non-Life Insurance
ASWORG	- Anti-Submarine Warfare Operations Research Group (U.S. Navy)
CAA	- Canadian Association of Actuaries
CAPP	- Conference of Actuaries in Public Practice
CAS	- Casualty Actuarial Society
CASSA	- Casualty Actuarial and Statistical Society of America
CIA	- Canadian Institute of Actuaries
CPC	- Certified Pension Consultant
CPI	- Consumer Price Index
CRVM	- Commissioners Reserve Valuation Method
CSI	- Commissioners Standard Industrial (Mortality Table)
CSO	- Commissioners Standard Ordinary (Mortality Table)
DJI	- Dow-Jones Industrial (stock price index)
DN	- *Disability Newsletter*
EA	- Enrolled Actuary
ENIAC	- Electronic Numerical Integrator and Calculator
ERISA	- Employee Retirement Income Security Act of 1974

ETS	- Educational Testing Service
F.A.I.A.	- Fellow of the American Institute of Actuaries
F.A.S.	- Fellow of the Actuarial Society of America
FASB	- Financial Accounting Standards Board
FCA	- Fellow of the Conference of Actuaries in Public Practice
FCAS	- Fellow of the Casualty Actuarial Society
FCIA	- Fellow of the Canadian Institute of Actuaries
FFA	- Fellow of the Faculty of Actuaries
FFAA	- Fellow of the Fraternal Actuarial Association
FIA	- Fellow of the Institute of Actuaries
FSA	- Fellow of the Society of Actuaries
FSPA	- Fellow of the American Society of Pension Actuaries
GAAP	- Generally Accepted Accounting Principles
HMO	- Health Maintenance Organization
HOLUA	- Home Office Life Underwriters Association
IAA	- International Actuarial Association
IACA	- International Association of Consulting Actuaries
ILI	- Institute of Life Insurance
IRIS	- Insurance Regulatory and Information System
IRS	- Internal Revenue Service
JAAA	- *Journal of the American Academy of Actuaries*
JIA	- *Journal of the Institute of Actuaries*
LIAA	- Life Insurance Association of America
LIAMA	- Life Insurance Agency Management Association
LIMRA	- Life Insurance Marketing and Research Association
LISRB	- Life Insurance Sales Research Bureau
LOMA	- Life Office Management Association
MAAA	- Member of the American Academy of Actuaries
MAMI	- Medico-Actuarial Mortality Investigation
MCA	- Member of the Conference of Actuaries in Public Practice
MSPA	- Member of the American Society of Pension Actuaries
NAIC	- National Association of Insurance Commissioners
NALU	- National Association of Life Underwriters
NCIC	- National Convention of Insurance Commissioners
NFC	- National Fraternal Congress
OASDI	- Old Age, Survivors and Disability Insurance
OEG	- Operations Evaluation Group
ORG	- Operations Research Group (U.S. Navy)
PBGC	- Pension Benefit Guaranty Corporation
PCAPP	- *Proceedings of the Conference of Actuaries in Public Practice*
PCAS	- *Proceedings of the Casualty Actuarial Society*
PCIA	- *Proceedings of the Canadian Institute of Actuaries*
PFAA	- *Proceedings of the Fraternal Actuarial Association*
R.A.I.A.	- *Record of the American Institute of Actuaries*

RSA - *Record of the Society of Actuaries*
SEC - Securities and Exchange Commission
SOA - Society of Actuaries
SOFASIM - Society of Actuaries Simulation Model
SSA - Social Security Administration
T.A.S.A. - *Transactions of the Actuarial Society of America*
TFA - *Transactions of the Faculty of Actuaries*
TICA - *Transactions of the International Congress of Actuaries*
TSA - *Transactions of the Society of Actuaries*
UNIVAC - Universal Automatic Computer

BIBLIOGRAPHY

Actuarial Society of America. *American—Canadian Mortality Investigation*. 2 vols. New York: A.S.A. with the Cooperation of the A.I.A. and the NCIC, 1918–1919.

_____. *Problems and Solutions, Associateship Examinations, Parts I and II, 1915–1919*. New York: A.S.A., 1921.

_____. *Report of Committee on Joint Investigation of Experience of American and Canadian Companies with Reference to Total and Permanent Disability Benefits*. New York: A.S.A., 1926.

Actuarial Society of America and the Association of Life Insurance Medical Directors of America. *Blood Pressure Study*. New York: A.S.A. and ALIMDA, 1940.

_____. *Impairment Study*. 1936 ed. and 1938 ed. New York: A.S.A. and ALIMDA, 1936 and 1939.

_____. *Joint Occupation Study 1928*. New York: A.S.A. and ALIMDA, 1929.

_____. *Medical Impairment Study 1929*. New York: A.S.A. and ALIMDA, 1932.

_____. *Occupational Mortality Ratings*. New York: A.S.A. and ALIMDA, 1929.

_____. *Occupational Study 1937*. New York: A.S.A. and ALIMDA, 1938.

_____. *Supplement to Blood Pressure Study*. New York: A.S.A. and ALIMDA, 1941.

_____. *Supplement to Medical Impairment Study*. New York: A.S.A. and ALIMDA, 1932.

The Actuary, SOA, February 1970–December 1982.

American Institute of Certified Public Accountants. *Accounting Principles Board Opinion No. 8—Accounting for the Cost of Pension Plans*. New York: AICPA, 1966.

_____. *"Audits of Life Insurance Companies*, (Draft)." [ca. 1970].

_____. *Audits of Stock Life Insurance Companies*. New York: AICPA, 1972.

Anderson, Arthur W. *Pension Mathematics for Actuaries*. Needham, Mass.: Arthur W. Anderson, 1985.

Association of Insurance and Financial Analysts. "Final Report of the Committee on Life Insurance Earnings Adjustment [ca. 1969]." AIFA.

Association of Life Insurance Medical Directors of America and the Actuarial Society of America. *Blood Pressure*. New York: ALIMDA and A.S.A., 1925.

_____. *Medico-Actuarial Mortality Investigation*. 5 vols. New York: ALIMDA and A.S.A., 1912–1914.

Athearn, James L. "New South Life: A Case Study." *Business and Economic Review* 19 (April 1973): 3–18.

Austrian, Geoffrey D. *Herman Hollerith, Forgotten Giant of Information Processing*. New York: Columbia University Press, 1982.

Baily, Francis. *The Doctrine of Life-Annuities and Assurances. Analytically investigated and practically explained*. 2 vols. London: John Richardson, 1812–1813.

Ball, Robert M. *Social Security, Today and Tomorrow*. New York: Columbia University Press, 1978.

Bartelson, Edwin L. *Health Insurance Provided through Individual Policies*. 1st ed., 2d ed. Chicago: SOA, 1963 and 1968.

Bashe, Charles J., et al. *IBM's Early Computers*. Cambridge: MIT Press, 1986.

Batten, Robert W. *Mortality Table Construction*. Englewood Cliffs, N.J.: Prentice-Hall, 1978.

Beard, Robert Eric, Teivo Pentikainen, and Erikki Pesonen. *Risk Theory*. London: Chapman and Hall, 1977.

Beatty, J. Gordon. "More Reminiscences of an Old Soldier and Actuary [ca. 1982]." Society of Actuaries Library, Schaumburg, Ill.

_____. "Reminiscences of an Old Soldier and Actuary [ca. 1977]." Society of Actuaries Library, Schaumburg, Ill.

Bell, W. D. *A Management Guide to Electronic Computers*. New York: McGraw-Hill, 1957.

Belth, Joseph M. *Participating Life Insurance Sold by Stock Companies*. Homewood, Ill.: Richard D. Irwin, 1965.

_____. *The Retail Price Structure in America Life Insurance*. Bloomington, Ind.: Bureau of Business Research, Graduate School of Business, Indiana University, 1966.

Berin, Barnet N. *The Fundamentals of Pension Mathematics*. New York: William M. Mercer, 1971.

Berkeley, Edmund Callis. *Giant Brains; or, Machines that Think*. New York: Wiley, 1949.

411

Bleakney, Thomas P. *Retirement Systems for Public Employees*. Homewood, Ill.: Richard D. Irwin, 1972.

Bowers, Newton L., Jr., Hans U. Gerber, James C. Hickman, Donald A. Jones, and Cecil J. Nesbitt. *Actuarial Mathematics*. Itasca, Ill.: SOA, 1986.

Bronson, Dorrance C. *Concepts of Actuarial Soundness in Pension Plans*. Homewood, Ill.: Richard D. Irwin, 1957.

Buley, R. Carlyle. *The American Life Convention, 1906–1952, A Study in the History of Life Insurance*. New York: Appleton-Century-Crofts, 1953.

Burt, Margaret Allen. "George B. Buck Consulting Actuaries, Inc.: The First 45 Years" 1976. Society of Actuaries Library. Schaumburg, Ill.

Butcher, Marjorie V., and Cecil J. Nesbitt. *Mathematics of Compound Interest*. Ann Arbor, Mich.: Ulrich's, 1971.

Calvert, Geoffrey N. *It's Time to Tell the Story to Employees*. Lyndhurst, N.J.: Alexander and Alexander, Inc., 1965.

_____. *New Realistic Projections of Social Security Benefits and Taxes*. Lyndhurst, N.J.: Alexander and Alexander, Inc., 1973.

Campbell, Paul A. *The Variable Annuity; Its Development, Its Environment and Its Future*. Hartford, Conn.: Paul A. Campbell, 1969.

Canadian Institute of Chartered Accountants. *Financial Reporting for Life Insurance Companies*. Toronto: CICA, 1972.

Canadian Life Insurance Association. Accounting. "Financial Reporting for Life Insurance Companies in Canada." 1974. Canadian Life and Health Association Library. Toronto, Ont.

Cannon, Walter Bradford. *The Wisdom of the Body*. New York: W. W. Norton and Company, Inc., 1932.

Carr, William H. A. *Perils, Named and Unnamed; The Story of the Insurance Company of North America*. New York: McGraw-Hill, 1967.

Chase, George C. "History of Mechanical Computing Machinery." *Annals of the History of Computing* 2 (1980): 198–226.

Chisholm, D. *On a New Method of Constructing a Table of the Probabilities of Survivorship, etc.* 1852.

Coward, Laurence E. *Pensions in Canada*. Don Mills, Ont.: C. C. H. Canadian Limited, 1964.

Davidson, Andrew R. *The History of the Faculty of Actuaries in Scotland 1856–1956*. Edinburgh: Faculty of Actuaries, 1956.

Dawson, Miles M. *Assessment Life Insurance*. New York: Spectator, 1896.

_____. *Practical Lessons in Actuarial Science*. 1st ed., 2d ed., 2 vols. New York: Spectator, 1898 and 1905.

De Moivre, Abraham. *Annuities on Lives*. 3d ed. London: A. Millar, 1750.

Derthick, Martha. *Policymaking for Social Security*. Washington, D.C.: The Brookings Institution, 1979.

Di Paolo, Frank P., ed. "Actuarial Feats and Foibles [ca. 1971]." Society of Actuaries Library. Schaumburg, Ill.

Edwards, Ralph E., ed. *The Actuarial Record*. v.1, no.1–v.3 no.12, 1964–1966. Society of Actuaries Library. Schaumburg, Ill.

Elston, James S. *Sources and Characteristics of the Principal Mortality Tables*. rev. ed., Actuarial Studies, no. 1. New York, A.S.A., 1932.

Farr, William. *English Life Table no. 3. London: H. M. Stationery Office, 1864.*

Faulkner, Edwin J. *Health Insurance*. New York: McGraw-Hill, 1960.

Finelli, John J. "Development of EDP Units." *The Computer Bulletin*, 4, no. 1 (June 1960).

Fisher, R. A. *Statistical Methods for Research Workers*. London: Oliver and Boyd, 1925.

Fraternal Actuarial Association. *Proceedings and History of the Fraternal Actuarial Association*, 1977–1980.

Freeman, Harry. *Mathematics for Actuarial Students. Part I and II*. London: Cambridge University Press, 1939.

Friedman, Annie N., and Lloyd K. Friedman. *On The Trail of Actuaries in Texas 1844–1964*. San Antonio: Watercress Press, 1988.

Gershenson, Harry. *Measurement of Mortality*. Chicago: SOA, 1961.

Griffin, Frank L., Jr. *"Wyco." The Building of a Professional Actuarial and Consulting Organization*. Cleveland, Ohio: The Wyatt Company, 1979.

Griffin, Frank L. Jr., and Charles L. Trowbridge. *Status of Funding Under Private Pension Plans*. Homewood, Ill.: Richard D. Irwin, 1969.

Hald, Anders. "On the Early History of Life Insurance Mathematics." *Scandinavian Actuarial Journal* 1–2 (1987) 4–18.

Hall, Henry Sinclair and S. R. Knight. *Higher Algebra*. London: Macmillan, 1889.

Henderson, Robert. *Actuarial Society Examinations in 1905 and the Fundamental Principles of Probability*. New York: Thrift, 1906.

_____. *Mathematical Theory of Graduation*. Actuarial Studies, no. 4. New York: A.S.A. 1938.

_____. *Mortality Laws and Statistics*. New York: John Wiley and Sons, Inc., 1915.

Henderson, Robert, and H. N. Sheppard. *Graduation of Mortality and Other Tables*. Actuarial Studies, no. 4. New York: A.S.A. 1919.

Herrick, Kenneth W. *Total Disability Provisions in Life Insurance Contracts*. Homewood, Ill.: Richard D. Irwin for S. S. Hueber Foundation for Insurance Education, University of Pennsylvania, 1956.

Hicks, Ernest L. *Accounting for the Cost of Pension Plans*. Accounting Research Study, no. 8. New York: AICPA, 1965.

Hunter, Arthur. *Total Permanent Disability Benefits in Relation to Life Insurance*. Actuarial Studies, no. 5. New York: A.S.A., 1920.

Hunter, Arthur, and James T. Phillips. *Disability Benefits in Life Insurance Policies*. Actuarial Studies, no. 5. New York: A.S.A., 1932.

Institute of Life Insurance and National Association of Insurance Commissioners. *The Nature of the Whole Life Contract*. New York: ILI and NAIC, 1974.

Jackson, Henry H. "Fragments" 1950. Society of Actuaries Library. Schaumburg, Ill.

Jones, David. *On the Value of Annuities and Reversionary Payments*. 2 vols. London: Baldwin and Craddock, 1843.

Jones, Nathan F. "Actuarial and Related Operations Models [ca. 1964]." Society of Actuaries Library, Schaumburg, Ill.

Jordan, Chester Wallace. *Life Contingencies*. 1st ed., 2d ed. Chicago: SOA, 1952 and 1967.

Journal of the Institute of Actuaries. v. 6, 1856–v. 91, 1965.

Kellam, William Porter. *Episodes in the Life of Charles Francis McCay*. Athens, Ga.: 1983.

Kellison, Stephen G. *Fundamentals of Numerical Analysis*. Homewood, Ill.: Richard D. Irwin, 1975.

_____. *The Theory of Interest*. Homewood, Ill.: Richard D. Irwin, 1970.

King, George. *Life Contingencies, Including Life Annuities and Assurances. Part II of Institute of Actuaries Text-Book of the Principles of Interest, Life Annuities and Assurances and Their Practical Application*. London: Charles and Edwin Layton, 1887.

Knight, Charles Kelly. "The history of life insurance in the United States to 1870." Ph.D. diss., University of Pennsylvania, 1920.

Kreader, J. Lee. "Rubinow, Isaac Max—Pioneering Specialist in Social Insurance." *Social Service Review* 50 (1976): 402–425.

Kulp, Clarence A., *Casualty Insurance*. New York: Ronald Press, 1928.

_____. *Casualty Insurance; An Analysis of Hazards, Policies, Insurers, and Rates*. 3d ed. New York: Ronald Press, 1956.

Linton, M. Albert. *Agents Earnings; A Study of the Relative Earnings of Soliciting Agents and General Agents*. Philadelphia: Provident Mutual Life Insurance Co., 1928.

_____. *Life Insurance Speaks for Itself*. New York: Harper and Brothers Publishers, 1937.

Maclean, Joseph B. *Life Insurance*. 1st ed. New York: McGraw-Hill Book Company, Inc., 1924.

Maclean, Joseph B., and Edward W. Marshall. *Distribution of Surplus*. Actuarial Studies, no. 6. New York: A.S.A., 1937.

McCahan, David. *Life Insurance Trends at Mid-Century*. Philadelphia: University of Pennsylvania Press, 1950.

McGill, Dan M. *Fulfilling Pension Expectations*. Homewood, Ill: Richard D. Irwin, 1962.

_____. *Fundamentals of Private Pensions*. 1st ed., 6th ed. Homewood, Ill.: Richard D. Irwin, 1955 and 1988.

Meares, Charles W. V. *Looking Back: A Memoir of New York Life*. New York: New York Life Insurance Company, 1985.

Meech, Levi W. *Economy in Mathematics; New Calculation Tables for Multiplication and Division*. Norwich, Conn.: H. Bill Publishing, 1894.

Michelbacher, Gustav F. *Casualty Insurance Principles*. New York: McGraw-Hill, 1930.

_____. *Multiple-Line Insurance*. New York: McGraw-Hill, 1957.

Michelbacher, Gustav F., and Thomas M. Neal. *Workmen's Compensation Insurance, Including Employer's Liability Insurance*. New York: McGraw-Hill, 1925.

Miller, John H. *With an Eye to Tomorrow*. New York: ILI, 1967.

_____. *Accident and Sickness Insurance Provided Through Individual Policies*. Chicago: SOA, 1956.

Miller, Morton D. *Elements of Graduation*. Actuarial Monographs, no. 1. A.S.A. and A.I.A., 1946.

Milne, Joshua. *A Treatise on the Valuation of Annuities and Assurances on Lives and Survivorships*; *On the Construction of Tables of Mortality; and on the Probabilities and Expectations of Life*. 2 vols. London: Longman, Hurst, Rees, Orme, and Brown, 1815.

Mitchell, Robert B. *From Actuarius to Actuary*. Chicago: SOA, 1974.

Moir, Henry. *Sources and Characteristics of the Principal Mortality Tables*. Actuarial Studies, no. 1. New York: A.S.A., 1919.

Moir, Henry, and M. M. Dawson. "Notes for Use in Preparation for the Fellowship Examination of the Actuarial Society of America—1906." Society of Actuaries Library, Schaumburg, Ill.

Morgan, William. *The Doctrine of Annuities and Assurance on Lives and Survivorships, Stated and Explained*. London: T. Cadell, 1779.

Morse, Philip M. *In at the Beginnings; A Physicist's Life*. Cambridge: MIT Press, 1977.

Munnell, Alicia H. *The Future of Social Security*. Washington, D.C.: The Brookings Institution, 1977.

Murphy, Ray D., and Percy C. H. Papps. *Construction of Mortality Tables from the Records of Insured Lives*. New York: A.S.A., 1922.

Myers, Robert J. *Medicare*. Homewood, Ill.: Richard D. Irwin, 1970.

_____. *Social Insurance and Allied Government Programs*. Homewood, Ill.: Richard D. Irwin, 1965.

_____. *Social Security*. 1st ed., 2d ed. Homewood, Ill.: Richard D. Irwin, 1975 and 1981.

National Association of Insurance Commissioners. Report of the Committee to Study the Need for a New Mortality Table and Related Topics. New York: Actuarial Society of America, 1939.

_____. "Report of the Committee to Study Non-Forfeiture Benefits and Related Matters" in Supplement to the *Proceedings of the National Association of Insurance Commissioners*. Kansas City; Mo.: NAIC, 1942.

New York. Insurance Department. Annual Report of the Superintendent. Albany, N.Y., 1860.

_____. Legislature. Joint Committee on Investigation of Life Insurance. Testimony taken before the Joint Committee of the Senate and Assembly of the State of New York to investigate and examine into the business and affairs of life insurance companies doing business in the state of New York. 10 vols. Albany, N.Y., 1905–1906.

Noback, Joseph C. *Life Insurance Accounting*. Homewood, Ill.: Richard D. Irwin, 1961.

Ogborn, Maurice Edward. *Equitable Assurances; The Story of Life Assurance in the Experience of the Equitable Life Assurance Society 1762–1962*. London: George Allen and Unwin Limited: 1962.

Parker, Donn B. *Crime by Computer*. New York: Scribner, 1976.

Pedoe, Arthur. *Life Insurance, Annuities and Pensions*. Toronto: University of Toronto Press, 1964.

Phillips, E. William. "A Note on the History of the Electronic Computer [ca. 1963]." Society of Actuaries Library. Schaumburg, Ill.

Price, Richard. *Observations on Reversionary Payments: On Schemes for Providing Annuities for Widows, and for Persons in Old Age: On the Method of Calculating the Values of Assurances on Lives: and on the National Debt*. 2 vols. 4th ed., 1783; 5th ed., 1791; 6th ed., 1803; 7th ed., 1812. London: T. Cadell.

_____. *Observations on Reversionary Payments*. 1st ed., 1769; 2d ed., 1772; 3d ed., n.d. London: T. Cadell.

Proceedings of the Canadian Institute of Actuaries. v. 1, 1965–1966–v. 12, 1980–1981.

Proceedings of the Casualty Actuarial Society. v. 2, 1915–1916–v. 51, 1964.

Proceedings of the Centenary Assembly of the Institute of Actuaries. 3 vols. 1950.

Proceedings of the Conference of Actuaries in Public Practice. v. 1, 1951–v. 14, 1964–1965.

Proceedings of the Fraternal Actuarial Association. v. 6, 1923–v. 48, 1976.

Record of the American Institute of Actuaries. v. 1, 1909–v. 37, 1948.

Record of the Society of Actuaries. v. 1, 1975–v. 12, 1986.

"Report of the Committee on New Recording Means and Computing Devices." Chicago: SOA, 1952, 1955 and 1957.

Report of the Consultant Panel on Social Security to the United States Congressional Research Service. Washington, D.C.: U. S. Government Printing Office, 1976.

Rietz, Henry Lewis. *Mathematical Statistics*. Chicago: Mathematical Association of America, 1927.

Robertson, A. Haeworth. *The Coming Revolution in Social Security*. McLean, Va.: Security Press, 1981.

Roelofs, Vernon W. "History of the Fraternal Actuarial Association, 1916–1980." *In Proceedings and History of the Fraternal Actuarial Association*. New York: Fraternal Actuarial Association, n.d.

Rubinow, Isaac Max. *The Quest for Security*. New York: Henry Holt and Company, 1934.

Russell, A. H. *Checking Calculations for Accountants, Clerks and Teachers*. London: Gregg Publishing Company, Limited, n.d.

Sable, Ronald L., and Robert E. Dallos. *The Impossible Dream; the Equity Funding Story, the Fraud of the Century*. New York. Putnam, 1975.

Schull, Joseph. *The Century of the Sun*. Toronto: Macmillan of Canada, 1971.

Shepherd, Pearce, and Andrew C. Webster. *Selection of Risks*. Chicago: SOA, 1957.

Simmonds, Reginald Claude. *The Institute of Actuaries, 1848–1948*. Cambridge: University Press, 1948.

Society of Actuaries. *Build and Blood Pressure Study*. 2 vols. Chicago: SOA, 1959.

_____. *Impairment Study 1951*. New York: SOA, 1954.

_____. *1967 Occupation Study*. Chicago: SOA, 1967.

Spiegelman, Mortimer. *Introduction to Demography*. New York: SOA, 1955.

Spurgeon, E. F. *Life Contingencies*. 1st ed., 2d ed., 3d ed. Cambridge: University Press, 1922, 1929, 1932.

Stalson, J. Owen. *Marketing Life Insurance: Its History in America*. Cambridge: Harvard University Press, 1942.

Sutton, William. *Interest including Annuities-Certain. Part 1 of Institute of Actuaries Text-Book of the Principles of Interest, Life Annuities, and Assurances and Their Practical Application*. London: Charles and Edwin Layton, 1882.

Thiesmeyer, Lincoln R., John E. Burchard, and Alan T. Waterman. *Combat Scientists*. Boston: Little, Brown, 1947.

Todhunter, Ralph. *Interest Including Annuities-Certain. Part 1 of Institute of Actuaries Text-Book of the Principles of Interest, Life Annuities, and Assurances, and Their Practical Application*. London: Charles and Edwin Layton, 1901.

Transactions of the Actuarial Society of America. v. 1, 1889–1890–v. 50, 1949.

Transactions of the Society of Actuaries. v. 1, 1949–v. 36, 1984.

Trowbridge, C.L., and Charles E. Farr. *The Theory and Practice of Pension Funding*. Homewood, Ill.: Richard D. Irwin, 1976.

Walford, Cornelius. *The Insurance Cyclopaedia: Being a Dictionary of the Definition of Terms Used in Connexion with the Theory and Practice of Insurance in all its Branches*. 6 vols. New York: J. H. and C. M. Goodsell, 1871–1880.

Willey, Nathan. *Principles and Practice of Life Insurance*. New York: Spectator, 1872.

_____. *Principles and Practice of Life Insurance*. 7th ed., rev. and enl. by Henry Moir. New York: Spectator, 1906.

Wolfenden, Hugh H. *The Fundamental Principles of Mathematical Statistics*. New York: A.S.A., 1942.

_____. *Population Statistics and Their Compilation*. Actuarial Studies, no. 3. New York: A.S.A., 1925.

_____. *Population Statistics and Their Compilation*. Appendix on "Some Theory in the Sampling of Human Populations," by W. Edwards Deming. rev. ed. Chicago: SOA, 1954.

_____. *The Real Meaning of Social Insurance*. Toronto: Macmillan Company of Canada Limited, 1932.

Wood, R. Norman. *Measuring the Investment Yield of Pension Funds*. Lyndhurst, N.J.: Alexander and Alexander, Inc., 1965.

Wright, Elizur. "Total Abstinence Life Insurance" 1845. Society of Actuaries Library. Schaumburg, Ill.

Index

In this index, names of persons are listed only if they appear in a setting more significant than that of an organization charter member list, for example. The charter member lists may be found for the Actuarial Society of America on page 51; for the American Institute of Actuaries on page 76; for the Casualty Actuarial Society on pages 90, 91; for the Fraternal Actuarial Association on page 99; and for the Conference of Actuaries in Public Practice on page 171. Company names appear only if in a context of importance in their own right rather than simply as an identification of a person. Page numbers listed in italics refer to illustrations.

-A-

AAA
  SEE American Academy of Actuaries
Abacus
  SEE calculators
Academy Newsletter, The
  SEE *Actuarial Update, The*
Accident and health insurance, 179, 180
Accounting Principles Board (APB), 266
Accounting profession, 196-198, 267
ACLI
  SEE American Council of Life Insurance
Actuarial Aptitude Test, 181, 182, 289
  SEE ALSO Life Office Management Association
Actuarial Club of Indianapolis, 381
Actuarial clubs, 297, 373-382
  British example, 373
  Club Profile, 381
  regional clubs, 378, 380
  relationship to CAS and SOA, 380, 381
  SEE ALSO
    Actuarial Club of Indianapolis
    Actuarial Society of Greater New York,
    Actuaries Club,
    Actuaries Club of Boston,
    Actuaries Club of Hartford,
    Actuaries Club of New York,
    Actuaries Club of the Southwest,
    Casualty actuarial clubs,
    Junior Actuaries Club of New York,
    Middle Atlantic Actuarial Club,
    Nebraska Actuaries Club,
    Pacific Coast Actuarial Club,
    Pacific States Actuarial Club,
    Senior Actuaries Club,
    Southeastern Actuaries Club,
    Toronto Actuaries Club,
    Winnipeg Actuaries Club,
    Wisconsin Actuaries Club
Actuarial education, 283-317
  alternate route, 309, 310, 316

continuing, 315, 316
cooperation in requirements, 308-312
developments 1949-1962, 306-308
early study notes, 297
history of in SOA, 312, 313
key changes of the 1970s, 311
1975 Rappaport/Plumley paper, 312
steps toward linkages, 313-315
seminars, 316
tuition and textbooks, 292-297
SEE ALSO
    actuarial examinations,
    actuarial organizations,
    Ball State University,
    Drake University,
    Georgia State University,
    Northeastern University,
    Pennsylvania State University,
    Universite Laval,
    University of California,
    University of Connecticut,
    University of Georgia,
    University of Iowa,
    University of Manitoba,
    University of Michigan,
    University of Minnesota,
    University of Nebraska,
    University of Texas,
    University of Toronto,
    University of Waterloo,
    University of Wisconsin
Actuarial Education and Research Fund (AERF), 228, 229, 368
Actuarial examinations, 283-317
  first fellow by examination, 284
  first to fail, 284
  Graduate Record Examination, 317
  jointly administered, 134, 299
  Language Aptitude Examination, 304
  multiple-choice questions, 304, 309
  preliminary examinations, 304

travel time, 308
SEE ALSO
    actuarial education
    Educational Testing Service
Actuarial humor, 391-405
Actuarial literature
    formal papers decline, 187
    index need, 234, 235
Actuarial newsletters, 231-235
    SEE ALSO
        Academy Newsletter, The,
        Actuarial Record, The,
        Actuarial Research Clearing House, The,
        Actuarial Review, The,
        Actuarial Update, The,
        Actuary, The,
        Disability Newsletter,
        Enrolled Actuaries Report
Actuarial notation, 61, 347, 348
Actuarial organizations
    A.I.A. and A.S.A. merger, 156-159
    consolidation attempt, 270
    Council of Presidents, 255
    early merger attempts, 28-33
    first four bodies, 43-103
    SEE ALSO
        Actuarial clubs,
        Actuarial Society of America,
        Actuarial Society of Australasia,
        American Academy of Actuaries,
        American Institute of Actuaries,
        American Society of Pension Actuaries,
        Canadian Association of Actuaries,
        Canadian Institute of Actuaries,
        Casualty Actuarial Society,
        Conference of Actuaries in Public Practice,
        Faculty of Actuaries,
        French Institute,
        Institute of Actuaries,
        International Congress of Actuaries,
        Mexican Institute of Actuaries,
        National Actuaries Institute,
        Society of Actuaries,
        Swiss Actuarial Association
Actuarial pioneers
    first woman, 27
    most influential, 1, 2
    SEE ALSO
        Canadian actuaries,
        consulting actuaries
Actuarial profession, 126-128
    accreditation, 187, 195, 196, 251
    before mechanical calculators, 331, 332
    challenges to traditional prerogatives, 196
    discipline, 262, 263

education and examinations, 284-289
expanding opportunities, 314
in 1888, 40
in 1858, 14, 15
in 1918, 101-103
in 1948, 159
in 1979, 276-278
in 1964, 205, 206
income tax formulation, 193
independence, 252, 253
in wartime, 92-94, 152-153, 349-361
journalist's view, 211, 212
minority recruiting, 239, 240
professional ethics, 70, 191, 192, 221, 239
professional opinion (public), 236-238, 259
relationship with CPAs, 197, 244-250, 265-267
research, 227-230, 277
social security impact on, 142
SEE ALSO
    actuarial clubs,
    actuarial education,
    actuarial examinations,
    actuarial organizations,
    calculators,
    computers,
    Enrolled Actuaries,
    statistics
Actuarial Record, The, 231
Actuarial Research Clearing House (ARCH), 231-233
Actuarial Review, The, 231, 233, 234, 395
Actuarial schools
    SEE actuarial education
Actuarial science,
    and statistics, 384
    early university courses, 297, 298
Actuarial Society of America, 43-60, 94, 168
    Associates, 59, 78, 290
    Canadian members, 81, 82, 145
    charter members, 37, 40, 51
    classification of members, 58-60
    complaints and discipline, 70
    Council, 46, 54-57, 62, 82, 94, 108, 135
    dinners, 54, 63
    domestic growth 1890-1898, 58
    dues 1909-1939, 363, 372
    education and exams. 1897-1928, 284-289, 296
    1896 meeting group, 64
    Fellows, 59, 78
    fiftieth anniversary, 153, 155
    final meeting, 46
    first employee, 62
    first Fellow by examination, 58
    first women members, 62, 63, 128
    fortieth anniversary, 40, 396
    inaugural meeting, 34, 46-52, 63, 394
    incorporation study, 82
    Joint Committee on Mortality, 111, 112

joint exams., 299, 300
joint meetings, 73, 117, 118
library, 116, 117
light side in, 394-398
membership 1889-1918, 101, 102
membership growth, 77, 180-182
membership in 1948, 159
membership overseas, 57, 58, 101
merger into SOA, 156-159
military service honor roll, 350
motto, 67
name, 48
new directions, 301-305
operations, 363-365
Scottish influence, 78-80
tenth anniversary, 102
three phases, 107, 108
twentieth anniversary, 1, 43, 102, 103
twenty-fifth anniversary, 59, 102, 103
two-timers, 290
wartime disruption, 359, 360
Yearbook, 52
SEE ALSO
    actuarial profession,
    mortality studies,
    Transactions of the Actuarial Society of America
Actuarial Society of Australasia, 357
Actuarial Society of Greater New York, 375
Actuarial soundness, 184, 185
Actuarial students
    1970s population trend, 316, 317
Actuarial Studies in Non-Life Insurance (ASTIN), 191, 276, 391
Actuarial textbooks
    SEE actuarial education
Actuarial Update, The, 231, 232, 272
Actuaries
    definitions, 401
    number in 1888, 40
    stock company, 135
    supply of, 180-182
    SEE ALSO
        actuarial humor,
        actuarial pioneers,
        actuarial profession
Actuaries Club, 373-375
Actuaries Club of Boston, 307, 378
Actuaries Club of Des Moines, 381
Actuaries Club of Hartford, 135, 373, 377, 378, 381
Actuaries Club of Indianapolis, 381
Actuaries Club of Little Rock, 381
Actuaries Club of London, 93, 378
Actuaries Club of New York, 239, 294, 373, 375, 376, 381
Actuaries Club of the Southwest, 306, 307, 381
Actuaries Club of Western Pennsylvania, 381
Actuaries' Table, 6, 22

Actuary, The, 231-234, 400
Adams, James Truslow, 135
Adams, Mary H., 232, 262
Adams, Samuel P., *301*
Adams, Warren R., 306, 316, 369
AERF
    SEE Actuarial Education and Research Fund
Aetna Life and Casualty, 35
Agency finance studies, 151, 152
AICPA
    SEE American Institute of Certified Public Accountants
Aid Association for Lutherans, 100
AIFA
    SEE Association of Insurance and Financial Analysts
Aiken, Howard H., 343
Ain, Samuel N., 222
AIPSO
    SEE Automobile Insurance Plan Service Office
Airline crashes, 383, 384
Aitken, William H., 307
ALC
    SEE American Life Convention
ALIMDA
    SEE Association of Life Insurance Medical Directors of America
Allison, Sinclair E., 289
Allstrom, Henry W., 289
Alvord, Morgan H., 184, 208
American Academy of Actuaries (AAA), 187, 196, 197, 213, 226, 235, 237, 248-250, 259-263, 267-269, 309, 311
    archives, 216
    dues 1969-1979, 372
    Enrolled Actuary membership, 268
    founding, 215-221
    initial membership, 219, 220
    1970s, 250-252
    operations, 372
    single membership class, 221
    SEE ALSO
        Academy Newsletter, The,
        Actuarial Update, The
        Journal of the American Academy of Actuaries
American Annuitants Mortality Tables, 112, 194
American Civil War, 34
    anecdotes, 360
    mortality experience, 19
American Council of Life Insurance (ACLI), 125
    SEE ALSO American Life Convention (ALC)
American Experience Table, 13, 24, 36, 38, 39, 48, 66, 70, 97, 100, 101, 108-111, 114, 133, 146-151, 194, 274
American Institute of Actuaries, 29, 52, 54, 66, 84, 85, 94, 101, 120, 152, 244, 245, 248, 265

Associates, 1909-1923, 290
Board of Governors, last, *158*
Canadian members, 81, 82, 145
charter Fellows, 40, 76
Constitution, 75
Contributing Members, 77, 366
dues 1909-1939, 366, 372
education and exams. 1897-1928, 77, 289, 290
first joint meetings, 73, 117, 118
first woman member, 62
founding, 72-78
joint exams., 378-380
librarian, 117
light side in, 398, 399
membership growth, 77, 78, 180-182
membership in 1918, 101
merger into SOA, 156-159
military service honor roll, 350
motto, 77
name, 74
new directions, 301-305
operations, 365-367
Scottish influence, 78-80
seal, 77
thirty-fifth anniversary, 73, 153, 155
twenty-fifth anniversary, 155
two-timers, 290
wartime disruption, 359, 360
American Institute of Certified Public Accountants (AICPA), 197, 225, 244, 266
American Life Convention (ALC), 83, 94, 250
American Management Association, 344
American Mathematical Society, 50, 95
American Men Table, 83, 101, 108-110, 112, 147, 194
American Remarriage Table, 1933, 295
American Society of Pension Actuaries (ASPA), 187, 222, 223, 268
American Statistical Association, 185
Ammeter, Hans, 404
Anderson, Arthur W., 265
Anderson, Buist M.
  Legal Notes, 80, 200
Anderson, Henry James, 8
Anderson, James C.H., 206, 241
Anderson, Lewis A., 97
Anderson, Roy R., 224
Anderson, William M., 191, 192, 209, 311, 312
Andrews, George H., 229
Angell, Charles H., 284
Annuities
  participating, 114
  single premium pricing, 113, 114
  SEE ALSO mortality studies
Annuity Table for 1949, 183
Anton, Debra, 371
APB
  SEE Accounting Principles Board

ARCH
  SEE *Actuarial Research Clearing House*
Arenberg, J. Theodore, 245
Arithmeter
  SEE calculators
Armstrong Investigation of 1905, 9, 23, 33, 48, 66-71, 128, 136, 177
  SEE ALSO insurance supervision
Arnold, Daniel M., 234
Arnold, O.J., 73, 75, 156
ASPA
  SEE American Society of Pension Actuaries
Assessment insurance, 15, 34-35, 48, 96
Asset and liability mismatching, 176
Association of Insurance and Financial Analysts (AIFA), 244
Association of Life Insurance Medical Directors of America (ALIMDA), 50, 64, 111, 236
Assurance Magazine
  SEE *Journal of the Institute of Actuaries*
ASTIN
  SEE Actuarial Studies in Non-Life Insurance
Athearn, Dr. James L., 239
Atlanta Actuarial Club, 381
Atomic bomb
  SEE nuclear era
Attwood, James A., 279
Austrian, Geoffrey D., 337
Automobile Insurance Plans Service Office (AIPSO), 226
Automobile liability insurance, 119, 120, 224, 386
  SEE ALSO casualty insurance
Aviation risks, 125, 126
Ayres, Leonard P., 94

-B-

Babbage, Charles, 331, 333, 343
Bailey, Arthur L., 386, 388
Bailey, Robert A., 386
Baillie, Donald C., 297, 387
Baily, Francis, 5, 283
Baker, Alfred, 297
Baker, Hugh C., 2, 14
Bakos, Thomas L., 118
Baldwin, Frank S., 336
Baldwin, R.D., 100
Ball, Robert M., 262
Ball State University, 307, 381
Ballantyne, Harry C., 257
Bankers Life Company, 35
Bank Loan Plan, 178
Barber, William P., 343, 344
Bard, William, 2, 6, 7, 15, 17
Barker, Jesse J., 47, 68
Barnard, William F., 97
Barnes, William, 20
Barnsley, Reginald C., 175, 207

Bartels, Bernard A., 372

Bartleson, Edwin L., 180

Bartlett, Daphne D., 262

Bartlett, Dwight K., III, 7, 228, 229, 257, 261

Bartlett, Professor William H.C., 21, 31, 37, 44

Bashe, Charles J., 347

Bassett, Preston C., 196, 197, 265, 267, 270, 279, 316

Bassford, Horace R., 123, 125, 126, *147*, 149, 150, 152, 161, 163, 165, 166, 298, 326, 334, 386

Basye, Walter, 98

Batten, Professor Robert W., 306, 311, 385

Baughmann, Charles B., 178

Bayes, Thomas, 386

Bayesian statistics
    SEE statistics

Beach, Henricka, 62

Beard, Robert E., 383

Beasley, Floyd T., 231

Beatty, J. Gordon, 107, 123, 146, 166, 207, 214, 360, 367, 374

Beatty, Samuel, 297

Beekman, John A., 229, 307

Beers, Henry S., 298, 303, 322

Beers, Josephine W., 378

Beers, William H., 29-31

Begault, A., 61

Beha, James A., 129

Bell, John H., 209, 345

Bell, W.D., 345

Belth, Professor Joseph M., 242, 243

Bennett, Michael, 307

Bera, Marsha M., 239

Berin, Barnet N., 311

Berkeley, E.C., 343, 344, 346

Bevan, John A., 357

Bicknell, William S., 306

Billings, Roger, 142, 143

Birkenshaw, John T., 214, 278

Bittel, W. Harold, 177, 247

Bitzer, J.F., 280

Black, Dr. Kenneth, Jr., 306

Blackadar, Alfred K., 36, 104, 284

Blagden, H.E., 210

Blair, B. Franklin, 399

Bleakney, Thomas P., 267, 269, 311

Boermeester, John M., 345, 348, 354

Bogen, Jules I., 153

Boggs, Hale, 218

Boom, Hendrik J., 298

Boothroyd, Herbert J., 239

Boschan, P., 163

Bowditch, Nathaniel, 2, 6, 7, 17

Bowerman, Walter G., 161, 194, 322, 337

Bowers, Newton L., Jr., 269, 306, 311, 384, 387

Bowles, George A., 146, 150

Bowles, Thomas P., Jr., 222, 238, 244

Bowman, William H., 273

Boynton, Edwin F., 251, 267, 269

Bradshaw, Thomas, 89

Bragg, John M., 178, 239, 277, 280, 281

Breiby, William, 326

Brender, Allan, 307

Brewer, William A., 29, 30

Brisbane, Arthur, 389

British North America Act
    SEE insurance supervision

Brockway, A.H., 291

Bronson, Dorrance C., 183-185, 188, 189, 192, 197, 207, 210, 218, 263

Brown, Arthur W., 354

Brown, Edward D., Jr., 169, 170, 173, 195

Brown, Helen E., 63

Brown, Professor John E., 306

Brown, M. David R., 267

Brown, Robert L., 307

Brownlee, Harold J., 234

Bruce, Harley N., 169, 172, 173

Bruce, Robert E., 218, 370

Bryce, George M., 217, 218

Buck, George B., 84, 85, 123, 160, 185

Buck, Norman F., 228

Buhlmann, Professor Hans, 386, 387

Buley, R. Carlyle, 83

Burchard, John E., 356

Bureau of War Risk Insurance, 354

Burke, Christine, 371

Burling, William H., 396

Burt, Margaret Allen, 84

Butcher, Marjorie VanEenam, 298

Buttolph, Henry W., 74, 75, 77

Bykerk, Cecil D., 306

-C-

C_1, C_2 and C_3 risks, 275

Calculators
    abacus, 333, 335
    arithmeter, 333, 334
    arithmometer, 334, *335*, 336
    binary calculator, 340
    desk calculators, 331, 334-337
    difference engine, 333
    Gore equipment, 338, *339*
    Hollerith machine, 337, 338
    Millionaire, 336, 337
    multiplication books, 331
    Nicholson method, 338
    Pierce system, 337
    Powers equipment, 337
    punched-card machines, 338
    slide rule, 331, 335
    tables of quarter squares, 331
    SEE ALSO computers

Calvert, Geoffrey N., 175, 184-188, 192, 257-259, 265, 267, 357, 358

Cammack, Edmund E., 70, 112, 113, 129, 160, 320
Campbell, Alistair M., 145, 161
Campbell, Donald F., Jr., 169, 173, 222
Campbell, G.C., 207
Campbell, James A., 209, 327, 328
Campbell, Paul A., 228
Canada Life Assurance Company, 14, 35
Canadian actuaries, 81, 200
    first, 14
Canadian Association of Actuaries, 145, 146, 213-216,
    371, 374, 378
Canadian Institute of Actuaries (CIA), 146, 196, 213,
    216, 237, 243, 250, 278, 311, 374, 375, 378
    dues 1969-1979, 372
    light side in, 401-403
    motto, 55, 214
    operations, 371, 372
Canadian Institute of Chartered Accountants, 249
Canadian Life Insurance Association, 250
Canadian Men Table, 194
Cannon, G.E., 280
Cannon, Dr. Walter B., 134
CAPP
    SEE Conference of Actuaries in Public Practice
Carlisle Table, 7, 8, 12
Carlson, Thomas O., 153, 154, 210, 388, 392
Carpenter, R.V., 160
Carr, William H.A., 383, 384
Carter, Edwin R., 77
CAS
    SEE Casualty Actuarial Society
Case, Daniel F., 247, 248
Case, R.L., Jr., 37
Castonguay, Claude, 306
Casualty Actuarial and Statistical Society of America
    (CASSA), 87
    SEE ALSO Casualty Actuarial Society
Casualty actuarial clubs,
    Casualty Actuaries of Greater New York, 380
    Casualty Actuaries of New England, 380
    Casualty Actuaries of the Bay Area, 380
    Casualty Actuaries of the Mid-Atlantic Region, 380
    Casualty Actuaries of the Northwest, 380
    Midwest Actuaries Forum, 380
    Southern California Casualty Actuarial Club, 380
    Southwest Actuarial Forum, 380
Casualty Actuarial Society (CAS), 84-92, 168, 223-227,
    237, 240, 251, 277, 278, 305, 311, 377, 380, 385
    charter Fellows, 89-91
    dues 1919-1979, 372
    education and exams. 1897-1928, 290-292
    Fellows, 1919-1924, 120
    first half-century, 201-204
    first woman president, 276
    first women members, 62, 128
    Guides to Professional Conduct, 192
    joint exams., 308
    joint meetings, 92, 271, 272, 314
    library, 199
    light side in, 391-394
    membership in 1918, 101
    membership in 1948, 159, 205
    membership in 1964, 205
    new directions, 305
    operations, 367, 368
    tenth anniversary, 118-120
    twelve charter members, *85*
    twentieth anniversary, 153-155
    twenty-fifth anniversary, 153-155, 392
    SEE ALSO
        Actuarial Review, The,
        casualty actuarial clubs,
        Proceedings of the Casualty Actuarial Society
Casualty actuaries, 1, 314
Casualty insurance, 86, 324
    loss reserves, 225, 311, 314, 384
Casualty reinsurance, 278
Cathles, Lawrence M., 78, 108, 155, 160, 289, 398
Celler, Emmanuel, 218
Certification of actuaries
    SEE
        actuarial profession,
        American Academy of Actuaries,
        Canadian Institute of Actuaries
Chamber of Life Insurance, 28, 29
Chan, Beda, 307
Chandler, Seth C., 41
Chang, Yuan, 276, 315
Charter Oak Life, 34, 38, 54
Chase, George C., 336
Chastain, Rita K., 371
Chennault, Gen. Claire L., 357
Cherriman, Professor John B., 14, 35, 41, 297
Chisholm, D., 284
Christian, Delos H., 239
Christiansen, Stephan L., 395
Christman, Joseph A., 326
Cillis, H., 37
Civil War
    SEE American Civil War
Clark, Professor John Emory, 297
Clark, Kenneth T., 275
Clark, Osman D., 51
Clarke, E.E., 279
Cochnower, H.W., 74
Cody, Donald D., 207, 260, 304, 354, 355
Coffin, William J., 30
Cole, Linden N., 316, 369
Coler, Wendell P., 98, 121
College of Insurance, 199, 200
College Retirement Equities Fund (CREF), 184
Collins, Russell M., Jr., 232, 279, 280
Collins, Sue Ann, 194

Combined Annuity Table, 113, 194
Combined Experience Table, 19, 22
Commissioners Reserve Valuation Method (CRVM), 149, 150
Commissioners Standard Industrial (CSI) Table, 148
Common stock, 185
    historical averages, 175, 176
    prices 1927-1933, 131
    valuation, 128
Compound interest, 22
    SEE ALSO interest rates
Computers, 190, 191, 348, 359
    ACE, 343
    consolidated functions approach, 344
    ENIAC, 343, 346
    Feranti computer, 345
    Harvard Mark I, 343
    IBM equipment, 337
    microcomputers, 347
    SOFASIM model, 229, 230, 346
    UNIVAC, 345, *346*
    SEE ALSO
        calculators,
        punched-card systems
Confederation Life Association, 14
Conference of Actuaries in Public Practice (CAPP), 197, 221, 222, 251, 270, 309, 311
    charter members, 171
    dues 1959-1979, 372
    formation, 169-173
    Guides to Professional Conduct, 192
    light side in, 404
    membership classes, 170
    membership in 1948-1964, 205
    operations, 370, 371
    twenty-fifth anniversary, 222
    SEE ALSO
    Proceedings of the Conference of Actuaries in Public Practice
Congleton, Richard, 251
Connecticut Mutual, 35, 40
Conover, Chase S., 169
Consulting actuaries, 155, 165, 180
    dual responsibility, 188
    first, 2, 13
    number in 1962, 205
    SEE ALSO Conference of Actuaries in Public Practice
Consumerism, 241
Consumer Price Index (CPI)
    SEE United States Consumer Price Index
Contribution plan, 24-27
    SEE ALSO dividends
Conway, Albert, 130
Cooper, S.H., 280
Copeland, John A., 169
Corbett, Gary, 243, 247, 268, 269, 310

Corbett, Henry R., 124
Corcoran, William M., 109, 110
Cosby, Byron J., 298, 307
Council of Presidents, 255, 270
Coutts, C.R.V., 342
Coward, Laurence E., 190, 210, 279
Cowell, Michael J., 385
CPI
    SEE United States Consumer Price Index
Craig, James D., 37, 40, 87, 88, 100, 110, 113, 117, 119, 131, 139, 143, 144, 160-162, 322, 323, 337, 396
Craig, James M., 68, 83, 92, 117, 119, 334
Credibility theory, 119, 202, 384-387
CREF
    SEE College Retirement Equities Fund
Crofts, Geoffrey, 307
Cross, Jerome R., *350*, 351
Cross, Rowland E., 268
Crowe, Ernest W., 163, 191
Cruess, Leigh, 194
Cueto, M.R., 208
Cumming, John B., 232
Cunneen, Grace, 371
Currie, Gilbert E., 18
Cushing, Robertson Macaulay, *350*, 351
Cushman, Emma Warren, 62, *63*

-D-

Dallos, Robert E., 263
Daughtrey, William Lamb, 351
Davenport, Isaac, 289
Davidson, Andrew R., 78, 79
Davies, Karl M., 346
Davis, George H., 193
Davis, Malvin E., 178, 191, 207, 344
Dawson, Miles Menander, 23, 24, 67, *68*, 70, 71, 87, 92, 95, 97, 101, 103-106, 172, 294, 295
Deas, R.G., 208
De Boer, Joseph A., 50, 104, 284, 298
Decker, Richard J., 226, 227
de Colmar, Thomas, 336
Deficiency reserves, 148, 150, 176, 177
de Finetti, Savage, 385
De Groot, Nicholas G., 12, 20, 30, 37
De Morgan, Professor Augustus, 92, 135, 192, 331, 332
Depression of 1929
    Canada, 144, 145
    United States, 131-138, 146, 153, 155, 179, 323, 324, 327, 363
Derthick, Martha, 262
DeVries, Walter L., 354, 356
Diamond, Peter A., 258
Dietrich, Richard Edward, 351, 352
Di Paolo, F.P., 280, 281, 348, 401
Disability experience, 102
    Hunter's Disability Table of 1911, 321
    1927-1930 actions to curb losses, 323, 324

1926 Committee Report, 321, 322, 323
Disability income benefits, 102, 113
   SEE ALSO income disability benefits
Disability Newsletter, The (DN), 231, 233, 330
Dividends
   contribution plan, 24-27
   illustrations, 242
   reversionary bonus, 9, 27
   three-factor method, 25
   tontine system, 33
   SEE ALSO surplus distribution
DN
   SEE *Disability Newsletter, The*
Dodd, Amzi, 29, 30
Dodd, Thomas J., 218
Dodson, James, 135
Donovan, James B., 195, 196, 217, 218
Dorweiler, Paul, 295
Dow, Harold E., 304
Doyle, Martina E., 377
Drake University, 306, 381
Draper, Frederick A., 97
Dreher, William A., 244
Driskill, Richard G., 307
Dropkin, Lester, 386
Dublin, Louis I., 100
Duncan, Robert M., 184, 185, 210
Dunlap, E.O., 161
Dyer, John K., Jr., 188, 189, 208, 212, 234, 266, 267

-E-

Eckler, Samuel, 183
Edgewater Beach Hotel, *132*, 158, 170
Educational Testing Service (ETS), 304, 309
Edwards, Ralph E., 231, 232
Eide, K. Arne, 259
Eidson, Colonel Harry T., 223
Elderton, W.P., 114
Eldridge, George D., 68, 97, 98, 121
Electronic data processing
   SEE computers
Elkin, J.M., 210
Elliott, Ezekiel B., 2, 13
Ellis, D.M., 210
Elston, James S., 115, 127, 160, 161, 294, 321
Emery, J.M., 74
Emory, Linda B., 273
Employee Retirement Income Security Act of 1974
   (ERISA), 264, 267-269, 312, 404
Engelfriet, Prof. Dr., 345
Enrolled Actuaries, 221, 251, 267-270
   SEE ALSO American Society of Pension Actuaries
Enrolled Actuaries Report, The, 231, 234, 270
Entz, John F., 2, 13, 29, 30, 36
Episcopal Corporation, 8
Equitable Life Assurance Society (in London), 6, 8
   bicentenary, 206

Equitable Life Assurance Society of New York, 13, 67,
   129, 363
   tontine field, 33, 37
Equity Funding Life Insurance Company, 262, 263
ERISA
   SEE Employee Retirement Income Security Act of
   1974
Espie, Robert G., 197, 358
ETS
   SEE Educational Testing Service
Evans, Percy H., 60, 113, 117, 299
Experience rating
   SEE Credibility theory

-F-

FAA
   SEE Fraternal Actuarial Association
Fackler, David Parks, 1, 3, 23-24, *25*, 26, 29-33, 37,
   44-48, 50, 52-54, 58, 59, 64, 66, 103, 104, 114, 118,
   284, 338, 347
   library, 118
Fackler, Edward B., 118, 121
Faculty of Actuaries, 14, 101, 155, 167, 168, 349
   influence on A.I.A. & A.S.A., 78-80
   women members, 27
   SEE ALSO *Transactions of the Faculty of Actuaries*
Fallow, Everett S., *85*, 298
Farley, Jarvis, 142, 143, 202, 250, 262, 329, 330, 354
Farr, Charles E., 234, 269, 311
Farr, Dr. William, 333, 347
FASB
   SEE Financial Accounting Standards Board
Fassel, Elgin G., 151, 156, 336
Federal income taxation (U.S.)
   SEE life insurance companies
Fellers, W.W., 282
Ferguson, C.C., 161
Ferguson, William A., 222
Ferrara, Giovanna, 276
Fewster, L. Blake, 145
Field, R.P., 50
Financial Accounting Standards Board (FASB), 250
Financial statements, 197, 198
Finelli, John J., 208, 344, 345
Finlaison, John, 135
Fire and marine insurance, 1, 86
Fischer, Carl H., 190, 298
Fisher, Sir Ronald A., 385
Fitzhugh, Gilbert W., 144, 208, 263, 264
Flynn, Benedict D., *85*, 87, 92, 119, 162
Fondiller, Richard, 367
Forbes, C.S., 87
Foster, Clark T., 184
Fowler, J.A., 4, 58
Frankel, Mary G., 60
Frankland, Frederick W., 284
Franklin, Benjamin, 92

Franklin, Lawrence M., 269
Fraser, John C., 193, 241
Fraternal Actuarial Association (FAA), 90-100, 198, 199, 251, 270, 309, 311
   charter members, 99
   dues 1919-1979, 372
   farewell to, 271
   first women members, 63, 128
   Guides to Professional Conduct, 192
   history of, 271
   library, 100
   membership in 1918, 101
   membership in 1948, 159, 205
   membership in 1964, 205
   operations, 368
   tenth anniversary, 120, 121
   SEE ALSO
      fraternal benefit societies,
      Proceedings of the Fraternal Actuarial Association
Fraternal benefit societies, 34, 52, 121
   disability experience, 320
   SEE ALSO Fraternal Actuarial Association
French Institute, 61
Friedman, Lloyd K. and Annie N., 306
Friend, Edward H., 253, 280
Fuhrer, J., 68
Futurism, 276

-G-

GAAP
   SEE Generally Accepted Accounting Principles
Gadient, Frank J., 217, 218
Galloway, C.T.P., 281
Garabedian, Harold A., 307
Gardner, Earl B., 354
Gardner, John R., 273
Garfin, Louis, 326
Geddes, G. W., 161
Generally Accepted Accounting Principles (GAAP), 244-250
Georgia State University, 306, 381
Gerber, Hans U., 282, 311, 384
Gerry, Frank E., 172, 217, 221
Gershenson, Harry, 307
Gibb, J.B., 78
Gibb, William T., III, 251
Gilbert, W.S., 401
Giles, L. Timothy, 346
Gill, Ardian C., 272, 403
Gill, Charles, 1, 2, 7, 9, 11-13, 15, 17, 19, 24, 41
Gillam, William S., 226
Girard Life Insurance, Annuity and Trust Company of Philadelphia, 8
Givens, Harrison, Jr., 281
Glover, Professor James W., 74, 140, 297, 369, 385

Gold, Melvin L., 178
Goldberg, Milton J., 399, 400
Goldman, L., 105
Goldsmith, Raymond W., 178
Gompertz, Benjamin, 135, 165
   biography, 194
   Gompertz's constant, 194
   law of mortality, 6
Goodrich, Clarence R., 128
Goodrich, Eloise Koch, 128, 130
Gore, J. Howard, 105, 298
Gore, John K., 64, 68, 105, 160, 338, 394
Gould, W.H., 74
Graham, George, 73, 110, 289
Graham, William J., 82, 83, *85*, 160, 161, 163
Grange, W.K., , 256
Gray, J.R., 208
Greeley, C., 280
Green, Edward A., 209, 399
Greene, Winfield W., *85*, 87, 92, 391, 392
Greenwood, J.A., 192
Gresham, John J., 22
Greville, T.N.E., 208, 298
Griffin, Frank L., Jr., 118, 184, 186, 188, 189, 196, 258, 265-267, 279, 400
Gross premium valuation
   SEE valuation
Groth, A.A., 210
Group life insurance, 82, 83, 102, 114, 121, 386
   mortality studies, 112
   T-rate minimums, 115
Groves, William E., 218
Grubbs, Donald S., 237, 265, 268
Guardian Life, 129
Guardian Mutual, 29, 34
Guertin, Alfred N., 146, *147*, 151, 176, 193, 298, 326
Guertin committees, 137, 146-149
Guertin laws, 272
Guest, Richard C., 151, 193
Gundy, Harry F., 161, 207, 279
Gustafson, Dale R., 246, 262

-H-

Hager, William D., 251
Haight, Arthur M., 173
Hald, Anders, 384
Hall, Clayton C., 43, 44, 47, 49, 58
Hall, H.S., 283
Hall, John W., 295
Hall, Samuel S., 284
Halley, Edmond, 135
   law of mortality, 6
Halmstad, David Garrick, 229, 281
Halvorson, William A., 206, 277
Hamilton, James A., 279, 400
Hammond, Dr. E. Cuyler, 195, 227
Hann, A.G., 74

Hann, Robert G., 105
Hansen, S., 207
Hanson, John, 222, 266
Hardcastle, Edward E., 75
Harper, Floyd S., 306
Hart, Senator Philip A., 242
Hart, Ward VanBuren, 135
Harvey, Augustus F., 334
Harvey, Charles J., 42
Harvey, Julian C., 334
Hasbrouck, Frank, 128, 129
Haugh, Charles J., 392
Hayes, Rea B., 234
Hazlehurst, Blackburn H., 264, 280, 281
Health insurance, 386
    SEE ALSO income disability benefits
Heath, Ethel M., 63, 128
Hegeman, John R., 83
Henderson, Robert, 70, 83, 84, 112, 129, 160, 284, 294, 295, 398
Henningsen, Victor E., 200, 227, 238, 255, 312, 367, 399
Hennington, Howard H., 196, 266, 267, 282, 354, 356
Herfurth, Carl E., 78, 326
Herman, James R., 101, 127, 157, 290, 375
Hewitt, Charles C., Jr., 229, 233, 262, 314, 358, 385, 389, 392
Hewitt, David L., 404
Heywood, Geoffrey, 256
Hickman, James C., 258, 269, 298, 306, 311, 314, 384, 388
Hickman, Herbert W., 131, 185
Hicks, Ernest L., 265, 266
Hicks, Orton H., 397
Higham, Charles D., 58, 117
Hill, J.S., 279
Hill, William B., 4
Hipp, Grady H., 129, 323
Hitchins, William R., 284
H^M Table, 83
Hobbs, Clarence W., 142, 154, 392
Hoffman, Frederick L., 87, 105, 106, 160, 161
Hogg, Robert V., 229
Hohaus, Reinhard A., 114, 124, 142, 144, 156-158, 160, 166, 170, 183, 190, 195, 207, 216, 217, 238, 290, 299, 376, 380
Hollenberg, Maximilian R., 114
Hollerith, Herman, 337, 338
Holloway, Lambert A., 354
Holmes, Benjamin T., 142, 166, 191, 297, 301, 303, 402
Holmes, H., 207
Holsten, Fred A., 354
HOLUA
    SEE Home Office Life Underwriters Association
Homans, I.S., 74
Homans, Sheppard, 13, 19, 20, 24, 25, 26-27, 39-31, 37, 41, 44, 46-48, 50, 58, 59, 61, 74, 97, 135

    SEE ALSO American Experience Table
Home Life, 129, 363
Home Office Life Underwriters Association (HOLUA), 116
Homes, Henry F., 37
Hoover, Herbert, 143
Hopkins, Hazel H., 371
Horn, Richard G., 248, 249
Hoskins, James E., 126, 127, 147, 162, 300, 302
Hoskins, Robert H., 232
Houser, Robert N., 272, 275
Howell, A. Charles, 265
Howell, Valentine, 132
Hrncsjar, Margaret, 365-367
Hsiao, William C., 258, 259
Hughes, Charles, 85, 289
Hughes, Norman M., 193
Hughey, M. Stanley, 229, 232
Humphrys, Richard, 177, 214
Hunter, Arthur, 46, 54, 68, 70, 72, 73, 78-80, 82, 88, 93, 98, 103, 105-109, 111, 112, 115, 116, 129, 138, 139, 160-163, 287, 292-294, 320, 324, 325, 337, 339, 352-354, 396, 397
    disability tables, 321, 322
Hunter, James, 301, 303
Hunter, Robertson G., 106, 114
Huntington, Robert W., 155, 395
Huse, Sylvester J., 266
Huston, F. Edward, 326
Hutcheson, William A., 29, 31, 78, 83-85, 95, 108, 155, 160, 287, 288, 321
Hutchings, Peter L., 239

-I-

IACA
    SEE International Association of Consulting Actuaries
Iliff, Charles W., 97, 121
Immerwahr, George E., 142, 184
Immunization, 274
Income disability benefits, 319-330
    Canadian experience, 327, 328
    1932 flight from coverage, 324
    noncancellable contracts, 328-330
    SEE ALSO disability income benefits
Income tax (U.S.),
    SEE life insurance companies
Individual life insurance
    design and pricing, 240, 241
    SEE ALSO
        nonforfeiture standards,
        policy cost comparisons,
        valuation standards
Inflation, 154, 178, 185, 187, 241, 257, 261, 269, 274, 277, 365
Influenza pandemic of 1918, 100, 101, 108, 109
Ingraham, Harold G., Jr., 243, 310

Institut Canadien des Actuaires,
SEE Canadian Institute of Actuaries
Institute of Actuaries, 13, 14, 18, 47-49, 94, 101, 166-168, 206, 255, 347, 349, 350, 373
Centenary Assembly, 69, 122, 123, 126, 142, 193, 356, 357
established, 14
fiftieth anniversary, 61
first North American Fellows, 14, 36
Jubilee Dinner, 283
Members' Handbook, 60
Staple Inn Hall, 14, 167, 123, 327, 342, 364, 366
Text-Book, 55, 57, 203, 294
women members, 27, 62
SEE ALSO *Journal of the Institute of Actuaries*
Institute of Life Insurance, 242
Insurance Accounting and Statistical Association, 345, 346
Insurance Act of the Dominion of Canada of 1910, 69
Insurance Company of North America, 4, 383
Insurance Monitor and Wall Street Review, 28, 29
Insurance Regulatory and Information System (IRIS), 278
Insurance Society of New York, 117
Insurance supervision, 15
British North America Act, 35
Canada, 35
Dominion Department of Insurance, 111
New York's expense limitation, 128-131, 151
state vs. federal, 29, 136, 137
United States, 36
SEE ALSO
Armstrong Investigation of 1905,
Elizur Wright,
nonforfeiture standards,
valuation standards
Insurance Times, The, 31, 37, 38
Intercompany mortality studies
SEE mortality studies
Interest rates, 138, 302
cyclic theory, 176
historical, 40, 49, 54, 114, 150, 151
SEE ALSO
compound interest,
investment yields
International Actuarial Association (IAA), 60, 61, 191, 276
SEE ALSO International Congress of Actuaries
International Association of Consulting Actuaries (IACA), 255, 256
International Congress of Actuaries, 52, 55, 60, 121-123
eighteenth (1968), 255, 279
eighth (1927), 115, 122, 123, 160
eleventh (1937), 122, 162, 163, 190
fifteenth (1957), 190, 208, 345, 379
fifth (1906), 105, 298
first (1895), 54, 61, 104, 121, 347
fourteeenth (1954), 190, 207
fourth (1903), 62, 74, 101, 104, 298, 306, 319, 363
National Reports, 191
nineteenth (1972), 255, 280, 348
ninth (1930), 122, 161
North American actuaries' papers, 61, 104-106, 160-164, 207-210
second (1898), 3, 61, 104
seventeenth (1964), 204, 205, 210, 388
seventh (1912), 106, 121
sixteenth (1960), 191, 209, 327
sixth (1909), 105
tenth (1934), 122, 125, 161, 325
third (1900), 62, 104
thirteenth (1951), 122, 190, 207
twelfth (1940), 122, 163, 164, 347
twentieth (1976), 255, 281, 348
twenty-first (1980), 255, 316
twenty-second (1984), 206
SEE ALSO *Transactions of the International Congress of Actuaries*
International Life Assurance Society, 20, 21
Investment yields, 54, 175, 176
Ireland, John, 189
Ireland, Oscar B., 18, 47, 82, 336
IRIS
SEE Insurance Regulatory and Supervision System

-J-

JAAA
SEE *Journal of the American Academy of Actuaries*
Jack, Colin E., *370*, 371
Jackson, E. Sydney, 213, 214, 217
Jackson, Henry H., 6, 26, 39, 92, 134, 135, 161, 165, 166, 167, 302, 347
Jackson, Paul H., 269, 279, 282, *370*
Jackson, Robert T., 259
Jacobson, R.I., 281
Jacoby, Oswald, 118, 359, 396-398
Jacquard, Joseph Marie, 337
Jahn, Fred S., 144
James, John F., 2, 8
James, Professor William, 293
Jellicoe, Charles, 19, 25, 26
Jelliffe, ----, 363
Jenkins, Wilmer A., 113, 151, 156, 183, 186, 191, 193, 208
Jewell, Professor William S., 387
Joffe, Solomon A., 7, 13, 24
John Hancock Mutual Life, 17, 34
Johnson, Oscar F., 101
Johnson, Samuel, 135
Johnson, William C., 320
Joint Board for the Enrollment of Actuaries, 267, 268

Jones, David, 61, 283, 347
Jones, Donald A., 298, 311, 384, 387, 388
Jones, Nathan F., 240, 241, 349, 354, 355, 388
Jones, Richard J., 354
Jordan, C. Wallace, 118, 307, 315
Journal of the American Academy of Actuaries (JAAA), 251, 252
Journal of the Institute of Actuaries (JIA), 18-19, 155
    Assurance Magazine, 14
    papers of North American actuaries, 17, 41, 42
    SEE ALSO Institute of Actuaries
Junior Actuaries Club of New York, 375

-K-

Kahn, P.M., 210, 279
Kattell, Sherman C., 148
Kaufman, Henry N., 337
Keeton, Professor Robert, 224
Keffer, Ralph, 386
Kellam, William Porter, 21
Kellison, Stephen G., 220, 225, 251, 306, 311, *370*, 372
Kellogg, A.W., 29
Kepler, Johannes, 333
Khury, C.K., 282
Kilbourne, Frederick W., 88, 225, 282, 392, 393
Kime, Virgil M., 74, 101
Kimeldorf, Professor George S., 387
King, Estella C., 62
King, George, 55, 61, 283, 336, 347
Klem, Walter, 17, 166, 180, 191, 205, 235, 236, 315, 343
Klugman, Stuart A., 229, 298, 384
Knauer, Virginia, 242
Knickerbocker Life, 34
Knight, Charles K., 8
Knight, Gardner F., 333, 334
Knight, S.R., 283
Knowler, Professor Lloyd A., 223, 298
Knowlton, Henry K., 230
Korean War, 173
Kormes, M., 279
Kraegel, W.A., 279
Kreader, J. Lee, 89
Krueger, Claudia M., 371
Kulp, Clarence A., 295

-L-

Laird, John M., 136, 137, 160, 161, 163, 296, 319, 336
Laird, Morton A., 401
Lamps, Dale E., 227
Lancaster, Edwin B., 244
Lander, Maxwell, 256, 357
Landis, Abb, 52, *89*, 97, 98, 103, 121, 198
Lange, Jeffrey T., 348
Langer, David, 239
Langstaff, James Miles, *350*, 351
Larson, Robert E., 306
Larus, John R., 83, 122, 127, 166, 180, 396

Lathrop, John B., 354
Lautzenheiser, Barbara J., 276
Lawson, Harold R., 178, 179, 215, 231, 281, 382, 399
Leach, ---, 363
Leapman, Donald J., 128, 375
Lebourveau, Allan F., 239
Lee, H. Douglas, 238
Lee, James Morgan, 360
Leslie, William, Jr., 92, 119, 162, 195, 359
Levinson, L., 209
Lew, Edward A., 183, 194, 209, 227, 228, 230, 275, 279, 349, 356, 382, 386
Lewis, Charlton T., 28, 29, 54, 105
Lewis, Sinclair, 389
LIAA
    SEE Life Insurance Association of America
LIAMA
    SEE Life Insurance Agency Management Association,
    Life Insurance Marketing and Research Association
Lidstone, George J., 60
Life Insurance Agency Management Association (LIAMA), 400
Life Insurance Association of America (LIAA), 250
Life insurance companies
    federal income taxation, 193
    financial statements, 197, 198, 244-250
    mutual, 4, 8
    number in 1888, 40
    rise of assessment, 34, 35
    stock, 8
    SEE ALSO fraternal benefit societies
Life Insurance Marketing and Research Association, 243, 400
Life insurance, history of, 288
Life insurance premiums
    early, 6-9
Life insurance products
    product revolution, 177, 178
    surrender values, 22, 23
    SEE ALSO
    group life insurance,
    individual life insurance,
    policy cost comparisions,
    universal life
Life Insurance Sales Research Bureau, 151
Life Office Management Association (LOMA), 302, 303
Life tables
    first, 38
    SEE ALSO mortality tables
Life Underwriters' Convention
    first attempts, 18, 19
LIMRA
    SEE Life Insurance Marketing and Research Association
Lincoln, Owen C., 72

Lincoln National Life, 115
Link, Robert F., 184, 259, 260
Linton, M. Albert, 70, 123, 129, 130, 133, 135, *140*, 142, 151, 162, 178, 207
Lipton, M.F., 210
Liscord, Paul, 233
Little, James F., 126, 163
Little Rock Actuarial Club, 381
LOMA
    SEE Life Office Management Association
London, Richard L., 307
Longley-Cook, Laurence H., 92, 203, 204, 207, 217, 218, 279, 308, 361, 378, 383, 387
Luckner, Warren R., 306
Lukacs, E., 163, 208
Lundborg, Ova, 386
Lyons, Daniel J., 131

-M-

Mabon, J.B., 162
Macaulay, Thomas B., 14, 42, 46, 48, 61, 82, 103, 104, 131, 145, 350, 398
MacCharles, F.D., 164
Macdonald, William Campbell, 117, 351
Macfarlane, William, 353, *354*
MacGinnitie, W. James, 224, 262
MacGregor, Kenneth R., 14, 35, 188
Mackenzie, Michael A., 297
MacKinnon, Will, 365
Maclean, Alexander T., 133
Maclean, Joseph B., 27, 71, 72, 79, 80, 98, 129, 152, 153, 198, 295, 303, 322, 324, 359
Madden, Madeline M., 220, 372
Maddex, Sir George, 166, 167, 183
Maglathlin, Ralph H., 196
Magoun, William N., *85*
Maguire, Ralph D., 386
Mahillon, L., 61
Mahoney, Michael J., 252
Malthus, Thomas Robert, 135, 301
Manhart case
    SEE pension plans
Manley, H.W., 34
Marples, William F., 187, 188, 210
Marshall, Edward W., 295, 343
Marshall, Ralph M., 295
Marshall, William A., 67, 68
Martin, D.B., 209
Martin, Grace A., 62, 128
Massachusetts Hospital Life Insurance Company, 2, 6, 7, 9
Massachusetts Mutual Life, 23
Masterson, Norton E., 201
Mathematical Association of America, 181, 308
Mathematical Miscellany, 11

Mathematical statistics
    SEE statistics
Matthews, A.N., 209
Maycrink, Emma C., 62
Mayerson, Allen L., 131, 187, 224, 298, 386, 387
Maynard, John C., 243, 249, 360
McAdam, Lucius, 27, 29, 30, 34, 37, 74, 75, 77, 104
McAndless, Alva J., 123, 155, 156, 193, *301*, 326
McCabe, William, 47, *49*, 284
McCarter, William C., 114
McCay, Professor Charles F., 2, 21, 22, 27, 40, 42
McClintock, Emory, 1, 11, 13, 17, 18, 29, 41, 44, 47, 48, *49*, 50, 58, 60, 61, 62, 64, 67, 68, 71, 95, 96, 103, 104, 112, 284, 300, 306, 333, 395
McClintock's Annuity Tables, 114
McConney, Edmund M., 35, 151, 166, *167*, 193, 238, 367, 380, 399
McCracken, Archie R., 253
McDiarmid, Fergus J., 54, 123, 175, 178, 186, 277
McGill, Dan M., 184, 187, 188, 189
McGiveran, Ben, 184
McGuinness, J.S., 209, 279, 282
McIntyre, Beatrice, 363
McKellar, J.A., 74
McKinnie, Arthur A., 367, 369, 372
McLean, John Victor, *350*, 351
McManus, Robert J., 291
Mead, Franklin B., *114-116*, 134, 160, 324
Meares, Charles W.V., 79, 353
Meech, Levi W., 30, 34, 38, 41
    multiplying book, 52, 331, *332*
Melnikoff, Meyer, 189
Menge, Walter O., 193, 207, 297, 388
Merchant's Magazine and Commercial Review, The, 21
Mereu, J.A., 282
Merriam, Walter A., 173
Merrill, Lieutenant Lewis, 19
Messenger, Hiram J., 105, 106, 319
Metropolitan Life, 58, 129, 143, 325, 334, 345, 346, 363
Mexican Actuarial Association, 205, 278
Mexican Association of Life Insurance Actuaries
    SEE Mexican Actuarial Association
Mexican Institute of Actuaries, 204
Mexican National University, 278
Meyer, Professor Balthaser H., 306
Michelbacher, Gustav F., *85*, 103, 154, 295, 307
Michie, Ian G., 214
Middle Atlantic Actuarial Club, 380
Miller, B.J., 47, *49*, 67
Miller, John H., 179, 180, 197, 216-218, 228, 233, 250, *254*, 281, 307, 310, 311, 320, 328-330
Miller, Morton D., 235, 238, 239, *254*, 255, 281, 295
Miller, Walter N., 241
Milliman, Wendell A., 155, 166, 184, 250, 251, 309, 310, 337
Milne, Joshua, 283

Mims, James Luther, 169, 172
Minor, E.H., 279
Missouri State Life, 138
Mitchell, Robert B., 232, 238
Moir, Henry, 23, 24, 66, 68, 71, 78-*80*, 83, 84, 105, 106, 108, 114, 133, 139, 160-162, 287, 294, 300, 398
Montgomery, John O., 272, 276
Montgomery Ward Company, 82
Moore, Ruth, 363
Moorhead, Ernest J., 231, 232, 237, 239, 241, 242, 258-260, 400
Morabito, Edith F., 365
Moran, Joseph W., 231
Morgan, W.G., 37
Morgan, William, 5, 283
Morris, Edward B., 70, 109, 112, 129, 323, 377
Morris, William O., 289, 399
Morrison, J. Edward, 191, 213
Morse, Dr. Philip M., 353, 355, 356
Mortality experience, 102
    Mutual Benefit Life, 38
    Mutual Life of New York, 11-13
    war experience, 19, 152
    SEE ALSO
        annuities,
        mortality studies,
        mortality tables
Mortality projection, 114
Mortality studies, 38, 39, 111-113, 193-195
    Actuarial Society of America members, 83
    American-Canadian Mortality Investigation, 66, 73
    Basic Table 1935-1954, 195
    Basic Table 1920-1934, 148
    Basic Table 1925-1932, 112
    Basic Table 1920-1926, 112
    Blood Pressure Study of 1925, 111
    Build and Blood Pressure Study of 1979, 230
    early intercompany, 29, 38, 63-66
    group life insurance, 112
    Joint Occupation Study of 1929, 111, 112
    Medical Impairment Study of 1929, 111
    Medico-Actuarial Mortality Investigation (MAMI), 64-66, 111, 338
    Mortality on Policies for Large Amounts, 112
    1959 Build and Blood Pressure Study, 194
    1951 Impairment Study, 194
    smoker and nonsmoker, 194, 227
    Specialized Mortality Investigation, 64, 116
    SEE ALSO
        mortality experience,
        mortality tables
Mortality tables
    SEE
    Actuaries' Table,
    American Annuitants Mortality Tables,
    American Experience Table,
    American Men Table,

Annuity Table for 1949,
Canadian Men Table,
Carlisle Table,
Combined Annuity Table,
Combined Experience Table,
Commissioners Standard Industrial Table (CSI),
H^M Table,
McClintock's Annuity Tables,
National Fraternal Congress Table of Mortality,
1980 Commissioners Standard Ordinary Table,
1958 Commissioners Standard Ordinary Table,
1941 Commissioners Standard Ordinary Table,
1937 Standard Annuity Table,
Northampton Table,
Table Z,
Thirty American Offices Table,
United States Annuitants 1918-1927,
X_{17} Table
SEE ALSO
    life tables,
    mortality studies
Morton, Alton P., 194, 208, 279
Mowbray, Professor Albert H., 73, 86, 87, 92, 103, 119, 140, 142, 160, 298, 326
Moyer, Ross, 367
Mullaney, Frank R., *85*
Muller, N., 280
Munnell, Alicia H., 262
Munson, Bartley L., 96, 242, 271
Murch, A.D., 208
Murphy, James J., 315
Murphy, Ray D., 112, 163, 173, 207, 295, 326
Murphy, T.B., 281
Murrin, Thomas E., 218, 250
Musher, Joseph, 189
Mutual Benefit Life Insurance Company, 11, 23, 326, 327, 337, 340
    mortality experience study, 38
Mutual funds, 179
Mutual life insurance, 26, 134, 135
Mutual life insurance companies
    SEE life insurance companies
Mutual Life of New York, 8, 11, 24, 26, 29, 37, 67, 321
    history, 21
Mutualization, 129
    Pacific Mutual Life case, 326
Myer, G.G., 280
Myers, Robert J., 13, *140*, 142, 143, 189, 207-210, 218, 232, 255-257, 261, 262, 280-282, 295

-N-

NAIC
    SEE National Association of Insurance Commissioners
Nail, T.M., 295

National Actuaries Institute, 28

National Association of Insurance Commissioners (NAIC), 36, 94, 146, 147, 177, 243, 272
SEE ALSO National Convention of Insurance Commissioners

National Association of Life Underwriters, 50, 177, 242, 243, 272

National Commission on Social Security Reform, 261, 262

National Convention of Insurance Commissioners (NCIC), 36, 66, 109, 110, 136, 323
SEE ALSO National Association of Insurance Commissioners

National Council on Compensation Insurance, 367

National Fraternal Congress (NFC), 97, 368

National Fraternal Congress Table of Mortality, 97

National Life of the United States, 138

National Reports, 210, 280, 281, 282

National Service Life Insurance Program, 354

Naylor, Carman A., 214, *219*

NCIC
SEE National Convention of Insurance Commissioners

Nebraska Actuaries Club, 306, 381

Nelson, Helen, 363

Nesbitt, Professor Cecil J., 184, 209, 229, 269, 282, 298, 304, 311, 384

Neumann, E.M., 164, 207

New England Mutual, 8, 9, 11, 23, 97, 334

Newman, Steven H., 229

New South Life case, 238, 239

New York Life, 35, 67, 116, 321, 325, 337, 363

New York Life Insurance and Trust Company, 2, 6, 7

New York's expense limitation statute
SEE insurance supervision

NFC
SEE National Fraternal Congress

Nicholas, Lewis A., *85*

Nichols, Walter S., 3, 41, 61, 82, 92, 93, 95, 103, 104, 292

Niessen, Abraham M., 185

1980 Commissioners Standard Ordinary (CSO) Table, 273, 274

1958 Commissioners Standard Ordinary (CSO) Table, 176, 177, 273

1941 Commissioners Standard Ordinary (CSO) Table, 148-152, 176

1937 Standard Annuity Table, 183, 194

Nitchie, Joseph H., 37, 50, 73, 74, 283, 284

Noback, Joseph C., 246

Nonforfeiture standards, 146-149, 272-274

Non-medical insurance, 113

Northampton Table, 7

Northeastern University, 307

Northwestern Mutual Life, 29, 334

November, William J., 194

Nuclear era, 173-175

Nulty, Eugenius, 7

-O-

Oakley, Colonel H.J.P., 114, 155

O'Connell, Professor Jeffrey, 224

O'Connor, John E., Jr., 369, *370*

Ogborn, M.E., 283

Ogden, S.N., 105

Old Age Survivors and Disability Insurance (OASDI)
SEE social security (U.S.)

Olmstead, Blair E., 338, 344

Olshen, Abraham C., 354, 356

Operations research, 311, 312, 354-356

Ormsby, Charles A., 273

Orr, Robert K., 87

-P-

Pacific Coast Actuarial Club, 378

Pacific Mutual Life, 138, 326

Pacific States Actuarial Club, 378

Page, B.A., 319

Panjer, Harry H., 307

Papps, Percy C.H., 25, 26, 287, 295, 299, 337, 374

Paradis, Gaston, 306

Parker, Donn B., 263

Parker, John G., 144, 152-153, 163, 300, 374

Parsons, R.D., 282

Partridge, Frances D., 63

Pascal, Blaise, 333

Paterson, John S., 36

Patrick, Gary, 229

Patterson, Professor Robert, 2, 4

Patterson, Robert M., 4

Patterson, W.D., 207

Pattison, George B., 289

PBGC
SEE Pension Benefit Guaranty Corporation

PCAS
SEE *Proceedings of the Casualty Actuarial Society*

Pedoe, Arthur, 125-128, 145, 162, 163, 173, 193, 276, 277, 297, 301, 302, 376, 402, 403

Peiler, Max H., 336

Peirce, Professor Benjamin, 20

Pennsylvania Company for Insurances on Lives and Granting Annuities, 4, 7

Pennsylvania State University, 307

Pension Benefit Guaranty Corporation (PBGC), 267, 269

Pension mathematics, 83-85, 269

Pension plans, 83-85, 123-125, 159, 182-189, 196, 197, 263-270
Federal Welfare and Pension Plans Disclosure Act, 195
group permanent contracts, 125, 189

in Canada, 190
Manhart case, 237, 269
pension trusts, 189
SEE ALSO
    American Society of Pension Actuaries,
    social insurance,
    social security (U.S.)
Pension Research Council, 184
Peoria Life, 138
Perryman, Francis S., 154, 203, 207, 348, 387
Peterson, Loren V., 306
Peterson, Ray M., 185, 188-190, 208
Pettengill, D.W., 208
PFAA
    SEE *Proceedings of the Fraternal Actuarial
    Association*
Phelps, John, 209, 210, *301*
Philadelphia, 4
Phillips, E. William, 193, 340, *341*, 342, 345
Phillips, George W., 29, 30, 37
Phillips, James T., 161, 179, 180, 190, 294, 322
Phillips, Thomas A., 140, 289
Phillips, W.N., 121
Phoenix Mutual Life, 35, 194, 337
Pierson, Israel C., 37, 46, *49*, 52, 61, 62, 102, 104, 347,
    363, 394
Pinney, Sydney D., 298, 392
Pipe, Sidney H., 97, 98, 120, 121, 163
Plumley, Peter W., 312, 313, 316, 369, *370*
Plummer, H.C., 331
Plymen, John, 354
Policy cost comparisions, 241-243
Poorman, William F., 125
Portch, Albert G., 94, 101
Posnak, Robert L., 246, 247
Pounder, Irvine R., 297
Premium notes, 9, 34
Premium rates
    SEE life insurance premiums
Premont, Professor Andre, 306
Presbyterian Ministers Fund, 2, 8, 21
Price, Dr. Richard, 5, 283, 386
Pricing and product design
    competitive problems, 113-115
Probability
    early examination, 284
Proceedings of the Casualty Actuarial Society (PCAS),
    92, 143
*Proceedings of the Centenary Assembly of the Institute
    of Actuaries*,
    SEE Institute of Actuaries
*Proceedings of the Conference of Actuaries in Public
    Practice (PCAPP)*, 221
*Proceedings of the Fraternal Actuarial Association
    (PFAA)*, 96, 368
Product revolution, 177, 178
Professional ethics
    SEE actuarial profession

Provident Mutual Life, 129
Prudential, 129, 337
Pruitt, Dudley M., 87, 120, 142, 143, 201-204, 290-292,
    305, 367, 392
Punched-card systems
    early mortality study, 64
    SEE ALSO computers

-Q-

-R-

Rae, William M., 176, 184, 186
R.A.I.A.
    SEE *Record of the American Institute of Actuaries*
Ramsay, Alexander G., 14, 46
Ramsey, Henry B., Jr., 250
Randall, Robert J., 239
Rappaport, Anna Maria, 312, 313
Reconstruction Finance Corporation, 138
*Record of the American Institute of Actuaries
    (R.A.I.A.)*, 143, 398
Record of the Society of Actuaries (RSA), 235, 313
Redington, Frank M., 176, 346
Reeder, Howard C., 366
Reid, E.E., 162
Reilly, Professor John F., 298
Reiter, Charles G., *53*
Remarriage tables,
    SEE American Remarriage Table, 1933
Reserves
    SEE
        mortality tables,
        valuation,
        valuation actuary,
        valuation standards
Reversionary bonus
    SEE dividends
Reynolds, Frank G., 307, 348
Rhodes, Edward E., 23, 60, 68, 69, 129, 134, 160, 161,
    193, 289, 326, 327, 330, 396
Rholl, Donald A., 270
Richardson, Charles F.B., 116, 137, 147, 151, 162, 210,
    273, 274, 275, 302
Richter, Otto C., 141, 142, 196
Rieder, Edward A., 343
Rietz, Professor Henry L., 103, 123, 140, 161, 169, 298,
    385
Rihouey, Adrienne M., 238
Risk classification, 252
Risk theory, 384
Ritcey, Lee F.S., 298
Ritchie, J.W., 208
Robb, Donald Hamilton, 351
Robbins, Rainard B., 39, 139, 142

Roberts, Joseph, 4, 6, 7, 17
Robertson, A. Haeworth, 256, 257, 262
Robertson, Richard S., 316
Roche, John Francis, 58, *63*, 284
Rodermund, Matthew, 225, 226, 233, 272, 391, 393, 394
Roeber, William F., 160, 295
Roelofs, Dr. Vernon W., 96, 271
Roffey, A.E., 281
Rogers, Oscar H., 111
Rollerson, Lloyd G., 214
Rolph, Dorothy, 62
Rood, Henry F., 166, 176, 191-193, 195, 196, 210, 215-218, *219*, 250, 357, 378
Roosevelt, Franklin D., 89, 136, 138, 140, 144, 189, 190
Rose, Douglas H., 100, 106, 284
Ross, James B., 228
Ross, K.H., 210
Rosser, H., 280
Roy, J., 281
RSA
    SEE *Record of the Society of Actuaries*
Rubinow, Isaac Max, 87-*89*, 92, 103, 119, 138, 153, 202
Rugland, Walter L., 198, 216, 217, 251
Rugland, Walter S., 238
Rutherford, Charles D., 114, 139
Ryall, Peter L.J., 307
Ryan, Sir Gerald H., 36, 55, 58
Ryan, Harwood E., 86, 92, 119
Ryan, Kevin M., 314
Rydgren, Adolph A., 198
Ryrie, George, 402, 403

-S-

St.John, Howell W., 12, 29, 44, 49, 53, 58, 61, 103, 104
Salzmann, Ruth E., 276
Sanderson, Frank, 105, 298
Sarason, Harry M., 301, 302, 398
Sartelle, E.J., 68
Scattergood, Claude E., 87, 367
Scheig, Henry F., 198, 199
Scheutz, Edward, 333
Scheutz, George, 333
Schmidt, William H., 279, 315, 316
Schuette, Donald R., 209, 306
Schull, Joseph, 145
Scott, Ellis W., 268
Seal, Hilary L., 184, 280
SEC
    SEE Securities and Exchange Commission
Securities and Exchange Commission (SEC), 250
See, Gary N., 220, 369, *370*, 372
Seeber, Robert R., 354
Seitz, Jacob C., 75, 77
Seltzer, Frederic, 282
Senior Actuaries Club, 373, 376, *377*, 378

Senior, Leon S., *85*
Settlement options, 114
Sewell, Edward H., 37
Shannon, Simon, 162, 164, 398
Shapiro, Arnold F., 307
Shapiro, Leslie S., 267, 268
Shaw, Samuel E., 399
Sheffler, William, 30
Shellard, Gordon D., 349, 352, 354, 356
Shepherd, Bruce E., 147, 193, 207, 375
Shepherd, Clinton O., 8, 19, 23, 40, 147, 148, 207
Shepherd, Pearce, 307
Sheppard, Herbert N., 105, 114
Sheppard, Norris E., 297
Shoemaker, Jacob, 2, 4, 5, 283
Shudde, Louis O., 193
Sibigtroth, J.C., 281
Siegfried, Charles A., 189, 229
Sillesky, J. Darrison, 269
Simmonds, Reginald C., 350, 373
Simon, LeRoy J., 233, 386
Simoneau, Paul W., 224
Single-premium annuities
    SEE annuities
Skelding, Albert Z., 367
Slater, R.E., 208
Slezak, L.F., 208
Sloan, Maryrose, 371
Sloat, Frederick P., 196, 266, 267
Smith, C., 282
Smith, Edward Buckey, 50, 58, 360
Smith, F. Eugene, 265
Smith, Henry W., 37, 47, 49, 294
Smith, J. Henry, 189, 208, 240
Smith, Victor R., 69, 155, 162, 163
Smith, William S., 36, 62
SOA
    SEE Society of Actuaries
Soble, Ronald L., 263
Social insurance, 88, 89, 138-143, 159, 202
    Townsend Plan, 141
    SEE ALSO
        pension plans,
        social security (U.S.)
Social security (U.S.), 89, 189, 190, 229, 241, 286, 323, 330
    decoupling, 259, 260
    mortality experience, 193
    OASDI trust funds, 260, 261
    old age benefits, 138-143, 170
    Speaker's Kit, 260
    trouble in, 256-262
    unemployment benefits, 143, 144
    SEE ALSO social insurance
Society of Actuaries (SOA), 242, 243, 251, 270, 308-312, 380

archives, 7, 35, 118, 301, 306, 342, 350, 360, 377, 378, 388, 402
arithmeter, 334
Board of Governors, first, *168*
constitution, 159
Director of Research, 230
dues 1949-1979, 369, 372
early days, 165-167
election procedures, 200, 253-255
Executive Directors, 220, 230, 369
expression of opinion, 50, 159, 232, 235-238, 242, 258, 259
faculty members, 168
first black female FSA, 239
first black male FSA, 239
first woman president, 276
future study of 1966, 235, 236
gifts to, *169*
Guides to Professional Conduct, 191, 192
inaugural meeting, 167, 367
Institute members, 168
joint exams., 308
joint meetings, 92, 271, 272, 314
library, 21, 50, 59, 155, 199, 200, 294, 345, 384
light side in, 399-401, 404, 405
membership growth, 180-182
membership in 1948 & 1964, 205
Memorial Fund, 228
merger of A.I.A. & A.S.A., 156-159
merger proposal with FAA, 271
minority recruiting, 239, 240
new Fellows, 1946-1963, 305
operations, 458, 459
Public Relations Committee, 223
seminars, 316
SOFASIM model, 229, 230, 346
twentieth anniversary celebration, 238
twenty-fifth anniversary celebration, 238
SEE ALSO
    actuarial education,
    actuarial examinations,
    actuarial profession
    Record of the Society of Actuaries
    Transactions of the Society of Actuaries
Sorensen, Gladys, 367
Southeastern Actuaries Club, 239, 306
Spanish-American War, 351
Speakman, F.M., 98, 121
Spiegelman, Mortimer, 193, 232, 307
Spoerl, Charles A., 207, 301-304, 307, 398
Sprague, Thomas B., 20, 27
Spurgeon, E.F., 336
Stagg, Ronald G., 110, 166, 367
Standard Nonforfeiture Law, 272, 273
Standard Valuation Law, 150, 151, 276
SEE ALSO
    valuation,
    valuation standards

Standen, W.T., 67
Stanton, Dorothy R., 377
Staple Inn Hall, *174*
    SEE ALSO Institute of Actuaries
Starr, William E., 103, 172
State Mutual Life, 23
Statistics, 383-389
Stearns, J.L., 210
Stebbins, Samuel N., 30, 37
Stephenson, Herbert R., 164
Stern, Henry Root, Jr., 212
Sternhell, Charles M., 241, 280, 349, 354
Stewart, Gathings, *301*
Stickell, Edward E., 208
Stilwell, Samuel E., 58
Stock life insurance companies
    SEE life insurance companies
Stock market
    SEE common stock
Stonecipher, David A., 178
Stowe, Hudson J., 164, 345
Straut, Frances, 62, 363, 364
Streeter, Gordon C., 346
Strong, H. Raymond, 218, 248, 309, 404
Strong, Wendell M., 117, 133, 160, 175, 287, 398
    Legal Notes, 80, 81, 200
Substandard underwriting
    SEE underwriting
Sun Life of Canada, 115, 131, 145
Surplus distribution, 8, 12
    SEE ALSO Dividends,
Surrender charges, 23
Surrender values
    SEE life insurance products
Susan Vallez, Jorge, 278
Sutton, William, 283
Swick, George B., 267, 395
Swiss Actuarial Association, 404, 405
Sylvester, James J., 331

-T-

Table Z, 148
Tarbell, Thomas F., 144, 338
T.A.S.A.
    SEE *Transactions of the Actuarial Society of America*
Tate's Arithmometer
    SEE Calculators
Tatlock, John, 52, 62, 67, 68, 294
Taylor, Charles A., 149
Taylor, Harmon R., 172, 173
Taylor, Robert D., 121, 169, 172
Taylor, Robert H., 331
Teachers Insurance and Annuity Association (TIAA), 184

Texas Life Convention, 307
TFA
  SEE *Transactions of the Faculty of Actuaries*
Theismeyer, Lincoln R., 356
Thirty American Offices Table, 38-40, 194
Thomas, B. Russell, 266, 281
Thompson, Carl E., 354
Thompson, John S., 34, 93, 136, 149, 162, 163, 295, 348
Thompson, S.M., 163
Thompson, William T., 33
TIAA
  SEE Teachers Insurance and Annuity Association
TICA
  SEE *Transactions of the International Congress of Actuaries*
Timpe, Ronald E., 280
Todhunter, Ralph, 283
Tontine dividend system
  SEE dividends
Tontine plans, 13, 37
Tookey, Clarence H., 166
Toronto Actuaries Club, 103, 145, 146, 297
Torrey, M.W., 68
Total abstainers, 9, *10*, 11
Townsend Plan
  SEE social insurance
Traber, Ralph E., 354
Transactions of the Actuarial Society of America, 52-54, 143
  advertising, 364-365
  Book Reviews and Notices, 81
  decline of papers, 187
  Legal Notes, 80, 200
  papers submission, 108
Transactions of the Faculty of Actuaries (TFA), 14, 349
Transactions of the International Congress of Actuaries, 61, 62
Transactions of the Society of Actuaries (TSA), 313
  Legal Notes, 80, 81, 200
  Reports Numbers, 194, 230, 236
Travelers, The, 35, 325, 337
Tressel, Harry S., 169, 172, 222, 370
Trinity College (Hartford), 298
Trowbridge, Charles Lambert, 183, 184, 188, 196, 232, 256, 257, 259, 260, 263, 265-267, 269, 272, 275, 281, 282, 305, 311, 315
TSA
  SEE *Transactions of the Society of Actuaries*
Tuckett, Harvey G. P., 2, 15, 41, 319
Turner, Samuel H., 248
Twin Cities Actuarial Club, 381

-U-

Underwriting
  numerical method, 116

substandard, 115, 116
  SEE ALSO
    aviation risks,
    risk classification
Unemployment insurance
  SEE social security (U.S.)
Union Mutual Life, 27, 35
Unisex
  SEE risk classification
United States Annuitants Table, 1918-1927, 112
United States Assurance Gazette, 13
United States Consumer Price Index (CPI), 365
United States Social Security Act of 1935
  SEE social security (U.S.)
Universal life, 241
Universite Laval, 306
University of California, 298
University of Connecticut, 381
University of Georgia, 22
University of Iowa, 298
University of Manitoba, 82, 145, 298
University of Michigan, 101, 284, 297
University of Minnesota, 379
University of Nebraska, 306, 381
University of Texas, 306, 381
University of Toronto, 82, 101, 145, 284, 285, 297
University of Waterloo, 307
University of Wisconsin, 306, 381
Unruh, Henry C., 272

-V-

Vachon, Francois J.F., 249
Vail, Henry Sherman, 50, 52, 74, 75, 77
Valuation
  gross premium, 8, 20, 198
  modified preliminary term, 20
  natural reserves, 247
  net level premium, 19, 20, 34
  preliminary term, 71, 72
  reserves and nonforfeiture values, 272
  statutory changes, 315
  SEE ALSO
    deficiency reserves,
    insurance supervision,
    mortality tables
Valuation actuary, 250, 382
  Canadian approach, 111, 148, 275
  early concept, 48
  SEE ALSO
    asset and liability mismatching
    C_1, C_2, and C_3 risks
Valuation standards, 146, 147, 274, 276
  SEE ALSO
    Commissioners Reserve Valuation Method,
    deficiency reserves,

Guertin committees,
1980 Commissioners Standard Ordinary Mortality Table,
1958 Commissioners Standard Ordinary Mortality Table,
1941 Commissioners Standard Ordinary Mortality Table,
Standard Valuation Law
VanCise, Joel G., 68, 221
Vanderhoof, Irwin T., 282
Vanular, John Henry, 351
Variable annuities, 185
Veit, Kenneth P., 282
Vogel, Julius, 270, 278
Vogt, Ernest R., 298, 403

-W-

Waites, G. Frank, 192
Wakefield, Gilbert, 301
Walford, Cornelius, 135, 333
Walker, Dwight A., 83
Walker, H., 281
Walker, Margaret, *301*
Walker, Sears C., 4
Walker, W.A., 266
Walsh, Richard S., 217
Walters, Mavis A., 262
War
    war clauses, 93, 94, 152
    SEE ALSO
        American Civil War,
        Korean War,
        Spanish-American War,
        World War I,
        World War II
Warren, D.B., 210
Warren, Professor Lloyd A.H., 298
Warters, Dennis N., 125, 139, 186, 189
Washburn, James H., 289
Washburne, Alva C., 284
Watson, Andrew D., 111, 125, 142
Watson, Charles Barry H., 220, 238, 248, 312, 369, *370*, 372
Watson, G.N., 209
Watt, W. Arthur, 86, 87
Weatherhead, Kenneth K., 167
Weaver, A.G., 280, 281
Weaver, Chalmers L., 184
Webb, R.M., 74
Webber, Lydia, 365
Webster, Andrew C., 80, 206, 209, 220, 231, 232, 236, 307, 399-401

Webster, G.R., 78
Weck, Frank A., 349, 356
Weeks, Rufus W., 44, 46, 47, 67-69, 138, 139
Weinberg, Mark, 206
Weinstein, Louis, 239
Welch, Archibald A., 53, 68, 69, 71, 396
Wells, Daniel H., 40, 47, 63, 64, 68, 69
Wells, Edward H., 209, 343
Western Empire Life, 145
Western Pennsylvania Actuarial Club, 381
Westfall, Dr., 298
Westwater, George T., 80
Wetterstrand, William H., 194, 307
Whitbread, F.G., 209
White, Cecil G., 214, 371
White, E.B., 394
Whiting, William D., 36, 37, 67, 117
Whitney, Albert W., *85*, 86, 87, 103, 106, 116, 38!
Whittaker, Edmund B., 79, 301, 302, 305
Wieder, John W., 224
Wigglesworth, Professor Edward, 8
Wilks, Prof. Samuel S., 356
Willey, Nathan, 294
William of Ockham, 55, 355
Williams, Frederick A., 204
Williamson, J.D., 163
Williamson, W. Rulon, 141, 142, 162-164, 184, 18!
Wiltsie, Donald J., 351
Windecker, Arthur A., 302
Wing, Asa, 46
Winnipeg Actuaries Club, 145
Winston, Frederick S., 13, 22, 26, 37, 38
Winter, B.A., 209, 210
Winters, Robert C., 245, 248, 249
Wisconsin Actuaries Club, 381
Wisdom, Eugene, 307
Wise, T.A., 211, 212
Withington, F.S., 74
Wittick, Herbert E., 224
Wolfe, Lee J., *85*
Wolfenden, Hugh H., 139, 142, 162, 163, 209, 29! 383, 387
Wolman, Leo, 143
Womersley, John R., 342, 343
Wood, Arthur B., 93, 117, 289
Wood, Charles F., 364
Wood, M.J., 210
Wood, R. Norman, 258, 265
Wood, W.A.P., 162
Wooddy, John C., 229, 230, 270, 274
Woodruff, Thomas C., 269
Woods, Cyril J., 186

Woodward, George B., 34, 47
Woodward, Joseph H., 92, 119, 120, 290, 291, 320
Woolhouse, W.S.B., 20, 389
Woolston, P.L., 74
Workmen's compensation insurance, 86, 116, 119, 120,
    385
World War I, 92-94, 350, 353, 359-361
    anecdotes, 360
World War II, 152, 153, 349, 359
    anecdotes, 360
Wright, Christopher, 334
Wright, Elizur, 2, 9-13, 17, 18, *20*, 21, 23, 24, 27-31, 34,
    36, 37, 39-41, 44, 48, 135, 246
    his arithmeter, 19, 333, 334
    policy valuation reform, 19-22
    surrender values reform, 22-24
Wright, Lucy Jane
    first woman actuary, 27, 28
Wright, Walter C., 47, 48, 334
Wulf, Alfredo, 204

-X-

X_{17} Table, 176, 177

-Y-

Yardley, Charles A., 232
Yates, H. Powell, 217
Young, Thomas E., 283
Young, William, 78

-Z-

Zillmer, August, 71
Ziock, Richard, 298
Zubay, Eli A., 306

OUR YESTERDAYS:
THE HISTORY OF THE ACTUARIAL PROFESSION
IN NORTH AMERICA, 1809–1979
Designed by Mark Becker
Composed by Impressions Unlimited
in English Times
Printed by Impressions Unlimited
on 50 lb. Lakewood
Bound by Bookbinders
in Gane's Stock Book Cloth